FOURTH
EDITION

JUVENILE DELINQUENCY

Theory, Practice and Law

FOURTH
EDITION

JUVENILE DELINQUENCY

Theory, Practice and Law

Larry J. Siegel, Ph.D.
University of Lowell

Joseph J. Senna, M.S.W., J.D.
Northeastern University

WEST PUBLISHING COMPANY
St. Paul   New York   Los Angeles   San Francisco

Art: Accurate Art and Thomas Mallon, Techart
Composition: Carlisle Communications, Ltd.
Copyediting: Marilynn Taylor
Cover Design: David Farr, ImageSmythe
Cover Painting: *Artist Crossing* by Leo Posillico
Index: Linda Buskus, Northwind Editorial Services

Library of Congress Cataloging-in-Publication Data
Siegel, Larry J.
    Juvenile delinquency :   theory, practice, and law   /   Larry J.
Siegel, Joseph J. Senna. — 4th ed.
        p.   cm.
    Includes bibliographical references and index.
    ISBN 0–314–78260–5 (hard)
    1. Juvenile delinquency—United States.   2. Juvenile justice,
Administration of—United States.   I. Senna, Joseph J.   II. Title.
HV9104.S53   1991
364.3′6′0973 —dc20   90–40932
                                                CIP

Photo Credits:
3   Kevin Horan/Picture Group, 4   David Burns/AP/Wide World Photos, 5   Mike Derer/AP/Wide World Photos, 9   AP/Wide World Photos, 10   AP/Wide World Photos, 25   Charles Harbutt/Actuality, Inc., 26   Stuart Rosner/Stock, Boston, 40   Joan Liftin/Actuality, Inc., 42   Michael Grecco/Stock, Boston, 51   John Giordano/Picture Group, 58   Deborah Copaken/Gamma-Liaison, 63   Charles Gatewood/Stock, Boston, 65   Andy Snow/Picture Group, 67   Courtesy of the Sellin Center for Studies in Criminology and Criminal Law, The Wharton School of the University of Pennsylvania. Photo by Bachrach Photos, 81   Jim Harrison/Stock, Boston, 93   Gale Zucker/Stock, Boston, 97   Tony Freeman/PhotoEdit, 104   AP/Wide World Photos, 125   Peter Menzel/Stock, Boston, 127   Arthur Grace/Stock, Boston, 134   Christopher Brown/Stock, Boston, 142   Virginia Blaisdell/Stock, Boston, 155   Jean-Claude Lejeune/Stock, Boston, 159   Mike Greenlar/Picture Group, 164   Robert Brenner/PhotoEdit, 169   Polly Brown/Actuality, Inc., 176   Courtesy of Terence P. Thornberry, 187   Martin J. Dain/Magnum, 190   Deborah Copaken/Gamma-Liaison, 195   Gamma-Liaison, 201   Gamma-Liaison, 203   Courtesy of Herman and Julia Schwendinger,

To my wife Therese J. Libby and my children, Julie, Andrew, Eric, and Rachel.

L.J.S.

To my wife Janet and my children, Christian, Stephen, Peter, and Joseph.

J.J.S.

Contents

KEY TERMS

juvenile justice system

chronic delinquent

chronic career offenders

persistence

desistance

criminologists

helping professions

ego identity

role diffusion

child savers

parens patriae

status offenses

Office of Juvenile Justice and Delinquency Prevention (OJJDP)

National Juvenile Justice Standards Project

recidivate

widening the net

NOTES

1. "A Victim's Progress," *Newsweek*, 12 June 1989, p. 5.

2. Bill Turque and Sue Hutchison, "Gang Rape in the Suburbs," *Newsweek*, 5 June 1989, p. 26.

3. Federal Bureau of Investigation, *Crimes in the United States, 1988* (Washington, D.C.: U.S. Government Printing Office. 1989), p. 174.

4. John Whitehead and Steven Lab, "A Meta-Analysis of Juvenile Correctional Treatment," *Journal of Research in Crime and Delinquency* 26:276–295 (1989).

5. Susan Crimmins and Michael Foley, "The Threshold of Violence in Urban Adolescents," Paper presented at the annual meeting of the American Society of Criminology, Reno, Nevada, November 1989.

6. Task Force on Education of Young Adolescents, *Turning Points, Preparing American Youth for the 21st Century* (New York: Carnegie Council on Adolescent Development, 1989). (Hereinafter cited as *Turning Points*).

7. *Ibid.*, p. 21.

8. Erik Erikson, *Childhood and Society* (New York: W.H. Norton, 1963).

9. Roger Gould, "Adult Life Stages: Growth toward Self-Tolerance," *Psychology Today* 8:74–78 (1975).

10. This section leans heavily on James Gilbert, *A Cycle of Outrage America's Reaction to the Juvenile Delinquent in the 1950's* (New York: Oxford University Press, 1986).

11. Harrison Salisbury, *The Shook-Up Generation* (New York: Harper, 1958).

12. Frederic Wertham, *Seduction of the Innocent* (Port Washington, N.Y.: Kennikat Press, 1953).

13. *Turning Points*, p. 24.

14. *Ibid.*

15. *Turning Points*, p. 27.

16. Lloyd Johnson, Patrick O'Malley, and Johnathon Bachman, *Illicit Drug Use, Smoking and Drinking by America's High School Students, College Students and Young Adults, 1975–1987* (Washington, D.C.: U.S. Government Printing Office, 1988).

17. *Turning Points*, p. 27.

18. Graeme Newman, *The Punishment Response* (Philadelphia: J.B. Lippincott, 1978), pp. 53–79; Philipe Aries, *Centuries of Childhood* (New York: Knopf, 1962). A detailed discussion of the history of childhood juvenile justice is contained in Chapter 13.

19. See, generally, David Rothman, *The Discovery of the Asylum* (Boston: Little, Brown, 1971).

20. Reports of the Chicago Bar Association Committee, 1899, cited in Anthony Platt, *The Child Savers: The Invention of Delinquency* (Chicago: University of Chicago Press, 1969) p. 119.

21. John L. Hutzler, *Juvenile Court Jurisdiction over Children's Conduct: 1982 Comparative Analysis of Juvenile and Family Codes and National Standards* (Pittsburgh: National Center for Juvenile Justice, 1982), p. 2.

22. *Ibid.*

23. Susan Dateman and Mikel Aickin, "Offense Specialization and Escalation among Status Offenders," *The Journal of Criminal Law and Criminology* 75:1246–75 (1985).

24. *Ibid.*

25. See, generally, Solomon Kobrin and Malcolm Klein, *National Evaluation of the Deinstitutionalization of Status Offender Programs—Executive Summary* (Los Angeles:

Social Science Research Institute, University of Southern California, 1982).

26. Barry Krisberg and Ira Schwartz, "Rethinking Juvenile Justice," *Crime and Delinquency* 29:333–64 (1983).

27. Martin Rouse, "The Diversion of Status Offenders, Criminalization, and the New York Family Court." Revised version of the paper presented at the American Society of Criminology, Reno, Nevada, November 1989.

28. American Bar Association Joint Commission on Juvenile Justice Standards, *Summary and Analysis* (Cambridge, Mass.: Ballinger, 1977), sect. 1.1.

29. National Advisory Commission on Criminal Justice Standards and Goals, *Juvenile Justice and Delinquency Prevention* (Washington, D.C.: U.S. Government Printing Office, 1977), p. 311.

30. Rouse, "The Diversion of Status Offenders, Criminalization, and the New York Family Court," p. 12.

31. Marc Miller, "Changing Legal Paradigms in Juvenile Justice," in Peter Greenwood, *The Juvenile Rehabilitation Reader* (Santa Monica, Calif.: Rand Corporation, 1985) p. V.44.

32. Thomas Kelley, "Status Offenders Can Be Different: A Comparative Study of Delinquent Careers," *Crime and Delinquency* 29:365–80 (1983).

33. Ira Schwartz, *(In)Justice for Juveniles: Rethinking the Best Interests of the Child,* (Lexington, Mass.: Lexington Books, 1989), p. 171.

34. *Ibid.*

35. Lawrence Martin and Phyllis Snyder, "Jurisdiction over Status Offenses Should Not Be Removed from the Juvenile Court," *Crime and Delinquency* 22:44–47 (1976).

36. *Ibid.,* p. 45.

37. Lindsay Arthur, "Status Offenders Need a Court of Last Resort," *Boston University Law Review* 57:631–44 (1977).

38. *Ibid.*

39. Kelley, "Status Offenders Can Be Different."

40. Charles Thomas, "Are Status Offenders Really So Different?" *Crime and Delinquency* 22:438–55 (1976).

41. Howard Snyder, *Court Careers of Juvenile Offenders* (Washington, D.C.: Office of Juvenile Justice and Delinquency Prevention, 1988), p. 65.

42. Randall Shelden, John Horvath, and Sharon Tracy, "Do Status Offenders Get Worse? Some Clarifications on the Question of Escalation," *Crime and Delinquency* 35:202–16 (1989).

43. Solomon Kobrin, Frank Hellum, and John Peterson, "Offense Patterns of Status Offenders," in D. Schichor and D. Kelly, *Critical Issues in Juvenile Delinquency* (Lexington, Mass.: Lexington Books, 1980), pp. 203–35.

44. Chris Marshall, Ineke Marshall, and Charles Thomas, "The Implementation of Formal Procedures in Juvenile Court Processing of Status Offenders," *Journal of Criminal Justice* 11:195–211 (1983).

45. Schwartz, *(In)Justice for Juveniles,* pp. 378–79.

46. Francis Cullen, Sandra Evans Skovron, Joseph Scott, and Velmer Burton, "Public Support for Correctional Treatment: the Tenacity of Rehabilitative Ideology," *Criminal Justice and Behavior* 17:6–18 (1990).

47. Rhena Izzo and Robert Ross, "Meta-Analysis of Rehabilitation Programs for Juvenile Delinquents," *Criminal Justice and Behavior* 17:134–42 (1990).

48. Dean Champion, "Teenage Felons and Waiver Hearing: Some Recent Trends, 1980–1988," *Crime and Delinquency* 35:577–85 (1989).

49. *Stanford v. Kentucky* and *Wilkins v. Missouri,* 109 S.Ct. 2969 (1989).

50. Sandra Skovron, Joseph Scott, and Francis Cullen, "The Death Penalty for Juveniles: An Assessment of Public Support," *Crime and Delinquency* 35:546–61 (1989).

51. See, generally, Edmund McGarrell, *Juvenille Correctional Reform: Two Decades of Policy and Procedural Change* (Albany, N.Y.: State University of New York Press, 1988); Barry Krisberg, Ira Schwartz, Paul Litsky, and James Austin, "The Watershed of Juvenile Justice Reform," *Crime and Delinquency* 32:5–38 (1986).

52. Mark Ezell, "Juvenile Arbitration: Net Widening and Other Unintended Consequences," *Journal of Research in Crime and Delinquency* 26:358–77 (1990).

53. Schwartz, *(In)Justice for Juveniles,* p. 17.

54. *Ibid.,* pp. 167–79.

2

Measuring Juvenile Delinquency

How common is juvenile delinquency? Who commits delinquent acts and where are they most likely to occur? Is the juvenile crime rate increasing or decreasing? These are some of the most important questions in the study of juvenile delinquency. Without answers to them, it would be impossible to determine the actual causes of delinquency and then devise effective strategies for its control. Therefore, criminologists and delinquency experts have long struggled to create valid methods of measuring the nature and extent of delinquency. Currently, three separate methods enjoy widespread acceptance and use: official data, self-report data, and victimization data.

Official data refers to information collected about crimes reported to the police; "official delinquents" are those youths who have been formally arrested. In contrast, **self-report data** comes from juvenile offenders themselves. It is collected in anonymous surveys or interviews, conducted in schools or juvenile institutions, that are directed at uncovering illegal activities that have gone undetected by the police. Self-reports allow researchers to determine the extent of unrecorded juvenile delinquency, the so-called "**dark figures of crime,**" and compare the personal characteristics of official delinquents with youths who have so far escaped detection. **Victim surveys** ask those who have witnessed crime firsthand to tell about their experiences. They can provide important information on such subjects as the rate of juvenile victimization and the percentage of all crimes in which victims claim they were preyed upon by a juvenile.

The sections below describe each of these methods in some detail and examine the information they provide on the nature and extent of delinquency. In the following chapter, these data sources will again be used to analyze the social forces that influence delinquency.

OFFICIAL STATISTICS

The term **official statistics** refers to the records of youths whose illegal activities have come to the attention of law enforcement agencies.[1] Youths with a public record are *official delinquents;* their actions are considered *official delinquency.* In contrast, "unofficial" delinquency is that which remains hidden and unknown. A youngster arrested by police for shoplifting has an official record; 1,000 youths who bought crack without getting arrested by police are unofficial or secret delinquents.

The accuracy of official statistics has been the source of much debate. For more than thirty years, critics have charged that official data can lead to a spurious view of delinquency, one dominated by the biases of police.[2] It has been alleged that local police departments make it a policy of arresting the poor and minority group members while letting middle-class white youths go with a warning.[3] If these allegations are true, the nature and extent of official delinquency is more reflective of police behavior than of youthful misbehavior.[4]

In contrast to these views, some criminologists believe that the accuracy of official statistics may be improving.[5] After more than twenty years of efforts to increase the sensitivity of police officers to civil rights, arrest statistics may now be less class and race biased and consequently a more valid indicator of the actual participation in delinquent acts.[6]

Regardless of which position is correct, official statistics continue to be widely used because they are one of the few comprehensive sources of information on the nature and extent of delinquency across the United States. And even if there are some built-in inaccuracies in this kind of data, the flaws are probably consistent over time, so that *trends* in delinquent behavior can be charted. That is, even if inaccurate, official statistics may be stable enough to show year-to-year changes in the amount of delinquent behavior and fluctuations in the delinquency rate.

The most widely used source of official crime and delinquency statistics has been the annual effort of the U.S. Justice Department's **Federal Bureau of Investigation (FBI)** to accumulate information gathered by the nation's police departments on the number of criminal acts reported by citizens and the number of persons arrested each year for criminal and delinquent activity. Called the **Uniform Crime Report (UCR)**, the FBI's effort constitutes our best known source of national crime and delinquency statistics.[7]

The Uniform Crime Reports

The FBI's Uniform Crime Report (UCR) is an annual survey of crime compiled from statistics sent to the FBI from over 15,000 police departments serving a majority of the population of the United States. Its major unit of analysis involves the **index crimes,** also known as **Part I offenses:** homicide and nonnegligent manslaughter, forcible rape, robbery, aggravated assault, burglary, larceny, arson, and motor vehicle theft (See Table 2.1). A record is compiled by cooperating police agencies every time one of these offenses is reported by a victim or a witness. The FBI receives quarterly tallies of these offenses and annually publishes the results. Data is broken down by city, county, standard metropolitan statistical area (SMSA), and geographical divisions of the United States. In addition to these statistics, the UCR provides information on the number and characteristics of individuals who have been arrested for these and all other criminal offenses (known as **Part II offenses**). The arrest data includes the age, sex, and race of all persons apprehended for both Part I and Part II offenses.

The UCR employs three methods to express crime data. First, the number of crimes reported to the police and arrests made are expressed as raw figures (for example, 1,432,916 motor vehicle thefts occurred in 1988). Second, percent changes in the amount of crime between years is computed (for example, motor vehicle theft increased 11.2 percent between 1987 and 1988). Finally, crime rate per 100,000 people are computed. That is, when the UCR indicates that the murder rate was 8.4 in 1988, it means that about eight people in every 100,000 fell victim to murder between January 1 and December 31, 1988. The equation used is:

Number of Reported Crimes/Total U.S. Population X 100,000 = Rate per 100,000

All three methods will be used in the following discussion, which reviews some of the most significant trends reported by the UCR.

TABLE 2.1 UCR Crimes and Definitions

CRIME	DEFINITION
Homicide	Causing the death of another person without legal justification or excuse.
Rape	Unlawful sexual intercourse with a female, by force or without legal or factual consent.
Robbery	Unlawful taking or attempted taking of property that is in the immediate possession of another, by force or threat of force.
Assault	Unlawful intentional inflicting, or attempted inflicting, of injury upon the person of another. *Aggravated assault* is the unlawful intentional inflicting of serious bodily injury or unlawful threat or attempt to inflict bodily injury or death by means of a deadly or dangerous weapon with or without actual infliction of injury. *Simple assault* is the unlawful intentional inflicting of less than serious bodily injury without a deadly or dangerous weapon or an attempt or threat to inflict bodily injury without a deadly or dangerous weapon.
Burglary	Unlawful entry of any fixed structure, vehicle, or vessel used for regular residence, industry, or business, with or without force, with the intent to commit a felony or larceny.
Larceny (Theft)	Unlawful taking or attempted taking of property other than a motor vehicle from the possession of another, by stealth, without force and without deceit, with intent to permanently deprive the owner of the property.
Motor Vehicle Theft	Unlawful taking or attempted taking of a self-propelled road vehicle owned by another, with the intent of depriving the owner of it permanently or temporarily.
Arson	Intentional damaging or destruction or attempted damaging or destruction by means of fire or explosion of the property without the consent of the owner, or of one's own property or that of another by fire or explosives with or without the intent to defraud.

CRIME TRENDS IN THE UNITED STATES

UCR data tells us that crime continues to be one of the leading social problems in the United States. The crime rate skyrocketed between 1960, when about 3.3 million crimes were reported to police agencies, and 1981, when 13.4 million crimes were recorded. Then, after four years of decline (1981 to 1984), the rate went up in 1985 and has continued to increase ever since. Currently, the FBI estimates that each year over 14 million serious crimes are reported to police.[8]

There are a number of possible explanations given for the fluctuations in the crime rate over the past decade. At first, the rather surprising decrease in the number of reported crimes between 1980 and 1984 was attributed to the decline in the teenage population. The U.S. population is steadily aging, the so-called "graying of America." Since young people are believed to be involved in much more criminal behavior than older Americans, the shift in the population was used to explain the declining crime rate in the early 1980s. Research indicates that changes in the age structure of U.S. society accounts for approximately 40 percent of the changes in the crime rate.[9] Consequently, crime rates should parallel the number of teens in the population.[10]

The increase in crime frequency and rate that began in 1984 is more of a puzzle since the teenage population has not suddenly begun to soar. One possible explanation is that the nation's drug abuse problem is responsible for an increased crime rate. There is consistent evidence that substance abusers commit a significant portion of all serious crimes and that the availability of drugs may account for the recent escalation in the crime rate.[11] Crime rate increases may also be a function of urban problems and the economic deterioration that has gone on in the nation's inner-city areas.[12]

Another explanation is that the actual number of crimes committed is relatively stable, but the public may now be more willing to cooperate with the police and report crime. Many jurisdictions have established citizens' crime councils, neighborhood watch groups, and community patrols. Recent increases in the crime rate may be more a matter of victim reporting practices than an actual change in crime patterns.

Crime Patterns

The Uniform Crime Reports also tell us something about the nature of violent and property crime patterns in the United States. First, there is a strong association between violent crime and population density. Urban areas have much higher violence and property crime rates than rural counties. Cities of 250,000 or more are considerably more prone to violence than small towns.

There are also regional differences in the crime rate. Western and southern regions have higher property crime rates than midwestern and northeastern regions; the violence rate in the West is the highest, followed by the Northeast and the South.

Violence is more likely to occur in warmer climates and during the hot summer months of July and August. And there is usually an upsurge of murder and robbery during the New Year's season. Property-crime trends follow a similar temperature and seasonal pattern.

In addition, the cost of crime is high. For example, in 1988, some $12.1 billion worth of property was stolen, and only $4.6 billion was recovered by police (about 39 percent).[13]

It has also been noted that the police consistently solve, or clear, about 20 percent of all reported crimes (a **clearance** is recorded when a person is arrested, charged, and turned over for prosecution). Serious violent crimes are much more likely to be cleared than property crimes. For example, 70 percent of reported murders are cleared, while only 15 percent of motor vehicle crimes are similarly resolved. Police are probably more successful in solving the most serious crimes because they are willing to devote more resources to violent personal crimes and also because the majority of these offenses involve a victim and assailant who were acquainted with or related to one another.

The fact that there are consistent and enduring social and ecological patterns in the crime rate is quite important to the study of delinquency. They indicate that **social forces** influence crime and delinquency. For example, if crime was a matter of individual choice, traits, or characteristics alone, such as an abnormal personality, low intelligence, or genetic defects, crime rates would be spread more evenly across time and geographic boundaries. That is, because there is no relationship between geographic locale and the presence of unusual or abnormal physical or mental traits, the crime rate should be the same in rural Kansas as it is in New York City or Los Angeles; similarly, it should be the same in October as it is in July. The fact that crime rates are higher in urban cities than in rural counties and in some seasons than in others tells us that there must be social forces operating at times in these congested metropolitan areas that produce and sustain criminality.

Measuring Official Delinquency

Because the UCR's *arrest statistics* are broken down by suspect's age, they have been widely used to measure the role of youths in the official crime rate.[14] Arrest data must be interpreted with caution, however. First, the number of teenagers arrested does not represent the actual number of youths who have committed delinquent acts, but only those caught and officially processed by the police. Some offenders are never counted because, in fact, they are never caught. Others are counted more than once since multiple arrests of the same individual for different crimes are counted separately in the UCR. Consequently, the total number of arrests does not equal the number of people who have been arrested. Put another way, if 2 million arrests of youths under 18 years of age were made in a given year, we could not be sure if 2 million individuals had been arrested once or if 500,000 chronic offenders had been arrested four times each.

The official statistics also cannot tell us the proportion of delinquent offenders who get caught. Though police generally solve about 20 percent of all crimes, there is no guarantee that the clearance rate is stable across age categories. It cannot be determined if the number of youths arrested represents a high proportion of their total criminal behavior, a low proportion, or one that is similar to that of people in other age categories. In other words, if the FBI reports that 1 million youths were arrested, we could not be certain whether they represent 20 percent, 50 percent, or 100 percent of all delinquents. Teenagers may face a greater apprehension probability than adults because they are easier targets than older, more experienced criminals.

In addition, arrest patterns are influenced by jurisdictional variations in police practices, use of discretion, and other law enforcement factors. Some police agencies may practice full enforcement, arresting all teens who violate the law, while others may follow a policy of discretion that encourages nonofficial handling of juvenile matters through social service agencies. This too can influence the arrest data.

With these issues in mind, what does the UCR tell us about delinquency?

TABLE 2.2 Serious Juvenile Arrests by Age

	JUVENILE	ADULT	% JUV.	% ADULT	RATIO
Murder	1,765	14,561	08%	92%	1:12
Rape	4,118	24,364	15%	85%	1:6
Robbery	24,337	87,007	25%	75%	1:3
Assault	38,536	265,954	13%	87%	1:7
Burglary	111,284	220,474	37%	63%	1:2
Larceny	351,133	811,619	32%	68%	1:2
Auto theft	61,301	91,715	38%	62%	1:2
Arson	6,216	8,289	40%	60%	1:1.5
Violence	68,756	391,886	17%	83%	1:5
Property	529,934	1,132,097	34%	66%	1:2
Total	598,690	1,523,983	31%	69%	1:2.3

Source: FBI, *Uniform Crime Reports, 1988*, p. 178.

Official Delinquency

Table 2.2 illustrates the number and percentage of arrests for serious crimes broken down by the legal status of offender. In 1988, about 2.1 million arrests were made for serious crimes, including about *600,000 juvenile arrests.*

According to UCR data, it appears that crime is a young person's game: property crime activity peaks at age 16, the peak age for violent crime arrests is 18, and the incidence continues unabated until age 30 (see Figure 2.1).[15] Both

FIGURE 2.1

The relationship between age and serious crime arrests

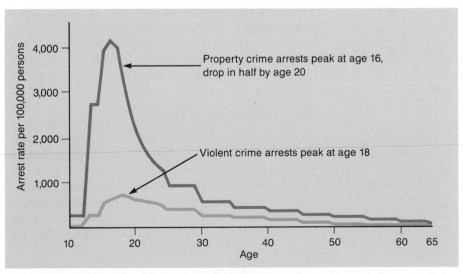

Source: FBI, *Uniform Crime Reports, 1988*, pp. 178–79.

TABLE 2.3 Arrests for Minor Crimes by Age

	JUVENILE	ADULT	% JUV.	% ADULT	RATIO
Vandalism	90,027	135,517	40%	60%	1:1.5
Sex offenses	12,585	65,654	14%	86%	1:6
Drug abuse	79,986	773,084	9%	91%	1:10
Liquor laws	124,024	368,361	25%	75%	1:3
Drunkenness	17,886	588,167	2%	98%	1:49
Disorderly conduct	88,813	484,767	15%	85%	1:6
Curfew violation	55,327	-------			
Runaway	124,709	-------			

Source: FBI, *Uniform Crime Reports, 1988,* p. 178.

the violence and property crime arrest rates decline dramatically in the over-30 population.

In addition to collecting information on the arrests made for serious crime, the FBI also examines the additional 8 million arrests made for other (Part II) criminal offenses ranging from forgery to suspicion. Some of these Part II crimes correspond to status (juvenile) offenses—curfew violations, running away, and underage drinking. In all, about *1 million juvenile arrests were made for Part II offenses.*

Table 2.3 lists some of the Part II crimes that youths are most likely to commit. As might be expected, all 180,000 arrests for running away and curfew violations involve youths under 18 years of age. Youths also made up a significant portion of those arrested for vandalism, minor assaults, and liquor law violations.

In contrast, adults were arrested disproportionately for the crime of driving while intoxicated: while over 1.2 million adult arrests for driving under the influence were recorded in 1988, only 17,000 youths under 18 were arrested for this crime. In all, delinquents account for about 16 percent of all arrests and 32 percent of the arrests for serious crime.

Juvenile Crime Trends

Since lurid crime stories sell newspapers and magazines, the media would have us believe that the nation is in the midst of a juvenile crime wave of epidemic proportions.[16] However, UCR arrest data paints a different picture. The total number of juveniles arrested by police has declined for more than a decade, and the percentage of crimes cleared in which a juvenile was arrested has undergone a similar decline. For example, in 1972, 27 percent of offenses known to police were cleared by an arrest of a minor under 18; by 1988, the percentage of arrestees 18 and under had decreased to about 18 percent.

It is actually not surprising that the total number of juvenile arrests has decreased, because the number of youths in the population has also declined. And

More than 1.5 million juveniles are arrested each year by local police.

as recent research by Philip Cook and John Laub shows, the *arrest rate* for juveniles in the population has remained extremely stable since 1971: approximately 103 total arrests and 38 index crime arrests per 1,000 youths in the population aged 13 to 17.[17] According to Cook and Laub, the percentage of youths engaging in criminal activity appears to be quite stable, so that the change in the youth arrest rate is more of a reflection of population trends in the United States than a function of changes in the everyday behavior of youth. Figure 2.2 illustrates these juvenile crime rate trends.

Taken in sum, UCR arrest statistics indicate that it is inaccurate to portray American youth as the most criminal in the nation's history. However, the fact that more than 1 million arrests of youths under 18 years of age are made annually makes it clear that the delinquency problem is not over or contained.

FIGURE 2.2
Juvenile crime rate trends

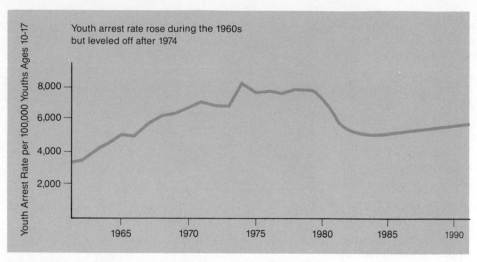

Youth arrest rate rose during the 1960s but leveled off after 1974

Youth Arrest Rate per 100,000 Youths Ages 10-17

Source: Bureau of Justice Statistics, *Report to the Nation on Crime and Justice* (Washington, D.C.:

SELF-REPORTS

The validity of official statistics has been a serious issue.[18] In addition to their problematic accuracy, official delinquency statistics do not tell us much about the personality, attitudes, and behavior of individual delinquents. Official statistics are useful for the examination of macro-level issues, such as trends in the relative frequency of delinquent behavior and geographic patterns of youth crime, but they are an inadequate source of micro-level information, such as the personality characteristics of delinquents. To address these deficiencies, criminologists have sought to develop alternative sources of delinquency statistics, of which the most commonly used are self-reports of delinquent behavior.

Self-report studies are designed to let youthful subjects personally reveal information about their violations of the law. A number of formats have been utilized: youths arrested by police are interviewed at the station house; an anonymous survey is simultaneously distributed to every student in a local high school; boys in a youth detention center are asked to respond to a survey; youths randomly selected from the population of teenagers are questioned in the privacy of their homes. Self-report studies can be conducted on a one-to-one basis through an interview or a self-administered questionnaire, but more commonly, they are conducted through a mass distribution of questionnaires. The subjects can be asked their identity or remain anonymous.

While the format can vary, the basic benefits and assumptions of self-report surveys remain constant: they can include all segments of the population (**cross-sectional data**) in order to avoid the class bias of official data; they can measure behavior that is rarely detected by police, such as drug abuse; and the promise of anonymity allows youths to describe their illegal activities honestly.

FIGURE 2.3
Sample self-report
survey

PLEASE INDICATE HOW OFTEN IN THE PAST 12 MONTHS YOU DID EACH ACT.
(Check the Best Answer.)

	Never Did Act	One Time	2-5 Times	6-9 Times	10-13 Times	14-17 Times	18 + Times
Stole something worth less than $50	_____	_____	_____	_____	_____	_____	_____
Stole something worth more than $50	_____	_____	_____	_____	_____	_____	_____
Snorted or sniffed heroin	_____	_____	_____	_____	_____	_____	_____
Injected heroin	_____	_____	_____	_____	_____	_____	_____
Used amphetamine pills (such as uppers, crystal meth, dex)	_____	_____	_____	_____	_____	_____	_____
Shot up amphetamines	_____	_____	_____	_____	_____	_____	_____
Got drunk on beer	_____	_____	_____	_____	_____	_____	_____
Got drunk on hard liquor	_____	_____	_____	_____	_____	_____	_____
Got drunk on wine	_____	_____	_____	_____	_____	_____	_____
Used marijuana (pot)	_____	_____	_____	_____	_____	_____	_____
Used downers (such as Valium, Librium, Darvon, Thorazine)	_____	_____	_____	_____	_____	_____	_____
Used psychadelics (such as LSD, mescaline)	_____	_____	_____	_____	_____	_____	_____
Used cocaine	_____	_____	_____	_____	_____	_____	_____
Been in a fistfight	_____	_____	_____	_____	_____	_____	_____
Carried a weapon such as a gun or knife	_____	_____	_____	_____	_____	_____	_____
Fought someone using a weapon	_____	_____	_____	_____	_____	_____	_____
Stole a car	_____	_____	_____	_____	_____	_____	_____
Used force to steal	_____	_____	_____	_____	_____	_____	_____
(For boys) Forced a girl to have sexual relations against her will	_____	_____	_____	_____	_____	_____	_____
Drove a car while drunk or high	_____	_____	_____	_____	_____	_____	_____
Damaged property worth more than $50	_____	_____	_____	_____	_____	_____	_____

Source: Self-report items created by Larry Siegel and Spencer Rathus.

Figure 2.3 is an example of a self-report survey. Subjects check off appropriate spaces to indicate how many times they have participated in illegal or deviant behavior. Other formats allow subjects to write in the precise number of times they engaged in each delinquent activity. Note that the sample survey limits the reporting period to the past twelve months, thereby focusing on relatively recent behavior; other surveys can question lifetime involvement.

Surveys measuring self-reported delinquency are also likely to contain items not directly related to delinquent activity: for example, items requesting information on such diverse topics as subjects' self-image, intelligence, personality, and attitudes toward family, friends, and school; leisure activities; and school activities. Self-report surveys also gather personal information on subjects' family background, social status, race, and sex. Reports of delinquent acts can then be used with this other information to create a much more complete picture of delinquent offenders than official statistics can provide.

In sum, criminologists have used self-report studies of delinquency frequently for over thirty years.[19] They are a valuable source of information on the delinquent activities of youths who have had formal contact with the juvenile justice system and those who have so far escaped official notice of their delinquent acts. The latter are referred to as "the dark figures of crime."

Self-Report Data

Most self-report studies indicate that the number of children who break the law is far greater than previously believed.[20] In fact, when truancy, alcohol consumption, petty theft, and soft drug use are included in self-report scales, delinquency appears almost universal.

Self-report studies indicate that the most common offenses are truancy, drinking alcohol, using a false identification (ID), shoplifting or larceny under five dollars, fighting, using marijuana, and damaging the property of others.[21]

Table 2.4 contains data from a national survey of juvenile misbehavior carried out on an annual basis by researchers at the University of Michigan's Institute for Social Research (ISR). This survey is one of the most methodologically sound and important sources of self-report data since it is conducted on a national level and involves a sample of over 3,000.[22]

During the twelve months prior to the survey, a surprising number of these "typical" teenagers reported involvement in serious criminal behavior: about 11

TABLE 2.4 Self-Reported Delinquent Acts—High School Class of 1988

| | PERCENT WHO COMMITTED ACT | | | | |
DELINQUENT ACT	Never	Once	Twice	3 or 4 Times	5 + Times
Used a weapon to steal	97.2	1.4	0.5	0.3	0.5
Stealing less than $50	66.6	15.1	7.2	5.3	5.9
Stealing more than $50	91.5	4.1	2.0	0.9	1.5
Shoplifting	69.6	12.9	6.4	4.9	6.1
Car theft (joyriding)	94.4	3.6	0.9	0.5	0.6
Stealing from cars	94.1	3.3	1.1	0.6	0.8
Breaking and entering	72.7	12.7	6.9	4.0	3.8
Arson	98.3	1.0	0.3	0.1	0.3
Damaged school property	85.8	7.8	3.2	1.6	1.6
Damaged work property	94.0	3.3	1.4	0.6	0.8
Got into trouble with police	77.5	12.8	6.2	2.4	1.1
N = 3297					

Source: Institute For Social Research, Ann Arbor, Michigan, 1990.

percent reported hurting someone seriously enough that the victim needed medical care (1 percent said they did this five times or more); about 34 percent reported stealing something worth less than fifty dollars and 9 percent stole something worth more than fifty dollars (about 2 percent said they did this five times or more); 31 percent reported shoplifting from a store; 14 percent had damaged school property. Of the youths reporting, about 23 percent said they got into trouble with the police for something they did.

A number of important conclusions can be drawn from the ISR data. If the ISR data accurately represents the national distribution of delinquent activities, then the juvenile crime problem is much greater than what official statistics lead us to believe. There are approximately 57 million American youth between the ages of 12 and 19. If 2 percent committed five or more theft offenses per year, that alone would amount to 5.7 million thefts. The 1 percent claiming five or more serious assaults (in which the victim needed medical attention) would account for 2.8 million assaults.

While these disturbing statistics show that the delinquency problem is far greater than indicated by the national arrest statistics, there is also little evidence that the delinquency rate is curving upward. A recent analysis by ISR statisticians indicates that with the exception of assault, patterns of self-reported delinquency have been rather stable since 1975.[23] Property crime rates, most notably shoplifting, may actually be in decline.

When the results of the ISR surveys are compared with various studies conducted over a twenty-year period, a uniform pattern emerges: teenagers' participation in theft, violence, and damage-related crimes seems to be stable. Although a self-reported crime wave has not occurred, neither has there been any visible reduction in teenage delinquency. And some research efforts indicate that these trends may actually have originated more than thirty years ago, since self-report data collected in the late 1970s is little changed from similar data obtained in the 1960s.[24] Thus, both official and self-report data suggest a stable teenage crime rate.

Validating Self-Reports

Critics of self-report studies frequently suggest that it is not feasible to expect young people to admit illegal acts candidly. None of them has anything to gain, and those taking the greatest risk are the ones with official records. On the other hand, some young people may exaggerate their delinquent acts or forget some of them or be confused. In addition, many self-reports may not use representative samples, while others contain items that are trivial and without real interest to police (for example, "used a false ID"). For these reasons, the use of self-reports has been criticized.

The most common technique for validating self-reports is to compare the answers that youths give on them with official police records. A typical approach is to ask youths if they have ever been arrested for or convicted of a delinquent act and then to check their **official records** against their self-reported responses. A number of studies using this method have found a remarkable degree of uniformity between self-reported answers and official records.[25]

There are other methods of testing the validity of self-reports: (1) the "known group method" compares incarcerated youths with "normal" groups to see whether the former report more delinquency;[26] (2) peer informants—friends who can verify the honesty of a subject's answers—are used;[27] (3) subjects are tested twice to see if their answers remain the same (testing across time); (4) the questions used are designed to select those who are lying—for example, "I have never done anything wrong in my life";[28] and (5) subjects are asked to take a polygraph to verify their answers.[29] In general, these efforts have been supportive of self-report techniques.

In what is considered the most thorough analysis of self-report validity, Michael Hindelang, Travis Hirschi, and Joseph Weis made use of data gathered in Seattle, Washington, and other sites.[30] They concluded that the problems of accuracy in self-reports are "surmountable"; that self-reports are more accurate than most criminologists believe; and that self-reports and official statistics are quite compatible. They state:

> the method of self-reports does not appear from these studies to be fundamentally flawed. Reliability measures are impressive and the majority of studies produce validity coefficients in the moderate to strong range.[31]

Despite the "clean bill of health" given self-reports by these preeminent sociologists, some serious questions about the true accuracy of the technique have recently emerged. Most damaging is the charge leveled by Stephen Cernkovich, Peggy Giordano, and Meredith Pugh that self-reports typically exclude the most serious chronic offenders in the teenage population.[32] Cernkovich, Giordano, and Pugh base their finding on comparisons made between samples of incarcerated youth and youths selected from the general teenage population. The researchers found significant differences in the offending patterns between the incarcerated youth and the neighborhood sample. They reported that "institutionalized youth are not only more delinquent than the 'average kid' in the general youth population but also considerably more delinquent than the most delinquent youth identified in the typical self-report survey."[33] Their conclusion was that self-reports may be measuring only nonserious, occasional delinquents while ignoring the hard-core chronic offender. The Cernkovich, Giordano, and Pugh research implies that self-reports are limited in their ability to provide data that can be used to accurately assess the delinquency problem.

Despite these criticisms, self-reports continue to be used as a standard method of delinquency research.[34] Their validity has been supported by studies indicating that the patterns and trends evident in official delinquency are also contained in self-report data.[35] Consequently, self-reports are considered an accurate indication of the "dark figures of crime."

VICTIMIZATION DATA

While the UCR and self-reports focus on the perpetrators of crime, there are also efforts to focus on crime victims.[36] The most important of these is a cooperative effort of the Bureau of Justice Statistics of the U.S. Department of Justice and the U.S. Census Bureau, called the National Crime Survey (NCS). The NCS is a massive annual house-to-house survey of the victims of criminal behavior in the United States that measures the nature of the crime and the personal characteristics of victims.

The total annual sample size of the NCS has been about 50,000 households containing about 100,000 individuals. The sample is broken down into subsamples of 10,000 households (22,000 individuals), and each group is interviewed twice a year; for example, people interviewed in January will be recontacted in July. The NCS has been conducted annually for more than ten years.

Victimization in the United States

The National Crime Survey provides yearly estimates of the total amount of personal contact crimes (such as assault, rape, and robbery) and household victimizations (such as burglary, larceny, and vehicle theft). According to victims' reports, about 35.8 million crimes occurred in the United States in 1988 (the last available data), an increase of about 1.3 percent from the previous year.[37] This includes about 6 million crimes of violence, 14 million personal thefts, and 15.8 million household crimes, such as burglary.

While at first glance these figures seem overwhelming, victimization rates seem to be relatively stable for most crime categories.[38] Estimates of criminal activity in the United States for the years 1973 through 1988 indicate that the crime rate seems to have peaked in the early 1980s (see Figure 2.4). In 1988, the violence rate increased slightly from the previous year (by 1.8 percent), the personal theft rate was essentially stable, and the household crime rate increased about 2.6 percent, for an overall increase of just under 2 percent.[39]

Many of the differences between the NCS data and official statistics can be attributed to the fact that many victims do not report their victimizations to police. About 50 percent of the crimes of violence, 72 percent of the personal crimes of theft, and 60 percent of the household crimes are not reported to law enforcement agencies.

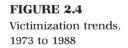

FIGURE 2.4
Victimization trends, 1973 to 1988

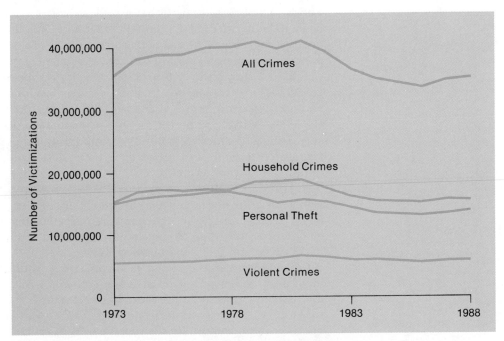

Source: Bureau of Justice Statistics, *Criminal Victimization, 1988.*

National crime survey data indicates that young people are much more likely to be the victims of crime than adults.

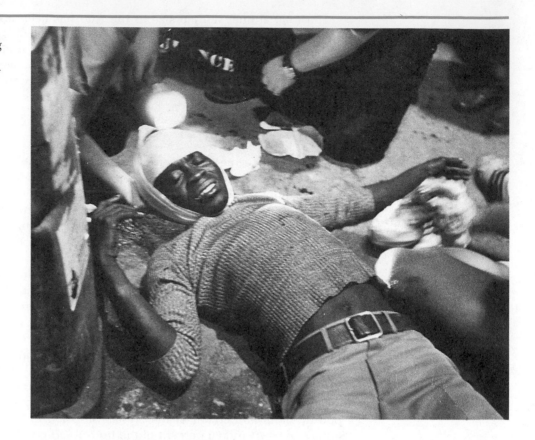

Young Victims

The National Crime Survey data indicates that young people are much more likely to be the victims of crime than adults. While it is common for the media to portray the elderly as particularly vulnerable to violent personal crime, it is actually teenagers who have the greatest risk of victimization.

Table 2.5 shows the victimization rates for crimes of violence and theft by age group.[40] Here we can see that the chance of victimization declines with age. Young teens are about ten times more likely to be the victims of violent crime and six times as likely to be the victims of theft than people over 65. What is both surprising and shocking is that this pattern holds for such serious crimes as rape, aggravated assault, and robbery; juvenile victimization is not just a matter of minor school yard assaults.

In addition to these age patterns, NCS data shows that male teenagers had a significantly higher (about two to one) chance of becoming victims than female teens (see Figure 2.5). Black teens had a greater chance of becoming the victims of violent crimes than teenagers of other racial groups; in contrast, white teens had the highest theft victimization rates.

Considering these findings, it is somewhat ironic that older women are the most likely to have a generalized fear of crime while teenage males and females are usually found to be the least fearful. While fear of crime is often difficult to measure, there are some indications that those who actually have the lowest risk of crime victimization are the most fearful of crime.[41]

TABLE 2.5 Victimization Rates for Persons Age 12 or Older, 1988

VICTIMIZATIONS FROM PERSONAL CRIMES PER 1,000 PERSONS AGE 12 OR OLDER

| | | | Crimes of violence | | | |
| | | | | Assault | | |
Age	Total	Robbery	Total	Aggravated	Simple	Crimes of theft
12-15	169.2	7.2	49.4	14.9	34.4	112.3
16-19	192.9	11.3	58.8	22.1	36.7	120.9
20-24	182.2	8.9	48.4	20.0	28.4	123.3
25-34	117.5	6.3	27.8	10.2	17.6	82.3
35-49	87.2	4.2	17.3	6.1	11.2	65.4
50-64	49.6	2.9	7.0	2.9	4.1	39.4
65 and over	22.4	1.7	2.4	.8	1.6	18.3

Source: Bureau of Justice Statistics, *Criminal Victimization, 1988*, p. 2.

FIGURE 2.5
Number of violent crimes per 1,000 population age 12 and older (rate)

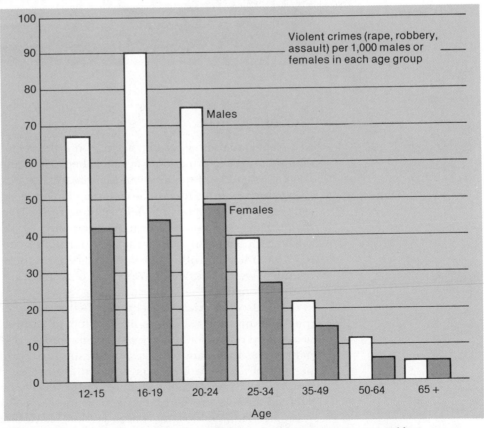

Source: Adapted from Bureau of Justice Statistics, *Criminal Victimization 1988*, Table 5.

While research indicates that the number of children kidnapped and killed by strangers may be less than previously believed, child abduction remains one of the most heinous of all crimes. The teen in this photo was later found dead.

Victim Patterns

NCS data can also tell us something about the relationship between victims and offenders. This information is available because victims of violent personal crimes, such as assault and robbery, can identify the age, sex, and race of their attackers.

In general, youths tend to be victimized by their peers: a majority of teens were victimized by other teens, while victims in the 20-and-over category identified their attackers as being 21 or more years old.

The NCS data also tells us that victimization is intraracial: black teens tended to be victimized by other black teenagers and whites by whites. And while most offenders were male, about 37 percent of teenage girls reported their attackers to be other females.

Teens also were victimized by people they knew or were acquainted with, and their victimization was more likely to occur during the day. In contrast, adults were more often victimized by strangers and at night. One explanation for this pattern was that many teenage victimizations occurred at school. For example, 34 percent of all the violent acts directed against the 12-to-15-year-old age group occurred on school grounds. These youths tend to be victimized in public places, such as schools and parks, by peers of the same sex, race, and age.

No aspect of child victimization is more disturbing than stranger homicide, a phenomenon discussed in the Focus on Delinquency.

Children Killed by Strangers

Though victim surveys tell us that youths are most likely to be victimized by people their own age, there has been a growing national concern over that most frightening of crimes: children who are abducted and killed by strangers. Public fears about this phenomenon have been fanned by some well-publicized cases, such as John Wayne Gacy's serial killing of more than forty teenage runaways and the Adam Walsh abduction-murder case, which was the subject of a well-received television docudrama starring Daniel J. Travanti. The fear that there are human beings who will kidnap and kill young children is enough to keep parents up at night devising ways to protect their young ones.

Despite the magnitude of public concern, until recently there has been relatively little information on the incidence of stranger abduction homicides. At one time, it was believed that thousands of children were kidnapped and murdered each year by strangers. The magnitude of these numbers prompted Gerald Hotaling, David Finkelhor, and Andrea Sedlak to conduct a sophisticated national survey of child abduction using a variety of data bases, including data from the FBI's Supplemental Homicide Reports and a national telephone survey of over 30,000 households, in order to obtain a clearer picture of the problem.

Preliminary findings indicate that while the problem is serious, the incidence of child abduction and murder is less than previously thought. Hotaling and his colleagues found that about 158 children are abducted and killed by strangers annually. Of these, fifty-two are clear-cut cases of stranger abduction and homicide and the rest are cases in which children were killed by strangers, but the circumstances were unclear.

The research indicates that 14 to 17 year olds account for nearly two out of three victims, giving them a risk nearly seven times greater than that faced by children from infancy to 9 years old. Girls were twice as likely as boys to be the victims of known stranger homicides, a pattern that contrasts with general homicide rates, which indicate that boys are more than twice as likely to be victims as girls. (However, boys are more likely to be the victims in cases where the circumstances were undetermined). While a greater number of white children fall victim to strangers each year than any other group, the rate of victimization of minority children is significantly higher (6.46 per million black children versus 1.79 per million white children). Finally, the research indicates another pattern that contradicts what we know about general murder patterns: stranger abduction homicides are greater in the northeast and lowest in the southern states.

What does this data tell us about children abducted and murdered by strangers? First, while the problem is not as common as previously believed, it is still an important social issue: every week in the United States as many as three children are abducted and killed by strangers. These horrible crimes permanently scar the victims' families and friends and probably take a greater toll on the general public than any other crime.

These findings also suggest that the prime target of these murders are not small children but older youths, perhaps runaways to large cities in the northeast or west.

These preliminary data will be expanded and refined in the years ahead. It is important that the nature and extent of this problem be accurately measured so that we can better deal with America's missing and exploited children.

Source: Barbara Allen-Hagen, *Stranger Abduction and Homicides of Children* (Washington, D.C.: Office of Juvenile Justice and Delinquency Prevention, 1989).

The Lifetime Likelihood of Victimization

An analysis of the National Crime Survey data indicates that sometime during their lifetime, about 80 percent of the 12 year olds in the United States will become victims of completed or attempted violent crimes, 99 percent will experience theft, and 40 percent will become injured during the course of the crime.[42]

TABLE 2.6 Lifetime Likelihood of Victimization, by Age

| | PERCENT OF PERSONS WHO WILL BE VICTIMIZED BY CRIME STARTING AT VARIOUS AGES | | | |
| | Total | Number of Victimizations | | |
	One or More Victimizations	One	Two	Three or More
Violent Crimes				
Current Age (in years)				
12	83%	30%	27%	25%
20	72	36	23	14
30	53	35	13	4
40	36	29	6	1
50	22	19	2	—
60	14	13	1	—
70	8	7	—	—
Robbery or Assault Resulting in Injury				
Current Age (in years)				
12	40%	30%	7%	2%
20	30	25	4	1
30	19	17	2	—
40	11	11	1	—
50	7	6	—	—
60	4	4	—	—
70	2	2	—	—
Personal Theft				
Current Age (in years)				
12	99%	4%	8%	87%
20	98	9	16	73
30	93	19	25	48
40	82	31	19	33
50	64	37	19	8
60	43	32	9	2
70	24	21	3	—

Source: Herbert Koppel, *Lifetime Likelihood of Victimization* (Washington, D.C.: Bureau of Justice Statistics Technical Report, 1987).

Even more startling, as Table 2.6 indicates, 52 percent of the 12 year olds will become the casualty of multiple acts of violence, and 95 percent will fall prey to multiple thefts.

As might be expected, personal characteristics also influence one's lifetime chances of becoming a crime victim. For example, while the overall probability of someday being a victim of robbery is about 30 percent, about 50 percent of black youths will become victims as opposed to only 25 percent of white youths. Similarly, the lifetime chances of being the victim of rape is estimated to be one in twelve for white females and one in nine for black females. Males have a much higher probability of being the victims of violent crimes, and blacks in general can expect to be victimized more frequently than whites. It also appears that living in an urban environment significantly increases one's chances of becoming a victim.

The lifetime prevalence rates mirror the annual rates supplied by the NCS. They indicate that crime and delinquency is a basic social issue, because like it or not, most of us will feel their impact.

CASE IN POINT

> You are a 17-year-old male. Your parents announce that they are interested in getting new jobs and trying to start their lives over again. They want to move to a different section of the country, relocate in a new home, and seek a new life-style.
>
> While at first you find this proposal startling, you accept the inevitable and try to make the best of a bad situation. You tell your parents that you are up for the move but that, as a teenager, you are the one who faces the greatest risk of being a crime victim. Therefore, you are the one who is most deeply affected by where and how they choose to live. Your parents are surprised by this information and claim they want to relocate to an environment that maximizes your safety. They tell you that since you are so well informed about crime information, you should given them input on where to move and what life-style is the safest.
>
> To what type of area would you advise them to move?
>
> What kind of life-style seems to be the safest?
>
> What are your chances of being a crime victim in the new location?

Are Delinquents and Victims One and the Same?

How can we explain the close association in personal characteristics between the victims and the perpetrators of teenage crime? One view is that both live within close proximity of one another and are therefore likely to have similar personal characteristics. Yet, the middle-aged and the elderly live in these areas, and they maintain lower victimization rates than teens. Another view is that since offenders must have easy access to their victims, they must by design share a similar life-style. It should not come as a surprise then that delinquents find it easier to prey upon their peers than upon members of any other age group.

A more intriguing view is that offenders and victims are so much alike because, in reality, they are the same people. For example, Joan McDermott found that the young victims of school crime were likely to strike back at other students in order to regain lost possessions or recover their self-respect.[43] In another study, Simon Singer found that the victims of violent assault were those most likely to become offenders themselves.[44] And there are a number of studies that show that youths who are the victims of child abuse are quite likely to later victimize their own children and families.[45] Gary Jensen and David Brownfield conclude:

> . . . for personal victimizations, those most likely to be the victims of crime are those who have been most involved in crime; and the similarity of victims and offenders reflects that association.[46]

Consequently, it may be wrong to consider delinquents and victims as two separate categories; the conditions that cause delinquency may effect most youths at some time in their lives.[47]

ALTERNATE DATA SOURCES

While official, self-report, and victim data are the main "building blocks" of delinquency research, they are by no means the only tools available to researchers. For example, public agency records have proven to be invaluable tools. School documents have been used to examine the association between academic achievement, disciplinary problems, teacher evaluations, and other educational variables. Hospital records have been employed to determine the association between delinquent behavior and reports of child abuse and neglect.

Another form of information comes from in-depth interviews with people who know delinquent youth and can provide background information on their behavior. For example, in one classic study, Sheldon and Eleanor Glueck interviewed the family members of known delinquents in order to examine the relationship between home atmosphere, family finances, family background, and youthful behavior patterns.[48]

It is also common for researchers to use data collected from an earlier project and reanalyze them to shed light on the delinquency problem; this is referred to as **secondary analysis**.[49] This type of analysis can be important because modern data analysis techniques can be applied to data collected before the advent of modern computing facilities and programming.[50]

SUMMARY

Official delinquency refers to youths who are arrested by police agencies. What is known about official delinquency comes from the FBI's Uniform Crime Report (UCR), an annual tally of crimes reported to police by citizens. In addition, the FBI gathers arrest statistics from local police departments. From these, it is possible to determine the number of youths who are arrested each year and to examine their racial and gender characteristics.

In 1988, about 1.5 million youths were arrested by police. This number actually represents a decline from previous years. In fact, from 1975 through 1988, juvenile crime has decreased substantially. The FBI's arrest statistics also include minor and status offense crimes.

Dissatisfaction with the validity of the UCR has prompted criminologists to develop other means of measuring the true amounts of delinquent behavior. Self-reports are anonymous surveys of youth in which subjects are asked to tell about their misbehavior. While self-reports indicate that many more crimes are committed than are known to the police, they also show that the delinquency rate is rather stable. Self-reports are the primary source of information on drug-abuse.

The third method of gathering information on delinquency involves the use of victim surveys. The National Crime Survey is an annual national survey of the victims of crime conducted by agencies of the federal government. It also indicates that the crime problem is far greater than official statistics would have us believe. However, NCS data also indicate that the crime problem has abated.

All three sources of crime statistics agree on one thing, however: young people commit more crime than adults. While the delinquency rate has declined, teens are proportionately more criminal than members of any other age group.

QUESTIONS FOR DISCUSSION

1. Have you ever been the victim of crime or delinquency and failed to report it to the police? If so, why?
2. Do you believe that the police treat certain ethnic and racial groups in a discriminatory fashion?
3. Do you believe that self-reports can be accurate?
4. Why are violence rates higher in cities than in rural or suburban areas?
5. Do you think that police alter crime statistics?

KEY TERMS

official data
self-report data
dark figures of crime
victim surveys
official statistics
Federal Bureau of Investigation (FBI)
Uniform Crime Report
index crimes

Part I offenses
Part II offenses
clearance
social forces
cross-sectional data
official records
secondary analysis

NOTES

1. The most commonly used statistics are the Federal Bureau of Investigation's annual compilation of crime data, referred to as the Uniform Crime Reports. The latest volume at the time of this writing is *Crime in the United States: Uniform Crime Reports, 1988* (Washington, D.C.: U.S. Government Printing Office, 1989). (Hereafter cited as *Uniform Crime Reports, 1988.*)

2. Patrick Jackson, "Assessing the Validity of Official Data on Arson," *Criminology* 26: 181–95 (1988); for an early criticism of official data, see Ronald Beattie, "Criminal Statistics in the United States," *Journal of Criminal Law, Criminology, and Police Science* 51:49–53 (1960).

3. For an important study, see Terence Thornberry, "Race, Socioeconomic Status, and Sentencing in the Juvenile Justice System," *Journal of Criminal Law and Criminology* 64:90–98 (1973).

4. See, for example, Irving Piliavin and Scott Briar, "Police Encounters with Juveniles," *American Sociological Review* 70:206 (1964).

5. For the most complete review, see Michael Hindelang, Travis Hirschi, and Joseph Weis, *Measuring Delinquency* (Beverly Hills, Calif.: Sage, 1981).

6. Walter Gove, Michael Hughes, Michael Geerken, "Are Uniform Crime Reports a Valid Indicator of the Index Crimes? An Affirmative Answer with Minor Qualifications," *Criminology* 23:451–501 (1985); Michael Hindelang, Travis Hirschi, and Joseph Weis, "Correlates of Delinquency: The Illusion of Discrepancy between Self-Report and Official Data," *American Sociological Review* 44:995–1014 (1979).

7. *Uniform Crime Reports, 1988.*

8. Associated Press, "Reports of Serious Crime Up 6% in '86," *Boston Globe*, 10 May 1987, p. 5.

9. Darrell Steffensmeir, "Is the Crime Rate Really Falling? An 'Aging' U.S. Population and Its Impact on the Nation's Crime Rate, 1980-1984," *Journal of Research in Crime and Delinquency* 24:23–48 (1987).

10. Darrell Steffensmeir, "Is the Crime Rate Really Falling? An 'Aging' U.S. Population and Its Impact on the Nation's Crime Rate, 1980-1984," pp. 38–39.

11. "Drug Use Forecasting Update," *NIJ Reports* (Washington, D.C.: National Institute of Justice, 1989).

12. David Wessel, "Poverty Rate Eased to 13.1% in 1988, but Income Disparities Widened Again," *Wall Street Journal* 19 October 1989, p. A2. See also National Research Council, *Common Destiny: Blacks and American Society* (Washington, D.C.: National Research Council, 1989).

13. *Uniform Crime Reports, 1988*, p. 156.

14. See, generally, Kimberly Kempf, *Measurement Issues in Criminology* (New York: Springer-Verlag, 1990).

15. *Report to the Nation on Crime and Justice* (Washington, D.C.: Bureau of Justice Statistics, 1983), p. 32. (Hereafter cited as *Report to the Nation*.)

16. "Youth Crime Plague," *Time*, June 1977, pp. 18–30.

17. Philip Cook and John Laub, "The (Surprising) Stability of Youth Crime," *Journal of Quantitative Criminology* 2:265–77 (1986).

18. Roger Hood and Richard Sparks, *Key Issues in Criminology* (New York: McGraw-Hill, 1970), p. 72.

19. A pioneering effort of self-report research is A. L. Porterfield's *Youth in Trouble* (Fort Worth, Texas: Leo Potishman Foundation, 1946). For a review, see Robert Hardt and George Bodine, *Development of Self-Report Instruments in Delinquency Research: A Conference Report* (Syracuse, N.Y.: Syracuse University Youth Development Center, 1965). See also Fred Murphy, Mary Shirley, and Helen Witmer, "The Incidence of Hidden Delinquency," *American Journal of Orthopsychiatry* 16:686–96 (1946).

20. For example, the following studies have noted the great discrepancy between official statistics and self-report studies: Maynard Erickson and LaMar Empey, "Court Records, Undetected Delinquency, and Decision Making," *Journal of Criminal Law, Criminology, and Police Science* 54:456–69 (1963); Martin Gold, "Undetected Delinquent Behavior," *Journal of Research in Crime and Delinquency* 3:27–46 (1966); James Short and F. Ivan Nye, "Extent of Unrecorded Delinquency, Tentative Conclusions," *Journal of Criminal Law, Criminology, and Police Science* 49:296–302 (1958).

21. In addition to the studies listed above, see David Farrington, "Self-Reports of Deviant Behavior: Predictive and Stable?" *Journal of Criminal Law and Criminology* 64:99–110 (1973); Michael Hindelang, "Causes of Delinquency: A Partial Replication and Extension," *Social Problems* 20:471–87 (1973).

22. The latest in this yearly series is Jerald Bachman, Lloyd Johnston, and Patrick O'Malley, *Monitoring the Future: Questionnaire Responses from the Nation's High School Seniors, 1988* (Ann Arbor, Mich.: Institute For Social Research, 1989).

23. D. Wayne Osgood, Patrick O'Malley, Jerald Bachman, and Lloyd Johnston, "Time Trends and Age Trends in Arrests and Self-Reported Illegal Behavior," *Criminology* 27:389–417 (1989).

24. Rosemary Sarri, "Gender Issues in Juvenile Justice," *Crime and Delinquency* 29:381–97 (1983).

25. Erickson and Empey, "Court Records, Undetected Delinquency, and Decision Making"; H. B. Gibson, Sylvia Morrison, and D. J. West, "The Confession of Known Offenses in Response to a Self-Reported Delinquency Schedule," *British Journal of Criminology* 10:277–80 (1970); and John Blackmore, "The Relationship between Self-Reported Delinquency and Official Convictions amongst Adolescent Boys," *British Journal of Criminology* 14:172–76 (1974).

26. Farrington, "Self-Reports of Deviant Behavior."

27. Gold, "Undetected Delinquent Behavior."

28. Robert Dentler and Lawrence Monroe, "Social Correlates of Early Adolescent Theft," *American Sociological Review* 26:733–43 (1961); Farrington, "Self-Reports of Deviant Behavior"; F. Ivan Nye and James Short, "Scaling Delinquent Behavior," *American Sociological Review* 22:326–31 (1957).

29. John Clark and Larry Tifft, "Polygraph and Interview Validation of Self-Reported Deviant Behavior," *American Sociological Review* 31:516–23 (1966).

30. Michael Hindelang, Travis Hirschi, and Joseph Weis, *Measuring Delinquency* (Beverly Hills, Calif.: Sage, 1981)

31. *Ibid.*, p. 114.

32. Stephen Cernkovich, Peggy Giordano, and Meredith Pugh, "Chronic Offenders: The Missing Cases in Self-Report Delinquency Research," *Journal of Criminal Law and Criminology* 76:705–32 (1985).

33. *Ibid.*, p. 706.

34. Michael Hindelang, Travis Hirschi, and Joseph Weis, *Measuring Delinquency* (Beverly Hills, Calif.: Sage, 1981).

35. Douglas Smith and Laura Davidson, "Interfacing Indicators and Constructs in Criminological Research: A Note on the Comparability of Self-Report and Violence Data for Race and Sex Groups," *Criminology* 24:473–87 (1986); Robert Sampson, "Sex Differences in Self-Reported Delinquency and Official Records: A Multiple Group Structural Modeling Approach," *Journal of Quantitative Criminology* 1:345–68 (1985).

36. The most recent data available are included in Joan M. Johnson and Marshall DeBerry, *Criminal Victimization 1988* (Washington, D.C.: Bureau of Justice Statistics, 1989).

37. Special thanks to Kristina Rose of the National Criminal Justice Reference Service for providing the latest available victim data.

38. Marshall DeBerry and Anita Timrots, *Criminal Victimization 1985*, (Washington, D.C.: Bureau of Justice Statistics, 1986).

39. U.S. Department of Justice, Preliminary National Crime Survey 1988 Results.

40. Data in this section come from Catherine Whitaker, *Teenage Victims* (Washington, D.C.: Bureau of Justice Statistics, 1986).

41. Randy LaGrange and Kenneth Ferraro, "Assessing Age and Gender Differences in Perceived Risk and Fear of Crime," *Criminology* 27:697–719 (1989).

42. Herbert Koppel, *Lifetime Likelihood of Victimization* (Washington, D.C.: Bureau of Justice Statistics, 1987).

43. Joan McDermott, "Crime in the School and in the Community: Offenders, Victims, and Fearful Youth," *Crime and Delinquency* 29:270–83 (1983).

44. Simon Singer, "Homogeneous Victim-Offender Populations: A Review and Some Research Implications," *Journal of Criminal Law and Criminology* 72:779–99 (1981).

45. Ross Vasta, "Physical Child Abuse: A Dual Component Analysis," *Developmental Review* 2:128–35 (1982).

46. Gary Jensen and David Brownfield, "Gender, Lifestyles, and Victimization: Beyond Routine Activities," *Violence and Victims* 3:85–101 (1986).

47. Jeffrey Fagan, Elizabeth Piper, and Yu-Teh Cheng, "Contributions of Victimization to Delinquency in Inner Cities," *Journal of Criminal Law and Criminology* 78:586–613 (1987).

48. Sheldon Glueck and Eleanor Glueck, *Unraveling Juvenile Delinquency* (New York: Commonwealth Fund, 1950).

49. David Stewart, *Secondary Research* (Beverly Hills, Calif.: Sage, 1984).

50. John Laub, Robert Sampson, and Kenna Kiger, "Assessing the Potential of Secondary Data Analysis: A New Look at the Glueck's *Unraveling Juvenile Delinquency* Data" in Kimberly Kempf, ed., *Measurement Issues in Criminology* (New York: Springer-Verlag, 1990).

3 Social Forces in Delinquency

W hat do the three major sources of delinquency statistics—official, self-report, and victim statistics—tell us about the social forces associated with delinquent behavior? Who are delinquents? Are they most likely male or female? Old or young? Rich or poor? Is their delinquency an unique act, or are they more often chronic or repeat offenders? Integrating information from the three main sources of delinquency statistics can help us provide answers to some of these highly relevant questions.

The measurement of social traits is essential for the study of delinquency. It can tell us much about the root causes of delinquency, and it can provide the raw material from which theories of delinquency are derived. If, for example, there exists a strong association between delinquent behavior and low social status, then poverty and economic deprivation must be considered in any explanation of the onset of delinquent behavior. If such an association is not found, then forces that are independent of the socioeconomic structure must be causing youthful law violations. The direction of social theory and the policies that rely on theories are controlled by what the crime data reveals.

This chapter will review the most important social and personal variables that have been linked to delinquent behavior: age, sex, race, class, and peer pressure. It will conclude with an analysis of the concept of the chronic or life-style delinquent offender.

AGE AND DELINQUENCY

There is general agreement that age is inversely related to criminality.[1] Official statistics tell us that young people are arrested at a disproportionate rate to their numbers in the population, and victim surveys generate similar findings for crimes in which the age of the assailant can be determined. Table 3.1 illustrates arrests for people at various ages compared to their percentage of the population. This is graphic proof of the age-crime relationship. While youths 15 to 18 collectively make up about 6 percent of the total U.S. population, they account for about 25 percent of the index crime arrests and 15 percent of the arrests for all crimes.[2] As a general rule, the peak age for property crime is believed to be 16 and for violence, 18. In contrast, adults 45 and over, who make up 30 percent of the population, account for only 6 percent of the index crime arrests.

Self-report data collected by the Institute of Social Research at the University of Michigan also indicates that people commit less crime as they mature. The results of a six-year-long nationwide survey of high school seniors found that the self-reported rate for such crimes as assault, gang fighting, robbery, stealing, and trespass declines substantially between ages 17 to 23.[3] As Table 3.2 shows, this pattern held for both males and females for the property, violent, and total crimes categories.

Victim data can also be used to evaluate the age-crime relationship. It is possible to derive some estimates of rates of offending by age for the violent personal crimes measured by the National Crime Survey (NCS) because the victims had the opportunity to view their attackers and estimate their age category. Research by the Hindelang Research Center in Albany, New York, shows that the estimated

TABLE 3.1 Arrests by Age Distribution of the United States

AGE	% OF POPULATION	% OF ARRESTS	% OF INDEX ARRESTS
Under 10	15%	.5%	1.1%
10–12	4%	1.3%	3.2%
13–14	3%	3.9%	7.9%
15	1.5%	3.3%	5.9%
16	1.5%	3.8%	6.3%
17	1.5%	3.3%	6.4%
18	1.5%	4.7%	5.9%
19	1.6%	4.8%	5.2%
20	1.7%	4.8%	4.6%
21	1.7%	4.8%	4.2%
22	1.7%	4.6%	3.9%
23	1.7%	4.4%	3.6%
24	1.8%	4.3%	3.4%
25–29	9%	17.5%	13.9%
30–34	8%	11.9%	9.4%
35–39	7%	7.7%	5.7%
40–44	6%	4.7%	3.2%
45–64	18%	7.6%	5.1%
Over 65	12%	.9%	.9%

Source: UCR arrest statistics, 1988, and U.S. Census Bureau *Population Projections*, 1989.

rates of offending for youths aged 18 to 20 is about three times greater than the estimated rate of adults 21 and over; youths 12 to 17 offended at a rate twice that of adults.[4] This relationship is even more pronounced when some specific crimes such as robbery and personal larceny are considered; for these offenses, the youthful offending rate is perceived to be almost six times the adult rate.

Age-Crime Controversy

The relationship between age and crime is highly important to delinquency experts. One of the major criticisms leveled against theories of delinquency causation is that they fail to adequately explain why many youngsters forego delinquent behavior as they mature, which is referred to as the **aging-out, desistance,** or **spontaneous remission** phenomenon. That is, well-known theories that account for the *start* or onset of delinquency rarely bother to explain why people *stop* committing crime as they mature. This theoretical failure is the subject of considerable academic debate.

One position, championed by respected criminologists Travis Hirschi and Michael Gottfredson, is that the age-crime relationship is a *constant* and therefore irrelevant to the study of crime. They find that regardless of race, sex, social class, intelligence, or any other social variable, people commit less crime as they age.[5]

TABLE 3.2 Self-Reported Illegal Behavior by Age and Gender: Percent Reporting One or More Offenses

	AGE						
	17	18	19	20	21	22	23
<u>Males</u>	%	%	%	%	%	%	%
Violence	35	28	22	21	14	17	09
Property	69	60	48	46	42	31	28
Any crime	74	65	55	53	46	41	30
<u>Females</u>	%	%	%	%	%	%	%
Violence	20	15	15	09	09	05	09
Property	45	35	29	28	19	23	17
Any crime	51	40	36	32	25	25	24

*Rounded to nearest whole number

Source: D. Wayne Osgood, Patrick O'Malley, Jerald Bachman, and Lloyd Johnston, "Time Trends and Age Trends in Arrests and Self-Reported Illegal Behavior," *Criminology* 27:398 (1989).

In fact, they argue that even the most chronic juvenile offenders will commit less crime as they age.[6] Since all people commit less crime as they age, age is irrelevant to the study of crime.

The Hirschi-Gottfredson concept of age and crime can be best understood through an example. Let's assume that children who drop out of high school will commit more delinquent acts than youths committed to their education (See Figure 3.1). According to Hirschi and Gottfredson, members of both groups will commit less crime as they age, but the crime rate of the dropouts will remain relatively higher than the rate of high school graduates at any given point in their respective life cycles. Consequently, the observed differences in their respective crime rates that first appeared in their early childhood will remain constant as they mature. By implication, it would be possible to compare the relative difference in the crime rate of dropouts and graduates (or any other two) groups by measuring their criminal activity at any single point in their lifetimes.

Those who oppose the Hirschi-Gottfredson view of the age-crime relationship suggest that age is an important determinant of crime and that there are factors directly associated with a person's age, such as life-style, economic situation, or peer relations, that need to be explained if the cause of crime is to be understood.[7] For example, David Farrington has shown that people begin to specialize in crime as they age and that crime patterns may undergo patterns or cycles that evolve over a person's lifetime. In addition, the probability that persons may become chronic or career criminals may be determined by the age at which they begin their offending careers.[8] There is evidence that the **age of onset** of a delinquent career has an important effect on its length: those who commit crime at very early ages are more likely to commit more crime for a longer duration. Consequently, it is important to follow delinquents over their life cycle *(longitudinal studies)* in order to fully understand how their age influences their offending patterns.[9]

FIGURE 3.1
Age by crime:
Dropouts vs.
graduates.

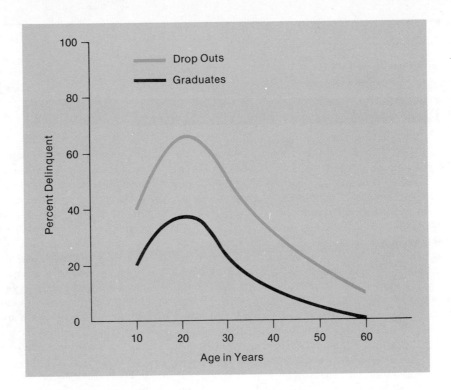

In summary, some criminologists believe that youths who get involved with delinquency at a very early age and who gain an official record will be the ones most likely to become career criminals; to these researchers, age is a key determinant of delinquency.[10] Those who are opposed to this view find that the age of onset is irrelevant and that all people commit less crime as they age; age, therefore, is inconsequential to the study of delinquency.[11]

The true role the age variable plays in the production of criminal careers has been the focus of many "lively" debates in the literature of crime and delinquency.[12] The research evidence indicates that there is a generalized decline in crime as a person matures but that there also may be some illegal acts, such as substance abuse, fraud, gambling, and drunkenness, whose incidence increases with age.[13] In addition, there may be a small segment of the chronic delinquent population whose criminal behavior remains intact as they reach adulthood. The age-crime association is discussed in the upcoming Focus on Delinquency.

GENDER AND DELINQUENCY

Crime and delinquency has long been considered a male-dominated phenomenon. To early criminologists, such as Cesare Lombroso and W. I. Thomas, the female offender was an aberration who engaged in crimes that usually had a

The Desistance Phenomenon

The debate over the age-crime relationship is a fierce one. But the fact remains that after the mid-teens, the crime rate declines. Research indicates that youths who quit committing crime rarely take it up again in their adulthood. What causes this decline?

There are a number of explanations for the "aging out" or desistance phenomenon. Some research by Edward Mulvey and John LaRosa found that desistance was linked to the realization by the youths that they were "going nowhere" and things had better change if they were going to become successful as adults. The Mulvey-LaRosa view is that desistance is a cognitive change occurring in the late teens when troubled youths were able to develop a long-term life view.

According to James Q. Wilson and Richard Herrnstein, the aging-out process is a function of the natural history of the human life cycle. Adolescent criminality coincides with the emergence of major sources of reinforcement for delinquent behavior—money, sex, and peers who defy conventional morality. At the same time, the child is becoming more independent of parents and other adults who enforce conventional standards. The new sense of energy and strength, coupled with a lack of economic and social skills and relationships with peers who are similarly vigorous and frustrated, create the conditions needed for a rise in criminality.

Why does the crime rate then decline? Wilson and Herrnstein find that small gains from petty crime lose their power to reinforce criminal behavior as youths mature and develop legitimate sources of money, sex, alcohol, and status. As adults, former delinquents develop increasingly powerful ties to conventional society, not the least of which is the acquisition of a family. Adult peers will further make crime an unattractive choice by expressing opinions in opposition to risk taking and law violation ("you're acting childishly"). The typical person also changes "from the egocentric and hedonistic focus of childhood to more abstract and principled guidelines to action." Along with this sense of maturity comes the ability to delay gratification and forego the immediate gains that law violations bring.

The "life cycle" view is supported in part by research conducted by Alicia Rand. Using data gathered from a group of delinquent youth followed over time, Rand found that some personal factors predicted desistance while others were correlated

continued

sexual connotation—prostitution, running away (which presumably leads to sexual misadventure), engaging in premarital sex, incorrigibility, and later, crimes of passion (killing a boyfriend or husband).[14] In the past, criminologists often ignored females, either assuming that they were rarely delinquent, or if they were, that their illegal acts were status-type offenses.

Official arrest statistics, victim data, and self-reports do in fact show that boys are significantly more delinquent than girls. UCR results typically show that the ratio for serious violent crime arrests is approximately eight to one and for property crime approximately four to one in favor of males.[15] Table 3.3 compares the representation of boys and girls in serious crime arrests. Overall, the ratio between male and female arrests is about four to one. However, with the exception of assault, teenage girls are arrested far less frequently for serious violent crime than boys (a ratio of one to eight). There is greater similarity between the sexes with respect to property offenses.

with persistent offending patterns. Youth who quickly got married, earned a high school diploma, and received vocational training within the armed services were the most likely to desist. In contrast, delinquent offenders who lived with a woman outside of marriage persisted in their criminal behavior almost four years longer than those who had never done so. And, as might be expected, delinquents who joined gangs were more likely to continue in their delinquency than those who remained unaffiliated. Rand also found that some expected associations between life-transition events and criminality did not exist: fatherhood, going to college, and joining the military were not related to desistance. In sum, youths who choose a more conventional life-style marked by marriage and productive military service are the most likely to forego criminal careers.

The life cycle explanation suggests that kids stop committing crime if they choose a conventional way of life. However, research conducted by Barry Glassner, Margaret Ksander, Bruce Berg and Bruce Johnson finds that the aging out of crime might also be linked to a very practical consideration: the fear of punishment. According to Glassner and his associates, youths are well aware that once they reach legal majority, punishment takes a decidedly more sinister turn. They are no longer protected by the kindly arms of the juvenile justice system. As one teenage boy told them:

When you're a teenager, you're rowdy. Nowadays, you aren't rowdy. You know, you want to settle down because you can go to jail now. [When] you are a boy, you can be put into a detention home. But you can go to jail now. Jail ain't no place to go.

Of course, not all juvenile criminals desist as they age; many go on to remain chronic offenders as adults. Yet, even people who actively remain in a criminal career will eventually slow down as they age. Crime is too dangerous, physically taxing, and unrewarding and punishments too harsh and long lasting to become a long-term way of life for most people.

Source: Kimberly Kempf, "Delinquency: Do the Dropouts Drop Back In?", *Youth and Society* 20:269–89 (1989); Alicia Rand, "Transitional Life Events and Desistance from Delinquency and Crime," in Marvin Wolfgang, Terence Thornberry, and Robert Figlio, eds., *From Boy to Man, from Delinquency to Crime* (Chicago: University of Chicago Press, 1987), pp. 134–63; Edward Mulvey and John LaRosa, "Delinquency Cessation and Adolescent Development: Preliminary Data," *American Journal of Orthopsychiatry* 56:212–24 (1986); James Q. Wilson and Richard Herrnstein, *Crime and Human Nature* (New York: Simon and Schuster, 1985), pp. 126–47; Barry Glassner, Margaret Ksander, Bruce Berg, and Bruce Johnson, "A Note on the Deterrent Effect of Juvenile Vs. Adult Jurisdiction," *Social Problems* 31:219–21 (1983), quote on p. 219.

Table 3.4 illustrates the male-female arrest patterns for some selected minor and status-type offenses. Although males also maintain a significant edge in arrests for these acts, one relationship does reverse this general pattern: girls are actually more likely than boys to be arrested for being runaways. There are two explanations for this. First, girls could simply be more likely than boys to run away from home. Or, police may view the female runaway as the more serious problem and therefore be more likely to process females through official justice channels. This may reflect paternalistic attitudes toward troubled girls, who are viewed by police as likely candidates for "getting in trouble."[16]

What have been the trends in female criminality in the past decade? While the total number of female arrests increased almost 30 percent, the number of girls under 18 who were arrested declined 14 percent, a pattern that was similar to that for male offenders. This pattern probably reflects the decreasing number of youths in the 10-to-18-year-old age bracket rather than any change in offending patterns.

Though girls are generally less delinquent than boys, many young females engage in theft and violence. This girl gang is formally named the "Tiny Diablas of the South Side Grape Street Watts", or (in Spanish) the "Watts Varrio Grapes" (WVG). The gang color is purple and their hand signal is similar to a sign language "g".

TABLE 3.3   Serious Juvenile Arrests by Gender

	MALE	FEMALE	% MALE	% FEMALE	RATIO
Murder	1,646	119	90%	10%	9:1
Rape	4,033	85	97%	3%	32:1
Robbery	22,535	1,802	93%	7%	13:1
Assault	32,684	5,852	84%	16%	5:1
Burglary	102,997	8,287	92%	8%	11:1
Larceny	258,747	92,386	72%	28%	2.5:1
Auto theft	54,984	6,317	88%	12%	7:1
Arson	5,624	592	90%	10%	9:1
Violence	60,898	7,858	89%	11%	8:1
Property	422,352	107,582	79%	21%	4:1
Total	483,250	115,440	80%	20%	4:1

Source: Uniform Crime Reports, 1988, pp. 180–82.

Self-report data allows us to further examine the issue. A few self-report studies have found that female delinquency is much higher than previously expected and that the ratio between male and female delinquency rates is actually quite low.[17] However, recent studies find that the self-reported sex ratios for serious index crimes, such as aggravated assault and grand theft, are similar to those reported in the official statistics.[18] In their national study, Jay Williams and Martin Gold found that boys are twice as likely as girls to be "frequently delinquent"

TABLE 3.4 Arrests for Status-Type Offenses by Gender

	MALE	FEMALE	% MALE	% FEMALE	RATIO
Vandalism	82,175	7,852	91%	9%	10:1
Sex offenses	11,701	884	94%	6%	13:1
Drug abuse	67,380	9,606	87%	13%	7:1
Liquor laws	90,739	33,285	73%	27%	4:1
Drunkenness	15,064	2,822	83%	17%	5:1
Disorderly conduct	71,652	17,161	79%	21%	4:1
Curfew violation	40,363	14,964	72%	28%	3:1
Runaway	55,386	69,323	44%	56%	1:1.3

Source: Uniform Crime Reports, 1988, pp. 180–82.

and that male delinquency was twice as serious as female delinquency.[19] Rosemary Sarri's survey of 1,735 midwestern youths found that while male-female ratios were quite similar for minor offenses, such as "lied about age" or "truancy," they were quite disparate for serious offenses, such as "theft of more than $50" and "breaking and entering."[20] Although Sarri found that the female crime rates for some serious crimes, such as "gang fights" and "hitting teachers," were higher than might be expected from the official data, males committed significantly more crimes in two-thirds of the categories surveyed. In sum, these efforts seem to indicate that the sex ratios in official and self-report data are quite similar.

RACIAL AND ETHNIC PATTERNS IN DELINQUENCY

The FBI also collects information on the race and ethnic origins of people arrested. The data shows that racial minorities are disproportionately represented in the arrest statistics. While black citizens make up about 12 percent of the population, they account for about 27 percent of all arrests and 34 percent of index crime arrests. Table 3.5 presents the relative involvement of black and white juveniles in the arrest data. It shows that black youths are arrested for a disproportionate number of serious crimes—murder, rape, and robbery. Overall, black youths comprise about 23 percent of the juvenile arrest statistics.

The UCR also lists arrests of Hispanic youths (who are *also* included as part of the white group). Since Hispanics number approximately 15 percent of the population, their arrest rates seem to be proportionate to their group size. In all, about 12 percent of Part I and Part II juvenile arrests involve Hispanic youths.

Table 3.6 lists arrests for minor and status offenses by race. Here we see that white youths are more likely than black youths to be arrested for minor crimes, such as liquor law violations and drug abuse, while blacks are more heavily represented in the disorderly conduct and curfew violation categories, perhaps because police are more likely to use formal measures to handle minority youths whose attitude and demeanor are not deferential to police authority.

TABLE 3.5 Serious Juvenile Arrests by Race

	WHITE	BLACK	% WHITE	% BLACK	RATIO
Murder	720	997	42%	58%	1:1.3
Rape	1,957	2,005	49%	51%	1:1
Robbery	8,079	15,662	33%	67%	1:2
Assault	20,198	17,295	54%	46%	1:1
Burglary	81,902	26,151	76%	24%	3:1
Larceny	249,723	89,755	73%	27%	3:1
Auto theft	35,458	23,614	59%	41%	1.5:1
Arson	5,079	994	83%	17%	6:1
Violence	30,954	35,959	46%	52%	1:1
Property	372,162	140,514	72%	25%	3:1
Total	452,407	187,089	69%	29%	2.3:1

Source: Uniform Crime Reports, 1988, pp. 187.

TABLE 3.6 Arrests for Status-Type Offenses by Race

	WHITE	BLACK	% WHITE	% BLACK	RATIO
Vandalism	72,610	15,460	81%	19%	4:1
Sex offenses	8,799	3,520	73%	17%	4:1
Drug abuse	43,088	32,048	57%	43%	1.3:1
Liquor laws	116,468	4,396	96%	04%	24:1
Drunkenness	16,227	1,153	94%	06%	16:1
Disorderly conduct	58,263	29,185	66%	34%	2:1
Curfew violation	44,219	8,766	84%	16%	5:1
Runaway	101,656	18,161	84%	16%	5:1

Source: Uniform Crime Reports, 1988, pp. 187.

Self-Report Differences

Official statistics show that minority youths are much more likely than white youths to be arrested for serious criminal behavior and that race is an important predictor of delinquent behavior. To many delinquency experts, this pattern merely reflects racism and discrimination in the juvenile justice system. In other words, black youths show up in the official statistics more often because they are more likely to be formally arrested by the police who, in contrast, will treat white youths informally.

One way to examine this issue is to compare the racial differences in self-reported data with those found in the official delinquency records. Charges of racial discrimination in the arrest process would be supported if there is insignificant racial difference in self-report data.

Early efforts by Leroy Gould in Seattle, Harwin Voss in Honolulu, and Ronald Akers in seven midwestern states found that the relationship between race and self-reported delinquency was virtually nonexistent.[21] This data was taken as evidence that racial differences in the UCR data were indeed a reflection of bias in police arrest practices.

Two recent self-report studies that make use of large national samples of youth have also found little evidence of racial disparity in offending. One conducted by the Institute for Social Research at the University of Michigan found that black youth self-report less delinquent behavior than whites.[22] And in an analysis of data obtained in a nationwide study of youth, social scientists at the Behavioral Science Institute in Boulder, Colorado, found that while black youths and white youths may be equally delinquent, black youths simply have a much greater chance of being arrested and taken into custody.[23] These and other self-report studies seem to indicate that the delinquent behavior rates of black and white teenagers are generally similar and that differences in arrest statistics may indicate a differential selection policy by police.[24]

Victim Data

National Crime Survey data has also been used to investigate racial differences in the crime rate. In general, black teens seem to be overrepresented in the serious and violent personal crimes of robbery, rape, and assault.[25]

John Laub and his colleagues compared racial characteristics of perpetrators identified by the victims of violent crime and found that both black male and female offenders aged 12 to 17 have a significantly higher perceived offending rate than their white counterparts.[26] However, the black offending rate for both males and females declined significantly over the ten-year period it was charted, while the rate for white youths remained rather stable; this trend was repeated in the other age categories.

Victim data must be interpreted with caution, however. First, the perceived racial characteristics of offenders may be confused by victims. Also, accounts from victims who actually view the offenders are available for relatively few incidents. In addition, a small number of chronic offenders may be responsible for a significant number of the total criminal offenses. If the crime rate for black male delinquents seems high, it could be because a few youths commit a disproportionate amount of crimes, rather than because a large percentage of that specific group commits many individual offenses.

Explaining Racial Patterns

Racial patterns in the delinquency rate have long been the subject of considerable controversy. One view is that the disproportionate amount of black official delinquency is a result of juvenile justice system bias. According to this view, police are more likely to arrest and officially process black youths while treating white offenders in a more charitable manner.[27] And as Donna Bishop and Charles Frazier have found, possession of a prior record, even if it is the product of bias, increases the likelihood that upon subsequent contact, police will formally arrest a suspect rather than release him or her with a warning or take some other "unofficial" action.[28]

Those who challenge this view find that while some bias on the part of the justice system does exist, there is enough similarity between official, victim-generated and self-report data to conclude that racial differences in the crime rate are real and not a result of a racially biased juvenile justice system.[29]

There have been a number of attempts to provide explanations for racial differences in the official crime data. One view, summarized by Daniel Georges-Abeyie, maintains that if the racial differences in the delinquency rate recorded by official data *are in fact valid*, they are a function of the ecological differences in American society: blacks reside in "natural areas" of crime that are characterized by (1) deteriorated housing; (2) limited or nonexistent legitimate employment and recreational opportunities; (3) anomic behavior patterns; (4) a local criminal tradition that actually existed prior to the current black ethnic group in residence; (5) abnormally high incidence of transient or psychopathological individuals; (6) a disproportionate number of opportunities to engage in criminal behavior or form delinquent subcultures; and (7) an area where poverty and limited wealth is the norm rather than the exception.[30]

Another view is that racial bias has produced a separate black culture split off from the white, middle-class dominated society. The black subculture has been solidified by harsh economic conditions and high teenage unemployment rates.[31] It has its own norms and values, culture, music, and speech patterns. Troy Duster found the existence of a permanent black teenage underclass whose membership lacks the basic job skills needed to ever allow them to enter the social mainstream: blacks are over three times as likely to be poor as whites; their median income is only half that of whites; their net worth is only one-twelfth that of whites; and black men are twice as likely to be jobless as white men.[32] Duster concludes that the lack of economic opportunity for blacks has been a direct influence on their crime and delinquency rates.[33]

In sum, the evidence on racial differences in the crime rate is still inconclusive. Official data indicates that black youths are arrested for more serious crimes than whites. However, a number of self-report studies conducted by some of the nation's most respected criminologists show that the differences between the races is insignificant and therefore official differences are an artifact of bias in the justice system.[34] If in fact the official data is valid, the participation of black youth in serious criminal behavior is generally viewed as a function of the socioeconomic position they hold in their environment and the racism they face in their lives.

SOCIAL CLASS AND DELINQUENCY

Another enduring debate among criminologists concerns the relationship between economic status and delinquent behavior. At first glance, the relationship ought to be an obvious one: youths without wealth or social standing who live in deteriorated inner-city areas should be the ones most likely to use criminal means to achieve their goals. Despite its inherent logic, available research data does not consistently support this relationship. There are many indicators of poverty and economic deprivation that do not correlate with crime. For example, there is little if any consistent evidence that unemployment rates are associated with crime rates.[35] And while there are many lower-class people who lead con-

Official delinquency rates are highest in deteriorated inner-city slums.

ventional and law-abiding lives, there are also a great number of middle-class delinquents and criminals.

Delinquency experts have produced a significant amount of confusing and contradictory evidence on the matter. Those who use official delinquency data persistently find **social class** to be a major predictor of delinquency. Juvenile arrest rates are highest in areas that are economically deprived and socially disorganized.[36] Theorists who have based their efforts on official police statistics maintain that those who think delinquency is spread throughout the social classes are just wishful thinkers; to many experts, "real" delinquency is a lower-class phenomenon.[37]

However, the first few self-report studies, specifically those conducted by **James Short** and **F. Ivan Nye,** did not find a direct relationship between social class and delinquency.[38] They found that socioeconomic class was related to official processing by police, court, and correctional agencies but not to the actual commission of delinquent acts. For example, Short and Nye found that delinquent behavior had no relationship to class when they used self-reports as the criterion of delinquency, but that social class was related to youths' chances of winding up in an institution if they were actually arrested. In addition, factors generally associated with lower-class status, such as broken homes, were found to be related to institutionalization but not to admissions of delinquency.

The pioneering work of Nye and Short sparked numerous self-report studies in the 1960s and 1970s, most of which supported their view of a weak or nonexistent relationship between class and delinquency.[39] Some of the most important work was conducted by sociologist Martin Gold. Although in his first few studies Gold found that delinquents were predominantly lower-class youth,[40] his later work with Jay Williams showed no statistically significant differences among classes (controlling for race and sex) in terms of the amount of admitted delinquency.[41] The only statistically significant relationship indicated that higher-status white males were more seriously delinquent than other white males.

In sum, the widespread use of self-reports in the 1960s and 1970s uncovered the rather startling fact that upper- and middle-class youth were as delinquent as their lower-class peers. Most researchers did conclude, however, that lower-class youths were more likely to receive official notice from the justice system. Therefore, they appear to be overrepresented as official delinquents. Middle-class delinquency, on the other hand, remained hidden.

The importance of this finding can be felt in its impact on delinquency theory. If delinquency is purely a lower-class phenomenon, then its cause must be rooted in the social forces that are to be found solely in lower-class areas: poverty, unemployment, social disorganization, culture conflict, and so on.[42] If, on the other hand, there are no class distinctions in delinquency, then its cause must be related to social and developmental factors that can be present in all classes: family problems, educational failure, peer influence, and so on.

Reassessing Class Differences

Is there a relationship between social class and delinquency? This issue is still critical for the study of delinquency. There is little question that the aggregate crime and delinquency rates of inner-city areas are much higher than those in wealthier suburban areas.[43] Yet, when samples of youths are surveyed in a population, there is little clear-cut evidence that the poorest youth in the sample are any more delinquent than the wealthiest. In the definitive statement on this issue, Charles Tittle, Wayne Villemez, and Douglas Smith reviewed thirty-five studies containing 363 separate estimates concerning the relationship between class and crime.[44] Their conclusion was that little if any support exists for the contention that delinquency is primarily a lower-class phenomenon. Consequently, Tittle and his associates argued that official statistics probably reflect class bias in the processing of lower-class youths. The Tittle review is usually cited by delinquency experts as the strongest statement that refutes the belief that lower-class youths are disproportionately delinquent and has been supported by a number of other research efforts.[45]

Those who find fault with Tittle's conclusions usually point to the inclusion of trivial offenses, such as using a false ID, in most self-report instruments. Although middle- and upper-class youths may appear to be as delinquent as those in the lower class, it is because they engage in significant amounts of what are actually status offenses. In one study, Delbert Eliott and Suzanne Ageton of the Behavioral Science Institute made use of a carefully drawn national sample of 1,726 youths ages 11 to 17 and a sophisticated self-report instrument. They found lower-class youths to be much more likely than middle-class youths to engage in serious delinquent acts, such as burglary, assault, robbery, sexual assault, and vandalism.[46] Moreover, lower-class youths were much more likely than middle-class youths to have committed "numerous" serious personal and property crimes (more than 200). These findings forced Eliott and Ageton to conclude that self-report data gives findings about class and crime that are actually similar to those of official data. Furthermore, the authors charge that studies showing middle- and lower-class youths to be equally delinquent rely on measures weighted toward minor crimes (for example, using a false ID or skipping school). When serious crimes, such as burglary and assault, are used in the comparison, lower-class youths are significantly more delinquent.

Adding to the confusion is the fact that the manner in which research is conducted produces significantly different outcomes. **Aggregate measures** of delinquency, which compare the delinquency rates in poor neighborhoods with those in wealthier areas (such as those using the Uniform Crime Reports and census tract data) usually show that residents of lower-class areas are more delinquent. In contrast, studies using individual-level self-report data show few class distinctions in the delinquency rate.

Though official delinquency rates seem higher in inner city urban areas, research indicates that youth crime is not unknown in suburbia. These gang members are strolling through a shopping mall in Ohio.

The way in which "social class" is measured may also influence research findings. While some researchers use such variables as "parental income" and "highest education level" as measures of social-class affiliation, others use "occupation," "employment status," "welfare status," and "housing quality"; each of these dissimilar measures can produce a different association between class and delinquency.[47]

So after more than four decades of research consensus has still not been achieved on the true relationship between class and delinquency. Chapters 5 and 7 review theories of delinquency that hold that social class is the key determinant of antisocial behavior; chapters 4 and 6 review theories of delinquency that do not strictly rely on a class-crime relationship.

THE CHRONIC JUVENILE OFFENDER

One of the most dramatic uses of official and unofficial data sources has been the "discovery" of the *chronic delinquent offender*. It has become generally recognized that a relatively few youthful offenders commit a significant percentage of all serious crimes in the community and that many of these same offenders grow up to become chronic adult criminals who contribute a significant share of the total adult crime rate.

Chronic offenders can be distinguished from conventional delinquent youths. The latter category contains youthful law violators who may be apprehended for a single instance of criminal behavior, usually of relatively minor seriousness—shoplifting, joyriding, petty larceny, and so on. The chronic offender is one who begins his or her delinquent career at a relatively young age (under 10 years old), has serious and persistent brushes with the law, is building a career in crime, and may be excessively violent and destructive. Moreover, chronics do not "age out" of crime but continue their law-violating behavior into their adulthood.[48]

A number of important research efforts have set out to chronicle the careers of serious delinquent offenders. Other experts have suggested policy changes designed to control their activities. The following sections describe both such initiatives.

"Delinquency in a Birth Cohort"

The concept of the chronic career offender is most closely associated with the research efforts of **Marvin Wolfgang** and his associates at the University of Pennsylvania.[49] In 1972, Wolfgang, Robert Figlio, and Thorsten Sellin published a landmark study, *Delinquency in a Birth Cohort,* that has had a profound influence on the very concept of the delinquent offender.

Wolfgang, Figlio, and Sellin used official records to follow the delinquent careers of a **cohort** of 9,945 boys born in Philadelphia, Pennsylvania, in 1945, until they reached 18 years of age in 1963. The authors' goal was to design a study that "would permit us to note the age of onset and the progression or cessation of delinquency. It would allow us to relate these phenomenon to certain personal or social characteristics of the delinquents and to make appropriate comparisons."[50]

Marvin Wolfgang

Official police records were used to identify delinquents. About one-third of the boys (3,475) had some police contact. The remaining two-thirds (6,470) had none. Each delinquent's actions were given a seriousness weight based on the Wolfgang-Sellin Delinquency Index, which provides a weighted score for every delinquent act.[51] The weighing of delinquent acts allowed the researchers to differentiate, for example, between a simple assault requiring no medical attention for the victim and a serious assault in which the victim needed hospitalization.

Wolfgang and his colleagues obtained data from school records, including subject intelligence-quotient (IQ) scores and measures of academic performance and conduct. Socioeconomic status was determined by locating the residence of each member of the cohort and assigning him the median family income for that area.

FINDINGS OF THE COHORT STUDY. The 3,475 boys in the sample who had at least one contact with the police during their minority committed 10,214 offenses. Race was found to be the most significant predictor of eventual police contact. Of the 2,902 nonwhite subjects, 1,458 had police contact (50.24 percent). Of the 7,043 white youths, 2,017 (28.64 percent) had similar records.[52] Wolfgang and his associates also noted that minority youths tended to fall in the lower-class category (84.2 percent of nonwhites and 30.8 percent of whites were from lower socioeconomic levels). However, when youths from the same socioeconomic levels were compared, nonwhites still had a higher level of police contact. After further analysis, the researchers were forced to conclude that no single variable predicted juvenile police contact better than racial background.[53]

Wolfgang found that school-related variables were significantly related to delinquent behavior. For one thing, the types of schools youths attended influenced whether they would eventually be picked up by police. A greater proportion of delinquents spent the major part of their school years in public schools, and fewer delinquents than nondelinquents attended parochial schools. Furthermore, 4 percent of delinquents, compared with 1 percent of nondelinquents, attended a public disciplinary institution.[54] Nondelinquents received more education than delinquents (11.24 years completed versus 9.96). While this relationship was consistent across racial lines, it was equally apparent that nonwhites averaged significantly less schooling than whites.

Another school-related factor, IQ, also distinguished delinquents from nondelinquents (see Chapter 4). The average IQ for nondelinquents was 107.87; for delinquents, it was 100.95. Again, this relationship was consistent across racial lines.

In a similar vein, school achievement levels were significantly related to delinquent activities: 12.8 percent of nondelinquents were rated "very low" on school achievement; 27.46 percent of delinquents received such negative ratings. Conversely, 19.48 percent of nondelinquents received a "very high" rating, while only 5.63 percent of delinquent youths received that rating. However, the researchers found major differences in school achievement between the races, with blacks doing considerably less well.[55]

CHRONIC OFFENDERS. The most well-known discovery of Wolfgang and associates was that of the so-called "chronic offender." The cohort data indicated that 54 percent (1,862) of the sample's delinquent youths were repeat offenders, while the remaining 46 percent (1,613) were one-time offenders. However, the repeaters could be further categorized as nonchronic recidivists and **chronic recidivists**. The former consisted of 1,235 youths who had been arrested more than once but less than five times and who made up 35.6 percent of all delinquents. The latter were a group of 627 boys arrested *five times or more* who accounted for 18 percent of the delinquents and 6 percent of the total sample of 9,945.[56]

It was the chronic offenders (known today as "the chronic 6 percent") who were involved in the most dramatic amounts of delinquent behavior; they were responsible for *5,305 offenses, or 51.9 percent of all offenses*. Even more striking was the involvement of chronic offenders in serious criminal acts. Of the entire sample, they committed 71 percent of the homicides, 73 percent of the rapes, 82 percent of the robberies, and 69 percent of the aggravated assaults.

Wolfgang and his associates found that arrest and juvenile court experience did little to deter the chronic offender. In fact, disposition was inversely related to chronic delinquency—the stricter the disposition youths received, the more likely they would be to engage in repeated delinquent behavior. Strict dispositions also increased the probability that further court action would be taken. Two factors stood out as encouraging recidivism—the seriousness of the original offense and the severity of disposition.

The researchers concluded that their analysis cast grave doubts on the efforts of the juvenile justice system to control or eliminate delinquent behavior:

> The judicial process and the correctional system do not seem to function effectively to restrain, discourage, or cure delinquency. Not only do a greater proportion of those who receive a severe disposition violate the law, but these violations are serious and rapid.[57]

BIRTH COHORT FOLLOW-UP. In a more recent analysis, Wolfgang and his associates followed a 10-percent sample of the original cohort (974 subjects) through their adulthood to age 30.[58] They divided the sample into three groups: those who had been juvenile offenders only; those who were adult offenders only; and persistent offenders (those who had offenses in both time periods). Those classified as chronic juvenile offenders in the original birth cohort made up 70 percent of the "persistent" group. They had an 80-percent chance of becoming adult offenders and a 50-percent chance of being arrested four or more times as adults. In comparison, subjects with no juvenile arrests had only an 18-percent chance of getting arrested as an adult. The chronic offenders also continued to engage in the most serious crimes. Though they accounted for only 15 percent of the follow-up sample, the former chronic delinquents were involved in 74 percent of all arrests and 82 percent of all serious crimes, such as homicide, rape, and robbery.

Although persistent delinquency did relate to adult criminality, there was a substantial drop in offensive behavior from the juvenile period to the adult period.[59] For example, more than half of the boys arrested twice as juveniles were never arrested as adults. While the pattern favored desistance, those youths who did commit crimes as adults were more likely to commit more serious, violent crimes than they did as juveniles.

BIRTH COHORT II. The juveniles who made up Wolfgang's original birth cohort were born in 1945. How have the behavior patterns of youths changed in subsequent years? To answer this question, Wolfgang and his associates Robert

Figlio and Paul Tracy conducted a new, larger birth cohort study of youths born in Philadelphia in 1958 and followed them until their maturity.[60] The 1958 cohort is larger than the original. There are 27,160 youths, of which 13,160 are males and 14,000 female.

What does this second cohort study reveal about delinquent behavior? For one thing, the proportion of delinquent youths in the second cohort (1,159 offenses per 1,000 subjects) was larger than that of the 1945 cohort (1,027). And since the second cohort involved more youths, those in the larger sample were involved in a total of 15,248 delinquent acts up to the age 18. However, the overall offending patterns in both cohorts were relatively similar; for example, about one third of the boys in both samples had at least one police contact before their eighteenth birthday.

The racial differences so apparent in the first cohort had less of an impact in the second. While a greater percentage of minority youth (42 percent) than white youth (23 percent) were delinquent, the differences between the races had declined since the earlier cohort data was analyzed (down two percent). The violent crime ratio, which was fifteen to one in the first cohort, had declined to about six to one in the second. In addition, the number of white chronic delinquents increased substantially (up five percent) while the number of chronic black offenders declined (down two percent).

Since the second cohort contains female subjects, it allows for comparing male and female delinquency patterns. As might be expected, males were two and a half times more likely to become involved in delinquent behavior than females. In addition, females who did get in trouble with the law were much more likely to be one-time offenders and less likely to be chronic delinquents. However, about seven percent of the delinquent females were classified as chronic recidivists (147 girls).

Of the males in the sample, chronic delinquents (five or more arrests for juveniles) made up 7.5 percent of the 1958 cohort (compared with 6.3 percent in 1945) and 23 percent of all delinquent offenders (compared with 18 percent in 1945). Chronic male delinquents continued to commit a disproportionate amount of crime. The 982 chronic male delinquents accounted for 9,240 offenses, or 61 percent of the total. They also committed a disproportionate amount of the most serious crimes: 61 percent of the homicides, 76 percent of the rapes, 73 percent of the robberies, and 65 percent of the aggravated assaults. The chronic female offender was less likely to be involved in serious crime.

It is interesting to note that the 1958 cohort, as a group, was involved in significantly more serious crime than the 1945 group. They committed more serious crimes (455 per 1,000) than the subjects in the first cohort (274 per 1,000); the violent crime ratio between the two samples was three to one.

The 1945 cohort study found that chronic offenders dominate the total juvenile crime rate and continue in their law-violating careers as adults. The newer cohort study is showing that the chronic delinquent syndrome is being maintained in a group of subjects who were born thirteen years later than the original cohort and, if anything, are more violent than their older brothers. Finally, the efforts of the justice system seem to have little preventive effect on the behavior of chronic offenders.

CHRONIC DELINQUENCY REVISITED. Wolfgang's pioneering effort to identify the chronic career offender has been supplemented by a number of other important research studies. Lyle Shannon also used the cohort approach to investigate career delinquency patterns.[61] He employed three cohorts totaling 6,127 youths born in 1942, 1949, and 1955 in Racine, Wisconsin. Shannon also encountered the phenomenon of the chronic career offender who engages in a disproportionate amount of delinquent behavior and later becomes involved in adult criminality. He found that less than 25 percent of each of the cohort's male subjects had five or more nontraffic offenses but accounted for 77 percent to 83 percent of all police contacts (by males) in their cohort. Similarly, from 8 percent to 14 percent of the persons in each cohort, respectively, were responsible for *all* the serious felony offenses. According to Shannon, if one wished to identify the persons responsible for about 75 percent of the felonies and much of the other crimes—then approximately five percent of each cohort—the persons with two or three felony contacts would be the target population. It is important to note that involvement of juveniles with the justice system did little to inhibit their adult criminality. Though most youths discontinued their criminal behavior after their teenage years, the few who continued are those who became well-known to the police when they were teenagers.

A number of other cohort studies have accumulated data that is supportive of the Wolfgang research. D. J. West and David Farrington's ongoing study of youths born in London during 1951 to 1954 has also showed that a small number of recidivists continue their behavior as adults and that arrest and conviction had little influence on their behavior other than to amplify the probability of their law violations: youths who had multiple convictions as juveniles tended to have multiple convictions as adults.[62] Similarly, Franklyn Dunford and Delbert Eliott employed a nationally selected sample of 1,725 youths to study the self-reported delinquency of chronic offenders who had remained undetected by police.[63] They were able to identify within their sample a *serious career offender type*, which they defined as a youth committing at least three serious felonies (such as aggravated or sexual assault, gang fights, car theft, or strong-arm robberies) two or more years in a row. In all, 70 of the subjects were classified as serious career offenders. Dunford and Eliott found that only 24 percent of the serious career offenders had ever been arrested, indicating that the problem of the chronic delinquent offender may actually be much greater than that found by studies that use police records exclusively to measure delinquent behavior.

The Chronic Offender in Court

These studies of **chronicity** depend largely on police records to define the chronic offender. A recent analysis by Howard Snyder of the National Center for Juvenile Justice of 69,000 youth who were processed to the juvenile court in Arizona and Utah reveals a similar delinquent career pattern.[64]

According to the Snyder research, the majority of youths (59 percent) were referred to juvenile court only once. Of the remaining 41 percent who recidivated, the majority were males whose first offense was robbery and aggravated assault. Conversely, those least likely to recidivate were females referred for underage drinking, truancy, shoplifting, or drug law violations.

Snyder found that juveniles who became chronic problems to the juvenile court started their careers at a relatively early age (9, 10, or 11) and their careers were more likely to contain a referral for a serious violent crime. The most chronic offenders, those with four or more court referrals (about 16 percent of the sample), accounted for over half of all petitions to juvenile court. Youths who had two juvenile court referrals by age 16 *had about a 70 percent chance of recidivating*.

Snyder's research confirms earlier cohort studies because it shows that a small group of persistent offenders account for a great deal of the offending in a particular jurisdiction. His data indicates that persistent offenders can be identified very early in their offending career, usually by age 15. Snyder suggests that rather than waiting for a fourth or fifth offense before classifying them as chronic offenders, programs be developed to focus resources on at-risk youth very early in their offending careers before they become locked into a criminal life-style.[65]

Understanding Chronic Offenders

There is little question that the concept of chronicity has become established within the study of delinquency. Yet many questions remain to be answered about chronic offenders. Foremost is how can potential repeat offenders be identified early in their careers so they can be made the target of social intervention strategies. A number of prominent criminologists have undertaken the task of identifying the personal traits of chronic offenders and predicting their future behavior. For example, using existing data on delinquent careers, Alfred Blumstein, David Farrington, and Soumyo Moitra found that youths could effectively be sorted into three categories: **innocents,** who were never involved with law enforcement; **desisters,** who suffered arrest but had a small chance of recidivating; and **persisters,** chronic offenders with a relatively high chance of repeat offending. They found that seven variables might be used to effectively predict chronic offending: conviction for crime prior to age 13; low family income; troublesome rating by teachers and peers at ages 8 to 10; poor public school performance by age 10; psychomotor clumsiness; low nonverbal IQ; and having a brother or sister convicted of a crime.[66] They argue that anticrime policies could be tailored around these traits, for example, by helping poor families attain higher incomes or giving youth with poor scholastic achievement special tutoring.

Offense Specialization

It is also important to develop more knowledge about the offending career patterns of chronic delinquent offenders. It is commonly believed that persistent offenders do not "specialize" in any one type of behavior but with few exceptions commit a variety of delinquent acts over their offending careers. For example, they commit a burglary, go on to steal a car, and then shoplift from a store. Those who do specialize seem to be involved in relatively minor status-type offenses, such as running away from home.[67]

There is, however, some recent evidence that over their lifetime, chronic offenders begin to specialize in particular forms of delinquency.[68] For example, Randall Shelden found that some chronic offenders specialized in serious crimes while others could be categorized as "chronic nuisance offenders" who were referred to court on status- and neglect-type petitions. The "nuisance" offenders appear to have significantly different offending patterns than the chronic serious offenders.[69]

In one important study using a very large sample of about 70,000 court-adjudicated youths in Arizona and Utah, David Farrington, Howard Snyder, and Terrence Finnegan found that about 20 percent of the group could be considered offense "specialists" who persistently committed one type of offense.[70]

Farrington and his associates found that the delinquent acts most likely to be the domain of "specialists" included running away from home, liquor violations, incorrigibility, burglary, motor vehicle theft, and drug violations. Not surprisingly, two of these are status offenses (which a desperate youth might repeatedly turn to for survival), two are criminal offenses that require some degree of skill (burglary and auto theft), and two involve substance abuse (and therefore might indicate habitual behavior). In addition, Farrington found that there was some tendency for youths who were repeatedly sent to juvenile court to *escalate* their delinquent activities; that is, kids who are continually petitioned to court for such serious offenses as robbery and aggravated assault tend to recidivate in ever increasing numbers.

Policy Implications of the Chronic Offender Concept

If relatively few chronic offenders commit a great portion of all delinquent acts and then progress into adult criminality, it follows that steps could be taken to limit their criminal opportunities. One approach would be to create programs to identify violent, persistent offenders at an early stage of their offending careers and then devote a significant share of juvenile justice resources to their treatment and control.[71] It might be possible to create special legal provisions requiring that young offenders who commit multiple serious crimes serve long periods of confinement. Such a policy might be justified because research indicates that delinquents who commit the most persistent and serious offenses during their adolescence are also the ones most likely to become adult offenders.[72] If we assume that even chronic persisters eventually age out of crime, locking them up for an extended period would reduce the time they had available for criminal enterprise.

Another approach is suggested by Peter Greenwood of the Rand Corporation. Greenwood conducted research that found that adult chronic offenders share seven characteristics, including a long history (beginning as a juvenile) of arrest, conviction, and incarceration; heroin or barbiturate use; and a poor employment record. Greenwood argues that if offenders with this background were given long prison sentences, the crime rate would decline significantly; this policy is referred to as **selective incapacitation**.[73]

These solutions are often troubling to civil libertarians since they involve the prediction of a person's future behavior. Is it not possible that some people will be unfairly punished because their background characteristics mistakenly indicate they are potential chronic offenders? Conversely, might not some serious offenders be overlooked because they have a conventional background? No prediction method is totally accurate, and error can involve a significant infringement on a person's civil rights. For example, Andrew Von Hirsch and Donald Gottfredson argue that Greenwood's method of predicting chronic offending is mistaken more than half the time.[74] Recent research by Scott Decker and Barbara Salert found that the Greenwood scale is highly inaccurate when used to predict individual cases of chronic offending.[75]

There is also the danger that early identification, arrest, and custody of youth will promote rather than inhibit their delinquent careers. For example, Pamela Tontodonato found that youths who have three arrests by age 15 have a greater likelihood of accumulating additional more serious arrests than those juveniles who accumulate arrests more slowly.[76] While an intensive law enforcement policy aimed at multiple offenders may have political appeal, it might actually produce a higher overall delinquency rate.

Despite any problems civil libertarians may have with the concept of the chronic career offender, it already has had a profound influence on the daily operations of the juvenile justice system. Few concepts have shaken the study of crime and delinquency as much as the "discovery" of the chronic delinquent offender. The belief that a few persistent offenders are responsible for a significant portion of the serious crime in a community has been translated into a number of policy initiatives within the juvenile justice system. First, it has strengthened the position of conservative policymakers who call for a "get tough" approach to juvenile delinquency. While it might seem futile, cruel, and expensive to lock up all juvenile offenders, it makes both economic and practical sense to incarcerate the few chronic offenders who are responsible for most of the crime problem.[77] This view has resulted in the development of tough new juvenile sentencing codes, as well as the transfer of serious delinquency cases to the adult court.

CASE IN POINT

You are a newly appointed judge in the county juvenile court.

A 12-year-old boy, Joseph L., is petitioned to court on a robbery charge. It seems that Joseph, a five-foot-four, 110-pound youngster, used a knife in a school yard robbery. You notice that this is already his fifth offense. He was arrested at age 9 on a petty larceny and six months later was picked up for breaking into a home. At age 10, he was again arrested on a break-in, and at 11, he assaulted a younger boy after school and beat him badly. Despite his youth, the boy seems defiant and unafraid when he is found to be a delinquent.

At the sentencing hearing, the prosecutor presents evidence that Joseph has all the character traits of a chronic offender: early onset of delinquency, multiple arrests, increased seriousness of offenses, a history of school failure, low intelligence, and siblings who are law violators. The prosecution demands a three-year placement in the state correctional facility for dangerous youth. Defense counsel asks for community supervision. She claims that the state's high-security juvenile facility usually houses much older offenders, many of whom are over 16. Placement will only exacerbate an already serious situation. Considering the boy's tender age, the case can better be handled by community treatment agencies.

The prosecutor counters that chronic offenders will not be impressed with leniency, and therefore, community treatment is a waste of time. Though the prosecutor agrees with the defense counsel's claim that placement with older delinquents will certainly diminish any chance of future rehabilitation, he believes that this youth has already proven himself beyond control. The need of society for safety outweighs the remote likelihood

continued

of rehabilitation. A period of incarceration is needed in this case to protect the public from a dangerous chronic offender.

Is it fair to place this child with older youth in a high-security treatment center?

Should the needs of society outweigh a child's right to treatment?

Should predictions of future behavior patterns influence the treatment of children?

SUMMARY

There are a number of consistent patterns in the delinquency rate that have proven to be stable over time. One of the most enduring relationships is between age and delinquency. Most experts agree that people commit less crime as they mature; this is called the aging-out process. One school of thought is that all people commit less crime as they age, while another is that some chronic offenders begin their criminal careers early in childhood and persist into adulthood.

There is general agreement that males are more delinquent than females. While the gender ratio is quite similar for petty or nonserious crimes, it is far greater for index or felony offenses. There are also racial differences in the arrest statistics. One view is that these differences reflect police bias in the arrest process, while another view is that black teens are actually more delinquent because of the effects of racism, poverty, and alienation.

There is also disagreement over the relationship between social class and delinquency. While some experts do not believe that class position influences crime rates, others believe that lower-class youth are much more likely to become delinquents and that delinquency rates are higher in lower-class neighborhoods. Recent evidence seems to support the latter position.

Finally, the chapter reviewed the nature and extent of chronic delinquency: kids who have multiple and persistent arrests. It is now believed that a few offenders account for a great majority of serious crimes and that they do not age out of crime.

QUESTIONS FOR DISCUSSION

1. What factors contribute to the aging-out process?
2. Why are males more delinquent than females? Is it a matter of life-style, culture, or physical properties?
3. Discuss the racial differences found in the crime rate. What factors account for the differences in the black and white crime rates?
4. Discuss the controversy surrounding the role social class plays in delinquency. Do you believe that middle-class youth are as delinquent as lower-class boys?
5. What can be done to control the chronic delinquent? Is it fair to punish someone because he or she fits the profile of a potential repeat offender?

KEY TERMS

aging-out	Marvin Wolfgang
desistance	cohort
spontaneous remission	chronic recidivists
age of onset	chronicity
social class	innocents
James Short	desisters
F. Ivan Nye	persisters
aggregate measures	selective incapacitation

NOTES

1. See, generally, David Farrington, "Age and Crime," in Michael Tonry and Norval Morris, eds., *Crime and Justice, An Annual Review*, vol. 7 (Chicago: University of Chicago Press, 1986, pp. 189–250.

2. Census data is from U.S. Department of Commerce, *Population Projections, 1989* (Washington, D.C.: U.S. Government Printing Office, 1990).

3. D. Wayne Osgood, Patrick O'Malley, Jerald Bachman, and Lloyd Johnston, "Time Trends and Age Trends in Arrests and Self-Reported Illegal Behavior," *Criminology* 27:389–419 (1989); Patrick O'Malley, Jerald Bachman, and Lloyd Johnston, "Period, Age and Cohort Effects on Substance Abuse among Young Americans: A Decade of Change, 1976–1986," *American Journal of Public Health* 78:1315–21 (1989); Darrell Steffensmeier, Emilie Allan, Miles Harer, and Cathy Streifel, "Age and the Distribution of Crime," *American Journal of Sociology* 94:803–31 (1989); Alfred Blumstein and Jacqueline Cohen, "Characterizing Criminal Careers," *Science* 237:985–91 (1987).

4. John Laub, David Clark, Leslie Siegel, and James Garofalo, *Trends in Juvenile Crime in the United States: 1973–1983* (Albany, New York: Hindelang Criminal Justice Research Center, 1987). Preliminary Draft.

5. Travis Hirschi and Michael Gottfredson, "Age and the Explanation of Crime," *American Journal of Sociology* 89:552–84 (1983).

6. Michael Gottfredson and Travis Hirschi, "The True Value of Lambda Would Appear to Be Zero: An Essay on Career Criminals, Criminal Careers, Selective Incapacitation, Cohort Studies, and Related Topics," *Criminology* 24:213–34 (1986); further support for their position can be found in Lawrence Cohen and Kenneth Land, "Age Structure and Crime," *American Sociological Review* 52:170–83 (1987).

7. David Greenberg, "Age, Crime, and Social Explanation," *American Journal of Sociology* 91:1–21 (1985).

8. Farrington, "Age and Crime," pp. 236–237.

9. *Ibid.*

10. Marvin Wolfgang, Robert Figlio, and Thorsten Sellin, *Delinquency in a Birth Cohort* (Chicago: University of Chicago Press, 1972); Lyle Shannon, *Assessing the Relationship of Adult Criminal Careers to Juvenile Careers: A Summary* (Washington, D.C.: U.S. Department of Justice, 1982); D. J. West and David P. Farrington, *The Delinquent Way of Life* (London: Hienemann, 1977); Donna Hamparian, Richard Schuster, Simon Dinitz, and John Conrad, *The Violent Few* (Lexington, Mass.: Lexington Books, 1978).

11. Rolf Loeber and Howard Snyder, "Rate of Offending in Juvenile Careers: Findings of Constancy and Change in Lambda," *Criminology* 28:97–109 (1990).

12. Travis Hirschi and Michael Gottfredson, "Age and Crime, Logic and Scholarship: Comment on Greenberg," *American Journal of Sociology* 91:22–27 (1985); Hirschi and Gottfredson, "All Wise after the Fact Learning Theory, Again: Reply to Baldwin," *American Journal of Sociology* 90:1330–33 (1985); John Baldwin, "Thrill and Adventure Seeking and the Age Distribution of Crime: Comment on Hirschi and Gottfredson," *American Journal of Sociology* 90:1326–29.

13. O'Malley, Bachman, and Johnston, "Period, Age, and Cohort Effects on Substance Use among Young Americans."

14. Cesare Lombroso, *The Female Offender* (New York: Appleton, 1920); W. I. Thomas, *The Unadjusted Girl* (New York: Harper & Row, 1923).

15. Chapter 5 will discuss the work of Albert Cohen (see note 10) and Richard Cloward and Lloyd Ohlin (see note 11), who stress delinquent behavior as a product of minority-youth culture.

16. For a discussion of sex bias, see Meda Chesney-Lind, "Guilty by Reason of Sex: Young Women and the Criminal Justice System." Paper presented before the American Society of Criminology, Toronto, 1980.

17. Helene Raskin White and Randy LaGrange, "An Assessment of Gender Effects in Self-Report Delinquency," *Sociological Focus* 20:195–213 (1987); Gary Jensen and Raymond Eve, "Sex Differences in Delinquency: An Examination of Popular Sociological Explanation," *Criminology* 13:427–48 (1976); Michael Hindelang, "Age, Sex, and the Versatility of Delinquent Involvements," *Social Problems* 18:522–35 (1979); James Short and F. Ivan Nye, "Extent of Unrecorded Juvenile Delinquency, Tentative Conclusions," *Journal of Criminal Law, Criminology and Police Science* 49:296–302 (1958).

18. White and LaGrange, "An Assessment of Gender Effects in Self-Report Delinquency," p. 302; see, generally, Michael Hindelang, Travis Hirschi, and Joseph Weis, *Measuring Delinquency* (Beverly Hills, Calif.: Sage, 1981).

19. Jay Williams and Martin Gold, "From Delinquent Behavior to Official Delinquency," *Social Problems* 20:209–29 (1972).

20. Rosemary Sarri, "Gender Issues in Juvenile Justice," *Crime and Delinquency* 29:381–97 (1983).

21. Leroy Gould, "Who Defines Delinquency: A Comparison of Self-Report and Officially Reported Indices of Delinquency for Three Racial Groups," *Social Problems* 16:325–36 (1969); Harwin Voss, "Ethnic Differentials in Delinquency in Honolulu," *Journal of Criminal Law, Criminology, and Police Science* 54:322–27 (1963); Ronald Akers, Marvin Krohn, Marcia Radosevich, and Lonn Lanza-Kaduce, "Social Characteristics and Self-Reported Delinquency," in Gary Jensen, ed., *Sociology of Delinquency* (Beverly Hills, Calif.: Sage, 1981), pp. 48–62.

22. Jerald Bachman, Lloyd Johnston, and Patrick O'Malley, *Monitoring the Future: Questionnaire Responses from the Nation's High School Seniors, 1986* (Ann Arbor, Mich.: Institute for Social Research, 1988), pp. 102–4.

23. David Huizinga and Delbert Elliott, "Juvenile Offenders: Prevalence, Offender Incidence, and Arrest Rates by Race," *Crime and Delinquency* 33:206–23 (1987). See also Dale Dannefer and Russell Schutt, "Race and Juvenile Justice Processing in Court and Police Agencies," *American Journal of Sociology* 87:1113–32 (1982).

24. Paul Tracy, "Race and Class Differences in Official and Self-Reported Delinquency," in Marvin Wolfgang, Terence Thornberry, and Robert Figlio, eds., *From Boy to Man, from Delinquency to Crime*, (Chicago: University of Chicago Press, 1987), p. 120.

25. Michael Hindelang, "Race and Involvement in Common Law Personal Crimes," *American Sociological Review* 43:93–109 (1978).

26. Laub, Clark, Siegel, and Garofalo, *Trends in Juvenile Crime in the United States: 1973–1983*.

27. Douglas Smith and Jody Klein, "Police Control of Interpersonal Disputes," *Social Problems* 31:468–81 (1984); Nathan Goldman, *The Differential Selection of Juvenile Offenders for Court Appearance* (New York: National Council on Crime and Delinquency, 1963); Aaron Cicourel, *The Social Organization of Juvenile Justice* (New York: John Wiley & Sons, 1968); Irvin Piliavin and Scott Briar, "Police Encounters with Juveniles," *American Journal of Sociology* 70:206 (1964); Dannefer and Schutt, "Race and Juvenile Justice Processing in Court and Police Agencies."

28. Donna Bishop and Charles Frazier, "The Influence of Race in Juvenile Justice Processing," *Journal of Research in Crime and Delinquency* 25:242–63 (1989).

29. For a general review, see William Wilbanks, *The Myth of a Racist Criminal Justice System* (Monterey, Cal.: Brooks-Cole, 1987).

30. Daniel Georges-Abeyie, cited in James Byrne and Robert Sampson, *The Social Ecology of Crime* (New York: Springer-Verlag, 1986).

31. Tom Joe, "Economic Inequality: The Picture in Black and White," *Crime and Delinquency* 33:287–99 (1987).

32. Troy Duster, "Crime, Youth Unemployment, and the Black Urban Underclass," *Crime and Delinquency* 33:300–16 (1987); Joe, "Economic Inequality: The Picture in Black and White."

33. Duster, "Crime, Youth Unemployment, and the Black Underclass," pp. 301–3.

34. Carl Pope and William Feyerherm, "Minority Status and Juvenile Processing: An Assessment of the Research Literature." A paper presented at the American Society of Criminology, Reno, Nevada, November 1989.

35. Robert Nash Parker and Allan Horwitz, "Unemployment, Crime, and Imprisonment: A Panel Approach," *Criminology* 24:751–73 (1986).

36. For a general review of these issues, see Byrne and Sampson, *The Social Ecology of Crime*.

37. John Braithwaite, "The Myth of Social Class and Criminality Reconsidered," *American Sociological Review* 46:36–57 (1981).

38. James Short and F. Ivan Nye, "Reported Behavior as a Criterion of Deviant Behavior," *Social Problems* 5:207–13 (1958).

39. F. Ivan Nye, James Short, and Virgil Olsen, "Socioeconomic Status and Delinquent Behavior," *American Journal of Sociology* 63:381–89 (1958); Robert Dentler and Lawrence Monroe, "Social Correlates of Early Adolescent Theft," *American Sociological Review* 26:733–43 (1961); John Clark and Eugene Wenninger, "Socioeconomic Class and Areas as Correlates of Illegal Behavior among Juveniles," *American Sociological Review* 27:826–34 (1962); William Arnold, "Continuities in Research: Scaling Delinquent Behavior," *Social Problems* 13:59–66 (1965); LaMar Empey and Maynard Erickson, "Hidden Delinquency and Social Status," *Social Forces* 44:546–54 (1966); Ronald Akers, "Socioeconomic Status and Delinquent Behavior: A Retest," *Journal of Research in Crime and Delinquency* 1:38–46 (1964); Voss, "Ethnic Differentials in Delinquency in Honolulu."

40. Martin Gold, "Undetected Delinquent Behavior," *Journal of Research in Crime and Delinquency* 3:35 (1966).

41. Williams and Gold, "From Delinquent Behavior to Official Delinquency."

42. For an analysis of inner-city delinquency see, Jefferey Fagan, Elizabeth Piper, and Melinda Moore, "Violent Delinquents and Urban Youths," *Criminology* 24:439–71 (1986).

43. Douglas Smith and G. Roger Jarjoura, "Social Structure and Criminal Victimization," *Journal of Research in Crime and Delinquency* 25:25–72 (1988).

44. Charles Tittle, Wayne Villemez, and Douglas Smith, "The Myth of Social Class and Criminality: An Empirical Assessment of the Empirical Evidence," *American Sociological Review* 43:643–56 (1978).

45. Gary Jensen and Kevin Thompson, "What's Class Got to Do with It? A Further Examination of Power-Control Theory," *American Journal of Sociology* 95:1009–23 (1990); Paul Tracy, "Race and Class Differences in Official and Self-Reported Delinquency," in Wolfgang, Thornberry, and Figlio, eds., *From Boy to Man, from Delinquency to Crime*, p. 118.

46. Delbert Eliott and Suzanne Ageton, "Reconciling Race and Class Differences in Self-Reported and Official Estimates of Delinquency," *American Sociological Review* 45:95–110 (1980). For a similar view, see generally Braithwaite, "The Myth of Social Class and Criminality Reconsidered."

47. David Brownfield, "Social Class and Violent Behavior," *Criminology* 24:421–38 (1986); see also Margaret Farnsworth, Terence Thornberry, Alan Lizotte, and Marvin Krohn, "Social Background and the Early Onset of Delinquency: Exploring the Utility of Various Indicators of Social Class Background", Working Paper No. 4, *Rochester Youth Development Study* (Albany, N.Y.: Hindelang Research Center, June 1990).

48. Arnold Barnett, Alfred Blumstein, and David Farrington, "A Prospective Test of a Criminal Career Model," *Criminology* 27:373–88 (1989).

49. Wolfgang, Figlio, and Sellin, *Delinquency in a Birth Cohort*.

50. *Ibid.*, p. 4.

51. See Thorsten Sellin and Marvin Wolfgang, *The Measurement of Delinquency* (New York: Wiley, 1964), p. 120.

52. *Ibid.*

53. Wolfgang, Figlio, and Sellin, *Delinquency in a Birth Cohort*, p. 54.

54. *Ibid.*

55. *Ibid.*

56. *Ibid.*, p. 57.

57. *Ibid.*

58. Wolfgang, Thornberry and Figlio, eds., *From Boy to Man, from Delinquency to Crime*; see also Paul Tracy and Robert Figlio, "Chronic Recidivism in the 1958 Birth Cohort." Paper presented at the American Society of Criminology meeting, Toronto, October 1982, p. 3. This and the next sections lean heavily on this work.

59. *Ibid.*, p. 34.

60. Paul Tracy, Marvin Wolfgang, and Robert Figlio, *Delinquency in Two Birth Cohorts, Executive Summary* (Washington, D.C.: U.S. Department of Justice, 1985).

61. Lyle Shannon, *Assessing the Relationship of Adult Criminal Careers to Juvenile Careers: A Summary* (Washington, D.C.: U.S. Department of Justice, 1982).

62. West and Farrington, *The Delinquent Way of Life*, p. 15. See also Hamparian, Schuster, Dinitz, and Conrad, *The Violent Few*.

63. Franklyn Dunford and Delbert Eliott, "Identifying Career Offenders Using Self-Reported Data," *Journal of Research in Crime and Delinquency* 21:57–86 (1984).

64. Howard Snyder, *Court Careers of Juvenile Offenders* (Washington, D.C.: Office of Juvenile Justice and Delinquency Prevention, 1988).

65. *Ibid.*, p. 66.

66. Alfred Blumstein, David Farrington, and Soumyo Moitra, "Delinquency Careers: Innocents, Desisters, and Persisters," in Michael Tonry and Norval Morris, eds. *Crime and Justice, An Annual Review*, vol. 6 (Chicago: University of Chicago Press, 1985), pp. 187–220.

67. Malcolm Klein, "Offence Specialization and Versatility among Juveniles," *British Journal Criminology* 24:185–94 (1984); see also, Kimberly Kempf, "Specialization and the Criminal Career," *Criminology* 25:399–420 (1987); Steven Lab, "Patterns in Juvenile Misbehavior," *Crime and Delinquency* 30:293–308 (1984).

68. Robert Bursik, "The Dynamics of Specialization in Juvenile Offenses," *Social Forces* 58:851–64 (1980).

69. Randall Shelden, "The Chronic Delinquent: Some Clarifications of a Vague Concept," *Juvenile and Family Court Journal* 40:37–44 (1989).

70. David Farrington, Howard Snyder, and Terrence Finnegan, "Specialization in Juvenile Court Careers," *Criminology* 26:461–85 (1988).

71. Jeffrey Fagan, "Social and Legal Policy Dimensions of Violent Juvenile Crime," *Criminal Justice and Behavior* 17:93–133 (1990).

72. Kimberly Kempf, "Crime Severity and Criminal Career Progression," *Journal of Criminal Law and Criminology* 79:524–40 (1988).

73. Peter Greenwood, *Selective Incapacitation* (Santa Monica, Calif.: Rand Corporation, 1982).

74. Andrew Von Hirsch and Donald Gottfredson, "Selective Incapacitation: Some Queries about Research Design and Equity," *New York University Review of Law and Social Change* 12:11–19 (1984).

75. Scott Decker and Barbara Salert, "Predicting the Career Criminal: An Empirical Test of the Greenwood Scale," *Journal of Criminal Law and Criminology* 77:215–36 (1986).

76. Pamela Tontodonato, "Explaining Rate Changes in Delinquent Arrest Transitions Using Event History Analysis," *Criminology* 26:439–59 (1988).

77. Kimberly Kempf, "Career Criminals in the 1958 Philadelphia Birth Cohort," *Criminal Justice Review* 15: In press (1990).

Theories of Delinquency

What causes delinquency? Social scientists have speculated on this problem for two hundred years. They have organized observed facts about delinquent behavior into complex theoretical models. A theory is a statement that explains the relationship between abstract concepts in a meaningful way. For example, if scientists observe that delinquency rates are usually higher in neighborhoods with high unemployment rates, poor housing, and inadequate schools, they might theorize that environmental conditions influence delinquent behavior. This theory suggests that social conditions can exert a powerful influence on human behavior.

Since the study of delinquency is essentially interdisciplinary, it is not surprising that a variety of theoretical models have been formulated to explain juvenile misbehavior. Each reflects the training and orientation of its creator. Consequently, theories of delinquency reflect many different avenues of inquiry, including biology, psychology, sociology, political science, and economics. Chapter 4 reviews theories that hold that delinquency is essentially an individual factor, caused either by personal choices and decision making or by psychological and biological aspects of human development. Chapters 5, 6, and 7 review sociological theories of delinquency. Chapter 5 reviews those theories that hold that youthful misbehavior is caused by a child's place in the social structure; Chapter 6 covers theories that regard the child's relationships with social institutions and processes as the key to understanding delinquency. Chapter 7 views how delinquents may be the victim of class conflict and struggle. Finally, Chapter 8 reviews theories devoted specifically to the female delinquent.

To the student, the variety of delinquency theories is often confusing. Logic dictates that the competing and contradictory theoretical models presented here cannot all be correct. Yet every branch of social science—sociology, psychology, political science, economics—contains competing theoretical models. Why people behave the way they do and how society functions are issues that are far from being settled. So do not lose patience! Recognize that theories of delinquency are attempts to bring together existing knowledge in an attempt to explain the onset and patterns of delinquent behavior. These explanations take on different perspectives because it is possible to look at the world differently and to create alternate explanations for similar facts and data. The variation in delinquency theories reflects their creators' visions of the world and interpretations of events.

4

The Individual Offender
Choice and Developmental Theories

The dynamic center of the whole problem of delinquency and crime will ever be the individual offender.

William Healy
The Individual Delinquent (1915)

In March 1989, Cameron Kocher was playing with friends at the home of Richard and Trudi Ratti, his next-door neighbors in a small Pennsylvania town. When scolded for making a mess, Cameron angrily went home. Soon after, a shot rang out of nowhere, striking and killing 7-year-old Jessica Ann Carr, who was playing in the yard. A little while later, Cameron returned to the Rattis' backyard with a bandage over his eye. While he claimed he had injured himself with a knife, police believed that the crescent-shaped cut was left by the telescopic sight of a .35-caliber hunting rifle. Prosecutors argued that Cameron went home and deliberately shot Jessica from a bedroom window with a gun that his father had taught him to use. Charged with murder, the 10-year-old Cameron could receive a life sentence if found guilty.[1]

Cases like Cameron's seem to indicate that some forms of delinquent behavior can be explained by an individual's psychological and physical traits, ranging from genetic defects to impulsivity and from impaired intelligence to psychosis. If they were not "abnormal," why would youths such as Cameron commit wanton and senseless acts of violence? Why would they use drugs generally known to be highly addictive and destructive? Why would they vandalize public buildings?

Conversely, if delinquents were a "product of their environment," as some suggest, how is it possible that many at-risk youths, residing in the most crime-filled neighborhoods, live conventional, law-abiding lives? Longitudinal research such as Wolfgang's cohort study have shown that relatively few youths in any population become hard-core delinquents.[2] There are even differences in behavior patterns among members of the same family. To some theorists, the facts that only a few youths in any area become chronic delinquents and that interfamily differences exist prove that delinquency cannot be viewed purely as a function of social or environmental factors. Consequently, some scholars argue that the onset of delinquency can be traced to factors deeply rooted in the individual, which may have been present at birth or developed early in childhood.

One such view of delinquency, referred to as **choice theory,** suggests that young offenders engage in antisocial activity because they believe their actions will be beneficial and profitable. Whether they join a gang, steal cars, or sell drugs, they are motivated by the reasoned belief that crime can be a relatively risk-free way to better their life-style. They have little fear of getting caught or of the consequences of punishment. Fantasies of riches produced by criminal acts fuel their antisocial activities.

However, it is evident that all youthful misbehavior cannot be traced to the profit motive and criminal entrepreneurship. Some delinquent acts, especially violent ones, seem irrational, selfish, and/or hedonistic. There are many forms of delinquency, such as substance abuse and vandalism, that appear more impulsive than rational. It is believed that these antisocial behaviors may be inspired by aberrant personal traits—physical and/or psychological—that govern behavioral choices. While some youths may choose to commit crimes simply because they desire conventional luxuries and power, others may be influenced by constitutional abnormalities, such as hyperactivity, low intelligence, biochemical imbalance, or genetic defects. This view of delinquency is referred to here generally as **developmental theory** because it links delinquency to biological and psychological traits and conditions that control human development.

Choice and developmental theory are linked together because they focus on individual mental and behavioral processes as the cause of delinquency. They share common ground because the motivation for choosing to commit a delinquent act may in fact stem from biological and/or psychological roots. While some delinquents may be purely a "product of their environment," others are motivated by forces ingrained within their own personalities and biological makeups.

This chapter first covers those theoretical models that focus on individual choice. Then, discussion turns to the view that the biological and psychological development of some youngsters makes them violent, aggressive, and antisocial. Finally, an attempt to integrate individual choice and development factors into a singular view of delinquent behavior causation will be analyzed.

CHOICE THEORY AND DELINQUENCY

The first formal explanations of crime and delinquency held that human behavior was a matter of choice. Since it was assumed that people had **free will** to choose their behavior, those who violated the law were motivated by personal needs: greed; revenge; survival; hedonism.

Over 200 years ago, **utilitarian** philosophers **Cesare Beccaria** and **Jeremy Bentham** founded what is today referred to as **classical criminology.** According to this view, people weigh the benefits and consequences of future actions before deciding to commit crime.[3] Most would cease their actions if the potential pain associated with a behavior outweighed its anticipated gain. Even law-violating behavior becomes attractive if the rewards seem far greater than the potential punishment.[4] For example, when a youth makes the decision to become a drug dealer, he or she weighs the possible benefits of drug dealing, such as a cash flow sufficient to buy cars, clothes, and other luxury items, with the potential penalties, such as arrest followed by a long period of confinement. If the potential drug dealer believes that the chances of apprehension are minimal and the potential punishment "manageable," he or she will more likely *choose* to become a dealer than if he or she believed that drug traffickers are almost always caught and punished by lengthy prison terms. Put simply, in order to deter or prevent crime, the potential criminal must be convinced that the pain of punishment outweighs the benefit of illegal gain.[5]

DEVELOPMENT OF CHOICE THEORY

The classical criminologists argued that punishment should be only severe enough to deter a particular offense and that punishments should be graded according to the seriousness of particular crimes: "let the punishment fit the crime." For example, Beccaria argued that it would be foolish to punish pickpockets and murderers in a similar fashion because this would encourage thieves to kill the victims or witnesses to their crimes.[6] The popularity of the classical approach was in part responsible for the development of the prison as an alternative to physical punishment and for the eventual creation of criminal sentences geared to the seriousness of crimes.[7] The classical approach dominated the policy of the U.S. justice system for about 150 years.

By the mid-twentieth century, the concept of the "rational criminal" was challenged by those who believed that crime and delinquency were products of social forces, such as environment and socialization. Breakthroughs in psychology and sociology showed that human behavior was often controlled by outside influences, such as family, school, and peer relations, and that the concept of "free will" was merely wishful thinking. Mental health professionals argued that delinquents should be treated and not punished for their misdeeds. Delinquents were viewed as troubled or "sick" individuals who needed **rehabilitation**, rather than punishment; this was known as the **medical model** of crime.[8] Rather than be punished in prisons for their crimes, youthful (and adult) criminals were offered rehabilitation in secure treatment facilities until they were deemed fit to return to society. Since this position was particularly amenable to the juvenile justice system's *parens patriae* philosophy, the concept of "punishing" delinquents all but disappeared during the twentieth century.[9]

Reviving the Rational Delinquent

In the past few years, the view that delinquents *choose* to violate the law has regained prominence as a theoretical approach to the study and control of delinquency. To some experts, the failure of treatment-oriented programs to prevent delinquency or rehabilitate known offenders shows that young law violators are not merely society's victims beset by a string of insurmountable social problems. If they were, educational enrichment, family counseling, job training programs, and the like should be more effective alternatives to crime. Instead of being viewed as social outcasts, delinquent youths are seen as processing information in order to make decisions: Will this act be good for me? Do I enjoy doing it? How will others view me? What are the consequences?[10]

The reasoning goes that youths, immune to the benefits of treatment, may be more receptive to the threat of punishments sufficiently severe to convince them to choose conventional over criminal behaviors. The well-known social scientists James Q. Wilson and Richard Herrnstein conclude in their controversial book *Crime and Human Nature* that delinquent behavior is deterrable if offenders experience firsthand the consequences attached to their behavior:

> That is, a person may become less likely to commit an offense either because he has learned (by experiencing punishment) that certain consequences of that offense are more likely than he had once supposed or because he has come to take more seriously the consequences (again, by having experienced them) that he knew were attached to that behavior.[11]

Wilson and Herrnstein, among others, have embraced the utility of punishment as a delinquency control mechanism. The **rational choice** view has also supported the emergence of profit-making teenage drug dealers. These young and well-armed entrepreneurs are seeking to cash in on a lucrative, albeit illegal, "business enterprise." Their behavior seems to be motivated by a chance to make big profits, and their techniques are well thought out and clearly "rational."

In sum, the rational choice theory views delinquents as individuals who are responsible for their actions and who might respond better to the fear of punishment than to the preventive influence of rehabilitatory treatment. Choice theory reemerged recently both as a force in the study of the causes of delinquency and as a guide for creating policies that can effectively control delinquent behavior.[12]

THE CONCEPT OF RATIONAL CHOICE

The concept that crime and delinquency are functions of the opportunities presented to motivated offenders has received widespread support from prominent social scientists.[13] Law-violating behavior is viewed as an event that occurs when an offender decides to take the chance of violating the law after considering his or her own personal situation (need for money, personal values, learning experiences, opportunities for conventional success), personal values (conscience, moral values, need for peer approval), and situational factors (how well the target is protected; whether people are at home; how wealthy the neighborhood is; what is the likelihood of getting caught; if apprehended, how much punishment will he or she receive). Accordingly, the decision to commit a specific type of crime and the subsequent entry into a delinquent life-style is a matter of personal decision making based on a weighing of available information; hence, the term *rational choice.*

Conversely, the decision to forego law-violating behavior may be based on the offender's perception that the economic benefits are no longer there or the probability of successfully completing a crime is less than the chances of being caught and punished. For example, the aging-out process may occur because older offenders desist after they realize that the risks of crime are greater than its potential profit.[14] The "solution" to delinquency, therefore, may be the formulation of policies that will cause the potential delinquent to choose conventional solutions rather than criminal.

Choosing Delinquency

Rational choice theorists believe that no matter how pathological or socially maladjusted youths may be, they process information that leads them to choose one target or crime method over another. The focus then is on the crime and not the offender. For example, why is a particular house in a wealthy middle-class suburb chosen by a teenage burglar? How does crime choice differ between neighborhoods and areas? Does the presence of lighting, security alarms, and/or guard dogs influence the decision to commit crime?

Rational choice theory views the concept of crime and criminality as two separate issues. Criminality is the "relatively stable differences among individuals in their propensity to engage in criminal or equivalent acts."[15] Crimes are events that are in violation of the criminal law. A "crime" may be committed because the target looks inviting, unprotected, and profitable. One becomes a delinquent or criminal because of personal factors ranging from having a sociopathic personality to growing up in a poverty area. Being a delinquent is a "status"; delinquency is an "event."

The reasons why one chooses to become a delinquent are quite distinct from the reasons a delinquent decides to break into a particular house one day or sell narcotics the next. According to sociologist Jack Katz, many youngsters choose crimes such as shoplifting and vandalism simply because they offer the attraction of "getting away with it"; delinquency is a thrilling demonstration of personal competence. In contrast, violent young offenders carry on like the avenging gods of mythology, choosing to have life or death control over their victims.[16]

Katz finds that the choice of committing crime is often linked to emotional upheaval: humiliation; righteousness; arrogance; ridicule; cynicism; defilement; and vengeance. The violence-prone teenagers interpret their victims' behavior as disrespectful and humiliating, and violence is a way of expressing their resulting rage. When the drunk at a party is told to "shut up and go home" because he is disturbing people, he responds, "So, I'm acting like a fool, am I?" and attacks his accusers. Public embarrassment leads to action: he must "sacrifice" or injure the body of the victim to maintain his "honor."[17]

ROUTINE ACTIVITIES

To some crime experts, the concept of the rational offender is insufficient to explain the cause of crime and delinquency. They argue that illegal behavior is not tied only to the rational and cunning acts of an offender but also depends on the behavior of potential victims and those who are charged with guarding them, such as police officers. Crime may occur not only because a criminal decides to break the law but also because a victim is in "the wrong place at the wrong time" and the police are not around.[18]

One of the most prominent of these works is *routine activity theory*, developed by Lawrence Cohen and Marcus Felson.[19] Cohen and Felson assume that the motivation to commit crime and the supply of offenders are constant.[20] Consequently, they believe that the volume and distribution of *predatory crime* (violent crimes against the person and crimes in which an offender attempts to steal an object directly) are closely related to the interaction of three variables that reflect the "routine activities" found in everyday American life: the availability of *suitable targets* (such as homes containing easily saleable goods); the absence of *capable guardians* (such as homeowners and their neighbors, friends, and relatives); and the presence of *motivated offenders* (such as unemployed teenagers). If each of these components are present, there is a greater likelihood that a predatory crime will take place.

Cohen and Felson have used the routine activities approach to explain the changes in the crime and delinquency rate since 1960. They argue that one reason the crime rate has increased is that the number of adult caretakers at home during the day (guardians) has been decreasing because of expanded female participation in the work force. Since mothers are at work and children are in day care, homes are left unguarded and become more "suitable targets." Similarly, with the growth of suburbia and the decline of the traditional neighborhood, the number of such familiar "guardians," such as family members, neighbors, and friends, has diminished.

Another influence on the crime rate is the growth of easily transportable wealth, which has created a greater number of available targets. Research has generally supported the fact that the more wealth a home contains, the more likely it will be victimized.[21] In one study, Cohen and his associates linked burglary rates to color television set purchases, reasoning that the more these high-priced, easily sold goods are available, the more offenders will be "motivated" to steal.[22]

Routine activities theory also links delinquency rates to social changes that increase the number and motivation of offenders. Robert O'Brien found that delinquency rates will increase if there is a surplus of youths of the same age all competing for a limited number of jobs and educational opportunities. For example, if during any given year there are "too many" 17-year-olds for the number of part-time and after-school jobs available, the supply of "motivated offenders" may be increased simply because there are many youths competing for a limited amount of legitimate resources.[23]

A critical component of the routine activities approach is that it gives equal weight to the role of both the victim and the offender in the crime process. While Cohen and Felson hold that predatory crime is a matter of rational choice, they also maintain that criminal opportunity is significantly influenced by the victim's life-style and behavior. Other research efforts have substantiated this claim. For example, Steven Messner and Kenneth Tardiff studied patterns of urban homicide and found that persons' life-styles significantly influenced their victimization: people who tended to stay at home were the ones most likely to be killed by family or friends, while those who went out more often were victimized by strangers.[24] In a recent study, Leslie Kennedy and David Forde found that lower-class young males who go out late at night to bars, work, class, or for a walk or drive are the most likely to become crime victims.[25] Put another way, the greater the opportunity there is for criminals and victims to interact, the greater the probability of crime; reduce the interaction and the opportunity for crime will decline.[26]

DETERRENCE THEORY

The core of choice theory is that youth choose to commit crimes. Deterrence theory holds that their choice can be controlled or deterred by the threat of punishment. Put another way, if kids come to fear the power of the law, to believe that their illegal behaviors will be met with certain and severe sanctions, they will choose to forego the benefits of outlawed activities, such as substance abuse and theft.[27]

One of the guiding principles of deterrence theory is that *the more severe, certain, and swift the punishment, the greater its deterrent effect.*[28] For example, there will be relatively little deterrent effect though a particular crime is punished quite severely if most people do not believe they will be caught.[29] Conversely, even a mild sanction may be sufficient to deter crime if people believe that punishment is certain. And, even the most severe sanctions will have little deterrent effect if they are slow, delayed, and easily put off.

Can a deterrence strategy work with juvenile offenders? The juvenile justice system has been reluctant to incorporate deterrence-based punishments on the grounds that they interfere with its stated *parens patriae* philosophy. Yet, in recent years, the increase in teenage violence, gang activity, and drug abuse has prompted a reevaluation of deterrence strategies. Consequently, police have been more willing to use aggressive tactics, such as gang busting units, to deter membership in drug trafficking gangs; juvenile court judges have been willing to waive youth to adult courts and place ever greater numbers of youth in secure treatment programs; legislators seem willing to pass more restrictive juvenile codes; and even the U.S. Supreme Court has upheld the use of the death penalty for youths over 16.[30]

Can deterrence strategies work? There is still considerable debate on this issue. A number of research studies have contributed data supportive of deterrence concepts. Evidence indicates that the threat of police arrest can deter property crimes.[31] Areas of the country in which punishment is more certain seem to have lower delinquency rates; the more likely people are to perceive that they will be punished for a crime, the less likely they are to engage in illegal activity.[32] However, the measurable deterrent effect of apprehension and punishment is usually slight and certainly less than projected by deterrence theory.[33] There is little reason to believe that crime and delinquency can be eliminated merely by the fear of legal punishment alone.[34] There is actually more evidence that fear of social disapproval and criticism from parents and friends may be a greater deterrent to crime than legal punishments.[35]

Deterring Delinquency

Deterring juvenile delinquency may present a greater problem than deterring adult criminality. Minors are subject to far more lenient sanctions than adults and by definition are less capable of making mature judgments about their behavior choices. Therefore, it seems futile to try to "deter" delinquency through fear of punishment. Research indicates also that many offenders are under the influence of drugs and/or alcohol when they break the law, a condition that might impair their decision-making ability.[36] Similarly, juveniles often commit crimes in groups, and peer pressure can outweigh the deterrent effect of the law.

Research by Maynard Erickson and Jack Gibbs suggests that deterrence efforts may have little success with delinquent offenders.[37] First, they found that youths do not report being deterred by the threat of a one-year jail sentence any more than they would be by losing spending money or having a 7:00 P.M. curfew. Second, adults do not seem willing to support a policy of harsh punishments sufficient to produce a deterrent effect.

Thus, while on the surface deterrence appears to have benefit as a delinquency control device, there is also reason to believe that it has limited demonstrable effectiveness.

Choice Theory in Review

Regardless of their form, choice theories have at their core a motivated offender who breaks the law because he or she perceives an abundance of benefits and an absence of threat. Increase the threat and reduce the benefits and the crime rate should decline.

This logic is hard to refute. After all, by definition a person who commits an illegal act but is not rational cannot be considered a criminal or delinquent but instead is "not guilty by reason of insanity."

To say that delinquents choose their crimes is for the most part entirely logical. Yet several questions remain unanswered by choice theorists. First, why do some people continually choose to break the law even after suffering its consequences, while others are content with living law-abiding yet unfulfilled lives; that is, how can "the good boy in the high crime area" be explained?[38] Conversely, why do billionaires like Ivan Boesky and Leona Helmsley break the law when they have everything to lose and little more to gain?

Choice theorists also have problems explaining seemingly irrational crimes, such as vandalism, arson, and even drug abuse. To say a teenager painted swastikas on a synagogue after making a "rational choice" seems inadequate to explain such a destructive, nonbeneficial act. Nor does the behavior of violent criminals like Robert Chambers, who strangled Jennifer Levin in what is referred to as the "preppie murder" case, lend itself to rational choice explanations.

It is also possible that the relationships observed by rational choice theorists can be explained in other ways. For example, while the high victimization rates in lower-class neighborhoods can be explained by an oversupply of "motivated offenders," they may also be due to other factors, such as social conflict and neighborhood disorganization.[39]

In sum, choice theories have utility as a way to understand criminal events and victim patterns. However, the question remains, why are some people "motivated" to commit crime and delinquency while others in similar circumstances remain law abiding? Why do some people choose crime over non-crime?

DEVELOPMENTAL THEORY

Why then do delinquents *choose* crime over law-abiding behavior? A faithful and loyal choice theorist would answer that selecting crime is a function of carefully weighing the benefits of criminal over noncriminal behavior. For example, a youth decides to commit a robbery if he believes he will make a good profit, have a good chance of getting away, and, even if caught, stand little chance of being severely punished.

A number of delinquency experts believe that this model is incomplete. They believe it is wrong to infer that all youths choose crime simply because they believe its advantages outweigh its risks. They argue that human behavioral choices are a function of an individual's mental and/or physical makeup. Most law-abiding youths have personal traits that fall within the "mainstream" of conventional society. In contrast, youths who choose to engage in repeated aggressive, antisocial, or conflict-oriented behavior manifest abnormal traits that influence their behavior choices.[40] Uncontrollable, impulsive behavior patterns place some youths at odds with society, and they soon find themselves in trouble with the law. While delinquents may choose their actions, the decision is a product of all but uncontrollable mental and physical properties and traits.

The view that delinquents are somehow "abnormal" is not a new one. Some of the earliest theories of criminal and delinquent behavior stressed that crime was a product of personal traits and that measurable physical and mental conditions, such as IQ and body build, determined behavior. This view is generally referred to today as *positivism*. Positivists believe that the scientific method can be used to measure the causes of human behavior and that behavior is a function of often uncontrollable factors, such as mental illness.

The issue of behavioral control is one significant difference between developmental and choice theories: while the former reasons that behavior is controlled by personal traits, the latter views behavior as purely a product of human reasoning. To choice theorists, reducing the benefits of crime by increasing the likelihood and severity of punishment will eventually lower the crime rate; developmental theorists focus less on the effects of punishment and more on the treatment of abnormal mental and physical conditions as a crime reduction method.

In the following sections, the primary components of developmental theory are reviewed.

The Origins of Developmental Theory

The first attempts to discover why criminal tendencies developed focused on the physical makeup of offenders. It was believed that biological traits present at birth predetermined whether people would live lives of crime.

The origin of this school of thought is generally credited to the Italian physician Cesare Lombroso (1835–1909).[41] Known as the father of criminology, Lombroso put his many years of medical research to use in his theory of **criminal atavism**.[42] Lombroso found that delinquents manifest physical anomalies that make them biologically and physiologically similar to our primitive ancestors. These atavistic individuals are savage throwbacks to an earlier stage of human evolution. Because of this link, the "born criminal" has such physical traits as enormous jaws, strong canines, flattened nose, and supernumerary teeth (double rows, as in snakes). Lombroso made such statements as, "It was easy to understand why the span of the arms in criminals so often exceeds the height, for this is a characteristic of apes, whose forelimbs are used in walking and climbing."[43]

Contemporaries of Lombroso refined the notion of a physical basis of crime. Raffaele Garofalo (1851–1934) shared Lombroso's belief that certain physical characteristics indicate a criminal or delinquent nature.[44] Enrico Ferri (1856–1929), a student of Lombroso, believed that a number of biological, social, and organic factors caused delinquency and crime. While Ferri accepted the validity of the biological approach to criminal activity, he attempted to interweave physical, anthropological, and social factors into his explanation of the causes of illegal behavior.[45] The English criminologist Charles Goring (1870–1919) challenged the validity of Lombroso's research and claimed instead that delinquent behaviors bore a significant relationship to a condition he referred to as "defective intelligence."[46] Consequently, Goring believed that delinquent behavior was inherited and could therefore be controlled by regulating the reproduction of families exhibiting such traits as "feeble-mindedness, epilepsy, insanity, and defective social instinct."[47]

Advocates of the psychobiological, or inheritance, theory studied the family trees of criminal and delinquent offenders. They traced the activities of several generations of families believed to have an especially large number of criminal members. The most famous of these studies involved the Jukeses and the Kallikaks. Richard Dugdale's *The Jukes: A Study in Crime, Pauperism, Disease, and Heredity* (1875) and Arthur Estabrook's later work *The Jukes in 1915* traced the history of the Jukes, a family responsible for a disproportionate amount of crime.[48]

Advocates of the body build or *somatotype* school argued that delinquents and criminals manifest distinct physiques that make them susceptible to particular types of delinquent behavior.[49] William H. Sheldon linked body type to delinquency.[50] *Mesomorphs* have well-developed muscles and an athletic appearance. They are active, aggressive, sometimes violent, and the most likely to become delinquents. *Endomorphs* have heavy builds and are slow moving. They are known for lethargic behavior. *Ectomorphs* are tall and thin and less social and more intellectual than the other types.

Recent studies of the relationship of body build and delinquency were conducted by Sheldon Glueck and Eleanor Glueck. The Gluecks used Sheldon's three body types and added a fourth, "balanced type," which includes bodies in which none of the other three types is discernibly dominant. In a lengthy research effort involving large samples of delinquent and nondelinquent boys, the Gluecks found that mesomorphs were disproportionately represented among delinquent boys (60.1 percent versus 30.7 percent). Conversely, only 14.4 percent of the delinquents were ectomorphic, but 39.6 percent of the nondelinquents were ectomorphic.[51]

These early views portrayed delinquent behavior as a function of a single factor or trait, such as body build or defective intelligence. They came under heavy criticism for their unsound methodology and lack of proper scientific controls. Many used captive offender populations and failed to compare experimental subjects with nondelinquents or *undetected* delinquents.[52] These omissions made it impossible to determine if biological traits produce delinquency or if police are more likely to arrest the mentally and physically abnormal. By the mid-twentieth century, biological theories had fallen out of favor as an explanation of delinquency.

MODERN DEVELOPMENTAL THEORY

For most of the twentieth century, delinquency experts scoffed at the notion that a youth's behavior was "controlled" by physical conditions present at birth. During this period, the majority of delinquency research focused on the social factors, such as poverty and family life, that were believed responsible for law-violating behavior. However, a small group of criminologists and penologists kept alive the biological tradition. With the publication of Edmond O. Wilson's *Sociobiology: The New Synthesis* in 1975, the biological perspective was given a new impetus.[53]

Wilson's *sociobiological* perspective views the gene as the ultimate unit of life that controls all human destiny. While the environment and experience do have an impact on behavior, most actions are controlled by a person's "biological machine." Most important, people are controlled by the innate need to have their genetic material survive and dominate others. Consequently, they do everything in their power to ensure their own survival and that of others who share their gene pool (relatives, countrymen, etc.). Even when they come to the aid of others ("reciprocal altruism"), people are motivated by the belief that their actions will be reciprocated and that their gene survival capability will be enhanced.

Although **sociobiology** has been criticized as methodologically unsound, it has had a tremendous effect on reviving interest in finding a physical basis for crime and delinquency. If biological (genetic) makeup controls all human behavior, it follows that physical and mental factors should also be responsible for determining whether a person chooses law-violating or conventional behavior.[54]

Two schools of thought have emerged in recent years. One, **biosocial theory**, maintains that the development of delinquency is an effect of the interaction of biological traits and social conditions. The second, psychological theory, leans more heavily on such issues as personality, mental illness, intelligence, and delinquency. These two views are discussed in detail below.

BIOSOCIAL THEORY

Biosocial theorists seek to explain the onset of delinquent behaviors, such as aggression and violence, from the standpoint of the physical qualities of the offenders themselves.[55] Though many have medical or natural science backgrounds, a number within their ranks are converts from the social science tradition.

Biosocial theorists charge that traditional social scientists ignore the biological basis for human behavior and disregard all the advances made in the sciences of biology and experimental psychology. Furthermore, most social scientists seem content to study reports of behavior, either through surveys or self-reports, rather than to observe the actual human behaviors they are allegedly concerned with.[56]

Modern biosocial theory rejects the traditional assumptions that all humans are born with equal potential to learn and achieve (**equipotentiality**) and that thereafter their behavior is controlled by social forces. While traditional social scientists suggest (either explicitly or implicitly) that all people are born equal and that parents, schools, neighborhoods, and friends control subsequent development, the biosocial perspective holds that no two people (with rare exceptions, such as identical twins) are alike and that the combination of human genetic traits and the environment produces individual behavior patterns. While biosocial theorists agree that environmental factors can have a powerful influence on behavior, they also remind us that it is unwise to ignore the influence of biological traits on behavior.

Although biosocial criminology has advanced in many different directions, it is possible to describe its major research efforts as being divided into three distinct areas of study; biochemical reactions, neurological dysfunction, and genetic influences.

Biochemical Factors

One area of biosocial research on delinquency concerns the relationship between antisocial behavior and biochemical makeup.[57] It is alleged that body chemistry, controlled by diet, blood chemistry, allergies, and so on, influences such personality traits as aggressiveness and depression.[58] These in turn have been linked to antisocial behavior.

Of particular interest is the diet of young offenders. It has long been accepted that an unusually high intake of such items as artificial food coloring, milk, and sweets can have a detrimental effect on behavior. Numerous studies have shown that institutionalized youths have had poor diets that were high in carbohydrates, and that there is a link between food intake, body chemistry, and behavior.[59] Some highly sophisticated experiments involving the diet of incarcerated youth show that ingesting a diet balanced in nutrients is significantly correlated with a reduction in antisocial behavior and scores on psychological inventories.[60] However, the relationship between sugar intake and abnormal behavior is far from settled; a number of controlled experiments have failed to substantiate any real link between the two variables.[61]

Some scientists believe that chronic under- or oversupply of vitamins, such as C and B3 and B6, may be related to restlessness and antisocial behavior in youths. Other vitamins and minerals linked to aggression include magnesium, copper, and zinc.

There have been a number of experiments to test whether delinquents and nondelinquents can be differentiated on the basis of their diets. Alexander Schauss compared a sample of incarcerated youths with a nondelinquent control group and found that the most significant factor separating the youths was the extremely high milk intake among the delinquents.[62]

In another study on the effect of diet on such crime-related acts as aggression and hostility, J. Kershner and W. Hawke evaluated the effect that a high-protein,

Biosocial theorists believe there may be an important relationship between diet and behavior.

low-carbohydrate, sugarless diet, supplemented by megavitamins, had on children labeled as behavior problems.[63] Kershner and Hawke asked the subjects' parents to evaluate their children on thirteen behavior qualities, including hyperactivity, aggression, and attention span. The researchers discovered that the children had significantly improved behavior patterns and that improved diet was the most important factor in producing positive change.

A number of efforts have continued to observe the effect of diet on behavior. For example, Stephen Schoenthaler conducted an experiment with 276 incarcerated youths to determine whether a change in the amount of sugar in their diet would have a corresponding influence on their behavior within the institutional setting.[64] In the experiment, a number of dietary changes were made: sweet drinks were replaced with fruit juices; table sugar was replaced with honey; breakfast cereals with high sugar content were eliminated; molasses was substituted for sugar in cooking; and so on. Schoenthaler found that these changes produced a significant reduction in disciplinary actions within the institution: the number of assaults, thefts, fights, and disobedient acts within the institution declined about 45 percent. It is important to note that these results were consistent when such factors as age, previous offense record, and race of the offender were considered.

In another experiment, Schoenthaler and his colleagues found that enriching students diets in New York City schools was correlated with improved school performance. Gradually eliminating synthetic (artificial), synthetic flavors, artificial preservatives (BHA and BHT), and reducing sucrose intake (by limiting ice cream and sweetened cereals) preceded improved scores on national achievement tests. Since school achievement has been consistently linked to delinquent behavior, any improvement in academic performance resulting from dietary changes may help reduce the rate of antisocial activities among the student population.[65]

The biochemical view of delinquency has been attacked as being methodologically unsound and unworkable because of the presumed cost of providing dietary supplements for actual and potential delinquents. Yet, despite these drawbacks, the relationship between diet and delinquency remains an intriguing one. As Schoenthaler concludes:

> the literature on diet policies and institutional criminal behavior certainly contains many legitimate limitations affecting external generalizations. Yet, one can conclude that official diet policies do impact official disciplinary rates in institutions for unknown reasons. Diet appears to be a significant factor in the presence or absence of juvenile antisocial behavior. Replication and subsequent interdisciplinary research to isolate the causes is certainly warranted.[66]

Neurological Dysfunction

Another focus of biosocial research on delinquency regards the **neurological,** or brain/nervous system, structure of offenders. One view is that the neuroendocrine system that controls brain chemistry is the key to understanding violence and aggression. Chemical imbalance in the central nervous system's chemical/hormonal activity has been linked to antisocial behavior and drug abuse.[67]

Another view is that neurological functions, commonly measured with an electroencephalogram (EEG) or a CAT scan are associated with aggression and violence. Research indicates that children exhibiting abnormal EEGs at birth may also suffer developmental problems, such as low IQ scores, later in life.[68] Children who manifest behavior disturbances may have identifiable neurological deficits, such as damage to the hemispheres of the brain.[69] One clinical analysis of death row inmates found that a significant number had suffered head injuries as children, resulting in damage to their central nervous systems and neurological impairment.[70] It is alleged that many antisocial youths have impaired brain activity that causes them to experience otherwise unexplainable outbursts of anger, hostility, and aggression.[71] Evidence has been found which links the ability of the brain to process information with schizophrenia, depression, and other mental illnesses.[72]

Numerous research studies have employed electroencephalograms to measure the brain waves and activity of delinquents and then compare them with those of law-abiding adolescents. In what is considered the most significant investigation of EEG abnormality and delinquency, a group of 335 violent delinquents were classified on the basis of their antisocial activities and measured on an EEG.[73] While youths who committed a single violent act had a 12-percent abnormality rate, the same as the general population, the habitually aggressive youths had a 57-percent abnormality rate, almost five times the normal rate. Behaviors believed to be highly correlated with abnormal EEG functions include poor impulse control, inadequate social ability, hostility, temper tantrums, destructiveness, and hyperactivity.[74]

MINIMAL BRAIN DYSFUNCTION. One neurological pattern of particular concern to biosocial criminologists is called **minimal brain dysfunction (MBD)**. This can be defined as an abnormality in the cerebral or brain structure that causes behavior injurious to a person's life-style and social adjustment. One specific type of MBD that has gained considerable interest is **learning disabilities (LD)**, a term that has been defined by the National Advisory Committee on Handicapped Children:

> Children with special learning disabilities exhibit a disorder in one or more of the basic psychological processes involved in understanding or using spoken or written languages. They may be manifested in disorders of listening, thinking, talking, reading, writing or arithmetic. They include conditions which have been referred to as perceptual handicaps, brain injury, minimal brain dysfunction, dyslexia, developmental aphasia, etc. They do not include learning problems which are due to visual, hearing or motor handicaps, to mental retardation, emotional disturbance, or to environmental disadvantages.[75]

The relationship between learning disabilities and delinquency has been highlighted by studies showing that arrested and incarcerated children have a far higher LD rate than children in the general population.[76] While it is estimated that approximately 10 percent of all youths have learning disorders, estimates of LD among adjudicated delinquents range from 26 percent to 73 percent.[77]

In a widely cited 1976 study, Charles Murray offered two possible explanations of the link between learning disabilities and delinquency.[78] One view, known as the *susceptibility rationale*, argues that the link is caused by certain side effects of learning disabilities, such as impulsiveness, poor ability to learn from experience, and inability to take social cues. In contrast, the *school failure rationale* assumes that the frustration caused by the LD child's poor school performance will lead to a negative self-image and consequent acting-out behavior.

A number of recent research efforts have found that the LD child may not be any more susceptible to delinquent behavior than the non-LD child. Research by Robert Pasternack and Reid Lyon found that the proposed link between learning disabilities and delinquency may be an artifact of bias in the way the juvenile justice system treats LD youths.[79] In another effort, Joel Zimmerman and his colleagues evaluated the self-reported delinquent behavior of LD and non-LD youth, they found that it was actually quite similar.[80] Similarly, Lynn Meltzer and her associates found that while a small number of delinquents had learning disabilities, the majority could not be classified as learning disabled.[81]

These findings can be interpreted as meaning that even though they are no more delinquent than non-LD children, when LD children get in trouble with the law, they often bring with them a record of school problems and low grades and a history of educational frustration. LD children's poor academic performance may work against them in the juvenile court. Consequently, the view that learning disabilities cause delinquency has been questioned, and the view that LD children are more likely to be arrested and officially labeled delinquent demands further inquiry. (See the Focus on Delinquency, page 98.)

Further research on the relationship between brain misfunctioning and delinquency is needed. Right now, as Diana Fishbein and Robert Thatcher report, efforts are being made to introduce new technologies in the measurement of brain function and behavior in order to investigate early detection, prevention, and control of maladaptive behaviors.[82]

Genetic Influences

Another area of concern for biosocial theorists is the genetic makeup of delinquents. It has been hypothesized that some youths inherit a genetic configuration that makes them predisposed to violence and aggression. In the same way that people inherit genes that control height and eye color, biosocial theorists believe that antisocial behavior characteristics may be inherited.[83]

Early theories of heredity suggested that delinquency proneness ran in families. However, because most families share a similar life-style and environment, as well as a similar gene pool, this type of study is inconclusive. Therefore, biosocial theorists have sought other methods to study the relationship of delinquency to genetic makeup. Research on the genetic basis of crime and delinquency received a boost when it was found that Richard Speck, convicted killer of eight Chicago nurses, had an unusual genetic structure. Speck possessed an extra male chromosome; instead of the normal forty-six XY structure, he had a forty-seven XYY chromosome makeup. Though numerous research studies failed to find conclusive proof that males with an extra Y chromosome were disproportionately violent and criminal, interest brought about by the Speck case boosted research on the genetic influences on delinquency.[84]

TWIN STUDIES. One method of studying the genetic basis of delinquency is to compare the behavior of twins to nontwin siblings. If a crime is an inherited trait, twins should be quite similar in their behavior because they share a common genetic makeup.

Identical monozygotic twins have identical genetic makeup and are closer in their personal characteristics than fraternal dizygotic twins.

However, because twins are usually brought up in the same household and share common life experiences, any similarity in their delinquent behavior might be a function of comparable environmental influences and not genetics at all. To guard against this happenstance, biosocial theorists have compared the behavior of identical monozygotic (MZ) twins with fraternal dizygotic (DZ) twins; while the former have an identical genetic makeup, the latter share only about 50 percent of their genetic combinations. Research has shown that MZ twins are significantly closer in their personal characteristics, such as intelligence, than are DZ twins.[85] Reviews of recent twin studies conducted by Sarnoff Mednick and Jan Volavka, and later by Lee Ellis, found that in almost all cases, MZ twins have behavior patterns more similar than that of DZ twins.[86] Overall, Mednick and Volavka found, 60 percent of MZ twins shared similar delinquent and criminal behavior patterns (if one was delinquent, so was the other), while only 30 percent of DZ twins were similarly related. Of particular importance is the work of Karl Christiansen in Denmark, who studied thousands of twin pairs and found MZ pairs more than twice as likely to be similar than DZ pairs.[87]

While this evidence seems to support a connection between genetic makeup and delinquency, there is little conclusive evidence that such a link actually exists. As Ellis points out, MZ twins are more likely to look alike and to share physical traits than DZ twins and they are more likely to be treated similarly. Consequently, shared behavior patterns may again be a function of experience and not heredity.

ADOPTION STUDIES. Another way to determine whether delinquency is an inherited trait is to compare the behavior of adopted children with that of their biological parents. If the criminal behavior of children is more like that of their

Attention Deficit Disorder

Many parents have noticed that their children do not pay attention to them—they run around and do things in their own way. Sometimes this inattention is a function of age; in other instances, it is a symptom of attention-deficit disorder (ADD), a condition in which a child shows a developmentally inappropriate lack of attention, impulsivity, and hyperactivity. The various symptoms of ADD are described in Table A.

About three percent of American children, most often boys, are believed to suffer from this disorder, and it is the most common reason children are referred to mental health clinics. The condition usually results in poor school performance, bullying, stubbornness, and a lack of response to discipline. While the origin of ADD is still unknown, suspected causes include neurological damage, prenatal stress, and even food additives and chemical allergies. ADD children are most often treated by giving them doses of stimulants, such as Ritalin and Dexedrine, which ironically help these children to control their emotional and behavioral outbursts.

A series of research studies now link ADD, minimum brain dysfunctions, such as poor motor function and below average written and verbal cognitive ability, to the onset and sustenance of a delinquent career. Research by Terrie Moffitt and Phil Silva seems to suggest that youths who suffer both ADD and MBD and who grow up in a dysfunctional family are the most vulnerable to chronic delinquency that continues into their adulthood. However, Moffitt and Silva found that ADD kids who did not suffer from other forms of impairment were at no more risk for delinquency than non-ADD kids. By implication, early diagnosis and treatment of ADD and MBD may enhance the life chances of at-risk youth.

Source: Terrie Moffitt and Phil Silva, "Self-Reported Delinquency, Neuropsychological Deficit, and History of Attention Deficit Disorder," *Journal of Abnormal Child Psychology* 16:553–69 (1988).

TABLE A   Symptoms of Attention Deficit Disorder

Lack of Attention

  Frequently fails to finish projects

  Does not seem to pay attention

  Does not sustain interest in play activities

  Cannot sustain concentration on schoolwork or related tasks

  Is easily distracted

Impulsivity

  Frequently acts without thinking

  Often "calls out" in class

  Does not want to wait his or her turn in line or games

  Shifts from activity to activity

  Cannot organize tasks or work

  Requires constant supervision

Hyperactivity

  Constantly runs around and climbs on things

  Shows excessive motor activity while asleep

  Cannot sit still; is constantly fidgeting

  Does not remain in his or her seat in class

  Is constantly on the go like a "motor"

Source: Adapted from American Psychiatric Association, *Diagnostic and Statistical Manual of the Mental Disorders, 3rd ed.* (Washington, D.C.: American Psychiatric Press, Inc. 1987), pp. 50–53.

biological parents, whom they have never met, than that of their adopted parents, who brought them up, it would indicate that the tendency toward delinquency is inherited rather than shaped by the environment.

Studies of this kind have generally supported the hypothesis that there is a link between genetics and delinquency.[88] Some of the most influential research in this area has been conducted by Sarnoff Mednick. In one study, Mednick, working with Bernard Hutchings, found that while only 13 percent of the adopted fathers of a sample of adjudicated delinquent youths had criminal records, 31 percent of their biological fathers had criminal records.[89] Analysis of a control group's background indicated that about 11 percent of all fathers will have criminal records. Hutchings and Mednick concluded that genetics played at least some role in creating delinquent tendencies, because the biological fathers of delinquents were much more likely than the fathers of noncriminal youths to be criminals themselves. Mednick reported similar results in another effort conducted with William Gabrielli.[90]

In addition to a direct link between heredity and delinquency, the literature also shows that behavior traits linked closely to delinquency may be at least in part inherited. For example, recent research by Jody Allberts-Corush and her associates shows that the biological parents of adopted hyperactive children are more likely to show symptoms of hyperactivity themselves than the adoptive parents.[91] And several studies have reported a higher incidence of mental impairment in parents of hyperactive children when compared to control groups. While all hyperactive children do not become delinquent, the link between the two has been long suspected.[92]

PSYCHOLOGICAL THEORY

There are also experts who view the cause of delinquency as essentially a psychological phenomenon.[93] After all, most behaviors labeled delinquent—for example, violence, theft, sexual misconduct—seem to be symptomatic of some underlying psychological problem. Psychologists point out that many delinquent youths have poor home lives, destructive relationships with neighbors, friends, and teachers, and conflicts with authority figures in general. These relationships seem to indicate a disturbed personality structure. Furthermore, numerous studies of incarcerated youths indicate that the youths' personalities are marked by negative, antisocial behavior characteristics. And since delinquent behavior occurs among youths in every racial, ethnic, and socioeconomic group, psychologists view it as a function of emotional and mental disturbance rather than purely a result of social factors, such as racism, poverty, and class conflict.

Considering the presumed relationship between personality disturbance and antisocial behavior, it is not surprising that psychologists have played a prominent role in the study of delinquency. While it is recognized that many delinquents do not manifest significant psychological problems, enough do to give clinicians a powerful influence on delinquency theory.

Because psychology is a complex and diversified discipline, there is more than one psychological perspective on crime. In fact, three prominent theoretical perspectives that link delinquency to mental processes exist: the psychodynamic, the behavioral, and the cognitive.[94]

Psychodynamic Theory

One long-held psychological view of delinquency is based on the pioneering work of the Austrian physician **Sigmund Freud** (1856–1939).[95] Freud's views are referred to as **psychoanalytic** (also known as **psychodynamic**) theory, and his method of treatment is called **psychoanalysis.**

Freud's early research led him to conclude that the human personality contains three major components. The *id* is the unrestrained, primitive, pleasure-seeking component with which each child is born. The *ego* develops through the reality of living in the world and helps manage and restrain the id's need for immediate gratification. The *superego* develops through interactions with parents and other significant people and represents the development of conscience and the moral rules that are shared by most adults.

Freud suggested that unconscious motivations for behavior come from the id's action to account for two primal needs—sex and aggression. Human behavior is often marked by symbolic actions that reflect hidden feelings about these needs. For example, stealing a car may reflect a person's unconscious need for shelter and mobility to escape from hostile enemies (aggression) or perhaps an urge to enter a closed, dark, womb-like structure that reflects the earliest memories (sex).

All three segments of the personality are in simultaneous operation. The id dictates needs and desires, the superego counteracts the id by fostering feelings of morality and righteousness, and the ego evaluates the reality of a position between these two extremes. If these components are properly balanced, the individual can lead a normal life. If one aspect of the personality becomes dominant at the expense of the others, however, the individual exhibits neurotic or even psychotic personality traits.

Freud also suggested that every person goes through a series of life stages that shape the personality. The first, experienced by the newborn infant, is the *oral stage.* This period is marked by receiving pleasure through eating, sucking, and chewing. In the second, the *anal stage,* occurring between 1 and 3 years of age, urinary and bowel movements replace sucking as a major source of pleasure. During this period, toilet training occurs and, for the first time, pressure is put on the child to conform to social rules.

The third influential stage is the *phallic stage,* in which children from ages 3 to 6 receive pleasure from fondling their genitals. During this period, the male child develops great unconscious feelings for his mother (the Oedipus complex) and the female child for her father (the Electra complex). Freud also identified two later stages, genital and latency, but these are considered less important for human development because, for all intents and purposes, the personality is formed by age 5.

Any trauma that occurs during any of these early life stages may have a lasting effect on the child's personality. For example, premature weaning during the oral stage may cause an individual to be fixated on oral pastimes such as smoking cigarettes and drinking alcohol. If toilet training is a frightening or frustrating experience, the child's superego may be damaged and sometimes a sadistic and cruel anal personality will develop.

Psychodynamic theory suggests that an imbalance in personality traits caused by a traumatic early childhood can produce a damaged adolescent personality. That is, deep-rooted problems developed early in childhood will cause long-term psychological problems. For example, if neglectful parents fail to develop a child's superego adequately, the id may become the predominant personality force. Later, the youth may demand immediate gratification, may lack compassion for and sensitivity to the needs of others, may disassociate feelings, may act aggressively and impulsively, and may demonstrate other psychotic symptoms. As a result, delinquent activity may become an outlet for violent and antisocial feelings. Thus, to explain antisocial behavior, psychodynamic theory focuses on traumas experienced during early developmental stages and the resulting personality imbalances.

According to this view, people who experience feelings of mental anguish and are afraid that they are losing control of their personalities are said to be suffering from *neuroses* in one form or another and are referred to as *neurotics*. Those people who have lost total control and who are dominated by their primitive id are known as *psychotics*. Their behavior may be marked by bizarre episodes, hallucinations, and inappropriate responses. *Psychosis* takes many forms, the most common being labeled *schizophrenia*, a condition marked by illogical thought processes and a lack of insight into behavior. According to the psychoanalytic view, the most serious types of youthful, antisocial behavior, such as murder, might be motivated by psychosis, while neurotic feelings would be responsible for less serious delinquent acts and status offenses, such as petty theft and truancy.[96]

The Psychodynamic Tradition and Delinquency

A number of modern psychoanalysts have employed Freud's model to explain the onset of antisocial behaviors. **Erik Erikson** speculated that many adolescents experience a life crisis in which they feel emotional, impulsive, and uncertain of their role and purpose.[97] To resolve this crisis, most youths achieve a sense of *ego identity*, a firm sense of who they are and what they stand for. However, some youths cannot adequately deal with their feelings of role conflict and experience a sense of *role diffusion*, feelings of uncertainty that make them susceptible to suggestion and at the mercy of others who might lead them astray. The clash between ego identity and role diffusion is precipitated by an **identity crisis**—a period of inner turmoil during which they examine inner values and make decisions about life roles. Using Erikson's approach, the behavior of youthful drug abusers might be viewed as an expression of confusion over their place in society, their inability to direct behavior toward useful outlets, and perhaps their dependency on others to offer them solutions to their problems.

Another psychoanalyst long associated with understanding delinquency, David Abrahamsen, views youth crime as a result of unresolved conflict between the ego and superego aspects of the personality:

> In the child between 4 and 6 years of age, incestuous unconscious feelings associated with resentment, fear and hatred are present. If [this] merging of Ego and Superego is unsuccessful, a regression to these earlier drives more or less takes place. This regression may be considered responsible for a great number of mental diseases, from neuroses to psychoses, and in many cases, it may be related to criminal behavior.[98]

Psychoanalysts like Abrahamsen view delinquents as id-dominated people who suffer from the inability to control impulsive, pleasure-seeking drives. Perhaps because they suffered unhappy experiences in childhood or had families who could not provide proper love and care, delinquents suffer from weak or damaged egos that make them unable to cope with conventional society.[99] In its most extreme form, delinquency may be viewed as a form of psychosis that prevents delinquent youths from appreciating the feelings of their victims or controlling their own impulsive needs for gratification. For example, psychoanalyst August Aichorn claimed that social stress alone could not produce such an emotional state. He identified *latent delinquents*—youths whose troubled family life led them to seek immediate gratification without consideration of right and wrong or the feelings of others.[100]

Psychiatrist Semour Halleck views delinquency as a manifestation of feelings of oppression and the inability of youths to do much about it. Criminality actually allows youths to strive by producing positive psychic results: helping them to feel free and independent; giving them the possibility of excitement and the chance to use their skills and imagination; providing the promise of positive gain; allowing them to blame others for their predicament (for example, the police); giving them a chance to rationalize their own sense of failure ("If I hadn't gotten into the trouble, I could have been a success").[101]

The views of psychoanalysts like Abrahamsen and Halleck are supported by research that shows that a number of serious, violent juvenile offenders suffer from some sort of personality disturbance. James Sorrells's well-known study of juvenile murderers, "Kids Who Kill," found that many homicidal youths could be described in such terms as "overtly hostile," "explosive or volatile," "anxious," and "depressed."[102] Likewise, Richard Rosner and his associates found that 75 percent of male adolescents accused of murder could be classified as having some mental illness, including schizophrenia.[103] Later in life, abused, depressed, suicidal children may grow up to vent their feelings in a homicidal rage.[104]

The psychoanalytic approach places heavy emphasis on the family's role in producing a delinquent child. When parents fail to maintain a stable, balanced home life, a child may adapt by turning inward and revamping his or her internal personality components. Antisocial youths frequently come from families in which parents are unable to give consistent love, set consistent limits, and provide the controls that allow children to develop the necessary personal tools to cope with their world.[105] The exploitive, destructive behavior of a youth may actually be a symbolic call for help. In fact, some psychoanalysts view delinquents' behavior as being motivated by an unconscious urge to be punished. Since these children believe they are unloved at home, the fault must be a result of their own inadequacy—hence they deserve punishment.

Behavioral Theory

Not all psychologists agree that behavior is controlled by unconscious mental processes determined by parental relationships developed early in childhood. Behavioral psychologists argue that a person's personality is learned throughout life during interaction with others. Based primarily on the works of the American psychologist John B. Watson (1878–1958) and popularized by Harvard professor B. F. Skinner, **behaviorism** concerns itself solely with measurable events and not with the unobservable psychic phenomenon described by psychoanalysts.

Behaviorists suggest that individuals learn by observing how people react to their behavior. Behavior is triggered initially by a stimulus or change in the environment. If a particular behavior is reinforced by some positive reaction or event, that behavior will be continued and eventually learned. However, behaviors that are not reinforced, or even punished, will be extinguished or become extinct. For example, if children are given a reward (ice cream for dessert) for eating their entire dinner, eventually they will learn to eat properly as a matter of habit. Conversely, if children are punished for some misbehavior, they will eventually learn to associate disapproval with that act and avoid it.

SOCIAL LEARNING THEORY. Not all behaviorists follow the teachings of Watson and Skinner strictly. Some hold that a person's learning and social experiences, coupled with his or her values and expectations, determine behavior. This is known as the *social learning* approach. The most widely read social learning theorists are Albert Bandura, Walter Mischel, and Richard Walters.[106] In general, they hold that children will model their behavior according to the reactions they receive from others, either positive or negative; the behavior of those adults they are in close contact with, especially parents; and the behavior they view on television and in movies. If a youth observes aggression, such as an adult slapping or punching someone during an argument, and the child also sees that the aggressive behavior is approved or rewarded, it becomes likely that the child will also react violently during a similar incident. Eventually, the child will master the techniques of aggression and become more confident that such behavior will bring tangible rewards.[107]

By implication, social learning suggests that a child who grows up in a home where violence is a way of life may learn to believe that such behavior is acceptable and rewarding. Even if parents tell children not to be violent and punish them if they are, the child will still model his or her behavior after observed parental violence. Thus, children, are more likely to heed what parents *do*, not what they *say*. Bonnie Carlson found that by middle childhood, some children have already acquired an association between their use of aggression against others and the physical punishment they receive at home. Often their aggressive responses are directed at other family members and siblings. Carlson's conclusion: the family serves as a training ground for violence, with physical punishment playing a prominent role in normalizing the child's use of violence during conflict situations with others.[108]

Bandura has suggested that adolescent aggression is a result of disrupted dependency relations with parents. This refers to the frustration and anger a child feels when parents provide poor role models and hold back affection and nurturance. He states:

A child who lacks close dependent ties to his parents can have little opportunity or desire to model himself after them and to internalize their standards of behavior. In the absence of such internalized controls, the child's aggression is likely to be expressed in an immediate, direct and socially unacceptable fashion.[109]

THE MEDIA AND DELINQUENCY. One aspect of social learning theory that has received a great deal of attention is the view that children will model their behavior after characters they observe on television or see in movies. This is of

There is evidence that watching violent television shows and movies can be related to aggression. The Teenage Mutant Ninja Turtles provide a violent image for very young viewers.

special concern since the content of both have been considerably violent for quite some time. Often the violence is of a sexual nature, and some experts fear that there is a link between sexual violence and the viewing of pornography. However, others cite evidence that TV shows and films that stress violence can increase levels of aggressive behavior regardless of their sexual content.[110]

Children are particularly susceptible to TV imagery. It is believed that many children consider television images "real," especially if they are authoritatively presented by an adult (as in a commercial). Of concern is the fact that some children, especially those who are considered "emotionally disturbed," may be unable to distinguish between fantasy and reality when watching TV shows.[111] This is especially important when we consider that systematic viewing of TV begins at 2.5 years of age and continues at a high level during the preschool and early school years; it has been estimated that children aged 2 to 5 watch TV 27.8 hours each week; children aged 6 to 11, 24.3 hours per week; and teens 23 hours per week.[112]

A number of recent research efforts indicate that watching violence on TV leads to increased level of violence in youth.[113] Such august bodies as the American

Psychological Association and the National Institute of Mental Health support the TV violence link.[114]

The issue is far from settled, however, since a number of research efforts dispute a TV-violent behavior link.[115] For example, Steven Messner's recent research indicates that areas that experience the highest levels of violent TV watching also have the lowest rates of violence.[116]

Cognitive Theory

One area of psychology that has received increasing recognition in recent years has been the **cognitive school**. Psychologists with a cognitive perspective focus on mental processes and the way people perceive and mentally represent the world around them, how they solve problems, and how they perceive their environment. The pioneers of this school were Wilhelm Wundt (1832–1920), Edward Titchener (1867–1927), and William James (1842–1920). The cognitive perspective contains several subgroups. *Gestalt* psychology is concerned with perception of the world in whole units rather than individual pieces. The *moral and intellectual development* branch is concerned with how adults morally represent and reason about the world. *Humanistic psychology* stresses self-awareness and "getting in touch with feelings."

MORAL AND INTELLECTUAL DEVELOPMENT THEORY. The moral and intellectual development branch of cognitive psychology is perhaps the most important for delinquency theory. Jean Piaget (1896–1980), the founder of this approach, hypothesized that people's reasoning processes develop in an orderly fashion, beginning at birth and continuing until they are 12 years old and older.[117] At first, during the *sensorimotor stage*, children respond to the environment in a simple manner, seeking interesting objects and developing their reflexes. By the fourth and final stage, the *formal operations* stage, they have developed into mature adults who can use logic and abstract thought.

Lawrence Kohlberg applied the concept of moral development to issues in criminology.[118] He suggests that people travel through stages of moral development, during which their decisions and judgments on issues of right and wrong are made for different reasons. It is possible that serious offenders have a moral orientation that differs from that of law-abiding citizens. Kohlberg's stage of development are:

- STAGE 1—Right is obedience to power and avoidance of punishment.
- STAGE 2—Right is taking responsibility for oneself, meeting one's own needs, and leaving to others the responsibility for themselves.
- STAGE 3—Right is being good in the sense of having good motives, having concern for others, and "putting yourself in the other person's shoes."
- STAGE 4—Right is maintaining the rules of a society and serving the welfare of the group or society.
- STAGE 5—Right is based on recognized individual rights within a society with agreed-upon rules—a social contract.
- STAGE 6—Right is an assumed obligation to principles applying to all humankind—principles of justice, equality, and respect for human personality.

Kohlberg classified people according to the stage on this continuum at which their moral development had ceased to grow. In studies conducted by Kohlberg and his associates, criminals were found to be significantly lower in their moral judgment development than noncriminals of the same social background.[119] The majority of noncriminals were classified in stages three and four, whereas a majority of criminals fell within stages one and two. Moral development theory, then, suggests that people who obey the law simply to avoid punishment or who have outlooks mainly characterized by self-interest are more likely to commit crimes than those who view the law as something that benefits all of society and who sympathize with the rights of others. Research efforts using delinquent youth have found that a significant number fell within the first two moral development categories, while nondelinquents were ranked higher.[120] In addition, higher stages of moral reasoning are associated with such behaviors as honesty, generosity, and nonviolence, which are considered noncompatible with delinquency.[121]

Psychological Traits and Delinquency

Each of the various perspectives and theories of psychology has its own view of how important psychological traits, such as sensation, perception, thought, memory, emotion, and motivation, develop. A number of these traits have been linked to the onset of delinquency. Of these, the two most prominent are personality and intelligence.

PERSONALITY AND DELINQUENCY. Personality can be defined as the reasonably stable patterns of behavior, including thoughts and emotions, that distinguish one person from another.[122] One's personality reflects characteristic ways of adapting to life's demands and problems. The way we behave is a function of how our personality enables us to interpret life events and make appropriate behavioral choices.

Can the cause of delinquency be linked to personality? There has been a great deal of research on this subject and an equal amount of controversy and debate over the findings.[123] In their early work, Sheldon and Eleanor Glueck identified a number of personality characteristics that characterize delinquents:

- self-assertiveness
- extroversion
- defiance
- ambivalence
- impulsiveness
- feeling unappreciated
- narcissism
- distrust of authority

- suspicion
- poor personal skills
- destructiveness
- mental instability
- sadism
- hostility
- lack of concern for others
- resentment[124]

The Glueck research is representative of the view that delinquents maintain a distinct personality whose characteristics increase the probability that they will be aggressive and antisocial and that their actions will involve them with agents of social control, ranging from teachers to police.

Since the Glueck findings were published, other research efforts have attempted to identify personality traits that increase the chances of a delinquent career.[125] For example, the well-known psychologist Hans Eysenck identified two important personality traits that he associated with antisocial behavior: extraversion and neuroticism. Extraverts are impulsive individuals who lack the ability to examine their own motives and behaviors; neuroticism is a trait in which a person is given to anxiety, tension, and emotional instability.[126] Youths who lack self-insight and are impulsive and emotionally unstable are likely to interpret events differently than youths who are able to make reasoned judgments of life events. While the former may act destructively (for example, by taking drugs), the latter will be able to reason that such behavior is ultimately destructive and life threatening.

A number of personality deficits have been identified in the delinquent population. A common theme is that delinquents are hyperactive, impulsive individuals with short attention spans (attention deficit disorder), conduct disorders, anxiety disorders, and depression.[127] These traits make them prone to problems ranging from psychopathology to drug abuse, sexual promiscuity, and violence.[128]

THE ANTISOCIAL PERSONALITY. It has also been suggested that delinquency may result from a personality pattern or syndrome commonly referred to as the **psychopathic** or **sociopathic** personality (the terms are used interchangeably).

Psychopathic (sociopathic) youths exhibit a low level of guilt and anxiety and persistently violate the rights of others. Although they may exhibit superficial charm and above-average intelligence, these often mask a disturbed personality that makes them incapable of forming enduring relationships with others and continually involves them in such deviant behaviors as truancy, running away, lying, substance abuse, and impulsivity. Psychoanalyst David Abrahamsen describes the genuine psychopath as someone who has never been able to identify with anyone. From an early age, the psychopath's home life was filled with frustrations, bitterness, and quarreling. Consequently, throughout life, he or she is unreliable, unstable, demanding, and egocentric. Hervey Cleckley, a leading authority on psychopathy, uses this definition:

> [Psychopaths are] chronically antisocial individuals who are always in trouble, profiting neither from experience nor punishment, and maintaining no real loyalties to any person, group, or code. They are frequently callous and hedonistic, showing marked emotional immaturity, with lack of responsibility, lack of judgment and an ability to rationalize their behavior so that it appears warranted, reasonable and justified.[129]

A number of factors have been found to contribute to the development of psychopathic/sociopathic personalities. They include having a psychopathic parent, a lack of love, parental rejection during childhood, and inconsistent discipline.[130] It has also been alleged that psychopathy has its basis in a measurable physical condition—psychopaths suffer from levels of arousal that are lower than those of the general population. Consequently, psychopathic youths may need greater-than-average stimulation to bring them up to comfortable levels. Youths diagnosed as psychopaths are believed to be thrill seekers who engage in violent, destructive behavior. For example, Lewis Yablonsky has described the psychopathic/sociopathic gang boy who engages in violent and destructive sexual escapades to compensate for a fear of responsibility and an inability to maintain interpersonal relationships.[131] And while the research of Helene Raskin White, Erich Labouvie, and Marsha Bates did not *directly* link delinquency to psychopathy, it did find that delinquents were more likely than nondelinquents to be sensation seekers who desired a hedonistic pursuit of pleasure, an extraverted life-style, partying, drinking, and a variety of sexual partners.[132] Psychologists have attempted to treat patients diagnosed as psychopaths by giving them adrenalin, which increases their arousal levels.

PERSONALITY TESTING. Psychiatrists and psychologists have developed *personality tests* designed to measure and analyze human personality traits quickly and efficiently. Personality tests have become significant tools in the effort to derive a psychological profile of the delinquent. The most widely used of these are **personality inventories**, which require subjects to respond to questions in a self-administered survey. Questions are made to appear ambiguous so that subjects cannot guess their true intent and meaning. Scale items might include such statements as "Sometimes I wake up cold and frightened," "Loud noises scare me," and "I like mechanic's magazines." Psychologists suggest that the way subjects answer these questions can be used to determine personality traits, such as hypochondria, schizophrenia, and psychopathy. Personality inventories are widely used because they measure a large variety of personality characteristics, are easily and uniformly administered, and can be scored by nonprofessionals. However, they have some limitations. It is uncertain why subjects answer particular questions the way they do. For example, subjects may deliberately try to give what they believe to be socially acceptable answers rather than tell the truth. Also, there is some question about the validity of subscales. For example, is it certain that a scale purporting to measure schizophrenia actually does so?

The most widely used psychological test is the Minnesota Multiphasic Personality Inventory, commonly called the MMPI. Developed by R. Starke Hathaway and J. Charnley McKinley, the MMPI has subscales that purport to measure many different personality traits, including psychopathic deviation (Pd scale), schizophrenia (Sc), and hypomania (overactivity, Ma).[133]

Elio Monachesi and R. Starke Hathaway pioneered the use of the MMPI to predict delinquent behavior.[134] They concluded that scores on some of the MMPI subscales, especially the Pd scale, predicted delinquency. In one major effort, they administered the MMPI to a sample of ninth-grade boys and girls in Minneapolis and found that Pd scores had a significant relationship to later delinquent involvement.[135] Similar studies have been conducted to classify both criminal and juvenile offenders, as well as substance abusers.[136]

Despite the time and energy put into using MMPI scales to predict delinquency, the results have proved inconclusive. Three surveys of the literature of personality testing, one by Karl Schuessler and Donald Cressey (covering the pre–1950 period), another by Gordon Waldo and Simon Dinitz (covering 1950–65), and a more recent one by David Tennenbaum, found inconclusive evidence that personality traits could indeed predict delinquent involvement.[137] However, the personality tests reviewed in these surveys often suffered methodological flaws so that any negative conclusions must be interpreted with caution. Some recent research efforts have successfully classified offenders and predicted their behavioral traits on the basis of personality inventory scores.[138] There exists sufficient evidence of an association between some delinquency and personality disturbance to warrant further research on this important yet sensitive issue.

MENTAL ABILITY AND DELINQUENCY. Psychologists are concerned with the development of intelligence and its subsequent relationship to behavior. Of particular importance to the study of delinquency is the allegation that there is an inverse relationship between IQ and youthful law violations. It has been charged that children with low IQs are responsible for a disproportionate share of delinquency. Questions surrounding IQ have been present throughout most of the twentieth century.

Early criminologists believed that low intelligence was a major cause of delinquency. If one could determine which individuals had low IQs, one might be able to identify potential delinquents before they committed socially harmful acts.[139] Since social scientists had a captive group of subjects in training schools and penal institutions, studies began to appear that measured the correlation between IQ and crime by testing adjudicated juvenile delinquents. Delinquent juveniles were believed to be inherently substandard in intelligence and thus naturally inclined to commit more crimes than more intelligent persons. Thus, juvenile delinquents were used as a test group around which numerous theories about intelligence were built.

When the newly developed IQ tests were administered to inmates of prisons and juvenile training schools in the first decades of the twentieth century, a large proportion of the inmates scored low on the tests. Henry Goddard found in his studies in 1920 that many institutionalized persons were what he considered "feeble-minded" and thus concluded that at least half of all juvenile delinquents were mental defectives.[140]

In 1926, William Healy and Augusta Bronner tested a group of delinquents in Chicago and Boston and found that 37 percent were subnormal in intelligence.[141] They concluded that delinquents were five to ten times more likely to be mentally deficient than normal boys.

These and other early studies were embraced as proof that low IQ scores identified potentially delinquent children and that a correlation existed between innate low intelligence and deviant behavior. IQ tests were believed to measure the inborn genetic makeup of individuals, and many criminologists accepted the predisposition of substandard individuals toward delinquency.

NURTURE THEORY. The rise of culturally sensitive explanations of human behavior in the 1930s led to the *nurture school* of intelligence. This view holds that intelligence must be viewed as partly biological but primarily sociological. Nurture theorists discredit the notion that people commit crimes because they have low IQ scores. Instead, they postulate that environmental stimulation from parents, relatives, social contacts, schools, peer groups, and innumerable others create a child's IQ level and that low IQs result from an environment that also encourages delinquent and criminal behavior.[142] For example, if educational environments could be improved, the result might be both an elevation in IQ scores and a decrease in delinquency.[143]

Studies challenging the assumption that people automatically committed delinquent acts because they had below-average IQs began to appear as early as the 1920s. John Slawson studied 1,543 delinquent boys in New York institutions and compared them with a control group of New York City boys in 1926.[144] He found that although 80 percent of the delinquents achieved lower scores in abstract verbal intelligence than the control group, they were about normal in mechanical aptitude and nonverbal intelligence. These results indicated the possibility of cultural bias in portions of the IQ tests. He also found that there was no relationship between the number of arrests, the types of offenses, and IQ. In 1931, Edwin Sutherland evaluated IQ studies of criminals and delinquents and noted significant variations in their findings.[145] The discrepancies were believed to reflect refinements in testing methods and scoring rather than differences in the mental ability of criminals.

These findings did much to discredit the notion that a strong relationship existed between IQ and criminality.

IQ AND DELINQUENCY TODAY. After many years of neglect, an often cited study by Travis Hirschi and Michael Hindelang revived interest in the association between IQ and delinquency.[146] After conducting a statistical analysis of a number of data sets, Hirschi and Hindelang concluded both that IQ tests are a valid predictor of intelligence and that "the weight of evidence is that IQ is more important than race and social class" for predicting delinquent involvement. Their most significant finding was that possession of a low IQ increases the likelihood of delinquent behavior. The IQ-delinquency association is most likely indirect: youths with low IQs do poorly in school, and school failure and academic incompetence are highly related to delinquency.

The Hirschi and Hindelang findings have been supported by a series of research studies conducted by Terrie Moffitt and his associates.[147] In one study, longitudinal data from a cohort of Danish youth indicated that children with a low IQ may be likely to engage in delinquent behavior because their poor verbal ability is a handicap in the school environment.[148]

Moffitt has also found that delinquency is related to indicators of limited mental ability in both official and self-reported samples of delinquents and that a high IQ can help protect at-risk children from delinquent involvement.[149] Working with Phil Silva and Jennifer White, Moffitt found that youths labeled "high risk" by teachers because of their early acting-out behavior in school (age 5) were less likely to become delinquents during their teen years if they had a relatively high IQ; low-IQ kids with early behavioral problems were much more likely to become chronic persisters.[150]

The case for an IQ-delinquency link is reviewed by James Q. Wilson and Richard Herrnstein in their book, *Crime and Human Nature*. Their conclusion:

> . . . there appears to be a clear and consistent link between criminality and low intelligence. That is, taking all offenders as a group and ignoring differences among kinds of crime, criminals seem, on the average, to be a bit less bright and to have a different set of intellectual strengths and weaknesses than do noncriminals as a group.[151]

While these studies support an IQ-delinquency association, there is also research, such as that conducted by Scott Menard and Barbara Morse, that finds that IQ level has negligible influence on delinquent behavior.[152] And, importantly, IQ research in general has been beset by charges that tests are culturally biased and therefore invalid.[153]

In sum, there is some, albeit inconclusive, evidence that youths with limited intellectual ability may be the ones more likely to engage in delinquent behaviors. Even those who believe IQ and crime are associated recognize that the linkage is indirect: intelligence is associated with poor school performance, which leads to delinquency.[154] As Wilson and Herrnstein put it, "A child who chronically loses standing in the competition of the classroom may feel justified in settling the score outside, by violence, theft, and other forms of defiant illegality."[155] Since the relationship runs from low IQ to poor school performance to frustration to delinquency, it is important for school officials to recognize the problem and plan programs to help underachievers perform better in school.

INTEGRATING DEVELOPMENTAL AND CHOICE THEORIES

In 1985, James Q. Wilson and Richard Herrnstein published their highly controversial book, *Crime and Human Nature*, which soon became one of the most talked about works in criminological literature.[156] Controversy has swirled around the fact that two prominent social scientists made convincing arguments in support of a link between biosocial factors, such as genetic makeup, IQ, and body build, and the onset of criminal behavior. However, what went almost unnoticed in their work was an attempt to integrate biosocial and psychological research with rational choice theory into a view of criminality they refer to as *crime as choice.*

According to Wilson and Herrnstein, human behavior is determined by its perceived consequences. Choosing between committing a crime and not committing it (referred to as "noncrime") will depend on perception of gains and losses:

> the larger the ratio of net rewards of crime to the net rewards of noncrime, the greater the tendency to commit the crime.[157]

The rewards for crime can be found in the form of material gain, sexual gratification, gaining revenge against an enemy, peer approval, and so on; the consequences can include pangs of conscience, revenge of the victim, disapproval of friends and associates, and the possibility of punishment. Noncrime rewards are usually gained in the future: they involve the maintenance of one's self-image, reputation, potential for a happier life, freedom, and so on.

The crime-noncrime choice is influenced by a number of factors. Decisions are reinforced by the desire to obtain basic rewards—food, clothing, shelter, sex—or learned goals—wealth, power, status. The choice of crime may be influenced by a person's perceived sense of inequity; those who feel cheated by society may turn to crime in order to "catch up." However, Wilson and Herrnstein's most "controversial" conclusion is that the crime-noncrime choice is influenced by biosocial factors, including low intelligence, mesomorphic body types, having a criminal father, impulsivity or extravertness, and having an autonomic nervous system that responds less slowly to stimuli.[158] Social factors include a turbulent family life, school experiences, and membership within a deviant teenage subculture. Having these traits will not by themselves guarantee that a person will become a delinquent or criminal; however, all things being equal, those who have them will be more likely to choose crime over noncrime in certain situations.

TABLE 4.1 Choice and Developmental Theories

THEORY	MAJOR PREMISE	STRENGTHS
Choice Theories		
Rational Choice	Law violating behavior is an event that occurs after offenders weigh information on their personal needs and the situational factors involved in the difficulty and risk of committing a crime.	Explains why high-risk youth do not constantly engage in delinquent acts. Relates theory to delinquency control policy. Is not limited by class or other social variables.
Routine Activities	Crime and delinquency is a function of the presence of motivated offenders, the availability of suitable targets, and the absence of capable guardians.	Can explain fluctuations in crime and delinquency rates. Shows how victim behavior influences criminal choice.
Deterrence Theory	People will commit crime and delinquency if they perceive that the benefits outweigh the risks. Crime is a function of the severity, certainty, and speed of punishment.	Shows the relationship between crime and punishment. Suggests a real solution to crime.
Developmental Theories		
Biosocial		
Biochemical	Crime, especially violence, is a function of diet, vitamin intake, hormonal imbalance, or food allergies.	Explains irrational violence. Shows how the environment interacts with personal traits to influence behavior.
Neurological	Criminals and delinquents often suffer brain impairment, as measured by the EEG. Attention deficit disorder and minimum brain dysfunction are related to antisocial behavior.	Explains irrational violence. Shows how the environment interacts with personal traits to influence behavior.
Genetic	Delinquent traits and predispositions are inherited. The criminality of parents can predict the delinquency of children.	Explains why only a small percentage of youth in a high-crime area become chronic offenders.
Psychological		
Psychodynamic	The development of the unconscious personality early in childhood influences behavior for the rest of a person's life. Delinquents have weak egos and damaged personalities.	Explains the onset of crime and delinquency. Shows why delinquency and drug abuse cut across class lines.
Behavioral	People commit crime when they model their behavior after others they see being rewarded for the same acts. Behavior is enforced by rewards and extinguished by punishment.	Explains the role of others in the crime process. Shows how family life and media can influence delinquency.

TABLE 4.1 *continued*

THEORY	MAJOR PREMISE	STRENGTHS
Cognitive	Individual reasoning processes influence behavior. Reasoning is influenced by the way people perceive their environment and by their moral and intellectual development.	Shows why delinquent behavior patterns change over time as people mature and develop their moral reasoning.
Integrated		
Wilson and Herrnstein's human nature theory	People choose to commit crime when they are biologically and psychologically impaired.	Shows how physical traits interact with social conditions to produce crime. Can account for noncriminal behavior in high-crime areas. Integrates choice and developmental theories.

DEVELOPMENTAL THEORY IN REVIEW

Developmental views have been the subject of criticism on the grounds that their research methodology is weak and inconclusive. Since they invariably employ adjudicated or incarcerated offenders, it is often difficult to determine whether findings represent the delinquent population or merely those most likely to be arrested and adjudicated by officials of the justice system. For example, in a recent review of heredity studies, Glenn Walters and Thomas White concluded:

> Our review leads us to the inevitable conclusion that current genetic research on crime has been poorly designed, ambiguously reported and exceedingly inadequate in addressing the relevant issues.[159]

Some critics also fear that developmental research can be socially damaging and politically naive. If a significant number of delinquents come from particular economic, racial, and ethnic groups, are we to conclude that a corresponding percentage of people in these groups share physical and mental traits that differ from the norm? To many social scientists, the implications of this work are unacceptable in light of what we know about racism, sexism, and class bias.

Critics also suggest that developmental theory is limited as a generalized explanation of delinquent behavior because it fails to account for the patterns of delinquency. Delinquent behavior trends seem to conform to certain patterns linked to social rather than individual factors—social class, seasonality, population density, age, gender, and so on. Social forces that appear to be influencing the onset and sustenance of delinquent behavior are not accounted for by explanations of delinquency that focus on the individual. For example, if, as is often the case, the delinquency rate is higher in one state, city or neighborhood than another, are we to conclude that youths in the high-crime area are more likely to be watching violent TV shows or eating more sugar-coated cereals than those in low-rate jurisdictions?

Developmental theorists contend that critics overlook the fact that their research gives equal weight to environmental and social as well as mental and physical factors.[160] According to this view, some people have particular developmental problems that place them at a disadvantage in society, limit their chances of conventional success, and heighten their feelings of anger, frustration, and rage. Though the incidence of these personal traits may be spread evenly across the social structure, families in one segment of the population have the financial wherewithal to help ameliorate the problem, while families in another segment lack the economic means and the institutional support needed to help their children. If developmental theorists are correct, delinquency rate differences are a result of differential access to the care and treatment needed to correct and compensate for developmental problems and not a reflection of the unequal distribution of these problems across the social structure.

In addition, developmental theorists believe that, like it or not, people are in fact different and may carry with them a differing potential for antisocial acts. For example, gender differences in the violence rate may be explained by the fact that after centuries of aggressive mating behavior, males have become naturally more violent than females.[161] Male aggression may be more a matter of genetic transfer than socialization or cultural patterns.

Theories that focus on individual human development and its relationship to choosing delinquent and other forms of antisocial behavior are still emerging and are likely to receive greater attention in the 1990s. In an important review, Rolf Loeber and Marc LeBlanc have pointed out that the study of the life span of the individual delinquent is critical if we are to understand why delinquents behave the way they do: Why do they begin committing antisocial acts? Why do they stop or desist? Why do some escalate the severity of their delinquency, that is, go from shoplifting to armed robbery, while others de-escalate? If they stop committing delinquent acts, what, if anything, causes them to begin again? Why do some delinquents "specialize" in certain types of crime, such as robbery, while others are "generalists" engaging in a "garden variety" of antisocial behaviors?[162] Loeber and LeBlanc believe that it is not sufficient to conclude that someone is a "delinquent" and that condition X is the cause of their "delinquency." To truly understand delinquency, we must find out why people behave the way they do at different points in their life cycle. The physical and mental abilities of adolescents undergo dramatic changes as they mature and so does their behavior; a valid theory of delinquency must be adequate to explain these changes and how they effect the evolution of a delinquent career over time.

INDIVIDUAL APPROACHES TO DELINQUENCY PREVENTION

Since many individual-oriented theorists are also practitioners and clinicians, it is not surprising that a great deal of delinquency prevention efforts have their basis in human development.

As a group, individual-oriented theories suggest that prevention efforts should be directed at strengthening a youth's home life and personal relationships. A

Head Start

One of the most well-known efforts to help youths achieve on an individual level, and in so doing reduce their potential for delinquency, is the Head Start program. Head Start programs were instituted in the 1960s as part of the Johnson Administration's War on Poverty. Today there are over 9,400 centers around the nation serving 500,000 children and their families on a budget of over $1 billion annually. They are government-funded efforts to provide underprivileged preschoolers with an enriched educational environment to develop their learning and cognitive skills. Children in these programs are given the opportunity to use pegs and pegboards, puzzles, toy animals, dolls, letters and numbers, and other materials that middle-class youths take for granted and that give them a leg up in the educational process.

There has been considerable controversy surrounding the success of the Head Start program. In 1970, the Westinghouse Learning Corporation issued a definitive evaluation of the Head Start effort and concluded that there was no evidence of lasting cognitive gains on the part of the participating children. Initial gains seemed to evaporate during the elementary school years, and by the third grade, the performance of the Head Start children was no different than that of their peers. However, more recent research has produced dramatically different results. One report found that by age 5, children who experienced enriched day care aver-

aged thirty points higher on their IQ scores than their peers who did not utilize the program. Other research that carefully compared Head Start children to similar youths who did not attend the program found that the former made significant intellectual gains: Head Start children were less likely to have been left back or placed in classes for slow learners; they outperformed peers on achievement tests, and were more likely to graduate from high school. In addition, research by Faith Lamb Parker shows that the Head Start program can have important psychological benefits for the mothers of participants, such as decreasing depression and anxiety and increasing feelings of life satisfaction.

If, as many experts believe, there is a close link between school performance (Chapter 11), family life (Chapter 9), and delinquency, programs such as Head Start can help some potentially delinquent youths avoid problems with the law. By implication, their success indicates that programs which help on the individual, personal level can be used to combat delinquency.

Source: Faith Lamb Parker, Chaya Piorkowski, and Lenore Peay, "Head Start as Social Support for Mothers: The Psychological Benefits of Involvement," *American Journal of Orthopsychiatry* 57:220–33 (1987); Seymour Sarason and Michael Klaber, "The School as a Social Situation," *Annual Review of Psychology* 36:115–40 (1985); Spencer Rathus, *Psychology,* 3rd ed. (New York: Holt, Rinehart and Winston, 1987), p. 308.

child cannot develop properly if parents cannot supply proper attention, love, care, discipline, and nutrition.

It is, therefore, not surprising that state and privately funded treatment centers have offered counseling and other mental health services to families referred by schools, welfare agents, and/or juvenile court authorities. In some instances, such intervention is focused on a particular family problem that has the potential for producing delinquent behavior, for example, alcohol and drug problems, child abuse, and sexual abuse. In other situations, intervention is more generalized and oriented toward developing the self-image of parents and children or improving discipline in the family (see the *Focus on Delinquency* above entitled "Head Start").

In addition, individual approaches have been used to prevent court-adjudicated youth from engaging in further criminal activities. This is sometimes referred to as *secondary* or *special prevention*. It has become almost universal for incarcerated and court-adjudicated youths to be given some sort of mental and physical evaluation before their term of correctional treatment is to begin. Such rehabilitation methods as psychological counseling and psychotropic medication (such as Valium or Ritalin) are often prescribed.[163] In some instances, these programs are "drop-in" centers that service youths who are able to remain in their homes, while other more intensive programs require residential care and treatment.[164] At the least, this illustrates that agents of the juvenile justice system believe that many delinquent youths and status offenders have psychological or physical problems and that their successful "cure" can reduce repeat criminal behavior. Faith in this treatment approach suggests widespread agreement among juvenile justice system professionals that the cause of delinquency can be traced to individual pathology; if not, why else bother treating them?

While the influence of psychological theory on delinquency prevention has been extensive, programs based on biological theory have been dormant for some time. However, institutions are beginning to sponsor demonstration projects designed to study the influence of diet on crime and to determine whether regulating the metabolism can influence behavior. Such efforts are relatively new and untested. Similarly, schools are making an effort to help youths with learning disabilities and other developmental problems. Delinquency prevention efforts based on biosocial theory are still in their infancy.

There is still some question about the effectiveness of individual treatment as a delinquency prevention technique. There has been little hard evidence that clinical treatment alone can prevent delinquency or rehabilitate known delinquents. Critics still point to the failure of the famous Cambridge-Somerville Youth Study as evidence that clinical treatment had little value. In that effort, 325 high-risk predelinquents were given intense counseling and treatment and their progress was compared with a control group that received no special efforts. A well-known evaluation of the project by Joan and William McCord found that the treated youths were more likely to become involved in law violation than the untreated controls.[165] By implication, the danger is that the efforts designed to help youths may actually stigmatize and label them, hindering their efforts to live conventional lives. Critics argue that the more we try to help youths, the more likely they will be to see themselves as different, outcasts, and troublemakers and to be caught in the widening net of justice.[166]

CASE IN POINT

You are a state legislator who is a member of the subcommittee on juvenile justice. Your committee has been asked to redesign the state's juvenile code because of public outrage over serious juvenile crime.

At an open hearing, a professor from the local university testifies that she has devised a surefire test to predict violence-prone delinquents. The procedure involves brain scans, DNA testing, and blood analysis. Used with

continued

samples of incarcerated adolescents, her procedure has been able to distinguish with 90 percent accuracy between youths with a history of violence and those who are exclusively property offenders. The professor testifies that if each juvenile offender were tested with her techniques, the violence-prone career offender could be easily identified and given special treatment (for example, separated from the general juvenile population and/or given a longer sentence).

Opponents argue that this type of testing is unconstitutional because it violates the youth's Fifth Amendment rights against self-incrimination and can unjustly label nonviolent offenders. Any attempt to base policy on biological makeup seems inherently wrong and unfair. Those who favor the professor's approach maintain that it is not uncommon to single out the insane or mentally incompetent for special treatment and these conditions often have a biological basis. It is better, they argue, that a few delinquents be unfairly labeled than serious, violent offenders ignored until it is too late.

Should special laws be created to deal with the "potentially" dangerous offender?

Should offenders be typed on the basis of their biological characteristics?

Is a 10-percent rate of inaccuracy too high to be considered for a basis of prediction? What would you do if the test were 100-percent reliable?

SUMMARY

Choice theory holds that people have free will to control their actions. Crime is a product of the weighing of the risks of crime against its benefits. If the risk is greater than the gain, people will choose not to commit crime. One way of creating fear is to make sure that the punishments associated with crime are severe, certain, and fast.

Choice theorists argue that delinquent behavior can be prevented if youths can be deterred from illegal acts. Consequently, they agree that the punishment for delinquency should be increased. One method is to transfer youths to the criminal courts or to grant the adult justice system original jurisdiction over serious juvenile cases. Similarly, some delinquent experts advocate the use of incapacitation for serious juvenile offenders—for example, using mandatory, long-term sentences for chronic delinquents.

Choice theorists also advocate tough juvenile sentencing. Some states now punish offenders according to the crimes they commit and not their need for treatment.

Developmental theory holds that personal and environmental factors dictate behavior choices, that delinquents do not choose to commit crimes freely but are influenced by forces beyond their control.

One of the earliest branches of developmental theory focused on the biological bases of delinquency. Cesare Lombroso originated the concept of the "born criminal" and linked delinquency to inborn traits. Following his lead were theories based on genetic inheritance and body build. While biological theory was in disrepute for many years, it has recently reemerged in importance. Biochemical, neurological, and genetic factors have been linked to aggressiveness and violence in youth. However, because biological theory has not been subjected to methodologically sound tests, the results remain problematic.

The second branch of developmental theory has a psychological orientation. Some theorists rely on Freud's psychoanalytic theory and link delinquency to ego development and personality. Others use a behavioral perspective. Social-learning theorists hold that children imitate the adult behavior they observe live or on television. Cognitive psychologists study the relationship between mental processes and behavior.

Many delinquency prevention efforts are based on psychological theory. It is common for judges to order delinquent youths to receive counseling and other mental health care. Recently, some adjudicated delinquent offenders have been given biochemical therapy.

QUESTIONS FOR DISCUSSION

1. Is there such a thing as the "criminal man"?
2. Is crime psychologically abnormal? Can there be "normal" crimes?
3. Apply Freud's theory to such delinquent acts as shoplifting and breaking and entering a house.
4. Can delinquent behavior be deterred by the threat of punishment? If not, how can it be controlled?
5. Should we incapacitate violent juvenile offenders for long periods of time—ten years or more?

KEY TERMS

choice theory
developmental theory
free will
utilitarian
Cesare Beccaria
Jeremy Bentham
classical criminology
rehabilitation
medical model
rational choice
life-style
deterrence
criminal atavism
sociobiology
biosocial theory

equipotentiality
neurological
minimal brain dysfunction (MBD)
learning disabilities (LD)
Sigmund Freud
psychoanalytic
psychodynamic
psychoanalysis
Erik Erikson
identity crisis
behaviorism
cognitive school
psychopath
sociopath
personality inventories

NOTES

1. "A Murder Rap at Age 10," *Newsweek* 14 August 1989, p. 24.

2. Marvin Wolfgang, Robert Figlio, and Thorsten Sellin, *Delinquency in a Birth Cohort* (Chicago: University of Chicago Press, 1972).

3. Jeremy Bentham, *A Fragment on Government and an Introduction to the Principles of Morals and Legislation*, ed. Wilfred Harrison (Oxford: Basic Blackwell, 1967).

4. See, generally, Ernest Van den Haag, *Punishing Criminals* (New York: Basic Books, 1975).

5. See, generally, James Q. Wilson, *Thinking about Crime* (New York: Basic Books, 1975).

6. Cesare Beccaria, *On Crimes and Punishments*, trans. Henry Paolucci, 6th ed. (Indianapolis: Bobbs-Merrill, 1977), p. 43.

7. F. E. Devine, "Cesare Beccaria and the Theoretical Foundations of Modern Penal Jurisprudence," *New England Journal on Prison Law* 7:8–21 (1982).

8. For an analysis of the rehabilitation philosophy, see Ted Palmer, *Correctional Intervention and Research* (Lexington, Mass.: Lexington Books, 1978).

9. Sanford Fox, "The Reform of Juvenile Justice: The Child's Right to Punishment," *Juvenile Justice* 25:2–9 (1974).

10. Mary Tuck and David Riley, "The Theory of Reasoned Action: A Decision Theory of Crime," in *The Reasoning Criminal*, ed. Derek Cornish and Ronald Clarke, (New York: Springer-Verlag, 1986), pp. 156–69.

11. James Q. Wilson and Richard Herrnstein, *Crime and Human Nature* (New York: Simon and Schuster, 1985), p. 396.

12. Wilson, *Thinking about Crime*; Van den Haag, *Punishing Criminals*; Andrew von Hirsch, *Doing Justice: The Choice of Punishments* (New York: Hill & Wang, 1976); Graeme Newman, *Just and Painful* (New York: Macmillan, 1983).

13. See, generally, Cornish and Clarke, *The Reasoning Criminal*; see also Philip Cook, "The Demand and Supply of Criminal Opportunities," in *Crime and Justice*, vol. 7, ed. Michael Tonry and Norval Morris (Chicago: University of Chicago Press, 1986), pp. 1–28; Ronald Clarke and Derek Cornish, "Modeling Offender's Decisions: A Framework for Research and Policy," in *Crime and Justice*, vol. 6, ed. Michael Tonry and Norval Morris, (Chicago: University of Chicago Press, 1985), pp. 147–87; Morgan Reynolds, *Crime by Choice: An Economic Analysis* (Dallas: Fisher Institute, 1985).

14. Neal Shover, *Aging Criminals* (Beverly Hills, Calif.: Sage, 1985).

15. Travis Hirschi, "Rational Choice and Social Control Theories of Crime," in Cornish and Clarke, *The Reasoning Criminal*, p. 114.

16. Jack Katz, *Seductions of Crime* (New York: Basic Books, 1988).

17. *Ibid.*, pp. 12–52.

18. James Massey, Marvin Krohn, and Lisa Bonati, "Property Crime and the Routine Activities of Individuals," *Journal of Research in Crime and Delinquency* 26: 378–400 (1989).

19. Lawrence Cohen and Marcus Felson, "Social Change and Crime Rate Trends: A Routine Activities Approach," *American Sociological Review* 44:588–608 (1979).

20. For a review, see James LeBeau and Thomas Castellano, "The Routine Activities Approach: An Inventory and Critique," (Center for the Studies of Crime, Delinquency and Corrections, Southern Illinois University, Carbondale, 1987).Mimeo.

21. Massey, Krohn, and Bonati, "Property Crime and the Routine Activities of Individuals," p. 397.

22. Lawrence Cohen, Marcus Felson, and Kenneth Land, "Property Crime Rates in the United States: A Macrodynamic Analysis, 1947–1977, with Ex-Ante Forecasts for the Mid–1980s," *American Journal of Sociology* 86:90–118 (1980).

23. Robert O'Brien, "Relative Cohort Size and Age-Specific Crime Rates: An Age-Period-Relative-Cohort-Size Model," *Criminology* 27:57–78 (1989).

24. Steven Messner and Kenneth Tardiff, "The Social Ecology of Urban Homicide: An Application of the 'Routine Activities' Approach," *Criminology* 23:241–67 (1985).

25. Leslie Kennedy and David Forde, "Routine Activities and Crime: An Analysis of Victimization in Canada," *Criminology* 28:137–52 (1990).

26. David Maume, "Inequality and Metropolitan Rape Rates: A Routine Activity Approach," *Justice Quarterly* 6:513–27 (1989).

27. Ernest Van den Haag, "The Criminal Law as a Threat System," *Journal of Criminal Law and Criminology* 73:709–85 (1982).

28. Beccaria, *On Crimes and Punishments*.

29. For the classic analysis on the subject, see Johannes Andenaes, *Punishment and Deterrence* (Ann Arbor: University of Michigan Press, 1974).

30. *Stanford v. Kentucky* and *Wilkins v. Missouri,* 1095.ct. 2969 (1989).

31. Carol Kohfeld and John Sprague, "Demography, Police Behavior, and Deterrence," *Criminology* 28:111–36 (1990).

32. Steven Klepper and Daniel Nagin, "The Deterrent Effect of Perceived Certainty and Severity of Punishment Revisited," *Criminolgy* 27:721–46 (1989).

33. See, generally, Raymond Paternoster, "The Deterrent Effect of Perceived and Severity of Punishment: A Review of the Evidence and Issues," *Justice Quarterly* 42:173–217 (1987).

34. Raymond Paternoster, "Absolute and Restrictive Deterrence in a Panel of Youth: Explaining the Onset, Persistence/Desistance, and Frequency of Delinquent Offending," *Social Problems* 36:289–307 (1989).

35. Donald Green, "Measures of Illegal Behavior in Individual-Level Deterrence Research," *Journal of Research in Crime and Delinquency* 26:253–75 (1989); Charles Tittle, *Sanctions and Social Deviance: The Question of Deterrence* (New York: Praeger, 1980).

36. Bureau of Justice Statistics, *Prisoners and Drugs* (Washington, D.C.: U.S. Government Printing Office, 1983); idem, *Prisoners and Alcohol* (Washington, D.C.: U.S. Government Printing Office, 1983).

37. Maynard Erickson and Jack Gibbs, "Punishment, Deterrence, and Juvenile Justice," in *Critical Issues in Juvenile Justice*, ed. David Shichor and Delos Kelly (Lexington, Mass.: Lexington Books, 1980). pp. 183–202.

38. Taken from the famous title of an article by Walter Reckless, Simon Dinitz, and Ellen Murray, "The Good Boy in a High Delinquency Area," *Journal of Criminal Law, Criminology, and Police Science* 48:18–26 (1957).

39. Massey, Krohn, and Bonati, "Property Crime and the Routine Activities of Individuals."

40. David Shantz, "Conflict, Aggression, and Peer Status: An Observational Study," *Child Development* 57:1322–32 (1986).

41. For an excellent review of Lombroso's work, as well as that of other well-known theorists, see, Randy Martin, Robert Mutchnick, and W. Timothy Austin, *Criminological Thought, Pioneers Past and Present* (New York: Macmillan, 1990).

42. Marvin Wolfgang, "Cesare Lombroso," in *Pioneers in Criminology*, ed. Herman Mannheim (Montclair, N.J.: Patterson Smith, 1970), pp. 232–71.

43. Gina Lombroso-Ferrero, *Criminal Man According to the Classification of Cesare Lombroso, 1911* (reprint, Montclair, N.J.: Patterson Smith, 1972), p. 7.

44. Edwin Driver, "Charles Buckman Goring," in *Pioneers in Criminology*, pp. 429–42.

45. See, generally, Thorsten Sellin, "Enrico Ferri," in *Pioneers in Criminology*, pp. 361–84.

46. Driver, "Charles Buckman Goring," pp. 434–35.

47. *Ibid.,* p. 440.

48. See Richard Dugdale, *The Jukes* (New York: Putnam, 1910); Arthur Estabrook, *The Jukes in 1915* (Washington, D.C.: Carnegie Institute of Washington, 1916).

49. Ernst Kretschmer, *Physique and Character,* trans. W. J. H. Spratt (London: Kegan Paul, 1925).

50. William Sheldon, *Varieties of Delinquent Youth* (New York: Harper Bros., 1949).

51. Sheldon Glueck and Eleanor Glueck, *Of Delinquency and Crime* (Springfield, Ill.: Charles C. Thomas, 1974), p. 2.

52. B. R. McCandless, W. S. Persons, and A. Roberts, "Perceived Opportunity, Delinquency, Race, and Body Build among Delinquent Youth," *Journal of Consulting and Clinical Psychology* 38:281–83 (1972).

53. Edmond O. Wilson, *Sociobiology: The New Synthesis* (Cambridge, Mass.: Harvard University Press, 1975).

54. Arthur Caplan, *The Sociobiology Debate: Readings on Ethical and Scientific Issues* (New York: Harper & Row, 1978).

55. For a thorough review of the biosocial perspective, see, Diana Fishbein, "Biological Perspectives in Criminology," *Criminology* 28:27–72 (1990).

56. See C. Ray Jeffrey, "Criminology as an Interdisciplinary Behavioral Science," *Criminology* 16:149–67 (1978).

57. See, generally, Leonard Hippchen, *The Ecologic-Biochemical Approaches to Treatment of Delinquents and Criminals* (New York: Van Nostrand Reinhold, 1978).

58. Elizabeth McNeal and Peter Cimbolic, "Antidepressants and Biochemical Theories of Depression," *Psychological Bulletin* 99:361–74 (1986); for an opposing view, see, "Adverse Reactions to Food in Young Children," *Nutrition Reviews* 46:120–21 (1988).

59. Leonard Hippchen, "Some Possible Biochemical Aspects of Criminal Behavior," *Journal of Behavioral Ecology* 2:1–6 (1981); Sarnoff Mednick and Jan Volavka, "Biology and Crime," in Norval Morris and Michael Tonry, eds., *Crime and Justice* v. 1 (Chicago: University of Chicago Press, 1980), pp. 85–159.

60. Stephen Schoenthaler, "Malnutrition and Maladaptive Behavior: Two Correlational Analyses and a Double-Blind Placebo-Controlled Challenge in Five States," in W. B. Essman, ed., *Nutrients and Brain Function* (New York: Karger, 1987).

61. Richard Milich and William Pelham, "Effects of Sugar Ingestion on the Classroom and Playgroup Behavior of Attention Deficit Disordered Boys," *Journal of Counseling and Clinical Psychology* 54:714–18 (1986).

62. Alexander Schauss and C. Simonsen, "A Critical Analysis of the Diets of Chronic Juvenile Offenders, Part I," *Journal of Orthomolecular Psychiatry* 8:149–57 (1979).

63. J. Kershner and W. Hawke, "Megavitamins and Learning Disorders: A Controlled Double-Blind Experiment," *Journal of Nutrition* 109:819–26 (1979).

64. Stephen Schoenthaler and Walter Doraz, "Types of Offenses Which Can Be Reduced in an Institutional Setting Using Nutritional Intervention," *International Journal of Biosocial Research* 4:74–84 (1983); idem, "Diet and Crime," *International Journal of Biosocial Research* 4:29–39 (1983).

65. Stephen Schoenthaler, Walter Doraz, and James Wakefield, "The Impact of a Low Food Additive and Sucrose Diet on Academic Performance in 803 New York City Public Schools," *International Journal of Biosocial Research* 8:185–95 (1986).

66. Stephen Schoenthaler, "Institutional Nutritional Policies and Criminal Behavior," *Nutrition Today* 24:16–24 (1985).

67. Diana Fishbein, David Lozovsky, and Jerome Jaffe, "Impulsivity, Aggression and Neuroendocrine Responses to Serotonergic Stimulation in Substance Abusers" (Paper presented at the meeting of the American Society of Criminology, Reno, Nevada, November 1989).

68. Leila Beckwith and Arthur Parmelee, "EEG Patterns of Preterm Infants, Home Environment, and later IQ," *Child Development* 57:777–89 (1986).

69. Kytja Voeller, "Right-Hemisphere Deficit Syndrome in Children," *American Journal of Psychiatry* 143:1004–9 (1986).

70. Dorothy Otnow Lewis, Johnathan Pincus, Marilyn Feldman, Lori Jackson, and Barbara Bard, "Psychiatric, Neurological, and Psychoeducational Characteristics of Fifteen Death Row Inmates in the United States," *American Journal of Psychiatry* 143:838–45 (1986).

71. See, generally, R. R. Monroe, *Brain Dysfunction in Aggressive Criminals* (Lexington, Mass.: D.C. Heath, 1978).

72. Adrian Raine, et al., "Interhemispheric Transfer in Schizophrenics, Depressives and Normals with Schizoid Tendencies," *Journal of Abnormal Psychology* 98:35–41 (1989).

73. D. Williams, "Neural Factors Related to Habitual Aggression—Consideration of Differences between Habitual Aggressives and Others Who Have Committed Crimes of Violence," *Brain* 92:503–20 (1969).

74. Charlotte Johnson and William Pelham, "Teacher Ratings Predict Peer Ratings of Aggression at Three-Year Follow-Up in Boys with Attention Deficit Disorder with Hyperactivity," *Journal of Consulting and Clinical Psychology* 54:571–72 (1987).

75. Cited in Charles Post, "The Link between Learning Disabilities and Juvenile Delinquency: Cause, Effect, and 'Present Solutions,'" *Juvenile and Family Court Journal* 31:59 (1981).

76. For a general review, see, Concetta Culliver, "Juvenile Delinquency and Learning Disability: Any link?" (Paper presented at the Academy of Criminal Justice Sciences, San Francisco, April 1988).

77. Joel Zimmerman, William Rich, Ingo Keilitz, and Paul Broder, "Some Observations on the Link between Learning Disabilities and Juvenile Delinquency," *Journal of Criminal Justice* 9:9–17 (1981); J. W. Podboy and W. A. Mallory, "The Diagnosis of Specific Learning Disabilities in a Juvenile Delinquent Population," *Juvenile and Family Court Journal* 30:11–13 (1978).

78. Charles Murray, *The Link between Learning Disabilities and Juvenile Delinquency: A Current Theory and Knowledge* (Washington, D.C.: U.S. Government Printing Office, 1976).

79. Robert Pasternak and Reid Lyon, "Clinical and Empirical Identification of Learning Disabled Juvenile Delinquents," *Journal of Correctional Education* 33:7–13 (1982).

80. Zimmerman, et al., "Some Observations on the Link between Learning Disabilities and Juvenile Delinquency."

81. Lynn Meltzer, Bethany Roditi, and Terence Fenton, "Cognitive and Learning Profiles of Delinquent and Learning-Disabled Adolescents," *Adolescence* 21:581–91 (1986).

82. Diana Fishbein and Robert Thatcher, "New Diagnostic Methods in Criminology: Assessing Organic Sources of Behavioral Disorder," *Journal of Research in Crime and Delinquency* 23:240–67 (1986).

83. L. Erlenmeyer-Kimling, Robert Golden, and Barbara Cornblatt, "A Taxometric Analysis of Cognitive and Neuromotor Variables in Children in Risk for Schizophrenia," *Journal of Abnormal Psychcology* 98:203–8 (1989).

84. A. A. Sandberg, G. F. Koeph, T. Ishiara, and T. S. Hauschka, "An XYY Human Male," *Lancet* 262:448–49 (1961); T. R. Sarbin and L. E. Miller, "Demonism Revisited: The XYY Chromosome Anomaly," *Issues in Criminology* 5:195–207 (1970).

85. Nancy Segal, "Monozygotic and Dizygotic Twins: A Comparative Analysis of Mental Ability Profiles," *Child Development* 56:1051–58 (1985).

86. Mednick and Volavka, "Biology and Crime"; Lee Ellis, "Genetics and Criminal Behavior," *Criminology* 10:43–66 (1982).

87. Karl O. Christiansen, "A Preliminary Study of Criminality among Twins," in *The Biosocial Bases of Criminal Behavior*, ed. S. A. Mednick and Karl O. Christiansen (New York: Gardner Press, 1977).

88. Remi Cadoret, Colleen Cain, and Raymond Crowe, "Evidence for a Gene-Environment Interaction in the Development of Adolescent Antisocial Behavior," *Behavior Genetics* 13:301–10 (1983).

89. Bernard Hutchings and Sarnoff Mednick, "Criminality in Adoptees and Their Adoptive and Biological Parents: A Pilot Study," in *Biosocial Bases of Criminal Behavior*.

90. William Gabrielli and Sarnoff Medinck, "Urban Environment, Genetics, and Crime," *Criminology* 22:645–53 (1984).

91. Jody Alberts-Corush, Philip Firestone, John Goodman, "Attention and Impulsivity Characteristics of the Biological and Adoptive Parents of Hyperactive and Normal Control Children," *American Journal of Orthopsychiatry* 56:413–23 (1986).

92. Wilson and Herrnstein, *Crime and Human Nature*, p. 121.

93. For a thorough review of this issue, see David Brandt and S. Jack Zlotnick, *The Psychology and Treatment of the Youthful Offender* (Springfield, Ill.: Charles C. Thomas, 1988).

94. Spencer Rathus, *Psychology* (New York: Holt, Rinehart & Winston, 1984).

95. See, generally, Sigmund Freud, *An Outline of Psychoanalysis*, trans. James Strachey (New York: Norton, 1963).

96. Seymour Halleck, *Psychiatry and the Dilemmas of Crime* (Berkeley, Calif.: University of California Press, 1971).

97. See, generally, Erik Erikson, *Identity, Youth, and Crisis* (New York: Norton, 1968).

98. David Abrahamsen, *Crime and the Human Mind* (New York: Columbia University Press, 1944), p. 137.

99. See, generally, Fritz Redl and Hans Toch, "The Psychoanalytic Perspective," in *Psychology of Crime and Criminal Justice*, ed. Hans Toch (New York: Holt, Rinehart & Winston, 1979), pp. 193–95.

100. August Aichorn, *Wayward Youth* (New York: Viking, 1935).

101. Halleck, *Psychiatry and the Dilemmas of Crime.*

102. James Sorrells, "Kids Who Kill," *Crime and Delinquency* 23:312–20 (1977).

103. Richard Rosner, et al., "Adolescents Accused of Murder and Manslaughter: A Five-Year Descriptive Study," *Bulletin of the American Academy of Psychiatry and the Law* 7:342–51 (1979).

104. Milton Rosenbaum and Binni Bennet, "Homicide and Depression," *American Journal of Psychiatry* 143:367–70 (1986).

105. Brandt and Zlotnick, *The Psychology and Treatment of the Youthful Offender*, pp. 72–73.

106. See Albert Bandura and Frances Menlove, "Factors Determining Vicarious Extinction of Avoidance Behavior through Symbolic Modeling," *Journal of Personality and Social Psychology* 8:99–108 (1965); Albert Bandura and Richard Walters, *Social Learning and Personality Development* (New York: Holt, Rinehart & Winston, 1963).

107. David Perry, Louise Perry, and Paul Rasmussen, "Cognitive Social Learning Mediators of Aggression," *Child Development* 57:700–11 (1986).

108. Bonnie Carlson, "Children's Beliefs about Punishment," *American Journal of Orthopsychiatry* 56:308–12 (1986).

109. Albert Bandura and Richard Walters, *Adolescent Aggression* (New York: Ronald Press, 1959), p. 32.

110. Edward Donnerstein and Daniel Linz, "The Question of Pornography," *Psychology Today* 20:56–59 (1986).

111. Joyce Sprafkin, Kenneth Gadow, and Monique Dussault, "Reality Perceptions of Television: A Preliminary Comparison of Emotionally Disturbed and Nonhandicapped Children," *American Journal of Orthopsychiatry* 56:147–52.

112. Daniel Anderson, Elizabeth Pugzles Lorch, Diane Field, Patricia Collins, and John Nathan, "Television Viewing at Home: Age Trends in Visual Attention Time with TV," *Child Development* 57:1024–33 (1986).

113. Lynette Friedrich-Cofer and Aletha Huston, "Television Violence and Aggression: The Debate Continues," *Psychological Bulletin* 100:364–71 (1986).

114. American Psychological Association, *Violence on TV. A Social Issue Release from the Board of Social and Ethical Responsibility for Psychology* (Washington, D.C.: American Psychological Association, 1985).

115. Johnathon Freedman, "Effect of Television Violence on Aggressiveness," *Psychological Bulletin* 96:227–46 (1984); idem, "Television Violence and Aggression: A Rejoinder," *Psychological Bulletin* 100:372–78 (1986).

116. Steven Messner, "Television Violence and Violent Crime: An Aggregate Analysis," *Social Problems* 33:218–35 (1986).

117. See, generally, Jean Piaget, *The Moral Judgment of the Child* (London: Kegan Paul, 1932).

118. Lawrence Kohlberg, *Stages in the Development of Moral Thought and Action* (New York: Holt, Rinehart and Winston, 1969).

119. L. Kohlberg, K. Kauffman, P. Scharf, and J. Hickey, *The Just Community Approach in Corrections: A Manual*

(Niantic, Conn.: Connecticut Department of Corrections, 1973).

120. Scott Henggeler, *Delinquency in Adolescence* (Newbury Park, Calif.: Sage, 1989), p. 26.

121. *Ibid.*

122. See, generally, Walter Mischel, *Introduction to Personality*, 4th ed. (New York: Holt, Rinehart and Winston, 1986).

123. D. A. Andrews and J. Stephen Wormith, "Personality and Crime: Knowledge and Construction in Criminology," *Justice Quarterly* 27:289–310 (1989); Donald Gibbons, "Comment-Personality and Crime: Non-Issues, Real Issues, and a Theory and Research Agenda," *Justice Quarterly* 27:311–24 (1989).

124. Sheldon Glueck and Eleanor Glueck, *Unraveling Juvenile Delinquency* (Cambridge, Mass.: Harvard University Press, 1950).

125. See, generally, Hans Eysenck, *Personality and Crime* (London: Routledge and Kegan Paul, 1977).

126. Hans Eysenck and M. W. Eysenck, *Personality and Individual Differences* (New York: Plenum, 1985).

127. David Farrington, "Psychobiological Factors in the Explanation and Reduction of Delinquency," *Today's Delinquent* 2:37–51 (1988).

128. Laurie Frost, Terrie Moffitt, and Rob McGee, "Neuropsychological Correlates of Psychopathology in an Unselected Cohort of Young Adolescents," *Journal of Abnormal Psychology* 98:307–13 (1989).

129. Harvey Cleckley, "Psychopathic States," in *American Handbook of Psychiatry*, ed. S. Aneti (New York: Basic Books, 1959), pp. 567–69.

130. Rathus, *Psychology*, p. 452.

131. Lewis Yablonsky, *The Violent Gang* (Baltimore: Penguin, 1971), pp. 195–205.

132. Helene Raskin White, Erich Labouvie, and Marsha Bates, "The Relationship between Sensation Seeking and Delinquency: A Longitudinal Analysis," *Journal of Research in Crime and Delinquency* 22:197–211 (1985).

133. See, for example, R. Starke Hathaway and Elio Monachesi, "The M.M.P.I. in the Study of Juvenile Delinquents," in *Mental Health and Mental Disorder*, ed. A. M. Rose (London: Routledge, 1956).

134. R. Starke Hathaway and Elio Monachesi, *Analyzing and Predicting Juvenile Delinquency with the M.M.P.I.* (Minneapolis: University of Minnesota Press, 1953).

135. *Ibid.*

136. Deborah Decker Roman and David Gerbing, "The Mentally Disordered Criminal Offender: A Description Based on Demographic, Clinical and MMPI," *Journal of Clinical Psychology* 45:983–90 (1989).

137. See Karl Schuessler and Donald Cressey, "Personality Characteristics of Criminals," *American Journal of Sociology* 55:476–84 (1950); Gordon Waldo and Simon Dinitz, "Personality Attributes of the Criminal: An Analysis of Research Studies, 1950–1965," *Journal of Research on Crime and Delinquency* 4:185–201 (1967); David Tennenbaum, "Research Studies of Personality and Criminality," *Journal of Criminal Justice* 5:1–19 (1977).

138. Donald Calsyn, Dourglass Roszell, and Edmund Chaney, "Validation of MMPI Profile Subtypes among Opioid Addicts Who Are Beginning Methadone Maintenance Treatment," *Journal of Clinical Psychology* 45:991–99 (1989).

139. L. M. Terman, "Research on the Diagnosis of Predelinquent Tendencies," *Journal of Delinquency* 9:124–30 (1925); idem, *Measurement of Intelligence* (Boston: Houghton-Mifflin, 1916). For example, see M. G. Caldwell, "The Intelligence of Delinquent Boys Committed to Wisconsin Industrial School," *Journal of Criminal Law and Criminology* 20:421–28 (1929); C. Murcheson, *Criminal Intelligence* (Worcester, Mass.: Clark University, 1926), pp. 41–44.

140. Henry Goddard, *Efficiency and Levels of Intelligence* (Princeton: Princeton University Press, 1920).

141. William Healy and Augusta Bronner, *Delinquency and Criminals: Their Making and Unmaking* (New York: Macmillan, 1926).

142. Kenneth Eels, et al., *Intelligence and Cultural Differences* (Chicago: University of Chicago Press, 1951), p. 181.

143. Sorel Cahahn and Nora Cohen, "Age Versus Schooling Effects on Intelligence Development," *Child Development* 60:1239–49 (1989).

144. John Slawson, *The Delinquent Boys* (Boston: Budget Press, 1926).

145. Edwin Sutherland, "Mental Deficiency and Crime," in *Social Attitudes*, ed. Kimball Young (New York: Henry Holt, 1973), chap. 15.

146. Travis Hirschi and Michael Hindelang, "Intelligence and Delinquency: A Revisionist Review," *American Sociological Review* 42:471–586 (1977).

147. Terrie Moffitt, William Gabrielli, Sarnoff Mednick, and Fini Schulsinger, "Socioeconomic Status, IQ, and Delinquency," *Journal of Abnormal Psychology* 90:152–56 (1981).

148. *Ibid.*, p. 155. For a similar finding, see L. Hubble and M. Groff, "Magnitude and Direction of WISC-R Verbal Performance IQ Discrepancies among Adjudicated Male Delinquents," *Journal of Youth and Adolescence* 10:179–83 (1981).

149. Terrie Moffitt and Phil Silva, "IQ and Delinquency: A Direct Test of the Differential Detection Hypothesis," *Journal of Abnormal Psychology* 97:1–4 (1988); E. Kandel, S. Mednick, L. Sorenson-Kirkegaard, B. Hutch-

ings, J. Knop, R. Rosenberg, and F. Schulsinger, "IQ as a Protective Factor for Subjects at a High Risk for Antisocial Behavior," *Journal of Consulting and Clinical Psychology*, 56:224–26 (1988); Christine Ward and Richard McFall, "Further Validation of the Problem Inventory for Adolescent Girls: Comparing Caucasian and Black Delinquents and Nondelinquents," *Journal of Consulting and Clinical Psychology* 54:732–33 (1986).

150. Jennifer White, Terrie Moffitt, and Phil Silva, "A Prospective Replication of the Protective Effects of IQ in Subjects at High Risk for Juvenile Delinquency," *Journal of Consulting and Clinical Psychology*, 37:719–24 (1989).

151. Wilson and Herrnstein, *Crime and Human Nature*, p. 148.

152. Scott Menard and Barbara Morse, "A Structuralist Critique of the IQ-Delinquency Hypothesis: Theory and Evidence," *American Journal of Sociology* 89:1347–78 1984).

153. *Ibid.*

154. Deborah Denno, "Sociological and Human Developmental Explanations of Crime: Conflict or Consensus," *Criminology* 23:711–41 (1985).

155. *Ibid.*, p. 171.

156. Wilson and Herrnstein, *Crime and Human Nature*.

157. *Ibid.*, p. 44.

158. *Ibid.*, p. 171.

159. Glenn Walters and Thomas White, "Heredity and Crime: Bad Genes or Bad Research," *Justice Quarterly* 27:455–85 (1989) at 478.

160. Ellis, "Genetics and Criminal Behavior," p. 58.

161. Lee Ellis, "The Evolution of the Nonlegal Equivalent of Aggressive Criminal Behavior," *Aggressive Behavior* 12:57–71 (1986).

162. Rolf Loeber and Marc LeBlanc, "Toward a Developmental Criminology," in *Crime and Justice: An Annual Review of Research*, vol. 12, ed. Norval Morris and Michael Tonry (Chicago: University of Chicago Press, 1990), pp. 375–473.

163. See, for example, Edward Pecukonis, "A Cognitive/Affective Empathy Training Programs as a Function of Ego Development in Aggressive Adolescent Females," *Adolescence* 25:61–67 (1990).

164. See, for example, Jennifer Chalmers and Michael Townsend, "The Effects of Training in Social Perspective Taking on Socially Maladjusted Girls," *Child Development* 61:178–90 (1990).

165. Joan McCord and William McCord, "A Follow-up Report on the Cambridge-Somerville Youth Study," *Annals* 322:89–98 (1959).

166. Edwin Schur, *Radical Nonintervention: Rethinking the Delinquency Problem* (Englewood Cliffs, N. J.: Prentice-Hall, 1973).

5

Social Structure Theories

Social Disorganization, Strain, and Cultural Deviance

In 1966, sociologist Oscar Lewis coined the phrase the **culture of poverty.** According to Lewis, the crushing burden of living in slum areas produces a large mass of urban poor whose wretched day-to-day living conditions are passed on from one generation to the next.[1] The culture of poverty is marked by apathy, cynicism, helplessness, and mistrust of such institutions as the police, courts, schools, and government. Mistrust of authority prevents slum dwellers from taking advantage of the few opportunities they do have. Consequently, there has developed a stable group of urban poor who have little chance of upward mobility or improvement; they are a permanent underclass.

The destructive social forces operating within a slum area are also believed responsible for leading its youthful residents toward delinquent behaviors and later into adult criminal careers. While middle- and upper-class children may engage in minor and occasional delinquent acts—vandalism, use of nonaddictive "recreational drugs" such as marijuana, petty theft, and motor vehicle violations—they refrain from the more serious acts of violence, theft, and gang membership. Even those middle-class youths who do engage in persistent delinquent acts eventually "age out" of criminality and become responsible citizens. Desistance is possible because members of the middle class are better able to organize their resources in education and in the marketplace.[2] These conventional behavior choices are simply not open or available to lower-class slum youths.

Considering their social and economic decay, it does not come as any surprise that deteriorated inner-city areas in such cities as New York, Miami, and Los Angeles are believed to be the spawning ground of youth gangs and groups. Without hope of earning money and achieving success through legitimate means, is it any wonder that inner-city youth turn to crime as a means of survival, self-esteem, and acquiring social standing among their peers?

Lower-class slum areas are the scene of the highest crime and victimization rates. Official delinquency rates for such crimes as robbery and larceny are much higher in urban areas than in suburban and rural areas. Likewise, victim and official record studies seem to indicate that lower-class youths are the most likely to commit the most serious delinquent and criminal acts.

Because of these conditions, many delinquency experts have held the view that delinquency is a function of social consequences faced by the lower class. They have formulated **social structure**-based theories that tie delinquency rates to socioeconomic conditions: areas that experience high levels of poverty and social disorganization will also experience high delinquency rates. Structural theories are not concerned with why an *individual* youth commits delinquent *acts* but why certain *ecological areas* experience high delinquency *rates.*

This chapter reviews theories that link the onset and sustenance of a delinquent career to the crushing problems faced by lower-class slum youths. First, however, we review some of the specific social problems faced by the lower class that have long been associated with delinquency.

LOWER-CLASS LIFE

Data gathered by a number of sources supports a bleak vision of a racially, socially, and economically **stratified** society. While most Americans have the financial means to enjoy the fruits of U.S. technology and achievement, about 13 percent of the population, or 30 million people, lives below the poverty line (estimated at about a $12,000 annual income for a family of four). Stratification effects are becoming sharper. The wealthiest Americans today enjoy a greater share of all money income than ever before (the top 5 percent gets 17 percent of all income), while the poorest Americans are receiving proportionately less (the bottom 20 percent gets 4.6 percent of all income).[3]

The poor in the United States often reside in deteriorated sections of the nation's largest cities. Because of their depressed financial status, they are deprived of a standard of living enjoyed by most other citizens. Some become members of a permanent *underclass*, supported by public welfare and private charity for their entire lives. They have no hope of achieving higher status within conventional society. They attend poor schools, live in substandard housing, and lack good health care. More than half the families are fatherless and husbandless, headed by a female who is the sole breadwinner; many are supported entirely by county welfare and Aid to Dependent Children (ADC). The Census Bureau estimates that about 20 percent of white children and 75 percent of black children are born out of wedlock; about 25 percent of all American families are single-parent households, and 88 percent of these are headed by a single mother.[4]

The problems of providing adequate care and discipline to children under these circumstances can be immense. One federal survey estimated that over 2 million latchkey children, about 7 percent of all American youth under 13, are left

About 30 million Americans live below the poverty line.

unattended after school every day.[5] Although there is little empirical evidence that living in a single-parent household alone is sufficient to produce delinquent behavior, it seems logical that the problems presented by raising a family in a deteriorated neighborhood are better met by two parents than one.[6]

Racial Disparity

The effects of poverty are most often felt by minority group members. As of 1990, it was estimated that 30 percent of black families, compared to 8 percent of white families, live in poverty; the median black family income was $18,100, compared to the median white income of $32,270; unemployment was 11.7 percent for blacks and 4.7 percent for whites; 32 percent of black teens and 13 percent of white teens in the labor force were unemployed.[7] A recent report by the National Research Council, a private, nonprofit group, found that black Americans are either losing ground or maintaining a second-class status in such critical areas as economic and educational status. For example, in 1950, the median family income for black families was about $7,500, while white families averaged about $15,000; by 1985, black income had doubled to about $15,000, but so had white income levels, to about $30,000. In 1960, 22 percent of black families were headed by a woman; by 1985, the rate had doubled to 44 percent; in contrast, white single-parent families remained stable (10 percent in 1940 to 13 percent in 1985). And while the number of high school graduates attending colleges has moved steadily upward (to about 60 percent), black college attendance peaked at 48 percent in 1977 and since then has fallen continuously to about 38 percent.[8]

The problems experienced by the urban poor are difficult to overcome; for black Americans, the situation has become desperate. In 1990, disturbing data was released by the nonprofit National Sentencing Project that highlights the seriousness of the situation: almost 25 percent of all black men 20 to 29 years of age are under some sort of correctional supervision; in comparison, about 6 percent of all young white men are under correctional supervision.[9] The report concluded that we "risk the possibility of writing off an entire generation of black men from having the opportunity to lead productive lives in our society."[10]

These alarming social data form the basis of social structure theory, the view that delinquency is a function of a youth's position in the socioeconomic structure of American society.

SOCIAL STRUCTURE THEORY

Social structure theories are based on the premise that a relationship exists between an individual's social and economic situation and the probability that he or she will engage in delinquent behavior. The lower youths are on the social scale, the fewer economic resources they possess, the more cultural hurdles they must face, and the greater their involvement will be with a delinquent way of life.

The structural approach has had a long tradition in the study of juvenile delinquency. Work in the area can be classified into three independent yet interrelated subgroups: **social disorganization, strain,** and **cultural deviance** (or **subcultural**) theories. Although they are closely related and overlap a great deal, enough difference exists between them to warrant separate analysis. Social disorganization theory regards the crime-producing influences such as poverty, substandard housing, and disrupted family lives that exist in the nation's poorest urban areas as the key to the cause of delinquency. Strain theories portray delinquency as a result of the frustration slum youths feel when they are locked out of the mainstream of American society yet desire middle-class benefits and luxuries. Cultural deviance theories view delinquency as a function of the prevailing cultural norms and values that emerge in lower-class, socially disorganized neighborhoods. All three are similar because they maintain that membership in the underclass is a prerequisite for serious delinquent behaviors. They differ in their description of the beliefs, values, attitudes, and goals of delinquent youth and how these personal sentiments influence law-violating behavior.

Each perspective will be analyzed in the next section.

SOCIAL DISORGANIZATION THEORY

Social disorganization theories link delinquency rates to neighborhood ecological characteristics. They seek to explain why crime rates are so high in areas that are characterized by urban decay and a breakdown in the fabric of social life. Why is it that localities with highly transient populations (so called "changing neighborhoods"), significant levels of unemployment, single-parent families, and families on welfare and ADC are also the ones that experience a considerable level of delinquent behavior? Is there some central element of community structure that influences its residents' behavior? As a group, these theories suggest that socially disorganized areas that are unable to provide essential services such as proper education, health care, and housing, in which the key social control agencies of society can no longer function effectively, are the ones that also experience the highest rates of crime and delinquency.

Shaw and McKay's Ecological Approach

The roots of the social disorganization tradition can be traced to the pioneering efforts of the Chicago school sociologists Clifford Shaw and Henry McKay.[11] During the 1920s, Chicago's history was typical of the transition taking place in many other urban areas. The city's wealthy, established citizens were concerned about the moral fabric of society. The prevailing belief was that foreign immigrants were crime-prone and morally dissolute. In fact, local groups were created with the very purpose of "saving" the children of poor families from moral decadence. It was popular to view delinquency as the property of inferior racial and ethnic groups.

Based in Chicago, Shaw and McKay sought to explain delinquency within the context of the changing urban ecology. They had collected extensive statistics on delinquency rates in the Chicago area. Included in their data were the records of

FIGURE 5.1
Social disorganization
theory

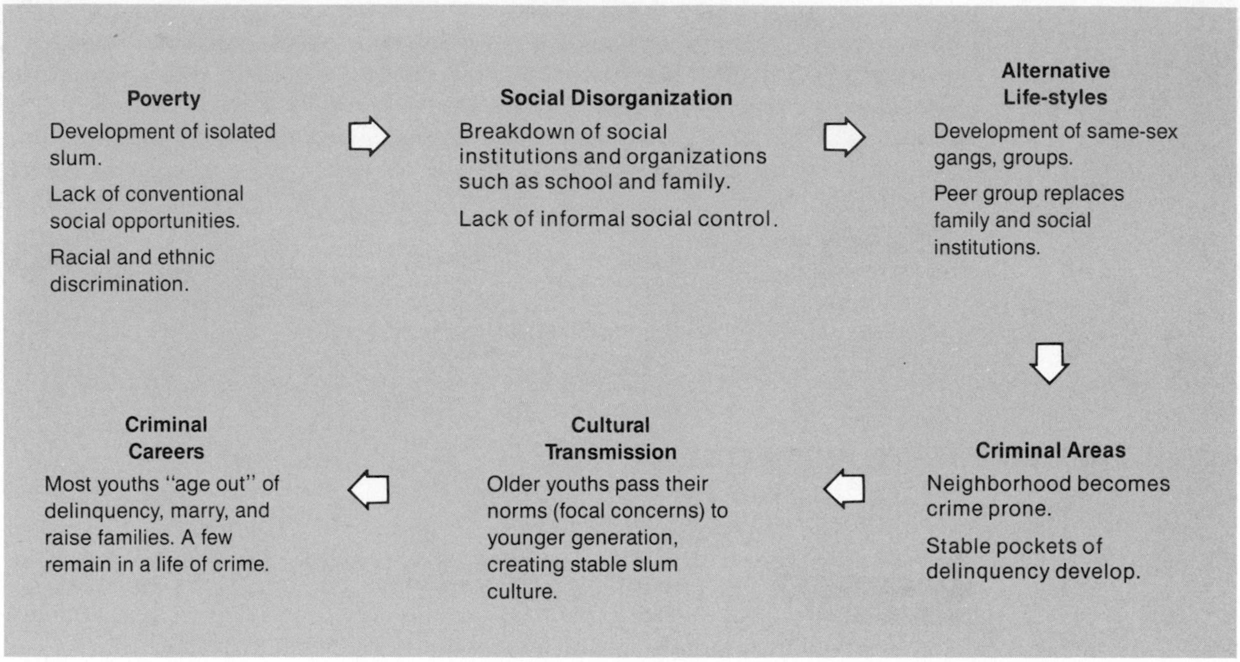

Poverty

Development of isolated slum.

Lack of conventional social opportunities.

Racial and ethnic discrimination.

Social Disorganization

Breakdown of social institutions and organizations such as school and family.

Lack of informal social control.

Alternative Life-styles

Development of same-sex gangs, groups.

Peer group replaces family and social institutions.

Criminal Careers

Most youths "age out" of delinquency, marry, and raise families. A few remain in a life of crime.

Cultural Transmission

Older youths pass their norms (focal concerns) to younger generation, creating stable slum culture.

Criminal Areas

Neighborhood becomes crime prone.

Stable pockets of delinquency develop.

almost 25,000 alleged delinquents brought before the Juvenile Court of Cook County during the period from 1900 to 1933.

Using their extensive data, they rejected the racial and cultural explanations of delinquency then popular and instead viewed the ecological conditions of the city itself as the real culprit in the creation of delinquent behavior. They saw that Chicago had developed into distinct neighborhoods, some marked by wealth and luxury, others by overcrowding, poor health and sanitary conditions, and extreme poverty. These slum areas were believed to be the spawning grounds of delinquency.

Shaw and McKay viewed delinquency as a product of the decaying **transitional neighborhood,** which manifested social disorganization and maintained conflicting values and social systems. In this environment, teenage gangs developed as a means of survival, economic gain, defense, and friendship. Also, gangs maintained a unique set of cultural norms and values that differed sharply from those of the general society. The gang leaders soon recruited younger members, passing on delinquent traditions and ensuring survival of the gang from one generation to the next. This view of delinquent behavior is known as **cultural transmission.**

Shaw and McKay identified the domicile of youthful delinquents in Chicago.[12] They noted that distinct ecological areas had developed in the city, comprising a series of five concentric circles, or zones, and that some of the zones had more delinquent behavior than others (see Figure 5.2). The areas of heaviest delinquency concentration appeared to be the transitional, inner-city zones of the city,

FIGURE 5.2
Shaw and McKay's
Concentric Zone
Model

The Growth of the City

where large portions of foreign-born citizens had recently immigrated. The zones farthest from the city's center were less prone to delinquency. Analysis of these data indicated a surprisingly stable pattern of delinquent activity in the five ecological zones over a sixty-five year period. What was most important to Shaw and McKay was that the high delinquency areas were unaffected by changes in their residents. Put another way, the delinquency proneness of an area remained constant regardless of who its inhabitants were. It seemed that there were high-risk areas and high-risk people.

ECOLOGICAL CAUSES OF DELINQUENCY. Shaw and McKay sought to explain the difference in the delinquency rates of slum and suburban communities through an analysis of the social values and social organization present in local communities. They found that clear-cut differences in social values existed in high- and low-delinquency areas.[13] Areas with high delinquency rates were marked by conflicting moral values and powerful attractions to deviant modes of behavior. While some lower-class youths were taught to strive for basic middle-class goals—education, hard work, and saving—others were taught that illegitimate activities, such as theft and drug dealing, were acceptable ways of getting ahead.

Youths who choose to admire deviant values eventually join with like-minded peers in law-violating groups and gangs. Because of their deviant way of life, gang boys quickly come in conflict with existing middle-class norms and laws. A "value conflict" occurs that sets delinquents and their peer group even farther from conventional society. The result is a fuller acceptance of deviant goals and behavior. Shut out of the "normal" stream of society, neighborhood street gangs become fixed institutions, recruiting new members and passing on delinquent traditions from one generation to the next.

High-crime rate areas also suffer from social disorganization. Under the burden of poverty and urban decay, distressed families and schools, which are normally the primary vehicles of socialization, are unable to function properly. For example, so many families in transitional areas have adult members profiting from illegal activities that even an intimate family life cannot insulate youths from delinquency. Under these circumstances, a close-knit family may actually enhance the lure of delinquency since children learn deviant values at home. In a socially disorganized neighborhood, social control and crime prevention agencies, such as police and community centers, have only limited utility because they are staffed and funded by outsiders who are not trusted by neighborhood residents.

By introducing a new variable—the ecology of the city—into the study of delinquency, Shaw and McKay paved the way for a whole generation of criminologists to focus on the social influences on delinquent behavior.

SOCIAL DISORGANIZATION THEORY TODAY

Since the Shaw and McKay era, social disorganization theory has continued to be a major perspective in the study of delinquent behavior. In the 1950s and 1960s, studies conducted by Bernard Lander in Baltimore, David Bordua in Detroit, and

Roland Chilton in Indianapolis generally showed that such ecological conditions as substandard housing, low income, and transient populations predicted a high incidence of delinquency.[14]

Today's research efforts go far beyond Shaw and McKay's simple techniques and make use of complex statistical models to determine the influence urban ecological conditions have on crime patterns.[15] There is a growing body of important research studies that indicate that the social context of a neighborhood has significant influence over its crime and delinquency rate.[16] Physically deteriorated, densely populated urban environments have been found to maintain a state of social disorder that weakens the ties people have to their primary groups (family and peers) and community.[17] There is a lack of the social support and neighborhood well-being that are needed to produce social competence and community integration (involvement with conventional social institutions, such as the school, church, and family).[18]

Instead of a sense of "community," large urban areas produce generalized feelings of alienation, which means that residents are psychologically separated from the surrounding society. People who live in these urban wastelands possess feelings of anonymity and find that their ties to others are weak or nonexistent. Beaten down by their environment, they become tolerant of bizarre or deviant behavior.[19]

Research shows that living within the lower-class culture can have serious psychological consequences. For example, males in these areas have been found to be intellectually inflexible and lacking in self-direction; they are unlikely to value freedom and self-direction in their children.[20]

This sense of community disorder encourages the presence of a criminal culture, while at the same time limiting resident's involvement in conventional community life.[21] It should come as no surprise then that deteriorated urban communities whose residents suffer the lack of basic human needs, including proper clothing, nutrition, and health care (resource deprivation), also experience the greatest rates of crime and delinquency.[22]

The Cycle of Disorganization

The view first articulated by Shaw and McKay, that delinquency rates within slums remain stable over time, has been displaced by the position that communities have an ecological life cycle that can have a profound influence on their residents; the stable patterns of inner-city delinquency depicted by Shaw and McKay may not actually exist.[23]

A number of research efforts have attempted to chart the relationship between community change and delinquency rates. Leo Scheurman and Solomon Kobrin found that urban communities go through cycles in which neighborhood deterioration precedes increasing rates of crime and delinquency.[24] Communities that may experience a rapid increase in antisocial behavior are likely to have the following characteristics: they are "middle-aged" rather than old; they are experiencing rapid increases in the number of single-parent families and unrelated people living together; they have undergone changes in land use from owner-occupied to renter-occupied units; and they have an economic base that has lost semiskilled and unskilled jobs (indicating a growing residue of discouraged workers who are no longer seeking employment).[25]

In a similar vein, Richard McGahey's analysis of delinquency-producing economic conditions in urban areas found evidence that neighborhoods with deteriorating employment opportunities for youth and adults were the most vulnerable to predatory crime.[26] Unemployment helped destabilize households. Unstable families are the ones most vulnerable to producing children who put a premium on violence and aggressiveness as a means of dealing with limited opportunity. A lack of employment opportunities also reduces the number of older people on the street, resulting in domination of street life by youth gangs. McGahey found that even the most deteriorated neighborhoods have a surprising degree of familial and kinship strength but that a consistent pattern of crime and neighborhood disorganization can soon overcome them.

Looking at this relationship from another perspective, Janet Heitgerd and Robert Bursik have found that areas that are adjoined to neighborhoods undergoing racial change will experience corresponding increases in their delinquency rates.[27] The authors speculate that this phenomenon may reflect community perceptions that racial conflict is inevitable in so-called "changing neighborhoods." Under these circumstances, the law-violating behavior of youth gangs is supported by neighborhood adults who view violence directed against outsiders as a means of protecting their property and way of life. These conditions may have helped trigger the nationally publicized incidents of racial conflict in New York's Howard Beach and Bensonhurst areas.

Relative Deprivation

Another ecological view is that the **relative deprivation** experienced by some members of society is a direct cause of their delinquent behavior. According to Judith and Peter Blau, income inequality in communities in which the poor and wealthy live in close proximity to one another leads to a sense of social injustice and anger, which in turn leads to expressions of hostility and criminal behavior.

According to the Blaus' model, youths growing up in an inner-city poverty area, such as those in New York, Chicago, and Los Angeles, will experience delinquency-producing **status frustration** since their neighborhoods are in close proximity to some of the most well-to-do areas in the United States. So while deprived teenagers can witness wealth and luxury firsthand, they cannot partake of its benefits through conventional means. Relative deprivation is experienced most acutely by black youths, since in American society, black citizens consistently suffer racial and economic deprivations that put them in a lower status with respect to the rest of society.[28]

Research supportive of the Blaus' relative deprivation model has been conducted by a number of criminologists. Richard Block found that in Chicago, the variable best able to predict crime rates was the proximity in which poor and wealthy people lived to one another.[29] Similar results were achieved both by Robert Sampson and Richard Rosenfeld in studies that used national crime rate data.[30] Sampson found, however, that juveniles may be more immune to economic conditions than adults and that some forms of antisocial behavior may be motivated by noneconomic factors, such as peer pressure, rather than by relative deprivation.[31]

Taken in sum, these studies indicate that youths living in deteriorated areas of the city who can easily see the benefits of higher social position without being able to enjoy them will resort to such crimes as homicide, robbery, and aggravated assault to satisfy their sense of social injustice.

STRAIN THEORY

Strain theorists agree that the socially disorganized urban slum is the source of delinquency in American society. However, the strain approach seeks to clarify the elements within lower-class culture that produce antisocial behavior patterns. According to this view, crime and delinquency are a result of the frustration and anger people experience over their inability to achieve legitimate social and financial success. Strain theorists believe that most people share similar values and goals but that the ability to achieve them is stratified by socioeconomic class. In middle- and upper-class communities, strain does not exist, since education and prestigious occupations are readily obtainable. In lower-class areas, strain occurs because legitimate avenues for success are all but closed to young people. When acceptable means for obtaining success do not exist, individuals may either use deviant methods to achieve their goals or reject socially accepted goals and substitute others for them.

In lower class areas strain occurs because social institutions cannot provide the means for achieving success.

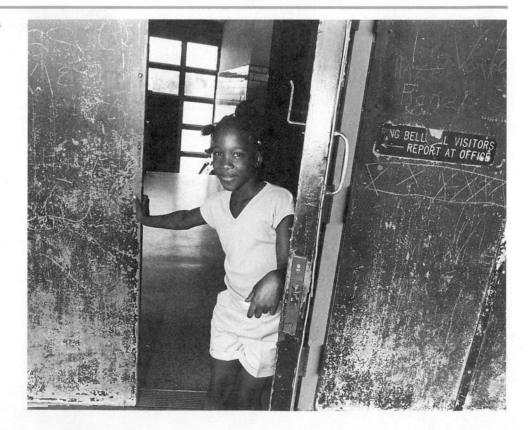

FIGURE 5.3

Strain theory

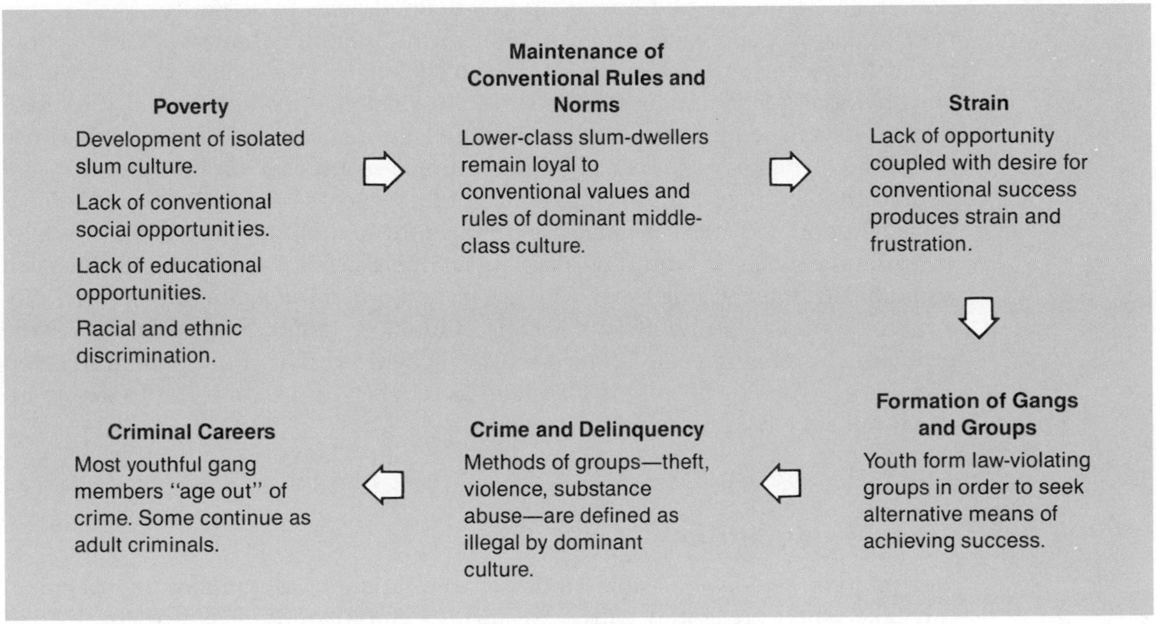

Poverty

Development of isolated slum culture.

Lack of conventional social opportunities.

Lack of educational opportunities.

Racial and ethnic discrimination.

Maintenance of Conventional Rules and Norms

Lower-class slum-dwellers remain loyal to conventional values and rules of dominant middle-class culture.

Strain

Lack of opportunity coupled with desire for conventional success produces strain and frustration.

Formation of Gangs and Groups

Youth form law-violating groups in order to seek alternative means of achieving success.

Crime and Delinquency

Methods of groups—theft, violence, substance abuse—are defined as illegal by dominant culture.

Criminal Careers

Most youthful gang members "age out" of crime. Some continue as adult criminals.

Strain theory holds that all Americans originally have conventional middle-class goals, values, and aspirations but that the frustration of underachievement causes lower-class citizens to substitute deviant for conventional values and behavior. Billions of dollars are spent each year trying to convince people to drive the right car, wear the right clothes, and live in the right neighborhood. It is certainly not surprising to conclude that lower-class youths, frustrated because they are shut out of the legitimate marketplace, will seek alternative means to get the luxuries that most Americans are taught to expect.

We now turn to the most important formulation of strain theory, Robert Merton's theory of anomie.

Merton's Theory of Anomie

Strain theory is most closely linked to the distinguished American sociologist Robert Merton.[32] In 1938, Merton proposed a revised version of the concept of **anomie**, which has proved to be one of the most durable theoretical concepts in twentieth-century social thought.[33] In his theory, Merton attempts to adapt the concept of anomie to conditions that exist in American society. French sociologist Emil Durkheim had first coined the term "anomie" to describe the "normlessness" and social malaise that occur during a breakdown of existing social rules, laws, and values.[34] Durkheim believed that an anomic condition results when the existing social structure can no longer establish and maintain controls over an individual's wants and desires. It is a breakdown of the rule of law. Under these conditions, deviant acts such as suicide and crime can be considered "normal" responses to existing social conditions.

Merton adapted anomie to explain all forms of deviance in modern American society. He argued that two elements of modern culture interact to produce potentially anomic conditions: culturally defined *goals* of acquiring wealth, success, and power and socially permissible *means*, including hard work, education, and thrift. According to Merton, American society is "goal-oriented," and wealth and material goods are coveted most of all. Merton's position is that the legitimate means to acquiring wealth are stratified across class and status lines. Those with little formal education and few economic resources soon find that they are denied the ability to acquire money and other success symbols legally.[35] Since socially mandated success goals are uniform throughout any society and access to legitimate means is bound by class and status, the resulting strain produces an anomic condition among those who are locked out of the legitimate opportunity structure. Consequently, they develop criminal or delinquent solutions to the problem of attaining goals.[36] Merton also recognized that some people rejected social goals, thereby becoming classified as rebels who are opposed to the mainstream of society.

Social Adaptations

Merton identified five possible modes of adaptation or adjustment an individual can take when presented with the various combinations of culturally defined goals and means: conformity, innovation, ritualism, retreatism, and rebellion. Each represents a way of coping with a balance or imbalance of goals and means.

CONFORMITY. Conformity occurs when an individual adheres to social goals and can attain them legitimately through conventional means. For example, middle-class, college-bound students will obey the law because they recognize that their future education and social position will land them a good job and they don't need to steal or commit other crimes to get what they want in life. This most common form of adaptation signals the absence of an anomic condition (and deviant behavior as well).

INNOVATION. Innovation occurs when an individual accepts the goals of society but rejects or is incapable of following legitimate means of attaining them. For example, when youths desire automobiles but lack money, the resulting conflict forces them to adopt an innovative solution to the problem: they steal cars.

Of the five adaptations, innovation is most closely associated with delinquent behavior. The inescapable demand to succeed that pervades American culture places such an enormous burden on those lacking economic opportunity that delinquent modes of adaptation are not a surprising result. This condition accounts for the high rate of delinquency in poverty areas, where access to legitimate means is severely limited. However, innovative adaptations can occur in any social class when members perceive the lack of appropriate means to gain social success they aspire to. For example, witness the recent insider trading scandal that rocked Wall Street in 1986 and 1987 and involved people who were already millionaires.

RITUALISM. Ritualism results from the diminution of goals and a rigid adherence to means. The maintenance of a strict set of manners and customs that serve no particular purpose is an example of ritualism. Such practices often exist in religious services, feudal societies, clubs, college fraternities, and organizations. Ritualists gain pleasure from traditional ceremonies that have neither a real purpose nor a goal.

RETREATISM. Retreatism entails a rejection of both the goals and the means of society. Merton suggests that people who adjust in this fashion are "in society but not of it."[37] Included in this category are "psychotics, psychoneurotics, chronic autists, pariahs, outcasts, vagrants, tramps, chronic drunkards, and drug addicts."[38] Often this posture results when an individual at first accepts socially acceptable goals but is denied the means to attain them. Because such people are also morally or otherwise incapable of using illegitimate means, they attempt to escape their lack of success by withdrawing, either mentally or physically.

REBELLION. A rebellious adaptation involves substitution of alternative sets of goals and means for the accepted ones of society. This adaptation is typical of revolutionaries, who wish to promote radical change in the existing social structure and who call for alternative life-styles, goals, and beliefs. For many years, revolutionary groups have abounded in the United States, some espousing the violent overthrow of the existing social order and others advocating the use of nonviolent, passive resistance to change society. The revolutionary orientation can be used as a reaction against a corrupt and hated regime or as an effort to create alternate opportunities and life-styles within the existing system.

Merton's adaptations apply to both deviant and nondeviant behavior. In our culture, innovation, retreatism, and rebellion seem most relevant to the understanding of delinquent behavior. Considering the apparent inequality in the social distribution of legitimate means, it is not surprising that large segments of our population react to the resulting anomic condition with innovations such as theft or extortion, with retreat into drugs or alcohol, or with rebellion by joining revolutionary or cultist groups.

Strain in Review

Strain theory holds that deviant behavior is caused by a person's inability to achieve culturally mandated goals; such as wealth, power, and prestige. Since members of all social classes desire these indicators of prosperity, but only members of the upper- and middle-classes can ever hope to achieve them, lower-class people are more likely to use unconventional or criminal means to gain success. Consequently, crime rates will be higher in lower-class areas.

Strain theory does not actually concern itself with the reason that any particular individual becomes delinquent. Instead, it attempts to explain the delinquency *rates* that exist in society. By acknowledging that our society unfairly distributes the legitimate means to achieving success, the concept of anomie helps explain the existence of high-delinquency areas and the apparent predominance of delinquent and criminal behavior among particular social and ethnic groups in our culture. In that respect, it is quite similar to social disorganization theory.

The most important criticism leveled at strain theory is that it does not explain how the distribution of goals and means evolved: what is it about American society—or any other society—that accounts for the way in which various patterns of attachment to goals and norms and of accessibility of institutionalized means are distributed within the system? In other words, strain theory does not explain the distribution of means in American society and therefore cannot tell us of the origin of people's motivations to commit crime.

CULTURAL DEVIANCE THEORIES

Cultural deviance theories combine elements of strain and social disorganization. They suggest that slum youths violate the law because they adhere to the unique, independent **subculture** existing within lower-class areas that is in conflict with the middle-class norms and values upon which the criminal law is based. Subcultures are groups that share in the overall culture of society but also maintain a distinctive set of values, norms, life-styles, and even language.[39] The lower-class subculture maintains values that include being tough, taking care of your own business, never showing fear, living for today, and never respecting authority.

FIGURE 5.4
Cultural deviance
theory

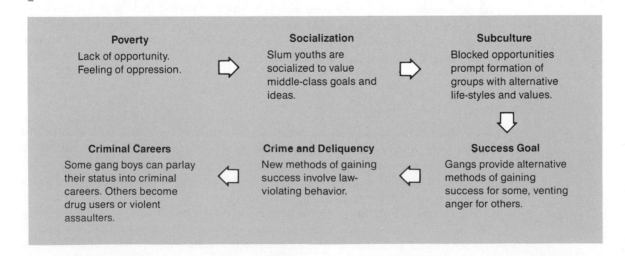

Poverty
Lack of opportunity.
Feeling of oppression.

Socialization
Slum youths are
socialized to value
middle-class goals and
ideas.

Subculture
Blocked opportunities
prompt formation of
groups with alternative
life-styles and values.

Criminal Careers
Some gang boys can parlay
their status into criminal
careers. Others become
drug users or violent
assaulters.

Crime and Deliquency
New methods of gaining
success involve law-
violating behavior.

Success Goal
Gangs provide alternative
methods of gaining
success for some, venting
anger for others.

This deviant subculture is appealing to many youths living in socially disorganized slums because conventional values, such as honesty, obedience, and hard work, make little sense when the only successful adult role models are the neighborhood gambler, drug dealer, or pimp. Even if at first they admire and strive for conventional values and success, the frustration they perceive at not obtaining them makes the subcultural values an attractive alternative. The delinquent subculture provides alternate forms of success and self-esteem by valuing highly goals that can be reached in their circumstances: joining a gang, selling drugs, being considered tough, bad, or street smart, and getting a "rep." The stable values of lower-class subculture can be contrasted with those of middle-class subcultures, such as "preppies," "yuppies," or "dinks," which require their members to buy a "Beemer" (BMW, for the uninitiated), join a health club, and eat sprouts.

According to this view then, delinquent youths are not rebelling against conventional rules (as strain theory holds) as much as they are obeying lower-class ones. As Joseph Weis and John Sederstrom interpret cultural deviance, "delinquent behavior is caused by proper socialization within a 'deviant' social group or culture. Juvenile delinquency is merely 'marching to a different drummer.' "[40]

Some of the most important cultural deviance theories are described in detail in the next sections.

Culture Conflict

In an early formulation of cultural deviance, Thorsten Sellin described the process of **culture conflict,** a clash between the criminal law of the middle class and the **conduct norms** of splinter groups.[41] These groups are formed by people who are living within conventional society but who do not hold full membership within it. Conduct norms are the rules governing daily life within these disenfranchised groups. Allegiance to the norms and values of unconventional groups will often cause conflict with the parent culture. For example, immigrants who follow the cultural norm of their homeland that demands that they take personal revenge for an injustice to family members will soon find themselves in trouble with U.S. authorities.

Marvin Wolfgang and Franco Ferracuti's well-known book the *Subculture of Violence* is another example of the cultural conflict view.[42] According to the Wolfgang and Ferracuti treatise, there is a subculture of violence in certain areas around the nation that contains norms separate from those of the dominant, parent culture. In the subculture, a potent theme of violence influences lifestyles, the socialization process, and interpersonal relationships. Violence is a subcultural norm especially among younger males. Because violence is an accepted part of their world, the violent do not feel guilty about their actions.

Focal Concern Theory

Sociologist **Walter Miller's** theory of lower-class culture is a well-known attempt to explain the gang activity found in lower-class environments as a function of cultural deviance. Miller portrays delinquent behavior as a "normal" reaction to the norms and values of a unique lower-class culture passed down from one generation to the next.[43]

Miller studied the daily activities of working-class males while conducting a delinquent gang control program in Boston.[44] He found that slum areas manifest a distinct cultural climate that remains stable over long periods of time. Because males in these areas are on the fringe of the established economic system with little chance for success within the legitimate social order, they seek to achieve personal satisfaction in their own neighborhoods and culture. Since so many families have absent fathers, young boys join single-sex groups and gangs that provide a family substitute and define the male role for adolescent boys.

According to Miller, a unique group of value-like **focal concerns**, which have evolved specifically to fit conditions in slum areas, have been embraced as cultural imperatives by gang youth. The major focal concerns that dominate life among the lower class are trouble, toughness, smartness, excitement, fate, and autonomy.

Trouble includes such behavior as fighting, drinking, and sexual misconduct. In lower-class communities, people are evaluated in terms of their actual, or potential, involvement in trouble-making activity. The attitude toward trouble is not always clear-cut. Sometimes it confers prestige, for example, when a man gets a reputation for being able to handle himself well in a fight. However, getting into trouble and having to pay the consequences can make a person look foolish and incompetent. In most instances, trouble-making escapades are designed with a goal in mind, such as stealing an automobile when the money to buy one is unobtainable.

Lower-class males also want local recognition of their physical and spiritual *toughness.* They refuse to be sentimental or soft and instead value physical strength, fighting ability, and athletic skill. Toughness involves a high tolerance of pain, disdain of fear, fighting skill, and the willingness to accept all manner of hardships without complaint; those males who cannot meet these standards risk getting a reputation for being weak, inept, and effeminate. *Smartness* means having streetwise savvy, which carries with it the ability to outfox and outcon the opponent. Smartness to the lower-class citizen means knowing essential survival techniques, such as gambling, conning, and outsmarting the law. The search for *excitement* involves gambling, fighting, getting drunk, sexual adventurism, and other risk-taking behaviors that of course can lead to "trouble." The consequences are a matter of *fate.* Lower-class citizens believe that their lives are in the hands of strong spiritual forces that guide their destinies. Getting lucky, finding good fortune, and hitting the jackpot are all dreams that are present daily in each slum dweller's life.

Getting lucky can mean a trip out of the ghetto and into the world of luxury and excitement. The belief in fate is behind the interest in playing the numbers, the horses, and the other forms of gambling that are so prevalent in the lower-class world. If fate is with you, one can achieve personal freedom and *autonomy.* Being in the control of others is an unacceptable weakness, incompatible with toughness.

Miller argues that by strictly satisfying the behavioral demands imposed by lower-class focal concerns, an adolescent is drawn into an ever-expanding pattern of delinquent behavior. By adhering to the cultural values, rules, and norms with which they are in close personal contact, lower-class youths often find that they are in conflict with representatives of the legal code. For example, proving their toughness may demand that lower-class youths engage in constant fighting, both individually and in groups. Smartness may lead them into theft and drug dealing. Excitement causes them to gamble, drink, and engage in premarital sex. Thus, obedience to unavoidable cultural demands, not a sense of alienation or anger, precipitates lower-class delinquent behavior.

Miller's model jibes with the view of lower-class life that portrays inner-city youngsters as being more concerned with their street "rep" than with getting an education and more enthused about crime than a legitimate occupation. It is supported by research showing that delinquents are "sensation seekers" who seek out parties, social drinking, and a hedonistic life-style. However, Miller does not explain how these deviant values developed nor how delinquents are able to ignore the influence of conventional values they are exposed to at home, school, and church and in the media.

Albert K. Cohen's Theory of Delinquent Subculture

Albert K. Cohen first articulated the theory of delinquent subculture in his 1955 book, *Delinquent Boys*.[45] Cohen's main purpose was to explain the disproportionate amount of official delinquent behavior found in slum neighborhoods. His central position is that delinquent behavior of lower-class youths is actually a protest against the norms and values of the middle-class American culture. Because social conditions make them incapable of achieving success in a legitimate fashion, lower-class youths experience a form of culture conflict that Cohen labels "status frustration." As a result, many of them join together in teenage gangs and engage in behavior that is *nonutilitarian, malicious*, and *negativistic*.[46] Cohen views delinquents as forming a separate subculture and possessing a value system directly in opposition to that of the larger society. He describes the subculture as one that takes "its norms from the larger culture but turns them upside down. The delinquent's conduct is right, by the standards of his subculture, precisely because it is wrong by the norms of the larger cultures."[47]

Family structure has a critical influence on delinquent behavior. Cohen argues that the relative position of a child's family in the social structure determines the quality of experiences and problems that the child will encounter later in life.[48] By implication, Cohen suggests that lower-class families are incapable of teaching their offspring proper socialization techniques for entry into the dominant middle-class culture. Lower-class families permanently cut off from the middle-class way of life produce children who lack the basic skills necessary to achieve social and economic success in our demanding society. Developmental handicaps produced by a lower-class upbringing include lack of educational training, poor speech and communication skills, and inability to delay gratification.[49]

MIDDLE-CLASS MEASURING RODS. One of the more significant handicaps that lower-class children face is the inability to positively impress such authority figures as teachers, employers, or supervisors. In our society, these positions tend to be held by members of the middle or upper class who have a difficult time relating to the lower-class youngster. Cohen calls the standards these authority figures set "**middle-class measuring rods**," and the conflict lower-class youths feel when they fail to meet these standards is a primary cause of delinquency.

According to Cohen, lower-class youth engage in behavior which runs afoul of middle class measuring rods.

Middle-class measuring rods develop because the most important institutions in our society—school, church, business, the military, the justice system, and so on—are dominated by agents of the middle class. Clients of these institutions (for example, students, workers, soldiers) are expected to display middle-class values and behaviors, such as verbal skills, ambition, neatness, cleanliness, good manners, and the ability to delay gratification. When lower-class youths cannot meet these criteria, their failures become part of an enduring public record that is consulted whenever they apply for a job, seek educational advancement, or wish to join a social organization. Failure to satisfy middle-class measuring rods is therefore not an isolated incident that, if not repeated, will be forgotten. It becomes an enduring part of the lower-class youth's permanent record that follows him or her throughout life and helps thwart personal ambitions.

DELINQUENT ORIENTATIONS. Cohen's central position is that lower-class boys who suffer the rejection of middle-class decision makers are deeply affected by their lack of social recognition.[50] In the typical case, they may elect to adopt one of three alternative behaviors: the "corner boy" role, the "college boy" role, or the "delinquent boy" role.

The stable corner-boy role is the most common response to middle-class rejection. The corner boy is not overtly delinquent but behaves in a way that is sometimes defined as delinquent. For example, he is a truant.[51] He hangs out in the neighborhood, engages in gambling, athletics, and other group activities, and eventually obtains a menial job. His main loyalty is to his peer group, on which he depends for support, motivation, and interest. His values, therefore, are those of the group with which he is in close, personal contact. The corner boy, well aware of his failure to achieve the standards of the American dream, retreats into the comforting world of his lower-class peers and eventually becomes a stable member of his society.

The college boy embraces the cultural and social values of the middle class. Rather than scorning middle-class measuring rods, he actively strives to be successful by middle-class standards. Cohen views this type of youth as one who is embarking on an almost hopeless path, since he is ill-equipped academically, socially, and linguistically to achieve the long-deferred rewards of middle-class life.

The delinquent boy adopts a set of norms and principles in direct opposition to middle-class society. Cohen describes a number of general properties of the delinquent subculture. For one thing, its members often manifest "short-run hedonism."[52] Delinquents are believed to live for today and to let tomorrow take care of itself. Although Cohen believes short-run hedonism is a characteristic of lower-class culture as a whole, he finds it especially applicable to delinquent groups.

Members of the delinquent subculture are also careful to maintain *group autonomy*. They resist efforts by family, school, or other sources of authority to control their behavior. Although some individual delinquents may respond to direction from others, the gang itself is autonomous, independent, and the focus of "attraction, loyalty, and solidarity."[53]

While members of the delinquent subculture often manifest negativistic and malicious behavior, Cohen believes they are still controlled to some degree by the norms and values of the generalized culture. They really want to be successful at school, jobs, and so on. To deal with the conflict inherent in this frustrating dilemma, the delinquent resorts to a process Cohen calls "reaction formation."[54] Symptoms of reaction formation include an overly intense response that seems to be disproportionate to the stimulus that triggers it. For the delinquent boy, this takes the form of "irrational," "malicious," "unaccountable" hostility to the enemy within the gates as well as without—the norms of respectable middle-class society.[55]

In a later work, Cohen (in conjunction with James Short) presented a refined version of his original theory that recognized that the original formulation of the delinquent subculture may have been too simplistic.[56] Cohen admitted that there is more than one type of delinquent subculture and that a more complex model is required to define delinquent adaptations. His later research identified the following five delinquent orientations:

1. *Parent male subculture.* The negativistic subculture originally identified in *Delinquent Boys.*
2. *The conflict-oriented subculture.* The culture of a large gang that engages in collective violence.
3. *The drug addict subculture.* Groups of youths whose lives revolve around the purchase, sale, and use of narcotics.
4. *Semiprofessional theft.* Youths who engage in the theft or robbery of merchandise for the purpose of later sale and monetary gain.
5. *Middle-class subculture.* Delinquent groups that rise because of the pressures of living in middle-class environments.[57]

In his revised theory, Cohen broadened the way delinquent subcultures can be explained by his original model.

Opportunity Theory

In their well-known 1960 work, *Delinquency and Opportunity*, Richard Cloward and Lloyd Ohlin added significantly to the knowledge of delinquent subcultures.[58] Cloward and Ohlin agree with the strain perspective of Robert Merton that socioeconomic class membership controls access to the legitimate means of achieving social goals.[59] However, they maintain that Merton's theory pays scant attention to the fact that even *illegitimate* means are unevenly distributed in the class structure. Cloward and Ohlin argue that some lower-class neighborhoods actually provide more opportunity for illegal gain than others do. These opportunities come in the form of access to rackets, organized crime, theft, and other high-payoff illegal activities. Cloward and Ohlin's view, therefore, is that in a particular urban area or neighborhood, *both* legitimate and illegitimate opportunities are differentially available.

THE DEVELOPMENT OF GANG SUBCULTURES. A key element of opportunity theory is the assumption that a strong relationship exists between the environment youths live in, its economic structure, and their subsequent behavior choices. This assumption incorporates cultural deviance and social disorganization elements with strain theory. For example, in wealthy or middle-class areas, educational and vocational opportunities abound, and youths can avail themselves of conventional means of getting ahead, such as going to college. However, in low-income socially disorganized areas, legitimate means are more difficult to come by, and therefore youths must seek illegitimate avenues of success.

Cloward and Ohlin propose that even illegitimate avenues of success are blocked for some youths. In fact, they are available only to children growing up in areas where "stable patterns of accommodation" exist between the criminal world and conventional society.[60] In these areas, adult criminals have worked out relationships with businesses, police, and court officials through bribery and corruption so that they are almost immune from prosecution. Their criminal activity—organized crime, drug trafficking, gambling—provides a stable income and an alternative avenue to legitimate success. Under adult tutelage, youths fit right into this model and form a *criminal subculture*. To prepare for adult crime, they join gangs specializing in theft, drug dealing, and other profitable criminal activities. Later, they become part of the even more profitable adult crime organizations.

Not all youths join criminal gangs. Some lower-class youths remain loyal to the values and rules of conventional society. Furthermore, some youths are temperamentally incapable of following either criminal or conventional rules. They take drugs and alcohol and stress playing it cool and being high and strung out. Cloward and Ohlin call their world the *retreatist subculture*.

Finally, opportunity theory recognizes that some poverty areas are so unstable and disorganized that even illegitimate means to success are blocked. Youths in these areas become members of the *conflict subculture*.[61] They form fighting gangs that provide the opportunity for success and ego gratification by enabling their members to show their bravery and strength and by allowing them to display fighting prowess.[62]

In sum, Cloward and Ohlin view urban delinquency as a function of the different opportunities youths have to attain both *legitimate* and *illegitimate* goals. Where opportunities for legal gain are blocked, criminal activity is attempted. When even criminal gain is unobtainable, then drug use or violence will ensue.

TESTING OPPORTUNITY THEORY. Several studies have been conducted to test opportunity theory. Judson Landis and Frank Scarpitti used self-report scales with 1,030 youths in Columbus, Ohio, and 515 boys at the Industrial School in Lancaster, Ohio. The industrial school boys exhibited greater perception of limited opportunity than did the public school boys; public school youths who admitted delinquency also perceived less opportunity than nondelinquents.[63] Similar research efforts have found support for opportunity theory.[64]

Despite this supportive evidence, there is also research data that conflicts with opportunity theory. For example, when testing samples of lower- and middle-class delinquents, Leon Fannin and Marshall Clinard found that subjects differed in their attitudes and values.[65]

> Lower-class boys felt themselves to be . . . tougher, more powerful, fierce, fearless, and dangerous than middle-class boys. Middle-class delinquents . . . conceived of themselves as being more loyal, clever, smart, smooth, and bad. . . . The lower class would like to be (ideal self) tougher, harder, and more violent than the middle class, while the latter would like to be more loyal, lucky, and firm.[66]

Lower-class youth then would be unlikely to perceive "blocked opportunities" because their actual goals—to be tough criminals—are easily achieved.

Other research efforts have found only a weak association between occupational expectations and delinquent behavior.[67] Critics suggest that this is because lower-class youth actually have modest aspirations and therefore are not likely to feel blocked or frustrated.[68] However, research findings do show that lower-class, minority youth who perceive that the system is stacked against them and that opportunities are unfairly distributed are more likely to commit crime than those who do not share these views. This supports Cloward and Ohlin's contention that "blocked opportunities" and not low aspirations cause delinquency.[69]

Another criticism of opportunity theory is that Cloward and Ohlin mistook the true nature of gang delinquency. Surveys of gang delinquency conducted subsequent to their research have shown that gangs are more pervasive than Cloward and Ohlin imagined, that more than one type of gang (conflict, violent, retreatist) exists in a particular area, that the commitment of gang boys to one another is less intense than opportunity theory would suggest, and that gangs do not seem to specialize in any particular type of behavior.

In sum, the work of Cloward and Ohlin is probably one of the most influential theoretical pronouncements of the twentieth century.[70] With its complexity and sophistication, it successfully blends the cultural deviance and strain perspectives. Though it has been superseded in importance by other theoretical models, it still retains an important place in delinquency theory and continues to receive attention from scholars and researchers.[71]

SOCIAL STRUCTURE THEORY AND DELINQUENCY PREVENTION

Social structure theories suggest that the best method of primary delinquency prevention is local community organization. The effort should be two-pronged. First, deteriorated neighborhoods must be refurbished in order to provide an environment that meets the basic needs of the residents. Second, educational and job opportunities must be created to provide legitimate alternatives to delinquent gangs.

Delinquency prevention through community organization was pioneered in Chicago by Clifford Shaw in the 1930s. In 1933, Shaw initiated the **Chicago Area Project,** which was designed to produce social change in communities that suffered from high delinquency rates and gang activity. The project attempted to have qualified local leaders coordinate social service centers that promoted community solidarity and counteracted existing social disorganization. More than twenty different projects were developed, featuring discussion groups, counseling services, hobby groups, school-related activities, and recreation. There is still some question whether these programs had a positive influence on the delinquency rate. While some evaluations indicated positive results, other studies indicated that the efforts of the Chicago Area Project had little influence on reducing juvenile criminality.[72]

In the 1950s, delinquency prevention programs sought to reach out to youths who were unlikely to make use of settlement houses or community centers. Instead of having troubled youths come to them, **detached street workers** set out into urban slums and created close relationships with juvenile gangs and groups in their own milieu.[73] The most well-known detached street worker program was Boston's **Mid-City Project.** There, trained social workers sought out and met with youth gangs three to four times a week on their own turf. Their goal was to modify the organization of the gang and allow gang members to devote activities to more conventional behaviors. The detached street workers tried to help gang members secure jobs and get educational opportunities. They acted as go-betweens for gang members with agents of the power structure—lawyers, judges, parole officers, and the like. Despite these efforts, an evaluation of the program by Walter Miller failed to show that it resulted in significant reduction in criminal activity.[74]

The heyday of delinquency prevention programs based on social structure theory was in the 1960s. The approach seemed to jibe politically with the New Frontier policies of the Kennedy administration and the Great Society/War on Poverty stance taken by the Johnson administration. A great deal of federal money was pumped into the delinquency prevention programs utilizing community organization and redevelopment techniques. The most ambitious of these was the New York City-based **Mobilization for Youth (MOBY).** Funded by more than $50 million, MOBY attempted an integrated approach to community development. Based securely on Cloward and Ohlin's concept of providing opportunities for legitimate success, MOBY organizers attempted to create new employment opportunities in the community, coordinated social services, and sponsored social action groups, such as tenant's committees, legal action services, and voter registration and political action committees. But MOBY died for lack of funding and amid serious questions about its utility and use of funds.

The concept of community organization and change to combat delinquency fell into disfavor in the 1970s and 1980s because of the failure of these early

TABLE 5.1 Social Structure Theories

THEORY	MAJOR PREMISE	STRENGTHS
Social Disorganization	The conflicts and problems of urban social life and communities control the crime rate.	Accounts for urban crime rates and trends.
Relative deprivation	Crime occurs when the wealthy and poor live in close proximity to one another.	Explains high crime rates in deteriorated inner city areas located near more affluent neighborhoods.
Strain theory	People who adopt the goals of society but lack the means to attain them seek alternatives such as crime.	Points out how competition for success creates conflict and crime. Suggests that social conditions and not personality can account for crime. Can explain middle- and upper-class crime.
Cultural deviance theory	Citizens who obey the street rules of lower-class life (focal concerns) find themselves in conflict with the dominant culture.	Identifies more coherently the elements of lower-class culture that push people into committing street crimes.
Cohen's theory of delinquent gangs	Status frustration of lower-class boys, created by their failure to achieve middle-class success, causes them to join gangs.	Shows how the conditions of lower-class life produce crime. Explains violence and destructive acts. Identifies conflict of lower class with middle class.
Cloward and Ohlin's theory of opportunity	Blockage of conventional opportunities causes lower-class youths to join criminal, conflict, or retreatist gangs.	Shows that even illegal opportunities are structured in society. Indicates why people become involved in a particular type of criminal activity. Presents a way of preventing crime.

projects and the exorbitant cost of transforming an entire neighborhood or area. They were replaced by programs of more modest scope that focused on individual change and rehabilitation.

Because the government rarely supports community revitalization efforts today, the trend has been for local citizens to take the initiative in the fight against crime and delinquency. Citizens have been working independently and in coop-

Middle-Class Delinquency

While most cultural explanations of delinquency focus on lower-class youths, the social structure approach can also be used to analyze middle-class youth crime. This phenomenon first came to the attention of authorities during the early 1960s, when the publication of self-report studies revealed a shockingly high delinquency rate in middle- and high-income areas. These findings surprised some criminologists who had long associated delinquent behavior with poor youths living in urban ghettos.

A number of reasons for the prevalence of middle-class delinquency have been put forth. On the one hand, the postwar baby boom produced a disproportionate number of teenage youths in the late 1950s and the 1960s, many of whom were members of families enjoying the newly won prosperity of that period. A good number of these affluent families left their traditional urban neighborhoods and moved to the suburbs. Traditional family ties and patterns changed, and long-held concepts of obedience and control broke down. Teenagers with time on their hands and money in the bank no longer felt the constraining hand of family, clan, and neighborhood, and they began to seek new forms of excitement and experience. In this search, delinquent behavior played no small part.

Moreover, child-rearing practices themselves changed in the postwar period. The so-called permissive school of thought led by Dr. Benjamin Spock influenced the disciplinary practices of many families. Schools began to try out innovative educational programs that stressed self-starting and self-discipline. At the same time, more than ever before, young people entered colleges and universities and delayed the period of entry into the work force. The period of adolescent inactivity was prolonged. Thus, middle-class youths were given more freedom than they had ever before enjoyed, but social norms constrained them from participating in meaningful social activity. The youth problem therefore extended to the very reaches of adult life.

Of the many early attempts to document and explain middle-class delinquency, Ralph England's work is among the most well known. England argued that American youngsters have gradually been removed from functional roles in the economy through restrictive apprenticeship codes, protective labor legislation, the compulsory education movement, and the growth of urbanization. Youths are no longer supposed to engage in productive labor, but they are also required not to loaf. They are discouraged from early marriages but allowed

continued

eration with local police agencies in neighborhood patrol and block watch programs. These programs organize local citizens in urban areas to patrol neighborhoods, watch for suspicious people, help secure the neighborhood, lobby for such improvements as increased lighting, report crime to police, put out community newsletters, conduct home security surveys, and serve as a hotline for crime information or tips. Block watches and neighborhood patrols have been more successful when they are part of general-purpose or multiissue community groups rather than when they focus solely on crime problems.

In sum, community crime prevention programs, and self-defense measures are flourishing around the United States. They are a response to the fear of delinquency and the perceived shortcomings of governmental agencies to insure community safety. They represent attempts to expand the "war on crime" to become a personal, neighborhood, and community concern.

to engage in premarital sex. They cannot vote but are expected to be civic-minded. They are given freedom but are not bound by the social ties that prevent privilege and freedom from deteriorating into license.

The tension produced by these conflicting demands and experiences helps create a teenage culture that maintains its own brand of values and behavior. Adults seeking teenage consumers for their products fuel and sustain this independent life-style. Advertising companies forcefully sell CD's, cosmetics, movies, and clothes specifically to teens. Adult identification of the teenage life-style, including such phenomena as recognizing teenage leaders and spokespersons who are familiar with teenage concerns, helps solidify the existence of this subculture.

England characterized middle-class teenage culture as hedonistic, intent on short-run gratification from fast cars, early sexual experience, parties, and so on. The relationship between these needs and delinquency is complex, but essentially, "if the teenager's urgent need for status affirmation is met by the teenage culture, then it becomes necessary for him to reject influences from the adult world which threaten it and to accept only those giving it support."

The threatening influences include any adult values, such as hard work and self-denial, that run counter to short-run, irresponsible hedonism. England characterized the middle-class delinquent as one engaging in illegal hedonistic acts, such as drinking, drug use, premarital sex, and petty theft.

Recent research indicates that a great deal of middle-class delinquency still occurs. Theorists have continued to view this as a function of a hedonistic teenage culture fueled by too much freedom, leisure, and wealth and a lack of adult control. Research with middle-class youth conducted by Helene Raskin White, Erich Labouvie, and Marsha Bates found that those who engaged in delinquency were indeed sensation seekers who enjoyed an hedonistic life-style, had extraverted personality structures, and enjoyed parties, drinking, and a variety of sexual partners. Middle-class delinquents also associate with peers who support and encourage antisocial acts. They are educational underachievers who do not expect to do well in school.

According to White and her colleagues, the problem of middle-class delinquency might be controlled or eliminated if school and other conventional institutions could find ways of offering youth legitimate alternatives for their need for excitement and stimulation.

Source: Helene Raskin White, Robert Pandina, and Randy LaGrange, "Longitudinal Predictors of Serious Substance Use and Delinquency," *Criminology* 25:715–40 (1987); Helene Raskin White, Erich Labouvie, and Marsha Bates, "The Relationship between Sensation Seeking and Delinquency: A Longitudinal Analysis," *Journal of Research in Crime and Delinquency* 22:197–211 (1985); Ralph England, "A Theory of Middle-Class Juvenile Delinquency," *Journal of Criminal Law, Criminology, and Police Science* 50:535–40 (1960).

CASE IN POINT

You have been appointed as a presidential advisor on urban problems.

The president informs you that he wants to create a major urban restructuring program in a large city that is aimed at reducing poverty, crime, and drug abuse. The area he has chosen for development is a large inner-city neighborhood with more than 100,000 residents. It suffers from disorganized community structure, poverty, and hopelessness. Predatory delinquent gangs run free and terrorize local merchants and citizens. The school system has failed to provide opportunities and educational experiences sufficient to dampen enthusiasm for gang recruitment. Stores, homes, and
continued

public buildings are deteriorated and decayed. Commercial enterprise has fled the area, and civil servants are reluctant to enter the neighborhood. There is an uneasy truce between the varied ethnic and racial groups that populate the area. Residents feel little can be done to bring the neighborhood back to life.

You are faced with suggesting an urban redevelopment program that can revitalize the area and eventually bring down the crime rate. You can bring any element of the public and private sector to bear on this rather overwhelming problem. Your budget is $500 million.

What programs do you feel could break the cycle of urban poverty?

Would reducing the poverty rate produce a lowered delinquency rate?

How might such conditions as cultural transmission and cultural deviance thwart your plans?

Is there a place for private industry in social reorganization?.

SUMMARY

Social structure theories hold that delinquent behavior is an adaptation to conditions that predominate in lower-class environments.

Social structure theory has three main branches. The first, social disorganization theory, suggests that deviant behavior develops in deprived areas where such social institutions as the family and school are too weak to control deviant behavior. Shaw and McKay viewed this development principally as a property of youthful street gangs. They found that delinquency rates vary widely throughout the city. The probability of adolescents becoming delinquent and getting arrested and later incarcerated depends on whether they live in a deteriorated inner-city area. Delinquency is a product of the socialization mechanisms within a neighborhood. Unstable neighborhoods have the greatest chance of producing delinquents. Delinquency is not the property of any one ethnic or racial group. Members of any racial or ethnic group will be delinquent if they live in the high-rate areas. Their crime rate will be reduced once they leave these areas.

The second branch of social structure theory is strain theory. This holds that lower-class youths may actually desire legitimate goals but that their unavailability causes rage, frustration, and substitution of deviant behavior.

Cultural deviance theory maintains that kids living in disorganized areas who perceive strain will create a unique culture within which they can find success and social support. Walter Miller argues that lower-class citizens maintain separate value systems or focal concerns. Albert Cohen finds that the youth culture is produced in part by a failure to measure up to "middle-class measuring rods." Sociologists Richard Cloward and Lloyd Ohlin have taken this idea one step further by suggesting that some neighborhoods even deny their residents the opportunity for illegal gain, thereby creating the rise of violence and drug-related subcultures.

In the 1960s, massive attempts were made by the federal government to transform socially disorganized areas in order to fight crime. When these efforts proved failures, the government withdrew support. Today, there are many local efforts to combat delinquency through fear-reduction techniques.

QUESTIONS FOR DISCUSSION

1. Is there a "transitional" area in your town or city?
2. Is it possible that a distinct lower-class culture exists? Do you know anyone who has the focal concerns Miller talks about?
3. Have you ever perceived anomie? What causes anomie?
4. Do middle-class youths become delinquent for the same reasons as lower-class youths?
5. Does "relative deprivation" produce delinquency?

KEY TERMS

culture of poverty
social structure
stratified
latchkey children
social disorganization
strain
cultural deviance
subcultural
transitional neighborhood
cultural transmission
urban ecological conditions
primary groups
alienation
anonymity
resource deprivation

relative deprivation
status frustration
Robert Merton
anomie
subculture
culture conflict
conduct norms
Walter Miller
focal concerns
Albert K. Cohen
middle-class measuring rods
Richard Cloward
Lloyd Ohlin
detached street workers
Mobilization for Youth (MOBY)

NOTES

1. Oscar Lewis, "The Culture of Poverty," *Scientific American* 215:19–25 (1966).
2. Herman Schwendinger and Julia Siegel Schwendinger, *Adolescent Subcultures and Delinquency* (New York: Prager, 1985).
3. National Research Council, *Common Destiny: Blacks and American Society* (Washington, D.C.: National Research Council, 1989).
4. Randolph Schmid, "A Trend Continues," *Boston Globe*, 5 November 1986, p. 3.

5. Associated Press, "2 Million Children Unattended, Study Finds," *Boston Globe* 6 February 1987, p. 6.

6. James Q. Wilson and Richard Herrnstein, *Crime and Human and Nature* (New York: Simon and Schuster, 1985).

7. U.S. Bureau of the Census Press Release, 10 January 1990; David Wessel, "Poverty Rate Eased to 13.1% in 1988, But Income Disparities Widened Again," *Wall Street Journal* 19 October 1989, p. A2; National Research Council, *Common Destiny: Blacks and American Society*.

8. National Research Council, *Common Destiny: Blacks and American Society*.

9. Marc Mauer, *Young Black Men and the Criminal Justice System: A Growing National Problem* (Washington, D.C.: Sentencing Project, 1990).

10. *Ibid.*, p. 4.

11. Clifford R. Shaw and Henry D. McKay, *Juvenile Delinquency and Urban Areas* (Rev. ed., Chicago: University of Chicago Press, 1972).

12. *Ibid.*, p. 52.

13. *Ibid.*, p. 170.

14. Bernard Lander, *Towards an Understanding of Juvenile Delinquency* (New York: Columbia University Press, 1954); David Bordua, "Juvenile Delinquency and 'Anomie': An Attempt at Replication," *Social Problems* 6:230–38 (1958); Roland Chilton, "Continuities in Delinquency Area Research: A Comparison of Studies in Baltimore, Detroit, and Indianapolis," *American Sociological Review* 29:71–73 (1964).

15. For a general review, see James Byrne and Robert Sampson, *The Social Ecology of Crime* (New York: Springer-Verlag, 1985).

16. Leo Carroll and Pamela Irving Jackson, "Inequality, Opportunity, and Crime Rates in Central Cities," *Criminology* 21:178–94 (1983).

17. Claude Fischer, *The Urban Experience* (New York: Harcourt Brace Jovanovich, 1984).

18. Cille Kennedy, "Community Integration and Well-Being: Toward the Goals of Community Care," *Journal of Social Issues* 45:6–77 (1989).

19. Charles Tittle, "Influences on Urbanism: A Test of Predictions from Three Perspectives," *Social Problems* 36:270 86 (1989).

20. Melvin Kohn, Atsushi Nqoi, Carrie Schoenbach, Carmi Shooler and Kazimierz Slomczynski, "Position in the Class Structure and Psychological Functioning in the United States, Japan, and Poland," *American Journal of Sociology* 95:964–1008 (1990).

21. Ora Simcha-Fagan and Joseph Schwartz, "Neighborhood and Delinquency: An Assessment of Contextual Effects," *Criminology* 24:667–703 (1986).

22. Kenneth Land, Patricia McCall, and Lawrence Cohen, "Structural Covariates of Homicide Rates: Are There Any Invariances across Time and Social Space?" *American Journal of Sociology* 95:922–63 (1990).

23. Robert Bursik and James Webb, "Community Change and Patterns of Delinquency," *American Journal of Sociology* 88:24–42 (1982).

24. Leo Scheurman and Solomon Kobrin, "Community Careers in Crime," in *Communities and Crime*, ed. Albert Reiss and Michael Tonry (Chicago: University of Chicago Press, 1986), pp. 67–100.

25. *Ibid.*, p. 96.

26. Richard McGahey, "Economic Conditions, Organization, and Urban Crime," in *Communities and Crime*, pp. 231–70.

27. Janet Heitgerd and Robert Bursik, Jr. "Extracommunity Dynamics and the Ecology of Delinquency," *American Journal of Sociology* 92:775–87 (1987).

28. Judith and Peter Blau, "The Cost of Inequality: Metropolitan Structure and Violent Crime," *American Sociological Review* 147:114–29 (1982).

29. Richard Block, "Community Environment and Violent Crime," *Criminology* 17:46–57 (1979).

30. Robert Sampson, "Structural Sources of Variation in Race-Age-Specific Rates of Offending across Major U.S. Cities," *Criminology* 23:647–73 (1985); Richard Rosenfeld, "Urban Crime Rates: Effects of Inequality, Welfare Dependency, Region, and Race," in Byrne and Sampson, *The Social Ecology of Crime*, pp. 116–30.

31. *Ibid.*, p. 668.

32. See, for example, Robert Merton, *Social Theory and Social Structure* (Glencoe, Ill.: Free Press, 1957).

33. Robert Merton, "Social Structure and Anomie," *American Sociological Review* 3:672–82 (1938).

34. For samples of his work, see Emil Durkheim, *The Rules of Sociological Method*, 8th ed. (Glencoe, Ill.: Free Press, 1950); idem, *Suicide* (Glencoe, Ill.: Free Press, 1951).

35. *Ibid.*, p. 680.

36. *Ibid.*

37. Robert Merton, "Social Structure and Anomie," in *The Sociology of Crime and Delinquency*, ed. Marvin Wolfgang, Leonard Savitz, and Norman Johnston (New York: Wiley, 1970), p. 242.

38. *Ibid.*

39. David Brinkerhoff and Lynn White, *Sociology*, 2nd ed. (St. Paul: West Publishing, 1988), p. 613.

40. Joseph Weis and John Sederstrom, *The Prevention of Serious Delinquency: What to Do?* (Washington, D.C.: U.S. Government Printing Office, 1981), p. 30.

41. Thorsten Sellin, *Culture Conflict and Crime*, Bulletin 41 (New York: Social Science Research Council, 1938).

42. Marvin Wolfgang and Franco Ferracuti, *The Subculture of Violence* (London: Tavistock, 1967).

43. Walter Miller, "Lower-Class Culture as a Generating Milieu of Gang Delinquency," *Journal of Social Issues* 14:5–19 (1958).

44. *Ibid.*, p. 6.

45. Albert Cohen, *Delinquent Boys* (New York: Free Press, 1955).

46. *Ibid.*, p. 25.

47. *Ibid.*, p. 28.

48. *Ibid.*

49. *Ibid.*, p. 86.

50. *Ibid.*, p. 128.

51. *Ibid.*, p. 129.

52. *Ibid.*, p. 30.

53. *Ibid.*, p. 31.

54. *Ibid.*, p. 133.

55. Albert Cohen and James Short, "Research on Delinquent Subcultures," *Journal of Social Issues* 14:20 (1958).

56. Cohen and Short, "Research on Delinquent Subcultures," p. 22.

57. *Ibid.*, pp. 25–31.

58. Richard Cloward and Lloyd Ohlin, *Delinquency and Opportunity* (New York: Free Press, 1960).

59. See Edwin Sutherland, *Principles of Criminology,* 4th ed. (Philadelphia: J. B. Lippincott, 1947).

60. Cloward and Ohlin, *Delinquency and Opportunity,* p. 159.

61. Clarence Schrag, *Crime and Justice, American Style* (Washington, D.C.: U.S. Government Printing Office, 1971), p. 67.

62. See, for example, Irving Spergel, *Racketville, Slumtown, and Haulburg* (Chicago: University of Chicago Press, 1964).

63. Judson Landis and Frank Scarpitti, "Perceptions Regarding Value Orientation and Legitimate Opportunity: Delinquents and Nondelinquents," *Social Forces* 84:57–61 (1965).

64. James Short, Ramon Rivera, and Ray Tennyson, "Perceived Opportunities, Gang Membership, and Delinquency," *American Sociological Review* 30:56–57 (1965).

65. Leon Fannin and Marshall Clinard, "Differences in the Conception of Self as a Male among Lower- and Middle-Class Delinquents," *Social Problems* 13:205–15 (1965).

66. *Ibid.*, p. 210.

67. Ronald Simons and Phyllis Gray, "Perceived Blocked Opportunity as an Explanation of Delinquency among Lower-Class Black Males: A Research Note," *Journal of Research in Crime and Delinquency* 26:90–101 (1989).

68. Ruth Kornhauser, *Social Sources of Delinquency: An Appraisal of Analytic Models* (Chicago: University of Chicago Press, 1978).

69. Simons and Gray, "Perceived Blocked Opportunity as an Explanation of Delinquency among Lower-Class Black Males," p. 99.

70. Francis Cullen, "Were Cloward and Ohlin Strain Theorists? Delinquency and Opportunity Revisited," *Journal of Research in Crime and Delinquency* 25:214–41 (1988).

71. *Ibid.*

72. For an intensive look at the Chicago Area Project, see Steve Schlossman and Michael Sedlak, "The Chicago Area Project Revisited," *Crime and Delinquency* 29:398–462 (1983).

73. See New York City Youth Board, *Reaching the Fighting Gang* (New York: New York City Youth Board, 1960).

74. Walter Miller, "The Impact of a 'Total Community' Delinquency Control Project," *Social Problems* 10:168–91 (1962).

6 Social Process Theories

Learning and Control

Outline

Not all sociologists view poverty, strain, cultural deviance, and social disorganization as the primary causes of delinquency. Some point to the self-report studies that show that middle-class youths also engage in delinquent acts, such as car theft, drug use, and vandalism, as proof that delinquency is not concentrated in lower-class areas but spread throughout the social structure. Differential arrest rates may be more reflective of police practices than a lower-class crime problem. Social structure theories also fail to explain the fact that most youths, even those in slum areas, do not become delinquents or adult criminals. If the presence of social disorganization and culture conflict alone caused delinquency, then how can the presence of many "good boys in a high crime area" be explained?[1]

If the culture of poverty alone does not cause delinquency, what does? One argument is that the onset of delinquency can be traced to the quality of a youth's **socialization** within the most significant social institutions he or she encounters: the family; the peer group; school; and the justice system. Each of these elements of the **social process** has a powerful influence on children's self-images, beliefs, values, and subsequently, their behavior.

According to this view, such factors as learning delinquent attitudes from peers, feeling alienated or detached from school, and experiencing conflict in the home help produce antisocial activity. Conflict-ridden social relationships help youth to become alienated from conventional social institutions, develop a poor self-image, and feel little attachment to a law-abiding life-style.

Social process theorists also dispute the existence of a value gap among the various social classes in American society. Even youths growing up in the most deteriorated urban areas learn the same values at home, school, and church as upper- and middle-class youths. Though lower-class kids face the burden of coping with economic hardships, family strain, delinquent peers, inadequate schools, low self-esteem, and racism, most are willing to obey legal and moral rules. Those that learn to cope do so because they enjoy a good home life, supportive friends, and caring teachers.

So, according to the social process view, delinquency can occur among any class of youth, rich or poor, whose socialization is weak and destructive. Unlike social structure theories, which focus on the law violations of the lower class, social process theories attempt to identify the factors within any class or status group that cause a youth to become involved in criminal behavior or to remain stable and law-abiding.

SOCIALIZATION AND DELINQUENCY

Social process theories are grounded in the extensive literature examining the relationship between socialization and delinquent behavior. Enumerable research studies have found that as a child matures, the elements within society that are entrusted with their care and nurturing must perform adequately lest their socialization become maladapted. Primary among these social institutions is the family. There is a consensus among experts that where parenting is inadequate, absent, or destructive, a child's normal maturation processes will be interrupted and damaged. And while there still exists much debate over which elements of the parent-child relationship are the most critical, there is little question that family relationships have a significant influence on antisocial behavior.[2]

In a similar vein, there exists an extensive literature linking delinquency to poor school performance, educational disabilities, boredom, and inadequate educational facilities. A youth who feels that teachers don't care or who has been made to feel like a hopeless academic failure is the one more likely to become involved in a delinquent way of life.[3]

Still another suspected element of deviant socialization is peer group relations that stress substance abuse, theft, and violence. Youths who form close relations with peers who engage in antisocial behavior may learn the techniques and attitudes that support delinquency and may also find themselves cut off from more conventional associates and institutions.[4]

In sum, social process theory portrays the delinquent youth as someone whose personality and behavior, formed in the crucible of social relationships and societal processes, is at odds with conventional society.

There are two sub-branches of the social process perspective. The first, **learning theory,** holds that delinquency is *learned* through close relationships with others. Both the techniques of crime and the attitudes necessary to support delinquency are learned.

The second branch, **social control theory,** views delinquency as a result of a youth's feeling cut off from the major institutions of society—family, peers, and school. Because the *bond* to these institutions is severed, the control that conventional society normally places on a youth is absent, and he or she feels free to exercise antisocial behavior choices.

LEARNING THEORIES

Learning theory stresses the learning of the attitudes, morals, skills, and behaviors needed to sustain a delinquent career (see Figure 6.1). Borrowing heavily from psychological views of social learning, such sociologists as Edwin Sutherland, Donald Cressey, Daniel Glaser, and David Matza have focussed their attention on the learning of delinquent values within the social context of family and peer groups. As a group, their theoretical position is that poverty or social class differences alone are not enough to explain delinquency. Youthful law violators must *learn* how to become delinquents and how to cope emotionally with the consequences of their behavior. We now turn to descriptions of the most important examples of learning theory.

Differential Association Theory

Edwin Sutherland, long considered the preeminent American criminologist, first formulated the theory of **differential association** in 1939 in his text *Principles of Criminology.*[5] The theory appeared in its final form in 1947. At that time, differ-

FIGURE 6.1

The learning theory perspective

Deviant Values

Significant others, such as parents and peers. hold values that condone criminal and delinquent behavior.

Exposure

Youths are exposed to deviant norms and values while in intimate contact with significant others.

Delinquent Behavior

Children learn the attitudes, techniques, values, and perceptions needed to sustain delinquent behavior.

Learning

Deviant norms and values are transferred to youths through a learning-type experience.

ential association was applied to all criminal and delinquent behavior patterns and has remained unchanged ever since. After Sutherland's death in 1950, his work was continued by his longtime associate Donald Cressey until his death in 1989. Cressey was so successful in explaining and popularizing his mentor's efforts that differential association remains one of the most enduring explanations of delinquent behavior.

There are a number of basic principles of differential association theory.[6] First, *criminal behavior is learned.* Delinquents are not born criminals, nor are they biologically or psychologically impaired. By suggesting that delinquent and criminal behavior is actually learned, Sutherland implied that it can be classified like any other learned behavior, such as writing, painting, or reading.

Second, *criminal behavior is learned in interaction with other persons in a process of communication.* Sutherland believed that delinquent behavior was learned actively. An individual does not become a delinquent simply by living in a crime-prone environment or by manifesting personal characteristics associated with delinquency, such as low IQ and family problems. Instead, criminal and other deviant behavior patterns are learned. Youths actively participate in the process with other individuals who serve as teachers and guides to delinquent behavior. Thus, delinquency cannot appear without the aid of others.

Third, *the learning of criminal behavior occurs principally within intimate personal groups.* Children's contacts with their closest social companions—family, friends, and peers—have the greatest influence on their learning of deviant behavior and attitudes. Relationships with these individuals can color and control the interpretation of everyday events and thus help youths overcome social controls so that they can embrace delinquent values and behavior. The intimacy of these associations far outweighs the importance of any other form of communications, for example, movies or television. Even on those rare occasions when violent films seem to provoke mass delinquent episodes, the outbreaks can be more readily explained as a reaction to peer group pressure than as a reaction to the films themselves.

Fourth, *the learning of criminal behavior includes techniques of committing the crime, which are sometimes very complicated, sometimes very simple, and the specific direction of motives, drives, rationalizations, and attitudes.* Because delinquent behavior is similar to other learned behavior, it follows that the actual

The learning of deviant values and behavior occurs principally within intimate personal groups.

techniques of criminality must also be acquired and learned. For example, young delinquents learn from their associates the proper way to pick a lock, shoplift, and obtain and use narcotics. In addition, delinquents must learn to use the proper terminology for their acts and then acquire the proper personal reactions to them. For example, getting high on marijuana and learning the proper way to "smoke a joint" are behavior patterns usually acquired from more experienced companions.[7] Moreover, delinquents must learn how to react properly to their criminal acts—when to defend them, rationalize them, or show remorse for them.

Fifth, *the specific direction of motives and drives is learned from various favorable and unfavorable definitions of the legal codes.* Since the reaction to social rules and laws is not uniform across society, youths constantly come in contact with people who maintain different views on the utility of obeying the legal code. When definitions of right and wrong are extremely varied, people experience what Sutherland referred to as *culture conflict*, which is the basis for the concept of differential association.

Sixth, *a person becomes delinquent if definitions favorable to violating the law exceed definitions unfavorable to it.* According to Sutherland's theory, individuals will become delinquent when they are in contact with persons, groups, or events that produce an excess of "definitions toward delinquency" and, concomitantly, when they are isolated from counteracting forces. A **definition toward delinquency** occurs, for example, when a youth is exposed to friends sneaking into a theater to avoid paying for a ticket or to friends talking about the virtues of getting high. A definition *against* delinquency occurs when friends or parents demonstrate their disapproval of crime. Of course, neutral behavior, such as reading a book, exists. It is neither positive nor negative with respect to law violation.[8]

Seventh, *differential associations may vary in frequency, duration, priority, or intensity.* Whether a child learns to obey the law or to disregard it is influenced by the quality of social interactions. Those of lasting duration will have greater influence than those that are briefer; frequent contacts have greater effect than rare and haphazard contacts.[9] Contacts made early in life will probably have greater and more far-reaching influence than those developed later on. Finally, "intensity" is generally interpreted to mean the importance and prestige attributed to the individual or groups from whom the definitions are learned. For example, the influence of a father, mother, or trusted friend will far outweigh the effect of more socially distant figures.

Eighth, *the process of learning criminal behavior by association with criminal and anticriminal patterns involves all the mechanisms involved in any other learning.* This statement suggests that the learning of criminal behavior patterns is similar to the learning of nearly all other patterns and is not a matter of mere imitation.

Finally, *while criminal behavior is an explanation of general needs and values, it is not explained by those needs and values, since noncriminal behavior is an explanation of the same needs and values.* By this principle, Sutherland suggests that the motives for delinquent behavior cannot logically be the same as those for conventional behavior. He rules out such motives as a desire to accumulate money or social status, a sense of personal frustration, a low self-concept, or any other similar motive as causes of delinquency. They are just as likely to produce such noncriminal behavior as getting a better education or working harder on a job. It is only the learning of deviant norms through contact with an excess of definitions toward criminality that produces delinquent behavior.

In sum, differential association theory holds that youth who are exposed to an excess of approved deviant attitudes and behavior at home and school and in their peer group will eventually incorporate these beliefs and judgments as part of their own personalities. Antisocial behavior is *learned* in the same manner as conventional behaviors are *learned.*

TESTING DIFFERENTIAL ASSOCIATION. There have been a number of important research efforts devoted to testing the validity of differential association. In one classic work, James Short tested a sample of 126 boys and 50 girls incarcerated in state training schools in order to measure the relationship between frequency, duration, priority, and intensity of interaction with delinquent peers and exposure to crime and delinquency.[10] Short used such measures as the number of friends a youth had who were delinquent, the degree to which a youth associated with criminals, and the intimacy of friendships with delinquents. He found that there was a consistent relationship between delinquent behavior and delinquent associations and that such associations were highly significant for both boys and girls. However, because the study was conducted with institutionalized youths regarded as seriously delinquent, it may not be applicable to the "average" law-violating child.

In a similar study, Albert Reiss and A. Lewis Rhodes attempted to determine whether delinquent behavior was associated with maintaining delinquent friendship patterns.[11] Using a sample of 378 white males grouped into friendship cliques, Reiss and Rhodes found that a boy's chance of committing a specific delinquent act depended on whether other members of his friendship group committed that same act. This pattern was related to social class. Delinquent boys from blue-collar families maintained delinquent friendship patterns. Among youths from white-collar backgrounds, this relationship held true only for less serious offenses.

Other research efforts have found that youths who are exposed to deviant definitions and attitudes are also the ones most likely to become delinquent.[12] For example, research has linked teenage drug use to peer approval and support for substance abuse.[13] The connection between the perception of differential associations and delinquency has been demonstrated with samples of youth of various races, ages, and classes.[14]

There has also been research efforts that show that youths may be deterred from delinquency by the threat of peer and family disapproval.[15] By implication, youths who believe their friends and family hold attitudes in support of deviance will feel free to violate the law; those who believe that their friends and family will condemn their behavior will be deterred from criminal violations.[16]

Despite these affirmations, efforts to verify differential association principles have not all been consistent.[17] Designing research to test the assumptions of differential association has proven to be a formidable task. It is difficult to conceptualize the principles of the theory, such as a *definition toward delinquency*, in a way that lends itself to empirical measurement.[18] There is also the problem of causal ordering: even if delinquent youth have many like-minded friends and also report exposure to an excess of prodelinquent definitions, it is difficult to determine whether these associations and definitions *caused* law-violating behaviors or were their result. That is, while it is possible that "innocent" youth are "seduced" into crime by exposure to the deviant attitudes of their more delinquent peers, it is also feasible that youngsters who continually break the law *later* develop a group of like-minded peers and associates who support their behavior.[19] To answer critics, researchers must develop more valid measures of differential associations. One possibility is that longitudinal analysis may be used to measure subjects repeatedly over time to determine if those exposed to excess definitions toward deviance eventually become deviant themselves.[20]

Despite these problems, differential association theory maintains an important place in the study of delinquent behavior. For one thing, it provides a consistent explanation of *all* types of delinquent and criminal behavior. Unlike the social structure theories discussed previously, it is not limited to the explanation of a single facet of antisocial activity, for example, lower-class gang activity. The theory can also account for the extensive delinquent behavior found even in middle- and upper-class areas, where youths may be exposed to a variety of prodelinquent definitions from such sources as overly opportunistic parents and friends.

Differential Reinforcement Theory

There have been a number of attempts to reformulate the concept of differential association.[21] The most important attempt has been the translation by Robert Burgess and Ronald Akers of Sutherland's model into a psychological learning theory format. They suggest that delinquent behavior, like all behavior, is shaped by the stimuli or reactions of others to that behavior.[22] Social behavior is learned through direct conditioning, or modeling of others' behavior. Likewise, behavior is strengthened through reward or positive reinforcement and weakened by loss of reward (negative punishment) or actual punishment (positive punishment). Youths who receive an excess of rewards over punishments for conforming behavior will be the most likely to remain nondelinquent—a process called **differential reinforcement.**

Reinforcements, both positive and negative, are usually received in group settings. The most powerful influences are the ones with which a person is in **differential association**—peers and family—but a youth may also be affected by school, social groups, clergy, and valued associates. Whether deviant or criminal behavior persists depends on the degree to which it has been rewarded or punished by these groups and the rewards or punishments they attach to its alternatives. Once people are initiated into crime-related activities, their behavior is influenced by a variety of factors: social reinforcement; exposure to deviant behavior models; association with deviant peers; lack of negative sanctions from parents and peers; and so on. The deviant behavior, originated by imitation, is sustained by social support.

In an empirical analysis of the differential reinforcement theory, Ronald Akers and his associates surveyed a large group of high school students on their alcohol and substance abuse patterns.[23] They found that survey items measuring differential association, differential reinforcement, and imitation of friends' behavior predicted significant amounts of marijuana use (39 percent) and alcohol abuse (32 percent). Similarly, a more recent study by Marvin Krohn and his associates found that differential reinforcement principles were effective for predicting the maintenance (or cessation) of a particular deviant behavior, cigarette smoking, in a sample of junior and senior high school boys measured over a three-year period.[24] Krohn found that reinforcement of smoking by parents and friends contributed to adolescent misbehavior.

Aker's work has emerged as an important way of viewing the onset and sustenance of a delinquent career. By suggesting that delinquent behaviors are a function of perceived rewards and punishments, it is one of the few prominent theoretical models that successfully integrates sociological and psychological variables.[25]

Neutralization Theory

Neutralization theory, sometimes referred to as *drift theory,* is identified with the writings of David Matza and his associate Gresham Sykes.[26] In furthering Sutherland's views, Sykes and Matza suggest that delinquents hold attitudes and values similar to those of law-abiding citizens but that they learn techniques that enable them to neutralize those values and attitudes temporarily and drift back and forth between legitimate and delinquent behavior. The techniques used by delinquents to weaken the hold of social values are learned through interaction with others.

Matza suggests that most individuals spend their lives behaving on a continuum somewhere between total freedom and total restraint. **Drift** is the process by which an individual moves from one extreme of behavior to another, behaving sometimes in an unconventional, free, or deviant manner and at other times with constraint and sobriety.[27]

Writing with Sykes, Matza subsequently rejected the notion that a delinquent subculture exists that maintains an independent set of values and attitudes in opposition to the values of the dominant culture. Rather, Matza and Sykes believe that most youths actually appreciate goal-oriented middle-class values but are conflicted because they see such views as being frowned upon by their peers. Therefore, middle-class beliefs remain unconscious or **subterranean** because juveniles are afraid to express them to members of their own peer group.[28]

TECHNIQUES OF NEUTRALIZATION. Since delinquents actually value middle-class norms and are not immune to the demands of conformity, they must develop a method to neutralize the guilt that comes from law violations. Sykes and Matza suggest that through a process of peer interaction, juveniles learn a distinct set of justifications for their behavior. These "neutralization techniques" allow youths to temporarily "drift away" from the rules of the normative society and participate in deviant behaviors.[29] Neutralization techniques include the denial of responsibility, the denial of injury, the denial of the victim, condemnation of the condemners, and appeal to higher loyalties:[30]

- *Denial of Responsibility.* Delinquents sometimes claim that their unlawful acts were simply not their fault, that the acts were due to forces beyond their control or were an accident.

- *Denial of Injury.* By denying the wrongfulness of an act, delinquents are able to rationalize their illegal behavior. For example, stealing is viewed as "borrowing," vandalism is considered mischief that has gotten out of hand. Society often agrees with delinquents, labeling their illegal behavior "pranks" and thereby reaffirming that delinquency can be socially acceptable.

- *Denial of the Victim.* Delinquents sometimes rationalize their behavior by maintaining that the victim of crime "had it coming." Thus, vandalism may be directed against a disliked teacher or neighbor, or homosexuals may be beaten up by a gang because their behavior is offensive.[31] Denying the victim may also take the form of ignoring the rights of an absent or unknown victim, for example, the unseen owner of a department store. It becomes morally acceptable for delinquents to commit crimes, such as vandalism, when the victims cannot be sympathized with or respected because of their absence.

- *Condemnation of the Condemners.* The delinquent views the world as a corrupt place with a dog-eat-dog moral code. Since police and judges are on the take, teachers show favoritism, and parents take out their frustrations on their children, it is ironic and unfair for these authorities to turn around and condemn youthful misconduct. By shifting the blame to others, delinquents are able to repress the feeling that their own acts are wrong.

- *Appeal to Higher Loyalties.* Delinquents argue that they are caught in the dilemma of being loyal to their own peer group while at the same time attempting to abide by the rules of the larger society. The needs of the group take

Delinquents argue that they must be loyal to their peer group rather than obey the rules of society.

precedence over the rules of society because the demands of the former are immediate and localized.[32]

In sum, the theory of neutralization presupposes a condition in which such slogans as "I didn't mean to do it," "I didn't really hurt anybody," "They had it coming to them," "Everybody's picking on me," and "I didn't do it for myself" are used by youths to rationalize accepted social norms and values so that they can enter, or "drift," into delinquent modes of behavior.

TESTING NEUTRALIZATION THEORY. Attempts have been made to verify the assumptions of neutralization theory empirically, but the results have so far been inconclusive. For example, Robert Ball found that samples of official and self-reported delinquents were more likely to use neutralization techniques than nondelinquents.[33] In a test of the attitudes incarcerated youths hold toward their misdeeds, Robert Regoli and Eric Poole also found that neutralization mitigated the conflict caused by law violations.[34]

A number of studies have attempted to test the validity of neutralization theory by comparing the values of delinquents with those of nondelinquents. If neutralization theory is valid, these groups should *not* differ in their values and attitudes (because, according to the theory, delinquents generally hold conventional values but are able to neutralize them before violating the law). Research has shown that gang youths do in fact value such middle-class behavior as "working for grades," "reading good books," and "saving one's money" as highly as nondelinquent youth, a finding that supports neutralization theory.[35] However, the evidence that delinquents and nondelinquents hold *identical* values and beliefs has not been substantiated.[36]

Despite these efforts, empirical verification of neutralization theory has been lacking because it is difficult to determine if delinquents neutralize law-violating behavior *before* or *after* they engage in it.[37] If youths neutralize their guilt after engaging in illegal activity, then neutralization theory loses its power as an explanation of the *cause* of delinquency and becomes a theory describing the *reactions* of juveniles to their misdeeds.

While the time ordering of neutralizations has been a problem for researchers, in a recent analysis, John Hamlin argues that neutralizations *should be considered* as postdelinquency rationalizations of behavior, used only when behavior is questioned or viewed as a major threat by others. Justifications and excuses neutralize guilt and enable youngsters to continue to feel good about themselves.[38] According to Hamlin's view then, neutralizations do not precede delinquency but are learned to help youngsters deal with the problems presented by getting caught!

Despite these concerns, the theory of neutralization is a major contribution to the literature of crime and delinquency. It is one of the few social theories that can account for the aging-out process. Neutralization theory implies that youths can forego criminal behavior when they reach their majority because, in reality, they never really rejected social norms. Once the needs and pressures of the postteenage world exert themselves—marriage, family, job—delinquents are less likely than ever to "drift" into illegitimate modes of behavior. The concept of neutralization also provides a logical explanation of why many otherwise law-abiding youths engage in occasional delinquent activities such as drug abuse; neutralization techniques like "everybody's doing it" and "no one is really hurt" helps make these behaviors morally acceptable. Because of these strengths, neutralization has endured as a view of delinquent behavior.

EVALUATING LEARNING THEORIES

Beginning with Sutherland's differential association model, learning theories have played an important role in the study of delinquent behavior. The empirical evidence that shows that delinquents learn deviant behaviors and attitudes from their intimate contacts has been used to support the view that "delinquents are made and not born." This view has had an important influence on policy efforts to reduce delinquent behavior. Numerous efforts have tried to expose kids either to the dangers of drug use and delinquency or conversely to the benefits of conventional behavior. You can observe learning principles in action the next time you see a TV ad exhorting youths to "just say no to drugs," practice "safe sex," or to stay in school until they graduate.

Critics of learning theory argue that delinquents are not influenced by significant others because, in fact, they rarely have close or meaningful relationships with other people. The learning approach is also criticized because research has not shown that the assimilation of deviant attitudes actually *precedes* delinquency and are not learned afterwards in order to justify behavior or assuage guilt. That is, rather than learning the techniques of delinquency from others, law-violating youths may later associate with equally criminal peers in order to learn how to deal comfortably with the consequences of their deviant life-style. It is important that research, especially projects relying on longitudinal designs (measuring kids' behavior over time), try to address these important methodological issues.

CONTROL THEORIES

Learning theories assume that youths originally scorn delinquent behavior but learn techniques that free them to engage in antisocial acts without regret or moral discomfort. In contrast, **control theories** suggest that many forms of delinquent behavior—using drugs, engaging in sexual acts, skipping school, fighting, getting drunk—are *always attractive* to almost every teenager. These acts represent the exciting, illicit, adventurous behavior that is glorified on television and in the movies and that serves as a theme for rock music.

Why then do most youths forsake the lure of illicit behavior, obey conventional rules, and grow up to be law-abiding adults? For a control theorist, the answer lies in the strength and direction of their ties with conventional groups, individuals, and institutions. Those who have close relationships with their parents, friends, and teachers and who maintain a positive self-image will be able to resist the lure of deviant behaviors. Rather than jeopardize their good standing in the community, they refuse to risk detection and punishment for delinquent offenses. On the other hand, youths without these social supports feel free to violate the law; if caught, they have nothing to lose. (See Figure 6.2.)

Containment Theory

Early versions of control theory speculated that delinquency was a product of weak self-concept and poor self-esteem. Youths who felt good about themselves were able to resist the temptations of the streets; their delinquent tendencies were "contained." As early as 1951, Albert Reiss described how delinquents had

FIGURE 6.2
The social control perspective

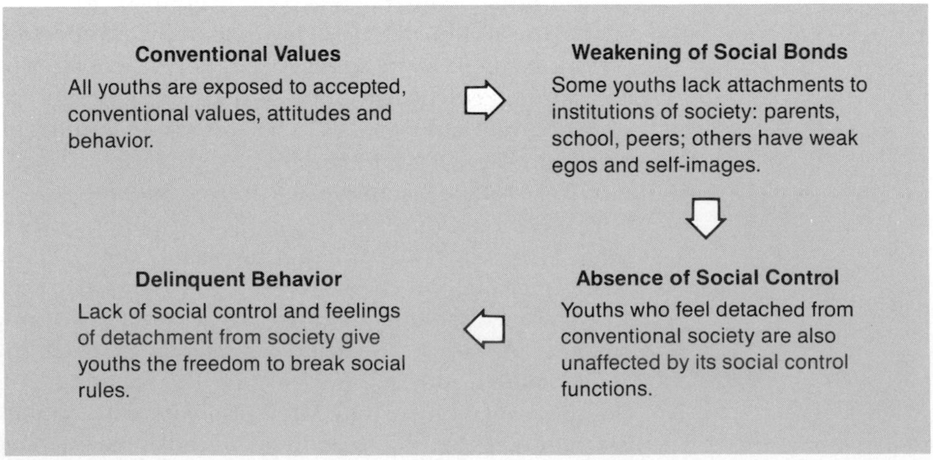

Conventional Values
All youths are exposed to accepted, conventional values, attitudes and behavior.

Weakening of Social Bonds
Some youths lack attachments to institutions of society: parents, school, peers; others have weak egos and self-images.

Absence of Social Control
Youths who feel detached from conventional society are also unaffected by its social control functions.

Delinquent Behavior
Lack of social control and feelings of detachment from society give youths the freedom to break social rules.

weak "ego ideals" and lacked the "personal controls" to produce conforming behavior.[39] In a similar vein, Scott Briar and Irving Piliavin described how delinquents have a weak **commitment to conformity.**[40] Briar and Piliavin concluded that youths who fear that apprehension for criminal activity will damage their self-image as well as their relationships with others will be most likely to conform to social roles; those who are less concerned about their social standing are free to violate social rules.

Walter Reckless's **containment theory** holds that society produces a series of pushes and pulls toward delinquency.[41] These in turn are counteracted by internal and external **containments,** which help insulate the individual from delinquency. The elements of containment include:

■ *Inner Containments.* Inner containments consist of the inner strength of an individual personality—for example, good self-concept, ego strength, high frustration tolerance, goal orientation, and tension-reducing capabilities.

■ *Outer Containments.* Outer containments are the normative constraints that societies and social groups ordinarily use to control their members. They consist of such factors as a sense of belonging, a consistent moral front, reinforcement of norms, goals, and values, effective supervision, discipline, and meaningful social roles.

■ *Internal Pushes.* Internal pushes involve such personal factors as restlessness, discontent, hostility, rebellion, mental conflict, anxieties, and the need for immediate gratification.

■ *External Pressures.* External pressures are adverse living conditions that influence deviant behavior. They include relative deprivation, poverty, unemployment, insecurity, minority status, limited opportunities, and inequalities.

■ *External Pulls.* External pulls are represented by deviant companions, membership in criminal subcultures or other deviant groups, and such influences as the mass media and pornography.

Simply put, containment theory suggests that the two containments act as a defense against youths' potential deviation from legal and social norms and insulate them from antisocial pulls, pushes, and pressures. Reckless suggested that of the two, inner containment, which depends on a positive self-image and sense of self-worth, is the more important. Since individuals spend much of their time away from the family and other sources of external containment, they must rely on their own inner strengths to control delinquent "pushes" and "pressures."

Reckless and his associates made an extensive effort to validate the principles of containment theory.[42] In a series of studies analyzing containment principles within the school setting, they concluded that the ability of nondelinquents to keep up a conventional status depends on their maintaining a positive self-image in the face of environmental pressures toward delinquency.[43]

Despite the success Reckless and his colleagues had in verifying their containment approach, their efforts have been criticized for lack of methodological rigor, and the validity of containment theory has been disputed.[44]

SELF-CONCEPT AND DELINQUENCY. Though the validity of containment theory has been challenged, it may be premature to dismiss "self-image" as a correlate of delinquency. Empirical research indicates that an important association between self-image and delinquency does in fact exist.[45] Research by Howard Kaplan found that youths with poor self-concepts are the ones most likely to engage in delinquent behavior and that successful participation in criminality helps raise their self-esteem.[46] According to Kaplan, delinquent activity occurs when illegal activity is viewed as a mechanism that can enhance self-concept: the boy who fails at school realizes that he will feel much better if he can reject the teacher's negative judgment by dropping out and joining a gang whose members value his cunning and fighting ability. Research by L. Edward Wells indicates that youth who maintain both the lowest self-image *and* the greatest need for approval are the ones most likely to seek self-enhancement from delinquency.[47]

In sum, while containment theory has been criticized, there is evidence that delinquent youth have lower self-esteem than nondelinquent youth and that a successful law-violating career may help enhance their self-image.

Social Control Theory

The predominant form of control theory today was first articulated by sociologist Travis Hirschi in his famous book *Causes of Delinquency.*[48]

Hirschi links delinquent behavior to the bond an individual maintains with society. When that bond weakens or breaks, the constraints that society puts on its members are lifted, and an individual may violate the law. Hirschi's control theory assumes that all individuals are potential delinquents and criminals and that social controls, not moral values, maintain law and order. Without controls and in the absence of sensitivity to and interest in others, a youth is free to commit criminal acts.[49]

Hirschi speculates that a consistent value system exists to which all people in society are exposed. Delinquents defy this moral code because their attachment to society is weak. Hirschi views the youthful law violator as someone who rejects social norms and beliefs and is thus morally free to engage in delinquent forms of behavior.

ELEMENTS OF THE SOCIAL BOND. Hirschi argues that the **social bond** a person maintains with society is divided into four main elements: attachment, commitment, involvement, and belief.

■ *Attachment.* Attachment refers to a person's sensitivity to and interest in others. Psychologists believe that without a sense of attachment, a person becomes a psychopath and loses the ability to relate coherently to the world. The acceptance of social norms and the development of a social conscience depend on attachment to and caring for other human beings. Hirschi views parents, peers, and schools as the most important social institutions with which a person should maintain ties. Attachment to parents is the most important. Even if a family if shattered by divorce and separation, a child must retain strong attachment to one or both parents. Without attachment to one's family, it is unlikely that feelings of respect for others in authority will develop.[50]

■ *Commitment.* Commitment involves the time, energy, and effort expended in pursuit of conventional lines of action. It embraces such activities as getting an education and saving money for the future. Control theory holds that if people build up a strong involvement in life, property, and reputation, they will be less likely to engage in acts that will jeopardize their position. Conversely, lack of commitment to conventional values may foreshadow a condition in which risk-taking behavior, such as delinquency, becomes a reasonable behavior alternative.

■ *Involvement.* An individual's heavy involvement in conventional activities does not leave time for illegal behavior. Hirschi believes that involvement—in school, recreation, and family—insulates a youth from the potential lure of delinquent behavior that idleness encourages.

■ *Belief.* People who live in common social settings often share a similar moral doctrine and revere such human values as sharing, sensitivity to the rights of others, and admiration for the legal code. If these beliefs are absent or weakened, individuals are more likely to share in antisocial acts.

Hirschi further suggests that the interrelationship of elements of the social bond influences whether an individual pursues delinquent or conventional activities. For example, boys or girls who feel kinship and sensitivity to parents and friends should be more likely to desire and work toward legitimate goals. On the other hand, youths who reject social relationships will probably lack commitment to conventional goals. In a similar fashion, youths who are highly committed to conventional acts and beliefs will be more likely to be involved in conventional activities, such as those associated with church, family, and school.

Hirschi's social control theory is important because it is applicable to youths in high, middle, and low socioeconomic groups. For example, in lower-class

Hirschi believes that involvement in conventional activities insulates a youth from the lures of delinquency.

settings, the social bond may weaken because of limited access to legitimate activities, lack of attachment to a poor school system, and an impaired commitment to unobtainable future goals. Middle- and upper-class youth may also find that their bonds to parents who are too busy with their upwardly mobile careers to care for them are weak and attenuated. They may find that their academic abilities fall below what is expected of people in their cultural circumstances or that their relatively secure financial status interferes with a true commitment to long-term goals. Thus, Hirschi's theory is neither culture-bound nor limited to explaining delinquency among youths in a particular social class.

RESEARCH ON SOCIAL CONTROL THEORY. The most powerful empirical support for social bond theory comes from the significant body of literature that indicates that poor familial, educational, and peer relationships are all related to delinquency. Over a twenty-year period, numerous studies have found that, as Hirschi predicted, delinquent youths have weak and strained relationships with their parents, experience school failure and lack interest in school activities, and exhibit inadequate peer group relations.

However, this evidence alone is not sufficient proof of the validity of social bond theory, because these relationships are also predicted by social learning theorists and social structure theorists. Consequently, one of Hirschi's most significant contributions to delinquency research is his attempt to test directly the principal hypothesis of control theory. He administered a complex self-report survey to a sample of over 4,000 junior and senior high school students in Contra Costa County, California.[51] In a detailed analysis of the data, Hirschi found considerable evidence to support the control theory model. We will now look at some of his more important findings in detail.

Hirschi measured attachment to society with such survey items as "Would you like to be the kind of person your father is?" and "When you come across things you don't understand, does you mother (father) help you with them?" Hirschi found that youths who were strongly attached to their parents were less likely to participate in delinquent behavior. This relationship also existed when race, social class, and the parents' own values were controlled.

Hirschi found that lower-class parents, even those who themselves are committing criminal acts, express allegiance to the law and conventional society. Thus, attachment to the parents counteracts delinquent behavior even when the parents themselves are delinquent.

Hirschi also found that lack of attachment to the school and to education, measured by items such as "Do you care what teachers think of you?" and "It is none of the school's business if a student wants to smoke outside the classroom," is a strong predictor of delinquent behavior. Poor school performance and academic incompetence affect this relationship significantly. Youths with poor basic academic skills are likely to become detached from school and involved in delinquency. Hirschi traces this important relationship as follows: "The causal chain runs from academic incompetence to poor school performance to disliking of school to rejection of the school's authority to the commission of delinquent acts."[52]

Hirschi also examined the attachment of youths to their friends and other peers, using such questions as "Would you like to be the kind of person your best friends are?" He found that youths who maintain close associations with friends are less likely to commit delinquent acts. Delinquent youths, on the other hand, often maintain weak and distant relationships with their peers. Hirschi did find that boys with a high stake in conformity who maintain delinquent friends are more likely to commit delinquent acts than boys with a high stake in conformity without delinquent friends. However, this relationship does not immediately contradict the control approach. First, only 22 percent of the high-stake boys had delinquent friends. Second, the greater a youth's stake in conformity, the less likely he was to maintain delinquent companions.

Among Hirschi's most important discoveries are the following:

- Contrary to subculture strain theories, the gang rarely recruits "good" boys or influences them to turn "bad."
- Boys who maintain middle-class values are relatively unaffected by the delinquent behavior of their friends, although having delinquent friends was generally related to criminality.
- The idea that delinquents have warm, intimate relationships with one another is a myth.
- "The child with little stake in conformity is susceptible to prodelinquent influences in his environment; the child with a large stake in conformity is relatively immune to these influences."[53]

Hirschi examined commitment to both deviant and conventional activities with questionnaire items dealing with frequency of smoking, drinking, and dating behavior, the level of educational aspiration (desire for a college education, for example), and the level of vocational expectation (blue-collar, white-collar, professional). Again Hirschi found evidence that commitment to conventional values is related to rejection of delinquent behavior. On the other hand, youths who drink and cruise around in cars are often involved in delinquency. He states, "The picture of the delinquent as a striver, either in word or deed, simply does not fit the data."[54]

Involvement in conventional activities was defined as time spent on homework, and involvement in unconventional activities was defined as hours a week spent riding around in cars. Again, Hirschi found that involvement in school inhibits delinquency. On the other hand, youths who smoke, drink, date, ride around in cars, and find adolescence "boring" are more prone to delinquency. However, this relationship is not as strong as Hirschi expected, and he found that boys who are involved in unconventional activities (smoking, drinking, and so on) are more likely to engage in delinquent acts regardless of their commitment to education and their involvement in school activities.

Hirschi measured a large variety of commonly held beliefs and values. In general, there was little difference in the beliefs of delinquents and nondelinquents. In fact, delinquents often respected middle-class attitudes. For example, Hirschi reports that children who do not personally care about good grades still believe that youths who do care about school and get good grades are taking a path preferable to their own.

Hirschi's data lends important support to the validity of control theory. While the statistical significance of his findings is sometimes less than he expected, his research data is extremely consistent. Only in very rare instances do his findings contradict the theory's most critical assumptions.

CORROBORATING RESEARCH. There have been many research studies that have been supportive of Hirschi's social control theory.[55] In general, research efforts have found that delinquents tend to have the strained relationships within the family, peer group and school that are indicative of a weakened social bond. These efforts can be grouped on the basis of the element of the theory they seek to support or corroborate.

Some have focused on the association between delinquency and the lack of familial *attachment*. For example, research by Patricia Van Voorhis and her associates found that such indicators of a disturbed and detached family life as intrafamily conflict, abuse of children, and a lack of affection, supervision, and family pride, were predictive of delinquent conduct.[56]

Another approach has been to show that delinquents have rejected social values and *beliefs*. John Cochran and Ronald Akers found that children who are involved in religious activities and hold conventional religious beliefs are less likely to become involved in substance abuses, such as drinking and using marijuana.[57]

There is also research by Robert Agnew and David Peterson that shows that youths *involved* in conventional leisure activities, such as supervised social activities and noncompetitive sports, are less likely to engage in delinquency than those youth who are involved in unconventional leisure activities and unsupervised, peer-oriented social pursuits.[58]

This type of data, while supportive, cannot by itself establish the validity of social control theory. Even if all delinquents had family, school, and peer group problems, it still would be possible that the strained relationships *were a result* of the youths' law violations and not their cause. For example, even if we find that few drug-using teens believe in God while abstainers regularly attend religious services, we would not be sure if sacrilegious behavior was a cause of substance abuse or if kids who get high on drugs eventually lose interest in religious beliefs. However, while not conclusive, the evidence has been in a direction that supports the hypothesis of control theory.

Hirschi's version of control theory has remained one of the pre-eminent theoretical approaches to the study of delinquency, receiving much praise and attention in the literature of the field. For many delinquency experts, it is perhaps the most important way of understanding the onset of youthful misbehavior.[59]

DISSENTING OPINIONS. While there has been significant empirical support for Hirschi's work, there has also been research studies that cast doubt on some or all of its elements. One area that has long been troublesome is Hirschi's contention that any attachment to significant others helps maintain the social bond. What about kids who are attached to delinquent peers and parents who engage in crime and drug abuse? Shouldn't their attachment promote rather than inhibit delinquent behavior? A number of research studies have indeed found that attachment to deviant peers and parents is, in fact, correlated with personal delinquency.[60] For example, Gary Jensen and David Brownfield found that youths who are emotionally attached to parents who use drugs are more likely to become drug users themselves.[61] Other research efforts indicate that attachment to delinquent friends is associated with personal delinquency.[62] There is evidence that delinquents are not lone wolves whose only personal relationships are exploitive and that their friendship patterns are quite close to those of conventional youth.[63]

Of a more serious nature are findings that indicate that social control theory has inadequacies limiting its power as a general theory of delinquency. One issue is whether the theory can explain all modes of delinquency or is restricted to particular groups of delinquents and forms of delinquent behavior. This problem was addressed in a research effort by Marvin Krohn and James Massey.[64] Using a sample of 3,065 junior and senior high school students, Krohn and Massey found that the element of "commitment" was a more powerful predictor of delinquency than "attachment" or "belief." They also found that social bond theory was better able to explain female delinquency than male delinquency and minor delinquency (such as alcohol and marijuana abuse) than more serious delinquent acts. Krohn and Massey concluded that Hirschi's model has utility as an explanation of the onset of delinquency, a period when youthful offenders are both engaging in petty offenses and questioning their commitment and attachment to social institutions.

Another research effort by Randy LaGrange and Helene Raskin White addressed one of the most important issues left unattended by Hirschi and his supporters: does elements of the bond and its influence on delinquency change over time?[65] Using samples of 12-, 15-, and 18-year-old boys, LaGrange and White found that there were indeed age differences in the way elements of the social bond influenced delinquency. They found that the processes hypothesized by Hirschi were most applicable to youths in their middle teens (15) than to older or younger adolescents. Midteens are more likely to be influenced by their parents and teachers than boys in the other two age groups, who are more deeply influenced by their deviant peers. LaGrange and White attribute this finding to the problems of midadolescence, when there is a great need to develop "psychological anchors" to conformity.

While the above-mentioned efforts support control theory in part, research by Robert Agnew puts into question its overall validity.[66] Using a sample of subjects measured over time, Agnew found evidence that, in contrast to Hirschi's theory, the weakening of the social bond is the result, not the cause, of antisocial behavior. Put another way, as kids get into trouble with the law, they may find that their parents reject them, schools withdraw their help, and they are shunned by their peers. While some delinquency may be caused in part by a weak bond, flaunting social rules and conventions may also help to weaken a youth's previously strong ties to society.[67]

EVALUATING SOCIAL CONTROL THEORY. While some research has given unqualified support to control theory, there are other efforts that question its validity. However, even its greatest detractors recognize that the theory might still be developed and fine-tuned and evolve into a valid explanation of delinquency.[68]

A number of questions remain unanswered: is the weakening of one particular element of the bond—attachment, belief, commitment, or involvement—the principal cause of delinquency? When it is weakened, does it trigger deficiencies in the other elements, or are they all weakened simultaneously? Once weakened, is it possible for the bond to strengthen itself? Some recent evidence on chronic offenders indicates that some may cease offending for quite some time and then later resume their criminal careers; this finding is not adequately explained by control theory.[69] Is delinquency episodic, or are delinquents perpetually involved in illegal behavior? Since most delinquents do not become adult criminals, can we assume that somehow their social bonds eventually are strengthened? How is this possible? Social control theory, therefore, remains an important arena for future research designed to refine its scope and direction.

INTEGRATED THEORIES

In recent years, delinquency experts have attempted to integrate some of the most salient features of a number of existing theoretical models into a single model in order to surmount some of the problems associated with the various forms of sociological theory. Put another way, an integrated theory of delinquency might combine the strain theory concept of status frustration with learning theory or social control ideas. In the sections below, some of the more prominent integrated theories are presented.

Social Development Theory

Joseph Weis and his associates have attempted to integrate some of the most important features of social control theory with elements of social structure theory.[70] Weis argues that control theory is useful when it describes how children become delinquent because of their inadequate socialization and alienation from important institutional forces, such as the family and school. And social structure theory can be useful because it accounts for the community context of delinquency. The two theoretical perspectives also complement one another in the area of the role of socialization. While control theory views delinquency as a result of inadequate relationships with such formal institutions as the school, family, and criminal justice authorities, social structure theories focus on the influence of informal peer groups and companions. Consequently, after reviewing the core premises of each type of theory, Weis found that both can contribute to an integrated model of delinquency.

According to Weis's **social development theory,** there is a positive relationship between community organization and social control, and both factors in turn exert influence on delinquent behavior. That is, in a low-income, disorganized community, social control is less effective because the frontline socializing institutions are weak: families are disorganized; educational facilities are inadequate; there are fewer material, social, and psychological resources; and respect for the law is inadequate. Because crime rates are traditionally higher in these areas, there exist more opportunities to commit crime, putting an even greater strain on the institutions of socialization. Within this context of weak social controls and community disorganization, legitimate social institutions are incapable of combating the lure of delinquent peer groups and gangs.

Weis's model of delinquency is illustrated in Figure 6.3, where we can see the direction of delinquency-producing relationships. Socialization within the family is influenced by the youth's sex, race, and economic status: children of a particular race and sex living within a certain area will have familial experiences different from those of another child with a different set of personal and economic characteristics. It is anticipated that males who are members of the lowest eco-

FIGURE 6.3

Overview of the social development theory of delinquency

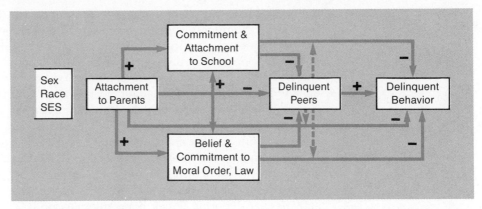

SES = Socioeconomic status.
Source: Joseph Weis and John Sederstrom, *Reports of the National Juvenile Assessment Centers, The Prevention of Serious Delinquency: What to Do* (Washington, D.C.: U.S. Department of Justice, 1981) p. 35.

nomic strata will have the highest potential for disrupted, unrewarding family lives and will experience a lack of attachment to their parents.

Opportunities for involvement in the family, plus specific parental skills, lead to a close attachment with parents. This attachment influences subsequent school experiences and beliefs and values. For those with strong family relationships, school will be a meaningful experience marked by academic success and commitment to education. Youths in this category are more likely to develop conventional beliefs and values, become committed to conventional activities, and form attachments to conventional others. But if a youth does not find participation in conventional activities rewarding, he or she will likely seek associations with other youths who are equally disillusioned and engage in deviant activities that promise alternative rewards. Together, these alienated youths are likely to influence one another in the pursuit of illegal gain and illicit experiences.

Weis's social development model combines features of social structure and social control theories. Like the former, it suggests that youths living in disorganized neighborhoods are the most likely to succumb to the lure of youth gangs and groups. And as suggested by the latter, it holds that commitment and attachment to conventional institutions, activities, and beliefs work to insulate youths from crime-encouraging influences, given the effect of their environment. This approach seems to have great power as an explanation of delinquent behavior. It deserves the serious attention of students of delinquency.

Elliott's Integrated Theory

Another attempt to integrate theories of delinquency has been proposed by Delbert Elliott and his colleagues, David Huizinga and Suzanne Ageton, of the Behavioral Research Institute in Boulder, Colorado.[71]

Elliott and his colleagues discount some aspects of "pure" strain, control, and learning theories. They contend that strain theory can account for some initial delinquent acts but does not adequately explain why some youths enter into delinquent careers while others forego them (since prolonged delinquency places the offenders' valued conventional roles in jeopardy). Similarly, control theory cannot explain prolonged delinquent involvement because there is no group support or rewards for this behavior (since control theorists, such as Hirschi, portray the delinquent as a loner without close bonds to peers or society). And learning theories usually portray the delinquent as a passive actor who simply reacts when confronted with delinquency-producing reinforcements.

Because these earlier models are flawed as general explanations of delinquency, Elliott and his colleagues integrate the strongest features of strain, social learning, and control theories into a single theoretical model. According to their view, perceptions of strain, inadequate socialization, and living in socially disorganized areas lead youths to develop weak bonds with conventional groups, activities, and norms. Weak conventional bonds and high levels of perceived strain lead some youth to seek out and become bonded to peer groups. From these delinquent associations come positive reinforcements for delinquent behaviors; delinquent peers help provide role models for antisocial behavior. Bonding to delinquent groups when combined with weak bonding to conventional groups and norms leads to a high probability of involvement in delinquent behavior.

Elliott and his colleagues tested their theoretical model with data taken from a national youth survey of approximately 1,800 youths who were interviewed annually over a three-year period. With only a few minor exceptions, the results generally supported their integrated theory. One difference was that some subjects reported developing strong bonds to delinquent peers even if they did not reject the values of conventional society. Elliott and colleagues interpret this finding as suggesting that youths living in disorganized areas may have little choice but to join with law-violating youth groups since conventional groups simply do not exist.[72] Elliott also found that initial experimentation with drugs and delinquency predicted both joining a teenage law-violating peer group and becoming involved with additional delinquency.

The picture Elliott draws of the teenage delinquent is not dissimilar to Weis's social development model: living in a disorganized neighborhood, feeling hopeless and unable to get ahead, and becoming involved in petty crimes eventually leads to a condition where conventional social values become weak and attenuated. Concern for education and family relations and respect for the social order are weakened. A deviant peer group becomes an acceptable substitute, and consequently, the attitudes and skills that support delinquent tendencies are amplified. The result: early experimentation with drugs and delinquency as a way of life.

Interactional Theory

A recent addition to theory integration is **Terence Thornberry's** interactional theory.[73] Thornberry agrees (with both Weis and Elliott) that the onset of crime can be traced to a deterioration of the social bond during adolescence, marked by a weakened attachment to parents, commitment to school, and belief in conventional values. Thornberry's theory similarly recognizes the influence of social class position and other structural variables: youths growing up in areas characterized by underclass status and social disorganization will also be the ones who stand the greatest risk of a weakened social bond and subsequent delin-

Terence P. Thornberry

FIGURE 6.4
Overview of the
interactional theory of
delinquency

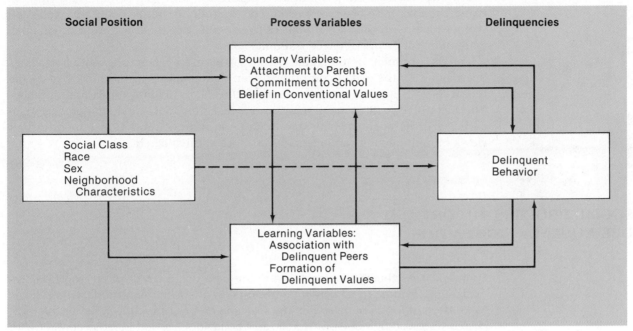

Source: Terence Thornberry, Margaret Farnsworth, Alan Lizotte, and Susan Stern, "A Longitudinal Examination of the Causes and Correlates of Delinquency" Working Paper #1, Rochester Youth Development Study. (Hindelang Criminal Justice Research Center, Albany, N.Y. 1987) p. 11.

quency. The onset of a criminal career is also supported by residence in a social setting in which deviant values and attitudes can be learned and reinforced by delinquent peers.

Thornberry's most important theoretical contribution is his theory's incorporation of elements similar to those of the **cognitive perspective** in psychology. This view, pioneered by Jean Piaget (1896–1980), holds that as people mature, they enter into separate stages of reasoning and sophistication.[74] Thornberry applies this concept when he suggests that criminality is a developmental process that takes on different meaning and form as a person matures. As he puts it, "The causal process is a dynamic one that develops over a person's life." During early adolescence, the family is the single most important determinant of whether a youth will adjust to conventional society and be shielded from delinquency. As the youth matures in midadolescence, the influence of the family is replaced by the "world of friends, school, and youth culture."[75] Finally, in adulthood, people's behavioral choices are shaped by their place in conventional society, their own nuclear family, and so on.

Thornberry's model is in its early stages of development and is being tested with a panel of Rochester, New York, youth who will be followed through their offending careers.[76]

The Future of Integrated Theory

The development of integrated theories, such as those constructed by Weis, Elliott, and Thornberry, is becoming more common in delinquency research. Ever more complex models that incorporate key concepts contained within existing theories have been proposed. For example, Frank Pearson and Neil Alan Weiner have synthesized elements of twelve different theories into a single intricate model of delinquency causation.[77]

The development of integrated theory is still in its infancy. Recent efforts have been aided by the use of computer-driven data analysis techniques that enable researchers to simultaneously investigate the effects of many individual variables. Theorists of the 1990s have many more research tools at their disposal than earlier experts, such as Shaw and McKay, could draw upon. Consequently, their views of delinquency can become ever more sophisticated.

SOCIAL PROCESS THEORY AND DELINQUENCY PREVENTION

Social process theory suggests that delinquency is a result of (1) improper socialization, leading to (2) conflict with important social institutions, which leads to (3) deviant forms of behavior. The *learning theory* branch holds that this process is triggered by values, attitudes, and behaviors learned in close contact with significant others. The *control theory* branch points to the youth's weakened relationship with the major deviance-controlling institutions—family, schools, and peers.

By implication, social process theories suggest that delinquency can be prevented by strengthening the relationship between youths and social institutions. This objective can be reached either by (a) strengthening and improving the institutions themselves or (b) helping youths to improve their personal relationships within the institutions. For example, the neighborhood school might approach the goal of delinquency control by improving teacher quality, expanding preschool education programs, developing relevant educational material, devising appropriate teaching methods, and developing individualized curriculum. Another approach is to make the youth who is manifesting problems in school the target of educational outreach programs. The first approach then aims at improving the social service delivery system, while the second is aimed at improving individual coping behavior.

Many primary prevention efforts have been aimed at improving the socialization of at-risk youth. For example, the Alternative Learning Project (ALP) instituted in Providence, Rhode Island, has helped educationally disillusioned youths develop learning experiences that create positive attachments with their school.[78] It utilized such features as a low student-teacher ratio (sixteen to one), individualized programs, emphasis on basic skills, special projects, tutoring, and courses at local colleges, An evaluation of the program indicated that 55 percent of its students go on to college and that absenteeism and dropout rates are greatly reduced. It is unlikely that such results would have been achieved without the ALP. In addition to these local efforts, the federal government has sponsored

TABLE 6.1 Social Process Theories

THEORY	MAJOR PREMISE	STRENGTHS
Social Learning Theories		
Differential Association Theory	People learn to commit crime from exposure to antisocial definitions.	Explains onset of criminality. Explains the presence of crime in all elements of social structure. Explains why some people in high-crime areas refrain from criminality. Can apply to adults and juveniles.
Differential Reinforcement Theory	Criminal behavior depends on the person's experiences with rewards for conventional behaviors and punishments for deviant ones. Being rewarded for deviance leads to crime.	Adds learning theory principles to differential association. Links sociological and psychological principles.
Neutralization Theory	Youths learn ways of neutralizing moral restraints and periodically drift in and out of criminal behavior patterns.	Explains why many delinquents do not become adult criminals. Explains why youthful law violators can participate in conventional behavior.
Control Theories		
Social Control Theory	A person's bond to society prevents him or her from violating social rules. If the bond weakens, the person is free to commit crime.	Explains onset of crime; can apply to both middle- and lower-class crime. Explains its theoretical constructs adequately so they can be measured. Has been empirically tested.
Containment Theory	Society produces pushes and pulls toward crime. In some people, they are counteracted by internal and external containments, such as a good self-concept and group cohesiveness.	Brings together psychological and sociological principles. Can explain why some people are able to resist the strongest social pressures to commit crime.
Integrated Theories		
Social Development Theory	Weak social controls produce crime. A person's place in the social structure influences his or her bond to society.	Combines elements of social structural and social process theories. Accounts for variations in the crime rate.
Elliott's Integrated Theory	Strained and weak social bonds lead youths to associate and learn from deviant peers.	Combines elements of learning, strain, and control theories.
Interactional Theory	Delinquents go through lifestyle changes during their offending career.	Combines sociological and psychological theories.

numerous national delinquency prevention efforts using the principles of social process theory. These include efforts at vocational training, such as the Job Corps and the Comprehensive Employment Training Act programs, as well as educational enrichment programs, such as Head Start for preschoolers and Upward Bound for high school students interested in a college education.

You have just been appointed the head of curriculum for the local school system.

The school board is interested in creating courses that will reduce the incidence of student delinquency and drug abuse. They fear that TV shows, popular music, and films that glorify the use of drugs teach kids that substance abuse and crime are exciting and socially desirable activities. They feel the school must present courses that can counteract the weight of these destructive influences.

You are faced with designing a program that can teach students to "say no" to drugs and crime. One of your advisors suggests that the best approach is to teach kids about the effects of drugs through media and live presentations in which former users discuss their experiences and problems. She believes that learning about the evils of drugs can counteract the pro-drug influence of commercial TV and rock and roll. In contrast, another advisor argues that the best approach is a series of workshops that help students develop a bond with their parents and community and learn the value of commitment to conventional behavior and actions. Such workshops would stress techniques of interfamily communications and life skills. While both of these approaches have merit, only one can be chosen to serve as the basis of the new course.

What type of information would you present to the students?

Can students learn not to commit crime and take drugs?

Who could best help students learn not to use drugs or engage in delinquency: other students? Parents? Teachers? Ex-offenders?

Prevention programs have also focused on providing services for youngsters who have been identified as delinquents or predelinquents. Such services usually include counseling, job placement, and legal services. One innovative program is the Massachusetts-based Discovery, which has been offered in juvenile detention centers since 1982. This highly structured program matches delinquent youth with college students who serves as confidants and counselors. The aim is to help juveniles develop a bond to conventional role models and teach them to review their lives and plan for the future.[79]

Prevention programs have also been aimed at strengthening the internal structure of families in crisis. Because attachment to parents is a cornerstone of all social process theories, it is an essential element of delinquency prevention. Efforts have been directed at helping the family become a living unit that provides care and support for its members. There have been efforts to create family structures that can encourage the positive self-image the child needs to resist the delinquency-promoting forces in his or her environment.[80]

Over the years, numerous local prevention programs have had as their objective goals that coincide with the premise of the social process approach. Many are demonstration programs that operate for a few years on funds provided by the federal government; others have become fixtures of state and local governments. Some efforts have been directed at primary prevention (before the onset of delinquency), while others are directed at secondary prevention (treating troubled youths) and tertiary prevention (helping ex-offenders "go straight"). Federal budget cutbacks have severely restricted these efforts, but local efforts keep these traditions alive.

While efforts to improve and supplement the socialization of youth seem appropriate means to counteract delinquency, there are still questions about socialization-oriented treatment efforts. Beginning with the well-known Cambridge- Somerville Youth Study in the 1930s, efforts to counsel and treat delinquent-prone youths have not resulted in lower recidivism rates.[81] Studies consistently show that treatment efforts fall far short of being helpful interventions. One reason may be that efforts by social agencies are simply insufficient to compensate for the years of family and social conflict experienced by young offenders. Another possibility is that the cause of delinquency is not related to socialization and therefore efforts to "reattach" youth to society and help them "learn" conventional attitudes are futile.

There have been review studies that conclude that rehabilitation efforts are of little value in combatting delinquency.[82] However, other reviews of existing programs suggest that some specific efforts may produce positive results.[83] A recent review of forty-six intervention programs by Rhena Izzo and Robert Ross found that rehabilitation efforts that stress such cognitive skills as role-playing, problem solving, and interpersonal negotiation may be the most promising.[84] So while "reattaching" a youth to society may be a difficult task, there is still reason for much optimism. The following Focus on Delinquency describes one such rehabilitation effort.

SUMMARY

Social process theories explain delinquency as a function of the human interactions that occur daily in society. As a group, they reject the view that delinquents are born criminals or that they are intellectually and psychologically impaired. In a similar vein, social process adherents take a dim view of theoretical models that blame delinquent behavior on the socioeconomic structure of society or on any of its class, racial, or social groupings.

Social process theories often stress the learning of delinquent or nondelinquent behavior. For example, Sutherland's theory of differential association suggests that delinquency is almost purely a learning process. Similarly, David Matza's neutralization approach describes how youngsters are able to learn techniques that can effectively neutralize the constraints of conventional values.

A second branch of social process theory is concerned with the forces of social control. Theorists such as Travis Hirschi view delinquency as a result of the inability of conventional institutions and relationships to restrain the behavior of youths.

While Hirschi's social control theory does not stress learning per se, it is evident that the weakening of the social bond is a long-term development that involves delinquent youths in an escalating process of antisocial behavior accompanied by a continuous diminution of their attachment to society. Like Hirschi's control theory, Walter Reckless's containment theory views the social control forces as having both internal and external dimensions.

A new theoretical model created by Joseph Weis, the social development theory, contains elements of both social process theory and social structure theory. Weis argues that a youth's place in the social structure, coupled with his or her interpersonal relationships, creates differential probabilities that youth will engage in delinquency. Similar integrated theories have been formulated by Delbert Elliott and Terence Thornberry.

Prevention programs based on social process theories usually prescribe treatment designed to strengthen family ties, improve school performance, or develop a youth's bond to society.

Country Roads Montpelier, Vermont

Kids run away from home and get into trouble with the law for a variety of reasons. The Country Roads program in Montpelier, Vermont, assumes that runaway and throwaway kids are neglected, abused, and have weak family ties. They may also be manifesting problems in the school and community, and they lack employment opportunities. Deviant behavior is a result of the child's inability to cope with life problems.

Using this view as a basis of its treatment orientation, Country Roads provides an emergency link between troubled youth and the community. They help kids resolve their problems by encouraging them to make mature decisions and take control of their lives.

The clientele is a mixed bag of males and females, almost all white, ranging in age from 13 to 19. The program was originally established to give temporary shelter to runaway youth in a rural Vermont county. However, during the past decade, program services have mushroomed.

Youths referred to Country Roads are handled on a twenty-four hour basis. After their emergency food, clothing, legal, and/or medical needs are met, clients begin working on their problems. Each youth must contact his or her parents within seventy-two hours. A formal signed consent of the parent must be obtained by a Country Roads counselor to place the youth in temporary shelter care. The program has a well-developed and trained network of thirty community residents who have been trained as Temporary Shelter Parents and who are financially reimbursed for housing young people. Although all counseling services are voluntary, youths are encouraged to make a commitment to some form of counseling, either individual, group, peer, or family. Roughly 80 percent of the families of youths provided with shelter at Country Roads have participated in counseling at the program.

New program components at Country Roads include:

1) Roadrunners: high school- and college-age volunteers who have been trained in crisis intervention and counseling techniques. They function as peer counselors and also organize recreational and educational programs for youths, provide them with information on drugs, sex, nutrition and health, and assist in program planning.

2) Parent's Support Group: provides an opportunity for parents to discuss their needs and concerns about their children with other parents.

3) Temporary Shelter Parent's Group: a training and support group for individuals, families, and couples who provide temporary shelter.

4) Special Aftercare Program: helps youths gain self-reliance in solving practical life problems. It consists of a series of workshops and group meetings that cover such things as finding an apartment, employment, nutrition, birth control, etc.

5) Young and Pregnant Women's Group: this group offers support, counseling, information, and education to young, pregnant women.

6) Youth Employment Project: seeks to place youths in jobs that provide them with meaningful roles and responsibilities.

Source: U.S. Department of Justice, *Report of the National Juvenile Justice Assessment Centers, Juvenile Delinquency Prevention: A Compendium of Thirty-six Program Models,* (Washington, D.C.: U.S. Department of Justice, 1981). Updated with personal communications with Country Roads, March 1990.

QUESTIONS FOR DISCUSSION

1. Identify the "processes" that produce delinquent behaviors.

2. Have you ever rationalized your deviant acts? What neutralization techniques did you use?

3. Discuss your "inner" and "outer" containments. Does self-esteem really influence behavior?

4. Comment on the statement "Delinquents are made, not born."

5. Does the integration of social process and social structure theories make sense?

KEY TERMS

socialization
social process
learning theory
social control theory
Edwin Sutherland
differential association
definition toward delinquency
differential reinforcement
differential association
neutralization theory
drift

subterranean
control theories
commitment to conformity
containment theory
containments
Travis Hirschi
bond
social bond
social development theory
Terence Thornberry
cognitive perspective

NOTES

1. Walter Reckless, Simon Dinitz, and Ellen Murray, "The Good Boy in a High Delinquency Area," *Journal of Criminal Law, Criminology and Police Science* 48:18–26 (1957).

2. Lawrence Rosen, "Family and Delinquency: Structure or Function," *Criminology* 23:553–73 (1985).

3. Kenneth Polk and Walter Schafer, eds., *Schools and Delinquency* (Englewood Cliffs, N.J.: Prentice-Hall, 1972).

4. Thomas Berndt, "The Features and Effects of Friendship in Early Adolescence," *Child Development* 53:1447–60 (1982).

5. Edwin Sutherland, *Principles of Criminology* (Philadelphia: J. B. Lippincott, 1939).

6. Edwin Sutherland and Donald Cressey, *Criminology*, 8th ed. (Philadelphia: J. B. Lippincott, 1970), pp. 75–77.

7. Howard Becker, *Outsiders* (New York: Free Press, 1963).

8. Sutherland and Cressey, *Criminology*, pp. 77–79.

9. *Ibid.*

10. James Short, "Differential Association as a Hypothesis: Problems of Empirical Testing," *Social Problems* 8:14–25 (1960).

11. Albert Reiss and A. Lewis Rhodes, "The Distribution of Delinquency in the Social Class Structure," *American Sociological Review* 26:732 (1961).

12. Elton Jackson, Charles Tittle, and Mary Jean Burke, "Offense-Specific Models of the Differential Association Process," *Social Problems* 33:335–56 (1986).

13. James Orcutt, "Differential Association and Substance Abuse: A Closer Look at Sutherland (with a Little Help from Becker)," *Criminology* 25:341–58 (1987).

14. Craig Reinerman and Jeffrey Fagan, "Social Organization and Differential Association: A Research Note from a Longitudinal Study of Violent Juvenile Offenders," *Crime and Delinquency* 34:307–27 (1988); Ross Matsueda and Karen Heimer, "Race, Family Structure, and Delinquency: A Test of Differential Association and Control Theories," *American Sociological Review* 52:826–40 (1987).

15. Donald Green, "Measures of Illegal Behavior in Individual-Level Deterrence Research," *Journal of Research in Crime and Delinquency* 26:253–75 (1989).

16. Charles Tittle, *Sanctions and Social Deviance: The Question of Deterrence* (New York: Praeger, 1980).

17. Reed Adams, "The Adequacy of Differential Association Theory," *Journal of Research in Crime and Delinquency* 11:1–8 (1974).

18. Jack Gibbs, "The State of Criminological Theory," *Criminology* 25:821–40 (1987).

19. Robert Burgess and Ronald Akers, "A Differential Association-Reinforcement Theory of Criminal Behavior," *Social Problems* 14:128–47 (1966).

20. Ross Matsueda, "The Current State of Differential Association Theory," *Crime and Delinquency* 34:277–306 (1988).

21. Donald Glaser, *Crime in Our Changing Society* (New York: Holt, Rinehart & Winston, 1978), p. 127; idem, "Criminality Theories and Behavior Images," *American Journal of Sociology* 61:433–44 (1956).

22. Robert Burgess and Ronald Akers, "Differential Association—Reinforcement Theory of Criminal Behavior," *Social Problems* 14:128–47 (1968).

23. Ronald Akers, Marvin Krohn, Lonn Lonza-Kaduce, and Marcia Radosevich, "Social Learning and Deviant Behavior: A Specific Test of a General Theory," *American Sociological Review* 44:636–55 (1979).

24. Marvin Krohn, William Skinner, James Massey, and Ronald Akers, "Social Learning Theory and Adolescent Cigarette Smoking: A Longitudinal Study," *Social Problems* 32:455–71 (1985).

25. M. William Minor, "The Neutralization of Criminal Offense," *Criminology* 18:103–20 (1980).

26. Gresham Sykes and David Matza, "Techniques of Neutralization: A Theory of Delinquency," *American Sociological Review* 22:664–70 (1957); David Matza, *Delinquency and Drift* (New York: Wiley, 1964).

27. Matza, *Delinquency and Drift*, p. 51.

28. Idem, "Subterranean Traditions of Youth," *Annals* 378:116 (1961).

29. Sykes and Matza, "Techniques of Neutralization," pp. 664–70.

30. *Ibid.*

31. See, for example, John Kitsuse, "Societal Reaction to Deviant Behavior," *Social Problems* 9:247–56 (1962).

32. For a vivid example of these values, see William F. Whyte, *Street Corner Society* (Chicago: University of Chicago Press, 1955).

33. Robert A. Ball, "An Empirical Exploration of Neutralization Theory," *Criminologica* 4:22–32 (1966). See also Minor, "The Neutralization of Criminal Offense."

34. Robert Regoli and Eric Poole, "The Commitment of Delinquents to Their Misdeeds: A Reexamination," *Journal of Criminal Justice* 6:261–69 (1978).

35. Robert Gordon, James Short, Desmond Cartwright, and Fred Strodtbeck, "Values and Gang Delinquency: A Study of Street Corner Groups," *American Journal of Sociology* 69:109–28 (1963).

36. Larry Siegel, Spencer Rathus, and Carol Ruppert, "Values and Delinquent Youth: An Empirical Reexamination of Theories of Delinquency," *British Journal of Criminology* 13:237–44 (1973).

37. Travis Hirschi, *Causes of Delinquency,* (Berkeley: University of California Press, 1969), p. 208.

38. John Hamlin, "Misplaced Role of Rational Choice in Neutralization Theory," *Criminology* 26:425–38 (1988).

39. Albert Reiss, "Delinquency as the Failure of Personal and Social Controls," *American Sociological Review* 16:196–207 (1951).

40. Scott Briar and Irving Piliavin, "Delinquency: Situational Inducements and Commitment to Conformity," *Social Problems* 13:35–45 (1965–66).

41. See Walter Reckless, *The Crime Problem* (New York: Appleton-Century-Crofts, 1967), pp. 469–83.

42. Among the many research reports by Reckless and his colleagues are Walter Reckless, Simon Dinitz, and Ellen Murray, "The Good Boy in a High Delinquency Area"; idem, "Self-concept as an Insulator against Delinquency," *American Sociological Review* 21:744–46 (1956); Walter Reckless and Simon Dinitz, "Pioneering with Self-Concept as a Vulnerability Factor in Delinquency," *Journal of Criminal Law, Criminology, and Police Science* 58:515–23 (1967); Walter Reckless, Simon Dinitz, and Barbara Kay, "The Self-Component in Potential Delinquency and Potential Non-Delinquency," *American Sociological Review* 22:566–70 (1957).

43. Reckless, Dinitz, and Kay, "The Self-Component in Potential Delinquency and Potential Non-Delinquency"; Frank Scarpitti, Ellen Murray, Simon Dinitz, and Walter Reckless, "The Good Boy in a High Delinquency Area:

Four Years Later," *American Sociological Review* 23:555–58 (1960).

44. Michael Schwartz and Sandra Tangri, "A Note on Self-Concept as an Insulator against Delinquency," *American Sociological Review* 30:922–26 (1965); Clarence Schrag, *Crime and Justice, American Style* (Washington, D.C.: U.S. Government Printing Office, 1971), p. 84.

45. Martin Gold, "Scholastic Experiences, Self-Esteem, and Delinquent Behavior: A Theory for Alternative Schools," *Crime and Delinquency* 24:290–308 (1978).

46. Howard Kaplan, *Deviant Behavior in Defense of Self* (New York: Academic Press, 1980); idem, "Self-Attitudes and Deviant Response," *Social Forces* 54:788–801 (1978).

47. L. Edward Wells, "Self-Enhancement through Delinquency: A Conditional Test of Self-Derogation Theory," *Journal of Research in Crime and Delinquency* 26:226–52 (1989); see also, John McCarthy and Dean Hoge, "The Dynamics of Self-Esteem and Delinquency," *American Journal of Sociology* 90:396–410 (1984); Edward Wells and Joseph Rankin, "Self-Concept as a Mediating Concept in Delinquency," *Social Psychology Quarterly* 46:11–22 (1983).

48. Hirschi, *Causes of Delinquency*.

49. *Ibid.*

50. *Ibid.*, p. 26.

51. Hirschi's data are examined in his *Causes of Delinquency*.

52. *Ibid.*, p. 132.

53. *Ibid.*, pp. 160–1.

54. *Ibid.*, p. 185.

55. LeGrande Gardner and Donald Shoemaker, "Social Bonding and Delinquency: A Comparative Analysis," *Sociological Quarterly* 30:481–500 (1989); Michael Hindelang, "Causes of Delinquency: A Partial Replication and Extension," *Social Problems* 21:471–87 (1973).

56. Patricia Van Voorhis, Francis Cullen, Richard Mathers, and Connie Chenoweth Garner, "The Impact of Family Structure and Quality on Delinquency: A Comparative Assessment of Structural and Functional Factors," *Criminology* 26:235–61 (1988).

57. John Cochran, "An Exploration of the Variable Effects of Religiosity of Adolescent Marijuana and Alcohol Use," *Journal of Research in Crime and Delinquency* 26:198–225 (1989).

58. Robert Agnew and David Peterson, "Leisure and Delinquency," *Social Problems* 36:332–48 (1989).

59. Michael Wiatroski, David Griswold, and Mary K. Roberts, "Social Control Theory and Delinquency," *American Sociological Review* 46:525–41 (1981).

60. Hindelang, "Causes of Delinquency: A Partial Replication and Extension."

61. Gary Jensen and David Brownfield, "Parents and Drugs," *Criminology* 21:543–54 (1983). See also, Wiatrowski, Griswold, and Roberts, "Social Control Theory and Delinquency."

62. Gardner and Shoemaker, "Social Bonding and Delinquency," p. 486.

63. Peggy Giordano, Stephen Cernkovich, and M. D. Pugh, "Friendships and Delinquency," *American Journal of Sociology* 91:1170–1202 (1986).

64. Marvin Krohn and James Massey, "Social Control and Delinquent Behavior: An Examination of the Elements of the Social Bond," *Sociological Quarterly* 21:529–43 (1980).

65. Randy LaGrange and Helene Raskin White, "Age Differences in Delinquency: A Test of Theory," *Criminology* 23:19–45 (1985).

66. Robert Agnew, "Social Control Theory and Delinquency: A Longitudinal Test," *Criminology* 23:47–61 (1985).

67. For a similar result, see A. E. Liska and M. D. Reed, "Ties to Conventional Institutions and Delinquency: Estimating Reciprocal Effects," *American Sociological Review* 50:547–60 (1985).

68. *Ibid.*, pp. 58–59.

69. Arnold Barnett, Alfred Blumstein, and David Farrington, "A Prospective Test of a Criminal Career Model," *Criminology* 27:373–88 (1989).

70. Joseph Weis and J. David Hawkins, *Reports of the National Juvenile Justice Assessment Centers, Preventing Delinquency* (Washington, D.C.: U.S. Department of Justice, 1981); Joseph Weis and John Sederstrom, *Reports of the National Juvenile Justice Assessment Centers, the Prevention of Serious Delinquency: What to Do* (Washington, D.C.: U.S. Department of Justice, 1981).

71. Delbert Elliott, David Huizinga, and Suzanne Ageton, *Explaining Delinquency and Drug Use* (Beverly Hills, Calif.: Sage, 1985).

72. *Ibid.*, p. 147.

73. Terence Thornberry, "Toward an Interactional Theory of Delinquency," *Criminology* 25:863–91 (1987).

74. See, for example, Jean Piaget, *The Grasp of Consciousness* (Cambridge, Mass.: Harvard University Press, 1976).

75. *Ibid.*, p. 886.

76. This research is known as the Rochester Youth Development Study.

77. Frank Pearson and Neil Alan Weiner, "Toward an Integration of Criminological Theories," *The Journal of Criminal Law and Criminology* 76:116–50 (1985).

78. J. Wall, D. Hawkins, D. Lishner, and M. Fraser, *Reports of the National Juvenile Justice Assessment Centers, Juvenile Delinquency Prevention: A Compendium of*

Thirty-six Program Models (Washington, D.C.: U.S. Department of Justice, 1981).

79. Norman Greenberg, "How College Students Can Help Delinquents," *Journal of Criminal Justice* 8:55–65 (1990).

80. Susan McPherson, Lance McDonald, and Charles Ryer, "Intensive Counseling with Families of Juvenile Offenders," *Juvenile and Family Court Journal* 34:27–34 (1983); see, generally, Gerald Patterson, "Performance Models for Antisocial Boys," *American Psychologist* 41:432–44 (1986); *idem, Coercive Family Process* (Eugene, Ore.: Castalia, 1982).

81. Joan McCord, "Crime in Moral and Social Contexts— The American Society of Criminology, 1989 Presidential Address," *Criminology* 28:1–26 (1990).

82. Steven Lab and John Whitehead, "An Analysis of Juvenile Correctional Treatment," *Crime and Delinquency* 34:60–83 (1988); Paul Lerman, *Community Treatment and Social Control* (Chicago: University of Chicago Press, 1975).

83. Carol Garrett, "Effects of Residential Treatment on Adjudicated Delinquents: A Meta-Analysis," *Journal of Research in Crime and Delinquency* 22:287–308 (1985).

84. Rhena Izzo and Robert Ross, "Meta-analysis of Rehabilitation Programs for Juvenile Delinquents," *Criminal Justice and Behavior* #12:134–142 (1990).

7 Social Reaction Theories

Labeling and Conflict

The two theoretical models discussed in this chapter, although quite different from one another, share one important characteristic differentiating them from all other theories of delinquency. While biosocial, psychological, and sociological theories of delinquency portray the youthful law violator as a rebel who for one reason or another cannot conform to the rules of society, labeling theory and conflict theory focus attention on the role that social institutions play in *producing* delinquent behaviors and how the application of the rule of law in American society influences delinquent behavior. The core element of these two views is that the politically powerful members of society control the behavior of the economically and socially deprived. How the power elite perceive and react to a behavior determines whether it will be considered legal or criminal. Similarly, people's personal identities and social standings are dictated by the perceptions of those who control them: teachers; bosses; police officers; psychiatrists; credit managers. If those who hold power react negatively toward an individual, his or her actions will be considered deviant or delinquent, and the individual will be subject to legal punishment.

The influence of both of these perspectives on delinquency theory and policy was first felt in the late 1960s and early 1970s. In this period of social ferment, many traditional social institutions began to be questioned and criticized. The role of the government became suspect because of the generally unpopular war in Vietnam and the corruption uncovered in the Nixon administration. Likewise, legal and academic scholars voiced growing suspicions of the juvenile justice system because of its alleged inefficiency and discriminatory practices. Even the educational system was criticized for its failure to provide equal opportunities for all members of society.[1]

Considering the climate of the times, it is not surprising that some social scientists began to question the role that powerful social institutions played in shaping the direction of the society and influencing public behavior. Scholars who were critical of big governmental, educational, corporate, and criminal justice agencies claimed that the efforts of these institutions actually helped produce crime and delinquency. Those holding power were accused of devoting their efforts to controlling the behavior of the lower class and protecting the interests of the wealthy and powerful.

Some scholars felt that those in power used their influence to control the criminal law for their own benefit.[2] While the illegal behaviors of the "have-not" members of society were heavily punished, the law violations of the upper classes—tax evasion, stock market manipulation, price fixing, political corruption, and so on—were often immune from prosecution or considered civil violations, resulting in the perpetrators being punished financially because of their status and position. Critics argued that those in power use their control over social institutions to stigmatize the powerless and brand them as outcasts from society. Even when sincere efforts were made to help the less fortunate, the outcome was to enmesh them further in a deviant or outcast status. For example, educational enrichment efforts, such as the Head Start program, were suspected of helping identify children as intellectually backward and in need of special attention; efforts to provide mental health services branded individuals as "sick" or "crazy." As a consequence of this critical inquiry, two potent themes emerged: (1) concepts of law and justice are differentially applied in American society, and (2) those who become involved with the justice system are soon branded deviants or outcasts and launched into a deviant "career."

This type of analysis was soon applied to the study of delinquent behavior. It was alleged that delinquency results from the reactions of politically powerful individuals and groups, especially government social control agencies, to society's less fortunate members. Delinquents are not inherently wrong or evil but kids who have had a deviant status conferred on them by those holding economic, political, and social power. A delinquent status results from interpersonal interactions in which youths are made to feel inferior or outcast because of socially unacceptable behavior. These reactions are stratified by class: while the lower-class youngster is arrested, tried, and punished, the middle-class youth is sent on his or her way by a benign, understanding police officer and/or juvenile court judge.[3] Thus, it is not the quality of the delinquent act itself that is important, it is the way society and its institutions react to the act. The purpose of social control is to maintain the status quo, ensuring that those in power will stay there indefinitely.

In this chapter, we will first review **labeling theory,** which maintains that official reactions to delinquent acts help label youths as criminals, troublemakers, and outcasts and help lock them in a cycle of escalating delinquent acts and social sanctions. Then, we will turn to conflict theory, which holds that the decision to confer a delinquent label is a product of the system of economic production and its destructive influence on human behavior.

LABELING THEORY

Labeling theory, is concerned less with what causes the onset of an initial delinquent act and more with the effect that official handling by police, court, and correctional agencies has on the future of youths who fall into the arms of the law. It is more a theory of delinquent career formation than a theory that predicts the onset of individual delinquent behaviors.[4]

According to labeling theory, youths may violate the law for a number of different reasons, including and not limited to poor family relationships, neighborhood conflict, peer pressure, psychological and/or biological abnormality, or prodelinquent learning experiences. Regardless of the cause, if a youth's delinquent behavior is detected by law enforcement or school officials, the offender will be given a negative social label that can follow him or her throughout life. These labels include "troublemaker," "juvenile delinquent," "mentally ill," "retarded," "criminal," "junkie," and "thief."

Even programs designed to be beneficial and reduce **stigma** tend to enmesh youth in the coils of the justice system, a process referred to as **net widening.**[5] As the delinquent progresses through the various stages of the justice system, the perception increases that this is a boy or girl who has failed and needs more control; the level of sanctions and labels escalate accordingly.[6]

The way labels are applied and the nature of the labels themselves are likely to have important future consequences for the delinquent. The degree to which youngsters are perceived as criminals may affect their treatment at home, at work, and at school. Young offenders may find that their parents consider them a detrimental influence on younger brothers and sisters. Their teachers may

Describe the behavior and personality of these girls who are members of a high school service club. Is your opinion influenced by the fact that they are actually members of a Los Angeles street gang?

place them in classes or in tracks reserved especially for behavior problems, thereby minimizing their chances of obtaining higher education. The delinquency label may also restrict eligibility for employment and negatively affect the attitudes of society in general. And depending on the severity of the label, the youthful offender will be subjected to official sanctions ranging from a mild reprimand to incarceration.

Beyond these immediate results, labeling theory argues that, depending on the visibility of the label and the manner and severity with which it is applied, youths will have an increasing commitment to delinquent careers. As the negative feedback from law enforcement agencies, parents, friends, teachers, and other figures strengthens the commitment, delinquents may begin to re-evaluate their own identities and come to see themselves as criminals, troublemakers, or "screwups." Through a process of identification and sanctioning, re-identification, and increased sanctioning, the identities of young offenders become transformed. They are no longer children in trouble; they are *delinquents*, and they accept that label as a personal identity—a process called **self-labeling** (we employ this term to mean personal acceptance and acknowledgement of a negative label).[7] (See Figure 7.1.)

The consequences of a negative label were identified in 1967 by the President's Commission on Law Enforcement and the Administration of Justice, which stated:

> The affixing of that label [delinquency] can be a momentous occurrence in a youngster's life. Thereafter he may be watched; he may be suspect; his every misstep may be evidence of his delinquent nature. He may be excluded more and more from legitimate activities and opportunities. Soon he may be designed and dealt with as a delinquent

FIGURE 7.1
Labeling theory

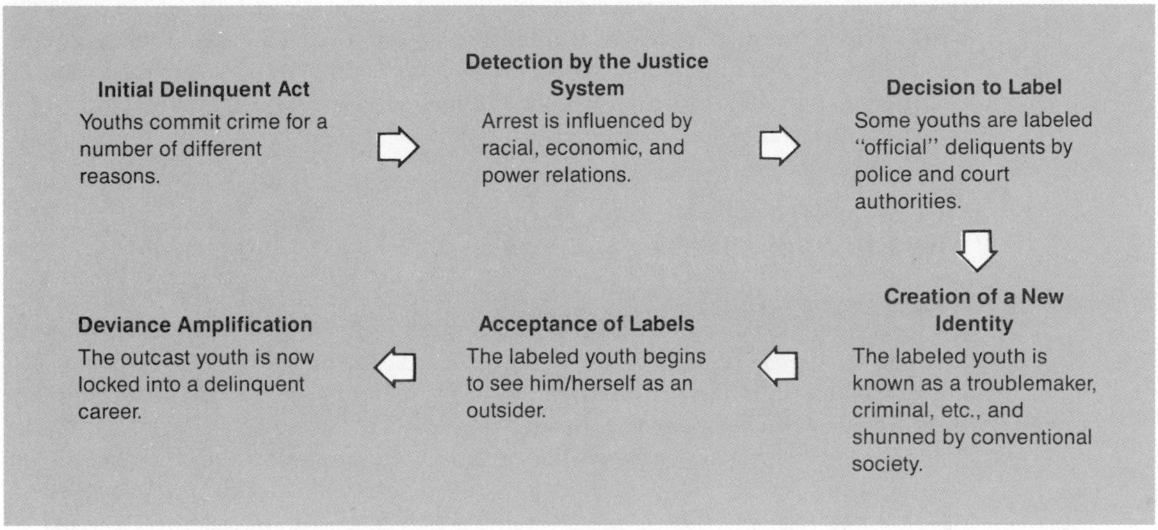

Initial Delinquent Act
Youths commit crime for a number of different reasons.

Detection by the Justice System
Arrest is influenced by racial, economic, and power relations.

Decision to Label
Some youths are labeled "official" deliquents by police and court authorities.

Creation of a New Identity
The labeled youth is known as a troublemaker, criminal, etc., and shunned by conventional society.

Acceptance of Labels
The labeled youth begins to see him/herself as an outsider.

Deviance Amplification
The outcast youth is now locked into a delinquent career.

and will find it very difficult to move into a law-abiding path even if he can overcome his own belligerent reaction and self-image and seeks to do so.[8]

These sentiments helped set the course for juvenile justice policy in the 1970s. Programs were created on a national level that attempted to insulate youths from the label-producing processes of the juvenile justice system. Policy initiatives included the **diversion** of offenders from juvenile court into alternative programs and the creation of nonsecure community-based treatment to replace traditional juvenile training schools and institutions (**deinstitutionalization**). Whenever possible, stigma producing activities were avoided, a philosophy of justice referred to as **nonintervention.**

The Nature of Crime and Delinquency

An important principle of the labeling approach is that the concepts of crime and delinquency are constantly changing. Acts are considered criminal and outlawed not because they are inherently evil but because people in power view them as harmful behaviors.[9] "Deviance is not a property inherent in certain forms of behavior," argues sociologist Kai Erikson. "It is a property conferred upon those forms by the audiences which directly or indirectly witness them."[10] **Howard Becker,** in what is probably the most well-known statmeent by a labeling theorist, states:

> Deviance is *not* a quality of the act the person commits, but rather a consequence of the application by others of rules and sanctions to an "offender." The deviant is one to whom that label has successfully been applied; deviant behavior is behavior that people so label.[11]

Becker argues that legal and social rules are created by "**moral entrepreneurs,**" people who are concerned about social morality and work to control its definition and application. Consequently, who is to be labeled and the forms labeling takes depend on social forces that vary considerably within cultures. Who is in power and how they interpret right and wrong play an important role in defining crime and delinquency. For example, during our own lifetimes, we have witnessed the legalization of abortions and, in some states, the decriminalization of marijuana. Becker and other labeling theorists helped us recognize that our concept of deviance has evolved over time.

The Effect of Labeling

The labeling approach focuses primarily on the social audience's reaction to persons and their behavior and the subsequent effects of that reaction, rather than on the cause of the deviant behavior itself. Furthermore, labeling theorists allege that the treatment of offenders in the labeling process depends far less on their behavior than on the way others view their acts.

In response to social transgressions, society assigns formal labels, such as "delinquent," "crazy," or "ex-con." Often, labels are bestowed during ceremonies designed to redefine the deviants' identity and place them apart from conventional society.[12] The net effect of this legal and social process is a *durable negative label and an accompanying loss of status.* The labeled deviant becomes a social outcast who is prevented from enjoying higher education, well-paying jobs, and other societal benefits.

We can see an example of this process in *stigma*-producing ceremonies, like those that sometimes occur in juvenile courts. In these courts, young offenders find, perhaps for the first time, that people in authority, in the person of the juvenile court judge, consider them incorrigible outcasts who must be separated from the right-thinking members of society. To reach that decision, the judge relies on the testimony of a parade of witnesses—parents, teachers, police officers, social workers, psychologists—all of whom may testify that the offenders are unfit to be part of conventional society.[13] As the label "juvenile delinquents" is conferred on them, their identities may forever be transformed from boys or girls who have done something bad, to "bad" girls or "bad" boys.[14]

Labeling theorists see these negative labels as creating a **self-fulfilling prophecy.**[15] If a child is reacted to negatively by parents, teachers, and others, he or she will view these negative labels as an accurate portrayal of his or her personality. If the labels are consistently applied, such children will join with their detractors and view themselves in a negative light. Eventually their behavior will begin to conform to these negative expectations. It is expected that labeled delinquents will seek out others who are similarly stigmatized because members of conventional society shun and avoid them.

The outcome of the labeling/stigmatization process is the development of a new, deviant identity. Individuals become what society says they are and then begin to behave in a predictable fashion. Delinquent youths will seek out others who sympathize with their plight and can identify with their needs. Their peers may help the labeled youths "reject their rejector": If conventional society cannot accept them, it's not their fault; besides teachers are stupid, cops dishonest, and parents just don't understand.

Primary and Secondary Deviance

The effect of the labeling process was refined by **Edwin Lemert** in his formulation of the **primary-secondary deviance** model.[16]

Lemert argues that deviant acts actually form two distinct classes, primary and secondary, each of which comprises a specific role orientation of the individual. Primary acts can be rationalized by the offender or considered a function of a socially acceptable role, such as using a false ID to buy beer. Primary deviance does not affect self-concept; primary deviants are not recognized by others as deviant, nor do they recognize themselves as such.

Lemert attaches little importance to primary deviance, but he argues that deviations become significant and secondary when they are used for bestowing social status and self-definition. This occurs because exposure to negative social labels results in "role reorganization." That is, if a person's deviant behavior is repetitive, highly visible, and subject to *severe social reaction*, he or she is likely to come to accept and incorporate this deviant identity as part of his or her personality: the drinker becomes an "alcoholic"; the boy who steals, a "thief." Thereafter, all life roles will be predicated on this new, stigmatized status.[17] Secondary deviance is a product of resocialization in which the deviant role becomes the central fact of existence and a person is transformed into one who "employs his behavior (deviant) or a role based upon it as a means of defense, attack, or adjustment to the overt and covert problems created by the consequent societal reaction to him."[18]

In sum, secondary deviance can be conceived as a behavior cycle (See Figure on page 191) in which a deviant act leads to a social reaction, then to self-conception as a "deviant," to increased, more serious deviant acts, and to greater and more severe social reactions, including legal reprisals, until identification with a deviant identity, which increases the probability of future deviant acts, has become complete.[19]

The Juvenile Justice Process and Labeling

The labeling hypothesis has received strong support in the literature of crime and delinquency. In an early work, Frank Tannenbaum first suggested that social typing, which he called the "dramatization of evil," transforms the offender's identity from a doer of evil to an "evil person."[20] Tannenbaum emphasized the role of the juvenile justice system in this scheme: "The entire process of dealing with young delinquents is mischievous insofar as it identifies *him* to *himself* and to the environment as a delinquent person."[21]

Theorists have continued to describe the impact of juvenile justice processing on delinquent labeling and consequent illegal behavior. For example, Aaron Cicourel contended that delinquents are in reality the finished products of the juvenile justice "assembly line."[22] Although they enter as children in trouble, they emerge as individuals transformed by decision makers into bearers of criminal histories, which are likely to reinvolve them in criminal activity. Arguing from a similar prospective, David Matza concludes that the apprehension of delinquents will lead sanctioning bodies to anticipate further illegal actions on their part.[23] Apprehended offenders are invested with all the behavioral characteristics associated with the labels, and although they have not necessarily demonstrated these characteristics by their own behavior, they become "perennial suspects."[24] As a result, labeled youthful offenders may begin to reconsider their own self-concepts. This reconsideration, Matza explains, relates directly to their interaction with the system and the treatment they receive at its hands.

These statements imply that labeling by the juvenile system turns the self-perception of a youthful suspect into that of a delinquent.[25] Processing by the juvenile authorities may cause a youth to enter into a delinquent career and be committed to criminal activity. Sociologist Harold Garfinkel has provided a concise analysis of this process in his description of the interactions that occur when the public identity of an offender is transformed via a "successful" degradation ceremony into "something looked on as lower in the social scheme of social types."[26] Garfinkel concludes that this process may be similar in form and function to what is currently practiced in juvenile court.

Labeling theory predicts two relationships with regard to juvenile justice processing: the delinquency label will be bestowed upon the powerless members of society in a discriminatory fashion, and the more frequent, prolonged, or decisive the contacts with the juvenile justice system, the more likely it is that an offender will ultimately accept the delinquency label as a personal identity and enter into a life of crime. These two relationships are discussed below.

Discrimination in the Labeling Process

Labeling theorists believe that the probability of being labeled a delinquent depends heavily on a youth's race, class, and gender. They point to studies that indicate that police are more likely to arrest and officially process males, minority group members, and those in the lower economic classes.[27] Similarly, they cite evidence that offenders whose families have economic or political power are likely merely to be given a warning by police officers, rather than processed to the juvenile court.[28] And the juvenile court is believed to respond more favorably to youths from middle-class homes than to those from the lower class. Many social scientists believe that youths from the lower classes, especially minorities, are the most likely candidates for delinquency labels and consequently are most likely to become enmeshed in a delinquent career. These sentiments have been supported by research studies, such as the one conducted by Donna Bishop and Charles Frazier, that have found that race has a direct effect on the decision to process a youth through the juvenile justice system. Bishop and Frazier found that after controlling for legal variables, such as prior adjudications, black youths have a greater chance of being tried by the juvenile court and, if found to be delinquent, are 9 percent more likely to be institutionalized or transferred to criminal court than whites.[29]

Despite this evidence, empirical research that *conclusively* proves that the juvenile justice system operates in a distinctly discriminatory fashion has heretofore been lacking.[30] In contradistinction to the labeling approach, there is also research evidence that juvenile justice processing is influenced more by acceptable legal factors, such as offense seriousness and prior record, than it is by extralegal or personal factors, such as racial or economic bias. For example, a study by Merry Morash found that police action with juveniles was not influenced by race or economic status.[31] Morash discovered that the factors that

Labeling theorists believe that the probability of being labeled depends heavily on a youth's race, class, and gender.

predicted formal police action were related to legal factors, including: a previous record of law-violating behavior; associating with delinquent peers; gang activity; group fighting; and drug involvement. Morash found that regardless of their race or class, kids who commit a lot of crime with their friends, use drugs, and get into fights will be the ones most likely to get arrested.

Similarly, Charles Corley, Stephen Cernkovich, and Peggy Giordano, using carefully drawn samples of neighborhood and institutionalized youth, found that juvenile court sanctions operate independently of sex, race, and age and were more dependent on legally permissible variables, such as offense seriousness.[32]

These recent studies indicate that a key proposition of the labeling perspective—that the powerless receive discriminatory treatment from middle-class representatives of conventional society—is still open to debate. Persons' actual behaviors may be more important factors in the labeling process than their personal characteristics and the attendant bias of social control agents.

The Effects of Official Labeling

The results of the few studies attempting to measure delinquents at the onset and conclusion of official contact have also been contradictory and inconclusive.[33] Some indicate that youths actually feel relief after the conclusion of their juvenile justice experience, rather than shame, stigma, or a diminution of their self-image, as labeling theorists would predict.[34]

A few research efforts have found that while youths who have had experience with the juvenile justice system are the ones most likely to maintain a delinquent self-concept, the relationship between sanctions and labels is far from clear. For example, Gary Jensen found that youths who experience arrest are the ones most likely to have negative self-images.[35] However, Jensen's research did not show that delinquent self-perceptions increase after police contact. It is possible, therefore, that youths with a poor self-concept may be more prone to arrest than other youths, and this factor may account for the interrelationship that Jensen discovered.[36]

Jack Foster, Walter Reckless, and Simon Dinitz found that most youth did not perceive any personal conflict with parents, teachers, or friends after being becoming officially labeled.[37] In fact, arrestees perceived only two significant areas of social liability: some expected the police to keep "an eye on them," and others believed their offense record would prejudice future employers.

Additional research has not supported the labeling theory contention that juvenile justice processing will amplify self-labels. Charles Thomas and Donna Bishop surveyed 2,147 Virginia youths at the beginning and end of the school year and found that formal sanctions by the juvenile justice system actually had very little impact on a child's self-image.[38] While it was true that youths who reported being officially labeled did view themselves more negatively than nondelinquents, the relationship between sanctions and an *escalation* or increase in delinquent self-image was very modest. Similarly, Richard Anson and Carol Eason found that male delinquents committed to the Georgia Department of Human Resources did not significantly increase their delinquent self-image after incarceration.[39]

How can these insignificant labeling effects be explained? Why does juvenile justice processing have little measurable influence on the self-image of court-processed youth? One possibility is that youths who suffer arrest and official processing have already had such long and active careers as undetected "secret deviants" that their experience with the juvenile justice system has little effect on their already damaged self-concepts and identities.

Another possible explanation is that the aggregate measurements used in most research studies mask individual differences among delinquents: while some delinquents are negatively influenced by punitive treatment, others who are placed in rehabilitation treatment may actually achieve benefits from the experience. Sociologist Stanley Cohen has written that the quality of treatment by the justice system helps categorize offenders into two distinct groups: one made up of unrepentant and antisocial offenders who are placed in programs that dish out harsh punishments (**exclusionary programs**), and another group made up of offenders who are placed in programs that continually encourage them to join the mainstream of social life (**inclusionary programs**). Since the experiences of members of these two groups are so different, the stigma generated by juvenile justice processing is cancelled out: while youths in the "excluded" group suffer deeply and increase negative labels, those in the "included" group derive benefits that help improve their self-images and actually *reduce labels*.[40]

In sum, there is little hard evidence that juvenile justice processing has a deep or lasting effect on a youth's self-image. The effects of growing up in a troubled or abusive family and attending a deteriorated school in a socially disorganized neighborhood may already be so overwhelming that processing by the juvenile justice system has little effect on the self-image of an already troubled youth.

Evaluation of Labeling Theory

While quite influential in the 1970s, labeling theory declined in its importance as a primary theory of delinquency. Four important criticisms of the labeling approach led to its decline:

1. Labeling theorists failed to explain the onset of the first or primary deviation. Why is it that some people engage in the initial deviant act that leads to their labeling, while others in the same social circumstances stick to conventional behaviors?[41] As criminologist Ronald Akers puts it, "One sometimes gets the impression from reading the literature that people go about minding their own business and then—'wham'—bad society comes along and slaps them with a stigmatized label."[42]

2. According to labeling theory, the over representation of males, minorities, and the poor in the crime rate is a function of discriminatory labeling by social control agents. However, empirical research has failed to consistently show that labels are bestowed in a discriminatory fashion.[43] For example, in a recent review of the literature, Charles Tittle and Debrah Curran found that about 40 percent of research studies indicate a racial effect on juvenile justice decision making, and 60 percent do not; about 33 percent of research studies show a class effect, and 67 percent indicate that class does not influence the labeling process.[44] Discrimination in the labeling process is a cornerstone of the theory because it indicates that the manner in which labels are bestowed is the key issue in determining criminality. If people were labeled only because they deserved negative social reactions (that is, they commited serious crimes), then the theory would lose its power since the labeling process would be an effect of crime, rather than its cause.[45]

3. Studies that evaluated the aftermath of labeling failed to show it had a deviance-amplification effect. Youngsters undergoing the labeling process were simply not as deeply affected by their experiences as labeling theorists would have us believe.[46]

4. Criminologists found that the labeling concept that "no act is inherently evil or criminal" is naive. This point was driven home by sociologist Charles Wellford, who argued rather conclusively that some crimes, such as rape and homicide, are almost universally sanctioned.[47] He says, "Serious violations of the law are universally understood and *are*, therefore, *in that sense*, intrinsically criminal."[48]

Labeling theory also suffered politically because of the conservative trend in the United States: instead of worrying about how the self-images of young offenders were being "damaged" by the justice system, the general public and academic community seemed more concerned with crime control and the best method of curbing delinquent youth. Enthusiasm for the theory was also dampened because efforts to reduce labels and stigma in the juvenile justice system seemed to have no appreciable effects on delinquency. In one influential study, *Beyond Probation: Juvenile Corrections and Chronic Delinquents*, sociologists Charles Murray and Louis Cox found that youths assigned to a treatment program designed to reduce labels were more likely to later commit delinquent acts than a comparison group who were placed in a traditional, more punitive, state training school. The implication was that the deterrent threat of punishment had a greater impact on youths than the feared influence of negative labels.[49]

Should labeling theory then be dropped from consideration as an "important" explanation of delinquency? According to Raymond Paternoster and LeeAnn Iovanni, that action would be premature.[50] Among the features of labeling theory that make it an important part of the study of delinquency are:

1. The labeling perspective identifies the role played by social control agents in the process of delinquency causation. Delinquent behavior cannot be fully understood if the agencies and individuals empowered to control and treat it are neglected.

2. Labeling theory recognizes that delinquency is not a disease or pathological behavior. It focuses attention on the social interactions and reactions that shape individuals and their behavior.

3. It distinguishes between delinquent *acts* (primary deviance) and delinquent *careers* (secondary deviance) and shows that these concepts must be interpreted and treated differently.

This third factor is critical considering what is known today about the delinquent career of the chronic offender. As you may recall, chronic offenders begin their antisocial activity early in their lives and persist in their delinquent activities despite being apprehended by police and punished by the juvenile court. The evidence indicates that sanctions tend to amplify rather than extinguish their deviant careers. Until recently, there has been scant attention paid to the parallels between these features of chronic offending and the theoretical concept of secondary deviance. That is, one factor that may create and sustain chronic offending and criminal careers is the negative labels some youths acquire and the subsequent onset of a secondary deviant identity.[51] In fact, the very definition of a chronic offender is a person who has been arrested and therefore labeled multiple times in his or her offending career. Who these youths are and why they begin to acquire a deviant identity are questions that are addressed by labeling theory. The ability of labeling theory to explain **deviance amplification,** the status factors that contribute to labeling choices, and secondary deviance may be of critical value in accounting for the criminal career patterns of the chronic offender.

CASE IN POINT

You are planning director for the state department of juvenile justice correctional services.

One of your main concerns in the effect of stigma on the criminal offending patterns of delinquent youth. Some of your advisors suggest that processing youths through the juvenile correctional justice system produces deviant identities that lock them into a criminal way of life. Rather than

continued

rehabilitate, the system produces hard-core delinquents who are likely to recidivate. They point to studies that show that an experience with the juvenile justice system has relatively little impact on chronic offenders and, if anything, is associated with escalating the seriousness of their criminal behavior.

Some of the more conservative members of your staff are opposed to making the reduction of stigma and labeling a top correctional concern. They remind you that an experience with the juvenile justice system may actually help deter crime. They point to studies that suggest that youth who have been processed through the correctional system are less likely to recidivate than youths who receive lesser punishments, such as community corrections or probation. In addition, they believe that hard-core, violent offenders deserve to be punished; excessive concern for the offender and not their acts ignores the rights of victims and society in general.

These opposing views have left you in a quandary. On the one hand, the system must be sensitive to the adverse effects of stigma and labeling. On the other hand, the need for control and deterrence must not be ignored. Despite your dilemma, you must come up with a plan that satisfies both positions.

What types of correctional programs might avoid excessive stigma yet control juvenile offenders?

Should more concern be given to control or to labeling?

CONFLICT THEORY

Unlike traditional theoretical perspectives, which try to explain why an individual violates the law, **conflict theory** focuses on why governments make and enforce rules of law and morality. Conflict criminologists, therefore, do not view delinquents as rebels who cannot conform to proper social norms, nor do they try to devise innovative ways of controlling youthful misbehavior. Their interests lie in other areas: identifying "real" crimes in society, such as profiteering, sexism, and racism; evaluating how the criminal law is used as a mechanism of social control; and turning the attention of citizens to the inequities in our society. (See Figure 7.2.)

It is not accidental that the emergence of conflict theory as an explanation of deviant behavior had its roots in the widespread social and political upheavals of the 1960s.[52] These forces included the Vietnam War, the counterculture movement, and various forms of political protest. Conflict theory flourished within this framework, because it provided a theoretical basis to challenge the legitimacy of the government's creation and application of law.

Another influence that helped bring conflict theory to the forefront was the apparent failure of more traditional theories of deviance to explain the challenges to government authority.[53] Experts on the causes of deviant behavior were at a loss to explain such phenomena as the increase in illicit drug use among middle-

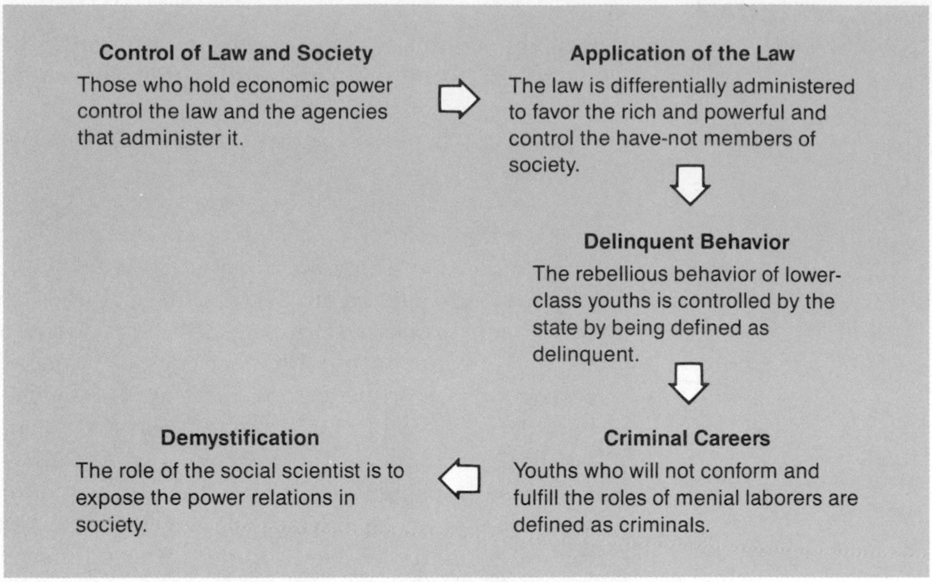

FIGURE 7.2
Conflict theory

Control of Law and Society
Those who hold economic power control the law and the agencies that administer it.

Application of the Law
The law is differentially administered to favor the rich and powerful and control the have-not members of society.

Delinquent Behavior
The rebellious behavior of lower-class youths is controlled by the state by being defined as delinquent.

Criminal Careers
Youths who will not conform and fulfill the roles of menial laborers are defined as criminals.

Demystification
The role of the social scientist is to expose the power relations in society.

class students, campus, prison, and urban rioting, and civil rights demonstrations and other protests against the government.

At the same time, critical thinkers hurled challenges at the academic world, the center of most theoretical thought in criminology. They claimed that it was archaic, conservative, and out of tune with recent changes in society.[54] Critical criminology began to challenge the fundamental role criminologists play in uncovering the causes of crime and delinquency. At a time of general turmoil in society, conflict theorists called for sweeping innovations in academic settings—including changes in the way courses were taught, grading, and tenure. Criminologists were asked to evaluate their own lives and activities in order to understand their personal role in the crime problem. Was it possible that they were acting as agents of the state, taking money from government agencies to achieve more effective repression of the poor and laboring classes?[55] These theorists called for a reappraisal of the entire field of law and criminology.[56]

There are a number of different views about what produces social conflict. "Pure" conflict theorists believe that conflict between the "have" and "have-not" members of society can occur in any social system. Other theorists view the capitalist system as it exists in American society as the primary cause of social and class conflict. The former view is usually referred to as **conflict criminology,** while the latter is called **Marxist** or **critical criminology.** While there is this significant dogmatic difference between groups of social conflict theorists, they do agree that those in power define the behavior of the poor as criminal and delinquent while shaping the law to define their own actions as acceptable and appropriate.

The conflict approach can also be contrasted with the labeling perspective. Conflict theorists charge that labeling advocates do not go far enough in exposing the crime-producing elements of American culture, that they seem content merely to analyze behavior of strange and different people. In contrast, conflict thinkers use historical research and political analysis to understand the social

Conflict theorists believe that the law protects the power of the ruling class at the expense of the poor and working classes.

relationships, power relations, and institutional arrangements that produce delinquent and criminal behavior.

Elements of Conflict Theory

The primary goal of conflict theory is to examine the relationship between the ruling class and the process by which deviance is defined and controlled in capitalist society. The most important of these concerns is the nature and purpose of social control. Conflict theorists believe that the state creates laws and rules designed to maintain the power and position of the power elite. Critical criminologist Robert Meier has suggested that the new criminology centers around a view of society in which an elite class uses the criminal law as a means of meeting and controlling threats to its status. Meier views the ruling class as a self-interested lot whose primary interest is self-gain.[57] Another well-known critical criminologist, Richard Quinney, argues, "Capitalist justice is by the capitalist class, for the capitalist class, and against the working class."[58]

Conflict theorists view the criminal law and justice system as a vehicle for controlling the poor, have-not members of society. It helps the powerful and rich to impose their particular morality and standards of good behavior on the entire society and to protect their property and physical safety from the "have-nots," even though the cost may be high in terms of the legal rights of those it perceives as a threat, and it extends the definition of illegal or criminal behavior to encompass those who might threaten the status quo.[59] The ruling elite draws the middle class into this pattern of control, leading it to believe that it also has a stake in controlling the behavior of the lower classes. The poor may or may not commit more crimes than the rich, but they certainly are arrested and punished more often.[60]

Conflict theorists seriously contradict the long-held presumption that the American system of law and justice is humane and fair to all citizens.[61] Conflict theory asks us to reevaluate many basic beliefs. For example, the fact that laws protecting private property may actually be designed to preserve the dominance of a ruling elite seems to strike at the very heart of our moral beliefs. For this reason alone, conflict theory has had a profound effect on twentieth-century criminological thought.

Demystification

Conflict theorists consider it essential to demystify law and science. This complex concept entails a number of different actions. For one thing, radical criminologists charge that an inordinate amount of scientific effort is devoted to unmasking the social conditions of lower-class citizens with the ostensible purpose of improving their lives. Such studies include views of lower-class family life, IQs, school performance, and so on. However, conflict criminologists argue that these efforts actually serve to keep the lower classes down by "proving" that they are more delinquent and less intelligent and that they have poorer school performance than the middle class. All the while, the tests and instruments used to conduct these studies are biased and inaccurate.[62] In this sense, **demystification** entails uncovering the real reasons behind scientific research.

Another aspect of demystification involves identifying the historical development of criminal law. By drawing attention to the "real" reasons such laws as tax codes and statutes prohibiting theft and drug use were created, people will understand the purpose and intent of these laws. If it is found that theft laws, for example, were originally created to maintain the wealth and capital of the rich, then those who violate the law should not perceive themselves as evil, immoral, or wrong, but rather as victims of an unjust system.

Finally, the demystification of capitalist society reveals the controlling nature of the "professional mystique."[63] It is alleged that our society grants inordinate power to professionals to judge and control the population. When teachers, doctors, lawyers, and psychologists judge persons to be crazy, stupid, sick, unfit, delinquent, or criminal, that label becomes their social identity. Radical criminologists charge that professionals often suppress and distort the truth, "unmasking" powerless people so that their position of social inferiority is maintained. The system quickly condemns those who speak against it as "subversive," traitorous," or "mentally ill."

The Conflict Concept of Delinquency

Conflict theorists view delinquency as a normal response by youth to the social conditions created by capitalist society.[64] In fact, the very creation of a unique legal category, delinquency, is a function of the class consciousness that occurred around the turn of the century.[65] In his book *The Child Savers*, Anthony Platt documents the creation of the delinquency concept and the role played by

Herman Schwendinger

Julia Schwendinger

wealthy child savers in forming the philosophy of the juvenile court. In a later work, Platt claims:

> The child-saving movement tried to do for the criminal justice system what industrialists and corporate leaders were trying to do by the economy—that is, achieve order, stability and control while preserving the existing class system and distribution of wealth.[66]

The roots of the juvenile delinquency concept can be traced to nineteenth-century efforts of powerful and wealthy citizens to control the behavior of weak and disenfranchised youths.[67]

Herman Schwendinger and Julia Schwendinger describe today's delinquent behavior as a function of the capitalist system. They argue that capitalism accelerates the trend toward replacing living labor with machines so that youths are removed from a useful place in the labor force.[68] This process prolongs their dependency and forces them to be controlled by socialization agencies, such as the family and, most important, the school. These social control agencies prepare youths for placement in the capitalist system by presenting them with behavior models that will help them conform to later job expectations. For example, rewards for good schoolwork correspond to the rewards a factory supervisor uses with subordinate employees. In fact, most schools are set up to reward and nurture youths who show early promise in such areas as self-discipline, achievement, and motivation and who are therefore judged likely to perform well in the capitalist system. Youths who are judged inferior as potential job prospects (the Schwendingers refer to them as "prototypic marginals") become known to the school community as "greasers," "dudes," and "hoods" and eventually wind up in delinquent roles.[69]

The Schwendingers also view the juvenile justice system as creating and sustaining delinquency. They claim that the capitalist state fails to control delinquents because it is actually in the state's own best interest to maintain a large number of outcast deviant youths. These youths can then be employed as low-paid factory labor in jobs no one else wants. It behooves capitalist managers to maintain an underclass of cheap labor to be employed in its factories and to buy inferior goods.

The capitalist system affects youths in each element of the class structure differently.[70] In the lowest classes, youths form delinquent gangs, which can be found in the most desolate ghetto areas of the nation. These violent street gangs serve outcast youths as a means of survival in a system that offers no other reasonable alternative. Other lower-class youths, who live in more stable areas, are usually on the fringe of criminal activity because the economic system excludes them from meaningful opportunity. Conflict theory also acknowledges middle-class delinquency. The alienation of individuals from one another, the never-ending competitive struggle, and the absence of human interest and feeling—all inherent qualities of capitalism—contribute to middle-class delinquency.[71] Since capitalism is such a dehumanizing system, it is not surprising that even middle-class youths turn to drugs, gambling, and illicit sex to find escape and excitement. Thus, conflict theory explains the various forms of delinquent behavior in our society. See the Focus on Delinquency entitled "Children and the Age Structure of Society."

There have been a number of recent attempts to create conflict theories specifically directed at the cause of delinquency. The following sections explore some of the more prominent examples.

Children and the Age Structure of Society

In a well-respected article, sociologist David Greenberg has attempted to use conflict analysis to describe how children's place in the socioeconomic structure determines their law-violating behavior.

According to Greenberg, delinquency is a function of the goals associated with a person's place in the human life cycle. During adolescence, personal goals focus on peer group relations and receiving acceptance from friends. Since young people are excluded from adult associations, these relationships take on even greater importance. As long as parents can provide support and funds for these relationships, they can develop along legitimate lines. However, those youths whose parents' economic positions make this support impossible may turn to delinquent behavior to support their lifestyles. The capitalist system hastens this process because it makes it difficult for teenagers to become part of the job market. As Greenberg states: "Adolescent theft then occurs as a response to the disjunction between the desire to participate in social activities with peers and the absence of legitimate sources of funds needed to finance this participation." Greenberg argues that this view helps explain the occurrence of middle-class delinquency. Even though the parents of middle-class youths are more likely to be able to provide them with funds than parents of lower-class youths, the cost of their leisure life-style is proportionately greater, so they will be unable to receive the economic support they need. The delinquency of females can be explained in a similar fashion.

As teenagers mature, their vulnerability to the expectations of peers is reduced because of involvements that provide an alternate source of self-esteem and gratification. Also, the opportunity for earning money legitimately increases. These two factors explain why the crime rate decreases with age.

Greenberg sees the school having a significant role in the delinquency equation. The educational experience deprives many adolescents of autonomy and freedom of movement. It demands a discipline and obedience that contradict the independent life-style teenagers crave. In addition, the educational system deprives low-achievement students of self-respect and holds them up for ridicule. Faced with this situation, some youngsters compensate by engaging in high-risk activities whose reward is a reputation for bravery and consequent increase in self-esteem. Of course, the risk-taking activities include such illegal acts as vandalism, drinking, and fighting. These pressures are reduced when a student drops out or graduates:

> When students drop out or graduate from high school, they enter a world that, while sometimes inhospitable, does not restrict their autonomy and assault their dignity in the same way the school does. The need to engage in crime to establish a sense of an autonomous self and to preserve moral character through risk taking is thus reduced.

Thus, leaving the educational environment reduces a major motivation for delinquency.

There are other class- and age-oriented motivations toward delinquency. Males may experience status anxiety when they perceive that their opportunities for economic success are limited and that they will not be able to fulfill the conventional male role of family breadwinner. Their anxiety is heightened when they observe that the adult males in their environment have high unemployment rates and cannot provide for their families.

Finally, the leniency afforded delinquents by the juvenile court–a function of the belief that they are not fully responsible for their actions—promotes their illegal activities. If for no other reason, youngsters engage in law violations because they know that this is their best opportunity to be treated leniently, that as adults they will be punished to the full extent of the law.

In sum, Greenberg views the removal of children from the labor force in twentieth-century America as a primary motive behind their law-violating behavior: "The high and increasing level of juvenile crime we are seeing in the present-day United States and in other Western countries originates in the structural position of juveniles in an advanced capitalist economy."

Source: David Greenberg, "Delinquency and the Age Structure of Crime," in *Crime and Capitalism* (Palo Alto, Calif.: Mayfield, 1981), pp. 118–39. Quotations from pp. 123, 130, 135.

Instrumental Theory

One of the few conflict models directed at explaining delinquency is **instrumental theory,** developed by Herman Schwendinger and Julia Schwendinger.[72] The Schwendingers' work seeks to explain, in theoretical terms, the paradox caused by the seeming lack of relationship between social class and delinquency. As noted in Chapter 3, many self-report surveys find that middle-class youths commit as many delinquent acts as lower-class youths, despite the commonsense view that poor, underprivileged children commit more crime. Although official record surveys, such as Wolfgang's cohort study, support a lower-class status-delinquency relationship, this has not been the case for most self-report studies.

The Schwendingers believe that this puzzling relationship can be explained by the nature of the delinquent experience itself. They find that delinquency is overwhelmingly concentrated within *stratified adolescent formations* that are relatively independent of social class; they refer to these as "stradom formations."

Stradom formations are adolescent social networks whose members have distinct dress, grooming, and linguistic behaviors. Many of us remember these groups from our high school experience and recall referring to someone as a "greaser," "hood," "preppie," "socialite," or "jock" based on their friendship patterns, dress, attitudes, and concerns (in fact, we ourselves may have been part of such a group).

According to instrumental theory, economically diverse communities produce three distinct adolescent groupings that emerge as early as the sixth to eighth grades. The "socialites" (sometimes called "soshes," "frats," "elites," or "preps") are predominantly middle-class youths who band together in cliques that remain intact throughout high school. These youths are the children of less affluent but still middle-class parents, who wish to imitate the life-style of the rich and affluent.[73]

At the other end of the economic spectrum are street-corner groups known as "greasers," "homeboys," "hodads," or "hoods." Falling between these two extremes are groups characterized by an independent life-style or intermediate status, for example, "surfers," "hot rodders," or "gremmies." Some intermediate groups have mixed identities, such as "sosh-surfers." Each of the three stradom formations is marked by a relatively high delinquency rate.

Not all youths become members of a stradom group. Some are involved in organized, adult-controlled activities—the science club, church groups, the 4-H club. Others, because of school achievements, are known as "brains" or "intellectuals"; still others are "turkeys," "clods," or "nerds." In general, nonstradom youths have lower delinquency rates.

Stradom groups may display a class bias and contain members of predominantly one class, but this does not prevent crossovers. For example, some hoods and greasers may come from middle-class backgrounds, while lower-class youths can become members of the socialite stradom; intermediary groups can be even more economically heterogeneous.

DELINQUENCY MODALITIES. According to the Schwendingers' theory, there is a natural history or life cycle of delinquency participation. As the stradoms undergo change, as their members mature, so do the varieties of their delinquent behavior.

At first, there occurs the *generalized modality* of delinquency. Occurring early in adolescence, it is marked by an indifference to the needs of others and a cynical attitude toward outsiders in general. Delinquency during this period includes petty thievery, vandalism, truancy, fighting, and other "less serious" delinquent acts.

By the end of junior high school, *ethnocentric delinquency* emerges. This is characterized by stradom rivalries and includes group fights and vandalism motivated by group rivalries and the placing of graffiti that proclaims the superiority of one's stradom over another. Conflict may be intra-stradom or inter-stradom.

In later adolescence, delinquency enters the *informal economic stage*. Now, for the first time, delinquent acts are instrumental—designed to bring economic reward to the offender. Criminal acts now involve burglary, larceny, robbery, drug sales, and so on. Violence and other acting-out behaviors are supported by this modality. Generally, development of the informal economic stage is dependent on the financial status of individuals and communities. Economically deprived youths are much more likely to be thrust into economic delinquency than middle-class stradom members. However, members of all groups help sustain delinquency because they are consumers of illegally gained materials, ranging from stolen auto parts to drugs.

In sum, stradom members are more likely to become delinquent than nonstradom youths, and lower-class street-corner groups are more likely to contain conventional delinquents than socialite and intermediate groups. However, since middle-class stradom members are more often delinquent than nonstradom lower-class youths, the relationship between class and delinquency is confounded. This explains the apparent failure of self-report studies to detect an economic bias in delinquency.

The Schwendingers' work is important for the study of delinquency. It disputes theories that view delinquency as a function of perceived normlessness or blocked opportunities when it recognizes that delinquent groups form early in adolescence before most youths are even aware of their limited social standing. Similarly, it accounts for middle-class delinquency, an issue left unexplained by the social structure view. While the theory does clash somewhat with social process theories, the differences are less pronounced. However, instrumental theory does not portray as an outcast the delinquent who has a weakened bond to social institutions, such as parents, school, peers, and society. In fact, the delinquent is viewed here as a socially entrenched member of a close peer-group association. Instead, according to the Schwendingers, delinquency is more a product of market relations and demands, societal relationships, and the changing life-style of adolescence.

Integrated Structural Marxist Theory

Mark Colvin and John Pauly have created an integrated conflict theory of delinquency that they label *integrated structural theory*.[74]

According to Colvin and Pauly, delinquency is a result of socialization within the family. However, family relations are actually controlled by the parents' location in the economic marketplace. The quality of one's work experience has been shaped by the historical interaction between competition among capitalists and the level of class struggle.[75] Wage earners who occupy inferior positions in the economic hierarchy will experience coercive relationships with their supervisors and employers. Negative experiences in the workplace create strain and alienation within the family setting, which in turn relates to inconsistent and overly punitive discipline at home. Juveniles who live in such an environment will become alienated from their parents and at the same time experience conflict with social institutions, especially the school. For example, youths growing up in family headed by parents who are at the bottom of workplace control structures are also the ones most likely to go to poorly funded schools, do poorly on standardized tests, and be placed in slow learning tracks; each of these factors has been correlated with delinquent behavior.

The subsequent feelings of alienation are reinforced by associations with groups of similarly alienated peers. In some cases, the peer group will be oriented toward patterns of violent behavior, while in other instances, the group will enable its members to benefit economically from criminal behavior.

According to integrated structural theory, it is naive to believe that a delinquency control policy can be formulated without regard for its basic root causes. Coercive punishments or misguided treatments cannot be effective unless the core relationships with regard to material production are changed. Those who produce goods must be given a greater opportunity to control the forms of production and, in so doing, given the power to shape their lives and the lives of their families.

Evaluation of Conflict Theory

The major achievement of conflict theory is its call to reevaluate the institutions and processes of society and government. Barry Krisberg and James Austin state that the social turmoil of the 1960s and 1970s—including the Vietnam War, Watergate, FBI and CIA plots, civil rights, and worldwide revolutionary struggles—has led many Americans to question conventional values and social arrangements. Official wisdom is simply not accepted without question any longer.[76]

Conflict theory does indeed question the many instances of misguided "official wisdom" that pervade our society, but despite its lofty goals and ideals, critics question its lack of empirical verification.[77] Most research has been by necessity historical and theoretical. Even when a specific Marxist theory of deviance has been attempted, such as Stephen Spitzer's "Toward a Marxian Theory of Deviance,"[78] it lacks the specific propositions sociologists require to test theories properly.[79]

In a similar vein, Jackson Toby argues that conflict theory is a simple rehash of the old tradition of helping the underdog.[80] He likens the ideas behind Marxist criminology to the ideas of such literary works as *Robin Hood* and Victor Hugo's *Les Miserables*, in which the poor stole from the rich to survive. In reality, Toby claims, most theft is for luxury, not survival. Moreover, he disputes the claim that the crimes of the rich are more reprehensible and less understandable than those of the poor. Criminality and immoral behavior occur on every social level, but Toby believes that the relatively disadvantaged contribute disproportionately to the crime and delinquency rates.

In general, criticism of conflict theory has aimed at undercutting its utopianism. To blame the state for all evil seems to ignore the great variety of human differences. Not all people react in the same way to social and economic conditions. Why is it that many people suffering the pains of capitalist existence refrain from committing crimes?

SOCIAL REACTION AND DELINQUENCY PREVENTION

Labeling and social conflict theories have had an important influence on delinquency prevention policy. These theoretical models have drawn attention to the biases that exist in the juvenile justice system and how an interface with the system can actually produce rather than eliminate delinquent behavior.

The philosophical underpinnings of these policies have described by Edwin Schur in his widely read book *Radical Nonintervention*. Schur captured the essence of the social reaction approach to delinquency by decrying rehabilitation that stigmatized youth:

> A great deal of the labeling of delinquents is socially unnecessary and counterproductive. Policies should be adopted, therefore, that accept a greater diversity in youth behavior; special delinquency laws should be exceedingly narrow in scope or else abolished completely, along with preventive efforts that single out specific individuals and programs that employ "compulsory treatment."[81]

Schur argued that the treatment orientation of the juvenile court, directed at dealing with the problems of the "whole" person and not his or her delinquent violations, helped enmesh many youths who were simply status offenders (for example, runaways, truants) into what was essentially a criminal signifying process. Thus, Schur called for an end to delinquency prevention programs that treated the individual and instead called for a focus on community action and collective solutions.

TABLE 7.1 Social Reaction Theories

THEORY	MAJOR PREMISE	STRENGTHS
Labeling Theory	Youths are locked into a delinquent career when their behavior is labeled by agents of the justice system and they reorganize their identities around a deviant role.	Explains delinquent careers and the role of social control agents in sustaining deviance.
Conflict Theory	Crime is a function of class conflict. The definition of the law is controlled by people who hold social and political power.	Accounts for class differentials in the delinquency rate. Shows how class conflict influences behavior.
Instrumental Theory	In early adolescence, delinquency cuts across class lines. However, lower-class youth are more likely to persist because of economic needs, while middle-class youths enter into conventional lifestyles.	Can account for the aging out process. Explains why it is often difficult to show class differences in self-reported delinquency.
Integrated Structural Theory	Delinquency is a function of family life, which is in turn controlled by the family's place in the economic system.	Explains the relationship between family problems and delinquency in terms of social and economic conditions.

The acceptance of this approach by policymakers had a dramatic influence on juvenile justice operations in the 1970s and 1980s. A massive effort was made on the local, state, and federal levels to limit the interface of youths with the juvenile justice system. One approach was to **divert** youths from official processing channels at the time of their initial contact with police authorities (see Chapter 15). It became common for police officers to refer children to community treatment facilities and clinics rather than to the juvenile court.

In a similar vein, children who were petitioned to juvenile court became eligible for an additional round of court-based diversion programs. For example, **restitution** allowed children to pay back the victims of their crimes for the damage (or inconvenience) they have caused instead of receiving an official delinquency label.

The federal government was a prime mover in the effort to divert as many children from the justice system as possible. The Office of Juvenile Justice and Delinquency Prevention sponsored numerous diversion and restitution programs around the nation. In addition, it made one of its most important priorities the removal of juveniles from adult jails and the discontinuation of housing status offenders and juvenile delinquents together. In sum, these programs were designed to limit, whenever possible, the juvenile's interaction with the formal justice system, to reduce stigma, and to make use of informal, nonpunitive treatment modalities.[82]

While diversion and restitution continue to be widely used, the impetus for the movement seems to have waned. Evaluation of existing programs has shown that they have little or not effect on the recidivism rate of their clients.[83] Also while numerous evaluations have been attempted, their findings have been mitigated by poor research designs and inconsistency of goals, procedures, and operations.

The philosophy of nonintervention has been criticized on a number of different levels. First, it institutionalized a practice that had been carried out informally for years. Police officers and probation officers commonly released children they felt were deserving of a second chance, and only a small percentage of all offenders were continued through the juvenile justice process.[84] Second, many diversion-program clients were young and first offenders who had been routinely released informally by the police; hard-core delinquents were not eligible for diversion programs. Finally, and perhaps most important, the diversion/restitution movement actually created new juvenile justice agencies whose need for clients developed a whole new stigmatizing mechanism; critics referred to this as widening the net.[85]

The variety of diversion, restitution, and deinstitutionalization programs will be discussed more fully in Chapters 16 and 18. They have had a profound influence on the way we view delinquency and plan for its prevention.

SUMMARY

Social reaction theories view delinquent behavior as a function of the influence that powerful members of society have on less fortunate youths. Two main branches of the theory are currently popular. Label-ing theory views deviant behavior as a product of the deviant labels society imposes on its least powerful citizens. Deviant labels mark people as social outcasts and create barriers between them and the general social order. Eventually, deviant labels transform the offenders' own personalities, so that they come to accept their new "criminal or delinquent" identities as personal ones.

Labeling theorists suggest that delinquent labels lock individuals outside the mainstream of society, thereby assuring that they will turn to additional illegal behavior for survival. Who is to be labeled and the type of labeling depends on a youth's position in the social structure. The poor and powerless are much more likely to be labeled than the wealthy and powerful.

Edwin Lemert has defined the difference between primary and secondary deviants. The former are people who cling to a conventional self-image; the latter are the people who have personally accepted the traits implied by deviant labels bestowed on them.

Despite popularity among criminologists, relatively few studies have empirically validated the labeling perspective. Research efforts aimed at the influence of juvenile justice processing on delinquent youths fail to find that labels produce their expected damaging results.

Conflict theory holds that the class conflicts present in modern society produce crime and delinquency. The law and legal systems are controlled by those in power, whose aim is to maintain their hold over society. Consequently, their activities are immune while the deviant behaviors of the lower-classes are severely punished. Delinquency occurs when lower-class youngsters rebel against the constraints placed on them by those in power. Middle-class crime is motivated more by rebellion than by economic need. The Schwendingers hold that role and economic position in capitalist societies influence delinquency modalities.

Social reaction and social control theories had an important effect on delinquency prevention policy in the 1970s. Efforts were made to eliminate, whenever possible, the stigma of the juvenile justice system. This resulted in efforts aimed at the diversion of offenders before trial, limiting detention and institutionalization.

QUESTIONS FOR DISCUSSION

1. What are some common labels used in the school setting? How can these hurt youths?
2. Can labels be beneficial to a person? What are some positive effects of labeling?
3. Is it possible to overcome labels? What methods could a person employ to counteract labels?
4. Are there laws that seem to be designed to protect the rich? Is it possible that laws are actually applied fairly?
5. Are there factors in our economy that make Marx's predictions about capitalism obsolete?
6. Discuss examples of the blind obedience we give to professionals, such as doctors, lawyers, and teachers.

KEY TERMS

Head Start program
labeling theory
stigma

net widening
self-labeling
diversion

deinstitutionalization

nonintervention

Howard Becker

moral entrepreneurs

self-fulfilling prophecy

Edwin Lemert

primary and secondary deviance

exclusionary programs

inclusionary programs

deviance amplification

conflict theory

conflict criminology

Marxist criminology

critical criminology

demystification

instrumental theory

stradom formations

divert

restitution

widening the net

NOTES

1. Charles Silberman, *Crises in the Classroom: The Remaking of American Education* (New York: Random House, 1971); idem, "Murder in the Classroom: How the Public Schools Kill Dreams and Mutilate Minds," *Atlantic* 255:82–94 (1970).

2. Richard Quinney, *The Social Reality of Crime* (Boston: Little, Brown, 1970); William Chambliss and Robert Seidman, *Law, Order, and Power* (Reading, Mass.: Addison-Wesley, 1971).

3. These sentiments are contained in some pioneering studies of police discretion, such as Nathan Goldman, *The Differential Selection of Juvenile Offenders for Court Appearance* (New York: National Council on Crime and Delinquency, 1963).

4. For a review of this position, see Anne R. Mahoney, "The Effect of Labeling upon Youths in the Juvenile Justice System: A Review of the Evidence," *Law and Society Review* 8:583–614 (1974). See also David Matza, *Becoming Deviant* (Englewood Cliffs, N.J.: Prentice-Hall, 1974).

5. Mark Ezell, "Juvenile Arbitration: Net Widening and Other Unintended Consequences," *Journal of Research in Crime and Delinquency* 26:358–77 (1989).

6. William Reese II, Russell Curtis, and Albert Richard, "Juvenile Justice as People-Modulating: A Case Study of Progressive Delinquent Dispositions," *Journal of Research in Crime and Delinquency* 26:329–57 (1989).

7. The self-labeling concept originated in Edwin Lemert, *Social Pathology* (New York: McGraw-Hill, 1951). See also Frank Tannenbaum, *Crime and the Community* (Boston: Ginn, 1936).

8. President's Commission on Law Enforcement and the Administration of Justice, *Task Force Report: Juvenile Delinquency and Youth Crime* (Washington, D.C.: U.S. Government Printing Office, 1967), p. 43.

9. Edwin Schur, *Labeling Deviant Behavior* (New York: Harper & Row, 1972), p. 21.

10. Kai Erikson, "Notes on the Sociology of Deviance," *Social Problems* 10:307–314 (1962).

11. Howard Becker, *Outsiders: Studies in the Sciology of Deviance* (New York: Macmillan, 1963), p. 9.

12. Harold Garfinkle, "Conditions of Successful Degradation Ceremonies," *American Journal of Sociology* 61:420–24 (1956).

13. M.A. Bortner, *Inside a Juvenile Court: The Tarnished Ideal of Individualized Justice* (New York: University Press, 1982).

14. Edwin Lemert, *Human Deviance, Social Problems, and Social Control* (Englewood Cliffs, N.J.: Prentice-Hall, 1967), p. 15.

15. Charles H. Cooley, *Human Nature and the Social Order* (New York: Scribner, 1902).

16. Lemert, *Social Pathology.*

17. *Ibid.*, p. 73.

18. *Ibid.*, p. 75.

19. Melvin Ray and William Downs, "An Empirical Test of Labeling Theory Using Longitudinal Data," *Journal of Research in Crime and Delinquency* 23:169–74 (1986).

20. Tannenbaum, *Crime and the Community.*

21. *Ibid.*, p. 27.

22. Aaron Cicourel, *The Social Organization of Juvenile Justice* (New York: Wiley, 1968).

23. Matza, *Becoming Deviant.*

24. *Ibid.*, p. 78.

25. Stanton Wheeler and Leonard Cottrell, "Juvenile Delinquency: Its Prevention and Control," in *Delinquency, Crime, and Social Processes*, ed. Donald Cressey and David Ward (New York: Harper & Row, 1969), p. 609.

26. Garfinkel, "Conditions of Successful Degradation Ceremonies," p. 424.

27. See, generally, Carl Pope, "Race and Crime Revisited," *Crime and Delinquency* 25: 347–57 (1979).

28. Goldman, *The Differential Selection of Juvenile Offenders for Court Appearance.*

29. Donna Bishop and Charles Frazier, "The Influence of Race in Juvenile Justice Processing," *Journal of Research in Crime and Delinquency* 25: 242–63 (1989).

30. See, for example, William Wilbanks, *The Myth of a Racist Criminal Justice System* (Cincinatti, Ohio: Anderson Publishing, 1986).

31. Merry Morash, "Establishment of a Juvenile Police Record," *Criminology* 22:97–111 (1984).

32. Charles Corley, Stephen Cernkovich, and Peggy Giordano, "Sex and the Likelihood of Sanction," *Journal of Criminal Law and Criminology* 80:540–61 (1989).

33. Paul Lipsett, "The Juvenile Offender's Perception," *Crime and Delinquency* 14:49 (1968).

34. Eloise Snyder, "The Impact of the Juvenile Court Hearing of the Child," *Crime and Delinquency* 17:180–82 (1971).

35. For an opposing view, see John Hepburn, "The Impact of Police Intervention upon Juvenile Delinquents," *Criminology* 15:235–62 (1977). See also Gary Jensen, "Labeling and Identity," *Criminology* 18:121–29 (1980).

36. For a similar view, see Suzanne Ageton and Delbert Elliot, *The Effect of Legal Processing on Self-Concept* (Institute of Behavioral Science, University of Colorado, 1973), cited in Mahoney, "The Effect of Labeling upon Youths in the Juvenile Justice System," pp. 607–8.

37. Jack Foster, Simon Dinitz, and Walter Reckless, "Perception of Stigma following Public Intervention for Delinquent Behavior," *Social Problems* 20:202 (1972).

38. Charles Thomas and Donna Bishop, "The Effect of Formal and Informal Sanctions on Delinquency: A Longitudinal Comparison of Labeling and Deterrence Theory," *Journal of Criminal Law and Criminology* 75: 1222–45 (1989).

39. Richard Anson and Carol Eason, "The Effects of Confinement on Delinquent Self-Image," *Juvenile and Family Court Journal* 37:39–47 (1986).

40. Stanley Cohen, *Visions of Social Control* (Cambridge: Polity Press, 1985).

41. Schur, *Labeling Delinquent Behavior*, p. 14.

42. Ronald Akers, "Problems in the Sociology of Deviance," *Social Forces* 46:463 (1968).

43. Peter Manning, "On Deviance," *Contemporary Sociology* 2:697–99 (1973).

44. Charles Tittle and Debra Curran, "Contingencies for Dispositional Disparities in Juvenile Justice", *Social Forces* 67:23–58 (1988).

45. Charles Wellford, "Labeling Theory and Criminology: An Assessment," *Social Problems* 22:335–47 (1975) at 337.

46. David Bordua, "On Deviance," *Annals* 312:121–23 (1969).

47. Wellford, "Labeling Theory and Criminology: An Assessment."

48. *Ibid.*

49. Charles Murray and Louis Cox, *Beyond Probation: Juvenile Corrections and Chronic Delinquents* (Beverly Hills, Calif.: Sage, 1979).

50. Raymond Paternoster and LeeAnn Iovanni, "The Labeling Perspective and Delinquency: An Elaboration of the Theory and an Assessment of the Evidence," *Justice Quarterly* 6:358–94 (1989).

51. Charles Tittle, "Two Empirical Regularities (Maybe) in Search of an Explanation: Commentary on the Age/Crime Debate," *Criminology* 26:75–85 (1988).

52. Gresham Sykes, "The Rise of Critical Criminology," *Journal of Criminal Law and Criminology* 65:211–17 (1974).

53. Robert Meier, "The New Criminology: Continuity in Criminological Theory," *Journal of Criminal Law and Criminology* 67:461–72 (1976).

54. See, for example, Dennis Sullivan, Larry Tifft, and Larry Siegel, "Criminology, Science and Politics," in *Criminal Justice Research*, ed. Emilio Viano (Lexington, Mass.: Lexington Books, 1978).

55. *Ibid.*, p. 10.

56. Meier, "The New Criminology," p. 463.

57. *Ibid.*

58. Richard Quinney, *Class, State, and Crime* (New York: Longman, 1977), p. 3.

59. Sykes, "The Rise of Critical Criminology," pp. 211–13.

60. *Ibid.*

61. Herman Schwendinger and Julia Schwendinger, "Delinquency and Social Reform: A Radical Perspective," in *Juvenile Justice*, ed. LaMar Empey (Charlottesville: University of Virginia Press, 1979), pp. 246–90.

62. Sullivan, Tifft, and Siegel, "Criminology, Science, and Politics," p. 11.

63. *Ibid.*

64. Robert Gordon, "Capitalism, Class, and Crime in America," *Crime and Delinquency* 19: 174 (1973).

65. Quinney, *Class, State, and Crime*, p. 52.

66. Anthony Platt, "The Triumph of Benevolence: The Origins of the Juvenile Justice System in the United States," in *Criminal Justice in America: A Critical Understanding*, ed. Richard Quinney (Boston: Little, Brown, 1974), p. 367. See also Anthony Platt, *The Child Savers* (Chicago: University of Chicago Press, 1969).

67. Barry Krisberg and James Austin, *Children of Ishmael* (Palo Alto, Calif.: Mayfield, 1978), p. 2.

68. Schwendinger and Schwendinger, "Delinquency and Social Reform," p. 250.

69. *Ibid.*, p. 252.

70. John Hagan, A.R. Gillis, and John Simpson, "The Class Structure and Delinquency: Toward a Power-Control Theory of Common Delinquent Behavior," *American Journal of Sociology* 90:1151–78 (1985).

71. John Hagan, John Simpson, and A.R. Gillis, "Class in the Household: A Power-Control Theory of Gender and Delinquency," *American Journal of Sociology* 92:788–816 (1987).

72. Herman Schwendinger and Julia Schwendinger, *Adolescent Subcultures and Delinquency* (New York: Praeger, 1985). See also idem, The Paradigmatic Crisis in Delinquency Theory," *Crime and Social Justice* 18:70–78 (1982); idem, "The Collective Varieties of Youth," *Crime and Social Justice* 5:7–25 (1976); idem, "Marginal Youth and Social Policy," *Social Problems* 24:184–91 (1976).

73. Idem, *Adolescent Subcultures and Delinquency*, p. 55.

74. Mark Colvin and John Pauly, "A Critique of Criminology: Toward an Integrated Structural-Marxist Theory of Delinquency Production," *American Journal of Sociology* 89:513–51 (1983).

75. *Ibid.*, p. 542.

76. Krisberg and Austin, *Children of Ishmael*, p. 4.

77. Carl Klockars, "The Contemporary Crises of Marxist Criminology," in *Radical Criminology: The Coming Crisis*, ed. James Inciardi (Beverly Hills, Calif.: Sage, 1980), pp. 92–123.

78. Stephen Spitzer, "Toward a Marxian Theory of Deviance," *Social Problems* 22:638–51 (1975).

79. Alan Horowitz, "Marxist Theory of Deviance and Teleology: A Critique of Spitzer," *Social Problems* 24:362 (1977).

80. Jackson Toby, "The New Criminology Is the Old Sentimentality," *Criminology* 16:516–26 (1979).

81. Edwin Schur, *Radical Nonintervention* (Englewood Cliffs, N.J.: Prentice-Hall, 1973), p. 88.

82. Malcolm Klein, "Deinstitutionalization and Diversion of Juvenile Offenders: A Litany of Impediments," in *Crime and Justice*, vol. 1, ed. Norval Morris and Michael Tonry (Chicago: University of Chicago Press, 1979).

83. William Selke, "Diversion and Crime Prevention," *Criminology* 20:395–406 (1982).

84. LaMar Empey, "Revolution and Counter Revolution: Current Trends in Juvenile Justice," in *Critical Issues in Juvenile Delinquency*, ed. David Shicher and Delos Kelly (Lexington, Mass.: Lexington Books, 1980), pp. 157–82.

85. James Austin and Barry Krisberg, "The Unmet Promise of Alternatives to Incarceration," *Crime and Delinquency* 28:3–19 (1982).

8 Theories of Female Delinquency

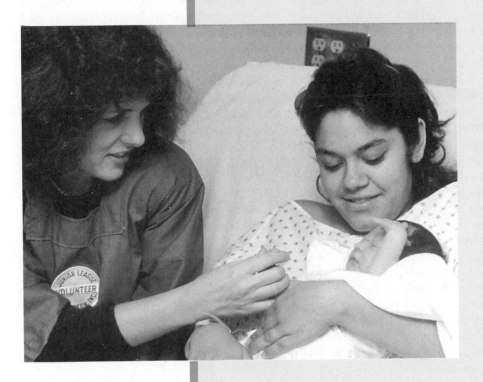

With but a few exceptions, prevailing theories of delinquent behavior tend to be male-dominated. Although a few of the theoretical models discussed so far also have relevance for **female delinquency,** the majority are directed solely at explaining the behavior of male law violators. Research seeking to examine supposedly "general" theories of delinquency have relied on methods verified with male subjects and used samples of male delinquents to test hypotheses.[1] Efforts to show that male-oriented theories have relevance for females have proven at best inconclusive.[2]

How can this theoretical bias be explained? For one thing, female delinquency was not taken seriously by early criminologists (the majority of whom were males). After all, official statistics show that girls are arrested far less often than boys and then for relatively minor offenses. Similarly, prison statistics indicate that about 96 percent of incarcerated inmates are males.

Early criminologists, such as Cesare Lombroso, viewed females as sexual delinquents who engaged in prostitution, had sexual relations while still in their minority, or were involved in acts that imply that sexual misconduct had occurred or soon will occur, such as running away from home, staying out late at night, and associating with older boys. Consequently, girls were considered neither violent nor responsible for major theft. Their delinquency was viewed as moral, emotional, or family-related, and such problems were not an important concern of traditional criminologists. In fact, the few "true" female delinquents were considered aberrations whose criminal or delinquent activity was a function of their abandoning accepted feminine roles and taking on masculine characteristics.[3]

In the aftermath of the women's movement, conceptions of female delinquency have been altered. First, there has been an ever-growing interest in a feminist approach to crime. While the female delinquency rate is still much lower than the male rate, there is little difference in their *crime patterns.* For example, larceny and burglary, the two most common forms of male criminality (as measured by the UCR) are also the most common types of female criminality. The stereotype of the female delinquent as a purely sexual deviant is no longer taken seriously.[4]

This chapter provides an overview of conceptions of female delinquency. It is divided into four sections: (1) developmental theories; (2) socialization theories; (3) liberal feminist theories; and (4) radical feminist theories.

DEVELOPMENTAL THEORIES

As you may recall, developmental theories view the cause of delinquency as stemming from the interaction of physical, psychological, and environmental conditions. There has been a long tradition of tracing the onset of female delinquency to traits that are uniquely "feminine." The argument is that biological and psychological differences in males and females can explain differences in their crime rates. The sections below briefly trace the history of this concept and discuss some modern views.

Early Views

The earliest conceptualizations of female offenders viewed them as a bizarre aberration. Since the female crime rate was so low and most girls were not delinquents, girls whose behavior deviated from what was appropriate for young girls and women were believed to be inherently evil or physically maladapted. Early positivist criminologists believed that the interplay between the biological characteristics of women and girls, the psychology of the "female mind," and the social order produced female delinquency.

With the publication in 1895 of his book *The Female Offender,* Cesare Lombroso extended his pioneering work on criminality to the study of female crimes.[5] Lombroso noted that women were lower on the evolutionary scale than men, more childlike, less sensitive, and less intelligent.[6] Women who committed crimes (most often prostitution and other sex-related offenses) could be distinguished from "normal" women by physical characteristics—excessive body hair, wrinkles, crow's feet, and abnormal craniums, for example.[7] In physical appearance, delinquent females appeared closer both to criminal and noncriminal men than to other women.

Lombroso's contention that women are lower on the evolutionary scale than men is puzzling when we consider that he viewed atavism or primitivism as the key element in producing criminal behavior and that the crime rate of females is lower than that of males. Lombroso explained this apparent inconsistency by arguing that most girls are restrained from committing delinquent acts by such counterbalancing traits as "piety, maternity, want of passion, sexual coldness, weakness, and undeveloped intelligence."[8] The delinquent female lacks these traits and is therefore unrestrained in her childlike, unreasoned passions. Lombroso also believed that much female delinquency was masked and hidden.

Lombroso did recognize, however, that there were far fewer female than male delinquents. He suggested that this was a function of the relative homogeneity and uniformity among females; the female "born criminal" was indeed a rare creature. But he also believed that if a girl did become a delinquent, her behavior might become even more vicious than that of males:

> What terrific criminals would children be if they had strong passions, muscular strength, and sufficient intelligence; and if, moreover, their evil tendencies were exasperated by a morbid physical activity! And women are big children; their evil tendencies are more numerous and more varied than men's, but generally remain latent. When they are awakened and excited, they produce results proportionately greater.
>
> Moreover, the born female criminal is, so to speak, doubly exceptional as a woman and as a criminal. For criminals are an exception among civilized people, and women are an exception among criminals, the natural form of retrogression in women being prostitution and not crime. The primitive woman was impure rather than criminal.
>
> As a double exception, the criminal woman is consequently a monster. Her normal sister is kept in the paths of virtue by many causes, such as maternity, piety, weakness, and when these counter influences fail, and a woman commits a crime, we may conclude that her wickedness must have been enormous before it could triumph over so many obstacles.[9]

Lombroso's writing had considerable influence on his contemporaries. There were a number of early-twentieth-century attempts to connect the cause of female delinquency with physical traits. For example, Cyril Burt in 1925 linked female delinquency to menstruation, a relationship later supported by Warren Middleton.[10] Similarly, William Healy and Augusta Bronner's research efforts found that about 70 percent of the delinquent girls they studied had abnormal weight and size characteristics.[11] This is sometimes referred to as the origin of the **masculinity hypothesis**—the belief that delinquent girls have excessive male characteristics.[12]

THE "UNADJUSTED GIRL." In the 1923 work *The Unadjusted Girl*, W. I. Thomas added a psychological dimension to the inherent biological nature of female delinquency.[13] Thomas believed that there are basic biological differences between men and women. In an earlier work, *Sex and Society*, he had argued that males are "katabolic," having an animal force that is destructive and aggressive and that produces creativity, while females are "anabolic," storing energy, being conservative and lethargic.[14]

Thomas found that human behavior is a function of **wish fulfillment,** which can be grouped into four independent categories: (1) desire for experience—new sensations, excitement, and adventure; (2) desire for security—fear of death, caution, conservatism; (3) desire for response—love, approval, appreciation; and (4) desire for recognition—social status, fame, and luxury.[15]

W. I. Thomas linked female delinquency to "wish fulfillment." Are these teenage prostitutes shown here impulsive, wish fulfilling thrill seekers?

According to Thomas, attempts to fulfill one's wishes can lead to a path of good or a path of evil. The choice is influenced by the opportunities available, individual temperament, and social pressures.[16] Many poor girls who have not been socialized with middle-class controls can become impulsive thrill seekers while attempting to satisfy their wishes. Female delinquency results from their unsocialized impulsiveness: unchecked desires for amusement, adventure, and luxury drives delinquent girls into the arms of men who take advantage of their naivete and eventually lead them to pregnancy, prostitution, and ruin.[17]

THE "DEVIOUS FEMALE." Otto Pollak published his most significant work, *The Criminality of Women*, in 1950.[18] Like the earlier developmental theorists, Pollak views the basis for female delinquency as wrapped up in the physiological differences between males and females. He suggests that female criminality has three distinct stages, each influenced by the onset of critical biological changes—menstruation, pregnancy, and menopause:

> Thefts, particularly shoplifting, arson, homicide, and resistance against public officials seem to show a significant correlation between the menstruation of the offender and the time of the offense. The turmoil of the onset of menstruation and the puberty of girls appears to express itself in the relatively high frequency of false accusations and—where cultural opportunities permit—of incendiarism. Pregnancy in its turn is a crime-promoting influence with regard to attacks against the life of the fetus and the newborn. The menopause finally seems to bring about a distinct increase in crime, especially in offenses resulting from irritability such as arson, breaches of the peace, perjury, and insults.[19]

Pollak argues that most female delinquency goes unrecorded because the female is the instigator rather than the perpetrator of illegal behavior. In keeping with his biological orientation, Pollak attributes this ability to physiological differences that enable girls and women to deceive men:

> Man must achieve an erection in order to perform the sex act and will not be able to hide his failure . . . and pretense of sexual response is impossible for him if it is lacking. Woman's body, however, permits such pretense to a certain degree and lack of orgasm does not prevent her ability to participate in the sex act. It cannot be denied that this basic physiological difference may well have a great influence on the degree of confidence which the two sexes have in the possible success of concealment and on their character pattern in this respect.[20]

According to Pollak, then, females are naturally more adept at concealing their true nature, having been forced from an early age to misguide men about their sexuality. This "natural" ability to be deceitful allows females to avoid the hazards of law violations by goading their male companions to commit crime at their behest.[21]

THE CHIVALRY HYPOTHESIS. Pollak's work inspired the **chivalry hypothesis.** This view says that gender differences in the delinquency rate can be explained by the fact that females are not less crime prone than males, but that their delinquency is "hidden" by the deference granted them by agents of the criminal justice system. Police and judges are deceived into maintaining a chivalrous attitude partly because they are gullible and easily misled by seemingly "innocent" young girls and partly because they have been taught to respect and defer to females. Those who believe in the chivalry hypothesis point to data that shows that while women make up about 12 percent of all arrestees, they account for less than 5 percent of inmates.

Psychodynamic Views

Sigmund Freud maintained that girls view their lack of a visible penis as a sign that they have been punished. Boys fear that they also can be punished by having their penis cut off and thus learn to fear women. From this conflict comes **penis envy** and the girl's wish to become a boy. Penis envy often produces an inferiority complex in girls, forcing them to make an effort to compensate for their defect. One way is to identify with their mother and accept a maternal role as wife and childbearer. Also, girls may become narcissistic and attempt to compensate for their lack of a penis by dressing well and beautifying themselves.[22]

Freud also found that if a young girl does not overcome her penis envy, neurotic episodes may follow: "If a little girl persists in her first wish—to grow into a boy—in extreme cases she will end as a manifest homosexual, and otherwise she will exhibit markedly masculine traits in the conduct of her later life, will choose a masculine vocation, and so on."[23]

Freud's concept of penis envy has been strongly questioned by more modern psychoanalysts who scoff at the notion that little girls feel inferior to little boys and charge that Freud's thinking was influenced by the sexist culture he lived in.[24]

Others using the psychoanalytic perspective have suggested that girls are socialized to be passive and need affection, helping to explain their low crime rate. However, this personality condition also makes some females susceptible to being manipulated by men; hence, their participation in sex-related crimes, such as prostitution.

This theme has been amplified by a number of psychoanalysts who link feminine crime and delinquency to sexuality. Peter Blos states:

> The girls' wayward behavior is restricted to stealing of the kleptomaniac type; to vagrancy; to provocative impudent behavior in public; and to frank sexual waywardness. In the girl, it seems delinquency is an overt sexual act, or to be more correct, a sexual acting out.[25]

Similarly, psychiatrist Walter Bromberg suggested that the sexual conflict that produces prostitution may be found in "every woman" and may be attributed to "conflicts surrounding enjoyment of sexuality."[26]

According to the psychoanalytic approach, therefore, female delinquency is a product of a young girl's psychosexual development. Female delinquency is viewed as a function of repressed sexuality, gender conflict, and abnormal socialization.

Current Biosocial Views

Modern biosocial theorists have continued the tradition of explaining female delinquency as a function of the interaction of physical and social traits unique to women and girls.[27] One biological factor long suspected as a cause of female criminality is premenstrual syndrome or *PMS:*

> For several days prior to and during menstruation, the sterotype has been that "raging hormones" doom women to irritability and poor judgement—two facets of premenstrual syndrome.[28]

The link between PMS and delinquency was popularized by Katharina Dalton, whose studies of English women led her to conclude that females are more likely to commit suicide and be aggressive and otherwise antisocial before or during menstruation.[29] While Dalton's research is often cited as evidence of the link between PMS and crime, methodological problems make it impossible to accept her findings at face value. Moreover, most other research efforts indicate that women do suffer anxiety prior to and during menstruation but that there is little evidence linking these conditions to crime or long-term psychological problems.[30] Criminologist Julie Horney impressively reviewed the literature on PMS and crime and found that existing evidence is inconclusive. Horney suggests there may be alternative explanations for a PMS-delinquency link; for example, it is possible that the psychological and physical stress of antisocial events produces early menstruation and not vice versa.[31]

HORMONAL DIFFERENCES. Some biosocial theorists link antisocial behavior to hormonal influences. Male-female dissimilarities have been associated with gender-related hormonal differences.[32] Walter Gove argues that testosterone levels are a key to understanding crime rate differences: the decline in this key hormone during the life cycle accounts for the aging-out process; its lower levels in females explains their lower delinquency rate.[33] The argument is that males' sex hormones (**androgens**) account for their more aggressive behavior.

Lee Ellis also links gender differences to the presence of androgens in males. These hormones cause areas of the brain to become less sensitive to environmental stimuli, making males more likely to seek high levels of stimulation and to tolerate more pain in the process. Androgens are also linked to brain seizures, which result in greater emotional volatility, especially when stresses occur. Ellis also believes that androgens effect brain structure itself (the left hemisphere of the neocortex), which effectively reduces sympathetic feelings towards others that help to inhibit the urge to victimize.[34]

There has been a great deal of research on the relationship of hormonal levels to aggression. In general, the research indicates that females who have naturally low androgen levels are more passive than males, while females who were exposed to male hormones, either before birth (in utero) or after, will take on characteristically male traits, including aggression. For example, research by Donald Baucom and his associates indicates that college women who had higher levels of the male hormone testosterone were more likely to engage in stereotypically male behaviors.[35]

SOCIALIZATION THEORIES

Socialization theories hold that the social and psychological development of a young girl, influenced and controlled by her family, her peers, and society, may be the key to understanding delinquent behavior. If she experiences psychological impairment, trauma, family disruption, and so on, a young woman will eventually be forced to engage in delinquent associations and criminality.

Are Females Naturally Less Aggressive?

Official and unofficial data sources generally show that male delinquents are more violent than female delinquents. Gender differences can be explained by a persistent double standard in socialization and culture: males are socialized to be more aggressive and are given peer and parental support for their belligerence. Fathers don't want their sons to be "sissies" and tell them, "If someone picks on you, fight back and they'll leave you alone." Girls are less likely to receive such parental advice.

Not all criminologists view gender differences as a matter of learning and enculturation. Biosocial theorists, for example, explain gender differences in delinquency by suggesting that females may be inherently less aggressive than males. As you may recall, one view is that the hormonal differences can explain the variance in male-female aggression rates because the violence-prone population is suspected of maintaining elevated amounts of the male sex hormones (androgens), such as testosterone.

Another biosocial approach links gender differences in aggression to the evolutionary process. Lee Ellis has suggested that males may be inherently more combative than females because of essential physical dissimilarities in the male and female reproductive systems. Like other biosocial theorists, Ellis links human behavior to the urge to reproduce and maintain the gene pool. He finds that males are naturally more aggressive because they wish to possess and control as many sex partners as possible in order to increase their chances of producing an offspring. Females have learned to control their aggressive impulses because multiple mates do not increase their chances of conception. They instead concentrate their efforts on acquiring things that will help them successfully rear their offspring, such as a reliable mate who will supply material resources.

While the weight of the evidence is that males are more aggressive than females, there is also evidence that females are more likely to act aggressively under some circumstances than others. For example, Ann Frodi and her associates found:

1. Males are more likely than females to report physical aggression in their behavior, intentions, and dreams.
2. Females are more likely to feel anxious or guilty about behaving aggressively, and these feelings tend to inhibit aggression.
3. Females behave as aggressively as males when they have the means to do so and believe that their behavior is justified.
4. Females are more likely to empathize with the victim—to put themselves in the victim's place.
5. Sex differences in aggression decrease when the victim is anonymous. Anonymity may prevent females from empathizing with their victims.

In sum, biosocial theorists find that qualities of male biological traits make them "naturally" more aggressive than females, and therefore, it should come then as no surprise that male delinquency rates are higher. However, the Frodi research shows that, depending on the circumstances, males and females can be equally aggressive.

Source: Lee Ellis, "The Victimful-Victimless Crime Distinction and Seven Universal Demographic Correlates of Victimful Criminal Behavior," *Personality and Individual Differences* 9:525–48 (1988); Lee Ellis, "Evolutionary and Neurochemical Causes of Sex Differences in Victimizing Behavior: Toward a Unified Theory of Criminal Behavior and Social Stratification," *Social Science Information* 28:605–36 (1989); Ann Frodi, J. Maccauley, and P. R. Thome, "Are Women Always Less Aggressive Than Men? A Review of the Experimental Literature," *Psychological Bulletin* 84:634–60 (1977).

The view that socialization influences antisocial behavior is not unique to explaining female delinquency, since we have already reviewed theories of male socialization. However, there have been a number of attempts to use the unique socialization experiences of females to distinguish the cause of their law violations from that of males.

Focus on Family Conflict

At mid-century, a number of writers began to focus on the socialization patterns of girls as a key determinant of their antisocial behavior. Perhaps the best-known work of this period was **Gisela Konopka's** *The Adolescent Girl in Conflict* (1966). Konopka incorporates many of the principles expounded by Freud but also emphasizes the influence of peers and socialization in causing deviant behavior.[36]

Konopka suggests that delinquency has its roots in a girl's feeling of uncertainty and loneliness. During her adolescence, a girl's major emotional need is to be accepted by members of the opposite sex. If normal channels for receiving such approval—family, friends, relatives—are impaired, she may fight isolation by joining a "crowd" or engaging in gratuitous sexual relationships. This behavior eventually leads to "rejection by the community, general experience of having no recognized success . . . and more behavior which increases the feeling of worthlessness."[37] Konopka identifies four major influences on loneliness and consequent delinquent behavior of girls:[38]

■ The onset of puberty in girls is traumatic because of the often cruel way in which it is received by parents and the fear it creates in the girl.

■ The social identification process can be dramatic and difficult because of a girl's competitiveness with her mother. In fatherless homes, girls have an especially hard time, since "the road to a healthy development toward womanhood through affection for the male and identification with the female simply does not exist."[39]

■ Changing the pattern of females' cultural position can create problems. Delinquent girls are believed to suffer from a lack of training and education. This locks them into low-paying jobs with little hope for advancement. These conditions lead girls to relieve their thwarted ambition by aggressive or destructive behavior.

■ The world presents a hostile picture to some young girls. Adult authority figures tell them what to do, but no one is there to listen to their needs.

Konopka emphasizes the effect of the family and society on female emotions as a primary influence on a girl's delinquent behavior. A number of authorities have shared Konopka's views since the publication of her study. One significant work, by Clyde Vedder and Dora Somerville, *The Delinquent Girl* (1970), also suggests that the delinquent behavior of girls is usually a problem of adjustment to family and social pressure.[40] In fact, the authors estimate that 75 percent of institutionalized girls have family problems. They also suggest that girls have serious problems in a male-dominated culture with rigid and sometimes unfair social practices.

Research on Female Socialization

There has been a great deal of research indicating that delinquent girls do in fact come from troubled, uncertain homes and are the victims of sexual and physical abuse. For example, Ames Robey and his associates studied the background and behavior of adolescent girls in a suburban juvenile court clinic. In their analysis of girls who manifested rebellious behavior, they often found sexual conflicts with both parents, sometimes marked by an erotic entanglement between father and daughter.[41]

William Wattenberg and Frank Saunders found a pattern of broken or disrupted homes in the backgrounds of female delinquents.[42] In their analysis of a sample of 4,533 youths contacted by the Youth Bureau of the Detroit Police Department, they found that girls were much more likely than boys to be charged with sex offenses, incorrigibility, and truancy. Girls were also likely to be described as aimless and nonenergetic. More revealing were the facts that girls often came from broken homes and that when police took them home, they were more likely than boys to be rejected by their parents.

Don Gibbons and Manzer Griswold had similar findings in their study of the delinquency referrals of an urban juvenile court.[43] More delinquent girls than boys were charged with ungovernable behavior, running away, and sex offenses (9.81 versus 4.7 percent). The girls were also more likely than boys to come from broken homes. This led Gibbons and Griswold to conclude that girls were more likely than boys to come before the court because of maladjustment.[44]

Gordon Barker and William Adams compared boys and girls in another setting, a state training school. They found that most of the male delinquents were incarcerated for burglary, robbery, and other theft-related offenses but that girls tended to be involved in incorrigibility, sex offenses, and truancy.[45]

Barker and Adams concluded that the boys were delinquent in order to gain status and demonstrate their masculinity by adventurous behavior. On the other hand, the girls were delinquent because of hostility toward parents and a consequent need to obtain gratification and attention from others.

In *Five Hundred Delinquent Women*, Eleanor Glueck and Sheldon Glueck examined the life histories of institutionalized female offenders.[46] A significant majority of the subjects had been involved in sexual deviance that began early in their teens. The Gluecks concluded that sexual delinquency and general behavior maladjustment developed in girls simultaneously with unstable home lives.[47] This finding is supported by Ruth Morris's often-cited study, which described delinquent girls as unattractive, poorly groomed youths who reside in homes marked by family tensions or absent parents.[48]

More recently, Meda Chesney-Lind found that a significant amount of female delinquency, which most often involves such acts as truancy, running away, and petty theft, can be traced to physical and sexual abuse in the home.[49] She writes, "Young women on the run from homes characterized by sexual abuse and parental neglect are forced, by the very statutes designed to protect them, into the life of an escaped convict."[50]

In sum, the socialization approach to female delinquency posits that family interaction and child-parent relations are the key to understanding the antisocial behavior of girls. If a girl grows up in an atmosphere of sexual tension, where hostility exists between her parents or where the parents are absent from the home, it is likely that she will turn to outside sources for affection and support. Unlike boys, girls have very narrowly defined behavioral patterns that they must follow. If their reaction to loneliness, frustration, and parental hostility is sexual activity, running away, staying out late at night, and so on, they are likely to be defined as delinquent or wayward. The socialization approach holds that the psychological pressure of a poor home life is likely to have an even more dam-

aging effect on females than males. Because girls are less likely than boys to have the support of close-knit peer associations, they are more likely to need close parental relationships in order to retain emotional stability. In fact, girls may become sexually involved with boys in order to receive support from them, a practice that tends only to magnify their problems.

LIBERAL FEMINIST THEORY

All of us, despite our differences, are constantly growing and trying to understand each other's oppression, be it as working-class women, black or brown women, gay women or, middle-class women. We are, by struggling, finding new ways of caring about each other, and it is this that gives us hope of having a movement, finally, which will provide for all of our needs.[51]

This statement represents the sentiments of women who were active participants in the feminist movement.[52] Feminist leaders fought to help women break away from their traditional role of homemaker and mother and secure for themselves economic, professional, educational, and social advancement. There is little question that the women's movement revised the way women perceive their roles in society, and it has significantly altered the relationship of women to many important social institutions.

The feminist movement also influenced thinking about the nature and extent of female delinquency. A number of scholars, including Rita Simon and Freda Adler, drew national attention to the changing pattern of female criminality and offered new explanations for its cause.[53] Their position is that economic conditions and sex-role differences influence female crime. Females are less delinquent than males because their social roles provide them with fewer opportunities to commit crime. As the role of girls and women becomes more similar to that of males, so too will their crime patterns. Female criminality is actually motivated by the same crime-producing influences as males.

"Sisters in Crime"

Freda Adler's book *Sisters in Crime* has been an influential source of information on how changing roles have influenced female crime and delinquency. Adler's major thesis is that by striving for social and economic independence, women have begun to alter social institutions, which until recently protected males in their position of power. "The phenomenon of female criminality," she claims, "is but one wave in this rising tide of female assertiveness."[54]

Adler argues that female delinquency is affected by the changing patterns of females' behavior. Girls are becoming increasingly involved in traditionally masculine crimes, such as stealing, gang activity, and fighting. Furthermore, Adler predicts that in the future, the women's liberation movement will produce even steeper increases in the rate of female delinquency because it creates an environment in which the social roles of girls and boys converge. Boys, she argues, have traditionally entered puberty ill-prepared for the world of aggression and competition they encounter in the activities of their peer groups. The consequent emotional strain leads them to engage in delinquent activities. Girls, on the other hand, have always maintained traditional, relatively static behavior patterns. These patterns have protected young girls from the pressures of transition into the adult world. However, Adler claims, "the modern girl . . . is passing from childhood to adulthood via a new and uncharted course. . . . She is partly pushed and partly impelled into fields previously closed to women . . . . Clearly, the developmental difficulties which encouraged male delinquency in the past are exerting a similar influence on girls."[55]

Adler proclaims that the changing female role will eventually produce female delinquents and criminals who are quite similar to their male counterparts:

> Women are no longer behaving like subhuman primates with only one option. Medical, educational, political, and technological advances have freed women from unwanted pregnancies, provided them with male occupational skills, and equalized their strengths with weapons. Is it any wonder that once women were armed with male opportunities, they should strive for status, criminal as well as civil, through established male hierarchical channels?
>
> In the cities . . . young girls are now taking to the streets just as boys have traditionally done. It has now become quite common for adolescent girls to participate in muggings, burglaries, and extortion rings which prey on schoolmates.[56]

Research on Liberal Feminist Theory

A number of recent studies have supported the determinist view of female delinquency.[57] The most notable may be **Rita Simon's** 1975 effort, *The Contem-*

porary Woman and Crime. While not specifically devoted to youth crime, Simon's work points to the consistent increase in the crime rate of females in general. Her comparison of arrest rates for the years 1953, 1963, and 1972 indicates that women's crime rates have increased dramatically and that the type of female criminality has changed. Simon suggests that women commit significantly more larceny, fraud, forgery, and embezzlement—all business- and economics-related crimes. Their violent crime rate has remained somewhat static. Simon explains that her findings are a function of the changing role of women:

> The same factors and conditions that explain women's increased participation in property offenses also serve to explain the slight decline or lack of increase in violent offenses during the same time period. The fact that women have more economic opportunities and more legal rights (divorces and abortions are easier to obtain) and that in recent years they have been developing a rhetoric which legitimizes their newly established socio-legal-economic status seems to lessen the likelihood that they will feel victimized, dependent, and oppressed. The diminishment of such feelings means that they will be less likely to attack their traditional targets: their husbands, lovers, pimps (that is, men with whom they are emotionally involved and dependent upon), and their babies (those recently born and those not yet delivered).[58]

Simon's view has been supported in part by Roy Austin's analysis of the effect the women's liberation and economic emancipation movement has had on the female crime rate.[59] Using 1966 as a jumping-off point (because the National Organization for Women was founded in that year), Austin's research shows that patterns of serious female crime (robbery and auto theft) correlate with indicators of female emancipation (namely, the divorce rate and participation in the labor force). While, as Austin admits, this research is not conclusive proof that female

The "Court-in" (beating up for fifteen seconds straight) is a part of this girl gang initiation ceremony.

crime is related to economic and social change, it certainly identifies behavior patterns that support that hypothesis.

In addition to these efforts, a number of self-report studies have supported liberal feminism by showing that gender differences in delinquency *patterns* are fading. That is, the delinquent acts committed most (petty larceny) and least often (heroin addiction, armed robbery) by girls is nearly identical to those reported most and least often by boys.[60] Research evidence uncovered in numerous self-report studies seems to indicate that the pattern of female delinquency, if not the extent, is now similar to that of male delinquents.[61]

There is growing evidence that social forces predictive of male delinquency, such as identification with a delinquent peer group, are also associated with female delinquency.[62] For example, Margaret Farnsworth found that with some forms of youthful misconduct, such as status offenses and violent crimes, male and female delinquency is motivated by the same social relationships (for example, family structure and function).[63] By implication, if the sex roles of males and females are made equivalent, there also may be greater similarity in their offending patterns.

Critiques of Liberal Feminism

Not all delinquency experts believe that changing sex roles actually influence female crime rates. Some argue that the delinquent behavior patterns of girls have remained static and have not been influenced by the women's movement. Others feel that there has been change but that the cause is something other than the feminist revolution. For example, Darrell Steffensmeier and Renee Hoffman Steffensmeier concluded that arrest data and juvenile gang studies show little increase in female violence or gang-related acts, that young female offenders do not seem to be catching up with males in terms of violent or serious crimes. They also found that gains in serious crimes by female offenders (as measured by the UCR) have leveled off. Earlier, the female crime rate had reflected the general increase in the overall crime rate occurring in the 1970s. In addition, the Steffensmeiers noted that self-reported studies show that female participation in most crime patterns has remained stable for the past ten years, with increases being in the area of drug use and alcohol abuse.[64]

Similarly, Joseph Weis has challenged the "invention" of the new female criminal. In a self-report study, he found that girls still engage in traditional female sex-role oriented behaviors, such as shoplifting, and are least involved in typically masculine crimes, such as fighting. Weis sees this as evidence that female crime patterns are not related to female liberation and calls such an equation "absurd": "after all, the women's movement is dedicated to stopping and preventing the kinds of explorations and victimization which comprise many criminal as well as noncriminal activities and relationships."[65]

These sentiments have been duplicated by other researchers, such as Carol Smart, who suggests that swings in the female crime rate have been recorded since the 1920s.[66] Smart maintains that the cause of female delinquency is so complex, as is the cause of all criminal behaviors, that it is meaningless to attribute it to a single cause, such as the women's movement.

In sum, the evidence indicates that gender differences in the crime rate have not changed as much as liberal feminist writers had predicted. Consequently, the argument that female crime and delinquency patterns will be elevated by the women's movement has not been given unqualified support.

RADICAL FEMINIST VIEWS

A number of feminist writers take a more revolutionary view of female criminality. Some can be categorized as **Marxist feminists** who view gender inequality as stemming from the unequal power of men and women in a capitalist society and the exploitation of females by fathers and husbands; women are considered a "commodity" worth possessing, like land or money.[67] In contrast, **radical feminists** view the cause of female delinquency as originating with the onset of male supremacy (**patriarchy**), the subsequent subordination of women, male aggression, and the efforts of men to control females sexually.[68] They focus on the social forces that shape women's lives and experiences in order to explain female criminality.[69] For example, they attempt to show how the sexual victimization of girls is a function of male socialization (for example, males learn to be aggressive and exploitive of women). Exploitation then acts as a trigger for behavior by female victims (for example, running away and substance abuse), which is labeled deviant or delinquent.[70] In a sense, the female delinquent is a victim herself.

There have been a number of theoretical models that have attempted to use a radical and/or Marxist feminist perspective to explain gender differences in the delinquency rate and the nature of female delinquency. In *Capitalism, Patriarchy, and Crime*, Marxist James Messerschmidt argues that capitalist society is marked by both patriarchy and class conflict. Capitalists control the labor of workers while men control women both economically and biologically.[71] This "double marginality" explains why females in a capitalist society commit fewer crimes than males: they are isolated in the family and have fewer opportunities to engage in elite deviance (white-collar and economic crimes); they are also denied access to male-dominated street crimes. Since capitalism renders women powerless, they are forced to commit less serious nonviolent, self-destructive crimes, such as becoming drug abusers. Supporting Messerschmidt's conclusions is the self-report data that shows girls report the same rates of substance abuse as males.

Meda Chesney-Lind has written extensively on the victimization of female delinquents by agents of the juvenile justice system. She found that police in Honolulu, Hawaii, were likely to arrest female adolescents for sexual activity and to ignore the same behavior among male delinquents.[72] Some 74 percent of the females in her sample were charged with sexual activity or incorrigibility, but only 27 percent of the boys suffered the same charges. Moreover, the court ordered physical examinations in over 70 percent of the female cases, but only about 15 percent of the males were forced to undergo this embarrassing procedure. Girls were also more likely to be sent to a detention facility before trial, and the length of their detention averaged three times that of the boys. Finally, a higher percentage of females than males were institutionalized for similar delinquent acts.

Chesney-Lind explains her data by suggesting that because female adolescents have a much narrower range of acceptable behavior than male adolescents, any sign of misbehavior in young girls is seen as a substantial challenge to authority and to the viability of the double standard of sexual inequality. Female delinquency is viewed as relatively more serious than male delinquency and therefore is more likely to be severely sanctioned.

Power-Control Theory

In one prominent radical feminist work, John Hagan and his associates have speculated that gender differences in the delinquency rate is a function of class differences and economic conditions that in turn influence the structure of family life. Hagan calls his view the **power-control theory**.[73]

According to this view, class position influences delinquency by controlling the quality of family life. In families that are paternalistic, fathers assume the traditional role of breadwinners, while mothers have menial jobs or remain at home to supervise domestic matters. Within the paternalistic home, mothers are expected to control the behavior of their daughters while granting greater freedom to sons. In such a home, the parent-daughter relationship can be viewed as a preparation for the "cult of domesticity," which makes girls' involvement in delinquency unlikely; hence, males exhibit a higher degree of delinquent behavior than their sisters.

On the other hand, in *egalitarian* families—those in which husband and wife share similar positions of power at home and in the workplace—daughters gain a kind of freedom that reflects reduced parental control. These families produce daughters whose law-violating behavior mirrors their brothers'. Ironically, these kind of relationships also occur in female-headed households with absent fathers. Similarly, Hagan and his associates found that when both fathers and mothers hold equally valued managerial positions, the similarity between the rates of their daughters' and sons' delinquency is greatest. By implication, middle-class girls are the most likely to violate the law because they are less closely controlled than their lower-class sisters.

Some of the theory's basic premises, such as the relationship between social class and delinquency, have been challenged. For example, power control theory holds that upper-class youth may engage in more petty delinquency than lower-class youth because they are brought up to be "risk takers" who do not fear the

TABLE 8.1 Theories of Female Delinquency

THEORY	MAJOR PREMISE	STRENGTH
Developmental Theory	Physical and psychological differences between males and females may explain the differences in their delinquency rates. Most important are hormonal traits and genetic makeup.	Explains the significant differences between male and female violence rates, which exist even among "at-risk" youths.
Socialization Theory	Girls are socialized to be more dependent than boys. Girls who lack love and affection at home will seek substitutes in the streets.	Shows why females are likely to engage in status offenses, such as running away.
Liberal Feminist Theory	Gender differences in the crime rate can be explained by the economic and social double standards that exist in American society. As educational, economic, and social differences between males and females evaporate, their delinquency rates should become similar.	Explains why female delinquency rates have risen faster than male delinquency rates.
Radical Feminist Theory	Female delinquency is a result of oppressive conditions suffered by young girls, including sex abuse, exploitation, and physical dominance by male authority figures. Capitalism favors male domination.	Shows how oppression and abuse lead to female delinquency.

consequences of their misdeeds. Some recent research indicates that such relationships may not exist.[74] However, on-going research by Hagan and his colleagues has tended to support the core relationship between family structure and gender differences in the delinquency rate.[75]

Power-control theory is important because it encourages a new approach to the study of delinquency, one that includes gender differences, class position, and the structure of the family. It also has value as an explanation of the relative increase in female delinquency because it incorporates the effects of the social changes occurring in the feminine role within its explanation of delinquency.[76] With the shift toward single-parent homes brought about by the significant numbers of unwed teenage mothers and the high divorce rate, the patterns Hagan has identified may also undergo change. The decline of the patriarchal family may produce looser family control over young girls, changing sex roles, and increased opportunities for delinquency.

SUMMARY

Female delinquency has become a topic of considerable interest to criminologists and other experts interested in youth crimes. It is believed that the nature and extent of female delinquent activities have changed, and it appears that girls are now engaging in more frequent and serious illegal activity.

Attempts to discover the cause of female delinquency can be placed in a number of different categories. Early efforts by Cesare Lombroso and W. I. Thomas and a later effort by Otto Pollak place the blame for female crime on the inherent biological nature of the female. Later, developmental theorists viewed a girl's psychological makeup and family environment as important factors in her misbehavior.

Socialization theorists portrayed the adolescent female offender as a troubled girl who lacked love at home and supportive peer relations. Both the socialization and developmental perspective portrayed the female delinquent as a sexual offender whose criminal activities were linked to destructive relationships with men.

More recent views of female delinquency incorporate the changes brought about by the women's movement. It is argued by such experts as Freda Adler and Rita Simon that as the social and economic roles of women change, so will their crime patterns. While a number of research studies support this view, there are theorists who question its validity. Though the female crime rate has increased and the nature of female delinquency is now patterned along the lines of male delinquency, the gender gap has not narrowed after more than a decade since the women's rights movement began. Hagan's power-control theory helps us understand why these differences exist and whether change may be forthcoming.

QUESTIONS FOR DISCUSSION

1. Are girls delinquent for different reasons than boys? Do they have a unique set of problems?
2. Are girls the victims of unfairness at the hands of the justice system, or do they benefit from "chivalry"?
3. Comment on Pollak's charge that women and girls are sneaky and cunning?
4. Do you think that PMS is a cause of delinquency?

KEY TERMS

female delinquency

masculinity hypothesis

wish fulfillment

chivalry hypothesis

penis envy

androgens

Gisela Konopka

Freda Adler

Rita Simon

Marxist feminists

radical feminists

patriarchy

power-control theory

NOTES

1. For a general review of this issue, see Kathleen Daly and Meda Chesney-Lind, "Feminism and Criminology," *Justice Quarterly* 5:497–538 (1988).

2. Douglas Smith and Raymond Paternoster, "The Gender Gap in Theories of Deviance: Issues and Evidence," *Journal of Research in Crime and Delinquency* 24:140–72 (1987).

3. Cesare Lombroso, *The Female Offender* (New York: Appleton, 1920).

4. Rita James Simon, *The Contemporary Woman and Crime* (Washington, D.C.: U.S. Government Printing Office, 1975).

5. Lombroso, *The Female Offender*.

6. *Ibid.*, p. 122.

7. *Ibid.*, pp. 51–52.

8. *Ibid.*, p. 151.

9. *Ibid.*, pp. 150–52.

10. Cyril Burt, *The Young Delinquent* (New York: Appleton, 1925); Warren Middleton, "Is There a Relation between Kleptomania and Female Periodicity in Neurotic Individuals?" *Psychology Clinic*, December 1933, pp. 232–47.

11. William Healy and Augusta Bronner, *Delinquents and Criminals, Their Making and Unmaking* (New York: Macmillan, 1926).

12. For a review, see Anne Campbell, *Girl Delinquents* (Oxford: Basic Blackwell, 1981), pp. 41–48.

13. W. I. Thomas, *The Unadjusted Girl* (New York: Harper & Row, 1923).

14. Idem, *Sex and Society* (Boston: Little, Brown, 1907).

15. Idem, *The Unadjusted Girl*.

16. *Ibid.*, p. 241.

17. *Ibid.*, p. 109.

18. Otto Pollak, *The Criminality of Women* (Philadelphia: University of Pennsylvania Press, 1950).

19. *Ibid.*, p. 158.

20. *Ibid.*, p. 10.

21. *Ibid.*, p. 4.

22. Sigmund Freud, *An Outline of Psychoanalysis*, trans. James Strachey (New York: Norton, 1949), p. 278.

23. Dorie Klein, "The Etiology of Female Crime: A Review of the Literature," in *The Criminology of Deviant Women*, ed. Fred Adler and Rita Simon (Boston: Houghton Mifflin, 1979), pp. 69–71.

24. Phyliss Chesler, *Women and Madness*, (Garden City, New York: Doubleday, 1972); Karen Horney, *Feminine Psychology* (New York: Norton, 1967).

25. Peter Blos, "Preoedipal Factors in the Etiology of Female Delinquency," *Psychoanalytic Studies of the Child* 12:229–42 (1957).

26. Walter Bromberg, *Crime and the Mind* (New York: Macmillan, 1965), p. 350.

27. See, generally, Ralph Weisheit and Sue Mahan, *Women, Crime and Criminal Justice* (Cincinnati, Ohio: Anderson Publishing, 1988).

28. Spencer Rathus, *Psychology*, 3rd ed. (New York: Holt, Rinehart and Winston, 1987), p. 88.

29. See, generally, Katharina Dalton, *The Premenstrual Syndrome* (Springfield, Ill.: Charles C. Thomas, 1971).

30. Karen Paige, "Effects of Oral Contraceptives on Affective Fluctuations Associated with the Menstrual Cycle," *Psychosomatic Medicine* 33:515–37 (1971).

31. Julie Horney, "Menstrual Cycles and Criminal Responsibility," *Law and Human Nature*, 2:25–36 (1978).

32. Eleanor Maccoby and Carol Jacklin, *The Psychology of Sex Differences* (Palo Alto: Stanford University Press, 1974).

33. Walter Gove, "The Effect of Age and Gender on Deviant Behavior: A Biopsychosocial Perspective," in A. S. Rossi, ed., *Gender and the Life Course* (New York: Aldine, 1985), pp. 115–44.

34. Lee Ellis, "Evolutionary and Neurochemical Causes of Sex Differences in Victimizing Behavior: Toward a Unified Theory of Criminal Behavior and Social Stratification," *Social Science Information* 28: 605–636 (1989).

35. D. H. Baucom, P. K. Besch, and S. Callahan, "Relationship between Testosterone Concentration, Sex Roles Identity, and Personality among Females," *Journal of Personality and Social Psychology* 48:1218–26 (1985).

36. Gisela Konopka, *The Adolescent Girl in Conflict* (Englewood Cliffs, N.J.: Prentice-Hall, 1966).

37. *Ibid.*, p. 40.

38. Peter and Lucille Kratcoski, *Juvenile Delinquency* (Englewood Cliffs, N.J.: Prentice-Hall, 1979), pp. 146–47.

39. Konopka, *The Adolescent Girl in Conflict*, p. 50.

40. Clyde Vedder and Dora Somerville, *The Delinquent Girl* (Springfield, Ill.: Charles C. Thomas, 1970).

41. Ames Robey, Richard Rosenwal, John Small, and Ruth Lee, "The Runaway Girl: A Reaction to Family Stress," *American Journal of Orthopsychiatry* 34:763–67 (1964).

42. William Wattenberg and Frank Saunders, "Sex Differences among Juvenile Court Offenders," *Sociology and Social Research* 39:24–31 (1954).

43. Don Gibbons and Manzer Griswold, "Sex Differences among Juvenile Court Referrals," *Sociology and Social Research* 42:106–10 (1957).

44. *Ibid.*, p. 110.

45. Gordon Barker and William Adams, "Comparison of the Delinquencies of Boys and Girls," *Journal of Criminal Law, Criminology, and Police Science* 53:470–75 (1962).

46. Eleanor Glueck and Sheldon Glueck, *Five Hundred Delinquent Women* (New York: Knopf, 1934).

47. *Ibid.*, p. 90.

48. Ruth Morris, "Female Delinquency and Relational Problems," *Social Forces* 43:82–89 (1964).

49. Meda Chesney-Lind, "Girls' Crime and Women's Place: Toward a Feminist Model of Female Delinquency." (Paper presented at the American Society of Criminology Meeting, Montreal, Canada, November 1987).

50. *Ibid.*, p. 20.

51. Deborah Babcox and Madeline Belken, *Liberation: NOW* (New York: Dell, 1971).

52. Leaders in the women's movement include Gloria Steinem, Germaine Greer, and Kate Millett. Earlier revolutionaries include Simone de Beauvoir and Gertrude Stein.

53. Simon, *The Contemporary Woman and Crime;* Freda Adler, *Sisters in Crime* (New York: McGraw-Hill, 1975).

54. Adler, *Sisters in Crime.*

55. *Ibid.*, p. 104.

56. *Ibid.*, pp. 10–11.

57. Rita James Simon, "Women and Crime Revisited," *Social Science Quarterly* 56:658–63 (1976).

58. *Ibid.*, pp. 660–61.

59. Roy Austin, "Women's Liberation and Increase in Minor, Major, and Occupational Offenses," *Criminology* 20:407–30 (1982).

60. Michael Hindelang, "Age, Sex, and the Versatility of Delinquency Involvements," *Social Forces* 14:525–34 (1971).

61. Martin Gold, *Delinquent Behavior in an American City* (Belmont, Calif.: Brooks/Cole, 1970) p. 118; John Clark and Edward Haurek, "Age and Sex Roles of Adolescents and Their Involvement in Misconduct: A Reappraisal," *Sociology and Social Research* 50:495–508 (1966); Nancy Wise, "Juvenile Delinquency in Middle-Class Girls," in *Middle Class Delinquency*, ed. E. Vaz (New York: Harper & Row, 1967), pp. 179–88; Gary Jensen and Raymond Eve, "Sex Differences in Delinquency: An Examination of Popular Sociological Explanations," *Criminology* 13:427–48 (1976).

62. Merry Morash, "Gender, Peer Group Experiences, and Seriousness of Delinquency," *Journal of Research in Crime and Delinquency* 23:43–67 (1986).

63. Margaret Farnsworth, "Male-Female Differences in Delinquency in a Minority-Group Sample," *Journal of Research in Crime and Delinquency* 21:191–212 (1986).

64. Darrell Steffensmeier and Renee Hoffman Steffensmeier, "Trends in Female Delinquency," *Criminology* 18:62–85 (1980). See also idem, "Crime and the Contemporary Woman: An Analysis of Changing Levels of Female Property Crime, 1960–1975," *Social Forces* 57:566–84 (1978); Darrell Steffensmeier and Michael Cobb, "Sex Differences in Urban Arrest Patterns, 1934–1979," *Social Problems* 29:37–49 (1981).

65. Joseph Weis, "Liberation and Crime: The Invention of the New Female Criminal," *Crime and Social Justice* 1:17–27 (1976).

66. Carol Smart, "The New Female Offender: Reality or Myth," *British Journal of Criminology* 19:50–59 (1979).

67. Julia Schwendinger and Herman Schwendinger, *Rape and Inequality* (Beverly Hills, Calif.: Sage, 1983).

68. For a review of feminist theory, see Sally Simpson, "Feminist Theory, Crime and Justice," *Criminology* 27:605–32 (1989).

69. *Ibid.*, p. 611.

70. Kathleen Daly and Meda Chesney-Lind, "Feminism and Criminology," *Justice Quarterly* 5:497–538 (1988).

71. James Messerschmidt, *Capitalism, Patriarchy and Crime* (Totowa, N.J.: Rowman and Littlefield, 1986); for a critique of this work, see Herman Schwendinger and Julia Schwendinger, "The World according to James Messerschmidt," *Social Justice* 15:123–45 (1988).

72. For some critical research, see Simon Singer and Murray Levine, "Power Control Theory, Gender and Delinquency: A Partial Replication with Additional Evidence on the Effects of Peers," *Criminology* 26:627–48 (1988).

73. John Hagan, A. R. Gillis, and John Simpson, "The Class Structure and Delinquency: Toward a Power-Control Theory of Common Delinquent Behavior," *American Journal of Sociology* 90:1151–78 (1985); John Hagan, John Simpson, and A. R. Gillis, "Class in the Household: A Power-Control Theory of Gender and Delinquency," *American Journal of Sociology* 92:788–816 (1987).

74. Gary Jensen and Kevin Thompson, "What's Class Got to Do with It? A Further Examination of Power-Control Theory," *American Journal of Sociology* 95:1009–23 (1990); Kevin Thompson, "Gender and Adolescent Drinking Problems: The Effects of Occupational Structure," *Social Problems* 36:30–44 (1989).

75. John Hagan, A. R. Gillis, and John Simpson, "Clarifying and Extending Power Control Theory," *American Journal of Sociology* 95:1024–37 (1990).

76. Meda Chesney-Lind, "Judicial Enforcement of the Female Sex Role: The Family Court and the Female Delinquent," *Issues in Criminology* 8:51–59 (1973).

Environmental Influences on Delinquency

Most delinquency theorists believe that children's relationships with elements of their social environment influence their behavior. More specifically, the interaction children have with their parents, peers, school, and substance abuse is thought to exert a powerful influence on their conventional or delinquent activities.

These social relationships are certainly not simple ones, and, therefore, they are subject to different interpretations, depending on the orientation of the observer. For example, a conflict theorist might view a child's school failure as a consequence of class conflict and discrimination. Conversely, a biosocial theorist might view the same incident of school failure as a function of a learning disability or some other neurological dysfunction. Although both experts conclude that children who do poorly in school are among the most likely to violate the law, the explanation of school failure and its relationship to delinquency is markedly different. In a similar fashion, the influence of family life and peer relations can also be viewed in a number of different ways, depending on the orientation of the observer.

Beyond their theoretical importance, the family, school, peer group, and drug abuse play critical roles in daily social life. They can escalate delinquency or help at-risk kids "desist." In fact, many delinquency prevention efforts focus on family, school, or peer group and drug abuse. For example, if the family is believed to be a cause of delinquency, family counseling and therapy may be used to prevent it. Similarly, gang control efforts have been used to counteract the influence of peer group pressure toward delinquency.

Part III contains four chapters devoted to the relationship these critical social forces have on delinquency. Among the special topics focused on are child abuse and neglect, school crime, gang violence, and teenage drug abuse.

By reading these chapters, you should develop a better understanding of the role schools, families, peers, and drugs play in delinquency behavior.

9

The Family and Delinquency

There seems to be little disagreement that a child who is growing up in a household characterized by conflict and tension, whose parents are absent or separated, and who lacks familial love and support will be susceptible to the delinquency-promoting forces in the environment (see Table 9.1).[1] Conversely, the effects of a supportive family life can be beneficial to children in any social environment or group. Even those children living in so-called "high-crime areas" may be better able to resist the "temptation of the streets" if they receive fair discipline, care, and support from parents who provide them with strong, positive role models.[2]

The assumed relationship between delinquency and family life is critical today because the traditional American family is rapidly changing. The extended family, once widespread because of the economic necessity of sharing housing with many family members, is now for the most part an anachronism. It has been replaced by the nuclear family, which has been described as a "dangerous hot-

TABLE 9.1   Theoretical Views on the Family and Delinquency

THEORY	MAJOR PREMISE
Choice Theory	Parents who don't teach children the consequences of rule-violating behavior will encourage them to be law violators. Parents may encourage delinquent behavior choices by promoting success at any cost; "greed is good."
Developmental Theory	The predisposition to commit crime may be inherited or encouraged by family activities, such as diet and living conditions. Some delinquency-promoting traits, such as low intelligence and impulsivity, may be inherited.[16] Family interaction influences personality traits that have been associated with delinquent behavior.[17]
Social Structure Theory	The area and environment children grow up in are controlled by their families' socioeconomic positions. The makeup of the family may be controlled by economic conditions.
Social Process Theory	The attachment of children to their families will negate delinquency-promoting inducements. Children who participate in family activities will be less likely to get involved with deviant peers and groups. Children may learn deviant values from parents.[18]
Social Reaction Theory	Some youths are actually labeled as deviants within their own families and made to feel like outcasts. Socioeconomic class position controls both the family's economic well-being and its child-rearing practices. Lower-class families are paternalistic and tend to control girls more than boys, freeing the latter to engage in delinquency.

house of emotions" because of the intensely close contact between parents and children, unrelieved by contact with other family members living nearby.[3]

Within the nuclear family, there are indications of breakdown. Much of the parental responsibility for child-rearing is delegated to baby-sitters, television, and day-care paraprofessionals. Despite such changes in structure, some families are able to adapt and continue functioning as healthy and caring units, producing well-adjusted children. Others have crumbled under the burden of such stresses, with severely damaging effects on the present and future lives of their children.[4] This is particularly true when child abuse and neglect become part of family life.

Because these domestic issues are so critical for understanding juvenile delinquency, this chapter is devoted to an analysis of the family's role as a delinquency-producing or delinquency-inhibiting social institution. The chapter first covers the changing face of the American family. It then reviews how family structure and function influence delinquent behavior. The relationship between child abuse and neglect is covered in some depth. Finally, programs designed to improve family functioning are reviewed.

THE CHANGING AMERICAN FAMILY

The fact that the family is so closely linked with delinquent behavior is critically important when the stress being placed on family functioning is considered. The divorce rate is now about one breakup for every two new marriages.[5] The very structure and definition of the family is undergoing change. The traditional concept of the **paternalistic family** in which there is a male breadwinner and a female who cares for the home and children simply does not exist. About 70 percent of all mothers of school-age children are now employed, up from 50 percent in 1970 and 40 percent in 1960.[6] Slightly over half of mothers with infants under one year of age are employed outside the home; by 1995, there will be 14.6 million preschool children and 37.4 million school-age children who have mothers working outside the home.[7]

People are waiting longer to marry and are having fewer children. **Single-parent households** have become common, and more unwed mothers than ever are deciding to keep and raise their children.

Caring for many of these children is an inadequate day-care system whose workers are often paid minimum wage. Of special concern are the hundreds of thousands of **family day-care** homes in which a single provider takes care of three to nine children. Several states do not license or monitor these small private centers. And even in those states that do mandate registration and inspection of day care, it is estimated that 90 percent or more are facilities that operate "underground." It is not uncommon for one adult to care for eight infants, an impossible task regardless of training or concern. According to Edward Zigler, a leading authority on day care, this condition is prima facie evidence that the development of many children is being compromised.[8]

The changing makeup of the American family has become a recognized and accepted fixture of modern life. The "typical" American family portrayed on such 1960s television shows as "Father Knows Best," "Ozzie and Harriet," and "Leave It to Beaver" is a thing of the past. Not surprisingly, the way the media depicts the American family has also changed with the times. Few eyebrows are raised today when a TV show depicts two single men living with a teenage girl and the plot device is that the characters are unsure which one is her father (as was the case with the 1990 sitcom "My Two Dads").

The American family is also undergoing stress that is the result of economic hardships. A study by the National Research Council indicates that close to 40 percent of black families and 20 percent of white families currently live below the poverty line.[9] The Council also estimates that one out of six white children and one out of two black children live in poverty; 44 percent of black families and 13 percent of white families were headed by a single mother.[10] The plight of these single parents is extremely desperate: about one fifth of all single mothers have incomes *below half of the poverty line.*[11]

The Effects of Family Conflict

Stress and conflict in the family have been linked to a number of delinquency-producing activities. For example, family stress makes it likely that many parents will act destructively toward their children. Abuse and neglect of children have become widespread and serious problems in the United States. More than two million children are being maltreated in a variety of ways, ranging from gross neglect and starvation to overt physical and mental cruelty. Each year, juvenile courts throughout the nation hear approximately 500,000 child neglect and abuse cases. As child abuse experts Richard Gelles and Murray Straus put it:

> Parent-to-child violence is so common and so widely approved that one needs few case studies to make the point. In general, the large majority of Americans believes that good parenting requires some physical punishment. . . . Among the thousands of people we have interviewed, it was the absence of physical punishment that was thought to be deviant, not the hitting of children.[12]

Children who are the victims of abuse suffer physical and psychological damage both at the time the abuse takes place and later in life. There is also evidence supporting a link between the abuse of young children and their subsequent violent and aggressive behavior as juvenile delinquents and status offenders.

It is believed that negative family environments contribute to the delinquent behavior of children chiefly because the family is the primary unit in which children learn the values, attitudes, and processes that guide their actions throughout their lives. Children with poor, detached home life often have problems at school and find it difficult to maintain positive peer relations.[13] Experts in the fields of juvenile delinquency, sociology, and psychology generally agree that "it is the social interaction between the child and those in its immediate environment that constitutes the vast majority of the steps contributing to the production of a healthy and normal young person. . . . The learning process is enhanced by environmental stimulation, . . . but the central developmental relationship occurs within the family."[14] Considering the significance of the family in the early development of children, it is not surprising that a national study group found:

Family life that is shattered by episodes of physical or emotional mistreatment may breed feelings of rejection among children and retard the youngsters' normal development. Thus, programs designed to insure that all children are raised in home situations beneficial to their healthy growth should be a major component of a community delinquency prevention plan.[15]

THE FAMILY'S INFLUENCE ON DELINQUENCY

Most delinquency experts agree that the family is a frontline defense against delinquency and that a disrupted family life may encourage any preexisting forces operating in a child's life to produce delinquency. However, the relationship between family functioning and delinquency is a complex one, and a variety of factors may be at work to influence a child's antisocial behavior. For example, Rolf Loeber and Magda Stouthamer-Loeber's extensive review of the literature uncovered four broad categories of family functioning that promote delinquent behavior: families disrupted by spousal conflict or breakup (broken homes); families that neglect their children's behavior and emotional problems (discipline and supervision); families that are involved in interpersonal conflict (family relationships); and families that contain deviant parents who may transmit their behavior to their children (parental criminality).[19] And of course, each of these factors may interact to intensify individual effects (for example, family conflict may lead to child neglect). We now turn to the specific types of family problems that have been linked to delinquent behavior.

Broken Homes

One of the most enduring controversies in the study of juvenile delinquency is the relationship between having a parent absent in the home and the onset of delinquent behavior. A number of prominent delinquency experts have contended that a **broken home** is a strong determinant of a child's law violating behavior. The connection seems self-evident, since a child is first socialized at home and from the beginning learns appropriate behavior, values, and beliefs from parents. Any disjunction in an orderly family structure should have a negative impact on the child's life. Family breakup should increase an effected adolescent's experience with such delinquency-promoting factors as greater autonomy, looser supervision, less involvement with parents, and greater susceptibility to peer pressure.[20] Children of single parents may be forced to "grow up too fast," increasing their desire for independence and freedom from parental supervision.[21]

A number of clinical studies of youth who have undergone family breakups indicate they are more likely to demonstrate behavior problems, inappropriate conduct, and hyperactivity when compared to children in intact families.[22] Consequently, family breakups are often associated with discord, conflict, hostility, and aggression—factors that seem to foster a delinquent orientation.

The relationship between broken homes and delinquency was found in early research conducted by Ashley Weeks and by Sheldon Glueck and Eleanor

Glueck.[23] Further research on the subject by Jackson Toby and Ruth Morris found that the influence of parental absence was greatest on girls and among white youths, compared with males and minorities.[24] There has also been evidence that children from middle- and upper- class homes are more deeply affected by parental absence than lower-class children.[25]

Despite the strong hypothetical case linking broken homes to delinquency, the bulk of empirical research on the matter has been inconclusive. Early studies used the records of police, courts, and correctional institutions to establish a link between broken homes and delinquency.[26] However, these studies were usually flawed by their use of "official" data. Because youths from broken homes may get arrested, petitioned to juvenile court, and institutionalized more often than youths from intact families, the use of official data may present an invalid picture of the association between broken homes and delinquency. Official statistics may reflect the fact that agents of the justice system treat children from disrupted households more severely because they cannot call on parents for support. The juvenile courts' *parens patriae* philosophy calls for official intervention when parental supervision is considered inadequate.

Clifford Shaw and Henry McKay were the first to provide important evidence that broken homes were not necessarily related to delinquency. In their analysis of youths in Chicago, they found that 36.1 percent of a school sample and 42.5 percent of a delinquent sample came from disrupted families—a finding that caused them to look skeptically on the contention that broken homes and delinquency were linked.[27]

Numerous subsequent studies, using both official and self-report data, also failed to establish any clear-cut relationship between broken homes and delinquent behavior.[28] Boys and girls from intact families seem as likely to *self-report* delinquency as those whose parents are divorced or separated. However, children from broken homes are still more likely to show up in the official statistics. Researchers concluded that the absence of parents has a greater effect on agents of the justice system than it does on the behavior of children:

> "In short, the presence of a father makes a major difference in preventing the child from getting into official trouble, even though it apparently has little or no effect on the child's amount of self-reported delinquent behavior."[29]

In sum, self-report studies have been used to challenge the association found in the official data between broken homes and delinquency. While youths from broken homes get arrested more often, they are no more likely than kids from intact homes to actually engage in delinquent behavior.[30]

BROKEN HOMES RECONSIDERED. In a well-known work, Lawrence Rosen and Kathleen Neilson reviewed the literature and concluded: "The concept of broken homes, no matter how it is defined or measured, has little explanatory power in terms of delinquency."[31] This statement seems to represent the consensus of opinion on the connection between broken homes and delinquency.

Although researchers have not found a definite relationship between a broken home and delinquency, it may be premature to dismiss the connection out of hand.[32] Since official delinquent behavior is generally of a more serious nature than the self-reported variety, it is possible that the influence of a broken home can have its greatest effect on particular types of offenses, perhaps those involving force or violence. Living in a broken home has also been related to specific acts of teenage rebelliousness that reflect poor control and supervision, such as running away, truancy, and joyriding.[33]

It seems logical that all circumstances being equal, children growing up with one parent rather than two will face more difficult socialization experiences. As James Q. Wilson and Richard Herrnstein point out, even if single mothers (or fathers) can make up for the loss of a second parent, it is simply more difficult to do so, and the chances of failure become increased.[34] Further research is needed to clarify this important relationship.

In addition to broken and disrupted homes, a number of other family factors have been related to the onset of delinquent behavior; the most important of these are discussed below:

Discipline and Supervision

It is generally agreed that inconsistent parental **discipline** is related to delinquent behavior.[35] Studies using both self-report and official samples show that families that are overly harsh or extremely lenient in their disciplinary practices are more likely to contain delinquent youths.[36] In one early study, F. Ivan Nye found that mothers who threatened discipline but failed to carry it out were more likely to have delinquent children than those who were consistent in their discipline.[37] Later research by Rolf Loeber and Thomas Dishion confirmed that boys who were reported to be assaultive by both parents and teachers could be characterized as growing up in homes that maintained poor problem-solving skills and used inconsistent discipline.[38] There is evidence that families that use harsh and inconsistent discipline also experience additional social problems related to delinquency, such as parental substance abuse and deviance.[39]

Youths who believe that their parents are aware and interested in their activities and companions and will closely supervise them and punish their misdeeds will be less likely to engage in criminal acts than those youths who believe that their antisocial behavior goes unnoticed. For example, Charles Tittle found that people are more likely to be deterred by fear of parental disapproval than by the threat of legal sanctions.[40] Similarly, Gary Jensen and Raymond Eve show that gender differences in the crime rate may be explained in part by the restrictive supervision received by many females.[41]

In sum, there is significant evidence that consistent discipline and close supervision are related to conventional behavior patterns in youth, while inconsistent and limited supervision is a strong predictor of delinquent behavior.[42]

Family Relationships

It is believed that children need a warm, close, supportive relationship with their parents. Researchers have found that youths who lack closeness with mothers or fathers or perceive a lack of family cohesiveness are more likely to engage in delinquent acts and status offenses.[43] Some studies indicate that it is closeness to the mother that regulates delinquent activity, while others point to the paternal relationship as the key factor. Research by Marvin Krohn and his associates indicates that *both* parents and children have independent impressions of family

It is believed that children need a warm, close, supportive relationship with their parents.

attachment and that perceived detachment from either party can be used to predict delinquent behavior.[44]

Research efforts have consistently supported the relationship between family conflict, hostility, low warmth and affection, and delinquency.[45] For example, Jill Leslie Rosenbaum found that the family background of incarcerated female delinquents was almost universally dysfunctional; some of the homes were described as "an animal-like environment."[46] Cindy Hanson and her associates found that the colder and more distant the father-son relationship, the greater the likelihood that children in the family would be arrested.[47] Similarly, Richard Smith and James Walters found that the factors that distinguished a sample of nondelinquents from a sample of incarcerated youths were associated with (1) lack of a warm, loving, supportive relationship with the father, (2) minimal paternal involvement with children, (3) high maternal involvement (delinquents reported being closer to their mothers and more often disciplined by mothers than fathers), and (4) broken homes.[48] Smith and Walters conclude that a stable, unbroken home characterized by loving, supportive parent-child relationships will help insulate a youngster from delinquency. John Laub and Robert Sampson found that the quality of family life, including measures of supervision, attachment to parents, and discipline, are far more important predictors of delinquent or conforming behavior than measures of family structure (such as absent parents, large families, or family income).[49]

While negative parent-child relationships are generally associated with delinquency, it is difficult to assess the direction the relationship takes. While it is often assumed that preexisting family problems cause delinquency, it may also be true that acting-out children put enormous stress on a family, causing the problems to occur.[50] In other words, the behavior of parents influences the behavior of children, which in turn influences the behavior of the parents, and on and on in an endless loop.[51] Parents of **beyond-control** youngsters have been found to be inconsistent rule-setters, less likely to praise, encourage and show interest in their children, and display high levels of hostile detachment.[52]

Parental Conflict

Research indicates that parents who have a marriage which is secure, maintains communication, and lacks conflict also produce children who are secure and independent.[53] Unfortunately, **intrafamily conflict** is a common experience in most American families.[54] Serious or excessive family conflict has also been linked to subsequent delinquency. Pioneering research by F. Ivan Nye found that conflict between parents is a better predictor of delinquency than a broken home. Nye concluded that a child's perception of his or her parents' marital happiness was a significant factor in the child's own self-reported delinquency.[55]

The more recent studies that have focused on the relationship between parental marital discord and delinquency have supported Nye's research. Most have found that children growing up in maladapted homes in which they witness violence and conflict tend to exhibit patterns of emotional disturbance, behavior problems, and social conflict.[56] In fact, one recent study found little difference in the behavior of children who had merely witnessed intrafamily violence and those who were child abuse victims.[57]

Related to perceptions of intrafamily conflicts is the level of communication between parent and child. A number of research efforts have found that children who feel inhibited with their parents and therefore refuse to discuss important issues with them are more likely to engage in deviant activities (such as smoking marijuana). Poor child-parent communications can be related to perceptions of disharmony in the home.[58]

Parental Criminality

A number of studies have found that the children of deviant or criminal parents are the most likely to engage in delinquent behavior themselves.[59] Some of the most important recent research, conducted by Donald J. West and David P. Farrington, found that a significant number of delinquent youths have parents who engage in criminal behavior themselves.[60] An in-depth study of 356 English youths conducted by West and Farrington found that 8.4 percent of the sons of noncriminal fathers had a multiple criminal offense record; in comparison, about 37 percent of youths with criminal fathers were multiple offenders![61] Maternal criminality was also found to be highly predictive of delinquent behaviors.

Homes that are conflict-ridden and lack communication are more likely to produce delinquent children.

John Laub and Robert Sampson found that parental criminality, especially substance abuse, has a strong influence on children's delinquent behavior:

> Parental deviance of both mother and father strongly disrupts family processes of social control, which in turn increases delinquency.[62]

These relationships can be explained in a number of different ways. Biosocial theorists claim that the link can be traced to genetic transference from parents to child. Psychologists look to the socialization of the child and their personality development. The link between parental criminality and child delinquency might also flow through the environment. Since parents and their offspring experience similar social and economic stimuli, it should come as no surprise that they respond in a similar fashion to them.

So while there is some agreement that criminal parents produce delinquent offspring, there is a great deal of difference about the nature and direction of the relationship.[63]

Family Structure

Another common association between family structure and delinquent behavior concerns family size, **birth order**, and age at childbearing. A number of studies have found that larger families are more likely to produce delinquents than smaller ones and that middle children are more likely to engage in delinquent acts than first- or last-born children. Criminologists attribute this phenomenon to the stretched resources of the large family and the relatively limited supervision parents can provide for each child. Middle children may suffer because they are the most likely to be home when large numbers of siblings are present (oldest children having presumably left the nest before the birth of their youngest brothers and sisters).[64] A research effort by Karen Wilkinson, B. Grant Stitt, and Maynard Erickson suggests that the relationship may be influenced by sibling gender: boys who have brothers are more likely to become delinquent than those who have sisters.[65]

It has also been alleged that early child rearing is associated with delinquency because younger, teenage mothers lack the economic and social resources of more mature parents. Some biosocial theorists maintain that the low birth weight and prenatal complications that are common in teenage pregnancies are associated with low IQ and personality disturbances, which in turn predict delinquency.[66] However, recent analysis of this issue by Merry Morash and Lila Rucker indicates that the association between early child rearing and delinquency may be more a social than biological factor. The children of teenage mothers are less likely to become delinquent if they have a live-in father who presumably can help provide support and nurturing. In contrast, poor households headed by unwed teenage mothers are more likely to produce delinquent children. Therefore, according to Morash and Rucker, the family's social situation and not its composition influence delinquency.[67]

These are but a few of the many research efforts that link the quality and structure of a child's family life with delinquency. It appears that a delinquent's home life tends to be disrupted, conflict ridden, and lacking in communication and affection. It is a family that does little to support and much to hinder a growing child's development. The delinquent child grows up in a large family and has parents who may drink, participate in criminal acts, be harsh and inconsistent disciplinarians, be cold and unaffectionate, have marital conflicts, and be poor role models. Thus, the *quality* of a child's family life seems a much more important predictor of delinquency than its structure.

CHILD ABUSE AND NEGLECT

Concern about the quality of family life has recently increased because of the disturbing reports that many children are physically abused and neglected by their parents and that this harsh treatment has serious consequences for their future behavior.

Parental abuse and neglect is not a modern phenomenon. From infanticide to severe physical beatings for disciplinary purposes, maltreatment of children has occurred throughout history. Some concern for the negative effects of such maltreatment was voiced in the eighteenth century in the United States, but concerted efforts to deal with the problem of endangered children did not begin until 1874.

In that year, residents of a New York City apartment building reported to a public health nurse that a child in one of the apartments was being abused by her stepmother. The nurse found a young child named Mary Ellen who was repeatedly beaten and chained to her bed and was malnourished from a continuous diet of bread and water. The child was obviously seriously ill, but the police agreed with her parents that the law entitled them to raise Mary Ellen as they saw fit.

In 1874 Henry Bugh and Etta Angell Wheeler persuaded a New York court to take a child, Mary Ellen, away from her mother on the grounds of child abuse. This is the first recorded case in which a court was used to protect a child. Mary Ellen is shown at age 9 when she appeared in court showing bruises from a whipping and several gashes from a pair of scissors. The other photograph shows her a year later.

Since no child protection agencies existed at that time, Mary Ellen's removal from her parents had to be arranged through the Society for Prevention of Cruelty to Animals (SPCA) on the ground that she was a member of the animal kingdom, which the SPCA was founded to protect. The intervention of the SPCA resulted in a legal suit and a jail sentence for Mary Ellen's parents, but more important, it led to the founding of the Society for Prevention of Cruelty to Children the following year, marking the extension of humane organizations from animals to humans.[68]

In the twentieth century, little legal or medical research into the problems of maltreated children occurred prior to the work of Dr. C. Henry Kempe of the University of Colorado. In 1962, Kempe reported the results of a survey of medical and law enforcement agencies that indicated that the child abuse rate was much higher than had previously been thought. He coined a new term, *the battered child syndrome*, which he applied to cases of nonaccidental physical injury of children by their parents or guardians.[69] Kempe's work sparked a flurry of research into the problems of the battered child, and a network of law enforcement, medical, and social service agencies was formed to deal with battered children.[70]

Professionals dealing with such children soon discovered the limitations of Kempe's definition as they came face to face with a wide range of physical and emotional abuse inflicted on children by their parents. As Kempe himself recognized in 1976,

The term "battered child" has been dropped. . . . When coined fifteen years ago, its purpose was to gain the attention of both physicians and the public. We feel, now, that enough progress has been made to move on to a more inclusive phrase—child abuse and neglect. The problem is clearly not just one of *physical* battering. Save for the children who are killed or endure permanent brain damage . . . the most devastating aspect of abuse and neglect is the permanent adverse effects on the developmental process and the child's emotional well-being.[71]

Thus, the definition has expanded, and **child abuse** is now a generic term that includes neglect as well as overt physical beating. Specifically, it now describes any physical or emotional trauma to a child for which no reasonable explanation, such as an accident or ordinary disciplinary practices, can be found. Child abuse is generally seen as a pattern of behavior rather than a single beating or an act of neglect. The effects of a pattern of behavior are cumulative. That is, the longer the abuse continues, the more severe the effect on the child.[72]

Although the terms *child abuse* and *neglect* are sometimes used interchangeably, they represent different forms of maltreatment. **Neglect** is the more passive term, referring to deprivations that children suffer at the hands of their parents—lack of food, shelter, health care, and parental love. *Abuse*, on the other hand, is a more overt form of physical aggression against the child, one that often requires medical attention. Yet the distinction between the two terms is often unclear. In many cases, both occur simultaneously in the same family.

Legally, each state has its own definition of child abuse. Despite the variety of these definitions, they all contain a combination of two or more of the following components: nonaccidental physical injury; physical neglect; emotional abuse or neglect; sexual abuse; abandonment.[73] Physically harmful actions by parents include throwing, shooting, stabbing, burning, drowning, suffocating, biting, and deliberately disfiguring their children; however, the greatest number of injuries come from beatings with various kinds of implements and instruments.[74]

Physical neglect results from parents' failure to provide adequate food, shelter, or medical care for their children, as well as failure to protect them from physical danger. Emotional abuse or neglect frequently accompanies physical abuse; it is manifested by constant criticism and rejection of the child, who as a result loses self-esteem.[75] Sexual abuse refers to the exploitation of children through rape, incest, and molestation by parents or legal guardians. Finally, abandonment refers to the situation in which parents physically leave their children with the intention of completely severing the parent-child relationship.[76]

The Extent of Child Abuse

How extensive is the incidence of child abuse and neglect? How many **endangered children** are there in the United States?[77]

Some of the first and most explosive indications of the severity of the problem came from a widely publicized 1979 national survey conducted by sociologists Richard Gelles and Murray Straus.[78] Gelles and Straus found that in a given year, between 1.4 million and 1.9 million children in the United States are subject to physical abuse from their parents. Their survey showed that physical abuse was rarely a one-time act; the average number of assaults per year was 10.5, and the median was 4.5.

In addition to parent-child abuse, Gelles and Straus found that 16 percent of the couples in their sample reported a violent act toward a spouse (husband or wife); 50 percent of multichild families reported attacks between siblings, and 20 percent had incidents where children attacked parents.[79] Gelles and Straus found the incidence of intrafamily violence so great that they directed their attention toward domestic violence in general, rather than limiting it to child abuse and neglect alone.[80]

Gelles and Strauss conducted a follow-up national survey of family violence in 1985 and found, somewhat surprisingly, that the incidence of very severe violence toward children may be on the decline. They estimate the decline between 1975 and 1985 may be as much as 47 percent.[81] Nonetheless, this means that approximately 1.5 million children were subjected to severe violence as late as 1985. And this research effort focused solely on two-parent families; had it included children from single-parent households, the estimate might have been increased.[82]

Reported Child Abuse

Not all child abuse cases are reported to authorities, but the number of reported cases is growing at a frightening pace.[83] Since 1976, the American Humane Association has collected reports of child-abuse incidents from all fifty states, three territories and the District of Columbia.[84] Most cases are reported to child protection agencies by family, relatives or neighbors (36 percent), while the remainder are reported by police (11 percent), school personnel (14 percent), medical personnel (11 percent), social service authorities (12 percent), and other sources.

As Figure 9.1 shows, the number of reported incidents increased dramatically, from 669,000 in 1976 to over 2.2 million in 1988 (the last data available), an increase of 466 percent. Of these reported cases, about 40 percent were later substantiated to involve abuse, while the remaining 60 percent were dropped as "unfounded."[85]

The Humane Association's survey also tells us something about the victims of child abuse. The average age of abused children is about 7 years old, a slight majority are females (52 percent), and about 67 percent are white. The average family reported for child maltreatment could be described as white (75 percent), the average age of the caretakers was 32, almost half were on welfare (48 percent), and it had two children. About 37 percent of the reported families were headed by single women, and women were the identified perpetrators of child abuse in 57 percent of the cases.[86]

FIGURE 9.1

National reporting of child abuse and neglect

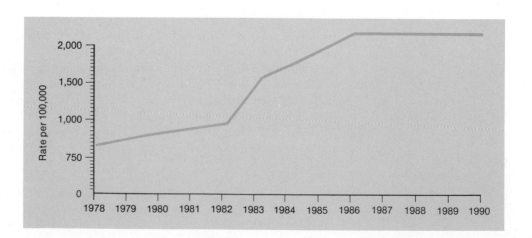

The Humane Association also found that about 3 percent of the reported abuse cases involved major physical injury and about 18 percent, minor physical injury; deprivation of life necessities made up the majority of cases (55 percent).

An extremely disturbing trend has been the meteoric rise in the number of reported sexual abuse cases. In fact, in 1976, less than 1 in 10,000 children was reported as being the victim of sexual abuse, while today the figure stands at more than 100 in 10,000. While this rapid rise could be caused by increased sexual abuse of children, it is more likely the result of greater public awareness of the problem, state efforts to encourage reporting, proliferation of sexual maltreatment programs, and expansion of the definition of sexual abuse.

Another important source of information on child abuse is the findings of the National Incidence and Prevalence of Child Abuse and Neglect Survey, sponsored by the U.S. Department of Health and Human Services. The findings of this survey are summarized in the Focus on Delinquency on the next page.

The Causes of Child Abuse and Neglect

Parental maltreatment of children is a complex problem with neither a single cause nor a single solution. It cuts across racial, ethnic, religious, and socioeconomic backgrounds, affecting the entire spectrum of society. Abusive parents cannot be categorized by sex, age, or educational level. They are persons from all walks of life, with varying cultural and economic backgrounds. However, although a number of general factors do seem to occur with some frequency in abusive or neglectful families and are described in this section, present research on the etiology of parental abuse is severely limited by a lack of research data on families in which abuse does not occur. Thus, efforts to isolate factors that either contribute to or lessen the incidence of abuse and neglect are hampered by an inability to make valid comparisons.[87]

Of all factors associated with child abuse, two are discussed most often: (1) parents who themselves suffered abuse as children tend to abuse their own children and (2) isolated and alienated families tend to become abusive. A cyclical pattern of family violence seems to be perpetuated from one generation to another within families. Evidence indicates that a large number of abused and neglected children grow into adolescence and adulthood with a tendency to engage in violent behavior. The behavior of abusive parents can often be traced to negative experiences in their own childhood—physical abuse, lack of love, emotional neglect, incest, and so on. These parents become unable to separate their own childhood traumas from their relationships with their children.[88]

In addition, abusive parents often have unrealistic perceptions of the appropriate stages of childhood development. When their children are unable to act "appropriately"—when they cry, throw food, or strike their parents—the parents may react in an abusive manner.[89] For such parents as these, "the axiom about not being able to love when you have not known love yourself is painfully borne out in their case histories. . . . They spend their days going around the house, ticking away like unexploded bombs. A fussy baby can be the lighted match."[90]

Parents may also become abusive if they are isolated from friends, neighbors, or relatives who can provide a lifeline in times of crisis:

> Potentially or actually abusing parents are those who live in states of alienation from society, couples who have carried the concept of the shrinking nuclear family to its most

The National Incidence of Child Abuse

The National Incidence and Prevalence of Child Abuse and Neglect survey was commissioned by the National Center on Child Abuse and Neglect, a component of the U.S. Department of Health and Human Services. Data was collected from child protection service (CPS) professionals from around the country. Based on their responses, the following estimates of the child abuse problem were formulated:

It was estimated that, in 1986, more than one million children nationwide (about 1,025,900) met the stringent requirement of having already experienced demonstrable harm as a result of abuse or neglect. These results represented a 64 percent increase in countable cases of abuse and neglect over the estimate of 625,100 provided by the 1980 incidence study. Only 40 percent of these children were known to CPS agencies through official, screened-in reports. The remainder were recognized as maltreated children by non-CPS professionals in various community agencies. This translates into an annual incidence rate of 16.3 children per 1,000 children in the nation who experienced demonstrable harm from abuse or neglect, of whom 6.5 children per 1,000 had been officially reported to CPS and accepted for investigation.

Even more children were identified as victims of abuse or neglect when the revised definitional standards were applied, which included children who had been endangered (but not yet demonstrably harmed) by abuse or neglect. By these standards, more than one and a half million children (about 1,584,700) were abused or neglected in 1986 throughout the United States. Again, less than half (46 percent) had been officially reported to (and screened-in by) CPS agencies. The remainder were children who were recognized as maltreated by some community professional in non-CPS agencies like those recruited for this study. This reflects 25.2 children per 1,000 in the United States endangered or already harmed as a result of abuse or neglect, 11.6 of whom were known to CPS agencies through official, screened-in reports.

Of likely child, family, and county characteristics, three had *no* effect on maltreatment countable un-

continued

extreme form, cut off as they are from ties of kinship and contact with other people in the neighborhood.[91]

Many abusive and neglectful parents describe themselves as highly alienated from their families and lacking close relationships with persons who could provide help and support in stressful situations.[92] The relationship between alienation and abuse may be particularly acute in homes where there has been divorce or separation or in which parents have never married: abusive punishment in single-parent homes has been found to be twice that of two-parent families.[93] Parents who are unable to cope with stressful life-styles marked by alcoholism, financial stress, poor housing conditions, recurring mental illness, mental retardation, and drug addiction or similar events are the ones most likely to maltreat their children.[94]

In sum, Richard Gelles and Murray Straus have described the abusive parent as follows:

der the original study definitions—child's race/ethnicity, family size, and county metrostatus. Race/ethnicity and county metrostatus were also not as sociated with maltreatment countable under the revised definitions. All other characteristics did show some relationship to the incidence or type of maltreatment and/or injury/impairment.

The child's sex affected maltreatment. Specifically, females experienced more abuse than did males (13.1 per 1,000 females versus 8.4 per 1,000 males), reflecting primarily a greater vulnerability to sexual abuse. There were 3.9 sexually abused females per 1,000 compared to 1.1 sexually abused males per 1,000. This higher rate of female sexual abuse was associated with a greater likelihood of female children experiencing "probable" injury and/or impairment—a category of harm that was more frequently assigned in cases of sexual abuse.

The incidence of abuse, particularly of physical abuse, increased with age; this increase essentially reflected the lower frequency of abuse among children from infancy to 2 years old compared to children in the other age brackets. When the youngest children were abused, however, they were more likely than older children to experience fatal injury, reflecting their greater vulnerability to physical harm. The distribution of moderate injuries/impairments was similar to that of abuse, and this level of harm was more prevalent in the older age brackets. The only form of neglect to vary with age was educa-tional, due in large part to the fact that this category was only defined for children of school age under both sets of definitional standards. There was, however, some tendency toward a higher incidence of educational neglect among the 15 to 17 year olds, at least under the revised definitions.

Family income had wide-ranging effects on both the incidence and severity of child maltreatment. Children from families earning less than $15,000 in 1986 were more likely than those from higher income families to experience maltreatment and injury. Whether under original or revised definitions, there were extensive differences between the groups, with the lower-income children always experiencing the greater frequency of maltreatment or injury.

Finally, under revised study definitions, family size was found to be associated with the incidence of maltreatment. Specifically, children from larger families (that is, those with four or more children) had higher estimated incidence of both abuse and neglect than did their counterparts from smaller families and were more likely to be regarded as endangered.

Source: Adapted from, *Study Findings, National Incidence and Prevalence of Child Abuse and Neglect* (Washington, D.C.: U.S. Department of Health and Human Services, 1988), pp. 1–10.

. . . a single parent who was young (under thirty), had been married for less than ten years, had his or her first child before the age of 18 and was unemployed or employed part-time. If he or she worked, it would be at a manual labor job . . . women are slightly more likely to abuse their children than men. The reason is rather obvious: women typically spend more time with children.[95]

It would be misleading to pinpoint any one of these factors as a definitive explanation of why abuse and neglect occur.

SUBSTANCE ABUSE AND CHILD ABUSE. Abusive and neglectful families suffer from severe stress, and it is therefore not surprising that they frequently harbor members who turn to drugs and alcohol. Research studies have found a strong association between child abuse and parental alcoholism.[96] In addition, there is evidence that a significant relationship exists between cocaine and heroin abuse and the neglect and physical abuse of children. A recent study of 108 cases of reported child abuse in Boston found that 64 percent involved some form of substance abuse, including parental involvement with cocaine (65 percent) and heroin (9 percent). Almost 90 percent of confirmed cases of abuse and neglect involving a victim under 1 year old occurred in families in which one or more members were drug users; about 68 percent of the abused infants were diagnosed as suffering congenital drug addiction themselves.[97]

It is now estimated that about 375,000 drug-exposed children are born each year.[98] A number of states, including Oklahoma, Massachusetts, Florida, and Utah, require child abuse reports in cases of drug dependence involving a child.[99] And courts are now considering child drug dependence as legally sufficient evidence to bring child abuse charges against parents.[100]

SOCIAL CLASS AND ABUSE. Official statistics show a high rate of reported abuse and neglect cases among lower economic classes, and this has led to the belief that parental maltreatment of children is predominantly a lower-class problem.[101] How can this lower-class predominance in child abuse statistics be explained?

One view is that the official statistics are generally accurate and that lower-class parents are in fact more abusive towards their children. Low-income families, especially those led by a single-parent, are often subject to greater levels of environmental stress and have fewer resources available to deal with such stress than families with higher incomes.[102] There seems to be a relationship between the burdens of raising a child absent adequate economic and social resources and the use of excessive force and discipline.

Another view is that child abuse rates are so high among the lower class because poor families are dealt with by public agencies that automatically report suspected cases of abuse. Higher-income families can afford private treatment, which shields their problems from public view.[103] Furthermore, courts and society in general are likely to look differently on abuse cases that involve well-educated suburban dwellers. It is also possible that attending physicians may label a child of middle-class parents "accident prone" under circumstances in which they would judge a lower-class child abused.[104] While this view seems plausible, research by Cecil Willis and Richard Wells indicates that police may actually be less likely to report child abuse by lower-class or minority families because they perceive that violence is more "normal" in these families and that black children "need" harsher discipline than white children.[105] The Willis and Wells research supports class differentials in the child abuse rate.

Robert Burgess and Patricia Draper offer a biosocial explanation for the class differences in child abuse.[106] They find that treatment of children is related to the actual "cost" to parents of perpetuating their genes through raising offspring. Higher rates of maltreatment in low-income families reflect the stress caused by the burdensome "investment" of resources lower-class parents make in raising their children. In contrast, middle-class parents devote a smaller percentage of their total economic resources to raising a family and therefore are less likely to perceive financial and social stress. According to this view, child abuse rates should be highest among lower-class families with large number of children: few resources must be spread among a large number of gene carriers, limiting the investment in each one's well-being. Burgess and Draper also note that higher abuse rates among emotionally and physically handicapped children may occur because these youngsters are "poor prospects for investment that will lead to their successful reproduction as adults."[107]

Sexual Abuse

One aspect of child abuse that has become an issue of growing national concern is sexual abuse. Sexual abuse can vary in content and style. It may range from rewarding a child for sexual behavior that is inappropriate for his or her level of development to using force or the threat of force for the purposes of sex. Sexual abuse can involve children who are well aware of the sexual content of their actions and others too young to have any real perception of what their actions mean. It can involve a variety of acts from inappropriate touching and fondling to forcible sexual penetration.

The incidence of sexual abuse is frightening. It has been estimated that perhaps one in ten boys and one in three girls have been the victim of some form of sexual exploitation. An often-cited survey by Diana Russell found that 16 percent of women reported sexual abuse by a relative and an additional 4.5 percent reported abuse by a father or stepfather.[108]

The effect of sexual abuse can be devastating. Abused children suffer disrupted ego and personality development.[109] Guilt and shame are commonly experienced by survivors, and psychological trauma sometimes continues into adulthood. The ego of the victim may be overwhelmed by rage and horror over the incident.[110] David Finkelhor and Angela Browne of the Family Violence Research Program at the University of New Hampshire have described the aftermath of sexual abuse as involving one of four dynamics:

1. *Traumatic sexualization*—is the process in which a child's sexual identity is shaped in an inappropriate and dysfunctional way by the result of the abuse episode.
2. *Betrayal*—refers to the discovery by the abused child that someone whom he or she trusted and upon whom he or she is dependent caused them harm.
3. *Powerlessness*—refers to the process in which the child's will, desires, and sense of competence are negated.
4. *Stigmatization*—refers to the negative connotations, such as shame and guilt, that are communicated to the child around his or her experiences and that then become incorporated into the child's self-image.[111]

The victim of child sexual abuse can experience a number of post-abuse traumas. Traumatic sexualization can lead children into such diverse behavior patterns as victimizing their peers, acting in a promiscuous and compulsive fashion, experiencing aversion to sex, or trading sex for affection.[112] It is common for victims to suffer frightening hallucinations, nightmares, and periods of profound rage.[113] Some victims find themselves sexualizing their own children in ways that lead them to sexual or physical abuse. Several studies have found a close association between sexual abuse and adolescent prostitution.[114] It has been estimated that 30 percent to 75 percent of women in treatment for substance abuse disorders have experienced childhood sexual abuse and rape.[115]

The Child Protection System: Philosophy and Practice

Although abusive parents are subject to prosecution in criminal courts under the traditional statutes against assault, battery, and homicide, they are most often dealt with in juvenile or family court. Specific neglect and abuse laws exist in each state, and they are generally more concerned with the care and protection of the child than with the punishment of the parents.

In 1974, Congress passed the **Child Abuse Prevention and Treatment Act**, which provides money to states to bolster their services to maltreated children and their parents. This act has been the impetus for all fifty states to improve the legal framework of their child protection systems. Many states now require the reporting of suspected neglect as well as abuse. State laws specifically prescribe procedures for the investigation and prosecution of cases. Most states have established specialized agencies to protect children. Most provide a **guardian** *ad litem* for the child (a lawyer appointed by the court to look after the interests of those who do not have the capacity to assert their own rights). States also ensure confidentiality of reporting and mandate professional training and public education programs.[116]

One major problem in enforcing abuse and neglect statutes is that maltreatment of children can easily be hidden from public view. Although state laws require doctors, teachers, and others who deal with children to report suspected cases to child protection agencies, many maltreated children are out of the law's reach because they are too young for school or because their parents do not take them to a doctor or a hospital. Parents abuse their children in private and, even when confronted, often accuse the children of lying or blame the children's medical problems on accidents of legitimate discipline. Thus, legal and social service agencies must find more effective ways to locate abused and neglected children and to provide procedures to handle such cases once they are found.

The number of confirmed cases of abuse and/or neglect that are petitioned to the juvenile or family court has more than doubled since 1980, probably due to the increase in sex abuse cases.[117] Unfounded accusations have become a significant problem, though, most likely because there has been a trend of spouses falsely accusing one another of physical and sexual abuse in divorce and custody cases.[118]

Once the court establishes jurisdiction in these cases, it is likely that the child will be separated from the parents, either temporarily or permanently. Furthermore, parents may be subject to criminal prosecution or supervision by law enforcement and social service agencies. In light of the frequency of this type of legal intervention in family life and its potentially negative effects on both the children and the parents, there is much disagreement as to when courts have the right to intervene and declare a child abused or neglected.[119]

Juvenile or family courts are generally guided by three interests: the role of the parents, protection for the child, and the responsibility of the state. Frequently, these interests conflict. In fact, at times, even the interests of the two parents are not in harmony. Ideally, the state attempts to balance the parents' natural right to control their children's upbringing with the child's right to grow into adulthood free from severe physical or emotional harm. This is generally referred to as the *balancing-of-the-interest approach*.

The legal system in the United States operates on a strong presumption of the autonomy of parents in matters affecting their children. Both common and statutory law have for centuries protected the primacy of the parental right to rear children free from undue intervention by the state. The interests of children, on the other hand, are less clearly understood and generally have not been recognized as legal rights.

LEGAL PROCESSING OF ABUSE CASES. Historical research shows child protection agencies were dealing with the problem of child abuse as early as the 1880s.[120] However, for most of the nation's history, courts have operated on the assumption that parents have the right to bring up their children as they see fit, but the awareness of the child abuse and neglect phenomenon has prompted judicial authorities to take increasingly bold steps to ensure the safety of children. The age-old assumption that the parent-child relationship is inviolate has been discarded. Unfortunately, because concerned state agents often lack the placement resources needed to make a significant adjustment in a child's life, children taken from the home may be shunted between foster homes and residential placement centers for unwanted, abused, or neglected youths.[121] Sometimes mere removal from the home is considered "treatment," when in reality it is simply warehousing. In far too many other cases, overworked social service agency staff find it impossible to keep up with the enormous number of cases which they must investigate and supervise. There are weekly media "horror" stories of children who are killed or maimed by parents because the local child care agency was too overworked to provide the proper degree of supervision or make follow-up investigations. Current cutbacks in state and local social service spending does not portend well for the child protection system.

Because the state has an interest in protecting children from harm and preventing future juvenile delinquency, it has removed children from homes, either temporarily or permanently, for neglect, extreme physical cruelty, lack of medical treatment, sexual abuse, drunkenness and debauchery, prostitution, adultery and cohabitation, mental illness, and the criminal conviction of a parent. But most substantiated child abuse cases do not result in either criminal prosecution or permanent removal of the child from the home. One estimate is that less than 5 percent of cases are criminally prosecuted.[122] The U.S. Department of Health and Human Services estimates that about 12 percent of all substantiated child abuse cases result in temporary or permanent foster care placements.[123] One reason is that removing the abuser may cause additional harm to the victim; in many cases, the remaining family members will blame the victim for the notoriety and stigma he or she caused and the fact that the imprisoned breadwinner may now be unable to support the family. As Judge Lindsay Arthur states: "Anger may be kept alive if the family is forever broken up, if the wound is kept open, instead of a return to some normalcy."[124] Surprisingly, the courts now seem more willing to remove sexually abused children from the home than those who face physical harm that could result in death.

THE PROCESS OF STATE INTERVENTION. At present, all fifty states have statutes requiring that persons suspected of abuse and neglect be reported. Many have gone as far as making failure to report child abuse a criminal offense.

Though such statutes are rarely enforced, there have actually been instances where teachers were arrested for failing to report cases involving abuse or neglect.[125]

Although procedures vary from state to state, most follow a similar legal process once a social service agency files criminal charges alleging abuse or neglect.[126] Parents have the right to counsel in all cases of abuse and neglect, and many states require the court to appoint an attorney for the child as well. The child's attorney, usually called a "guardian *ad litem*," often acts as an advocate for the child's welfare as well as providing legal assistance.

When an abuse or neglect petition is filed, an *advisement hearing* is held to notify the parents of the nature of the charges against them. If the parents admit the allegations, the court enters a consent decree and the case is continued for disposition. Approximately half of all cases are settled by admission of the advisement hearing. If the parents deny the petition, an attorney is appointed for the child and the case is continued for a pretrial conference.

At the *pretrial conference*, the attorney for the social service agency presents an overview of the case and summarizes the evidence. Such matters as admissibility of photographs and written reports are settled. The parents' attorney also reviews the facts of the case and reveals the evidence that will be used. At this point in the process, the attorneys can plea-bargain. As a result, about three-fourths of the cases that go to pretrial conference are settled by a consent decree. Thus, eighty-five out of every one hundred petitions filed will be settled at either the advisement hearing or the pretrial conference.

Of the fifteen remaining cases, five will generally be settled before trial. Usually, no more than ten cases out of every one hundred will actually reach the *trial stage* of the process. These few cases are tried with the regular adversary process, and the allegation of abuse and neglect is almost always readily proved. However, in recent years, some well-publicized trials, including the McMartin Day Care Center case (the longest trial in U.S. history), have resulted in not-guilty verdicts. In this case, as in others, some jurors believed that prosecutors were so anxious to get a conviction that they led young children to believe they were abused while the physical evidence told another story; children often retract their testimony. Consequently, prosecutors are now more likely to pursue cases brought to their attention very soon after the abuse took place and in which sound medical evidence of sexual abuse exists; these legal factors have also been associated with a high probability of conviction.[127]

From the perspective of both the child and the parents, the most crucial part of an abuse or neglect proceeding is the *disposition hearing*, an entirely separate process held after the adjudication. The social service agency presents its case plan, which includes recommendations for returning the child to the parents, any conditions the parents must meet, a visitation plan if the child is to be taken from the parents, and so on. The plan is discussed with the parents, and an agreement is reached by which the parents commit themselves to following it.

Periodically, *review hearings* are held to determine if the conditions of the case plan are being met. Parents who fail to cooperate are warned that they may lose their parental rights. Most abuse and neglect cases are concluded within a year. Either the parents lose their rights and the child is given a permanent placement, or the child is returned to the parents and the court's jurisdiction ends.

You are an investigator with the county Bureau of Social Services.

A case has been referred to you by the middle school's head guidance counselor. It seems that a young girl, Emily M., has been showing up to school in a dazed and listless condition. She has had a hard time concentrating in class, and seems withdrawn and uncommunicative. The 13-year-old has missed more than a normal share of school days and has often been late to class. Last week, she seemed so lethargic that her homeroom teacher sent her to the school nurse. A physical examination revealed that she was malnourished and in poor physical health. She also had evidence of bruising that could only come from a beating. Emily told the nurse that she had been punished by her parents for doing poorly at school and for failing to do her chores at home.

When her parents were called in to school to meet with the principal and head guidance counselor, they claimed that they are members of a religious order that strongly believes that children should be punished severely for their misdeeds. Emily had been placed on a restricted diet as well as beaten with a belt to correct her misbehavior. When the guidance counselor asked them if they would be willing to go into family therapy, they were furious and told her to "mind her own business." It's a sad day, they said, when "God-fearing American citizens cannot bring up their children according to their religious beliefs." The girl is in no immediate danger insofar as her punishment has not been life threatening.

The case is then referred to your office. When you go to see the parents at home, they refuse to make any change in their behavior and claim they are in the right and you are representative of all that is wrong with society. The lax discipline you want imposed leads to drugs, sex, and other teenage problems.

Should you get a court order removing Emily from her house and requiring the parents to go into counseling?

Should you report the case to the district attorney's office so it could proceed against her parents criminally under the state's Child Protection Act?

Should you take no further action, reasoning that Emily's parents have the right to discipline their child as they see fit?

Should you talk with Emily and see what she wants to happen?

THE ABUSED CHILD IN COURT. One of the most significant problems associated with the prosecution of child abuse and sexual abuse cases is the trauma that a child must go through in a court hearing. Children get confused and frightened and may change their testimony, resulting in dropped charges or mistrial. As one expert, Judge Lindsay Arthur of the National Council of Juvenile and Family Court Judges, put it:

The system may interview the child time and again, each time making her relive the experience, keeping the wound open. It may force her down to court waiting rooms, where she sits uncomfortably without even the accoutrements of a dentist's office for hours and then often to be told that the case was continued and to come back next week. She may be put on a witness stand, in a big formal room, with what seems like a thousand eyes staring at her, and a bailiff in full uniform ready to lock her up and a judge in a black robe towering above her. She may find that the newspapers and television are full of her name and pictures and stories about what happened to her, which they obtained from the official records. And this may make her the focus of her classmates with all the brutal teasing that can involve.

The system may also suddenly arrest her father and just as suddenly release him. It may plea-bargain away her future hope of rehabilitation without even talking to her, in the name of speedy justice.[128]

State jurisdictions have instituted a number of innovative procedures to minimize the trauma to the child. About twenty states allow the videotaping of children's testimony at a preliminary hearing in order to spare them the trauma of testifying in open court.[129] In addition to preliminary hearing videotapes, about half of the states now allow children to testify at trial by one- or two-way closed-circuit television. One-way systems permit the child to testify in a separate room in which only the judge, counsel, technicians, and in some cases the defendant are present.[130] Two-way systems permit the child to see the courtroom and the defendant over video monitors. In addition, thirty-three states (including nineteen that allow closed-circuit TV) permit the use of videotaped testimony at trial.[131]

While it is important for children testifying in abuse cases to feel comfortable and unafraid, protecting the child sometimes comes into conflict with the defendant's right to secure a fair trial. In the case of *Coy vs. Iowa*, the U.S. Supreme Court limited the protection available to child sex abuse victims at the trial stage. In *Coy*, two girls were allowed to be cross-examined behind a screen that separated them from the defendant. The court ruled that the screen violated the defendant's right to confront witnesses and overturned his conviction.[132] However, in her supporting opinion, Justice Sandra Day O'Connor made it clear that ruling out the protective screen did not bar the states from using videotapes or closed-circuit TV. Then in an important case, *Maryland v. Sandra Ann Craig*, the Court ruled that the use of one-way closed circuit television to receive the testimony of a victim of abuse was permissible if there was a prior determination that the child was suffering from serious emotional distress which would prevent the child from communicating in court. The Court ruled that the procedure used in Maryland was legally acceptable: the child prosecutor and defense counsel withdraw to another room where the child is examined and cross-examined. The judge, jury, and defendant remain in the courtroom where the testimony is displayed. Although the child cannot see the defendant, the defendant remains in electronic communications with counsel and can provide information upon which to raise objections.[133]

Children in sexual abuse cases are also now allowed to use anatomically correct dolls to enact happenings that they cannot describe verbally. Similarly, nine states have relaxed their laws of evidence to allow out-of-court statements by the child to a social worker, teacher, or police officer to be used as evidence (this would otherwise be considered hearsay). However, seven of the states that allow such statements require corroboration by others if the child does not testify.

The prevalence of sexual abuse cases has created new problems for the justice system. Accusations are often made in conjunction with marital disputes and

Here Dr. Elizabeth Morgan is released from jail after 25 months in captivity for failing to produce her daughter to the child's father for visitation rights.

separations. The nationally publicized case in which Dr. Elizabeth Morgan spent more than two years in a Washington, D.C., jail rather than reveal the whereabouts of her daughter illustrates the problem of sex abuse accusations in divorce and custody cases. Morgan had accused her ex-husband of abuse and refused him visitation rights even when ordered to do so by a district court judge. It took an act of Congress to secure Morgan's release from jail. Cases such as this makes it incumbent for the justice system to develop techniques that can get at the truth of the matter without creating a lifelong scar on the child's psyche.

DISPOSITION OF ABUSE AND NEGLECT CASES. Just as there is widespread disagreement about when state intervention into family life is appropriate, there is also considerable controversy over what forms of post-conviction intervention are helpful in abuse and neglect cases. Most often, children are separated from their parents, usually on a temporary basis. Children are removed from their homes in approximately half of all neglect proceedings. Placement of these children in foster care is intended to be temporary, but half of the children are likely to remain in foster care for three years or more.[134] Furthermore, children are likely to be shifted from one temporary home to another during this period, which severely deprives them of a stable home, may put them in situations where they may continue to be seriously abused or even killed, and may increase the risk of the negative psychological impact of destroying the parent-child relationship.

Ultimately, the court has the power to terminate the rights of parents over their children on a permanent basis, but because the effects of destroying the family unit are serious and far-reaching, the court does so only in the most severe cases. Most states distinguish between procedures to authorize temporary deprivation of custody and those resulting in permanent termination of parental rights. In general, moreover, much stricter statutory requirements exist for permanent termination than for temporary loss of custody rights.[135]

In the vast majority of abuse and neglect cases, permanent removal of the child is not warranted. Parents and children are required to participate in treatment programs that seek to rehabilitate the family and prevent a recurrence of the maltreatment. Such programs attempt to alter the psychological, social, and environmental factors that are at the root of the problem. Social casework, mental health services, day-care centers, homemaker services, parent effectiveness training, group therapy, and foster grandparent programs are among some of the most frequently utilized efforts to help children and parents avoid potential abuse or neglect situations. One of the most important and most difficult goals of such treatment services is to reduce the isolation of parents by helping them improve their relationships with others (family, friends, professionals) who may be able to provide help and support in crisis situations.

A widely used self-help therapeutic technique for abusive parents is Parents Anonymous. Parents Anonymous groups are guided by professional therapists who help parents find more appropriate ways of dealing with explosive family situations. Both parents are encouraged to attend, even if only one is actively engaged in the abuse, and the group helps them recognize their potential to be good parents without resorting to abuse.[136]

Despite such treatment programs, much more help is needed to deal effectively with the problem of child abuse and neglect. Even today, more organized services are available in the United States to prevent cruelty to animals than to children.[137] Furthermore, the efficacy of treatment programs is questionable. A three-year evaluation of thirteen child abuse and neglect service programs concluded that the chance of future abuse was lessened in only 42 percent of the cases by the time the treatment ended. In addition, acts of severe abuse or neglect recurred among 30 percent of the parents while they were in treatment.[138]

There has been an ongoing effort to improve the child protection system and reduce the chance of further abuse. Jurisdictions have expedited case processing, instituted court procedures designed not to frighten child witnesses, coordinated investigations between various social service and law enforcement agencies, and assigned an advocate or guardian *ad litem* to support the child in need of protection.

Legal Considerations

The courts have been active in recent years in providing legal guidelines that control procedures for state intervention in family matters. In the past, parents were given a free hand in bringing up their children. For example, in the case of

Prince v. Massachusetts, reaffirmed in the case of *Ginsberg v. New York*, the Supreme Court stated:

> First of all, constitutional interpretation has consistently recognized that the parents' claim to authority in their own household to direct the rearing of their children is basic in the structure of our society. It is cardinal with us that the custody, care, and nurture of the child reside first in the parents, whose primary function and freedom include preparation for obligations the state can neither supply nor hinder.[139]

As a result of this hands-off policy, the state has in the past given parents a free hand in the areas of medical care and privacy for their children, as well as in such areas as discipline, limits on speech, searching of a child's belongings, and even choosing a child's religion. In recent years, however, the state has considered children's rights primarily in the realms of medical care and privacy.

Legally, cases of child abuse or neglect are considered separate from the parents' right to reasonable discipline and control over their children. The most drastic action the state may take in instances of parental abuse is to remove the child from the home permanently and terminate parental rights and privileges. In *Lassiter v. Department of Social Services* and *Santosky v. Kramer*, the Supreme Court recognized the child's right to be free from parental abuse and set down guidelines for a termination-of-custody hearing.[140]

In general, states will seek termination if parents are abusive, mentally ill, or neglectful. And, in a number of recent cases, courts have held that children who are not protected from abusive parents can, under certain circumstances, sue the state for damages.

ABUSE AND DELINQUENCY

The immediate effects of abuse and neglect are evident—physical injury, malnutrition, emotional depression, death. Less obvious are the potential effects of maltreatment on its young victims. It encourages them to use aggression as a means of solving problems. It prevents them from feeling empathy for others. It diminishes their ability to cope with stress. It makes them vulnerable to the aggression and violence in the culture.

Definitive support for a direct causal relationship between an abusive childhood and delinquency is lacking, but researchers generally agree that abuse and neglect may have a profound effect on behavior in later years. Exposure to excessive physical aggression and emotional chaos in early life provides a foundation for several varieties of violent and antisocial behavior. In fact, sociologists Richard Gelles and Murray Straus state that "with the exception of the police and the military, the family is perhaps the most violent social group, and the home the most violent social setting, in our society."[141]

Aggressive, delinquent behavior is the means by which many abused or neglected children act out their hostility toward their parents. Some join gangs, which furnish a sense of belonging and allow pent-up anger to be expressed in group-approved delinquent acts.

A 1975 Philadelphia study found that 82 percent of the juvenile offenders in the sample were abused as children; 43 percent remembered being knocked unconscious by a parent. A research project among two hundred juveniles in a detention center in Denver reported that 72 percent remembered being seriously injured by their parents. Statements of one hundred of these juveniles, confirmed by their parents or other reliable sources, revealed that 84 percent were significantly abused before the age of 6, and 92 percent were bruised, lacerated, or fractured within one and a half years prior to their apprehension for delinquency.[142] Likewise, studies of persons convicted of murder reveal "a demonstrable association between homicide and maltreatment in early childhood."[143] Among children who kill or who attempt murder, the most common factor is said to be "the child's tendency to identify himself with aggressive parents and pattern after their behavior."[144] One study of several cases of murder and murderous assault by juveniles indicated that in all cases, "one or both parents had fostered and condoned murderous assault."[145] Similarly, C.H. King found that adolescent boys who had committed homicide as teenagers reported being beaten more often than their brothers and sisters.[146]

A number of empirical studies link delinquency with severe physical punishment and/or abuse. Jeanette Abrams found such a relationship in a sample of over 1,300 high school youths.[147] A similar project studied the records of 5,392 children referred to the Arizona State Department of Economic Security for child abuse or neglect. Of the total cases, 873, or 16.2 percent, had been referred to juvenile court, again indicating a substantial link between abuse and neglect and subsequent delinquency.[148] In addition, a study of incarcerated youths in Texas found that 29 percent of the sample had been physically abused. In a similar study in Arkansas, the figure was 86 percent.[149]

Another study compared the child abuse records of matched samples of 109 delinquent and nondelinquent youths in New Haven, Connecticut.[150] Looking at the records of the major hospital serving the area, the study found that 8.6 percent of the delinquents and only 1 percent of the nondelinquents had required hospital service for abuse. Furthermore, 36 percent of the delinquents, as compared with 21.6 percent of the nondelinquents, had received treatment for head and face injuries, which are considered instances of possible abuse.

One other large-scale study of the link between child abuse and delinquency is noteworthy. Psychiatrist Richard Jenkins evaluated the records of 1,500 youths referred to a mental health clinic in Chicago. Of these, 445 had been referred by the juvenile court for aggressive and assaultive delinquency. A second group of 231 youths had been sent by the court because of their records of property offenses.[151] Jenkins found that the assaultive and aggressive juveniles came from families that were punitive and rejecting and that used extreme and inconsistent measures of physical punishment. The property offenders generally had family backgrounds marked by poverty and by neglectful parents who were frequently alcoholic, promiscuous, and irresponsible.

Cohort Studies

An important way of studying the relationship between child abuse and delinquency is to select a cohort of youth who had been reported for child abuse and neglect early in their lives and then compare them with a similar cohort of nonabused youth. One such study was conducted by Jose Alfaro in New York, who found that (a) a significant number of children (50 percent) who were reported to area hospitals as abused children later grew up to become delinquents; (b) a significant number of boys (21 percent) and girls (29 percent) petitioned to juvenile courts had earlier been referred to clinics as abuse cases; (c) abuse/neglect cases were later overrepresented in violent delinquency, including homicide, rape and assault; and (d) the families of reported abuse/neglect cases tended to be larger, single-parent households with a large number of illegitimate children.[152]

In an important recent study, Cathy Spatz Widom compared 908 abuse cases with a control group of 667 nonabused youth. Widom found that overall, 29 percent of those who were abused and neglected later developed adult criminal records as compared to 21 percent of the control groups. This ratio was *less* than might be expected, considering the assumed abuse-delinquency relationship. Widom found that race, sex, and age impacted the abuse-delinquency relationship: the highest risk group were older, black males who had suffered abuse; about 67 percent of this group went on to become adult criminals. In contrast, only 4 percent of young, white females became adult offenders.[153]

Such research findings indicate that not all abused or neglected children eventually become violent delinquents. Many do not, and many seriously delinquent youths come from what appear to be model homes. They do suggest, however, that many youths who break the law, especially through acts of violence, have a history of maltreatment as children. Efforts to combat maltreatment are vital, therefore, for preventing both the immediate harm caused by abuse and for reducing the possibility that the victims will settle into patterns of violent, aggressive criminal behavior throughout their lives.

THE FAMILY AND DELINQUENCY PREVENTION

Since the family is believed to play such an important role in the production of youth crime, it follows that improving family functioning can help prevent delinquency. Consequently, it is common to find counselors working with the families of antisocial youth as part of a court-ordered treatment strategy. Family counseling and therapy is almost mandatory when the child's acting-out behavior is suspected to be the result of family-related problems, such as child abuse or neglect.[154] Some jurisdictions have created family counseling services that are integrated within the juvenile court.[155]

Another approach to involving the family in delinquency prevention is to attack the problem before it occurs. The most widely cited program is the one created at the *Oregon Social Learning Center (OSLC)* by *Gerald R. Patterson* and his associates.[156] Patterson's long research into the life-styles of antisocial children convinced him that poor parenting skills are associated with antisocial behavior occurring in the home and at school. Family disruption and coercive exchanges between parents and children led to increased family tension, poor academic performance, and negative peer relations. The primary cause of the problem seemed to be that parents did not know how to deal with their children in an effective manner. They sometimes ignored their children's behavior, while at other times, the same childish actions would result in explosive rage. Some parents would discipline their children for reasons that had little to do with the children's behavior but reflected their own frustrations and conflicts.

Children in turn would react to indifferent parenting in a regular progression from learning to be noncompliant at home to learning to be physically assaultive. Their "coercive behavior," which included whining, yelling, and temper tantrums, may be acquired by other family members, thus exacerbating an already explosive situation. Eventually, family conflict would escalate and flow out of the home into the school and social environment.

The OSLC program uses behavior modification techniques to help parents of antisocial children acquire proper care and disciplinary methods. Parents are asked to select several particular behaviors for change. Staff counselors first analyze family dynamics and then work with parents to construct a change program. Parents are asked to closely monitor the particular behaviors and to count the weekly frequency of their occurrence. OSLC personnel teach both prosocial skills to reinforce positive behaviors and constructive disciplinary methods to discourage negative ones. Incentive programs are initiated in which a child can earn points or praise for such desirable behaviors as being cooperative, doing chores, and so on. Points can be exchanged for an allowance, prizes, or privileges. Parents are also taught effective disciplinary techniques that stress firmness and consistency, rather than "nattering" (low-intensity nonverbal or negative verbal behaviors, such as scowling or scolding) or explosive discipline, such as hitting, humiliating remarks, or screaming. One important technique is the "time out" in which the child is removed for brief isolation in a quiet room. Parents are taught the importance of setting rules and sticking to them.

Most evaluations indicate that the OSLC methods can be highly successful.[157] One program that uses these techniques is the Family Teaching Center in Helena, Montana.

This program is based on the premise that children learn disruptive, violent, and delinquent behaviors through daily interactions with members of their natural communities—parents, kin, peers, and teachers. Delinquency is learned through reinforcement in social interactions; deviant behaviors will continue to occur only so long as they are supported by others. When taught how their responses support problem behaviors, parents can learn to change their interactions and therefore prevent children's delinquent and oppositional behaviors.

The program serves working and middle-class, two-parent and single-parent families with aggressive or out-of-control children ages 4 to 12. The family is the starting point for therapeutic intervention. Initially, therapists meet the family in the home, observing the family's interactive style and administering a self-concept scale to the child. Therapists also instruct parents in the use of a parent daily report instrument that the Family Teaching Center staff uses in monitoring the child's behavior.

Parents attend a series of six to seven weekly evening classes that focus on child management skills. They learn to: 1) pinpoint and observe problems and prosocial behavior; 2) use social activity and tangible reinforces to strengthen appropriate behavior; 3) apply mild punishment in a nonabusive and corrective manner; 4) modify or extend the basic treatment strategies to other children in the family or to new problems; and 5) evaluate their effectiveness using data they collect.

After treatment, the families enter a one-year "fadeout" follow-up period during which the Family Teaching Center staff maintains periodic telephone contact.

The Family Teaching Center also has a school involvement program. School contact begins after the parents have completed several instructional sessions. Depending on the child's need and the school's desire to participate in the program, interventions may consist of an individualized child-school program collaboratively arranged by the Family Teaching Center therapist, school teachers, and social service personnel.[158]

A similar program is Homebuilders of Tacoma, Washington.[159] Homebuilders attempts to strengthen the family unit through parenting training and communication skills. These skills can increase attachment between parents and children and can prevent a further deterioration of the family unit, out-of-home placement, and juvenile delinquency.

Homebuilders began in 1974 as part of a National Institute of Mental Health grant awarded to an affiliated group of five social, educational, and medical service agencies in Tacoma. Homebuilders functions under Catholic Community Services of Tacoma, a nonprofit social service agency. The program is now classified as a mental health program licensed through the State of Washington. According to the current program director the program functions on the same basic premise today as it did at its inception.

Families experiencing a variety of problems are accepted for service if at least one family member expresses a desire to keep the family together and no key family member absolutely refuses to participate. Homebuilders is a short-term, intensive, in-home, family-systems-based approach designed to improve family interactions and preserve the family structure. Therapists interview in the homes of families in crisis and remain until relative stability is achieved. The first session may last up to eight hours, and staff may spend the night at the family's home. Therapists stay involved with a family from three weeks to six months. To maximize the therapists' availability to clients, they are limited to no more than two new cases per month and may have no more than three families on their caseload at one time.

Homebuilders uses a parent effectiveness training procedure, "active listening," to elicit information in a supportive manner. When possible the Homebuilders therapist involves representatives from the local youth services bureau or other community service agency to tie the family into a network of social services and to provide the family with support when the crisis is over.

Clients have their therapists' home phone number, and these therapists are on call twenty-four hours a day, seven days a week in case of crisis.

A service recently added to Homebuilders is family intervention on behalf of youthful sex offenders. The target population is 12 to 14 year-olds and involves having a staff member in the home twenty-four hours a day and twenty hours of therapy a week. In some situations, the staff member even attends school with the client. After six months, the child is released to outpatient counseling, which occurs once a week.

The success rate of the Homebuilders program, along with its sex offender portion, runs very high. The overall program success rate, based on keeping these children in the home and out of out-of-home placements, including psychiatric hospitals, is estimated at 90 percent.

Ongoing research and evaluation is needed to formulate the best methods to use with particular problem areas. For example, what works for 10-year-olds who steal may not be the best method to use with assaultive teenagers.

SUMMARY

Family relationships have long been linked to the problem of juvenile delinquency. Early theories viewed the broken home as a cause of youthful misconduct, but recent research indicates that divorce, separation, or the death of parents play a smaller role in influencing delinquent acts than previously thought. Other expects have suggested that the quality of family life has the greatest influence on a child's behavior. Keeping this in mind, studies have explored the effect of discipline, parental misconduct, and family harmony on youth crime.

Concern over the relationship between family life and delinquency has been heightened by reports of widespread child abuse and neglect. Cases of abuse and neglect have been found in every level of the economic strata, and it has been estimated that almost two million youths are subject to abuse each year from their parents.

Two factors are seen as causing child abuse. First, parents who themselves suffered abuse as children tend to abuse their own children. Second, isolated and alienated families tend to become abusive.

Local, state, and federal governments have attempted to alleviate the problem of child abuse. The major problem has been the issue of state interference in the family structure and the lack of monetary support for services. At present, all fifty states have statutes requiring that suspected cases of abuse and neglect be reported.

A number of studies have linked abuse and neglect to juvenile delinquency. Studies show that a disproportionate number of court-adjudicated youths had experienced child abuse or neglect. While the evidence so far is not conclusive, it suggests that there exists a strong relationship between child abuse and neglect and subsequent delinquent behavior.

QUESTIONS FOR DISCUSSION

1. What is the meaning of the terms *child abuse* and *child neglect*?
2. Social agencies, police departments, and health groups all indicate that child abuse and neglect are increasing. What is the incidence of such action by parents against children? Are the definitions of *child abuse* and *child neglect* the key elements in determining the volume of child abuse cases in various jurisdictions?
3. What causes parents to abuse their children?
4. What is meant by the *child protection system?* Do courts act in the best interest of the child when they allow an abused child to remain with the family?

KEY TERMS

paternalistic family
single-parent households
family day care
poverty

broken home
discipline
beyond control
intrafamily conflict

birth order
child abuse
neglect

endangered children
Child Abuse Prevention and Treatment Act
guardian *ad litem*

NOTES

1. For general reviews of the relationship between families and delinquency, see Alan Jay Lincoln and Murray Straus, *Crime and The Family* (Springfield: Ill.: Charles C. Thomas, 1985); Rolf Loeber and Magda Stouthamer-Loeber, "Family Factors as Correlates and Predictors of Juvenile Conduct Problems and Delinquency," *Crime and Justice, An Annual Review of Research*, vol. 7, ed. Michael Tonry and Norval Morris (Chicago: University of Chicago Press, 1986), pp. 29–151. (Herein cited as "Family Factors.").

2. Scott Henggeler, ed., *Delinquency and Adolescent Psychopathology: A Family Ecological Systems Approach* (Littleton, Mass.: Wright-PSG, 1982).

3. Ruth Inglis, *Sins of the Fathers: A Study of the Physical and Emotional Abuse of Children* (New York: St. Martin's Press, 1978), p. 131.

4. See Joseph J. Costa and Gordon K. Nelson, *Child Abuse and Neglect: Legislation, Reporting, and Prevention* (Lexington, Mass.: D.C. Heath, 1978), p. xiii.

5. Ian Robertson, *Sociology* (New York: Worth, 1988), p. 363.

6. S. E. Shank, "Women and the Labor Market: The Link Grows Stronger," *Monthly Labor Review* 111:3–8 (1988).

7. Edward Zigler, "Addressing the Nation's Child-Care Crisis: The School of the Twenty-First Century," *American Journal of Orthopsychiatry* 59:484–91 (1989).

8. *Ibid.*, p. 486.

9. National Research Council, *Common Destiny: Blacks and American Society* (Washington, D.C.: National Research Council, 1989).

10. *Ibid.*

11. Edward Zigler, "Addressing the Nation's Child-Care Crisis: The School of the Twenty-First Century," pp. 488–89.

12. Richard Gelles and Murray Straus, *Intimate Violence* (New York: Simon and Schuster, 1988), p. 27.

13. Deborah Cohn, "Child-Mother Attachment of Six-Year-Olds and Social Competence at School," *Child Development* 61: 152–62 (1990).

14. National Advisory Commission on Criminal Justice Standards and Goals, *Juvenile Justice and Delinquency Prevention* (Washington, D.C.: U.S. Government Printing Office, 1976), p. 78.

15. *Ibid.*, p. 92.

16. J. C. Schwartz, "Childhood Origins of Psychopathology," *American Psychologist* 34:573–80 (1979).

17. Michael Rutter, *Changing Youth in a Changing Society* (Cambridge, Mass.: Harvard University Press, 1980).

18. D. J. West, *Who Becomes Delinquent?* (London: Heinemann, 1973).

19. Loeber and Stouthamer-Loeber, "Family Factors," pp. 39–41.

20. Scott Hongeller, *Delinquency in Adolescence* (Newbury Park, Calif.: Sage, 1989) p. 48.

21. Sadi Bayrakal and Teresa Kope, "Dysfunction in the Single-Parent and Only-Child Family," *Adolescence* 25:1–7 (1990).

22. C. Patrick Brady, James Bray, and Linda Zeeb, "Behavior Problems of Clinic Children: Relation to Parental Marital Status, Age, and Sex of Child," *American Journal of Orthopsychiatry* 56:399–412 (1986).

23. Sheldon Glueck and Eleanor Glueck, *Unraveling Juvenile Delinquency* (Cambridge, Mass.: Harvard University Press, 1950); Ashley Weeks, "Predicting Juvenile Delinquency," *American Sociological Review* 8:40–46 (1943).

24. Jackson Toby, "The Differential Impact of Family Disorganization," *American Sociological Review* 22:505–12 (1957); Ruth Morris, "Female Delinquency and Relation Problems," *Social Forces* 43:82–89 (1964).

25. Roland Chilton and Gerald Markle, "Family Disruption, Delinquent Conduct, and the Effects of Subclassification," *American Sociological Review* 37:93–99 (1972).

26. For a review of these early studies, see Thomas Monahan, "Family Status and the Delinquent Child: A Reappraisal and Some New Findings," *Social Forces* 35:250–58 (1957).

27. Clifford Shaw and Henry McKay, *Report on the Causes of Crime*, vol. 2, *Social Factors in Juvenile Delinquency* (Washington, D.C.: U.S. Government Printing Office, 1931), p. 392.

28. John Laub and Robert Sampson, "Unraveling Families and Delinquency: A Reanalysis of the Gluecks' Data," *Criminology* 26:355–80 (1988); Lawrence Rosen, "The Broken Home and Male Delinquency," in *The Sociology of Crime and Delinquency*, ed. M. Wolfgang, L. Savitz, and N. Johnston (New York: Wiley, 1970), pp. 489–95.

29. Richard Johnson, "The Broken Home Revisited: A Cause of Delinquent Behavior?" (Paper presented at the Academy of Criminal Justice Sciences, Philadelphia, March 1981).

30. Loeber and Stouthamer-Loeber, "Family Factors," p. 78.

31. Lawrence Rosen and Kathleen Neilson, "Broken Homes," in *Contemporary Criminology*, ed. Leonard Savitz and Norman Johnston (New York: Wiley, 1982), pp. 126–35.

32. *Ibid.*, p. 14.

33. Joseph Rankin, "The Family Context of Delinquency," *Social Problems* 30:466–79 (1983).

34. James Q. Wilson and Richard Herrnstein, *Crime and Human Nature* (New York: Simon and Schuster, 1985) p. 249.

35. Gerald Patterson and Magda Stouthamer-Loeber, "The Correlation of Family Management Practices and Delinquency," *Child Development* 55:1299–1307 (1984).

36. Gerald R. Patterson, *A Social Learning Approach: Coercive Family Process*, vol. 3 (Eugene, Ore.: Castalia, 1982).

37. F. Ivan Nye, *Family Relationships and Delinquent Behavior* (New York: Wiley, 1938).

38. Rolf Loeber and Thomas Dishion, "Boys Who Fight at Home and School: Family Conditions Influencing Cross-Setting Consistency," *Journal of Consulting and Clinical Psychology* 52:759–68 (1984).

39. Laub and Sampson, "Unraveling Families and Delinquency," p. 370.

40. Charles Tittle, *Sanctions and Social Deviance* (New York: Praeger, 1980).

41. Gary Jensen and Raymond Eve, "Sex Differences in Delinquency: An Examination of Popular Sociological Explanation," *Criminology* 13:427–48 (1976).

42. Stephen Cernkovich and Peggy Giordano, "Family Relationships and Delinquency," *Criminology* 25:295–321 (1987).

43. Keith Warren and Ray Johnson, "Family Environment, Affect, Ambivalence, and Decisions about Unplanned Adolescent Pregnancy," *Adolescence* 24:630–41 (1989).

44. Marvin Krohn, Susan Stern, Terence Thornberry, and Sung Joon Jang, *Family Processes and Initiation of Delinquency and Drug Use: The Impact of Parent and Adolescent Perceptions* (Albany, N.Y.: Hindelang Research Center, unpublished working paper, n.d.).

45. Hongeller, *Delinquency in Adolescence*, p. 39.

46. Jill Leslie Rosenbaum, "Family Dysfunction and Female Delinquency," *Crime and Delinquency* 35:31–44 (1989) at 41.

47. Cindy Hanson, Scott Henggeler, William Haefele, and J. Douglas Rodick, "Demographic, Individual, and Familial Relationship Correlates of Serious and Repeated Crime among Adolescents and Their Siblings," *Journal of Consulting and Clinical Psychology* 52:528–38 (1984) at 536.

48. Richard Smith and James Walters, "Delinquent and Nondelinquent Males' Perceptions of Their Fathers," *Adolescence* 13:21–28 (1978).

49. Laub and Sampson, "Unraveling Families and Delinquency," p. 375.

50. Hanson, et al., "Demographic, Individual, and Familial Relationship Correlates of Serious and Repeated Crime among Adolescents and Their Siblings."

51. Hongeller, *Delinquency in Adolescence*, p. 42.

52. Paul Robinson, "Parents of 'Beyond Control' Adolescents," *Adolescence* 13:116–19 (1978).

53. Paul Howes and Howard Markman, "Marital Quality and Child Functioning: A Longitudinal Investigation," *Child Development* 60:1044–51 (1989).

54. Judith Smetana, "Adolescents' and Parents' Reasoning about Actual Family Conflict," *Child Development* 60:1052–67 (1989).

55. F. Ivan Nye, "Child Adjustment in Broken and Unhappy Unbroken Homes," *Marriage and Family* 19:356–61 (1957); idem, *Family Relationships and Delinquent Behavior* (New York: Wiley, 1958).

56. Michael Hershorn and Alan Rosenbaum, "Children of Marital Violence: A Closer Look at the Unintended Victims," *American Journal of Orthopsychiatry* 55:260–66 (1985).

57. Peter Jaffe, David Wolfe, Susan Wilson, and Lydia Zak, "Similarities in Behavior and Social Maladjustment among Child Victims and Witnesses to Family Violence," *American Journal of Orthopsychiatry* 56:142–46 (1986).

58. Louise Biron and Marc LeBlanc, "Family Components and Home-Based Delinquency," *British Journal of Criminology* 17:157–68 (1977); Denise Kandel, "On Variations in Adolescent Subcultures," *Youth and Society* 9:373–84 (1973).

59. For an early review, see Barbara Wooton, *Social Science and Social Pathology* (London: Allen and Unwin, 1959).

60. Donald J. West and David P. Farrington, "Who Becomes Delinquent?" in *The Delinquent Way of Life* (London: Heinemann, 1977); Donald J. West, *Delinquency, Its Roots, Careers, and Prospects* (Cambridge, Mass.: Harvard University Press, 1982).

61. West, *Delinquency*, p. 114.

62. Laub and Sampson, "Unraveling Families and Delinquency," p. 375.

63. Wooton, *Social Science and Social Pathology*; H. Wilson, "Juvenile Delinquency, Parental Criminality, and Social Handicaps," *British Journal of Criminology* 15:241–50 (1975).

64. G. Rahav, "Birth Order and Delinquency," *British Journal of Criminology* 20:385–95 (1980); D. Viles and D. Challinger, "Family Size and Birth Order of Young Offenders," *International Journal of Offender Therapy and Comparative Criminology* 25:60–66 (1981).

65. Karen Wilkonson, B. Grant Stitt, and Maynard Erickson, "Siblings and Delinquent Behavior," *Criminology* 20:223–40 (1982).

66. Deborah Denno, "Victim, Offender, and Situational Characteristics of Violent Crime," *Journal of Criminal Law and Criminology* 77:1142–58 (1987).

67. Merry Morash with Lila Rucker, "An Exploratory Study of the Connection of Mother's Age at Childbearing to Her Children's Delinquency in Four Data Sets," *Crime and Delinquency* 35:45–93 (1989).

68. Daniel Glaser, *Crime in Our Changing Society* (New York: Holt, Rinehart & Winston, 1978) p. 246. See also Lois Hochhauser, "Child Abuse and the Law: A Mandate for Change," *Harvard Law Journal* 18:200 (1973); Douglas J. Besharov, "The Legal Aspects of Reporting Known and Suspected Child Abuse and Neglect," *Villanova Law Review* 23:458 (1978).

69. C. Henry Kempe, C. H. Kempe, F. N. Silverman. B. F. Steele, W. Droegemueller, and H. K. Silver, "The Battered-Child Syndrome," *Journal of the American Medical Association* 181:17–24 (1962).

70. Vincent J. Fontana, "The Maltreated Children of Our Times," *Villanova Law Review* 23:448 (1978).

71. Ray E. Helfer and C. Henry Kempe, eds., *Child Abuse and Neglect: The Family and the Community* (Cambridge, Mass.: Ballinger, 1976), p. xix.

72. Brian G. Fraser, "A Glance at the Past, a Gaze at the Present, a Glimpse at the Future: A Critical Analysis of the Development of Child Abuse Reporting Statutes," *Chicago-Kent Law Review* 54:643 (1977–78).

73. *Ibid.*

74. Vincent J. Fontana, "To Prevent the Abuse of the Future," *Trial* 10:14 (1974).

75. See especially Inglis, *Sins of the Fathers*, chap. 8.

76. Ruth S. Kempe and C. Henry Kempe, *Child Abuse* (Cambridge, Mass.: Harvard University Press, 1978), pp. 6–7.

77. National Advisory Commission on Criminal Justice Standards and Goals, *Juvenile Justice and Delinquency Prevention* (Washington, D.C.: United States Government Printing Office, 1977); Institute of Judicial Administration, American Bar Association Juvenile Justice Standards Project, *Standards Relating to Abuse and Neglect* (Cambridge, Mass.: Ballinger, 1977).

78. Murray Straus, Richard Gelles, and Suzanne Steinmetz, *Behind Closed Doors: Violence in the American Family* (Garden City, N.Y.: Anchor Books, 1980); Richard Gelles and Murray Straus, "Violence in the American Family," *Journal of Social Issues* 35:15–39 (1979).

79. *Ibid.*, p. 24.

80. Straus, Gelles, and Steinmetz, *Behind Closed Doors*.

81. Gelles and Straus, *Intimate Violence*, pp. 108–9.

82. Richard Gelles and Murray Stauss, *Is Violence toward Children Increasing? A Comparison of 1975 and 1985 National Survey Rates* (Durham, N.H.: Durham Family Violence Research Program, 1985).

83. E. Newberger, C. M. Newberger, and R. Hampton, "Child Abuse: The Current Theory Base and Future Research Needs," *Journal of Child Psychiatry* 22:262–68 (1983).

84. American Humane Association, *Annual Report 1984, Highlights of Official Child Neglect and Abuse Reporting* (Denver: American Humane Association, 1986).

85. Robin Alsop and Katy Bond, American Humane Association, personal communication, 14 February 1990.

86. American Humane Association, *Annual Report 1984*, p.13.

87. Fraser, "A Glance at the Past, A Gaze at the Present, a Glimpse of the Future," p. 644.

88. Carolyn Webster-Stratton, "Comparison of Abusive and Nonabusive Families with Conduct-Disordered Children," *American Journal of Orthopsychiatry* 55:59–69 (1985).

89. Fontana, "To Prevent the Abuse of the Future," p. 16; idem, "The Maltreated Children of Our Times," p. 451; Brandt F. Steele and Carl B. Pollock, "A Psychiatric Study of Parents Who Abuse Infants and Small Children," in *The Battered Child*, ed. Ray Helfer and C. Henry Kempe (Chicago: University of Chicago Press, 1968), pp. 103–45.

90. Inglis, *Sins of the Fathers*, p. 68.

91. *Ibid.*, p. 53.

92. Brandt F. Steele, "Violence within the Family," in Helfer and Kempe, *Child Abuse and Neglect*, p. 13.

93. William Sack, Robert Mason, and James Higgins, "The Single-Parent Family and Abusive Punishment," *American journal of Orthopsychiatry* 55:252–59 (1985).

94. Fontana, "The Maltreated Children of Our Times," pp. 450–451. See also Blair Justice and Rita Justice, *The Abusing Family* (New York: Human Sciences Press, 1976); Steele, "Violence within the Family," p. 12; Nanette Dembitz, "Preventing Youth Crime by Preventing Child Neglect," *American Bar Association Journal* 65:920–23 (1979).

95. Gelles and Straus, *Intimate Violence*, p. 85.

96. Richard Famularo, Karen Stone, Richard Barnum, and Robert Wharton, "Alcoholism and Severe Child Maltreatment," *American Journal of Orthopsychiatry* 56:481–85 (1987).

97. Jordana Hart, "Child Abuse Found Tied to Drug Use," *Boston Globe*, 2 June 1989, p. 23.

98. Abigail English and Marcia Henry, "Legal Issues Affecting Drug-Exposed Infants," *Youth Law News* 11:1–2 (1990).

99. Abigail English, "Prenatal Drug Exposure: Grounds for Mandatory Child Abuse Reports?" *Youth Law News* 11:3–8 (1990).

100. In re Troy D., 263 Cal Rptr. 869 (Cal. App. 4th Dist. 1989).

101. David Gil, "Violence against Children," *Journal of Marriage and the Family* 33:644–48 (1971).

102. Richard Gelles, "Child Abuse and Violence in Single-Parent Families: Parent Absence and Economic Deprivation," *American Journal of Orthopsychiatry* 59:492-501 (1989).

103. Karla McPherson and Laura Garcia, "Effects of Social Class and Familiarity on Pediatricians' Responses to Child Abuse," *Child Welfare* 62:387–93 (1983).

104. S. Bittner and E. H. Newberger, "Pediatric Understanding of Child Abuse," *Pediatrics in Review* 7:197–207 (1981); see also E. H. Newberger and P. Bourne, "The Medicalization and Legalization of Child Abuse," *American Journal of Orthopsychiatry* 48:593–607 (1978).

105. Cecil Willis and Richard Wells, "The Police and Child Abuse: An Analysis of Police Decisions to Report Illegal Behavior," *Criminology* 26:695–716 (1988).

106. Robert Burgess and Patricia Draper, "The Explanation of Family Violence," in *Family Violence*, ed. Lloyd Ohlin and Michael Tonry, (Chicago: University of Chicago Press, 1989), pp. 59–117.

107. Ibid., pp. 103–4.

108. Diana Russell, *Sexual Exploitation: Rape, Child Sexual Abuse, and Workplace Harassment* (Beverly Hills, Calif.: Sage, 1984).

109. Herman Daldin, "The Fate of the Sexually Abused Child," *Clinical Social Work Journal* 16:20–26 (1988).

110. Gerald Ellenson, "Horror, Rage, and Defenses in the Symptoms of Female Sexual Abuse Survivors," *Social Casework: The Journal of Contemporary Social Work* 70:589–96 (1989).

111. David Finkelhor and Angela Browne, "The Traumatic Impact of Child Sexual Abuse: A Conceptualization," *American Journal of Orthopsychiatry* 55:530–41 (1985).

112. David Goldston, Dawn Turnquist, and John Knutson, "Presenting Problems of Sexually Abused Girls Receiving Psychiatric Services," *Journal of Abnormal Psychology* 98:314–17 (1989).

113. Ellenson, "Horror, Rage, and Defenses in the Symptoms of Female Sexual Abuse Survivors," pp. 589–91.

114. Magnus Seng, "Child Sexual Abuse and Adolescent Prostitution: A Comparative Analysis," *Adolescence* 24:665–75 (1989); Dorothy Bracey, *Baby Pros: Preliminary Profiles of Juvenile Prostitutes* (New York: John Jay Press, 1979).

115. Maria Root, "Treatment Failures: The Role of Sexual Victimization in Women's Addictive Behavior," *American Journal of Orthopsychiatry* 59:543–49 (1989).

116. Besharov, "The Legal Aspects of Reporting Known and Suspected Child Abuse and Neglect," pp. 459–460; Glaser, *Crime in Our Changing Society*, p. 246. For a survey of each state's reporting requirements, abuse and neglect legislation, and available programs and agencies, see Costa and Nelson, *Child Abuse and Neglect*.

117. American Humane Association, *Highlights of Official Child Neglect and Abuse Reporting 1984*, p. 30; David Finkelhor, "Removing the Child—Prosecuting the Offender in Cases of Sexual Abuse: Evidence from the National Reporting System for Child Abuse and Neglect," *Child Abuse and Neglect* 7:195–205 (1983).

118. "False Accusations of Abuse Devastating to Families," *Crime Victims Digest* 6 (2):4–5 (1989).

119. Judith Areen, "Intervention between Parent and Child: A Reappraisal of the State's Role in Child Neglect and Abuse Cases," *Georgetown Law Review* 63:887–88 (1975).

120. Linda Gordon, "Incest and Resistance: Patterns of Father-Daughter Incest, 1880–1930," *Social Problems* 33:253–67 (1986).

121. A. Haeuser, J. Stenlund, and L. Daniel, "Policy Program Implications in the Child Delinquency Correlation," in R. Hunner and Y. E. Walker, *Exploring the Relationship between Child Abuse and Delinquency* (Montclair, N.J.: Allanheld, Osmun, 1981), p. 15.

122. Patricia Tjaden and Nancy Thoennes, "Predictors of Criminal Prosecution in Intrafamily Child Abuse and

Neglect," (Paper presented at the Annual Meeting of the American Society of Criminology, Reno, Nevada, November 1989).

123. Finkelhor, "Removing the Child," p. 199.

124. Lindsay Arthur, "Child Sexual Abuse," *Juvenile and Family Court Journal* 37:12 (1986); see also Judith Herman, Diana Russell, and Karen Trocki, "Long-Term Effects of Incestuous Abuse in Childhood," *American Journal of Psychiatry* 143:1293–96 (1986).

125. Martha Brannigan, "Arrests Spark Furor over the Reporting of Suspected Abuse," *Wall Street Journal*, 7 June 1989, p. B8.

126. For a complete discussion of procedures used in neglect cases, see Michael S. Wald, "State Intervention on Behalf of 'Neglected Children': A Search for Standards for Placement of Children in Foster Care and Termination of Parental Rights," *Stanford Law Review* 28:626–706 (1976).

127. Tausha Bradshaw and Alan Marks, "Beyond a Reasonable Doubt: Factors That Influence the Legal Disposition of Child Sexual Abuse Cases," *Crime and Delinquency* 36:276–85 (1990); Tjaden and Thoennes, "Predictors of Criminal Prosecution in Intrafamily Child Abuse and Neglect".

128. Lindsay Arthur, "Child Sexual Abuse: Improving the System's Response," *Juvenile and Family Court Journal* 37:27–36 (1986).

129. *Ibid.*

130. These procedures are discussed in *Coy v. Iowa* 108 S.Ct. 2804 (1988).

131. *Ibid.*

132. *Coy v. Iowa* 108 S.Ct. 2798 (1988).

133. *Maryland v. Craig* 58 LW5044 (1990).

134. Wald, "State Intervention on Behalf of 'Neglected Children'," pp. 626–27.

135. Keith E. Galliher, "Termination of the Parent-Child Relationship: Should Parental I.Q. Be an Important Factor?" *Law and the Social Order* 4:855–59 (1973).

136. Brian G. Fraser, "A Pragmatic Alternative to Current Legislative Approaches to Child Abuse," *American Criminal Law Review* 12:123 (1974–75); and Costa and Nelson, *Child Abuse and Neglect*, pp. xvi–xvii.

137. Mark Miller and Judith Miller, "The Plague of Domestic Violence in the U.S.," *USA Today* 108:28 (1980).

138. Steele, "Violence within the Family," p. 23.

139. *Ibid.*

140. 452 U.S. 18, 101 S.Ct. 2153 (1981), 455 U.S. 745, 102 S.Ct. 1388 (1982).

141. Richard Gelles and Murray Straus, "Violence in the American Family," *Journal of Social Issues* 35:15 (1979).

142. National Center on Child Abuse and Neglect, Department of Health, Education, and Welfare, *1977 Analysis of Child Abuse and Neglect Research* (Washington, D.C.: U.S. Government Printing Office, 1978), p. 29.

143. Steele, "Violence within the Family," p. 22.

144. L. Bender and F. J. Curran, "Children and Adolescents Who Kill," *Journal of Criminal Psychopathology* 1:297 (1940) cited in Steele, "Violence within the Family," p. 21.

145. W. M. Easson and R. M. Steinhilber, "Murderous Aggression by Children and Adolescents," *Archives of General Psychiatry* 4:1–11 (1961), cited in Steele, "Violence within the Family," p. 22; see also J. Duncan and G. Duncan, "Murder in the Family: A Study of Some Homicidal Adolescents," *American Journal of Psychiatry* 127:1498–1502 (1971); C. King, "The Ego and Integration of Violence in Homicidal Youth," *American Journal of Orthopsychiatry* 45:134–45 (1975); James Sorrells, "Kids Who Kill," *Crime and Delinquency* 23:312–26 (1977).

146. King, "The Ego and the Integration of Violence in Homicidal Youth."

147. Jeanette Abrams, "Adolescent Perceptions of Parental Discipline and Juvenile Delinquency," in *Exploring the Relationship between Child Abuse and Delinquency*, ed. R. J. Hunter and Y. E. Walker (Montclair, N.J.: Allanheld, Osmun, 1981) pp. 252–65.

148. F. G. Bolton, J. Reich, and S. E. Guiterres, "Delinquency Patterns in Maltreated Children and Siblings," *Victimology* 2:349–59 (1977).

149. Chris Mouzakitia, *An Inquiry into the Problem of Child Abuse and Juvenile Delinquency* (Little Rock, Ark.: Graduate School of Social Work, University of Arkansas, n.d.); Steven Charles Wick, *Child Abuse and Causation of Juvenile Delinquency in Central Texas* (Seattle, Wash.: URSA Institute, n.d.). (These studies were originally reported in Charles Smith, David Berkman, and Warren Fraser, "The Shadows of Distress," *A Preliminary National Assessment of Child Abuse and Neglect and the Juvenile Justice System* [Washington, D.C.: U.S. Government Printing Office, 1980], pp. 129–49.)

150. Dorothy Lewis, David Balla, Shelly Shanok, and Laura Snell, "Delinquency, Parental Psychopathology, and Parental Criminality: Clinical and Epidemiological Findings," *Journal of the American Academy of Child Psychiatry* 15:665–78 (1976).

151. Richard Jenkins, "The Varieties of Adolescents' Behavior Problems and Family Dynamics," *American Journal of Psychiatry* 124:1440–45 (1968).

152. Jose Alfaro, "Report of the Relationship between Child Abuse and Neglect and Later Socially Deviant

Behavior," *Exploring the Relationship between Child Abuse and Delinquency*, pp. 175–219.

153. Cathy Spatz Widom, "Child Abuse, Neglect, and Violent Criminal Behavior," *Criminology* 27:251–71 (1989).

154. Leonard Edwards and Inger Sagatun, "Dealing with Parent and Child in Serious Abuse Cases," *Juvenile and Family Court Journal* 34:9–14 (1983).

155. Susan McPherson, Lance McDonald, and Charles Ryer, "Intensive Counseling with Families of Juvenile Offenders," *Juvenile and Family Court Journal*, 34:27–34 (1983).

156. See, generally, Gerald Patterson, "Performance Models for Antisocial Boys," *American Psychologist* 41:432–44 (1986); idem, *Coercive Family Process* (Eugene, Ore.: Castalia, 1982).

157. N. A. Wiltz and G. R. Patterson, "An Evaluation of Parent Training Procedures Designed to Alter Inappropriate Aggressive Behavior in Boys," *Behavior Therapy* 5:215–21 (1974).

158. *Reports of the National Juvenile Justice Assessment Centers, Juvenile Delinquency Prevention: A Compendium of thirty-six Program Models*. (Washington, D.C.: U.S. Department of Justice, March 1981). Updated with personal communication, Program Director, Family Teaching Center, March 1990.

159. *Ibid.*, updated with personal communication Program Director, Homebuilders, March 1990.

10 Peers and Delinquency

Juvenile Gangs and Groups

No issue confronting the study of delinquency is more important today than the growing problem of juvenile gangs and groups. After years of inactivity, violent juvenile gangs have reemerged in major cities around the country. While some are made up of only a few loosely organized neighborhood youth, others have thousands of members who cooperate in highly complex, illegal enterprises. It is believed that a significant portion of all drug distribution in the nation's inner cities is gang controlled; gang violence accounts for thousands of deaths each year.

There has been a concerted effort by law enforcement groups to contain gangs and reduce their criminal activity. Efforts range from setting up treatment-oriented settlement houses to deploying tactical gang control units that conduct **"gang sweeps"** (mass arrests). The problem of gang control is a difficult one: gangs flourish in inner-city areas that offer lower-class youth few conventional opportunities. Members are resistant to offers of help that cannot deliver legitimate economic hope. Though police may arrest and courts may incarcerate gang members, there always seems to be a new crop of young recruits ready to take the place of their fallen comrades. Those sent to prison quickly join up with branches of their street gang that have formed behind bars. And upon their release from prison, gang boys find their former groups only too willing to have them return to active membership.

This chapter discusses the nature and extent of gang and group delinquency. It begins with a discussion of adolescent peer relations. It then explores the definition, nature, and structure of delinquent gangs. Theories of gang formation, the extent of gang activity, and gang-control efforts are also discussed.

ADOLESCENT PEER RELATIONS

Psychologists have long recognized that as children mature, the nature of their friendship patterns also evolve. While in early childhood parents are the primary source of influence and attention, between the ages of 8 and 14, children begin to seek out a stable peer group; both the number and variety of friendships increase as children go through adolescence. Soon friends begin having a greater influence over decision making than parents.[1] By their early teens, children report that their friends give them emotional support when they are feeling bad and that they can confide intimate feelings to peers without worrying about their confidences being betrayed.[2]

As they go through adolescence, children form **cliques,** small groups of friends who share activities and confidences.[3] They also belong to **crowds,** loosely organized groups of children who share interests and activities. While clique members share intimate knowledge, crowds are brought together by mutually shared activities, such as sports, religion, and hobbies. Popular youths can be members of a variety of cliques and crowds.

In later adolescence, peer approval has a major impact on socialization. The most popular youths do well in school and are socially astute. In contrast, children who are rejected by their peers are more likely to display aggressive behavior and disrupt group activities by bickering or antisocial behavior.[4]

Peer relations, then, are a significant aspect of maturation. Peers exert a powerful influence on youth and pressure them to conform to group values. Peers guide children and help them learn to share and cooperate, cope with aggressive impulses, and discuss feelings they would not dare to bring up at home. With peers, youths can compare their own experiences and learn that others have similar concerns and problems; they realize they are not alone.[5]

Peer Relations and Delinquency

Delinquency experts have long debated the relationship between peer group interaction and delinquency. Two opposing viewpoints exist on the subject. Control theorists such as Travis Hirschi argue that delinquents are as detached from their peers as they are from other elements of society. While delinquent youths may acknowledge that they have "friends," their actual personal relationships are cold and exploitive. In an often-cited work, James Short and Fred Strodtbeck described the importance delinquent youths attach to their peer groups, while at the same time they observed how delinquents lack the social skills to make their peer relations rewarding or fulfilling.[6]

In contrast, there are those experts who view supportive peer relations as a key influence on delinquent behavior. For example, structural theories as a group link delinquency to the rewards gained by lower-class males when they begin associating with like-minded peers in the form of **law-violating youth groups** and **gangs**. Kids who find it difficult to achieve success in conventional society are open to achieving status in a same-sex peer group whose members reward them for being "tough," "cool," and "bad." Peers help them learn the knowledge and attitudes needed to perform illegal acts and then make them feel good by telling them their actions are righteous.

This perspective has been supported by research showing that youths who are loyal to delinquent friends, belong to a gang, and have "bad companions" are the ones most likely to commit crime.[7] Peggy Giordano, Stephen Cernkovich, and M. D. Pugh found that both delinquents and nondelinquents actually had similar types of friendship patterns.[8] Delinquent youth reported that their peer relations contained elements of caring and trust and that they could be open and intimate with their friends. Delinquent youth also reported getting more intrinsic rewards from their peers than nondelinquents, more conflict with their friends, more feelings of jealousy and competition, and, not unexpectedly, more pronounced feelings of loyalty in the face of trouble. In a similar vein, A. R. Gillis and John Hagan found that delinquents are more willing in some instances to be supportive and render aid to family and friends than are nondelinquents. Delinquents are intensely loyal to a few close associates, while nondelinquents seem more generally interested in helping other juveniles.[9]

These findings support the view that delinquents' peer group relations play an important part in their life-styles and stand in contrast to those who suggest that youthful law violators are loners without peer group support.

GROUPTHINK. What is it about group behavior that provokes delinquency? Psychologists find that the collective decisions made by group members are often unrealistic. They tend to be fueled by misperceptions of external threats to the group's cohesiveness. Under stress, group members do not consider all their options carefully and instead become more concerned with protecting members from outsiders.[10]

Group decision-making processes, called **groupthink** by psychologist Irving Janis, also help provide an atmosphere that is conducive to antisocial behavior.[11] According to this view, groups maintain five characteristics that affect their members' decision making:

1. *Feeling of invulnerability.* The group's solidarity helps convince its members that they are beyond the reach of the law because of their numbers and power.

2. *Group belief in rightness.* Kids who belong to groups perceive their conduct is "right" because others they are closely associated with and whom they admire are behaving the same way.

3. *Discrediting information opposed to the group's decisions.* Groups tend to support their members' decisions and behaviors by discrediting contrary evidence. For example, though they read or hear about the dangers of drug use, group leaders decide that government information about drug effects is a scam designed to scare members into conformity.

4. *Pressures to conform.* Groups demand conformity. Consequently, kids may engage in behavior that is against their better judgment simply because they are afraid of offending other members and violating group norms.

5. *Stereotyping of members of the outgroup.* The group views nonmembers as weak, stupid, and deserving of their fate. This frees members to violate others' rights without risk to their conscience.

If Janis's view of groupthink is correct, then it is easy to see how group decision-making processes might lead teenagers to make decisions that encourage and support law-violating behavior.

TEENAGE GANGS

As youths move through adolescence, they gravitate toward cliques that provide them with support, assurance, protection, and direction. Peer group membership allows them to devalue enemies, achieve status, and develop self-assurance. In some instances, the peer group provides the social and emotional basis for antisocial activity. In this instance, the clique is transformed into a gang.

The delinquent gang is a topic of considerable interest to many American citizens. Such a powerful mystique has grown up around gangs that mere mention of the word "gang" evokes images of black-jacketed youths roaming the streets at night in groups bearing such colorful names as the Mafia Crips, the Bounty Hunters, and the Savage Skulls. Such films, television shows, and novels as *The Warriors*, *Blackboard Jungle*, *The Wanderers*, *Outsiders*, *Amboy Dukes*, *West Side Story*, and *Colors* have popularized the teenage gang.[12]

Considering their importance, information about gangs is surprisingly lacking. We are not sure how many gangs actually exist, how many gang members there are, or how much crime is gang related. The secretive, constantly changing nature of the juvenile gang is probably one reason for this lack of knowledge; the danger in collecting the information is another.

What Are "Gangs"?

What exactly is a delinquent gang? Despite the familiarity of gangs to the American public, delinquency experts are often at odds over the precise definition of a "gang." The term is sometimes used broadly to describe any congregation of youths who have joined together to engage in delinquent acts. Some police departments use narrower definitions, designating as gangs only cohesive groups that hold and defend territory or "turf."[13] Some experts distinguish between *group delinquency* and *gang delinquency*. The former consists of a short-lived alliance that was created to commit a particular crime or engage in a random violent act. In contrast, gangs are long-lived, complex institutions that have a distinct structure and organization, including identifiable leadership, division of labor (some members are fighters, others burglars, while some are known as deal makers), rules, rituals, and possessions (such as headquarters and weapons).

Some of the core elements generally included in the "gang" concept include formation in **interstitial** areas (the "cracks" that form in the fabric of society) and the maintenance of standard group processes, such as recruiting new members, goal setting (such as controlling the neighborhood drug trade), assigning roles (appointing someone to negotiate with rivals), and status development (grooming young members for leadership roles).[14]

Gangs can also be defined by their criminal activity: some are devoted to violence and protection of their neighborhood boundaries or turf; others are devoted to theft; some specialize in drug trafficking; some gangs are primarily social groups concerned with recreation rather than crime.[15] Table 10.1 provides definitions of teen gangs by leading experts.

NEAR GROUPS AND YOUTH GROUPS. The standard definition of gangs and gang behavior imply that they are cohesive groups that maintain rules and customs and develop ongoing traditions. Not all gang experts share this view. Sociologist Lewis Yablonsky believes gangs can best be described as **"near groups"**. According to Yablonsky, human collectives tend to range from highly cohesive, tight-knit organizations to mobs with anonymous members who are motivated by emotions and disturbed leadership. Because teenage gangs fall between the two extremes, they can be described as near groups. They usually are characterized by: diffuse role definition; limited cohesion; impermanence; minimal consensus of norms; shifting membership; disturbed leadership; and limited definitions of membership expectations.[16]

In Yablonsky's view, the gang maintains only a small core of totally committed members who need the gang for satisfaction and other personal reasons. These core members work constantly to keep the momentum of the gang going. On a second level are affiliated youths, who participate in gang activity only when the mood suits them. At a third level are peripheral members, who participate in a particular situation or fight but who usually do not identify with the gang.

Sociologist **Walter Miller** suggests that *law-violating youth group* is a more appropriate term than "gang" to identify collective youth crime.[17] He says, "A law-

TABLE 10.1   Definition of Teen Gangs

Frederick Thrasher

A gang is an interstitial group originally formed spontaneously and then integrated through conflict. It is characterized by the following types of behavior: meeting face to face, milling, movement through space as a unit, conflict, and planning. The result of this collective behavior is the development of tradition, unreflective internal structure, esprit de corps, solidarity, morale, group awareness, and attachment to local territory.

Malcolm Klein

Any denotable adolescent group of youngsters who (a) are generally perceived as a distinct aggregation by others in their neighborhood; (b) recognize themselves as a denotable group (almost invariably with a group name); and (c) have been involved in a sufficient number of delinquent incidents to call forth a consistent negative response from neighborhood residents and/or enforcement agencies.

Desmond Cartwright

An interstitial and integrated group of persons who meet face to face more or less regularly and whose existence and activities are considered an actual or potential threat to the prevailing social order.

Walter Miller

A youth gang is a self-formed association of peers, bound together by mutual interests, with identifiable leadership, well-developed lines of authority, and other organizational features, who act in concert to achieve a specific purpose or purposes that generally include the conduct of illegal activity and control over a particular territory, facility, or type of enterprise.

G. David Curry and Irving Spergel

. . . law-violating behavior committed by juveniles and adults in or related to groups that are complexly organized although sometimes diffuse, sometimes cohesive with established leadership and membership rules. The gang also engages in a range of crime but significantly more violence within a framework of norms and values in respect to mutual support, conflict relations with other gangs, and a tradition of turf, colors, signs, and symbols. Subgroups of the gang may be differentially committed to various delinquent or criminal patterns, such as drug trafficking, gang fighting, or burglary.

Source: Frederick Thrasher, *The Gang* (Chicago: University of Chicago Press, 1927), p. 57; Malcolm Klein, *Street Gangs and Street Workers* (Englewood Cliffs, N.J.: Prentice-Hall, 1971), p. 13; Desmond Cartwright, Barbara Tomson, and Hersey Schwarts, eds., *Gang Delinquency* (Monterey, Calif.: Brooks/Cole, 1975), pp. 149–50; Walter Miller, "Gangs, Groups, and Serious Youth Crime," in *Critical Issues in Juvenile Delinquency*, ed. David Schicor and Delos Kelly (Lexington, Mass.: Lexington Books, 1980); G. David Curry and Irving Spergel, "Gang Homicide, Delinquency, and Community," *Criminology* 26:382 (1988).

violating youth group is an association of three or more youths whose members engage recurrently in illegal activities with the cooperation and/or moral support of their companions."[18] Miller recognizes the loose affiliations found in many youth groups. He employs such terms as *cooperation* and *moral support* to convey the idea that collective activities rarely include all group members. While

Miller also acknowledges "formal" delinquent gangs, he recognizes that formal gangs represent only one element of collective youth crime, which also includes cliques, networks, bands, corner groups, and so on. In sum, Miller sees the gang problem as one in which the formal street gang plays only a small part.

THE STUDY OF JUVENILE GANGS AND GROUPS

The study of juvenile gangs and groups was prompted by the Chicago School sociologists in the 1920s. Researchers such as Clifford Shaw and Henry McKay were concerned about the nature of the urban environment and how it influenced young people. Delinquency was believed to be a product of unsupervised groups made up of children of the urban poor and immigrants.

Frederick Thrasher, a colleague of Shaw and McKay, initiated the study of the modern gang in his analysis of more than 1,300 youth groups in Chicago. His report on this effort, *The Gang*, was first published in 1927.[19] Thrasher found that the social, economic, and ecological processes that affect the structure of great metropolitan cities create interstitial areas, or cracks in the normal fabric of society, characterized by weak family controls, poverty, and social disorganization. According to Thrasher, groups of youths develop spontaneously in interstitial areas to meet such childhood needs as play, fun, and adventure—activities that sometimes lead to delinquent acts.

The slum area presents many opportunities for conflict between youth gangs themselves and between youth gangs and adult authority. If this conflict continues, the group becomes more solidified and its activities become primarily illegal. The group thus develops into a gang, with a name and a structure oriented toward delinquent behavior.

To Thrasher, the gang provided the young, lower-class boy with an opportunity for success. Since adult society does not meet the needs of slum dwellers, the gang solves the problem by offering what society fails to provide—excitement, fun, and opportunity. The gang is not a haven for disturbed youths but rather an alternative life-style for normal boys.

Gangs at Mid-Century

In the 1950s and early 1960s, the threat of gangs and gang violence swept into the public consciousness. It was unusual for a week to go by without a major city newspaper featuring a story on the violent behavior of "bopping gangs" and their colorful leaders and names—the Egyptian Kings, the Young Lords, the Blackstone Rangers. Social service and law enforcement agencies directed major efforts to either rehabilitating or destroying the gangs. Movies, such as *The Wild Ones* and *Blackboard Jungle*, were made about gangs, and the play *West Side Story* romanticized violent gangs.

In his 1967 work, *Juvenile Gangs in Context*, Malcolm Klein summarized existing knowledge about gangs.[20] He concluded that gang membership was a way for individual boys to satisfy certain personal needs that were related to the development of youths caught up in the emotional turmoil typical of the period between adolescence and adulthood. A natural inclination to form gangs is reinforced by the perception that the gang represents a substitute for unobtainable middle-class rewards. The experience of being a member of a gang will dominate a youngster's perceptions, values, expectations, and behavior. Finally, the gang is self-reinforcing:

> It is within the gang more than anywhere else that a youngster may find forms of acceptance for delinquent behavior—rewards instead of negative sanctions. And as the gang strives for internal cohesion, the negative sanctions of the "outside world" become interpreted as threats to cohesion, thus providing secondary reinforcement for the values central to the legitimization of gang behavior.[21]

As the 1960s came to a close, the gang menace seemed to have suddenly disappeared. Some experts attributed the decline of gang activity to successful gang-control programs. For example, in the successful **detached street worker program**, a social worker was attached directly to an individual gang to rechannel the energies of gang boys in useful directions.[22] Others believe that gang activity was curtailed because police gang-control units infiltrated gangs, arrested leaders, and constantly harassed members.[23] In addition, juvenile court judges are generally more willing to incarcerate gang youth and give them more severe sentences than delinquent youth who were not gang members.[24]

Another explanation for the decline in gang activity was the growing political awareness that took on national proportions during the 1960s. Many gang leaders renounced crime for social or political activities; such organizations as the Black Panthers, civil rights groups, and anti-Vietnam War groups recruited gang members. In addition, many gang members were drafted into the U.S. Army. Still another explanation is that gang activity diminished during the 1960s because many gang members became active users of heroin and other drugs, which curtailed their group-related criminal activity.[25]

Gangs Reemerge

Gang activity began anew in the early 1970s. Walter Miller comments on the New York scene:

> All was quiet on the gang front for almost ten years. Then, suddenly and without advance warning, the gangs reappeared. Bearing such names as Savage Skulls and Black Assassins, they began to form in the South Bronx in the spring of 1971, quickly spread to other parts of the city, and by 1975, comprised 275 police-verified gangs with 11,000 members. These new and mysteriously emerging gangs were far more lethal than their predecessors—heavily armed, incited and directed by violence-hardened older men, and directing their lethal activities far more to the victimization of ordinary citizens than to one another.[26]

The rise of the teenage youth gang that Miller first noticed in the mid-70s has continued ever since. Why did the gang phenomenon reemerge? The most compelling reason may be the involvement of youth gangs in drug distribution and sales.[27] While in an earlier era, neighborhood gangs relied on group loyalty and emotional involvement with "turf" and their peer "family" to encourage membership, modern gang boys are lured by the quest for drug profits. Some gangs are more similar to traditional drug-dealing organized crime families, whom they have replaced in some areas, than to the youth gangs of yore. The traditional weapons of gangs—chains, knives and homemade guns—have been replaced by the "heavy artillery" drug money can buy: Uzi and AK-47 automatic weapons. It is ironic that the efforts made by the FBI and other federal agencies to crack down on traditional organized crime families have opened the door to a younger, more violent generation of youth gangs that control the drug trade on a local level and will not hesitate to use violence to maintain and expand their authority.

Another reason for the increase in gang activity has been the nationalization of gangs. At one time, gang activity was restricted to the nation's largest cities, especially Philadelphia, New York, Detroit, Los Angeles, and Chicago.[28] Today, these cities still maintain large gang populations. For example, authorities in Los Angeles claim that there are 600 gangs in operation containing approximately 70,000 members in Los Angeles County alone.[29] Chicago police estimates indicate that city has 135 gangs with over 14,000 members.[30]

However, smaller cities such as Cleveland and Columbus, Ohio, Omaha, Nebraska, and Milwaukee, Wisconsin, which had not experienced serious gang problems before saw the emergence or importation of gangs.[31] The nationalization of gangs has occurred in part because big-city gangs have sent "representatives" to organize chapters in distant areas and/or have taken over existing local gangs. For example, police in Miami have reported that Chicago gang leaders have moved into Dade County and demanded cooperation and obedience from local gangs. Two major Chicago gangs, the Black Gangster Disciples and their rivals, the Vice Lords, have established branches in Milwaukee; police there estimate that there are now 2,000 active and 6,000 peripheral members in that city.[32] Members of Los Angeles' two largest gangs, the Crips and the Bloods, have set up shop as far away as Omaha, Nebraska, with the result that local police departments with little experience in gang control are confronted with well-organized gang activities. However, not all middle-size cities have experienced the establishment of gang "chapters" from Los Angeles or New York. C. Ronald Huff found that gangs in Columbus, Ohio, were mostly homegrown, originating from local dance and rap groups and neighborhood street corner hanging-out groups.[33]

MODERN GANGS

There are thousands of gangs in operation around the country today containing more than a million members. The "gang," however, cannot be viewed as a uniform or homogenous social concept. Modern gangs are usually organized around behaviors and themes that make each one somewhat unique. Nonetheless, many share enough similarities to enable them to be categorized. In their early work, Cloward and Ohlin recognized that some gangs "specialized" in violent behavior, others were *retreatists* that actively engaged in substance abuse, while a third type were criminal gangs that devoted their energy to crime for profit.[34] Today, experts have characterized gangs according to their drug use and criminal tendencies. For example, Jeffrey Fagan analyzed gang behavior in Chicago, San Diego, and Los Angeles and found that most gangs fall into one of four categories:

1. *Social gang*—is involved in few delinquent activities and little drug use other than alcohol and marijuana. Membership is more interested in the social aspects of group behavior.
2. *Party gang*—concentrates on drug use and sales, while forgoing most delinquent behavior, save vandalism. Drug sales are designed to fund members' personal drug use.
3. *Serious delinquent gang*—engages in serous delinquent behavior while eschewing most drug use. Drugs are used only on social occasions.
4. *Organized gang*—heavily involved in criminality and drug use and sales. Criminality and drugs are linked; drug use and sales reflect a systemic relationship with other criminal acts. For example, violent acts are used to establish control over drug-sale territories. Highly cohesive and organized, these gangs are on the verge of becoming formal criminal organizations.[35]

Fagan's findings have been duplicated by other gang observations conducted around the United States. For example, after observing gangs in the Columbus, Ohio, area, C. Ronald Huff found that they could be organized into "hedonistic gangs" (similar to "party gangs"), "instrumental gangs" (similar to the "serious delinquent gang"), and "predatory gangs" whose heavy crime and crack use make them similar to the "organized gangs" found by Fagan in Chicago and on the West Coast.[36] These more recent gang observation efforts seem to validate Cloward and Ohlin's research findings from thirty years ago.

In the sections below, some of the most important features of modern gangs are discussed in detail.

Location

The gang problem was traditionally considered an urban, lower-class phenomenon. Two types of urban areas are gang-prone. The first, the **transitionary neighborhood,** is marked by rapid population change in which diverse ethnic and racial groups find themselves living side by side and in competition with one another.[37] This area was first described by Frederick Thrasher as follows:

> "In nature, foreign matter tends to collect and cake in every crack, crevice, and cranny—interstices. There are also fissures and breaks in the structure of social organizations. The gang may be regarded as an interstitial region in the layout of the city."[38]

By *interstitial*, Thrasher meant the shifting, changing, or transitional neighborhoods of the larger cities. Intergang conflict and homicide rates are high in these areas that house the urban "underclass."[39]

The second gang area is the "**stable slum,**" a neighborhood where population shifts have slowed down, permitting patterns of behavior and traditions to develop over a number of years. Most typical of these areas are the slums in New York and Chicago and the Mexican-American *barrios* of the Southwest and California.[40] The stable slum more often contains the large, structured gang clusters that are the most resistant to attempts by law enforcement and social service agencies to modify or disband them.

SHIFTING GANG LOCALES. The transitionary neighborhoods and the stable slums are not the only environments that produce gangs. In recent years, there has been a massive movement of people out of the central city into outlying communities and suburbs. Many of these people have been from the upper- or middle-class, but lower-income residents have also been affected. In some cities, once-fashionable outlying neighborhoods have declined, and downtown, central-city areas have undergone extensive urban renewal. Central, inner-city districts of major cities like New York and Chicago have become devoted to finance, retail stores, restaurants, and entertainment.[41] Two aspects of this development inhibit gang formation: first, there are few residential areas and thus few adolescent recruits, and second, there is intensive police patrol. In some areas, such as Miami and Boston, slums or ghettos have shifted from the downtown areas to outer-city, ring-city, or suburban areas—that is, to formerly middle-class areas that are now in decay. Suburban housing projects are also gang-prone. While today gangs are still located in areas of urban blight, these neighborhoods are often at some distance from their traditional inner-city locations.[42] Even though gang areas have shifted their locale, the ecological patterns that produce them remain unchanged.[43]

Age

The ages of gang members range widely, perhaps as much as from 8 to 55, with an average of 17 to 18.[44] Gang experts believe that the average age has been increasing yearly.[45] The aging of youth gangs may be explained in part by the changing structure of the American economy. There has been a loss of desirable unskilled jobs that could attract older gang boys and an concommitant increase in low-level drug dealing opportunities that require a gang affiliation. As a result, gang affiliations can last indefinitely, so it is not unusual to see intergenerational memberships with parents, children, and even grandchildren affiliating with the same gang.[46] However, older members who continue their membership into middle-age (called "veteranos" or "OG's" (old guys) in Hispanic gangs) are usually infrequent participants in gang activities.[47]

Data on the average age of gang members has been collected by the Chicago police.[48] The modal age of active gang members is from 16 to 19. The Chicago data indicates that females begin their gang activity earlier than males but abandon it as they approach their twenty-first birthdays. Perhaps females mature faster or are accepted by gang members at an earlier age. Males may have more problems assuming a gang role at an early age and leaving gangs as they mature.[49] Small gangs are more likely to have restricted age ranges, with all members being within two and three years of each other. Larger gangs sometimes have youthful and adult cliques and therefore a much larger age range.

There is also some evidence that some gangs are being formed or led by adults.[50] Some may be armed services veterans who, after their discharge, have resumed their former gang membership, bringing with them increased knowledge of combat and weapons. Organized crime figures also use gang boys for some duties because they are less liable to receive severe criminal penalties if apprehended by law enforcement agents.[51]

Gender

Of the more than 1,000 groups included in Thrasher's original survey, only half a dozen were female gangs. This may have been an accurate portrayal of gang membership in the 1920s, but a change has taken place. Though female gangs may not function independently, female units or auxiliaries of boys' groups appear to be quite common in major cities. For example, Klein reports on one or two such groups associated with each male gang he observed in Los Angeles.[52] Walter Miller cites two of seven groups he studied in Boston as female.[53]

Females are involved in gang activities in one of three ways: as part of auxiliaries, or branches, of male gangs; as part of sexually mixed gangs; or as part of autonomous gangs. Of these, the first form has been the most common. Often, the units will take on a feminized version of the male gang name, such as Devil's Disciples or Lady Disciples. New York City police estimated that half the city's gangs have female branches, but their members comprise only 6 percent of the total gang population. Chicago police found that only one in twenty youths linked to street gang activity were females.[54] A general estimate that gangs are 90 percent or more male is probably accurate for all cities where gangs are active.[55]

Conflicting evidence on the role of female gang members is provided by Glen Weisfeld and Roger Feldman's in-depth interview of a former gang leader whom they call "Tom Nichols."[56] Tom reported that many girls in his Chicago neighborhood belonged to gangs, each girl's gang operating as a sort of ladies' auxiliary to a particular boys' gang. The girls' gangs actually fought each other, but they were not likely to use weapons, such as guns or knives. Fights between individual gang members were usually caused by sexual jealousy, theft of personal belongings, an insulting remark, betrayal to the police, or the suspicion that one of these acts had occurred. Tom Nichols's portrayal of female gangs seems accurate today, though police departments in southern California report that violence and drug dealing by female gangs is on the upswing.

Formation

It has long been suggested that gangs form in order to defend their turf from outsiders, and therefore, gang formation involves a sense of territoriality. Most gang members live in close proximity to one another, and their sense of belonging and loyalty extends only to their small area of the city. At first, a gang may form when members of a newly immigrated ethnic minority join together for self-preservation. As the group gains numerical domination over an area, the gang may view the area as its territory or turf, which needs to be defended. Defending turf involves fighting rivals who wish to encroach on the territory and make it their own.

Once formed, gangs grow when youths who admire the older gang boys and wish to imitate their life-style "apply" and are accepted for membership. Sometimes the new members will be given a special diminished identity within the gang, which reflects their inexperience and apprenticeship status. Joan Moore and her associates found that once formed, youth cliques (*klikas*) in Hispanic gangs remain together as unique groups with separate names (for example, the Termites), separate identities, and distinct experiences and have more intimate relationships among themselves than among the general gang membership.[57] She likens klikas to a particular class in a university, such as the class of '87—not a separate organization but one that has its own unique life experiences.

Moore also found that gangs can expand by including members' kin, even if they do not live in the immediate neighborhood, and rival gang members who wish to "come aboard" because they admire the gang's way of doing things. Adding outsiders gives the gang the ability to advance its borders and take over new territory. However, it also brings with it new problems, since outsider members and the grasp for new territory usually result in greater conflicts with rival gangs.

Leadership

Most experts describe gang leaders as cool characters who have earned their position by a variety of abilities—fighting prowess, verbal ability, athletic distinction, and so on. For example, William Whyte describes the gang leader as

> [the] focal point for the organization of his group. In his absence, the members of the gang are divided into a number of small groups. There is no common activity or general conversation. When the leader appears, the situation changes strikingly. The small units form into one large group. . . . The members do not feel that the gang is really gathered until the leader appears. . . . The leader is the man who acts when the situation requires action. He is more resourceful than his followers. . . . The leader need not be the best baseball player, bowler, or fighter, but he must have some skill in whatever pursuits are of interest to the group.[58]

Other experts emphasize that gang leadership is rarely held by one individual and that it varies with particular activities, such as fighting, sex, and negotiations. In fact, in some gangs, each age level of the gang has its own leaders. Older members may be looked up to, but they are not necessarily considered leaders by younger members. In his analysis of Los Angeles gangs, Malcolm Klein observed that many gang leaders shrink from taking an authority role and actively deny leadership. Klein overheard one gang boy claim, "We got no leaders, man. Everybody's a leader, and nobody can talk for nobody else."[59] The most plausible explanation of this ambivalence is the boy's fear that during times of crisis, his decisions will conflict with those of other leaders and he will lose status and face.

Barry Krisberg studied gangs in Philadelphia and discovered that leaders stressed the concept of "hustling," emphasizing individual gain and success.[60] He found that many gang leaders were not even aware of outside philosophies, racial groups, leaders, or ideas. They did not plan actions in advance because announcing future goals would lock them into a position where their inability to achieve would be an overt admission of failure. Furthermore, gang leaders maintained a mirror image of the values of the larger society—for example, they espoused, "Do unto others before they do unto you." The basic theme of the gang leader was survival in the urban jungle.

Thus, the experts do not agree about the nature of gang leadership. Some view it as transient in nature, while others view it as steady and in the hands of the toughest, smartest, and most able boys.

Communications

Gangs today seek recognition both from their rivals and the community as a whole. Image and reputation depend on the gang's ability to communicate to the rest of the world.

Wall graffiti is a major form of gang communication.

One major source of gang communication is **graffiti.** These wall writings are especially elaborate among Latino gangs, who call their inscriptions "placasos" or "placa," meaning sign or plaque.[61] Latino gang graffiti will usually contain the writer's street name and the name of the gang. There are frequent assertions of strength or power, such as by the use of the term "rifa," which means to rule, and "controllo," indicating that the gang controls the area. Another common inscription is "p/v," meaning "por vida"; this refers to the fact that the gang expects to control the area "for life." If the number 13 is used, it signifies that the gang is "loco" or wild.

Crossed-out graffiti indicates that a territory is being contested by a rival gang, while undisturbed writing indicates that the gang's power has gone unchallenged.

Gangs also communicate by ritualistic argot (speech patterns) and hand signs. Flashing or tossing gang signs in the presence of rivals is often viewed as a direct challenge that can escalate into a verbal or physical confrontation. In Chicago, gangs call this *representing.* Gang boys will proclaim their affiliation ("Latin King Love!", "Stone Killers!") and ask victims, "Who do you ride?" or "What do you be about?"; an incorrect response will provoke an attack.[62] False representing can be used to intentionally misinform witnesses and victims; it can be used to expose imposters or neutrals trying to make safe passage through gang-controlled territory.

Still another method of communication is clothing. In some areas, gang members communicate their membership by wearing jackets with the name of their gang embroidered on the back. In Boston neighborhoods, certain articles of clothing, for example sneakers or jackets with a particular logo, are worn to identify gang membership. *Sneaker trees,* into which gang members throw dozens of pairs of sneakers whose laces have been tied together, are used to designate gang turf; one gang area is called "Addidas Park."[63] In Los Angeles, the two major black gangs are the Crips and the Bloods, each containing many thousands of members. Crips can be identified by the color blue and wear some article of blue clothing—hat, belt, or jacket—to communicate their allegiance; their rivals, the Bloods, identify with the color red.[64] In one 1988 incident, a Crips member was shot while waiting in line to see the gang film *Colors* by a member of the Bloods who, after viewing the film, was apparently upset by the way his gang had been depicted; the victim's blue handkerchief gave away his gang affiliation to his assailant.[65]

It is also common for gang boys to tattoo themselves with the name of their gangs or a gang sign. This shows permanent loyalty to the gang and warns the community of their membership in a powerful and violent organization.

Figure 10.1 illustrates hand signs and symbols of Los Angeles gangs.

Criminality

There are numerous patterns of gang criminality. As you may recall, each gang "specializes" in a different kind of criminal activity. Criminal gangs frequently engage in felony assaults, robberies, and other kinds of theft; in contrast, drug-

FIGURE 10.1
Hand signs and logos
of Los Angeles gangs

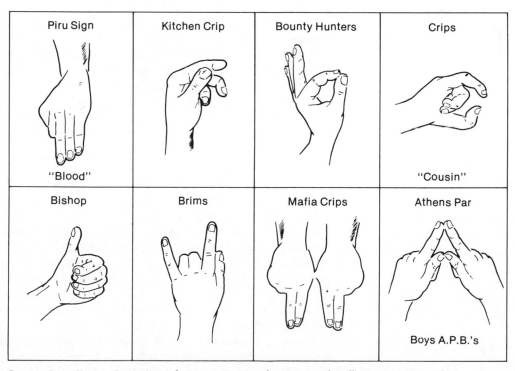

Source: Jerry Kaono, Operation Safe Streets, Los Angeles County Sheriff's Department, n.d.

FIGURE 10.1

Hand signs and logos
of Los Angeles
gangs—*continued*

oriented gangs concentrate on the sale of marijuana, PCP, cocaine (crack), and amphetamines (ice); organized gangs use violence to control a drug territory.

While gangs have been linked to drug sales, including crack cocaine, that is by no means their only criminal activity. In fact, research by Malcolm Klein and his associates has questioned whether gangs actually are as instrumental in the crack trade as the media contends.[66] Klein found that gang boys engage in retaliatory violence against rivals who they accuse of being insulting. They also engage in personal disputes, chance altercations, and turf battles.[67] Once an insult is perceived or a challenge offered, the gang's honor cannot be restored until the "debt" is repaid. Police efforts to "cool down" gang disputes only delay the inevitable revenge, a beating or a **drive-by shooting**. On occasion, though it is more common in movies than in reality, large-scale street fights between rival gangs are held in order to settle turf disputes.

Retaliation is also directed against gang members who step out of line. If subordinates disobey orders, perhaps by using rather than selling drugs, they may be subject to harsh disciplinary action by other gang members. Violence is used to maintain the gang's internal discipline and security.

Other common gang crimes include extortion, called "turf tax," which involves forcing people to pay for protection from dangerous neighborhood youths (presumably members of the gang). **Prestige crimes** occur when gang boys steal or assault someone, even a police officer, for the purpose of gaining prestige in the gang and neighborhood. Their action may be part of an initiation right, an effort to establish a special reputation or to secure a position of responsibility and a leadership role with their show of daring, or a response to a challenge from a rival (proving they are not "chicken").

There is a growing fear of gang crime and violence, and though the exact amount is often difficult to tally, the number of gang-related homicides most likely exceeds 1,000 annually.[68]

FIGURE 10.1

Hand signs and logos of Los Angeles gangs—*continued*

Ethnic and Racial Composition

Most gangs seem to be racially exclusive. Although Lewis Yablonsky reports racially mixed violent gangs, the majority of gang observers all view gangs as racially homogeneous groups: all white (English, Italian, Irish, Slavic, and/or German origin), all black (African origin), all Hispanic (Mexican, Puerto Rican, Panamanian, Colombian, and from other Spanish-speaking countries), and/or all Asian (Chinese, Japanese, Korean, Taiwanese, Samoan, and American Indian).[69] Moreover, most intergang conflict appears to be among groups of the same ethnic and racial background.[70]

The ethnic distribution of gangs corresponds to the geographic area in which they are located. For example, in Philadelphia and Detroit, the overwhelming number of gang members are black. In New York and Los Angeles, Hispanic gangs predominate, and San Francisco's small gang population is mostly Asian; Asian gangs are also of major importance in New York and Boston.[71]

Each type of racial and ethnic gang has its own characteristics, as described next.

BLACK GANGS. The first black teenage gangs were organized in the early 1920s and specialized in common street crime activities.[72] Since they had few rival organizations in their inner-city locales, they were able to concentrate on criminal activity rather than on defending turf. By the 1930s, the expanding number of rival gangs spawned competition, and inner-city gang warfare became commonplace.

In Los Angeles, today a hot spot of gang activity, the first black youth gang formed in the 1920s was the Boozies, named after the family that provided a significant portion of their membership. This gang virtually ran the inner city until the 1930s, when rivals began to challenge its criminal monopoly. In the next twenty years, a number of black gangs, including the Businessmen, the Home Street Gang, the Slauson Gang, and the Neighborhood Gang, emerged and met with varying degrees of criminal success.

In the 1970s, the dominant Crips gang was formed and began to spread over much of Los Angeles. Other neighborhood gangs merged into the Crips or affiliated with them by adding "Crips" to their name, so that the Main Street Gang became the Main Street Crips. The Crips's dominance has since been challenged by their arch rivals, the Bloods. Both of these groups, whose total membership may exceed 25,000 boys, have an organization that resembles an organized crime family and are heavily involved in drug trafficking.

Black gangs, especially those in Los Angeles, have some unique characteristics. Their members frequently use nicknames to identify themselves, often based on a personal characteristic: "Little .45" might be the street name used by someone whose favorite weapon is a large handgun. While TV shows portray gangs wearing particular attire and jackets, black gangs usually favor nondescript attire in order to reduce police scrutiny. However, black gang members frequently sport distinctive hairstyles, featuring shaving, cornrows, shaping, and/or braids. Tattooing is popular, and members often wear scarves or "rags" to identify their gang affiliation.

It is also common for black gang members to mark their territory with distinctive graffiti. The messages are crude rather than sophisticated: drawings of guns, dollar signs, proclamations of individual power, and profanity.

HISPANIC GANGS. Hispanic gangs are made up of boys whose ethnic ancestry can be traced to one of a variety of Spanish-speaking cultures, ranging from Puerto Rico to Mexico. They are known for their fierce loyalty to their original or "home" gang; this affiliation is maintained even if they move to a new neighborhood that contains a rival gang.[73] To be admitted into the gang usually involves an initiation ritual in which boys are required to show their fearlessness and prove their *machismo* or manliness. The most common test requires novices to fight several established members or to commit some crime, such as a purse snatching or robbery. The code of conduct associated with membership means never informing on a brother or even a rival, facing death or prison without betraying the sense of honor.

In some areas, such as Miami, Hispanic gangs are rigidly organized with a fixed leadership hierarchy. However, in the largest concentration of Hispanic youth gangs in southern California, leadership is fluid. During times of crisis, those with particular skills will assume command on a situational basis.[74] For example, one boy will lead in combat, while another will negotiate drug deals.

Hispanic gang boys are known for their distinctive dress codes. Some wear knit dark-colored watch caps pulled down over the ears with a small roll at the bottom. Others wear a folded bandana over the forehead and tied in back. Another popular headpiece is the "stingy brim" fedora or a baseball cap with the wearer's nickname and gang affiliation written on its turned-up bill. Members also favor tank-style T-shirts and/or open Pendleton shirts, which give them quick access to weapons. Members also proclaim their affiliations by marking off territory with colorful and intricate graffiti. Hispanic gang graffiti appears in very stylized lettering, frequently making use of three-dimensional designs, and proclaims members' organizational pride and power.

Hispanic gangs have a strong sense of territory or turf, and a great deal of gang violence is directed toward warding off any threat to their neighborhood control. Slights by rivals, including put-downs, stare-downs ("mad-dogging"), defacing gang insignia, and territorial intrusions, can set off a violent and bloody gang confrontation. Today, gangs carry out these vendettas with high-powered automatic weapons, a far cry from the zip guns and gravity knives of the past. The following Focus on Delinquency describes the formation and activities of Hispanic gangs in East Los Angeles and black gangs in Detroit.

ASIAN GANGS. Asian gangs are prominent in cities with large Asian populations, including New York, Los Angeles, San Francisco, Seattle, and Houston. In an important work, Ko-lin Chin has described the formation and nature of Chinese youth gangs.[75] According to Chin, the earliest gangs, formed in San Francisco in the 1950s, were known as the Bugs and were made up of American-born Chinese youth. Later, the **Wah Ching** (Youth of China) was formed by foreign-born youth to protect members from the American-born Chinese. Members of the Wah Ching broke away and formed Yo Le, which later became known as the Joe Fong Boys.

The Wah Ching and the Joe Fong Boys now operate in many major U.S. cities. Activities of these Chinese gangs were brought to the national attention in 1977, when a shoot-out in San Francisco's Golden Dragon restaurant left five dead and eleven wounded.

Chin finds that the factors that promote Chinese gang delinquency include: a lack of employment opportunities; perceptions of school failure and incompetence; and family stress and conflict. Another critical determinant of gang formation is the learning of criminal values from adult criminal role models who are members of Chinese secret societies, or **triads,** and self-help associations, or **tongs.**[76]

In addition to Chinese gangs, Samoan gangs, primarily the Sons of Samoa, have operated on the West Coast, as have Vietnamese gangs, whose influence has been felt in Los Angeles, New York, and Boston. These Asian gangs tend to victimize members of their own ethnic group, and because of group solidarity and distrust of outside authorities, relatively little is known about their activities.

ANGLO GANGS. The first American youth gangs were made up of white ethnic youth of European backgrounds, especially Irish and Italian immigrants. It was common to see white ethnic youth gangs competing with black and Hispanic gangs in the nation's largest cities.

Today, the number of organized white gangs is dwindling, though sporadic organized activity is not uncommon. However, while traditional white gangs have

Changing Gang Structures: Los Angeles and Detroit

There is evidence that the nature of gang organization is constantly shifting and reflects the political and economic conditions of the domain in which it exists. Political turmoil can create new avenues of gang activity, such as neighborhood organizations and activism, while economic downturns can influence the pace of their criminal activity.

One important study of shifting gang activities was Joan Moore's pioneering studies of Chicano gangs in East Los Angeles. Moore found that the gang is not necessarily associated with delinquent or criminal behavior in Mexican-American communities. Aggressive male youth groups were a feature of the Mexican community as far back as the nineteenth century. The early barrio gangs were made up of young laborers whose behavior was more oriented around sports and socializing than criminality.

Then in the 1940s, the *pachuco* fad swept through the community; its advocates wore outlandish outfits ("zoot suits") and spoke a unique version of Spanish-English slang. A well-publicized murder case and some urban disturbances helped brand the *pachucos* as vicious "ratpacks." Though most zoot-suiters (who can be compared to the new wavers or punks of today) were not gang members or necessarily involved in crime, the local press focused attention on them as a major social problem, and a popular stereotype was created. Mexican-American youth became suspect regardless of their actual interest in gangs.

In the 1950s, increasing stigmatization and isolation encouraged the development of deviance. Drug use, which had been quietly tolerated in an earlier generation, was now the target for police crackdowns, and many barrio residents went to prison. Mexican-Americans gained the stereotype of "evil dope dealers," and the early naivete of the street life-style (*cholo*) of the gang boys was finally destroyed.

In the 1960s, the Chicano political movement had an important influence on gangs. First, gangs were romanticized as social bandits in the tradition of earlier Mexican opposition to Anglo author-

continued

all but disappeared from the American scene, their place has been taken by derivatives of the English **punk** and **skinhead** movement of the 1970s. In England, these youth, generally the daughters and sons of lower-class parents, sported wildly dyed hair, often shaved into "Mohawks," military clothes and Iron Cross earrings and favored high-topped military boots. Music was a big part of their lives, and the band that characterized their life-style was the Sex Pistols, led by Johnny Rotten and Sid Vicious. Their creed was antiestablishment, and their anger was directed towards foreigners who they believed were taking their jobs.

The punker-skinhead style was brought over to the United States by bands that replicated the Sex Pistols's antisocial music, stage presence, and dress; these included the Clash, the Dead Kennedys, and Human Sexual Response. The music, philosophy, and life-style of these rock bands inspired the formation of a variety of white youth gangs. However, unlike their British cousins, American ity. Second, gangs (and their adult ex-offender members, the *pintos*) began to be viewed as the fighting branch of the movement who protected the community from the police. Protecting the community (*la raza*) was an extension of protecting their turf or neighborhood. The youth gang and its extensions became enmeshed in community affairs, and their problems with the law came to be identified with the problems of the community as a whole.

In the last ten years, there has been significant change in the nature of the Chicano gang. The image of the gang altered within the community and its purpose was similarly reoriented. There were a number of reasons for this transformance. Publicity about violent Mexican-American prison gangs, such as La Familia, helped create the image that all Chicano gangs were criminally oriented. Street kids, or *cholos*, began to be viewed as a liability of the Chicano movement. When political activism cooled, street demonstrations ended, so there was little need for gang members to act as community protectors. Federal and state funds for community development were curtailed, and the gangs became more closely identified with criminals than with social activists. A new wave of Mexican immigrants rejected the gang culture, and community leaders asked for police protection from the gangs. As gang isolation increased, so too did gang violence and criminality. So from leaders in a sociopolitical movement, gang members ended up belonging to an ostracized underclass.

Carl Taylor recently studied the drug dealing gangs of Detroit. Taylor also found that gang priorities and activities have shifted. At one time, the leading Detroit gangs, Young Boys, Inc., and Pony Down, were involved in violent turf battles and petty street crime. In the 1980s, the gangs were under extreme pressure from police. Their most senior leaders were imprisoned. Instead of dissolving, the Detroit gangs shifted their operations to super secret and sophisticated drug dealing. To avoid police attention, gang members forgo flashy cars, clothes, and colors and concentrate on highly organized and profitable crack dealing. Detroit gangs are now attracting middle-class recruits, who are lured by quick profits. There has also been an increased number of independent female gangs, whose members are as well armed as their male peers.

In sum, gangs are not unchanging, unified organizations. Like modern corporations, they are more than willing to take on new product lines, develop marketing campaigns, and go with the socioeconomic flow.

Source: Carl Taylor, *Dangerous Society* (East Lansing, Mich.: Michigan State University Press, 1990); Joan Moore, "Isolation and Stigmatization in the Development of an Underclass: The Case of Chicano Gangs in East Los Angeles," *Social Problems* 33:1–12 (1985).

white gang members are often alienated middle-class youths rather than poor, lower-class kids who are out of society's mainstream. Many perceive the United States as a country in decline that will not be able to provide them with an adequate standard of living. Other characteristics of youths in Anglo gangs are heavy drug use, experience with physical and sexual abuse in the home, and feelings of alienation and anger.[77]

There are a number of emerging Anglo gang types. "Punkers" or "stoners" dress in the latest "heavy metal" rock fashions and engage in drug- and violence-related activities. There are also skinhead groups that are devoted to racist, white supremacist activities. Satanic gangs engage in demonic rituals and become obsessed with occult themes, suicide, ritual killings, and animal mutilations. Their members get seriously involved in devil worship, tattoo themselves with occult symbols, and gouge their bodies to draw blood for satanic rituals.

Members of a white skin-
head gang.

CAUSES OF GANG DELINQUENCY

What causes youth to join gangs?[78] Though gangs flourish in lower-class, inner-city areas, it cannot be assumed that membership is solely a function of lower-class subcultural identity: many lower-class youth do not join gangs, and middle-class kids are found in suburban skinhead and stoner groups. What, then, are the assumed causes of gang formation?

The Anthropological View

In a classic work, **Herbert Block** and **Arthur Niederhoffer** suggested that gangs provide a mechanism for bridging the gap between the freedom of childhood and the responsibilities of adulthood.[79] Young people of all societies go through an adolescent period in which they seek adult status. Societies vary in the amount of aid they grant adolescents during this period. When assistance from adults is inadequate, adolescents will provide their own. The development of gangs is one means. In the United States, upper- and middle-class youths are more easily able to identify with adults, so the transition to adulthood can be attained without gangs. Lower-class youths find the transition more difficult because adult support is usually lacking.

The cornerstone of the Block-Niederhoffer theory is that gang processes and functions are similar to the puberty rites of primitive cultures, and like their primitive counterparts, they help the child bridge the gap between childhood and adulthood. Block and Niederhoffer cite a number of gang behavior patterns that are similar to primitive puberty rites.

For example, many gang boys display tattoos and other identifying marks, and some gangs make tattooing an integral part of initiation ceremonies. Gangs also adopt uniforms—especially jackets with the name of the gang on them, motorcycle jackets, and boots. Another form of decoration is scars, which gang members view as measures of their toughness and recklessness. Some boys will scar themselves with the name of their girlfriend to show solidarity with their mates. This is similar to activities of young men in island cultures.

In the puberty rites of primitive societies, the novice theoretically emerges as a new person with a new name and language. New names are a badge of honor among street gangs, and gangs frequently create a unique jargon. Primitive societies also have specific rights involving separation from home, transition to manhood, and incorporation into the adult world. The gang allows the adolescent to separate from his parents' control and helps bridge the gap to maturity. Thus, the gang serves as a substitute family. The adolescent gang is preeminently a male sanctuary. Girls are usually kept at arm's length from the group, which congregates nightly at the same clubhouse or street corner.

Many gangs put new members through a period of hazing as an initiation to the gang to make sure they have "heart." This feature is also similar to primitive tribal rites. Finally, in primitive societies, initiation into a cult is viewed as the death of childhood. By analogy, younger boys in lower-class urban areas yearn for the time when they can join the gang and really start to live. Membership in the adolescent gang "means the youth gives up his life as a child and assumes a new way of life."[80] Gang names themselves are suggestive of "primitive totemic ancestors" because they usually are symbolic (Jaguars and Egyptian Kings, for example).

In conclusion, Block and Niederhoffer suggest that the gang transforms its members into something different from nonmembers. Because of their highly charged, explosive nature, gangs crystallize in visible and overt form the traits that are repressed or dormant in nongang teenagers.

The Sociocultural View

The most widely held view among sociologists is that sociocultural factors (discussed in Chapter 5) contribute to the formation of gangs. Youth who are alienated from the larger culture and cannot obtain success goals through conventional means join a gang as a substitute source of achievement and belonging. In a classic 1964 work, Irving Spergel found that the gang gives lower-class youths a means of attaining personal reputations and consequent status among their peer group that they cannot achieve in school or conventional society.[81] Almost thirty years later, Wayne Wooden found a similar pattern of gang formation among white youths who join punk rock or heavy metal stoner gangs.[82]

Overall, the sociocultural view assumes that gangs are a status-generating medium for boys whose aspirations cannot be realized by legitimate means.

The Psychological View

A minority position on the formation of gangs is that they serve as an outlet for psychologically diseased youth. One proponent of this view is Lewis Yablonsky, whose theory of violent-gang formation holds that violent gangs recruit their members among the more **sociopathic** youths living in disorganized slum communities.[83] Yablonsky views the "sociopathic" youth as one who lacks "social feelings." He "has not been trained to have human feelings or compassion or responsibility for another."[84] Yablonsky supports this contention by pointing to the eccentric, destructive, and hostile sexual attitudes and behavior of gang youths, who are often violent and sadistic. He sums up the sociopathic character traits of gang boys as: (1) a defective social conscience marked by limited feelings of guilt for destructive acts against others; (2) limited compassion or empathy for others; (3) the acting out of behavior dominated by egocentrism and self-seeking goals; and (4) the manipulation of others for immediate self-gratification (for example, sexually exploitative modes of behavior) without any moral concern or responsibility.

Sociopathic youth are most often drawn to violent gangs, which provide a vehicle for these violent, hostile youths to act out their aggressions and personal problems. Membership in violent gangs is fluid.

In sum, there is no clear-cut agreement on why youths join gangs. The decision to form a gang may have elements of culture, social status, personality, and economic needs.

CONTROLLING GANG ACTIVITY

In recent years, gang control has often been left to the resources of local police departments. Three basic forms of gang control can be found:

- The **youth service program,** in which traditional police personnel, usually from the youth unit, are given responsibility for gang control. No personnel are assigned exclusively or mainly to gang-control work.
- The **gang detail,** in which one or more traditional police officers, usually from youth or detective units, are assigned exclusively to gang-control work.
- The **gang unit,** established solely to deal with gang problems, to which one or more officers are assigned exclusively to gang-control work.[85]

In most police agencies, these special units share control efforts with other departmental personnel, such as patrol officers or investigators. Together, they are involved in such activities as information processing on youth gangs and gang leaders, prevention efforts such as mediation programs, enforcement efforts to suppress criminal activity and apprehend those who are believed to have committed crimes, and follow-up investigations directed at the apprehension of gang members alleged to have committed crimes. For example, the Chicago Police Department has a gang crime section that maintains intelligence on gangs and trains officers to deal with gang problems. Through its Gang Target Program, it identifies street gang members and enters their names in a computer that is programmed to alert the unit if the youth is picked up or arrested.

Other police departments also sponsor general prevention programs that can help control gang activities, including school-based lectures, police-school liai-

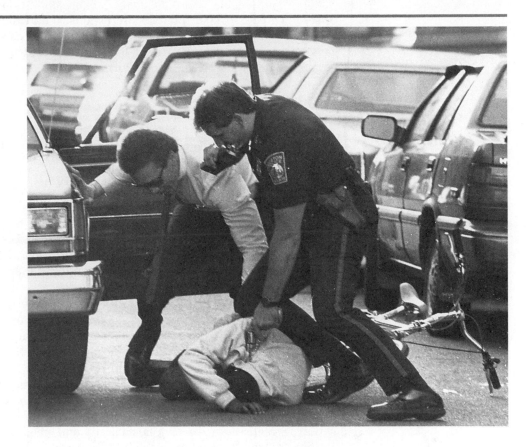

Boston cops battle youth gang violence.

sons, information dissemination, recreation programs, and street worker programs, including counseling, working with parents, and community organization.

Some police departments engage in **gang-breaking** activities, in which police will focus on the gang leaders and make special efforts to arrest, prosecute, convict, and incarcerate them whenever possible. For example, Los Angeles police conduct intensive anti-gang "sweeps" in which more than one thousand officers are put on the street in an effort to round up and intimidate gang boys. Police say that the sweeps let the gangs know "who the streets belong to" and show neighborhood residents that someone cares.[86] Despite such efforts, the police response to the gang and youth group problem seems fragmented at best; even in Los Angeles, gang membership and violence remain at all-time highs. Few departments have written policies or procedures on how to deal with youths, and many do not provide gang-control training.

Criminologists Mark Moore and Mark A. R. Kleiman suggest that gang sweeps and other "traditional" police tactics will not work on today's drug gangs. Instead, they argue that gangs should be viewed as organized criminal enterprises and should be dealt with as traditional "organized crime families." They suggest a policy of: (1) developing informants through criminal prosecutions, payments, and witness protection programs; (2) relying heavily on electronic surveillance and long-term undercover investigations; and (3) using special statutes that create criminal liabilities for conspiracy, extortion, or engaging in criminal enterprises.[87] Of course, such policies are expensive and difficult to implement and may be needed only against the most sophisticated gangs. However, the largest gangs present the greatest threat to urban life and therefore may be suitable targets for more intensive police efforts.

Community Control Efforts

In addition to law enforcement programs, there have been a number of community-based gang control efforts. During the late nineteenth century, social workers of the YMCA were active in working with youth in Chicago gangs.[88] During the 1950s, at the height of perceived gang activity, the detached street worker program was developed in major centers of gang activity.[89] This unique approach sent social workers into the community to work with gangs on their own turf. The workers attached themselves to a gang, participated in its activities, and tried to get to know its members. The purpose was to act as an advocate of the youths, to provide them with a positive role model, to help orient their activities in a positive direction, and to treat individual problems. Gang control efforts were common features of such community programs as the Chicago Area Project and the Mobilization for Youth Program. Detached street worker programs are sometimes credited with curbing gang activities in the 1950s and 1960s, although their effectiveness has been challenged on the grounds that they helped legitimize delinquent groups by turning them into neighborhood organizations.[90]

These pioneering efforts have continued with the upswing in gang activity. In Philadelphia, the House of Umoja project began when members of the Fattah family, concerned about the safety of one of their children who was a gang member, began taking other gang kids into their home and instilling them with pride in their African heritage and culture. The House of Umoja helped more than seven hundred youths, providing fifteen to twenty-five at a time with food, shelter, surrogate parenting, and employment opportunities. It also sponsored cultural programs and the Black Youth Olympics.

In some areas, citywide coordinating groups help orient gang-control efforts. For example, the Chicago Intervention Network operates field offices around the city in low-income, high-crime areas and provides a variety of services, including neighborhood watches, parent patrols, alternative youth programming, and family support efforts. These efforts have not significantly reduced gang activity, and more effective approaches remain to be developed.

SUMMARY

Gangs are a serious and growing problem in many cities, yet relatively little is known about them. Most gang members are males, aged 14 to 21, who live in urban ghetto areas. Ethnic minorities make up the majority of gang members. Gangs can be classified by their structure, behavior, or status. Some are believed to be social, others are criminally oriented, and still others are violent.

Gangs developed early in the nation's history and reached their heyday in the 1950s and early 1960s. After a lull of ten years, gang operations seem to be on the rise. Millions of crimes, including hundreds of murders, are believed to be committed annually by gangs. A recent development has been the control by gangs of the drug trade in many urban areas. Large gangs numbering in the thousands have set up a national crack and cocaine distribution network.

Gang and delinquent group membership may be in the millions.

We are still not sure what causes gangs. One view is that they serve as a bridge between adolescence and adulthood in communities where adult control is lacking. Another view suggests that gangs are a product of lower-class social disorganization and that they serve as an alternative means of advancement for disadvantaged boys. Still another view is that some gangs are havens for psychotic and disturbed youths.

Police departments have tried a number of gang-control techniques, but efforts have not been well organized. There are relatively few training efforts designed to help police officers deal with gangs. Community and other approaches are needed to control the gang problem.

QUESTIONS FOR DISCUSSION

1. Do gangs serve a purpose? Differentiate between a gang and a fraternity.
2. Discuss the differences between violent, criminal, and drug-oriented gangs.
3. How do gangs in suburban areas differ from inner-city gangs?
4. Do delinquents have cold and distant relationships with their peers?

KEY TERMS

gang sweeps
cliques
crowds
law-violating youth groups
gangs
groupthink
interstitial
near groups
Walter Miller
detached street worker
transitionary neighborhood
stable slum
drive-by shooting
prestige crimes

graffiti
Wah Ching
triads
tongs
punk
skinhead
Herbert Block
Arthur Niederhoffer
sociopathic
youth service program
gang detail
gang unit
gang-breaking

NOTES

1. Thomas Berndt, "The Features and Effects of Friendships in Early Adolescence," *Child Development* 53:1447–69 (1982).
2. Thomas Berndt and T. B. Perry, "Children's Perceptions of Friendships as Supportive Relationships," *Developmental Psychology* 22:640–48 (1986).
3. Spencer Rathus, *Understanding Child Development* (Holt, Rinehart and Winston, 1988), p. 462.
4. *Ibid*, p. 463.
5. *Ibid.*
6. James Short and Fred Strodtbeck, *Group Process and Gang Delinquency* (Chicago: Aldine, 1965).
7. Cindy Hanson, Scott Henggeler, William Haefele, and J. Douglas Rodick, "Demographic, Individual, and Family Relationship Correlates of Serious Repeated Crime among Adolescents and Their Siblings," *Journal of Consulting and Clinical Psychology* 52:528–38 (1984).
8. Peggy Giordano, Stephen Cernkovich, and M. D. Pugh, "Friendships and Delinquency," *American Journal of Sociology* 91:1170–1202 (1986).

9. A. R. Gillis and John Hagan, "Delinquent Samaritans: Network Structure, Social Conflict, and the Willingness to Intervene," *Journal of Research in Crime and Delinquency* 27:30–51 (1990).

10. G. Keinan, "Decision Making under Stress: Scanning of Alternatives under Controllable and Uncontrollable Threats," *Journal of Personality and Social Psychology* 52:639–44 (1987).

11. Irving Janis, *Groupthink: Psychological Studies of Policy Decisions and Fiascoes* (Boston: Houghton Mifflin, 1982).

12. Other well-known gang-related media images include the motorcycle gangs depicted in the movies *The Wild Ones* and *Hell's Angels on Wheels*, the neighborhood street toughs in *Saturday Night Fever*, and the futuristic gangs in the *Mad Max* series and *Clockwork Orange*; see also David Dawley, *A Nation of Lords* (Garden City, N.Y.: Anchor, 1973).

13. Walter Miller, *Violence by Youth Gangs and Youth Groups as a Crime Problem in Major American Cities* (Washington, D.C.: U.S. Government Printing Office, 1975).

14. *Ibid.*, p. 20.

15. Jeffery Fagan, "The Social Organization of Drug Use and Drug Dealing among Urban Gangs," *Criminology* 27:633–69 (1989).

16. Lewis Yablonsky, *The Violent Gang* (Baltimore: Penguin, 1966), p. 109.

17. Walter Miller, "Gangs, Groups, and Serious Youth Crime," in *Critical Issues in Juvenile Delinquency*, ed. David Schicor and Delos Kelly (Lexington, Mass.: Lexington Books, 1980).

18. *Ibid.*

19. Frederick Thrasher, *The Gang* (Chicago: University of Chicago Press, 1927).

20. Malcolm Klein, ed., *Juvenile Gangs in Context* (Englewood Cliffs, N.J.: Prentice-Hall, 1967), pp. 1–12.

21. *Ibid.*, p. 6.

22. Irving Spergel, *Street Gang Work: Theory and Practice* (Reading, Mass.: Addison-Wesley, 1966).

23. Miller, *Violence by Youth Gangs*, p. 2.

24. Marjorie Zatz, "Los Cholos: Legal Processing of Chicano Gang Members," *Social Problems* 33:13–30 (1985).

25. *Ibid.*, pp. 1–2.

26. *Ibid.*

27. Irving Spergel, "Youth Gangs: Problem and Response" (University of Chicago School of Social Service Administration, Chicago, 1989, unpublished mimeo).

28. "LA Gang Warfare Called Bloodiest in 5 Years," *Boston Globe*, 18 December 1986, p. A4.

29. National School Safety Center, *Gangs in Schools, Breaking Up Is Hard to Do* (Malibu, Calif.: Pepperdine University, 1988) p. 7 (hereinafter cited as *Gangs in Schools*).

30. Jean Latz Griffin, "Radio Appeal to Push for Chicago Gang Truce," *Boston Globe*, 27 November 1986, p. A10; Aurelio Rojas and Alice Crane, "Drug Trade Blamed for Widening Gang Wars in Los Angeles Area," *Manchester Union Leader* 14 December 1986, p. 6D.

31. John Hagedorn, *People and Folks: Gangs, Crime, and the Underclass in a Rustbelt City* (Chicago: Lake View Press, 1988).

32. *Gangs in Schools*, p. 8.

33. C. Ronald Huff, "Youth Gangs and Public Policy," *Crime and Delinquency* 35:524–37 (1989).

34. Richard Cloward and Lloyd Ohlin, *Delinquency and Opportunity* (New York: Free Press, 1960).

35. Jeffery Fagan, "The Social Organization of Drug Use and Drug Dealing among Urban Gangs," *Criminology* 27:633–69 (1989).

36. Huff, "Youth Gangs and Public Policy," pp. 528–29.

37. Saul Bernstein, *Youth in the Streets: Work with Alienated Youth Gangs* (New York: Associated Press, 1964).

38. Thrasher, *The Gang*, p. 20.

39. William Julius Wilson, *The Truly Disadvantaged* (Chicago: University of Chicago Press, 1987).

40. James Diego Vigil, *Barrio Gangs* (Austin, Texas: University of Texas Press, 1988).

41. Miller, *Violence by Youth Gangs*, pp. 17–20.

42. Jerome Needle and W. Vaughan Stapleton, *Reports of the National Juvenile Justice Assessment Centers, Police Handling of Youth Gangs* (Washington, D.C.: Office of Juvenile Justice and Delinquency Prevention, 1983), p. 12.

43. *Ibid.*

44. *Gangs in Schools*, p. 7.

45. Spergel, "Youth Gangs: Problems and Response," p. 7.

46. *Gangs in Schools*, p. 7.

47. Jeffery Fagan, "The Social Organization of Drug Use and Drug Dealing among Urban Gangs," p. 639.

48. LeRoy Martin, "Collecting, Organizing, and Reporting Street Gang Crime" (Chicago Police Department, Chicago, 1988) p. 38 (Hereinafter cited as "Street Gang Crime").

49. *Ibid.*, p. 39.

50. Miller, *Violence by Youth Gangs*, pp. 21–22.

51. Kevin Cullen, "Gangs Are Seen as Carefully Organized," *Boston Globe*, 7 January 1987, p. 17.

52. Malcolm Klein, *The Landino Hills Project* (Los Angeles: Youth Studies Center, University of Southern California, 1968).

53. Walter Miller, "The Impact of a 'Total Community' Delinquency Control Project," *Social Problems* 10:168–69 (1962).

54. Martin, "Street Gang Crime," p. 37.

55. Miller, *Violence by Youth Gangs*, p. 23.

56. Glenn Weisfeld and Roger Feldman, "A Former Street Gang Leader Re-interviewed Eight Years Later," *Crime and Delinquency* 28:567–81 (1982).

57. Joan Moore, Diego Vigil, and Robert Garcia, "Residence and Territoriality in Chicano Gangs," *Social Problems* 31:182–94 (1983).

58. William F. Whyte, *Street Corner Society* (Chicago: University of Chicago Press, 1955).

59. Malcolm Klein, "Impressions of Juvenile Gang Members," *Adolescence* 3:59 (1968).

60. Barry Krisberg, "Gang Youth and Hustling: The Psychology of Survival," *Issues in Criminology* 9:115–29 (1974).

61. Los Angeles County Sheriff's Department, *Street Gangs of Los Angeles County, White Paper,* (Los Angeles County Sheriff's Department, Los Angeles, n.d.), p. 14.

62. Martin, "Street Gang Crime."

63. Patricia Wen, "Boston Gangs: A Hard World," *Boston Globe*, 10 May 1988, p. 1.

64. Rick Graves and Ed Allen, *Black Gangs and Narcotics and Black Gangs* (Los Angeles County Sheriff's Department, Los Angeles, n.d.).

65. Associated Press, "Calif. Youth Slain Outside Theater Showing 'Colors'," *Boston Globe*, 26 April 1988, p. 6.

66. Malcolm Klein, Cheryl Maxson, and Lea Cunningham, " 'Crack,' Street Gangs, and Violence" (Center for Research on Crime and Social Control, University of Southern California, 1990).

67. Martin, "Street Gang Crime," p. 20.

68. Cheryl Maxson and Malcolm Klein, "Street Gang Violence: Twice as Great, or Half as Great?" (Paper presented at the American Society of Criminology Meeting, Reno, Nevada, November 1989).

69. Miller, *Violence by Youth Gangs*, pp. 2–26.

70. Malcolm Klein, "Violence in American Juvenile Gangs," in *Crimes of Violence*, ed. Donald Muvihill, Melvin Tumin, and Lynn Curtis, *National Commission on the Causes and Prevention of Violence*, vol. 13 (Washington, D.C.: U.S. Government Printing Office, 1969) p. 1429.

71. Cullen, "Gangs Are Seen as Carefully Organized," p. 17.

72. The following description of ethnic gangs leans heavily on the material developed in *Gangs in Schools*, pp. 11–23.

73. James Vigil, *Barrio Gangs* (Austin, Texas: University of Texas Press, 1988).

74. Los Angeles County Sheriff's Department, *Street Gangs of Los Angeles County*.

75. Ko-lin Chin, *Chinese Subculture and Criminality: Nontraditional Crime Groups in America* (Westport, Conn.: Greenwood Press, 1990).

76. Ibid., pp. 98–101.

77. Wayne Wooden, "Profile of Stoner Gang Members in the California Youth Authority" (Paper presented at the American Society of Criminology Meeting, Reno, Nevada, November 1989).

78. For an excellent review of theories of gang formation, see Patrick Jackson, "Theories and Findings about Youth Gangs," *Criminal Justice Abstracts*, June 1989, 313–327.

79. Herbert Block and Arthur Niederhoffer, *The Gang: A Study in Adolescent Behavior* (New York: Philosophical Library, 1958).

80. Ibid., p. 113.

81. Irving Spergel, *Racketville, Slumtown, and Haulburg: An Exploratory Study of Delinquent Subcultures* (Chicago: University of Chicago Press, 1964).

82. Wayne Wooden, "Contemporary Youth Identities: Problems and Issues" (Paper presented at the Western Society of Criminology Meeting, Las Vegas, Nevada, February 1990).

83. Yablonsky, *The Violent Gang*, p. 237.

84. Ibid., pp. 239–41.

85. Needle and Stapleton, *Police Handling of Youth Gangs*, p. 19.

86. Scott Armstrong, "Los Angeles Seeks New Ways to Handle Gangs," *Christian Science Monitor*, 23 April 1988, p. 3.

87. Mark Moore and Mark A. R. Kleiman, *The Police and Drugs* (Washington, D.C.: National Institute of Justice, 1989), p. 8.

88. Barry Krisberg, "Preventing and Controlling Violent Youth Crime: The State of the Art," in *Violent Juvenile Crime*, ed. Ira Schwartz (Minneapolis: Hubert H. Humphry Institute of Public Affairs, University of Minnesota, n.d.).

89. See, generally, Irving Spergel, *Street Gang Work*.

90. For a revisionist view of gang delinquency, see Hedy Bookin-Weiner and Ruth Horowitz, "The End of the Youth Gang," *Criminology* 21:585–602 (1983).

11 Schools and Delinquency

DETROIT BOARD OF EDUCATION

CODE OF STUDENT CONDUCT
METAL DETECTOR SEARCH
PROCEDURE

ATTENTION: STUDENTS

NOTICE OF SEARCH

STUDENTS ENTERING THIS BUILDING MAY BE ASKED TO SUBMIT TO A METAL DETECTOR SEARCH PROCEDURE TO ENSURE THAT WEAPONS AND OTHER DANGEROUS OBJECTS ARE NOT BROUGHT INTO THE BUILDING. THIS IS IN ACCORDANCE WITH ARTICLE III, SECTION 4 (b) OF THE CODE OF STUDENT CONDUCT. John

April 25, 1986

"Many of the underlying problems of delinquency, as well as their prevention and control, are intimately connected with the nature and quality of the school experience."[1]

Because the schools are responsible for educating virtually everyone during most of the formative years and because so much of an adolescent's time is spent in school, it seems logical that there is some relationship between delinquent behavior and what is happening—or not happening—in classrooms throughout the United States. This relationship was pointed out as early as 1939, when a study by the New Jersey Delinquency Commission found that of 2,021 inmates of prisons and correctional institutions in that state, two out of every five had first been committed for truancy.[2]

Numerous studies have confirmed that school and educational success is as important a contributing factor to delinquent behavior as the effects of either family or friends[3] (see Table 11.1). In addition, the school itself has been the scene of a significant amount of violence and theft. Consequently, educators are as concerned about combating crime within the schools as they are about creating an educational experience that will reduce general delinquent involvement.

This chapter examines the relationship between the school and delinquency. We will first explore how educational achievement and delinquency are related and what factors in the school experience appear to contribute to delinquent behavior. Next, we turn to delinquency within the school setting itself— vandalism, theft, violence, and so on. Finally, we look at the educational system's attempt to prevent and control delinquency.

EDUCATION AND AMERICAN YOUTH

The school plays a significant role in shaping the values and norms of American children. In contrast to earlier periods, when formal education was a privilege of the upper classes, the American system of compulsory public education has made schooling a legal obligation so that most school-age children are attending classes. In contrast to the earlier, agrarian days of U.S. history, when most adolescents shared in the work of the family and became socialized into adulthood as part of the work force, today's young people, beginning as early as age 3 or 4, spend most of their time in school. The school has become the primary instrument of socialization, the "basic conduit through which the community and adult influences enter into the lives of adolescents."[4]

Because young people spend a longer time in school, the period of their adolescence is prolonged. As long as students are still economically dependent on their families and have not entered the work world, they do not consider themselves, nor do others consider them, "adults." The responsibilities of adulthood come later to modern-day youths than they did to those in earlier generations, and some experts see this prolonged childhood as a factor that contributes to the irresponsible, childish, often irrational behavior of many juveniles who commit delinquent acts.[5]

Another significant aspect of the educational experience of American youths is that it is overwhelmingly a peer experience. Children spend their school hours

TABLE 11.1 Theoretical Views on Schools and Delinquency

VIEW	EDUCATIONAL IMPACT
Choice theory	People commit crime because of poor social control. The school can educate youths about the pains of punishment and through disciplinary procedures teach youths that behavior transgressions lead to sanctions. Education can stress moral development.
Developmental theory	The school can compensate for psychological and biological problems. For example, youths with low IQs or learning disabilities can be put in special classes to ease their frustration and reduce their delinquency-proneness.
Social structure theory	The school is a primary cause of delinquency. Middle-class school officials penalize lower-class youths, intensifying their rage, frustration, and anomie.
Social process theory	A lack of bond to the school and nonparticipation in educational activities can intensify delinquency-proneness. The school fails to provide sufficient definitions toward conventional behavior to thwart delinquency.
Labeling theory	Labeling by school officials solidifies negative self-images. The stigma associated with school failure locks youths into a delinquent career pattern.
Conflict theory	Schools are designed to train lower-class youngsters for menial careers and upper-class youths to be part of the privileged society. Rebellion against these roles promotes delinquency.

with their peers, and most of their activities after school take place with school friends. Young people rely increasingly on school friends and consequently become less and less interested in adult role models. Often, the norms and values of the peer culture are at odds with those of adult society and a pseudoculture with a distinct social system develops, offering a united front to the adult world.[6] Law-abiding behavior or conventional norms may not be among the values promoted in such an atmosphere. Youth culture may instead admire bravery, defiance, and having fun at the expense of hard work.

In addition to its role as an instrument of socialization, the school has become a primary determinant of economic and social status in American society.[7] In this highly technological age, education is the key to a "successful" job. No longer can parents ensure the status of their children through social class origin alone. Educational achievement has become of equal, if not greater, importance as a determinant of economic success.

Schools, then, are geared toward success defined in terms of academic achievement, which provides the key to profit and position in society. Virtually all adolescents must participate in the educational system, not only because it is required by law but also because the notion of success is defined in terms of possession of a technical or professional skill that can be acquired only through formal education.

This emphasis on the value of education is fostered by parents, the media, and the schools themselves. Regardless of their social or economic background, most children grown up believing that education is the key to success.[8] A national study of education found that a significant majority of youths who were asked how they would feel about having to leave school said, irrespective of social class, they would "try hard" or "do anything" to stay in school.[9]

American Educational Problems

Despite their apparent acceptance of the value of education, many youths do not meet acceptable standards of school achievement. Whether failure is measured by test scores, not being promoted, or dropping out, its incidence continues to be a major social problem in American society. A single school failure often leads to a pattern of chronic academic failure.[10]

After a twenty-year reform effort, there is little indication that the educational experience has improved. A government-funded study of the academic achievement among 9-, 13-, and 17-year-olds found that children only slightly improved their reading skills between 1971 and 1990 and showed no improvement in writing. Most troubling was the fact that the youngest group tested, fourth graders who were 9 years old, actually experienced a decline in reading ability during the 1980s.[11]

While minority groups have made up ground, they still lag white students in achievement. The percentage of black and Hispanic 13-year-olds who are one or more years behind their expected grade level is far higher than white students; underachievement figures for all three groups are troubling.[12]

Minority dropout rates are also higher; for example, almost 60 percent of Hispanic students never receive a high school diploma.[13] The lack of educational opportunity experienced by minority students is unacceptable in our society, which must dedicate itself to improving the quality of academic experience for all students.

The educational problems being faced by the nation's youth have been associated with serious social problems. High school dropouts will earn $200,000 less than graduates over their lifetimes, pay $78,000 less in taxes, and have double the unemployment rate and a much greater chance of being on public welfare.[14]

Because the school plays such an important role in socialization and the problems of the educational system have become so acute, the links between school failure, academic and social aspirations, and delinquency have become a topic of significant national importance.

THE EDUCATIONAL EXPERIENCE AND DELINQUENCY

There is a large body of research that indicates that an educational experience characterized by poor **academic performance** is directly associated with delinquent behavior. The general consensus developed over thirty years of research is

that students who are chronic underachievers in school are also among the most likely to be delinquent.[15] In fact, it is common for researchers to find that school failure is a stronger predictor of delinquency than such personal variables as economic class membership, racial or ethnic background, or peer group relations. Studies that compare the academic records of delinquents and nondelinquents, including their scores on standardized tests of basic skills, failure rates, teacher ratings, and other measures, have found that delinquents are often educationally deficient, a condition that may lead to their leaving school and becoming involved in antisocial behavior.[16] Though this pattern could also be the result of teacher bias toward classroom "troublemakers" or the impact of a self-fulfilling prophecy (kids labeled "behavior problems" by teachers also are perceived to be deserving of lower grades), there is evidence that teacher evaluations are accurate and reflect the poor academic performance of law-violating youth.[17]

Nowhere is the relationship between academic performance and delinquency more apparent than in studies of chronic offending. Lyle Shannon found that school failure and dropping out were significantly related to both self-reported and official measures of chronic delinquency.[18] David Farrington and Donald J. West also found that chronic delinquents did poorly in school. While 33 percent of youths in their sample who felt school was "of little use to them" were recidivists, only 7 percent of those who saw some benefit in school were repeat offenders.[19]

Marvin Wolfgang's cohort study also closely links chronic delinquency to school failure.[20] Only 9 percent of the chronic offenders graduated from high school, compared with 74 percent of nonoffenders. Chronic offenders also had significantly more disciplinary actions and remedial/disciplinary placements than nonoffenders.[21]

The long-term consequences of school failure may be equally acute. One survey of prison inmates found that 42 percent of incarcerated felons had twelve or more years of education, compared with about 80 percent of the general population.[22]

In summary, the relationship between poor school achievement and delinquent behavior is well documented in the literature of crime and delinquency. Recent research finds that chronic delinquents experience an alarming rate of school failure. While this data cannot by itself confirm that school failure *causes* delinquency to occur, it certainly supports theories that include academic underachievement as a major correlate of delinquency.

RELATING SCHOOL FAILURE TO DELINQUENCY

While there is general agreement that school failure and delinquency are related, there is some conflict over the nature and direction of the relationship. One view is that there is a "common cause" for both school failure and delinquency and that therefore it is erroneous to conclude that school failure precedes and causes antisocial behavior. For example, some delinquency experts contend that delinquents have lower IQs than nondelinquents, a factor that might also explain their poor academic achievement. Similarly, delinquency might be caused by a tumultuous family life, which can also be a cause of school failure. In sum, it is possible that the observed relationship between school failure and delinquency is actually the result of another underlying social problem.

A second view is that the school experience is a direct cause of delinquent behavior. According to this view, children who perform poorly in school will feel frustrated and angry, fail to see a future, and eventually conclude that they will never achieve success through conventional means. Educational failure that begins early in the academic career elicits negative responses from important people in children's lives: parents consider them "failures" who are unworthy of attention; achievement-oriented peers shun them. These reactions may lead nonachieving students to delinquency.

Some experts believe that the school experience may have only an indirect impact on delinquent behavior. For example, a suspected result of academic failure is a loss of **self-esteem.** Studies using a variety of measures of academic competence and self-esteem clearly demonstrate that good students have better attitudes about themselves than do poor students.[23] Concomitantly, several research efforts corroborate the finding that low self-esteem contributes to delinquent behavior.[24]

Some of the factors related to a child's school experience that are believed to have either a direct or indirect influence on delinquency are discussed in some detail below.

Social Class Bias

During the 1950s, research by Albert Cohen indicated that delinquency was fundamentally a phenomenon of working-class students who were poorly equipped to function in middle-class schools. Cohen referred to this phenomenon as a failure to live up to "**middle-class measuring rods.**"[25] Jackson Toby reinforced this concept of class-based delinquency by contending that the disadvantages of lower-class children in school (for example, lack of verbal skills, lack of parental education, lack of motivation) are a direct result of their position in the social structure and implicitly foster their delinquency.[26]

Some theorists contend that the high incidence of failure among lower-class youths is actually a result of the schools themselves. Martin Gold described the school experience as a frightening world in which conditions for success and failure are clear and ever present. Constant testing and comparing and the threat of failure make school a difficult experience for at-risk lower-class youth.[27]

Schools, by their failure to counterbalance the handicaps of low-income and minority children, may actively contribute to academic failure. Research data confirms not only that such children begin school at lower levels of achievement but also that, without help, their performance progressively deteriorates the longer they are in school. If this is true, the school itself becomes an active force in the generation of delinquency.[28]

Not all experts, however, agree with the social class bias hypothesis. Some find that kids who do poorly in school, regardless of their socioeconomic background, are more likely to be delinquent that those who perform well in school.[29] Arthur Stinchcombe showed that a discrepancy between students' future goal aspirations and their present school performance is more important in determining delinquency than is social class position. Kids who aspired to middle-class occupations but lacked the academic skills to achieve them were the most likely to later succumb to the lure of law-violating behaviors. Thus, according to Stinchcombe's **articulation hypothesis,** "the key fact is the future of students, not their origins. Since we know that origins partly determine futures, social class will be an important variable, but in an unusual way."[30]

Although students from all social strata who suffer academic failure appear prone to delinquency, lower-class students may be at a particular disadvantage, having to compete academically while coping with overwhelming economic disadvantages. Lower-class youths may be overrepresented as school failures because teachers tend to stereotype them and expect disruptive behavior from them, strengthening the relationship between the lower class and official delinquency.

Tracking

"Placement in noncollege tracks of the contemporary high school means consignment to an educational oblivion without apparent purpose or meaning."[31] Many researchers have looked at academic tracking—dividing the students into groups according to ability and achievement level—as a contributor to student delinquency. There is evidence that beginning as early as the *first grade,* a students' positions in the academic structure may influence their placement in subsequent classes and the entire pattern of their educational careers.[32] Studies overwhelmingly indicate that, compared with those in college tracks, lower-track students experience greater academic failure and progressive deterioration of achievement, participate less frequently in the extracurricular life of the school, have an increased tendency to drop out, engage in more frequent misbehavior in school, and commit more delinquent acts. These differences are at least partially caused by assignment to a low academic track, whereby these students are effectively locked out of a chance to achieve educational success.

Some effects of tracking as it relates to delinquency are:[33]

■ *Self-fulfilling prophecy.* Low-track students from whom little achievement and more misbehavior are expected tend to live up to these often unspoken assumptions about their behavior.

■ *Stigma.* The labeling effect of placement in a low-track leads to loss of self-esteem, which increases the potential for academic failure and troublemaking both in school and out.

■ *Student subculture.* Students segregated in lower tracks develop a value system that often rewards misbehavior rather than the academic success they feel they can never achieve.

■ *Future rewards.* Low-track students are less inclined to conform. Because they see no future rewards for their schooling, their futures are not threatened by a record of deviance or low academic achievement.

■ *Grading policies.* Low-track students tend to receive lower grades than other students, even for work of equal quality, based on the rationale that students who are not college-bound are "obviously" less bright and do not need good grades so they can get into college.

■ *Teacher effectiveness.* Teachers of high-ability students make more of an effort to teach in an interesting and challenging manner than those who instruct lower-level students.

In one analysis, Delos Kelly and William Pink showed that school officials begin stereotyping and tracking students in the lowest grade levels.[34] Educators sometimes separate youths into special groups that bear innocuous names but may carry with them the taint of failure and academic incompetence ("Bluebirds" versus "Blackbirds"). Junior and senior high school students may be tracked separately in individual subjects, based on the perceived ability of the students. Classes may be labeled in descending order as: advanced placement, academically enriched, average, basic, and remedial. And as Jeannie Oakes found in her national study of tracking, it is common for students to have all their courses in only one or two tracks.[35]

The effects of negative school labels (e.g., "school failure," "delinquent," or "low tracker") become cumulative over time. A student's academic failure often means that he or she is probably destined to fail again, and over time, the repeated instances of failure can help to produce the career of the "misfit," delinquent, or dropout.[36] Consequently, a tracking system keeps certain students from any hope of achieving academic success, thereby causing a lack of motivation, failure and rebellion, which may be fertile ground for delinquent behavior.[37]

Another disturbing outcome of tracking is that students are often stigmatized as academically backward if they voluntarily attend a program or institution designed to help underachievers.[38] Teachers consider remedial reading programs as dumping grounds for youths with "bad attitudes," and consequently, educators expect youths who attend special-education programs to be disruptive in the classroom.[39] Even more serious charges against tracking have been leveled by Oakes, whose landmark study, *Keeping Track*, has helped expose the problems associated with the practice. She found that

> Tracking seems to retard the academic progress of many students—those in average and low groups. Tracking seems to foster low self-esteem among these same students and promote school misbehavior and dropping out. Tracking also appears to lower the aspirations of students who are not in the top groups. And perhaps most important, in view of all the above, is that tracking separates students along socioeconomic lines, separating rich from poor, whites from nonwhites. The end result is that poor and minority children are found far more often than others in the bottom tracks. And once there, they are likely to suffer far more negative consequences of schooling than are their more fortunate peers.[40]

Charges have also been made by parent groups around the nation that racial and ethnic minorities are overrepresented in low achievement tracks while advanced programs are reserved for white youths. Because of these concerns a few school systems, such as those in San Diego and Denver, have eliminated tracking. Schools in Chelsea, Massachusetts, in cooperation with Boston University to improve school performance, will eliminate all remedial reading classes in grades one through five and require eighth and ninth graders to enroll in courses traditionally restricted by gender such as home economics, mechanics, and bookkeeping. The Holyoke, Massachusetts school system plans to replace tracking with a cooperative approach of team learning and team teaching.

Student Alienation

Alienation of students from the educational experience is another primary factor in the link between schools and delinquency. Alienation and academic failure are closely related, for it is unlikely that a child who is doing poorly in school will perceive school as a rewarding or meaningful experience.[41]

Student alienation can be produced by a number of different factors. For example, the isolation and impersonality that result from the large size of many modern public schools is believed to contribute to student alienation and is therefore linked to delinquent behavior. Although larger schools are more economical to construct, their climate is often impersonal, and relatively few students can find avenues for meaningful participation. The resulting resentment can breed an environment in which violence and vandalism are likely to occur. Smaller schools offer a more personalized environment in which students can experience more meaningful interaction with the rest of the educational community. Furthermore, teachers and other school personnel have the opportunity in a smaller school to deal with early indications of academic or behavior problems and thus act to prevent delinquency.

In addition to impersonality, students can be alienated from the traditional student role that continues to operate in the schools. They are passive, docile receivers of knowledge and are seldom encouraged to take responsibility for their own learning. In many schools, students have little voice in decision making. Some of them therefore feel excluded from the educational process, and such alienation may at times result in withdrawal from or overt hostility toward the school and all that it represents.

Looking at this issue from another perspective, schools that encourage warm, personal student-teacher relationships have also experienced increased developmental achievement. "Warm" teachers have been found to assist underachievers to do better in school; lower-class youth who report a positive experience with teachers have been found to be more successful when they finish school than students who fail to develop supportive relationships.[42] The role teachers can play as a significant other in the lives of troubled youth is only beginning to receive proper recognition.

Irrelevant Curriculum

One cause of dissatisfaction among many students is their inability to see the relevance or significance of what they are taught in school.[43] The gap between their education and the real world leads them to feel that the school experience is little more than a waste of time.[44]

Many students, particularly those from low-income families, believe that school has no payoff in terms of their future. Because the legitimate channel appears to be meaningless, "the illegitimate alternative becomes increasingly more attractive and delinquency sometimes results."[45]

Rebelliousness in school has been linked to the perception that school is irrelevant to future job prospects. Students who do not plan to attend college or to use their high school educations directly in their careers are particularly susceptible to feelings of educational irrelevancy; in contrast, those who have expectations of a college education and commitment to long-term goals are less likely to engage in delinquency.[46]

Alienation is a problem particularly among low-income and minority students because American schools are predominantly white, middle-class institutions. Although all states have had compulsory education statutes for several decades, today's schools are oriented toward middle-class youths and exclude lower-class youths, whose needs and values are ignored. Current methods of instruction as well as curriculum materials reflect middle-class mores, language, and customs and have little meaning for the disadvantaged child.[47]

For some students, then, school is alien territory—a place where they feel unwelcome either because they lack academic skills or because they are different from the role models that the school holds out to them. Disruption of classes, vandalism, and violence in schools may in fact be part of an effort to obtain enjoyment in an otherwise lifeless and unfriendly environment.[48]

There is evidence that in many schools, alienated youths form a subculture and work in concert to subvert the educational system. This subculture participates in a higher-than-normal amount of delinquent behavior. Individualized treatment efforts will have little effect if they do not take these subcultural influences into account.[49]

Dropping Out

Delinquency is not the only self-destructive alternative available to academically or socially alienated students. They can also **drop out** of school.

While it is generally recognized that dropping out of school carries with it many negative social consequences, there has actually been much debate over the impact dropping out has on delinquent behavior. Surprisingly, the bulk of research efforts points to a decline in delinquent behavior once a child leaves the school environment. Strain theory holds that once the pressure and conflict of the school experience ends, the probability of continued delinquency among disaffected students should be reduced. This hypothesis was tested by Delbert Elliott and Harwin Voss in an often-cited study of 2,600 male and female students during their four years in high school. Elliott and Voss found:

- The rate of delinquency is significantly higher among those who drop out of school than among those who do not.

- Dropouts' reasons for being delinquent while still in school are often rooted in the school experience itself (limited academic achievement, feelings of alienation from school, association with delinquent classmates, for example).

- The rate of delinquency for dropouts increases during the period immediately preceding their leaving school, but once they drop out, both police-recorded and self-admitted delinquency decline rapidly.[50]

Sociologist Daniel Glaser also notes that this phenomenon seems to cut across socioeconomic lines: "In *every* neighborhood and *every* socioeconomic class, most of those who are first arrested *while still in school* are less frequently arrested after they drop out."[51]

Several other research efforts are consistent with the results of the Elliott and Voss study.[52] However, in an important work, Terence Thornberry, Melanie Moore, and R. L. Christenson examined data gathered in Philadelphia to determine the effect of dropping out on the delinquency rate.[53] Their results were in sharp contrast to earlier research efforts. Thornberry and his associates found that dropouts were more likely to engage in antisocial behavior immediately after dropping out and then repeat their criminal behavior throughout their early twenties. This finding was consistent for youths of various social backgrounds and races and held up when marital status and employment record were controlled. Thornberry and his associates conclude that these findings are in synch with the control theory view that severing ties with conventional society helps establish a youth in a delinquent way of life.

There are several other indicators that support the dropout-delinquency connection. A recent government sponsored survey of more than 12,000 arrestees in twenty major cities found that more than 50 percent dropped out of school before the twelfth grade.[54] As Table 11.2 shows, black, white, and Hispanic arrestees all exhibited a consistent lack of educational attainment. The rate of dropping out among Hispanic arrestees is especially disturbing: 60 percent or more of Hispanic youth who get in trouble with the law have dropped out of

TABLE 11.2   Percentage of Arrestees Who Completed Less Than Twelve Grades of School*

	MALES				FEMALES		
City	Black	White	Hispanic	City	Black	White	Hispanic
San Antonio	55	50	81	San Antonio	**	42	74
Kansas City	58	70	**	Kansas City	51	**	**
St. Louis	64	70	**	St. Louis	52	38	**
Philadelphia	55	54	69	Philadelphia	56	42	**
Dallas	56	69	86	Dallas	46	49	**
Cleveland	55	52	**	New Orleans	48	44	**
New Orleans	60	34	**	New York	57	54	64
New York	55	36	65	Indianapolis	36	64	**
Indianapolis	60	68	**	Chicago	48	**	**
Miami	46	57	68	Detroit	54	67	**
Chicago	56	50	65	Portland	51	65	**
Detroit	62	47	**	Birmingham	52	55	**
Portland	46	54	71	Los Angeles	29	42	72
Birmingham	49	57	**	Phoenix	47	50	74
Los Angeles	34	38	72	San Diego	31	46	71
Houston	52	34	75				
Omaha	36	54	**				
Phoenix	36	37	74				
San Diego	34	37	61				
Ft. Lauderdale	45	28	**				

*Data based on voluntary self-reports, 1988. Sample sizes for males are: black—5,622, white—2,936, Hispanic—1,794. Sample sizes for females are: black—1,533, white—1,169, Hispanic—438.
**Less than twenty cases.

Source: National Institute of Justice/Drug Use Forecasting Program (Washington, D.C.: U.S. Government Printing Office, 1989).

school before completing the twelfth grade. It comes as no surprise then that surveys of prison inmates also show that a significant number left school before the completion of the high school curriculum.[55]

DROPPING OUT AND EDUCATIONAL POLICY. The dropout problem has serious implications for educational policy in the United States. The wisdom of having compulsory education statutes seems questionable if there is evidence that delinquency rates actually *decline* after students leave school. Forcing unwilling teenagers to stay in school might be counterproductive, and delinquency might decline if trouble-prone students are allowed to assume a productive place in the work force. In other words, for many youths, leaving school can actually have the beneficial effect of escape from a stressful, humiliating situation that has little promise of offering them any future benefits.

Sociologist Jackson Toby for one suggests that lowering the dropout age to 15 or less might improve the educational climate of public schools at the same time that it makes schools safer places for students and staff. Toby reasons that a great deal of school crime is committed by youths who are forced to remain in school with little desire to further their education. If these problem students were removed from the academic scene, remaining students would be able to pursue their education in a climate conducive to scholarship and learning and teachers could be more concerned with the curriculum and less with maintaining security.[56]

If, in contrast, the recent literature indicates accurate, allowing students to leave school before graduation may hold little promise of short- or long-term benefits and therefore must be avoided at all costs. If, as the evidence seems to suggest, dropouts pursue a long-term criminal career, then it would be beneficial to design school programs that encourage students to stay in school and improve their academic performance.

DELINQUENCY WITHIN THE SCHOOL

It has become common to view school as a highly dangerous place in which intruders or students victimize teachers and other pupils, vandalize property, and disrupt the educational process. A number of national surveys have documented the seriousness of the problem. One conducted by the National Institute of Education found that although teenagers spend only 25 percent of their time in school, 40 percent of the robberies and 36 percent of the physical attacks involving members of this age group occur in school.[57] Victim surveys show that each year, nearly 3 million attempted or completed street crimes, including assault, rape, robbery, and theft, take place inside schools or on school property.[58]

One disturbing trend has been the spread of weapons on school grounds, ranging from pocket knives to Uzi machine guns. To give an idea of how serious this problem is, California officials reported that between July 1, 1987, and June 30, 1988, 8,539 weapons were confiscated from students, including 789 guns, 4,408 knives, 2,216 explosives, and 1,126 "other weapons."[59] During the 1986-1987 school year, Nashville schools reported 107 weapons-related suspensions while Detroit had 519 disciplinary actions for weapons possession.[60] These figures may be only the tip of the iceberg, since most weapons violations go unreported. One survey of students in Baltimore found that 64 percent said they knew someone who had carried a handgun to school, 60 percent said they knew someone who had been shot, threatened, or robbed at gunpoint, and almost half the males admitted carrying a handgun to school at least once.[61]

The Nature of School Crime

Who are the victims of school crime? Young persons between the ages of 12 and 15 incur the highest risk, for in this group are the victims of 68 percent of the robberies and 50 percent of the assaults taking place on school grounds. The risk of being victimized is highest for minority students in largely white schools and for white students in minority-dominated schools.[62]

It has become common for schools to experience criminal activity. This photo captures the scene after intruders caused $500,000 damage in a Salem, Massachusetts high school.

Teachers are also victims in the school setting. A poll taken by the National Education Association found that about 5 percent of teachers were physically attacked and 29 percent had property stolen or damaged in a twelve-month period.[63]

Who commits school crime? Nationally, most offenders are students currently enrolled in the school, but in major cities, the most common offender is a trespasser or **intruder.** Rule and law violators are often **truants** who come to school late and wander the hallways looking for trouble. Another type is the predator who does not belong to the school community at all. Others are marginal members of the school community, described by Jackson Toby as including "an angry parent intent on beating up the child's teacher; friends or enemies of enrolled students; suspended students who prefer a warm, dry school building to the streets."[64] According to Toby, intruders who have little connection to the school are heavy contributors to big-city school violence, and schools must develop security measures to prevent their entry onto school grounds.

What kind of schools experience high crime and victimization levels? According to Gary Gottfredson and Denise Gottfredson, the most critical factor is if the school is experiencing *social disorganization*, which can be defined as

a high proportion of students behind grade level in reading, many students from families on welfare, a high proportion of minority students; and such community characteristics as high unemployment, high crime, much poverty and unemployment, and many female-headed households.[65]

The Gottfredsons found that schools whose administrators cooperate with teachers, that have highly regarded principals, are perceived to be fair and to have well-defined rules, and allow students a say in the way the school is run will have lower rates of many crimes. However, the Gottfredsons' research indicates that school disruption and victimization are not easy concepts to understand: several types of victimization can be found in every school, and no single factor can account for all forms of school problems.

School Crime and the Community

A number of researchers have observed that school crime and disruption is a function of the community in which the school is located. In other words, crime in schools does not occur in isolation from crime in the community.[66]

An important analysis by Joan McDermott raises some interesting questions about school crime and its victims.[67] McDermott found that crime and fear in schools reflect the same patterns that exist in the outside neighborhood environment. Schools in high-crime areas experience more crime than schools in safer areas; there is less fear in schools in safer neighborhoods than in high-crime areas. Thus, the school cannot be viewed independently from the neighborhood in which it is located. In fact, students who report being afraid in school are actually *more* afraid of being in city parks or streets or subways.

McDermott also discovered that perpetrators and the victims of school crime cannot be divided into two separate groups. Many young offenders have been victims of delinquency themselves and fear being victimized again. It is possible, McDermott concludes, that violent and theft-related crimes in the school have "survival value" and can be viewed as "rational responses to situations." The victim of school crime may find that striking back at another, weaker victim is emotionally satisfying or simply a method of regaining lost possessions or self-respect.

Using data collected from the school system in Boston, Daryl Hellman and Susan Beaton also found that school problems are linked to crime and disruption in the community and may stem from external environmental factors.[68] Hellman and Beaton found that measures of school disruption, such as suspension rates, are significantly related to such community variables as family structure (communities with high percentages of two-parent families experience fewer school problems), housing quality, population density, and stability. School problems were not related to income level, employment, or the racial composition of the community.

McDermott's analysis suggests that it may be futile to attempt to eliminate school crime without considering the impact that prevention efforts will have on the community:

> The school-community link suggests additional problems with some in-school crime prevention strategies. Law-and-order approaches, such as tighter security, stricter rule enforcement, and fortress-like alterations in a school's physical plant, may reduce acts of crime and violence in school, only to displace them to the community. Similarly, expelling or suspending troublemakers puts them on the street with nothing to do. Lowering the level of crime in schools may have no real impact on reducing the total amount of crime committed by young people.[69]

Similarly, Hellman and Beaton suggest that as communities undergo change (for example, when they experience increases in labor force participation and the number of nonfamily households), both school disruption and community crime increase.[70] Consequently, the school environment must be restructured (for example, by lowering student-teacher ratios or by taking steps to keep intruders out of school buildings) to combat community influences.

Preventing School Crime

A number of school-based delinquency prevention efforts have been carried out around the nation. One approach has been to ensure the physical safety of the school facility by mechanical security devices, such as surveillance cameras, electronic barriers to keep out intruders, and roving security guards. In Detroit schools, a portable metal detector is set up when security guards believe that trouble is imminent and hand searches are conducted in a nearby holding room.[71] To prevent students from bringing weapons on campus, Montgomery, Alabama, requires students to carry clear plastic or mesh bookbags; in Baltimore, students must leave bookbags and coats in lockers during the school day.[72] Critics claim that even though these methods are effective, they reduce staff and student morale.

Another approach used successfully by some school administrators is to set up and enforce strict disciplinary codes. Some school districts, such as Providence, Rhode Island, have adopted policies that require students caught with a weapon be suspended for 60 days; New York City adds notification of police to the sus-

School administrators can make and enforce rules to assure a safe, educational environment. This can include the right to search students' lockers.

pension order.[73] Some districts suspend such students for the remainder of the school year or longer; the California education code mandates that a student who uses a weapon in school may not attend a public school in the state until a hearing is held and the board of education is shown that the student is no longer a risk.[74] After numerous acts of violence were committed in the Boston school system, law violators are now sent to a center for evaluation and counseling and kept separate from the law-abiding school population.[75] Experts have applauded efforts to create clear-cut policies banning weapons and mandate that school-based violence be reported to the police.[76]

Other programs have been designed to improve the standards of the teaching staff and administrators and the educational climate in the school, increase the relevance of the curriculum, and provide law-related education classes.[77]

One Chicago-based program uses existing discipline and legal standards to combat school crime. Researchers found that teachers were not aware of existing codes of school conduct. They also found that more than half of the teachers were verbally abused by students and that student fights were common. The research team is developing a new disciplinary code in conjunction with teachers and parents. One proposed change is an in-school suspension room to cut down on the number of suspended students who are free to roam the neighborhood.[78]

These efforts remain local in scope, but as a whole, they point toward successful strategies to reduce school crime.

Legal Issues

While educational officials have attempted to restore order within the school, their actions often run into opposition from the courts, which are concerned with maintaining the legal rights of minor children. The U.S. Supreme Court has sought to balance the right of students to maintain civil liberties with the school's mandate to provide a reasonable and safe educational environment. In some instances, the Court has sided with students, while in others, the balance has shifted toward the educational establishment. The main issues concerning the rights of children and the schools include compulsory attendance, free speech in school, and school discipline.

COMPULSORY SCHOOL ATTENDANCE. In the United States, compulsory school attendance statutes have been in effect for more than half a century.[79] Children are required by law to attend school until a given age, normally 16 or 17.[80] Violations of compulsory attendance laws generally result in complaints that can lead to court action. Often, however, children are truant because of emotional problems or learning disabilities. They are then brought into the court system for problems beyond their control. Many of them might be better off leaving school at an earlier age than the compulsory education law allows. On the other hand, emotionally disturbed and nonconforming children are pushed out of many school systems and thereby deprived of an education. Whether these children have a right to attend school is unclear. Many school systems ignore the difficult student, who may be classified as "bad" or "delinquent."

In 1925, the Supreme Court determined that compulsory education did not necessarily have to be provided by a public school system and that parochial schools could be a reasonable substitute.[81] From that time through the 1970s, the courts upheld the right of the state to make education compulsory. Then, in 1972, in the case of *Wisconsin v. Yoder*, the Supreme Court made an exception to the general compulsory education law by holding that traditional Amish culture was able to give its children the skills that would prepare them for adulthood within Amish society. Thus, their removal from school after the completion of the eighth grade was justified.[82] It is not clear, however, whether this decision speaks directly to the issue of compulsory education or whether it is simply another instance of the freedom of religion. Therefore, the state's role in requiring school attendance is still unsettled.

FREE SPEECH. Freedom of speech is granted and guaranteed in the First Amendment to the U.S. Constitution. The right has been divided into two major categories as it affects children in schools. The first category involves what is known as **passive speech,** a form of expression not associated with the actual speaking of words. Examples include the wearing of armbands or political protest buttons. The most important Supreme Court decision concerning a student's right to passive speech was in 1969 in the case of *Tinker v. Des Moines Independent Community School District.*[83] This case involved the right to wear black armbands to protest the war in Vietnam. High school students, aged 16 and 17, were told they would be suspended if they demonstrated their objections to the war by wearing black armbands. They went ahead and attended school wearing the armbands and were suspended. According to the Court, in order for the state (in the person of a school official) to justify prohibiting an expression of opinion, it must be able to show that its action was caused by something more than a mere desire to avoid the discomfort and unpleasantness that accompany the expression of an unpopular view. Unless it can be shown that the forbidden conduct will interfere with the discipline required to operate the school, the prohibition cannot be sustained. In the *Tinker* case, the Court said there was no evidence that the school authorities had reason to believe that the wearing of armbands would substantially interfere with the work of the school or infringe on the rights of other students.[84]

This decision is significant because it recognizes the child's right to free speech in a public school system. Justice Abe Fortas stated in his majority opinion, "Young people do not shed their constitutional rights at the schoolhouse door."[85] *Tinker* established two things: (1) a child is entitled to free speech in school under the First Amendment of the Constitution, and (2) the test used to determine whether the child has gone beyond proper speech is whether he or she materially and substantially interferes with the requirements of appropriate discipline in the operation of the school.

The concept of free speech articulated in *Tinker* was used again in the 1986 case of *Bethel School District No. 403 v. Fraser.*[86] This case upheld a school system's right to suspend or otherwise discipline a student who uses obscene or profane language and gestures. Matthew Fraser, a Bethel high school student, used sexual metaphors in making a speech nominating a friend for student office, and was subsequently suspended. His statement included these remarks:

Mary Beth Tinker and her brother, John Tinker, display the black armbands they wore to school to protest U.S. involvement in Vietnam in 1965 despite a school rule that prohibited armbands. When the Tinkers were suspended, they appealed to the Supreme Court, which ruled that under the First Amendment schools cannot punish students for expressing an opinion.

I know a man who is firm—he's firm in his pants, he's firm in his shirt, his character is firm—but most . . . of all, his belief in you, the students of Bethel, is firm.

Jeff Kuhlman is a man who takes his point and pounds it in. If necessary, he'll take an issue and nail it to the wall. He doesn't attack things in spurts—he drives hard, pushing and pushing until finally—he succeeds.

Jeff is a man who will go to the very end—even the climax, for each and every one of you.

So vote for Jeff for A.S.B. vice-president—he'll never come between you and the best our high school can be.

The Court found that a school has the right to control lewd and offensive speech that undermines the educational mission. The Court drew a distinction between the sexual content of Fraser's remarks and the political nature of Tinker's armband. It ruled that the pervasive sexual innuendo of the speech interfered with the school's mission to implant "the shared values of a civilized social order" in the student body.

In a 1988 case, *Hazelwood School District v. Kuhlmeier*, the Court extended the right of school officials to censor "active speech" when it ruled that the principal could censor articles in a student publication.[87] In the present case, students had written about their personal experiences with teenage pregnancy and parental divorce. The majority ruled that censorship was justified in this case because school-sponsored publications, activities, and productions were part of the curriculum and therefore designed to impart knowledge. Control over such school-inspired activities could be differentiated from the armband action Tinker and other students initiated on their own accord. In a dissent, Justice William Brennan accused school officials of favoring "thought control."

SCHOOL DISCIPLINE. Most states have statutes permitting teachers to use corporal punishment to discipline students in public school systems. Under *in loco parentis*, discipline is one of the assumed parental duties given the school system. In two decisions, the Supreme Court upheld the school's right to use corporal punishment. In the case of *Baker v. Owen*, the Court stated:

> We hold that the Fourteenth Amendment embraces the right of parents generally to control the means and discipline of their children, but that the state has a countervailing interest in the maintenance of order in the schools . . . sufficient to sustain the right of teachers and school officials must accord to students minimal due process in the course of inflicting such punishment.[88]

In 1977, the Court again spoke on the issue of corporal punishment in school systems in the case of ***Ingraham v. Wright,*** which upheld the right of teachers to use corporal punishment.[89] The facts in this case were that James Ingraham and Roosevelt Andrews, two students, sustained injuries as a result of paddling in the Charles Drew Junior High School in Dade County, Florida. The legal problems raised in the case were (1) whether corporal punishment by teachers was a violation in this case of the Eighth Amendment against cruel and unusual punishment and (2) whether the due process clause of the Fourteenth Amendment required that the students be given proper notice and a hearing prior to receiving corporal punishment. The Court held that neither the Eighth Amendment nor the Fourteenth Amendment was violated in this case. Even though Ingraham suffered hematomas on his buttocks as a result of twenty blows with a wooden paddle and Andrews was hurt in the arm, the Court ruled that such punishment was not a constitutional violation. The Court established the standard that only reasonable discipline was allowed in school systems, but it excepted the degree of punishment administered in this case. The key principle in *Ingraham* is that the reasonableness standard that the Court articulated represents the judicial attitude that the scope of the school's right to discipline a child is by no means more restrictive than the rights of the child's own parents to impose corporal punishment.

Other issues involving the legal rights of students include their due process rights when interrogated, if corporal punishment is to be imposed, and when suspension and expulsion are threatened. When students are questioned by school personnel, no warning as to their legal rights to remain silent or right to counsel need be given. However, when school security guards, on-campus police officials, and public police officers question students, such constitutional warnings are required. In the area of corporal punishment, procedural due process established with the case of *Baker v. Owen* requires that students at least be forewarned about the possibility of corporal punishment as a discipline. In addition, the *Baker* case requires that there be a witness to the administration of corporal punishment and allows the student and the parent to elicit reasons for the punishment.

With regard to suspension and expulsion, the Supreme Court ruled in 1976 in the case of *Goss v. Lopez* that any time a student is to be suspended up to a period of ten days, he or she is entitled to a hearing.[90] The student does not, however, have a right to counsel or a right to confront or cross-examine witnesses. The Court went on to state in *Goss* that the extent of the procedural due process requirements would be established on a case-by-case basis. That is, each case would represent its own facts and have its own procedural due process elements.

In summary, schools have the right to discipline students, but students are protected from unreasonable, excessive, and arbitrary discipline.

CASE IN POINT

As principal of the suburban regional high school, you are faced with a growing drug-use problem among the student body. There is evidence of dealing on campus, and parents have complained that their kids are bringing home drugs they bought at school. Last week, a 15-year-old overdosed and almost lost her life. At a school board meeting, angry parents charge that this kind of behavior may be okay in the city but this is a suburban community to which people come to get away from drugs and delinquency. There is some angry talk that if you can't handle the situation, then a new school chief should be found who can.

The local police offer a solution for the drug problem: institute a tough security policy that makes use of hidden cameras in public areas, such as the parking lot and cafeteria; allow random searches of student lockers and desks; hire a security director who will search students suspected of selling or possessing drugs; turn over to the police all evidence for prosecution; and suspend students possessing drugs on campus for the school year. Some teachers feel these draconian policies are misplaced in a suburban school. The relatively few offenders should be placed in counseling programs. Instead of security guards, the school should hire a drug awareness education teacher and teach kids about the dangers of taking drugs.

Should a school drug-prevention program stress law enforcement or education?

Is it fair to search student lockers at random?

Are hidden cameras an intrusion of student privacy or a needed security measure?

THE ROLE OF THE SCHOOL IN DELINQUENCY PREVENTION

In 1983, the National Commission on Excellence in Education reviewed the nation's educational system and published its findings in *A Nation at Risk*.[91] The report highlighted the significant security problems faced by educators and focused efforts towards reducing fear on school campuses. Since then, educators have attempted to play a role in delinquency prevention in two areas: (1) controlling vandalism and crime within the school itself and (2) creating programs that will have a beneficial influence on youths and provide them with opportunities for conventional success in the outside world. Some of these efforts are listed in Table 11.3.

Despite these and other well-publicized efforts, skepticism still remains about whether the American school system, viewed by critics as overly conservative and archaic, can play a significant role in delinquency prevention. There is a danger that the pressure being placed on schools to improve the educational experience of students can produce unforeseen problems for staff members. Pressure to show that the school is doing a good job can create an atmosphere of faculty desperation. For example, efforts to improve student performance on standardized tests have given rise to faculty cheating, resulting in criminal prosecutions of teachers for encouraging students to cheat on standardized tests and providing them with answer sheets.[92]

Some experts contend that no significant change in the lives of youths is possible by merely changing the schools. The entire social and economic structure of society must be altered if schools are to help students realize their full potential. Alexander Liazos, for example, asserts that schools are primarily perpetrators of the status quo and that delinquency in schools is simply a refusal to

---

TABLE 11.3   School-Based Delinquency Prevention Strategies

1. Teacher training programs for parents
2. Policies and practices to ensure that schools and classrooms reflect the best examples of justice and democracy in their organization and their operation and in the rules and regulations governing student conduct
3. A guarantee of literacy for elementary school students
4. Special language services for bicultural students
5. Career preparation in schools
6. Effective supportive services in schools
7. Alternative education programs for deviant students
8. Opening schools for community activities
9. Alternative education programs for students who require them
10. Community education programs
11. Alternatives to suspension of troublesome students
12. Codes of rights and responsibilities drawn up by all elements of the school community (students, teachers, parents, and administrators)
13. Curriculum reform, especially the use of apprenticeship programs and law-related education
14. Police, school, and community liaison programs
15. Teacher education in appropriate disciplinary techniques and sensitivity to special students
16. Proper training of school security personnel
17. Improved counseling and guidance programs
18. Creation of a more personalized atmosphere in schools through architectural design and use of smaller buildings
19. Student and parental involvement in programs to combat violence and vandalism in schools

---

fit into the mold in which schools attempt to place students. "There are no possible solutions *in* schools," he contends, "as long as schools must prepare students for alienated work."[93] Therefore, according to Liazos, it will take a restructuring of the entire society before delinquency can be dealt with effectively: "We cannot focus on schools as the problem or the solution. We need to change the economy and the society and the ruling groups that control them. We must create a true democracy where the people control all institutions."[94]

Preventing Delinquency

How to make schools more effective instruments of delinquency prevention has also been a topic for study. One approach is to improve the educational experience of at-risk youth in order to shield them from peer inducements toward drug use and crime. Special classes and individualized educational programs that foster success rather than failure have been created for nonadjusting students. An effort has been made to help students learn to deal constructively with failure when it does occur in their academic experience.

More personalized student-teacher relationships have been recommended. This effort to provide young persons with caring, accepting adult role models will, it is hoped, strengthen their bond to the educational process. School counselors who act as liaisons between the family and the school have been effective in preventing delinquency. These counselors try to ensure cooperation between the parents and the school and to secure needed services—academic, social, or psychological—for troubled students before serious delinquency becomes a problem.

A number of experimental programs have attempted to prevent or reduce delinquency by manipulating factors in the learning environment. One such project, known as Project PATHE (Positive Action through Holistic Education) was operated in four middle and three high schools in South Carolina and sought to reduce delinquency by increasing students' stakes in conformity by strengthening their commitment to school, success experiences in school, attachment to conforming members of the educational community, and participation in school activities. By encouraging their sense of social competence, belonging, and usefulness, the project sought to promote the development of students in a positive direction. To achieve these goals, teams made up of staff members, students, parents, and community members were created in each school and trained to implement changes and revise school policies; in so doing, the team concept involved diverse segments of the community in school improvement programs.[95]

Other recent school-based programs have attempted to train student leaders to become role models for younger students who may be having academic or social problems. For example, the Peer Leadership Program in the Schenectady County, New York, school system trained peer leaders to conduct small group sessions with fourth through sixth graders in order to help them develop healthy attitudes, coping skills, and more positive self-images.[96]

Two new experimental programs that are considered to have important potential for reducing school crime and neighborhood delinquency, **Cities in Schools** and Law-Related Education, are set out in detail in the following Focus on Delinquency.

School-Based Prevention Programs

Cities in Schools

Cities in Schools (CIS), a major public-private partnership in thirty-one cities, works to reduce school violence and prevent students from dropping out of school. Three central principles guide CIS: a relationship must be established between a troubled youth and a caring adult, the youth and service provider must be held accountable, and fragmented services must be coordinated and made available to youth and their families.

Students are referred to CIS because of low academic achievement, poor attendance, disruptive behavior, or family problems. Counselors, social workers, and volunteers work with students to improve their personal, educational, and social development skills; provide employment skills; and reinforce positive behavior.

The CIS approach has produced a number of excellent programs that have made a difference for high-risk youth. In 1988, Federated Department Stores, Inc., received the Presidential Award for Private Sector Initiatives for its Rich's Academy partnership with CIS in Atlanta. In Charlotte-Mecklenburg County, North Carolina, where CIS operates in five schools, more than one hundred IBM professionals serve as mentors and tutors to the program's 260 student participants. A dropout prevention counselor, Department of Social Services social worker, Recreation Department staff member, and court counselor work at each school site.

This demonstration project was designed to be replicated by states and localites. CIS is in the process of developing training materials to assist additional communities in replicating the program.

Law-Related Education

Law-Related Education (LRE) helps students understand responsibilities and rights associated with everyday life. It teaches youth about good citizenship, helps them become more accountable for their actions, and promotes respect for the law. In 1988, LRE added a drug component to its curriculum to stress to youth that they will be held accountable for illegal drug use.

Since 1978, the Office of Juvenile Justice and Delinquency Prevention (OJJDP) has funded a national LRE effort that is implemented by five grantees: the American Bar Association, Center for Civic Education/Law in a Free Society, Constitutional Rights Foundation, National Institute for Citizen Education in the Law, and Phi Alpha Delta Public Service Center. Today, more than 580 school districts nationwide and more than 1.9 million students participate in LRE programs. As of September 1988, forty states had developed statewide LRE programs in their schools; twenty-one states were testing the new drug curriculum; and 43,947 teachers, lawyers, and other individuals had received LRE training. It is anticipated that by 1991, LRE will be institutionalized in all fifty states.

This project is intended to provide information to states and local jurisdictions about law-related education curriculums. The information developed through this project is suitable for replication.

Source: Office of Juvenile Justice and Delinquency Prevention, *Fiscal Year 1988 Annual Report* (Washington, D.C.: U.S. Government Printing Office, 1989) pp. 82–83.

Schools may be unable to reduce delinquency single-handedly, but a number of viable alternatives to their present operations could aid in a communitywide effort at lessening the problem of juvenile crime.

SUMMARY

For several decades, criminologists have attempted to explain the relationship between schools and delinquency. Although no clear causal relationship can be established, research points to many definite links between the delinquent behavior of juveniles and their experiences within the educational system.

Contemporary youths spend much of their time in school because education has become increasingly important as a determinant of social and economic success. Educational institutions are one of the primary instruments of socialization, and it is believed that this role is bound to affect the amount of delinquent behavior among school-age children.

Those who claim a causal link between schools and delinquency cite two major factors in the relationship. The first is academic failure, which arises from a lack of aptitude, labeling, or class conflict and which results in tracking. The second factor is alienation from the educational experience, which is the result of such realities as the impersonal nature of the schools, the traditionally passive role assigned to students, and students' perception of their education as irrelevant to their future lives.

Student misbehavior, which may have its roots in the school experience itself, ranges from minor infractions of school rules (for example, smoking and loitering in halls) to serious crimes, such as assault, burglary, arson, drug abuse, and vandalism of school property.

Dissatisfaction with the educational experience frequently sets the stage for more serious forms of delinquency both in school and out. Some dissatisfied students choose to drop out of school as soon as they reach the legal age, and research has shown a rapid decline in delinquency among those who do drop out.

School administrators have attempted to eliminate school crime and prevent delinquency. Among the measures taken are security guards, electronic surveillance, and teacher training. Major curriculum revision is now being undertaken to make the school experience more meaningful.

QUESTIONS FOR DISCUSSION

1. Was there a delinquency problem in your high school? If so, how was it dealt with?
2. Should disobedient youths be suspended from school? Does this solution hurt or help?
3. What can be done to improve the delinquency prevention capabilities of schools?
4. Is school failure responsible for delinquency, or are delinquents simply school failures?

KEY TERMS

academic performance

self-esteem

middle-class measuring rods

articulation hypothesis

stereotype

tracking

labeling

alienation

drop out

intruder

truants

passive speech

Tinker v. Des Moines Independent Community School District

Hazelwood School District v. Kuhlmeier

Ingraham v. Wright

Cities in Schools (CIS)

NOTES

1. U.S. Senate Subcommittee on Delinquency, *Challenge for the Third Century: Education in a Safe Environment* (Washington, D.C.: U.S. Government Printing Office, 1977), p. 1.

2. *Justice and the Child in New Jersey,* Report of the New Jersey Juvenile Delinquency Commission (1939), p. 110, cited in Paul H. Hahn, *The Juvenile Offender and the Law* (Cincinnati, Ohio: Anderson, 1978).

3. Delbert S. Eliott and Harwin L. Voss, *Delinquency and the Dropout* (Lexington, Mass.: Lexington Books, 1974), p. 204.

4. Kenneth Polk and Walter E. Schafer, eds., *Schools and Delinquency* (Englewood Cliffs, N.J.: Prentice-Hall, 1972), p. 13.

5. Herman Schwendinger and Julia Schwendinger, *Adolescent Subcultures and Delinquency,* (New York: Praeger, 1985).

6. James S. Coleman, *The Adolescent Society* (New York: Free Press, 1961), p. 4.

7. Material in this section is based in part on Polk and Schafer, *Schools and Delinquency,* pp. 10–14, 22, 68–69, 166–67.

8. Albert J. Reiss, Jr., and Albert Lewis Rhodes, *A Sociopsychological Study of Adolescent Conformity and Deviation,* U.S. Office of Education Cooperative Research Project Number 501 (1959), cited in Polk and Schafer, *Schools and Delinquency,* p. 167.

9. *Ibid.*

10. *Ibid.,* p. 68.

11. Ina Mullis, National Assessment for Educational Progress, *The Reading Report Card* (Princeton, N.J.: Educational Testing Service, 1990); *The Writing Report Card* (Princeton, N.J.: Educational Testing Service, 1990).

12. *Ibid.*

13. Task Force on Education of Young Adolescents, *Turning Points, Preparing American Youth for the 21st Century* (New York: Carnegie Council on Adolescent Development, 1989), p. 27.

14. *The Forgotten Half: Pathways to Success for America's Youth and Young Families* (Washington, D.C.: William T. Grant Foundation, 1988).

15. Task Force on Juvenile Delinquency, *Juvenile Delinquency and Youth Crime* (Washington, D.C.: U.S. Government Printing Office, 1967), p. 51. See also Alexander Liazos, "Schools, Alienation, and Delinquency," *Crime and Delinquency* 24:355–61 (1978); Sheldon Glueck and Eleanor Glueck, *Unraveling Juvenile Delinquency* (New York: Commonwealth Fund, 1950); Kenneth Polk and David S. Halferty, "Adolescence, Commitment, and Delinquency," *Journal of Research in Crime and Delinquency* 4:82–86 (1966); Travis Hirschi, *Causes of Delinquency* (Berkeley, Calif.: University of California Press, 1969); LaMar T. Empey and Steven G. Lubeck, *Explaining Delinquency* (Lexington, Mass.: D.C. Heath, 1971); Polk and Schafer, *Schools and Delinquency.*

16. Frank W. Jerse and M. Ebrahim Fakouri, "Juvenile Delinquency and Academic Deficiency," *Contemporary Education* 49: 108–9 (1978).

17. Lee Jussim, "Teacher Expectations: Self-Fulfilling Prophecies, Perceptual Biases, and Accuracy," *Journal of Personality and Social Psychology* 57:469–80 (1989).

18. Lyle Shannon, *Assessing the Relationship of Adult Criminal Careers to Juvenile Careers: A Summary* (Washington, D.C.: U.S. Government Printing Office, 1982).

19. Donald J. West and David P. Farrington, *The Delinquent Way of Life* (London: Heineman, 1977), p. 76.

20. Marvin Wolfgang, Robert Figlio, and Thorsten Sellin, *Delinquency in a Birth Cohort* (Chicago: University of Chicago Press, 1972).

21. Ibid., p. 94.

22. Bureau of Justice Statistics, *Prisons and Prisoners* (Washington, D.C.: U.S. Government Printing Office, 1982), p. 2.

23. Martin Gold, "School Experiences, Self-Esteem, and Delinquent Behavior: A Theory for Alternative Schools," *Crime and Delinquency* 24:294–95 (1978).

24. *Ibid.*

25. Albert K. Cohen, *Delinquent Boys* (New York: Free Press, 1955). See also Kenneth Polk, Dean Frease, and F. Lynn Richmond, "Social Class, School Experience, and Delinquency," *Criminology* 12:84–85 (1974).

26. Jackson Toby, "Orientation to Education as a Factor in the School Maladjustment of Lower-Class Children," *Social Forces* 35:259–66 (1957).

27. Gold, "School Experiences, Self-Esteem, and Delinquent Behavior," p. 292.

28. *Ibid.*, pp. 183–5.

29. Polk, Frease, and Richmond, "Social Class, School Experience, and Delinquency," p. 92.

30. Arthur L. Stinchcombe, *Rebellion in a High School* (Chicago: Quadrangle Press, (1964), p. 70.

31. Kenneth Polk, "Class, Strain, and Rebellion among Adolescents," in Polk and Schafer, *Schools and Delinquency*, pp. 34–54.

32. Adam Gamoran, "Rank, Performance, and Mobility in Elementary School Grouping," *Sociological Quarterly* 30:109–23 (1989).

33. Based on Walter E. Schafer, Carol Olexa, and Kenneth Polk, "Programmed for Social Class: Tracking in High School," in Polk and Schafer, *Schools and Delinquency*, pp. 34–54.

34. Delos Kelly and William Pink, "School Crime and Individual Responsibility: The Perpetuation of a Myth," *The Urban Review* 14:47–63 (1982).

35. Jeannie Oakes, *Keeping Track, How Schools Structure Inequality* (New Haven, Conn.: Yale University Press, 1985), p. 48.

36. *Ibid.*, p. 57.

37. Delos Kelly, *Creating School Failure, Youth Crime, and Deviance* (Los Angeles: Trident Shop, 1982), p. 11.

38. Delos Kelly and W. Grove, "Teachers' Nominations and the Production of Academic Misfits," *Education* 101:246–63 (1981).

39. Delos Kelly, "The Role of Teacher's Nominations in the Perpetuation of Deviant Adolescent Careers," *Education* 96:209–17 (1976).

40. Oakes, *Keeping Track*, p. 40.

41. Hirschi, *Causes of Delinquency*, pp. 113–24, 132.

42. Joseph Galbo, "The Teacher as Significant Adult: A Review of the Literature," *Adolescence* 24:549–55 (1989).

43. D. Hawkins and T. Lam, "Teachers' Practices, Social Development, and Delinquency," in *Prevention of Delinquent Behavior*, ed. J. D. Burchard and S. N. Burchard (Newbury Park, Calif.: Sage, 1987).

44. "Learning into the 21st Century," Report of Forum 5, White House Conference on Children (Washington, D.C.: 1970).

45. Polk and Schafer, *Schools and Delinquency*, p. 72.

46. Hirschi, *Causes of Delinquency*, pp. 170–83.

47. Polk and Schafer, *Schools and Delinquency*, p. 23.

48. Mihaly Czikszentmihalyi and Reed Larson, "Intrinsic Rewards in School Crime," *Crime and Delinquency* 24:322 (1978).

49. Polk and Schafer, *Schools and Delinquency*, p. 28.

50. Eliott and Voss, *Delinquency and the Dropout*.

51. Daniel Glaser, *Crime in Our Changing Society*, (New York: Holt, Rinehart & Winston, 1978) p. 164.

52. Daniel Glaser, *Strategic Criminal Justice Planning* (Washington, D.C.: U.S. Government Printing Office, 1975), Tables 3–2, 3–3, and 3–4, cited in Glaser, *Crime in Our Changing Society*, p. 163.

53. Terence Thornberry, Melanie Moore, and R. L. Christenson, "The Effect of Dropping Out of High School on Subsequent Criminal Behavior," *Criminology* 23:3–18 (1985).

54. Joyce Ann O'Neil and Eric Wish, *Drug Use Forecasting* (Washington, D.C.: U.S. Government Printing Office, 1989).

55. Christopher Innes, *Profile of State Prison Inmates, 1986* (Washington, D.C.: Bureau of Justice Statistics, 1988).

56. Jackson Toby, *Violence in Schools* (Washington, D.C.: National Institute of Justice, 1983).

57. National Institute of Education, U.S. Department of Health, Education and Welfare, *Violent Schools—Safe Schools: The Safe Schools Study Report to the Congress*, vol. 1 (Washington, D.C.: U.S. Government Printing Office, 1977).

58. *Weapons in Schools* (Washington, D.C.: Office of Juvenile Justice and Delinquency Prevention, 1989), pp. 1–3.

59. *Weapons in Schools*, p. 1.

60. *Ibid.*

61. *Ibid.*, p. 2.

62. *Violent Schools—Safe Schools*, vol. 1.

63. National Education Association, *Nationwide Teacher Opinion Poll 1981* (Washington, D.C.: National Education Association, 1982).

64. Jackson Toby, "Violence in Schools," National Institute of Justice Research Brief (Washington, D.C., 1983), p. 2.

65. Gary Gottfredson and Denise Gottfredson, *Victimization in Schools* (New York: Plenum Press, 1985) p. 18; see also G. Roy Mayer, Tom Butterworth, Mary Nafpakititis, and Beth Sulzer-Azaroff, "Preventing School Vandalism and Discipline: A Three-Year Study," *Journal of Applied Behavior Analysis* 16:355–69 (1983).

66. James Q. Wilson, "Crime in Society and Schools," in *Violence in Schools: Perspective, Programs and Positions*, ed. J. M. McPartland and E. L. McDill (Lexington, Mass.: D. C. Heath, 1977) p. 48.

67. Joan McDermott, "Crime in the School and in the Community: Offenders, Victims, and Fearful Youth," *Crime and Delinquency* 29:270–83 (1983).

68. Daryl Hellman and Susan Beaton, "The Pattern of Violence in Urban Public Schools: The Influence of School and Community," *Journal of Research in Crime and Delinquency* 23:102–27 (1986).

69. McDermott, "Crime in the School," p. 281.

70. Hellman and Beaton, "The Pattern of Violence in Public Schools," pp. 122–3.

71. *Weapons in Schools*, p. 2.

72. *Ibid.*

73. *Ibid.*

74. *Ibid.*

75. Bella English, "Hub Program to Counsel Violent Pupils," *Boston Globe*, 24 February 1987, p. 1.

76. C. Ronald Huff, "Youth Gangs and Public Policy," *Crime and Delinquency* 35:534–37 (1989).

77. Jackie Kimbrough, "School-Based Strategies for Delinquency Prevention" in *The Juvenile Rehabilitation Reader*, ed. Peter Greenwood (Santa Monica, Calif.: Rand Corporation, 1985), pp. IX.1–IX.22.

78. Office of Juvenile Justice and Delinquency Prevention, *Using the Law to Improve School Order and Safety* (Washington, D.C.: U.S. Department of Justice, 1989).

79. S. Arons, "Compulsory Education: The Plain People Resist," *Saturday Review* 15:63–69 (1972).

80. *Ibid.*

81. See *Pierce v. Society of Sisters*, 268 U.S. 610, 45 S.Ct. 571, 69 L.Ed. 1070 (1925).

82. 406 U.S. 205, 92 S.Ct. 1526, 32 L.Ed.2d 15 (1972).

83. 393 U.S. 503, 89 S.Ct. 733 (1969).

84. *Ibid.*

85. *Ibid.*, p. 741.

86. Bethel School District No. 403 v. Fraser, 478 U.S. 675, 106 S.Ct. 3159, 92 L.Ed.2d 549 (1986).

87. Hazelwood School District v. Kuhlmeier, 484 U.S. 260, 108 S.Ct. 562, 98 L.Ed.2d 592 (1988).

88. 423 U.S. 907, 96 S.Ct. 210, 46 L.Ed.2d 137 (1975).

89. 430 U.S. 651, 97 S.Ct. 1401 (1977).

90. 419 U.S. 565, 95 S.Ct. 729 (1976).

91. National Commission on Excellence in Education, *A Nation at Risk* (Washington, D.C.: U.S. Government Printing Office, 1983): see also U.S. Department of Justice, *Disorder in Our Public Schools* (Washington, D.C.: U.S. Government Printing Office, 1984); National Council on Crime and Delinquency, *Suppression of Drug Abuse in Schools Program: First Year Evaluation.* (Sacramento, Calif.: California Criminal Justice Planning Counsel, 1986).

92. Gary Putka, "Cheaters in Schools May Not Be Students but Their Teachers," *Wall Street Journal*, 2 November 1989, p. 1.

93. Alexander Liazos, "Schools, Alienation, and Delinquency," *Crime and Delinquency* 24:355–61 (1978).

94. *Ibid.*

95. Denise Gottfredson, "An Empirical Test of School-Based Environmental and Individual Interventions to Reduce the Risk of Delinquent Behavior," *Criminology* 24:705–31 (1986).

96. Ronald Kingsley, "A Peer Connection Program: An In-School Resource for High-Risk, Delinquency-Prone Students," *Juvenile and Family Court Journal* 40:25–29 (1989).

12 Drugs and Delinquency

There is no more serious environmental problem confronting American society today than that of teenage **substance abuse** and its association with youth crime and delinquency. Almost every town, village, and city in the United States has some type of drug problem. Los Angeles, New York City, and Washington, D.C., are not the only areas in which drug abuse has become an imminent threat to social order; police have confiscated millions of dollars worth of drugs in small towns like Willow Springs, Missouri, and Waynesboro, Georgia.[1]

Drug abuse has become a significant national concern; when surveyed by the Gallup Poll, 11 percent of the American public listed drugs *as the most important* problem facing the country (exceeded only by concern for the economy, 12 percent, and excessive government spending, 12 percent); in 1980, only 2 percent of the public listed drugs as their top anxiety.[2] This fivefold increase in concern about drugs took place during a decade when (a) surveys of school age children show that the *overall use of illegal drugs declined substantially* and (b) American teens report that they consider drugs (54 percent) and alcohol (12 percent) the biggest problems they face.[3]

Despite such encouraging trends, *there is still cause for alarm*: while American youth have not turned into a pack of drug-crazed zombies, it is evident that far too many are still involved with drugs and alcohol. Self-report surveys indicate that more than half of high school seniors have tried drugs and more than 90 percent use alcohol.[4] Equally troubling is the association between drug use and crime: drug users commit a significant amount of all crimes, and a large portion of known criminals are drug abusers.[5] The consistent drug-crime pattern makes teenage substance abuse a key national concern.

This chapter addresses some of the most important issues involving teenage substance abuse. It first reviews the kinds of drugs kids are using today and how often they are using them. It then goes into the why of drug abuse: who uses drugs and what are the suspected causes of substance abuse. After describing the association between drug abuse and criminal and delinquent behavior, the chapter concludes with a review of the efforts being made to control the use of drugs in the United States.

SUBSTANCES OF ABUSE

A wide variety of substances that are generically referred to as "drugs" are sold and used by teenagers. Some are addicting, others not. Some provide hallucinations; other cause a depressing, relaxing stupor; and a few give an immediate, exhilarating uplift. This section will discuss some of the most widely used substances that, because of the danger they present for the user and their association with illegal activity, have been banned from private use.

Marijuana

Commonly called "pot," "grass," "ganja," "maryjane," "dope," and a variety of other names, **marijuana** is produced from the leaves of *Cannabis sativa*, a plant that grows throughout the world. Hashish (hash) is a concentrated form of cannabis made from unadulterated resin from the female plant.

Marijuana is the illicit drug most commonly used by teenagers. Smoking large amounts of pot or hash can cause drastic distortions in auditory and visual perception, even producing hallucinatory effects. Small doses produce an early excitement ("high") that gives way to a sedated effect and drowsiness. Pot use is also related to decreased physical activity, overestimation of time and space, and increased food consumption. When the user is alone, marijuana produces a quiet, dreamy state. When used in a group, it is common for users to become giddy and lose perspective. Though marijuana is nonaddicting, its long-term effects have been the subject of much debate.

Cocaine

Cocaine or "coke" is an alkaloid derivative of the coca leaf that was first isolated 1860. When originally discovered, it was considered a medicinal breakthrough that could relieve fatigue, depression, and various other symptoms, and it quickly became a staple of popular patent medicines. When its addictive qualities and dangerous side effects became apparent, its use was controlled by the Pure Food and Drug Act of 1906.

Cocaine is the most powerful natural stimulant known. Its use produces euphoria, laughter, restlessness, and excitement. Overdoses can cause delirium, increased reflexes, violent manic behavior, and possible respiratory failure.

Cocaine can be sniffed, or "snorted," into the nostrils or injected. The immediate feeling of euphoria or rush is short-lived, and heavy users may snort coke as often as every ten minutes.

A number of deadly derivatives of cocaine have become popular on the street in recent years. Mixing cocaine and heroin is a highly dangerous combination called "speedballing." **Freebase** is a chemical produced by treating street cocaine with a liquid to remove the hydrochloric acid with which pure cocaine is bonded during manufacture. The freebase is then dissolved in a solvent, usually ether, which crystallizes the purified cocaine. The resulting crystals are crushed and smoked through a special glass pipe, providing a high more immediate and powerful than snorting street-strength coke. **Crack**, like freebase, is processed street cocaine. Its manufacture involves using ammonia or baking soda to remove the hydrochlorides and create a crystaline form of cocaine base that can then be smoked. However, unlike freebase, crack is not a pure form of cocaine and contains both remnants of hydrochloride along with additional residue from the baking soda (sodium bicarbonate). In fact, crack gets its name from the fact that the sodium bicarbonate often emits a crackling sound when the substance is smoked.

Also referred to as "rock," "gravel," and "roxanne," crack seemed to be introduced and gain popularity on both coasts simultaneously in the mid-1980s. It is relatively affordable, can provide a powerful high, and is considered to be highly psychologically addictive.

Cocaine and its derivatives continue to be the fastest growing drug problem. In recent years, cocaine supplies have expanded while costs have dramatically declined; it should not be surprising that the popularity of cocaine, crack, and freebase has concomitantly increased.

Selling crack vials.

Heroin

Narcotic drugs have the ability to produce insensibility to pain and to free the mind of anxiety and emotion. Users experience a rush of euphoria, relief from fear and apprehension, release of tension, and elevation of spirits. After experiencing this uplifting mood for a short period, the user becomes apathetic and drowsy and nods off. Heroin, the most commonly used narcotic in the United States, is produced from opium, a drug derived from the opium poppy flower. Dealers cut the drug with neutral substances, such as sugar (lactose), so that "street heroin" is often only 1 to 4 percent pure.

Heroin is probably the most dangerous commonly used narcotic. Users rapidly build up a tolerance for it, fueling the need for increased doses in order to feel the desired effect. Some users will change their method of ingestion to get the required "kick." At first, heroin is usually sniffed or snorted; as tolerance builds, it is "skin-popped" and then finally injected or "mainlined."

Through the progressive use of heroin, the user becomes an **addict**—a person with an overpowering physical and psychological need to continue taking a particular substance or drug by any means possible. If addicts can't get a supply of heroin sufficient to meet their habit, they will suffer withdrawal symptoms. These include irritability, emotional depression, extreme nervousness, pain in the abdomen, and nausea.

Alcohol

Despite concern for "harder" drugs, alcohol remains the drug of choice for most teenagers. More than 80 percent of high school seniors report using alcohol in the past year, and more than 90 percent say they have tried it sometime during their lifetime.[6] It is also estimated that upwards of 20,000,000 Americans are problem drinkers and that at least half of these are **alcoholics**.

The cost of alcohol abuse is quite high. Alcohol may be a factor in nearly half of America's murders, suicides, and accidental deaths.[7] Alcohol-related deaths number 100,000 a year, far more than those associated with all other illegal drugs combined. The economic cost of America's drinking problem is equally staggering. An estimated $117 billion is lost each year, including $18 billion from premature deaths, $66 billion in reduced work effort, and $13 billion for treatment efforts.[8]

Considering these anticipated problems, why do so many youths drink alcohol to excess? Youths who use alcohol report that it reduces tension, diverts worries, enhances pleasure, improves social skills, and transforms experiences for the better.[9] While these reactions may follow the limited use of alcohol, higher doses act as a sedative and depressant. Long-term use has been linked with depression and numerous physical ailments ranging from heart disease to cirrhosis of the liver (though there is research linking moderate drinking to reduction in the probability of heart attack).[10] And while many teens think that drinking stirs their romantic urges, the weight of the scientific evidence indicates that alcohol decreases sexual response.[11]

Anesthetics

Anesthetic drugs are used as nervous system depressants. Local anesthetics block nervous system transmissions; general anesthetics act on the brain to produce a generalized loss of sensation, stupor, or unconsciousness.

The most widely abused anesthetic drug is **phencyclidine (PCP)**, also known on the street as "angel dust." PCP can be sprayed on marijuana or other plant leaves and smoked, drunk, or injected. Originally developed as an animal tranquilizer, PCP causes hallucinations and a spaced-out feeling that induces heavy users to engage in extremely violent acts. The effects of PCP can last up to two days; the danger of overdose is extremely high.

Inhalants

Some substance-abusing youths inhale vapors from lighter fluid, paint thinner, cleaning fluid, and model airplane glue to reach a drowsy, dizzy state sometimes accompanied by hallucinations. The psychological effect produced by inhaling these substances is a short-term sense of excitement and euphoria followed by a period of disorientation, slurred speech, and drowsiness. Amyl nitrate ("poppers") is a commonly used volatile liquid sold in capsules that are broken and inhaled.

Sedatives

Sedatives, most commonly of the barbiturate family, are able to depress the central nervous system into a sleeplike condition. On the illegal market, sedatives are called "goofballs" or "downers" or are known by the color of the capsules— "reds" (Seconal), "blue dragons" (Amytal), and "rainbows" (Tuinal).

Sedatives can be prescribed by doctors as sleeping pills. Illegal users employ them to create relaxed, sociable, and good-humored feelings; overdoses can cause irritability, repellent behavior, and eventual unconsciousness. Barbiturate overdoses are probably the major source of drug overdose deaths.

Tranquilizers

Tranquilizers have the ability to relieve uncomfortable emotional feelings by reducing levels of anxiety and promoting relaxation. Legally prescribed tranquilizers, such as Ampazine, Thorazine, Pacatal, and Sparine, were originally designed to control the behavior of people suffering from psychoses, aggressiveness, and agitation. Less powerful tranquilizers, such as Valium, Librium, Miltown, and Equanil, are used by the average citizen to combat anxiety, tension, fast heart rate, and headaches. The use of increased dosages of illegally obtained tranquilizers can lead to addiction, and withdrawal can be painful and hazardous.

Hallucinogens

Hallucinogens are drugs, either natural or synthetic, that produce vivid distortions of the senses without greatly disturbing the viewer's consciousness. Some produce hallucinations, and others cause psychotic behavior in otherwise normal people.

One common hallucinogen is mescaline, named after the Mescalero Apaches, who first discovered its potent effect. Mescaline occurs naturally in the peyote, a small cactus that grows in Mexico and the southwestern United States. After initial discomfort, mescaline produces vivid hallucinations in all ranges of colors and geometric patterns, a feeling of depersonalization, and out-of-body sensations.

A second group of hallucinogens are synthetic alkaloid compounds, such as psilocybin. These compounds can be transformed into a **D-lysergic acid diethylamide-25**, commonly called LSD. This powerful substance (eight hundred times more potent than mescaline) stimulates cerebral sensory centers to produce visual hallucinations in all ranges of colors, to intensify hearing, and to increase sensitivity. Users often report a scrambling of sensations; they may "hear colors" and "smell music." Users also report feeling euphoric and mentally superior, though to an observer they appear disoriented and confused. Unfortunately, anxiety and panic may occur during the LSD experience, and overdoses can produce psychotic episodes, flashbacks, and even death.

Stimulants

Stimulants ("uppers," "beans," "pep pills", "ice") are synthetic drugs that arouse the central nervous system. They produce an intense physical reaction: increased blood pressure, breathing rate, and bodily activity and elevation of mood. One widely used stimulant, **amphetamine**, produces such psychological effects as increased confidence, euphoria, fearlessness, talkativeness, impulsive behavior, and loss of appetite.

The commonly used stimulants are Benzedrine ("bennies"), Dexedrine ("dex"), Dexamyl, Bephetamine ("whites"), and Methedrine ("meth," "speed," "crystal meth").

Methedrine is probably the most widely used and most dangerous amphetamine. Some people swallow it; heavy users inject it for a quick rush. Long-term heavy use can result in exhaustion, anxiety, prolonged depression, and hallucinations. A new form of methamphetamine is a crystallized substance with the street name of "ice". Popular on the West Coast and in Hawaii, it originated in Asian labs where it is called "batu" by Filipinos, "shaba" by the Japanese, and "hirropon" by the Koreans. Smoking this crystal causes weight loss, kidney damage, heart and respiratory problems, and paranoia—symptoms of its better known competitor, crack.[12]

Steroids

Teenagers use highly dangerous anabolic **steroids** to gain muscle bulk and strength for athletics and body building.[13] Black-market sales of these drugs now approach $1 billion annually. While not physically addicting, steroids can become almost an obsession among teens who desire athletic success. Long-term users may spend up to four hundred dollars a week on steroids and may support their habit by dealing the drug.

Steroids are dangerous because of the significant health problems associated with long-term use: liver ailments; tumors; hepatitis; kidney problems; sexual dysfunction; hypertension; and mental problems such as depression. Steroid use runs in cycles, and other drugs, such as Clomid, Teslac, and Halotestin, which carry their own dangerous side effects are used to curb the need for high dosages. Steroid users often share needles, which makes them high risks for contracting the AIDS virus.

DRUG USE TODAY

Drug abuse has become an alarming social problem in the United States. However, each type of illegal substance presents a different problem to legal authorities. Government-sponsored drug surveys show that cocaine and its derivatives, such as crack, are the country's fastest-growing drugs.[14] Indicators of cocaine use, such as drug-related deaths, arrests, emergency-room overdose admissions, and possession arrests, have all increased faster than for any other drug. While "crack" or "rock" use is not widespread, its concentration in large urban areas has contributed to a growing urban crime rate.

Surveys also show that marijuana continues to be the most widely used drug but that its popularity has peaked. Distributors have felt the heat of increased law enforcement efforts and attempts to eradicate crops; higher prices have hurt business.

As marijuana's popularity declines, synthetic (laboratory-made drugs) have become more popular. Some western states report that methamphetamine ("speed," "crank") use is increasing and that its low cost and high potency has encouraged manufacturers ("cookers") to increase production and distribution efforts. Other synthetics include PCP and LSD, whose use is not widespread nationally but focused in particular areas of the country. For example, California leads the nation in the manufacture of PCP; about two-thirds of all PCP laboratories seized are in California. One drug enforcement official has stated, "Los Angeles is to PCP what Santa Cruz, Bolivia, is to cocaine."[15]

Synthetics are currently popular because labs can be easily hidden in rural areas and traffickers do not have to worry about border searches or payoffs to foreign growers and middlemen. Users like synthetics because they are cheap and produce powerful, long-lasting highs that can be greater than those provided by more expensive drugs, such as cocaine. Their manufacture is extremely profitable: the estimated street value of one gallon of PCP is $153,600, or $1,200 an ounce.[16] Despite such cost, the use of synthetics is disturbingly high: in the late 1980s, more than half of all juvenile arrestees who tested positively for drugs did so for PCP.[17]

While heroin use has stabilized in most of the country, there are an estimated 500,000 addicts. Heroin abuse seems to be concentrated in only a few areas. New York City, where half of all addicts reportedly reside, experienced 9,000 heroin-related deaths in 1981; by 1987, the number had increased to almost 17,000.[18]

Despite the concern over these "hard drugs," the most persistent teenage substance abuse problem today is alcohol. While teenage alcoholism is sometimes considered "less" of a social problem than other types of substance abuse, it actually produces far more deaths and social problems. Teenage alcohol abusers suffer depression, anxiety, and other symptoms of mental distress. It is now well established that alcoholism runs in families, so that it is possible today's teenage abusers will be the parents of the next generation of teenage alcoholics.[19]

Teenage Drug Use

While there is little question that the national concern over teenage drug use is well placed, there are some indications that the overall teenage substance abuse rates have *declined* over the past decade. This rather surprising conclusion is drawn from the national surveys of teenage drug and alcohol use prepared by a variety of government and private agencies. The most widely cited is the annual survey of teenage drug use sponsored by the National Institute on Drug Abuse (NIDA) and conducted by social scientists at the University of Michigan's Institute for Social Research (ISR).[20]

Since 1975, the Michigan research team has annually surveyed about 16,000 students on over 125 high school campuses around the country. Each participant (and the research team reports that students are enthusiastic participants) is queried about his or her lifetime, monthly, and annual use of sixteen commonly abused drugs and substances (including cigarettes and alcohol). In addition to the annual survey, about 2,400 members of each class surveyed are followed up for ten years after high school to determine the lifetime incidence of their drug usage.

The most recent survey available (1989) continues to show a decade-long *decline* in the use of almost all classes of illegal substances. As Tables 12.1 and 12.2 show, the decreases applied to the number of students who report "ever using" any of the survey drugs and also to current use of drugs (in the past thirty days). Among the most encouraging trends is that lifetime crack use has declined from a high of 5.4 percent in 1987 to 4.7 percent today; unfortunately, the number of students reporting using crack in the last thirty days has remained stable (about 1.4 percent). What is probably the most encouraging trend has been a reported decrease in drinking. While a large percentage of American teens still drink, the portion of high school seniors indicating that they had consumed any alcoholic beverage during the prior thirty days had fallen from 72 percent in 1980 to 60 percent in 1989; the proportion reporting heavy drinking experiences is down from a high of 41 percent in 1983 to 33 percent in 1989.

While the survey findings are generally positive, there are a few trouble spots. PCP use has increased slightly (though levels are still down from their peak in the late 1970s). Use of inhalants has remained stable, as has cigarette smoking despite thirty years of efforts to warn the public about its danger.

Despite this encouraging trend, substance abuse among teenagers remains *disturbingly high*. About 50 percent of all students have tried some type of drug, including 44 percent who used pot and 10 percent who used cocaine (5 percent used crack). Alcohol abuse is still a major youth problem; more than 90 percent of all high school students reported using alcohol. If we assume that there are almost 20 million high school-age youth, then it is likely that 10 million have tried drugs.

There are also indications that drug use is beginning at a very early age. For example, a recent survey in New Jersey shows that almost three fourths (71 percent) of the marijuana users reported having first used the drug prior to the tenth grade, as did a majority of youths using hallucinogens, amphetamines, barbiturates, and tranquilizers.[21] Considering the severity of this problem, it should come as no surprise that the National Association of State Alcohol and Drug Abuse Directors found that each year, more than 1.3 million youths are admitted to alcohol-treatment programs and more than 400,000 receive drug treatment.[22]

Why Has Teenage Drug Use Declined?

If the ISR results are valid, teenage drug use has undergone a period of significant decline. How can this social change be explained? One reason for the suspected drop in teenage drug use can be attributed to changes in perceptions about the harmfulness of such drugs as cocaine and marijuana; as students come to view these drugs as harmful, the incidence of their use has declined. In 1980,

TABLE 12.1 Trends in Lifetime Prevalence of Eighteen Types of Drugs

	PERCENT EVER USED					
	Class of 1975	Class of 1976	Class of 1977	Class of 1978	Class of 1979	Class of 1980
Approx. N =	(9400)	(15400)	(17100)	(17800)	(15500)	(15900)
Any illicit drug use	55.2	58.3	61.6	64.1	65.1	65.4
Adjusted version	–	–	–	–	–	–
Any illicit drug other than marijuana	36.2	35.4	35.8	36.5	37.4	38.7
Adjusted version	–	–	–	–	–	–
Marijuana/hashish	47.3	52.8	56.4	59.2	60.4	60.3
Inhalants	NA	10.3	11.1	12.0	12.7	11.9
Inhalants adjusted	NA	NA	NA	NA	18.2	17.3
Amyl and butyl nitrites	NA	NA	NA	NA	11.1	11.1
Hallucinogens	16.3	15.1	13.9	14.3	14.1	13.3
Hallucinogens Adjusted	NA	NA	NA	NA	17.7	15.6
LSD	11.3	11.0	9.8	9.7	9.5	9.3
PCP	NA	NA	NA	NA	12.8	9.6
Cocaine	9.0	9.7	10.8	12.9	15.4	15.7
Crack	NA	NA	NA	NA	NA	NA
Other cocaine	NA	NA	NA	NA	NA	NA
Heroin	2.2	1.8	1.8	1.6	1.1	1.1
Other opiates	9.0	9.6	10.3	9.9	10.1	9.8
Stimulants	22.3	22.6	23.0	22.9	24.2	26.4
Stimulants adjusted	NA	NA	NA	NA	NA	NA
Sedatives	18.2	17.7	17.4	16.0	14.6	14.9
Barbiturates	16.9	16.2	15.6	13.7	11.8	11.0
Methaqualone	8.1	7.8	8.5	7.9	8.3	9.5
Tranquilizers	17.0	16.8	18.0	17.0	16.3	15.2
Alcohol	90.4	91.9	92.5	93.1	93.0	93.2
Cigarettes	73.6	75.4	75.7	75.3	74.0	71.0

31 percent of the youth surveyed believed cocaine was harmful, while in 1989 that number had increased to 55 percent. Considering the widespread publicity linking drug use, needle sharing and the AIDS virus, it comes as no surprise that kids today see drug taking as more dangerous and risky than in the 1970s.

In addition, youths report greater disapproval of drug use among their friends, and peer pressure may help account for lower use rates. National ad campaigns to "just say no to drugs" and to stop friends from drinking and driving may be helping reduce peer approval of substance abuse. Even commercial films aimed at teenagers, such as *Say Anything*, make it a point to show that teens disapprove of drunk drivers and that a "designated driver" should be appointed at parties where alcohol is served.

TABLE 12.1 *continued*

	PERCENT EVER USED								
Class of 1981 (17500)	Class of 1982 (17700)	Class of 1983 (16300)	Class of 1984 (15900)	Class of 1985 (16000)	Class of 1986 (15200)	Class of 1987 (16300)	Class of 1988 (16300)	Class of 1989 (16700)	'88—'89 change
65.6	65.8	64.1	-	-	-	-	-	-	
–	64.4	62.9	61.6	60.6	57.6	56.6	53.9	50.9	−3.0
42.8	45.0	44.4	–	–	–	–	–	–	
–	41.1	40.4	40.3	39.7	37.7	35.8	32.5	31.4	−1.1
59.5	58.7	57.0	54.9	54.2	50.9	50.2	47.2	43.7	−3.5
12.3	12.8	13.6	14.4	15.4	15.9	17.0	16.7	17.6	+0.9
17.2	17.7	18.2	18.0	18.1	20.1	18.6	17.5	18.6	+1.1
10.1	9.8	8.4	8.1	7.9	8.6	4.7	3.2	3.3	+0.1
13.3	12.5	11.9	10.7	10.3	9.7	10.3	8.9	9.4	+0.5
15.3	14.3	13.6	12.3	12.1	11.9	10.6	9.2	9.9	+0.7
9.8	9.6	8.9	8.0	7.5	7.2	8.4	7.7	8.3	+0.6
7.8	6.0	5.6	5.0	4.9	4.8	3.0	2.9	3.9	+1.0
16.5	16.0	16.2	16.1	17.3	16.9	15.2	12.1	10.3	−1.8
NA	NA	NA	NA	NA	NA	5.4	4.8	4.7	−0.1
NA	NA	NA	NA	NA	NA	14.0	12.1	8.5	−3.6
1.1	1.2	1.2	1.3	1.2	1.1	1.2	1.1	1.3	+0.2
10.1	9.6	9.4	9.7	10.2	9.0	9.2	8.6	8.3	−0.3
32.2	35.6	35.4	NA	NA	NA	NA	NA	NA	NA
NA	27.9	26.9	27.9	26.2	23.4	21.6	19.8	19.1	−0.7
16.0	15.2	14.4	13.3	11.8	10.4	8.7	7.8	7.4	−0.4
11.3	10.3	9.9	9.9	9.2	8.4	7.4	6.7	6.5	−0.2
10.6	10.7	10.1	8.3	6.7	5.2	4.0	3.3	2.7	−0.6
14.7	14.0	13.3	12.4	11.9	10.9	10.9	9.4	7.6	−1.8
92.6	92.8	92.6	92.6	92.2	91.3	92.2	92.0	90.7	−1.3
71.0	70.1	70.6	69.7	68.8	67.6	67.2	66.4	65.7	−0.7

Source: University of Michigan, Institute for Social Research, 9 February 1990.

While perceptions of harmfulness and peer disapproval are correlated with declines in drug use, kids actually report that it is easier to obtain drugs today than ever before. Though the perceived availability of cocaine is at an all-time high, so too is its perceived risk. The change then is one in demand and not in supply.

ARE THE SURVEY RESULTS VALID? While these trends are encouraging, student drug surveys must be interpreted with caution. First, it may be over optimistic to expect that heavy crack, ice, and PCP users are going to cooperate with a drug use survey. Even if willing, they are the ones who are more than likely to be absent from school during testing periods.

TABLE 12.2 Trends in Thirty-Day Prevalence of Eighteen Types of Drugs

| | PERCENT WHO USED IN LAST THIRTY DAYS | | | | | |
| | Class of 1975 | Class of 1976 | Class of 1977 | Class of 1978 | Class of 1979 | Class of 1980 |
Approx. N =	(9400)	(15400)	(17100)	(17800)	(15500)	(15900)
Any illicit drug use	30.7	34.2	37.6	38.9	38.9	37.2
Adjusted version	–	–	–	–	–	–
Any illicit drug other than marijuana	15.4	13.9	15.2	15.1	16.8	18.4
Adjusted version	–	–	–	–	–	–
Marijuana/hashish	27.1	32.2	35.4	37.1	36.5	33.7
Inhalants	NA	0.9	1.3	1.5	1.7	1.4
Inhalants adjusted	NA	NA	NA	NA	3.2	2.7
Amyl and butyl nitrites	NA	NA	NA	NA	2.4	1.8
Hallucinogens	4.7	3.4	4.1	3.9	4.0	3.7
Hallucinogens adjusted	NA	NA	NA	NA	5.3	4.4
LSD	2.3	1.9	2.1	2.1	2.4	2.3
PCP	NA	NA	NA	NA	2.4	1.4
Cocaine	1.9	2.0	2.9	3.9	5.7	5.2
Crack	NA	NA	NA	NA	NA	NA
Other cocaine	NA	NA	NA	NA	NA	NA
Heroin	0.4	0.2	0.3	0.3	0.2	0.2
Other opiates	2.1	2.0	2.8	2.1	2.4	2.4
Stimulants	8.5	7.7	8.8	8.7	9.9	12.1
Stimulants adjusted	NA	NA	NA	NA	NA	NA
Sedatives	5.4	4.5	5.1	4.2	4.4	4.8
Barbiturates	4.7	3.9	4.3	3.2	3.2	2.9
Methaqualone	2.1	1.6	2.3	1.9	2.3	3.3
Tranquilizers	4.1	4.0	4.6	3.4	3.7	3.1
Alcohol	68.2	68.3	71.2	72.1	71.8	72.0
Cigarettes	36.7	38.8	38.4	36.7	34.4	30.5

Since the dropout rate among drug users is so high, it is also likely that the most deviant and drug-dependent portion of the youth population is omitted from the sample. Research by drug expert Eric Wish indicates that more than half of all people arrested dropped out of school before the twelfth grade (when the ISR survey is conducted) and more than two-thirds of these arrestees are drug users.[23] Wish found that the number of juvenile arrestees who test postively for cocaine is many times higher than those reporting recent use in the ISR survey. For example, while about 3.4 percent of the seniors report using cocaine in the prior thirty days, about 22 percent of young arestees in Washington, D.C., and 18 percent in Phoenix tested positively for cocaine.[24] High school drug surveys are clearly excluding some of the most drug-prone kids.

TABLE 12.2 *continued*

PERCENT WHO USED IN LAST THIRTY DAYS

Class of 1981 (17500)	Class of 1982 (17700)	Class of 1983 (16300)	Class of 1984 (15900)	Class of 1985 (16000)	Class of 1986 (15200)	Class of 1987 (16300)	Class of 1988 (16300)	Class of 1989 (16700)	'88–'89 change
36.9	33.5	32.4	–	–	–	–	–	–	
–	32.5	30.5	29.2	29.7	27.1	24.7	21.3	19.7	– 1.6
21.7	19.2	18.4	–	–	–	–	–	–	
–	17.0	15.4	15.1	14.9	13.2	11.6	10.0	9.1	– 0.9
31.6	28.5	27.0	25.2	25.7	23.4	21.0	18.0	16.7	– 1.3
1.5	1.5	1.7	1.9	2.2	2.5	2.8	2.6	2.3	– 0.3
2.5	2.5	2.5	2.6	3.0	3.2	3.5	3.0	2.7	– 0.3
1.4	1.1	1.4	1.4	1.6	1.3	1.3	0.6	0.6	0.0
3.7	3.4	2.8	2.6	2.5	2.5	2.5	2.2	2.2	0.0
4.5	4.1	3.5	3.2	3.8	3.5	2.8	2.3	2.9	+ 0.6
2.5	2.4	1.9	1.5	1.6	1.7	1.8	1.8	1.8	0.0
1.4	1.0	1.3	1.0	1.6	1.3	0.6	0.3	1.4	+ 1.1
5.8	5.0	4.9	5.8	6.7	6.2	4.3	3.4	2.8	– 0.6
NA	NA	NA	NA	NA	NA	1.3	1.6	1.4	– 0.2
NA	NA	NA	NA	NA	NA	4.1	3.2	1.9	– 1.3
0.2	0.2	0.2	0.3	0.3	0.2	0.2	0.2	0.3	+ 0.1
2.1	1.8	1.8	1.8	2.3	2.0	1.8	1.6	1.6	0.0
15.8	13.7	12.4	NA	NA	NA	NA	NA	NA	NA
NA	10.7	8.9	8.3	6.8	5.5	5.2	4.6	4.2	– 0.4
4.6	3.4	3.0	2.3	2.4	2.2	1.7	1.4	1.6	+ 0.2
2.6	2.0	2.1	1.7	2.0	1.8	1.4	1.2	1.4	+ 0.2
3.1	2.4	1.8	1.1	1.0	0.8	0.6	0.5	0.6	+ 0.1
2.7	2.4	2.5	2.1	2.1	2.1	2.0	1.5	1.3	– 0.2
70.7	69.7	69.4	67.2	65.9	65.3	66.4	63.9	60.0	– 3.9
29.4	30.0	30.3	29.3	30.1	29.6	29.4	28.7	28.6	– 0.1

Source: University of Michigan, Institute for Social Research, 9 February 1990.

To account for these presumably absent heavy users, the ISR researchers compared drug use among the general high school population with drug use by kids who are frequently truant and have poor grades. They reasoned that these poor performers are the most like the dropouts. While the poor students did use drugs more than the general high school population, they too have reduced their substance abuse. This suggests that improvements cut across all segments of the teenage population.

In sum, national surveys show promising trends in teenage drug use. It is also possible that because they do not include dropouts and arrestees, high school surveys are overlooking a large portion of the overall teenage drug problem. And while there is evidence that drug use is declining, even in the at-risk population, arrest data presents a disturbing pattern of drug use among delinquent youth.

WHY DO KIDS TAKE DRUGS?

To most people, the "why" of teenage drug abuse remains a puzzle: Why do youths engage in an activity that is sure to bring them overwhelming personal problems? It is hard to imagine that even the youngest drug users are unaware of the social, physical, and legal problems associated with substance abuse. While it is easy to understand the dealers' desire for quick profits, how can we explain the users' casual disregard for long- and short-term consequences?

One explanation ties drug abuse to poverty, social disorganization, and feelings of hopelessness. The involvement in drug use by young minority-group members has been tied to such factors as racial prejudice, "devalued identities," low self-esteem, poor socioeconomic status, and the stress of living in the harsh urban environment.[25] The association between drug use, race, and poverty has been linked to the high level of mistrust, negativism, and defiance found in lower socioeconomic areas.[26]

Youths living in a deteriorated inner-city slum area, where feelings of alienation and hopelessness run high, often come in contact with established drug users who teach them that drugs provide an answer to their feelings of personal inadequacy and stress.[27] Perhaps they will join with peers to learn the techniques of drug use; their friendships with other drug-dependent youth give them social support for their habit. Recent data acquired by Terence Thornberry and his associates as part of the Rochester Youth Development study does in fact show that a youth's association with friends who are committed to delinquent values increases the probability of drug use.[28]

Peer networks that support drug use may be the most significant influence on long-term substance abuse. Shared feelings and a sense of intimacy lead the youth to become fully enmeshed in what has been described as the "drug-use subculture."[29] But not all ghetto residents become drug addicts. Cloward and Ohlin have explained this as a function of slum dwellers' differential access to illegitimate sources of income or prestige. Those who cannot function as fighters or thieves may seek to lose themselves in the drug world.

Another explanation is that drug users come from the most unstable elements of the ghetto. An often-encountered personal characteristic of lower-class abusers is a poor family life and troubled adolescence. The majority of drug users have had unhappy childhoods that included harsh physical punishment and parental neglect and rejection.[30] It is also common to find substance abusers within large families with parents who are divorced, separated, or absent.[31]

Are There Personal Traits Associated with Substance Abuse?

Yet not all drug-abusing youth reside in lower-class slum areas; the problem of middle-class substance abuse is very real. To explain drug usage across the social structure, some experts have linked substance abuse to personality disturbances and emotional problems, which can strike kids in any economic class. Psychodynamic explanations of substance abuse suggest that drugs help youths control or express unconscious needs and impulses. Drinking alcohol may reflect a young teen's need to remain dependent on an overprotective mother, an effort to reduce the emotional turmoil of adolescence, or an attempt to cope with unconscious homosexual impulses.[32]

Research on the psychological characteristics of narcotics abusers does in fact reveal the presence of a significant degree of personal pathology. Personality testing of known users suggests that a significant percentage suffer from psychotic disorders, including various levels of schizophrenia. Studies have found that addicts suffer personality disorders characterized by a weak ego, low frustration tolerance, anxiety, and fantasies of omnipotence. Still another view is that addicts exhibit psychopathic or sociopathic behavior characteristics forming what is called an "addiction-prone personality."[33]

It is also possible that a precondition for substance abuse may have a genetic basis. Research has shown that the biological children of alcoholics reared by nonalcoholic adoptive parents more often develop alcohol problems than the natural children of the adoptive parents.[34]

Social psychologists suggest that drug abuse patterns may also result from the observation of drug abuse by significant others, such as parents or peers. Having a history of family drug and alcohol abuse has been found to be a characteristic of violent teenage sexual abusers.[35] Youths who learn from others that drugs provide pleasurable sensations may be the most likely to experiment with illegal substances; a habit may develop if the user experiences lower anxiety, fear, and tension levels.[36] For example, L. Thomas Winfree, Curt Griffiths, and Christine Sellers found that both Native American and white youths who report that their best friends use drugs and alcohol and who like to discuss the benefits of alcohol and drug use with their friends are the most likely to be substance abusers themselves.[37]

DRUG-INVOLVED YOUTH

What are the patterns of teenage drug use? Are all abusers similar, or are there different types of drug involvement? Research indicates that drug-involved youth do take on different roles, life-styles, and behavior patterns, which are described below.[38]

Adolescents Who Distribute Small Amounts of Drugs

Many adolescents who are involved with the use and distribution of small amounts of drugs do not commit any other serious delinquent acts. Most of these petty dealers occasionally sell marijuana, ice, and PCP to support their own drug use. Their customers are almost always known to them and include friends, relatives, and acquaintances. Deals are arranged over the phone, in school, or in public hangouts and meeting places; however, the actual distribution takes place in more private arenas, such as at home or in cars.

Petty dealers do not consider themselves "seriously" involved in drugs. They make claims such as:

. . . I don't consider it dealing. I'll sell hits of speed to my friends and joints and nickel bags [of marijuana] to my friends, but that's not dealing.

Petty dealers are insulated from the juvenile justice system because their activities rarely result in apprehension and sanction. In fact, few adults take notice of their activities because they are able to maintain relatively conventional lifestyles. However, in several jurisdictions, agents of the justice system are cooperating in the development of educational programs to provide nonusers with the skills to resist the "sales pitch" of the petty dealers they meet at school or in the neighborhood.

Adolescents Who Frequently Sell Drugs

A small number of adolescents, most often multiple-drug users or heroin or cocaine users, are high-rate dealers who bridge the gap between adult drug distributors and the adolescent user. Though many are daily users, they are not "strung-out junkies" and maintain many normal adolescent functions, such as going to school and socializing with friends.

Frequent adolescent dealers often have adults who "front" for them: sell them drugs for cash. The teenagers distribute the drugs to friends and acquaintances. They then return most of the proceeds to the suppliers while keeping a "commission" for themselves. They may also keep drugs for their own personal use, and in fact some consider their drug dealing as a way of "getting high for free."

Frequent dealers are more likely to sell drugs in public and can be seen in known drug hangouts in parks, schools, or other public places. Deals are irregular, so the chances of apprehension are slight.

Teenage Drug Dealers Who Commit Other Delinquent Acts

A more serious type of drug-involved youth are those who use and distribute multiple substances and also commit both property and violent crimes. Though these youngsters make up about 2 percent of the teenage population, they commit 40 percent of the robberies and assaults and about 60 percent of all teenage felony thefts and drug sales. There are few gender or racial differences among these youth: girls are as likely as boys to become high-rate persistent drug-involved offenders, white youths as likely as black youths, middle-class adolescents raised outside cities as likely as lower-class city children.[39]

In cities, these youths are frequently hired by older dealers to act as street-level drug runners. Each member of a "crew" of three to twelve boys will handle small quantities of drugs, perhaps three bags of heroin, which are received on consignment and sold on the street; the supplier receives 50 percent to 70 percent of the drugs' street value. The crew members also act as lookouts, recruiters, and guards. While they may be recreational drug users themselves, crew members refrain from addictive drugs, such as heroin; some major suppliers will only hire "drug-free kids" to make street deals. Between drug sales, the young dealers commit robberies, burglaries, and other thefts.

Most youngsters in the street drug trade have few success skills and either terminate their dealing or become drug dependent themselves. A few develop

Affluent teenage drug dealers often wear symbols of their wealth and success.

excellent entrepreneurial skills. Those that are rarely apprehended by police earn the trust of their older contacts and advance in the drug business. They develop their own crews and handle more than a half million dollars a year in drug business. Some are able to afford the BMW or Mercedes-Benz, jewelry, and expensive clothes that signify success in the drug trade.

DRUG-INVOLVED GANGS. It is also common for youth involved in teenage gangs to become serious suppliers of narcotics. At one time, control of the drug trade was maintained by traditional organized crime families who used their control of the Asian heroin market as a principle source of mob income. Over the years, the monopoly that organized crime families held over the American drug trade has been broken. Law enforcement efforts to jail crime bosses coupled with the popularity and growth of the trade in cocaine and synthetic drugs (which are less easily controlled by a single source) have shattered their distribution monopoly. Stepping into the void have been local gangs that have used their drug income to expand their bases and power. Prominent among these groups are biker gangs, such as the Hell's Angels, Outlaws, and Bandidos, which have become active in the manufacture and distribution of synthetic drugs. Jamaican Posse and Latino gangs control a large part of the East Coast cocaine business, while Chinese groups now import much of the nation's heroin supply.

There has also been an emergence of teenage gang members as major players in the drug trade. Most prominent are the two largest Los Angeles youth gangs, the Bloods and the Crips, whose total membership is estimated to be more than 20,000 members (though actual membership is probably impossible to determine).

In Los Angeles itself, these drug-dealing gangs maintain "rock houses" or "stash houses." The houses receive drug shipments arranged by gang members who have the overseas connections and financial backing needed to wholesale drugs. The wholesalers pay the gang for permission to deal in their territory and hire members as a security force. Lower-echelon gang members help transport the drugs and work the houses, retailing cocaine and other drugs to neighborhood youths. Each member makes a profit for every ounce of "rock" sold. Police estimate that youths who work in rock houses will earn seven hundred dollars and up for a twelve-hour shift.[40]

The Los Angeles gangs have sent members to set up cocaine and crack distribution networks in states as far away as Minnesota, Colorado, Arizona, Texas, and Maryland. Violent confrontations occurring when local gangs have challenged the presence of these California-based outsiders have involved the use of Uzi and AK-47 automatic weapons. However, like other "business entrepreneurs," these teenage drug dealers are seeking new markets for their "product." As one Kansas City police official put it, "They are just like any other businessmen. They do market research. They come in and see who the players are."[41] Retail drug prices are higher in the nation's interior than they are on the coasts, where supplies are greater. In Kansas City, for example, a kilogram of cocaine sells for upwards of $22,000, compared to $8,000 in Los Angeles.[42] It makes good "business sense" to open "franchises" where the potential profits are so great.

There is also a new spirit of cooperation between Crips and Bloods factions designed to facilitate the drug trade. Gangs cooperate in the purchase of legitimate businesses, such as car washes and liquor stores, in order to "launder" drug money. It is possible that the "war on drugs" will produce the same atmosphere that prompted the growth of organized crime during Prohibition in the 1920s. Los Angeles street gangs may follow in the path of New York's "Five Families" and Al Capone and the Chicago mob and become the leaders of a new version of organized crime.

Adolescents Who Cycle in and out of the Justice System

Some drug-involved youth are failures at both dealing and crime. They do not have the savvy to join gangs or groups and instead begin committing unplanned, opportunistic crimes that increase their chances of arrest. They are heavy drug users, which both increases apprehension risk and decreases their value for organized drug-distribution networks.

Drug-involved "losers" can earn a living by steering customers to a seller in a "copping" area, "touting" drug availability for a dealer, or acting as lookouts. However, they are not considered trustworthy or deft enough to handle drugs or money. They may bungle other criminal acts, which solidifies their reputation as undesirable:

> Buster is almost always stoned on 'ludes' and beer. He is continually getting caught robbing and is in and out of treatment centers. Once, he and another boy robbed [sic] a jewelry store. They smashed the window with a brick and the window fell on them, knocking them both out. The store owner called the cops and an ambulance.[43]

A drug career often ends tragically in an overdose.

Though these persistent offenders get involved in drugs at a very early age, they receive little attention from the justice system until they have developed an extensive arrest record. By then, they are approaching the end of the their minority and will either spontaneously desist or become so deeply entrenched in the drug-crime subculture that little can be done to treat or deter their illegal activities.

Drug-Involved Youth Who Continue to Commit Crimes as Adults

Though about two-thirds of substance-abusing youths continue to use drugs after they reach adulthood, about half desist from other criminal activities. Those who persist in both substance abuse and crime maintain the following characteristics:

- they come from poor families;
- their families include other criminals;
- they do poorly in school;
- they started using drugs and committing other delinquent acts at a relatively early age;
- they use multiple types of drugs and commit crimes frequently; and
- they have few opportunities in late adolescence to participate in legitimate and rewarding adult activities.[44]

There is also some evidence that these drug-using persisters have low nonverbal IQs and poor physical coordination. Nonetheless, there is still little scientific evidence that indicates why some drug-abusing kids drop out of crime while others remain active into adulthood.

DRUG USE AND CRIME

The drug-crime connection has been firmly established. It is realized on a number of different levels. Violence erupts when rival drug cartels use their automatic weapons to settle differences and establish territorial monopolies. In New York City, authorities report that crack gangs will burn down their rival's headquarters even if people living on the premises are not connected to the drug trade; it is estimated that between 35 percent and 40 percent of New York's homicides are drug-related.[45]

Addicts also commit many crimes in order to pay for their habits. One study conducted in Miami found that in order to purchase drugs, 573 narcotics users *annually* committed more than 200,000 crimes, including 6,000 robberies, 6,700 burglaries, and 70,000 larceny offenses; similar research with a sample of 356 addicts accounted for 118,000 crimes annually.[46] If such proportions hold true, then it is possible that the nation's estimated 500,000 heroin addicts alone commit over one hundred million crimes each year, and this estimate ignores the criminal activity of cocaine and crack abusers.

The relationship between drugs and crime is dramatically illustrated by the extent of substance abuse among criminal suspects and those already convicted of crimes.

There have been a number of efforts to measure drug use by people immediately upon their arrest for crime. The federal government's **Drug Use Forecasting (DUF)** program tests arrestees in major cities in order to determine their drug involvement. The results have been startling. In some cities such as San Diego, New York, Philadelphia, and Washington, D.C., more than 70 percent of all arrestees test positively for some drug, and this association crosses both gender and racial boundaries.[47] As Table 12.3 indicates, a significant portion of youth and young adult arrestees aged 15 to 20 test positively for single and multiple drug use. In San Diego, Miami, Philadelphia, New York, Portland, and other cities, more than 70 percent of young male arrestees are drug dependent; female offenders tested almost as high for drugs. This data indicates that young offenders are quite likely to be substance abusers and that the drug-crime connection only begins to decline after age 36.[48]

It is possible that most criminals and delinquents are not actually drug users but that police are just more likely to apprehend muddled-headed substance abusers than clear-thinking abstainers. A second and probably more plausible interpretation of the existing data is that the drug abuse-crime connection is so powerful because that most criminals and delinquents are in fact substance abusers. Some may commit crimes to support a drug habit. Others may become violent while under the influence of drugs or alcohol, which lowers inhibitions and in-

TABLE 12.3 Any Drug Use by Male and Female Arrestees*

City	% Positive Any Drug (Male / Female)	\	% Positive By Age					\	% Positive By Race			
			15-20	21-25	26-30	31-35	36+		Black	White	Hispanic	Other
Birmingham	72 / 65		58 / **	75 / **	86 / **	69 / **	62 / **		74 / 58	69 / 75	** / **	** / **
Chicago	80 / 77		70 / **	83 / 84	84 / 82	88 / **	74 / **		82 / 77	71 / **	72 / **	** / **
Cleveland	68 / No data for females		55 / —	76 / —	76 / —	76 / —	58 / —		71 / —	60 / —	** / —	** / —
Dallas	66 / 65		57 / 66	66 / 61	77 / 76	77 / 60	52 / 55		69 / 63	63 / 68	49 / **	** / **
Detroit	68 / 81		63 / **	68 / 84	69 / 82	65 / **	75 / **		70 / 81	57 / 82	** / **	** / **
Ft. Lauderdale	62 / No data for females		58 / —	82 / —	64 / —	63 / —	49 / —		72 / —	54 / —	** / —	** / —
Houston	65 / No data for females		54 / —	76 / —	79 / —	76 / —	41 / —		71 / —	56 / —	60 / —	** / —
Indianapolis	54 / No data for females		65 / —	50 / —	62 / —	** / —	33 / —		47 / —	61 / —	** / —	** / —
Kansas City	54 / 70		41 / **	66 / 67	59 / **	62 / **	** / **		61 / 74	42 / **	** / **	** / **
Los Angeles	75 / 76		65 / 67	74 / 75	83 / 84	80 / 78	72 / 69		82 / 88	72 / 77	74 / 59	24 / **
Miami	75 / No data for females		76 / —	78 / —	69 / —	89 / —	68 / —		77 / —	67 / —	77 / —	** / —
New Orleans	70 / 55		66 / 32	76 / 53	78 / 65	74 / 71	58 / 48		73 / 54	54 / 59	** / **	** / **
New York	83 / 80		70 / 70	87 / 80	93 / 83	86 / 85	74 / 77		86 / 83	82 / 79	81 / 74	** / **
Omaha	56 / No data for females		** / —	54 / —	73 / —	** / —	** / —		59 / —	57 / —	** / —	** / —
Philadelphia	81 / 79		82 / **	83 / 76	85 / 90	90 / 85	59 / 68		82 / 80	69 / 85	87 / **	** / **
Phoenix	63 / 60		74 / 57	68 / 58	67 / 71	67 / 69	41 / 40		75 / 84	60 / 60	64 / 49	47 / 45
Portland	74 / 78		75 / 69	80 / 80	77 / 79	78 / 88	63 / 71		83 / 86	70 / 75	74 / **	66 / 70
St. Louis	56 / 44		41 / **	62 / **	70 / **	57 / **	48 / 28		55 / 56	56 / 21	** / **	** / **
San Antonio	63 / 51		58 / **	73 / **	64 / 63	60 / **	58 / 36		62 / **	53 / 58	68 / 38	** / **
San Diego	82 / 79		72 / 88	86 / 89	86 / 78	86 / 84	72 / 55		85 / 89	83 / 78	79 / 62	** / **

■ Males
□ Females

*Positive urinalysis, January through December 1988   **Less than twenty cases

Source: National Institute of Justice/Drug Use Forecasting Program, *Annual Report*, 1990. (Washington, D.C.: National Institute of Justice 1990).

creases aggression levels. The drug-crime connection may also be a function of the violent world of drug distributors who regularly use violence in doing business.

Explaining Drug Use and Delinquency

The general association between delinquency and drug use has been well established in research efforts using cross-cultural samples.[49] However, it is still far from certain whether drug use *causes* delinquency, whether delinquent behavior patterns *lead* youth to engage in substance abuse, or whether both drug abuse and delinquency are a *function* of some other variable that is responsible for both behaviors, such as a personality disorder.[50]

Some of the most sophisticated research on this topic has been conducted by Delbert Elliott and his associates at the Institute of Behavioral Science at the University of Colorado.[51] Using data from the National Youth Survey, a longitudinal study of self-reported delinquency and drug use, Elliott and his colleagues David Huizinga and Scott Menard found a strong association between delinquency and drug use.[52] However, they too find that the direction of the relationship is unclear. As a general rule, drug abuse appeared to be a *type* of delinquent behavior and not a cause of delinquency. Most youth become involved in delinquency before they were initiated into drugs; it was difficult to conclude that "drugs cause crime."

According to the Elliott research, both drug use and delinquency seem to reflect a developmental problem. Rather than causing one another, both drug use and delinquency seem to be part of a disturbed socialization and life-style. This research does reveal some important associations between substance abuse and delinquency:

1. Alcohol abuse seems to be a cause of marijuana and drug abuse since most drug users started with alcohol and youth who abstain from alcohol almost never take drugs.

2. Marijuana use is a cause of polydrug use: about 95 percent of kids who use more serious drugs, such as crack, started on pot; only 5 percent of serious drug users never smoked pot.

3. Kids who commit felonies started off by committing minor delinquent acts. There are few (1 percent) delinquents who report committing felonies only.

The Elliott research has been supported by a number of other studies that also found that delinquency and substance abuse are actually part of a general pattern of deviance. Helene Raskin White, Robert Padina, and Randy LaGrange found that both forms of deviance are related to symptoms of social disturbance, such as association with a antisocial peer group and educational failure.[53] Eric Wish found a pattern of deviance escalation in which troubled youth start by committing petty crimes and drinking alcohol and then proceed to both harder drugs and more serious crimes. According to Wish, both drug abuse and delinquency are part of an urban underclass life-style characterized by limited education, few job skills, unstable families, few social skills, and patterns of law violations.[54]

By implication, these studies indicate that restricting or reducing substance abuse may have *little* effect on delinquency rates because drugs are a *symptom* and not a *cause* of youthful misbehavior.

DRUG CONTROL STRATEGIES

The United States is in the midst of a well-publicized "war on drugs." Billions are being spent each year to reduce the importation of drugs, deter would-be drug dealers, and treat users. Yet, as most of us suspect drug control efforts have been less than successful. Though the overall incidence of drug abuse has declined, there has been a concentration of drug use in the nation's poorest neighborhoods with a consequent association between substance abuse and crime.

A number of different drug control strategies have been tried with varying degrees of success. Some are designed to deter drug use by stopping the flow of drugs into the country, apprehending and punishing dealers, and cracking down on street-level drug deals. Another approach is to prevent drug use by educating would-be users and convincing them to "say no to drugs." A third approach is to treat known users so they can terminate their addictions. Some of the more important of these efforts are discussed below.

Deterrence Strategies

One approach to drug control is to deter the sale and importation of drugs through the systematic apprehension of large-volume drug dealers, coupled with the enforcement of strict drug laws that carry heavy penalties. This approach is designed to punish known drug dealers and users and deter those who are considering entering the drug trade.

A major effort has been made to cut off supplies of drugs by destroying overseas crops and arresting members of drug cartels; this approach is known as **source control**. The federal government has been in the vanguard of encouraging exporting nations to step up efforts to destroy drug crops and prosecute dealers. Three South American nations, Peru, Bolivia, and Colombia, have agreed with the United States to coordinate control efforts.

However, translating words into deeds is a formidable task. Drug lords are willing and able to fight back through intimidation, violence, and corruption when necessary. The United States was forced to invade Panama with 20,000 troops in 1989 to stop its leader, General Manuel Noriega, from cocaine dealing.

Adding to control problems is the fact that the drug trade is an important source of foreign revenue and destroying the drug trade undermines the economy of Third World nations. For example, about 60 percent of the raw coca leaves used to make cocaine for the United States is grown in Peru. The drug trade supports 200,000 Peruvians and brings in over $3 billion annually. In Bolivia, which supplies 30 percent of the raw cocaine for the U.S. market, 300,000 people are supported with profits from the drug trade; coca is the country's single leading export. About 20 percent of Colombia's overseas exports are made by the Medellin and Cali drug cartels, which refine the coca leaves into cocaine before shipping it to the United States.[55] And even if the government of one nation would be willing to cooperate in vigorous drug suppression efforts, suppliers in other nations, eager to cash in on the seller's market, would be encouraged to turn more acreage over to coca, poppy, or marijuana production.

Law enforcement efforts have also been directed at interdicting drug supplies as they enter the country. Border patrols and military personnel using sophisticated hardware have been involved in massive interdiction efforts; many impressive billion-dollar seizures have been made. Yet the United State's borders are so vast and unprotected that meaningful interdiction is impossible. And even if all importation were shut down, homegrown marijuana and laboratory-made drugs, such as ice, LSD, and PCP, could become the drugs of choice. Even now, their easy availability and relatively low cost are increasing their popularity among teenagers.

There have also been efforts to bust large-scale drug rings. The long-term consequence has been to decentralize drug dealing and encourage teenage gangs to become major suppliers. Ironically, it has proven easier for federal agents to infiltrate and prosecute traditional organized crime groups than to take on drug-dealing gangs.

Police can also target, intimidate, and arrest street-level dealers and users in an effort to make drug use so much of a hassle that consumption is cut back and the crime rate reduced. While some street-level enforcement efforts have had success, others are considered failures. "Drug sweeps" have clogged courts and correctional facilities with petty offenders while proving a costly drain on police resources. There are also suspicions of a displacement effect: stepped-up efforts to curb drug dealing in one area or city simply encourages dealers to seek out friendlier "business" territory.[56]

Even if police are successful in eliminating existing drug networks, it is possible that a new set of dealers will emerge. In Chicago, a police undercover program called Operation SKID (School Kids in Danger) turned up a new variety of drug dealers: school bus drivers who deal drugs along their bus routes![57]

Punishment Strategies

If law enforcement agents cannot deter drug abuse, how successful are the courts in trying and punishing drug dealers and traffickers? There have been a number of initiatives making the prosecution and punishment of drug offenders a top priority. State prosecutors have expanded their investigations into drug importation and distribution and created special prosecutors to focus on drug dealers. Some states, such as New Jersey and Pennsylvania, report that these efforts have resulted in sharp increases in the number of convictions in drug-related cases.[58] Once convicted, drug dealers can get very long sentences. Research by the federal government tells us that the average sentence for drug offenders sent to federal prison is about six years.[59]

However, these efforts often have their downside. Defense attorneys consider the use of delay tactics to be sound legal maneuvering in drug-related cases. Courts are so backlogged that prosecutors are anxious to plea-bargain. The consequence of this legal maneuvering is that about 25 percent of people convicted on federal drug charges are granted probation or some other form of community release.[60]

Even so, state prisons have become jammed with inmates, many of whose convictions are drug related. In order to relieve overcrowded conditions, many drug offenders sent to prison do not serve their entire sentence. The average prison stay is slightly more than one year, or about one third of the original sentence. In fact, of all criminal types, drug offenders spend the least amount of their sentence behind bars.[61]

PUNISHING TEENAGE ABUSERS. How have teenage drug abusers fared in court? Despite the leveling off of teenage drug use, there is evidence that drug and alcohol offenses makeup a significant portion of the juvenile court's docket. One study conducted by the National Center for Juvenile Justice analyzed nearly 393,000 court records from 696 courts in 15 states in order to develop a picture of youthful substance abusers.[62] The records show that drug and alcohol cases accounted for about 14 percent of the delinquency cases handled by the courts, about six per every 1,000 youths aged 10 to 17 living in the courts' jurisdictions.

Though about half of these cases involved repeat offenders, judges were less likely to handle drug and alcohol cases formally than other delinquency matters (formal handling involves placing the case on the court's docket for a subsequent waiver or adjudicatory hearing; informally handled cases are either dismissed, diverted to another agency, or result in informal probation or voluntary placement outside the home). Fewer youths charged with drug and alcohol offenses were placed in a treatment facility than youths charged with other delinquency offenses. The study also found that repeat offenders were handled more formally than first offenders. Similarly, youths charged with driving while intoxicated were subject to out-of-home placement at a far higher rate than youths charged with merely being in possession of or drinking alcohol. There were also jurisdictional differences. Some courts formally handled over 80 percent of its drug cases, while others petitioned only 12 percent for formal trials.

Another research study of 534,000 cases petitioned to the nation's juvenile courts in 1984 and 1985 found that drug cases were the fastest growing segment of the juvenile court docket. This data indicates that the number of drug cases climbed 20 percent in one year (from 28,000 to 33,000) and that the number of drug cases per 1,000 youths increased almost 22 percent.[63] This national survey found that about 69 percent of drug cases were formally processed, and of these, 17 percent received some form of incarceration and 43 percent, probation.[64]

Drug Prevention Strategies

A third approach to reducing substance abuse has been prevention programs that help kids to "say no" to drugs. One of the most familiar is the "McGruff, the Crime Dog" advertisements sponsored by the federal government's National Citizen's Crime Prevention Campaign. This friendly symbol, which is familiar to 99 percent of children between the ages of 6 and 12, has been used extensively in the media to warn kids about the dangers of drug use and crime victimization. A multimedia drug prevention kit containing antidrug materials and videos has been distributed to almost every school district in the nation. A drug prevention curriculum featuring a McGruff puppet and an audio cassette has been distributed to over 75,000 elementary teachers, and more than 1.5 million McGruff antidrug comic books are being given away to students. There is some indication that students who participate in this program learn and improve their antidrug attitudes, teachers like the program, and parents endorse the content and need for the program.[65]

Another familiar program is **Drug Abuse Resistance Education, or DARE.** This program is an elementary school course designed to give students the skills for resisting peer pressure to experiment with tobacco, drugs, and alcohol. It is unique because it employs uniformed police officers to carry the antidrug message to the students before they enter junior high school. The program has five major focus areas:

1. Providing accurate information about tobacco, alcohol and drugs;
2. Teaching students techniques to resist peer pressure;
3. Teaching students respect for the law and law enforcers;
4. Giving students ideas for alternatives to drug use; and
5. Building the self-esteem of students.

DARE is based on the concept that young students need specific analytical and social skills to resist peer pressure and say no to drugs. Instructors work with children to raise their self-esteem, provide them with decision-making tools, and help them identify positive alternatives to substance abuse. So far, police in more than eight hundred jurisdictions have received DARE training, and they have presented the program to more than three million students.[66]

Community Strategies

Another type of drug control effort relies on the involvement of local community groups to lead the fight against drugs. Representatives of various local government agencies, churches, civic organizations, and similar institutions are being brought together to create drug prevention awareness programs. Their activities often include the creation of drug-free school zones (which encourage police to keep drug dealers away from the vicinity of schools); Neighborhood Watch programs, which are geared to spotting and reporting drug dealers; and citizen patrols, which frighten dealers away from children in public housing projects. One federally funded program, administered by the Congress of National Black Churches, is a comprehensive community effort that uses local black churches as the structure within which community involvement with traditional criminal justice agencies and other service providers is organized and coordinated. The program's main initiatives are as follows:[67]

■ Summon, focus, and coordinate the leadership of the black churches to support a unified message and structural plan to enable and assist high-risk target communities to more effectively combat the problem of drug abuse and drug-related crime;

■ Use the leadership authority of key ministers in each target community, in conjunction with the local mayors, to forge a communitywide task force to support the plan and specifically tailored strategies aimed at reducing the supply and demand for drugs and the crime associated with drugs;

■ Mobilize groups of community residents to plan, review, refine, and participate in implementing these specific strategies and helping families and individuals cope with the crises created by drug abuse and drug crime; and

■ Create a national communications network between these target communities to allow for the exchange of information and comparison of results regarding the effectiveness of various strategies and to form a more uniform consciousness of collective action in the fight against drug abuse and drug crime.

Treatment Strategies

There are a number of approaches to treat known users. One view is that users have low self-esteem, and treatment efforts use various techniques to build up

A counseling session at the J-Cap drug treatment program, Queens, New York.

the adolescent's sense of him or herself. Another approach has been to involve users in worthwhile programs that include outdoor activities, wilderness training, and after-school community programs.[68]

More intensive efforts use group therapy approaches in which leaders, many of whom have had prior experience as substance abusers, try to give users the skills and support that can help them reject the social pressure to use drugs. These programs are based on the Alcoholics Anonymous (AA) approach, which holds that users must find within themselves the strength to stay clean and that peer support from those who understand their experiences can be a successful means of achieving a drug-free life.

There are also residential programs for the more heavily involved, and a large network of drug-treatment units geared to juveniles has been developed. Some are detoxification units that use medical procedures to wean patients from the more addicting drugs. Others are therapeutic communities that attempt to deal with the psychological causes of drug use. Hypnosis, aversion therapy (getting users to associate drugs with unpleasant sensations, such as nausea), counseling, biofeedback, and other techniques are often used.

Despite their good intentions, there has been little evidence that these residential programs can efficiently terminate teenage substance abuse. Many are restricted to families whose health insurance will pay for short-term residential care; when the insurance coverage ends, children are released before their treatment program is complete. Adolescents do not often enter these programs voluntarily and have little motivation for changing.[69] A stay can help stigmatize residents as "addicts," even though they never used hard drugs; while in treatment, they may be introduced to hard-core users who they will associate with upon release. The following Focus on Delinquency describes one program currently used in the State of Washington.

Project ADAPT

Project ADAPT is a three-and-a-half-year-old demonstration project funded by the National Institute on Drug Abuse that combines behavioral skill training, supportive network development, and involvement in prosocial activities to facilitate the community reentry of youths following placement in a Washington state correctional facility. Project ADAPT accepts youths from Echo Glen, a state juvenile facility that serves both boys and girls ages 11 to 18. This project serves only those youths from the two nearest urban counties. The average age of ADAPT participants is 15; 75 percent are male, 52 percent are white, 35 percent are black, and 13 percent are of other racial/ethnic backgrounds.

Project ADAPT's creators agree with Hirschi's control theory (Chapter 6) that a strong bond consisting of attachment to conventional others, commitment to conventional lines of action, and belief in the conventional moral order inhibits frequent drug use and delinquency. It is hypothesized that the bond is produced from social processes in the family, school,

peer group, and the community that involve: 1) opportunities for involvement in conventional activities and interactions with others; 2) actual involvement and interaction in conventional activities; 3) acquisition of skills for successfully participating in these activities and interactions; and 4) the rewards forthcoming from performance in conventional activities and interactions. If these conditions are not present in the environment, adolescents are less likely to develop bonds of commitment, attachment, and belief in conventional roles. In the absence of such bonds, frequent drug use and crime become preferable alternatives.

The goals of Project ADAPT are: 1) to reduce the likelihood of association with drug-using peers in the community; 2) to reduce drug-dependent or addictive behavior patterns; 3) to reduce criminal activities; and 4) to prevent later need for drug treatment and correctional services.

The purpose of Project ADAPT is to create conditions for bonding once incarcerated youths return to

continued

WHAT THE FUTURE HOLDS

The United States is willing to go to any lengths to fight the drug war. There has been stepped-up law enforcement efforts, prevention programs, and drug treatment projects. Yet, all drug control strategies are doomed to fail as long as youth want to take drugs and dealers find that their sales efforts are a lucrative source of income. Prevention, deterrence, and treatment strategies ignore the core reasons that the drug problem exists: poverty, hopelessness, boredom, alienation, and family disruption. As the gap between rich and poor widens and the opportunities for legitimate advancement decrease, it should come as no surprise that adolescent drug use continues. It is a sad fact that a smaller percentage of the poor and minority group members is attending college today than ten years ago. The social failures of American society are being translated into teenage substance abuse.

the community by enhancing their opportunities, skills, and rewards for prosocial involvement. The project aims to increase subjects' skills in participating in prosocial activities through systematic training in social networking, impulse control, drug refusal, consequential thinking, relapse coping, and problem-solving skills. The program uses a case management system to help participants generalize and maintain skills across life situations, to increase opportunities for involvement in prosocial relationships and activities, and to provide coordinated posttreatment rewards for prosocial involvement and negative consequences for antisocial involvement in community environments.

Project ADAPT's intervention approach combines behavioral skill training with supportive network development and involvement in prosocial activities. The intervention is conducted in two phases: reentry preparation and aftercare. The reentry preparation phase involves participation in a ten-week-long goal-setting and skill-training group and work with an ADAPT case manager while participants are still in the institution. During this phase, group members are introduced to the two goals of the program: staying out of trouble and having fun. They work with their case managers to personalize these goals and develop plans for meeting these goals upon their return to the community.

During the aftercare phase, participants continue contact with their case managers for six months after release from Echo Glen. The case manager works to reintegrate clients into the family or alternative placement; provides skill practice; helps enroll them in school, find jobs, and obtain needed services; assists them in finding prosocial activities and developing a supportive social network; and reinforces the use of skills and the development of supportive activities and contacts.

The ADAPT intervention combines intensive case management services with small caseloads and flexible case management hours to maximize effectiveness of aftercare coordination. The average caseload consists of six to eight clients for each fulltime case manager. This intensive and coordinated program requires a high level of commitment on the part of the skill trainers and case managers.

Source: Kevin Haggerty, Elizabeth Wells, Jeffery Jenson, Richard Catalano, and J. David Hawkins, "Delinquents and Drug Use: A Model Program for Community Reintegration," *Adolescence* 94:311–329 (1989).

Some commentators have called for the legalization of drugs. While this approach can have the short-term effect of reducing the association between drug use and crime (since presumably the cost of drugs would decrease), it may also have grave social consequences. In the long-term, drug use might increase, creating an overflow of nonproductive, drug-dependent people who must be cared for by the rest of society. The problems of teenage alcoholism should serve as a warning of what can happen when controlled substances are made readily available. Nonetheless, as Kathryn Ann Farr has suggested, the implications of drug decriminalization should be further studied: what effect would a policy of **partial decriminalization** (for example, legalizing small amounts of marijuana) have on drug use rates? Would a get-tough policy help to "widen the net" of the justice system and actually deepen some youths' involvement in substance abuse? Can society provide alternatives to drugs that will reduce teenage drug dependency?[70] The answers to these questions have so far proven elusive.

The president has appointed you the new "drug czar" to lead the fight against drugs.

You have $10 billion with which to fight a campaign against drugs. You know that drug use is unacceptably high, especially among poor, inner-city kids, that a great deal of all criminal behavior is drug related, and that drug-dealing gangs are expanding around the United States.

At an open hearing, drug control experts express their policy strategies. One group favors putting the money into hiring new law enforcement agents who will patrol borders, target large dealers, and make drug raids here and abroad. They also call for such "get tough" measures as the creation of strict drug laws, the mandatory waiver of young drug dealers to the adult court system, and the death penalty for drug-related gang killings.

A second group believes that the best way to deal with drugs is to spend the money on community treatment programs, expansion of the number of beds in drug detoxification programs, and funding research on how to clinically reduce drug dependency.

A third group argues that neither punishment nor treatment can restrict teenage drug use and that the best course is to educate at-risk kids about the dangers of substance abuse and then legalize all drugs but control their distribution. This course of action will both help reduce crime and violence among drug users and help balance the national debt, since drugs could be heavily taxed.

Should drugs be legalized?

Can law enforcement strategies reduce drug consumption?

Is treatment an effective drug control technique?

SUMMARY

Drug abuse has been closely linked to juvenile delinquency. Among the most popular drugs of abuse are marijuana, cocaine and its derivative, crack, ice, LSD, and PCP. However, the most commonly used drug is alcohol, which contributes to almost 100,000 deaths per year.

There is some question about the trends in teenage substance abuse. Self-report surveys indicate that fewer teenagers are using drugs today than ever before. However, surveys of arrestees indicate that a significant proportion are current drug users and that many are high school dropouts. This indicates that surveys of current high school students may be missing the most delinquent and drug-abusing students.

There are a variety of kids who use drugs. Some are occasional users who might sell to friends. Others are seriously involved in both drug abuse and delinquency; many of these are gang members. There are also kids who are "losers" who filter in and out of the juvenile justice system. A small percentage of teenage users remain involved with drugs into their adulthood.

Despite years of research it is not certain whether drug abuse causes delinquency. Many kids who break the law later abuse drugs. Some experts believe that there is a "common cause" for both delinquency and drug abuse, such as alienation, anger, and rage.

There have been many attempts to control the drug trade. Some have attempted to inhibit the importation of drugs from overseas, others are aimed at closing down major drug rings, and a few have attempted to stop street-level dealing. There have also been attempts to treat known users through rehabilitation programs and to reduce juvenile use by education efforts. Communities beset by drug problems have also mounted grassroots drives to reduce the incidence of drugs. So far, these efforts have not been totally successful, though the overall use of drugs may have, in fact, declined.

KEY TERMS

substance abuse

marijuana

cocaine

freebase

crack

addict

alcoholics

phencyclidine (PCP)

D-lysergic acid diethylamide-25 (LSD)

amphetamine

ice

steroids

Drug Use Forecasting (DUF)

source control

Drug Abuse Resistance Education (DARE)

partial decriminalization

QUESTIONS FOR DISCUSSION

1. Discuss the differences between the various categories and types of substances of abuse. Is the term "drugs" too broad to have real meaning?

2. Why do you think kids take drugs? Do you know anyone with an addiction prone personality?

3. What policy might be the best strategy to reduce teenage drug use: source control? reliance on treatment? national education efforts? community level enforcement?

4. Under what circumstances, if any, might the legalization or decriminalization of drugs be beneficial to society?

5. Do you consider alcohol a "drug"? Should greater control be placed on the sale of alcohol? Should all liquor and beer advertisements be banned?

NOTES

1. James Baker, "The Newest Drug War," *Newsweek*, 3 April 1989, p. 20.

2. Katherine Jamieson and Timothy Flanagan, *Sourcebook of Criminal Justice Statistics, 1988* (Washington, D.C.: U.S. Government Printing Office, 1989), p. 182 (herein after cited as *Sourcebook, 1988*).

3. *Sourcebook 1988*, p. 182.

4. University of Michigan, Institute for Social Research News Release, 28 February 1989 (herein after cited as ISR).

5. U.S. Department of Justice, *Drugs and Crime Facts, 1988* (Washington, D.C.: Bureau of Justice Statistics, 1989), pp. 3–4.

6. "Drugs—The American Family in Crisis," *Juvenile and Family Court*, Special Issue 39:45–46 (1988).

7. *Ibid.*

8. *Ibid.*

9. D.J. Rohsenow, "Drinking Habits and Expectancies about Alcohol's Effects for Self Versus Others," *Journal of Consulting and Clinical Psychology* 51:752–56 (1983).

10. William Castelli, cited in G. Kolata, "Study Backs Heart Benefits in Light Drinking," *New York Times*, 3 August 1988, p. A24.

11. Spencer Rathus, *Psychology*, 4th ed. (New York: Holt, Rinehart, Winston, 1990), p. 161.

12. Mary Tabor, " 'Ice' in an Island Paradise," *Boston Globe* 8 December 1989, p. 3.

13. Paul Goldstein, "Anabolic Steroids: An Ethnographic Approach," Narcotics and Drug Research, Inc., March 1989.

14. Bureau of Justice Assistance, *FY 1988 Report on Drug Control* (Washington, D.C.: U.S. Government Printing Office, 1989).

15. Matt Lait, "California's New Role: Leading PCP Supplier," *Washington Post*, 17 April 1989, p. 1.

16. *Ibid.*

17. *Ibid.*, p. 11.

18. *Ibid.*, p. 10.

19. Robert Brooner, Donald Templer, Dace Svikis, Chester Schmidt, and Spyros Monopolis, "Dimensions of Alcoholism: A Multivariate Analysis," *Journal of Studies on Alcohol* 51:77–81 (1990).

20. Data in this section comes from the 1989 ISR news release of 9 February 1990.

21. *FY 1988 Report on Drug Control*, p. 23.

22. *Ibid.*

23. Joyce Ann O'Neil and Eric Wish, *Drug Use Forecasting, Cocaine Use* (Washington, D.C.: U.S. Government Printing Office, 1989), p. 7.

24. Eric Wish, "U.S. Drug Policy in the 1990s: Insights from New Data from Arrestees," *International Journal of the Addictions*. In press.

25. G. E. Vallant, "Parent-Child Disparity and Drug Addiction," *Journal of Nervous and Mental Disease* 142 (1966):534–39.

26. Charles Winick, "Epidemiology of Narcotics Use," in *Narcotics*, ed. D. Wilner and G. Kassenbaum (New York: McGraw-Hill, 1965), pp. 3–18.

27. C. Bowden, "Determinants of Initial Use of Opioids," *Comprehensive Psychiatry* 12 (1971):136–40.

28. Terence Thornberry, Margaret Farnworth, Marvin Krohn, and Alan Lizotte, *Peer Influence and the Initiation to Drug Use* (Albany, N.Y.: Hindelang Criminal Justice Research Center, n.d.).

29. Richard Cloward and Lloyd Ohlin, *Delinquency and Opportunity: A Theory of Delinquent Gangs* (Glencoe, Ill.: Free Press, 1960).

30. D. Baer and J. Corrado, "Heroin Addict Relationships with Parents during Childhood and Early Adolescent Years," *Journal of Genetic Psychology* 124:99–103 (1974).

31. See S. F. Bucky, "The Relationship between Background and Extent of Heroin Use," *American Journal of Psychiatry* 130:709–10 (1973); I. Chien, D. L. Gerard, R. Lee, and E. Rosenfield, *The Road to H: Narcotics Delinquency and Social Policy* (New York: Basic Books, 1964).

32. Rathus, *Psychology*, p. 158.

33. Jerome Platt and Christina Platt, *Heroin Addiction*, (New York: Wiley, 1976), p. 127.

34. D. W. Goodwin, "Alcoholism and Genetics," *Archives of General Psychiatry* 42:171–74 (1985).

35. J. S. Mio, G. Nanjundappa, D. E. Verlur, and M. D. De-Rios, "Drug Abuse and the Adolescent Sex Offender: A Preliminary Analysis," *Journal of Psychoactive Drugs* 18:65–72 (1986).

36. G. T. Wilson, "Cognitive Studies in Alcoholism," *Journal of Consulting and Clinical Psychology* 55:325–31 (1987).

37. L. Thomas Winfree, Curt Griffiths, and Christine Sellers, "Social Learning Theory, Drug Use, and American Indian Youths: A Cross-Cultural Test," *Justice Quarterly* 6:393–417 (1989).

38. The following sections lean heavily on Marcia Chaiken and Bruce Johnson, *Characteristics of Different Types of Drug-Involved Youth* (Washington, D.C.: National Institute of Justice, 1988) (Herein after cited as *Characteristics*).

39. *Ibid.*, p. 12.

40. Rick Graves and Ed Allen, *Narcotics and Black Gangs* (Los Angeles County Sheriff's Department, Los Angeles, n.d.)

41. Scott Armstrong, "Los Angeles Gangs Go National," *Christian Science Monitor*, 19 July 1988, p. 3.

42. *Ibid.*

43. *Ibid.*, p. 13.

44. *Characteristics*, p. 14.

45. *FY 1988 Report on Drug Control*, p. 19.

46. James Inciardi, "Heroin Use and Street Crime," *Crime and Delinquency* 25:335–46 (1979); James Inciardi, *The War on Drugs* (Palo Alto, Calif.: Mayfield, 1986); see also

W. McGlothlin, M. Anglin, and B. Wilson, "Narcotic Addiction and Crime," *Criminology* 16:293–311 (1978); George Speckart and M. Douglas Anglin, "Narcotics Use and Crime: An Overview of Recent Research Advances," *Contemporary Drug Problems* 13:741–69 (1986); Charles Faupel and Carl Klockars, "Drugs-Crime Connections: Elaborations from the Life Histories of Hard-Core Heroin Addicts," *Social Problems* 34:54–68 (1987).

47. Eric Wish and Joyce O'Neil, *Drug Use Forecasting Research Update* (Washington, D.C.: National Institute of Justice, 1989).

48. *Drug Use Forecasting Annual Report* (Washington, D.C.: National Institute of Justice, 1990); see also Eric Wish, Mary Toborg, and John Bellassai, *Identifying Drug Users and Monitoring Them during Conditional Release* (Washington, D.C.: National Institute of Justice, 1988), p. 11.

49. W. David Watts and Lloyd Wright, "The Relationship of Alcohol, Tobacco, Marijuana, and Other Illegal Drug Use to Delinquency among Mexican-American, Black, and White Adolescent Males," *Adolescence* 25:38–54 (1990).

50. Speckart and Anglin, "Narcotics Use and Crime,"; Faupel and Klockars, "Drugs-Crime Connections."

51. Delbert Elliott, David Huizinga, and Susan Ageton, *Explaining Delinquency and Drug Abuse* (Beverly Hills: Sage, 1985).

52. David Huizinga, Scott Menard, and Delbert Elliott, "Delinquency and Drug Use: Temporal and Developmental Patterns," *Justice Quarterly* 6:419–55 (1989).

53. Helene Raskin White, Robert Padina, and Randy LaGrange, "Longitudinal Predictors of Serious Substance Use and Delinquency," *Criminology* 25:715–740 (1987).

54. Wish, "U.S. Drug Policy in the 1990s."

55. Drug Enforcement Administration, *National Drug Control Strategy* (Washington, D.C.: U.S. Government Printing Office, 1989).

56. Mark Moore, *Drug Trafficking* (Washington, D.C.: National Institute of Justice, 1988).

57. "Bus Drivers: Dealing while Working," *Newsweek* 11 December 1989, p. 71.

58. *FY 1988 Report on Drug Control*, p. 103.

59. Carol Kaplan, *Sentencing and Time Served* (Washington, D.C.: Bureau of Justice Statistics, 1987).

60. *Ibid.*, p. 2.

61. Stephanie Minor-Harper and Christopher Innes, *Time Served in Prison and on Parole* (Washington, D.C.: Bureau of Justice Statistics, 1988).

62. Office of Juvenile Justice and Delinquency Prevention, *Juvenile Courts Vary Greatly in How They Handle Drug and Alcohol Cases* (Washington, D.C.: Office of Juvenile Justice and Delinquency Prevention, 1989).

63. Howard Snyder, Terrence Finnegan, Ellen Nimick, Melissa Sickmund, Dennis Sullivan, and Nancy Tierny, *Juvenile Court Statistics* (Pittsburgh: National Center for Juvenile Justice, 1988).

64. *Ibid.*, p. 15.

65. *FY 1988 Report on Drug Control*, p. 50.

66. *Ibid.*

67. *Ibid.*, p. 52.

68. Eli Ginzberg, Howard Berliner and Miriam Ostrow, *Young People at Risk, Is Prevention Possible?* (Boulder, Colo.: Westview Press, 1988), p. 99.

69. *Ibid.*, p. 99.

70. Kathryn Ann Farr, "Revitalizing the Drug Decriminalization Debate", *Crime and Delinquency* 36:223–37 (1990).

Juvenile Justice Advocacy

Part IV provides a general overview of the juvenile justice system, its process, history, and legal rules.

Since 1900, juveniles who violate the law have been treated differently from adults. They have their own court, legal rules, and processes. The separation of juvenile and adult offenders reflects a concern for the plight of children in society. Since many experts believe children can be reformed or rehabilitated, it makes sense to treat their law violations more leniently than those of adults. Care, protection, and treatment are the bywords of the juvenile justice system. Of course, to some influential critics, the serious juvenile offender is not deserving of these privileges. Consequently, there have been recent efforts to "toughen up" the juvenile justice system and treat some delinquents much like adult offenders. While juveniles are supposed to be treated separately from adults, these differences are often blurred both by the need to maintain public order and by the need to protect juveniles from the people allegedly trying to help them. The rhetoric of juvenile justice and its reality are often at odds.

Chapter 13 reviews the history of juvenile justice and describes its development and evolution. Chapter 14 provides an overview of the juvenile justice system and describes its major components and processes, goals, and institutions. It also describes the organization of juvenile court and its processes.

13

The History and Philosophy of Juvenile Justice

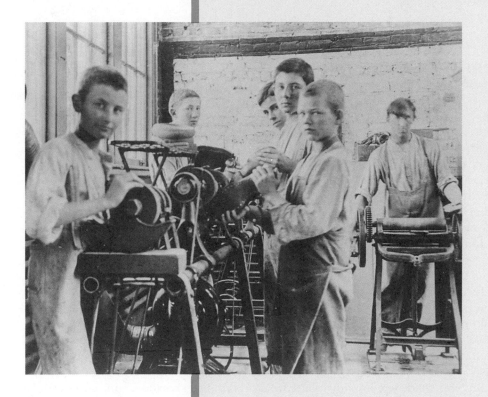

This chapter analyzes the history of dealing with at-risk children.[1] How has the role of children changed from the Middle Ages to the present time? Where did the term *delinquency* originate? What historical developments led to the first modern juvenile court in Chicago in 1899? Included is a discussion of the social welfare movement, the notion of treating children separately, and the establishment of legislation to segregate delinquent children from adult criminal offenders. The chapter concludes with a look at the period from the turn of the century to the mid-1960s and provides a timeline of major events in the history of juvenile justice.

THE CARE OF CHILDREN IN THE MIDDLE AGES

Little is known about the day-to-day lives of children between 700 A.D. and 1500 A.D. During this period, the concept of childhood as we know it today did not exist. Children were not seen as a distinct social group with unique needs and behaviors.

In the early centuries of the Middle Ages, family life was paternalistic.[2] The father was the final authority on all family matters and exercised complete control over the social, economic, and physical well-being of his wife and children. Ordinarily, if the father's will was not obeyed, his children and wife were subject to severe punishment, even death. The concept of the father's dominance had its roots in Roman law, which gave a father unlimited authority over his family. This included the right of life and death over all family members, the power to sell members of the family, the right to veto marriages, and the right to recover stolen children.

Much of what we know about family life in this period concerns upper-class, landholding families. In these, the nuclear family—father, mother, and children—was viewed as a small segment of a larger clan. This larger group, or extended family, was made up of many loosely related families sharing a common heritage and tradition. In England, for example, the Yorks, Tudors, and Lancasters were all powerful congregate family groups. These families sought to expand their power and influence over rivals by intermarriage. The importance of improving and expanding the family influenced marriage, inheritance, and child-rearing practices. Marriages were not made for love or affection; they were made for family interest, to strengthen alliances, and to improve one's possessions. Thus, love was subjugated to duty to family and relatives.

Other practices also greatly influenced the daily life of children during the Middle Ages. **Primogeniture** required that the oldest surviving male child inherit family lands and titles. He could then distribute them as he saw fit to younger siblings. However, there was no absolute requirement that he distribute portions of the estate, so when this was not done, many youths were forced to fend for themselves. They entered religious orders, became soldiers, or sought wealthy patrons. Primogeniture often caused intense family rivalries that led to blood feuds and tragedy among family members. For example, a mother might die in childbirth, leaving behind an infant who was the sole heir to a family estate and title. If the child's father remarried and produced offspring who had no hope of substantial titles or inheritance, conflicts might arise over the inheritance rights of the first-born infant and subsequent siblings, creating feuds between individual family members.

The **dower system** mandated that a family bestow money, land, or other wealth on a potential husband or his family in exchange for his marriage to their daughter. In return, the young woman received a promise of financial assistance, called a jointure, from the groom's family. It provided her with a lifetime income if she outlived her mate. The dower system had a significant impact on the role of the female in medieval society and consequently on the role of children. It ensured that marriages would be contracted only within a social class and not across classes. It gave the woman's father control over whom she married because he could threaten to withhold funds. It placed the female in the role of being an economic drain on the family. A father with many daughters and few sons might find himself financially unable to obtain suitable marriages for his daughters. As a result, in many instances, the youngest girls entered convents, became unwanted, or were left at home.

Little is known about the peasant family during the Middle Ages. It did not maintain the same ties to a powerful kinship group as did the wealthy families. Although it too had a patriarchal family structure, a great portion of the family's time was devoted to work and survival. Consequently, the peasant father's influence was weaker than that of the wealthy landowner. Children were expected to assume adult roles early in life. They went into domestic or agricultural service on great estates or were apprenticed in trades or crafts. To some degree, this system of control over children lifted the burden from parents and placed the children in the care of wealthy families.

CHILD CARE IN THE FIFTEENTH AND SIXTEENTH CENTURIES

Medieval features of the family had an important effect on child-rearing practices during the fifteenth and sixteenth centuries. For instance, newborn children were almost immediately handed over to wet nurses, who breast-fed and cared for them during the early years of their lives. These women often lived away from the family so that parents had little contact with their children. Even the wealthiest families employed wet nurses, because it was considered demeaning for a noblewoman to nurse. Swaddling, a common practice, entailed wrapping a newborn entirely in bandages. The bandages prevented any movement and enabled the wet nurse to manage the child easily. It was thought that this practice protected the child, but it most likely contributed to high infant mortality rates because the child could not be kept clean.

Discipline was severe during this period. Young children of all classes, both peasant and wealthy, were subjected to stringent rules and regulations. They were beaten severely for any sign of disobedience or ill-temper. Many children during this time would be considered abused if they lived in today's world. The relationship between parent and child was remote. Children were expected to enter the world of adults and to undertake responsibilities early in their lives, sharing in the work of siblings and parents.

The roots of the nonpersonal relationship between parent and child can be traced to high mortality rates, which made sentimental and affectionate relationships risky. It would have been foolish for parents to invest emotional effort in relationships that could so easily be terminated by violence, accidents, or disease. Parents often thought that children must be toughened to ensure their survival in a hostile world. Close family relationships were viewed as detrimental to this process. Also, since the oldest male child was viewed as the essential and important element in a family's well-being, younger male and female siblings were considered economic and social liabilities. Often children and others thought to be suffering from disease or retardation were abandoned to churches, orphanages, or foundling homes.[3]

In summary, then, lack of parental affection, physical and emotional remoteness, severe physical punishments and other discipline, rigid social class structure, and conflict, suspicion, hostility, and alienation among family groups all characterized child care in the Middle Ages. These conditions are the most significant features precipitating the children's court movement in Great Britain in the seventeenth and eighteenth centuries.

THE DEVELOPMENT OF CONCERN FOR CHILDREN

Throughout the seventeenth and eighteenth centuries, a number of developments in England heralded the historical march towards the recognition of the rights of children. In many instances, these events eventually affected the juvenile legal system as it emerged in America. They include: (1) changes in family style and child care, (2) the effect of the English Poor Laws in America, (3) the apprenticeship movement, and (4) the role of the chancery court.[4]

Changes in Family Structure

Family structure and the role of children began to change after the Middle Ages as the influence of the great families began to wane. Extended families, which were created over centuries, gave way to the nuclear family structure with which we are familiar today. It became more common for marriage to be based on love and mutual attraction between men and women than on parental consent and male dominance. But parents still kept their rigid discipline over children. Control of a child's actions was considered essential for proper maintenance of the family structure. At this time, the concept of childhood as an independent status was developing and the needs of children were beginning to be understood.

In an effort to provide more controls over children, schools began to flourish in many large cities during this time.[5] Their structure and subject matter were quite different from those that exist today. The subject matter included grammar, Latin, law, and logic. Children often began to study at an early age. During the latter part of the seventeenth century, grammar and boarding schools emerged. Children were sent to school very early in England. The growth of this scholastic movement was directly related to the emphasis such philosophers as John Locke and Jean Jacques Rousseau put on the learning process. Teachers in these institutions often ruled by fear, and flogging was their main method of discipline.

Students were often beaten for academic mistakes as well as moral lapses. Such brutal treatment involved both the rich and the poor and extended to all levels of educational life, including boarding schools and universities. Only toward the end of the eighteenth century, when the Enlightenment, stressing the rights of human beings, emerged, did this treatment abate throughout the continent of Europe. It remained in full force in Great Britain, however, where the child's position in society was that of a second-class citizen.

Toward the close of the eighteenth century, the work of such philosophers as Voltaire, Rousseau, and Locke began to herald a new age for childhood and family.[6] The Enlightenment stressed a humanistic view of life, freedom, family, reason, and law. The philosophers suggested that the ideal person was sympathetic to others and receptive to new ideas. These new beliefs influenced the life-style of the family. The father's authority was tempered, discipline in the home became more relaxed, and the expression of love and affection came to be of deep concern to family members. Upper- and middle-class families began to devote attention to child-rearing.

As a result, toward the end of the eighteenth and the beginning of the nineteenth centuries, children began to emerge as a readily distinguishable group with independent needs and interest, at least in the wealthier classes. Parents often took greater personal interest in their upbringing. In addition, serious questions arose over the treatment of children in school. Public outcries led to a decrease in excessive physical discipline there. Restrictions were placed on the use of the whip, and in some schools, the imposition of academic assignments or the loss of privileges replaced corporal punishment. Nonetheless, not all customs underwent positive change. Girls were still undereducated, parents were still excessively concerned with the moral and religious development of their children, physical punishment was still primary, and schools continued to mistreat children. Yet the changes in England in this period paved the way for today's family structure of child care.

Poor Laws

While children of the upper classes were involved in educational programs, poor children in the cities and counties had different experiences. As early as 1535, the English passed statutes known as **Poor Laws**.[7] These laws allowed for the appointment of overseers to bind out destitute or neglected children as servants. The Poor Laws forced children to serve during their minority in the care of families who trained them in agricultural, trade, or domestic services. The Elizabethan Poor Laws of 1601 were a model for dealing with poor children for more than two hundred years. These laws created a system of church wardens and overseers who, at the consent of justices of the peace, identified vagrant, delinquent, and neglected children and took measures to put them to work. Often this meant placing them in poorhouses or workhouses or apprenticing them to masters.

The Apprenticeship Movement

Apprenticeship in Great Britain existed through almost the entire history of the country.[8] It was a practice that placed children in the care of adults who trained them to discharge various duties and obtain skills. Voluntary apprentices were bound out by parents or guardians who wished to secure training for their children. Involuntary apprentices were compelled by the authorities to serve until they were 21 or older. The master-apprentice relationship was similar to the parent-child relationship in that the master had complete responsibility for and authority over the apprentice. If an apprentice was unruly, a complaint could be made and the apprentice could be punished. Apprentices were often placed in rooms or workshops separate from other prisoners and were generally treated differently from those charged with a criminal offense. Even at this early stage, the conviction was growing that the criminal law and its enforcement should be applied differently to children.

Chancery Court

The concept of *parens patriae* and the chancery court system played significant parts in shaping juvenile justice in Great Britain. The **chancery court** existed throughout the Middle Ages. It was concerned primarily with protecting property rights, although its authority extended to the welfare of children generally. The major issues in medieval cases that came before the chancery courts concerned guardianship, the uses and control of property, and the arrangement of people and power in relation to the monarchy. Agents of the chancery courts were responsible for controlling and settling problems involving rights to estates and guardianship interests with regard to the hierarchy of families and the state. These courts were founded on the proposition that children and other incompetents were under the protective control of the king. Thus, the Latin phrase *parens patriae* referred to the role of the king as the father of his country. As Douglas Besharov states, "The concept apparently was first used by English kings to justify their intervention in the lives of the children of their vassals—children whose position and property were of direct concern to the monarch."[9] In the famous 1827 English case *Wellesley v. Wellesley,* a duke's children were taken away from him in the name and interest of *parens patriae* because of his scandalous behavior.[10] Thus the concept of *parens patriae* became the theoretical basis for the protective jurisdiction of the chancery courts acting as part of the crown's power.

As time passed, the crown used *parens patriae* more and more to justify its intervention in the lives of families and children by its interest in their general welfare. However, as Douglas Rendleman points out, "the idea of *parens patriae* was actually used to maintain the power of the crown and the structure of control over families known as feudalism.[11]

The chancery court dealt with the property and custody problems of the wealthier classes. It never had jurisdiction over children charged with criminal conduct. Juveniles who violated the law were handled within the framework of the regular criminal court system. Nonetheless, the concept of *parens patriae,* which was established with the English chancery court system, grew to refer primarily to the responsibility of the courts and the state to act in the best interests of the child. The idea that the state—and particularly the juvenile court in the twentieth century—should act to protect the young, the incompetent, the neglected, and the delinquent subsequently became a major influence on the development of the American juvenile justice system.

CHILDREN IN COLONIAL AMERICA

While England was using its chancery courts and its Poor Law system to deal with unfortunate children, the American colonies were struggling with similar concepts. Initially, the colonies were a haven for poor and unfortunate people looking for religious and economic opportunities denied them in England and Europe. Along with early settlers, many children came not as citizens but as indentured servants, apprentices, or agricultural workers. They were recruited from the English workhouses, orphanages, prisons, and asylums that housed vagrant and delinquent youths during the sixteenth and seventeenth centuries.[12]

At the same time, the colonies themselves produced illegitimate, neglected, abandoned, and delinquent children whose parents were absent or could not care for them. The colonies' initial response to caring for such unfortunate children was to adopt a court system and Poor Law system similar to the English one. Involuntary apprenticeship and the indenturing and binding out of children became an integral part of colonialization in America. For example, Poor Law legislation was passed in Virginia in 1646 and in Massachusetts and Connecticut in 1673.[13] Under the laws, poor and dependent children were required to serve apprenticeships.

The master in colonial America acted as a natural parent, and in certain instances, apprentices would actually become part of the nuclear family structure. If they disobeyed their masters, apprentices were punished by local tribunals. If masters abused apprentices, courts would make them pay damages, return the children to the parents, or find new guardians. Maryland and Virginia developed an orphan's court that supervised the treatment of youth placed with guardians and insured that they were not mistreated or taken advantage of by their masters. These courts did not supervise children living with their natural parents, leaving intact the parents' right to care for their children.[14]

The apprenticeship system eventually eroded under the pressure of national growth prompted by the War of Independence, the rise of the industrial revolution, and the ever-increasing European immigration. The concepts of *parens patriae* and the chancery court system came to be unacceptable in America because they represented the ideas of monarchy and feudalism that were being rejected in the establishment of the new nation. After the American Revolution, many poor youths sought jobs in mills and factories and lived in boarding homes and industrial settlements provided by mill owners.

By the beginning of the nineteenth century, the apprenticeship system could no longer compete with the factory system. Yet the problems of how to deal effectively with growing numbers of dependent youths increased. Early American settlers were firm believers in hard work, strict discipline, and education. These principles were viewed as the only reliable method for salvation. A child's life was marked by work alongside parents, some schooling, prayer, more work, and further study. In keeping with the family interest in hard work and discipline, the Factory Act of the early nineteenth century limited the hours children were permitted to work and the age at which they could begin to work. It also prescribed a minimum amount of schooling to be provided by factory owners.[15] Often, these statutes were violated, and conditions of work and school remained troublesome issues well into the twentieth century. Nevertheless, the statutes were a step in the direction of reform.

Controlling Children

As in England, moral discipline was rigidly enforced. Stubborn-child laws were passed that made it a legal requirement for children to obey their parents.[16] It was not uncommon in the colonies for children who were disobedient or disrespectful to their families to be whipped or otherwise physically chastised. Children were often required to attend public whippings and executions because they served as important forms of moral instruction. Parents often referred their children to published works and writings on behavior and discipline and expected them to follow their precepts carefully. However, the early colonists viewed family violence as a sin and child protection laws were passed as early as 1639 (in New Haven, Connecticut). These laws were generally symbolic and rarely enforced. They expressed the community's commitment to God to oppose sin; offenders usually received lenient sentences.[17]

While most colonies adopted a protectionist stance, there were actually few cases of child abuse brought before the courts. The absence of child abuse cases may reflect the nature of life in what were essentially extremely religious households. Children were productive laborers and respected by their parents. In addition, large families provided many siblings and kinfolk who could care for children and relieve stress-producing burdens on parents.[18]

Another view is that children were harshly punished in early American families but that the "acceptable" limits of discipline were so high that few parents were charged with assault. Any punishment that fell short of maiming or permanently harming a child was considered within the ambit of parental rights.[19]

DEVELOPMENTS IN THE NINETEENTH CENTURY

As the nineteenth century began, delinquent, neglected, dependent, and runaway children were not treated as separate groups.[20] Children were often charged and convicted of crimes, including capital offenses, and the harsh sentences that were imposed were similar to those imposed on adults. The adult criminal code also applied to children, and no juvenile court was in existence before the end of the nineteenth century.

Throughout the early nineteenth century, various pieces of legislation were introduced to humanize criminal procedures for children. The concept of probation, introduced in Massachusetts in 1841, was geared toward helping young people avoid the trauma of a prison experience.[21] The many books and reports written during this time made the subject of juvenile child care one of intense public interest.

Despite this interest, there were no special facilities for the care of youths in trouble with the law, nor were there separate laws or courts to control their behavior. As in England, children in America during this time were subject to adult criminal procedures and adult punishments. Youths who committed petty crimes, such as stealing, gambling, or minor damage to property, were viewed as wayward or victims of neglect and were placed in community asylums or homes. Youths who were involved in serious crimes were subject to the same punishments as adults—prisons, whipping, or death. The criminal laws of the eighteenth and the nineteenth centuries in both England and the United States provided severe and often brutal punishments for convicted offenders. Children, like adults, were even subject to the death penalty.

To understand how the contemporary juvenile justice system evolved, we must ask what important factors in nineteenth-century America led to reform in the field of child care. A number of significant events nourished and supported the eventual development of the juvenile justice system in the United States: urbanization; child-saving; the concept of *parens patriae;* the reform school movement; and the development of Society for the Prevention of Cruelty to Children.

Urbanization

Especially during the first half of the nineteenth century, the United States experienced rapid population growth, primarily because of an increase in the birthrate and continuing increases in European immigration. The growing numbers of young people eligible for apprenticeship programs overwhelmed this system of work and training. In the South, slavery eliminated the need for fieldhands and servants. To accommodate groups of dependent and destitute youths, local jurisdictions developed systems of almshouses, poorhouses, and workhouses. In crowded, unhealthy conditions, they accepted the poor, the insane, the diseased, and vagrant and destitute children. The overseers responsible for them placed many children in institutions.

In addition, increased urbanization and industrialization led to the belief that certain segments of the population, namely youths in urban areas and immigrants, were prone to criminal deviance and immorality. The children of these classes were considered a group that might be "saved" by state intervention.[22] Intervention into the lives of these potentially "dangerous classes" to help alleviate their burdens became acceptable for wealthy, civic-minded citizens. Such efforts included shelter care for youths, educational and social activities, and the development of settlement houses.

The Child-Saving Movement

The problems generated by large-scale urban growth, fueled by immigration, sparked tremendous interest in the difficulties faced by "new" Americans. The main focus, however, was on extending government control over a whole range of youthful activities that had previously been left to private or family control, including idleness, drinking, vagrancy, and delinquency.

The parties interested in the care of unfortunate children became known as **child savers.** Prominent among these were penologist Enoch Wines, Judge Richard Tuthill, Lucy Flowers of the Chicago Women's Association, Sara Cooper of the National Conference of Charities and Corrections, and Sophia Minton of the New York Committee on Children.[23] They believed that poor children presented a threat to the moral fabric of American society and should be controlled because their behavior could lead to the destruction of the nation's economic system.

Child-saving organizations influenced state legislatures to enact laws giving courts the power to commit children who were runaways, committed criminal acts, and who were out of the control of parents to specialized institutional programs. The most prominent of the institutional care facilities developed by

This engraving depicts the work of the Children's Aid Society.

child savers was the **House of Refuge** in New York, opened in 1825.[24] It was founded on the concept of protecting youths by taking potential criminals off the streets and reforming them in a family-like environment.

When the House of Refuge opened, the majority of children admitted were status offenders placed there because of vagrancy or neglect. However, the institution was run more like a prison, with a work schedule, study schedule, strict discipline, and absolute separation of the sexes. Such a harsh program led to runaways, with the result that the House of Refuge was forced to take a more lenient approach. Children entered the house by court order, sometimes over parental objections, for vagrancy or delinquency. Their stay depended on need, age, and skill. Once there, youths were required to do piecework provided by local manufacturers or to work part of the day in the community.

Despite criticism of the program, the concept enjoyed expanding popularity. In 1826, the Boston City Council founded the House of Reformation for juvenile offenders. Similar institutions were opened in Massachusetts and New York in 1847.[25] To these schools, which were both privately and publicly funded, the courts committed children found guilty of criminal violations, as well as those beyond the control of their parents. Because the child-saving movement regarded both convicted offenders and parents of delinquent children in the same category, they sought to have the reform schools establish control over the children. As Robert Mennel states, "By training destitute and delinquent children, and by separating them from their natural parents and adult criminals, refuge managers believed they were preventing poverty and crime."[26]

Parens Patriae and Its Legal Challenges

The philosophy of *parens patriae* was extended to refuge programs, which were given parental control over a committed child. Robert Mennel has summarized this attitude:

> The doctrine of *parens patriae* gave refuge managers the best of two worlds, familial and legal: it separated delinquent children from their natural parents, and it circumvented the rigor of criminal law by allowing courts to commit children, under loosely worded statutes, to specially created schools instead of jails.[27]

Once a refuge received a child, procedures of criminal law no longer applied.

But this process of institutional control over children in the name of the state and family did not proceed without some significant legal challenges. In 1838, a young child's father attempted to free her from the Philadelphia House of Refuge, which claimed the right of parental control over her because of unmanageable behavior. The girl's father argued that her commitment without a trial by jury was unconstitutional. In its decision in the case, *Ex Parte Crouse,* the court held that the House of Refuge was specifically planned to reform, restrain, and protect children from depraved parents or their environment.[28] A statutory procedure without a trial in the interest of the child was legal. As a result, the *Crouse* case gave the state almost complete authority to intervene in parent-child relationships. The court stated:

> The right of parental control is a natural, but not an unalienable one. It is not accepted by the Declaration of Rights out of the subjects of ordinary legislation; and it consequently remains subject to the ordinary legislative power which, if wantonly or inconveniently used, would soon be constitutionally restricted, but the competency of which, as the government is constituted, cannot be doubted.[29]

The *Crouse* decision demonstrated that children could be deprived of the constitutional liberties guaranteed to adults.

Another, more significant, case was decided in favor of the parent and child against the state. The case was *O'Connell v. Turner.*[30] In 1870, the Illinois courts committed Daniel O'Connell to the Chicago Reform School on the ground that he was a vagrant or destitute youth without proper parental care. The parents attacked the child's commitment because he was not convicted of a crime and had been apprehended and confined under a general grant of power to arrest for simple misfortune. The basic legal problem was whether children could be committed to reform schools in the absence of criminal conduct or because of gross misconduct on the part of their parents.

The law was held to be unconstitutional, and on subsequent appeal, the court ordered Daniel O'Connell discharged. As Justice Thornton noted in the case: "The warrant of commitment does not indicate that the arrest was made for a

The House of Refuge was one of the earliest juvenile institutions in the United States to offer residents vocational training.

criminal offense. Hence, we conclude that it was made under the general grant of power to arrest and confine for misfortune."[31] The fact that the court distinguished between criminal acts and those arising from misfortune was significant, for all legislation dealing with misfortune cases was subsequently appealed as a direct result of the *O'Connell* decision. Also, as Sanford Fox indicates, the *O'Connell* case changed the course of events in Illinois. The Chicago Reform School was closed in 1872, and the case encouraged procedural due process reform for committed youths.[32]

The Development of Juvenile Institutions

Despite the *O'Connell* decision, state intervention in the lives of children continued throughout the latter portion of the nineteenth century and well into the twentieth century. The child savers influenced state and local governments to create institutions, called reform schools, exclusively devoted to the care of vagrant and delinquent youths. State institutions opened in Westboro, Massachusetts, in 1848 and in Rochester, New York, in 1849.[33] These were soon followed by institutional programs in other states—Ohio in 1850 and Maine, Rhode Island, and Michigan in 1860.[34] Children lived in congregate conditions and spent their days working at institutional jobs, learning a trade where possible and receiving some basic education. They were racially and sexually segregated, discipline was harsh and often involved whipping and isolation, and the physical care was of poor quality. For example, Beverly Smith's historical research found that girls admitted to the Western House of Refuge in Rochester, New York, were often labeled as deviant or criminal but were in reality abused, orphaned, and neglected. They too were subject to harsh working conditions, strict discipline, and intensive labor before their release.[35]

Some viewed houses of refuge and reform schools as humanitarian answers to poorhouses and prisons for vagrant, neglected, and delinquent youths, but many remained opposed to such programs. For example, as an alternative, New York philanthropist Charles Brace helped develop the **Children's Aid Society** in 1853.[36] Brace's formula for dealing with neglected and delinquent youths was to rescue them from the harsh environment of the city and provide them with temporary shelter care. He then sought to place them in private homes throughout the nation. This program was very similar to the foster home programs of today. As Fox points out, "The great value to be placed on family life for deviant and crime-prone children was later explicitly set forth in the juvenile court act."[37]

Although the child reformers provided services for children, they were unable to stop juvenile delinquency. Most reform schools were unable to hold youthful law violators and reform them. Institutional life was hard. Large numbers of children needing placement burdened the public finances supporting such programs. So while state control over vagrant, delinquent, and neglected children became more widespread after the Civil War, it also became more controversial. As the nation grew, it became evident that private charities and public organizations were not caring adequately for the growing number of troubled youths.

The SPCC Movement

In 1874, the first **Society for the Prevention of Cruelty to Children (SPCC)** was established in New York; by 1900, there were three hundred such societies in the United States.[38] Leaders of the SPCCs were concerned that neglected and abused boys would grow up to join the ranks of the "dangerous classes"—lower-class

The House of Refuge in New York was built in 1824, opened in 1825, and burned in 1838. It housed young boys found to be "juvenile delinquents."

criminals. Mistreated young girls might become sexually promiscuous women. SPCC membership was swelled by the growing post-Civil War crime rate and concern about a rapidly shifting and changing population. There was also true concern for the welfare of children who were subject to cruelty and neglect at home and at school.

SPCC groups influenced state legislatures to pass statutes protecting children from exploitive or neglectful parents, including those who did not provide them with adequate food and clothing or employed them to beg or work in places where liquor was sold.[39] Criminal penalties and provisions were created for removing children from the home. In some states, such as New York, agents of the SPCC could actually arrest abusive parents, while in others, they would inform the police about suspected abuse cases and accompany officers when they made an arrest.[40]

Individual reform groups continued to lobby for government control over children, but the commitment of children under the doctrine of *parens patriae* without due process of law began to be questioned. Why should parents have their children taken away from them? What was in the best interest of a child in terms of proper parental care? Should minors be imprisoned for being vagrants? What right did the state have to place in reform school children who had not violated the criminal law? These and other questions began to plague reformers and those interested in the plight of children. Institutional deficiencies, the detention of delinquent children in adult jails and prisons, the handling of poor, dependent, ignorant, and noncriminal delinquents by inadequate private child welfare organizations without due process, and the religious segregation of children all formed the basis for the idea that a juvenile court should be established.

ESTABLISHMENT OF THE ILLINOIS JUVENILE COURT

Against the background of the early reform efforts of the child savers, the well-known **Illinois Juvenile Court** Act was passed in 1899. This was a major event in the history of the juvenile justice movement in the United States. Its significance was such that by 1917, juvenile courts had been established in all but three states.

What exactly did the passage of the Illinois Juvenile Court Act mean? The traditional interpretation is that the reformers had the highest motives and passed legislation that would serve the best interests of the child. Justice Abe Fortas took this position in the 1967 *In re Gault* case:

> The early reformers were appalled by adult procedures and penalties and by the fact that children could be given long prison sentences and mixed in jails with hardened criminals. They were profoundly convinced that society's duty to the child could not be confined by the concept of justice alone. . . . The child—essentially good, as they saw it—was to be made to feel that he was the object of the state's care and solicitude, not that he was under arrest or on trial. . . . The idea of crime and punishment was to be abandoned. The child was to be treated and rehabilitated, and the procedures from apprehension through institutionalization were to be clinical rather than punitive.[41]

The child savers were imbued with a positivistic philosophy and emphasized individual values and judgments about children and their care. Society was to be concerned with where children came from, what their problems were, and how these problems could be handled in the interests of the children and of the state.

Interpretations of its motives and effects differ, but unquestionably the Illinois Juvenile Court Act established juvenile delinquency as a legal concept and the juvenile court as a judicial form. Sections of this act are reproduced in Table 13.1.

The Illinois Juvenile Court Act for the first time made a major distinction between children who were dependent and neglected and those who were delinquent. Delinquent children were those under the age of 16 who violated the laws. The act also established a court specifically for children and an extensive probation program whereby children were to be the responsibility of probation officers. In addition, the legislation allowed children to be committed to institutions and reform programs under the laws and control of the state.

Among the most important provisions of the act were:

■ A separate court was established for delinquent, dependent, and neglected children.

TABLE 13.1   The Illinois Juvenile Court Act of 1899

Section 1. Definitions. This act shall apply only to children under the age of sixteen (16) years not now or hereafter inmates of a State institution, or any training school for boys or industrial school for girls or some institution incorporated under the laws of this State, except as provided in sections twelve (12) and eighteen (18). For the purposes of this act the words *dependent child* and *neglected child* shall mean any child who for any reason is destitute or homeless or abandoned; or dependent upon the public for support; or has not proper parental care or guardianship; or who habitually begs or receives alms; or who is found living in any house of ill fame or with any vicious or disreputable person; or whose home, by reason of neglect, cruelty or depravity on the part of its parents, guardian or other person in whose care it may be, is an unfit place for such a child; and any child under the age of eight (8) years who is found peddling or selling any article or singing or playing any musical instrument upon the streets or giving any public entertainment. The words *delinquent child* shall include any child under the age of 16 years who violates any law of this State or any city or village ordinance. The word *child* or *children* may mean one or more children, and the word *parent* or *parents* may be held to mean one or both parents, when consistent with the intent of this act. The word *association* shall include any corporation which includes in its purposes the care or disposition of children coming within the meaning of this act . . . .

§ 3. Juvenile Court. In counties having over 500,000 population the judges of the circuit court shall, at such times as they shall determine, designate one or more of their number whose duty it shall be to hear all cases coming under this act. A special courtroom, to be designated as the juvenile courtroom, shall be provided for the hearing of such cases, and the findings of the court shall be entered in a book or books to be kept for that purpose and known as the "Juvenile Record," and the court may, for convenience, be called the "Juvenile Court."

§ 4. Petition to the Court. Any reputable person, being resident in the county, having knowledge of a child in his county who appears to be either neglected, dependent or delinquent, may file with the clerk of a court having jurisdiction in the matter a petition in writing, setting forth the facts, verified by affidavit. It shall be sufficient that the affidavit is upon information and belief . . . .

§ 6. Probation Officers. The court shall have authority to appoint or designate one or more discreet persons of good character to serve as probation officers during the pleasure of the court; said probation officers to receive no compensation from the public treasury. In case a probation officer shall be appointed by any court, it shall be the duty of the clerk of the court, if practicable, to notify the said probation officer in advance when any child is to be brought before the said court; it shall be the duty of the said probation officer to make such investigation as may be required

TABLE 13.1   *continued*

by the court; to be present in court in order to represent the interests of the child when the case is heard; to furnish to the court such information and assistance as the judge may require; and to take such charge of any child before and after trial as may be directed by the court.

§ 7. **Dependent and Neglected Children.** When any child under the age of sixteen (16) years shall be found to be dependent or neglected within the meaning of this act, the court may make an order committing the child to the care of some suitable State institution, or to the care of some reputable citizen of good moral character, or to the care of some training school or an industrial school, as provided by law, or to the care of some association willing to receive it embracing in its objects the purpose of caring or obtaining homes for dependent or neglected children, which association shall have been accredited as hereinafter provided. . . .

§ 9. **Disposition of Delinquent Children.** In the case of a delinquent child the court may continue the hearing from time to time and may commit the child to the care and guardianship of a probation officer duly appointed by the court and may allow said child to remain in its own home, subject to the visitation of the probation officer; such child to report to the probation officer as often as may be required and subject to be returned to the court for further proceedings, whenever such action may appear to be necessary, or the court may commit the child to the care and guardianship of the probation officer, to be placed in a suitable family home, subject to the friendly supervision of such probation officer; or it may authorize the said probation officer to board out the said child in some suitable family home, in case

provision is made by voluntary contribution or otherwise for the payment of the board of such child, until a suitable provision may be made for the child in a home without such payment; or the court may commit the child, if a boy, to a training school for boys, or if a girl, to an industrial school for girls. Or, if the child is found guilty of any criminal offense, and the judge is of the opinion that the best interest requires it, the court may commit the child to any institution within said county incorporated under the laws of this State for the care of delinquent children, or provided by a city for the care of such offenders, or may commit the child, if a boy over the age of ten (10) years, to the State reformatory, or if a girl over the age of ten (10) years, to the State Home for Juvenile Female Offenders. In no case shall a child be committed beyond his or her minority. A child committed to such institution shall be subject to the control of the board of managers thereof, and the said board shall have power to parole such child on such conditions as it may prescribe, and the court shall, on the recommendation of the board, have power to discharge such child from custody whenever in the judgment of the court his or her reformation shall be complete; or the court may commit the child to the care and custody of some association that will receive it, embracing in its objects the care of neglected and dependent children and that has been duly accredited as hereinafter provided. . . .

§ 11. **Children under Twelve Years Not to Be Committed to Jail.** No court or magistrate shall commit a child under twelve (12) years of age to a jail or police station, but if such child is unable to give bail it may be committed to the care of the sheriff, police officer or probation officer. . . .

Source: Illinois Statutes 1899, Section 131.

■ Special legal procedures were to govern the adjudication and disposition of juvenile matters.

■ Children were to be separated from adults in courts and in institutional programs.

■ Probation programs to assist the court in making decisions in the best interests of the state and the child were to be developed.

Were They Really Child Savers?

The child-saving movement has come under significant reappraisal by modern scholars (see the following Focus on Delinquency). In his ground-breaking book,

Conscience and Convenience: The Progressive Era

David Rothman's important work, *Conscience and Convenience*, is an analysis of the social policies developed during what is referred to as the Progressive Era (1900–1920) of U.S. history.

According to Rothman, the Progressive Era was marked by a great deal of social change prompted by appeals to the conscience of the nation. Reformers were shocked by exposés of how society treated its less fortunate members. They were particularly concerned about what was going on in prisons and mental institutions. The poor, ill, and unfortunate were living in squalor, beaten and mistreated by their "keepers." Progressive reformers lobbied legislators and appealed to public opinion in order to force better conditions. Their efforts helped establish the probation and parole system and other liberal correctional reforms.

The question Rothman poses is whether reformers acted out of conscience or convenience. Did beneficial change really occur, or was it simply a matter of making control over minorities, immigrants, and the lower class in general easier and more "convenient"?

The development of the juvenile court is a case in point. Its operational philosophy reflected the core value of the Progressive Era reformers: individualized treatment. Because each child was considered unique, the cause of his or her delinquency, whether it was a poor home life, destructive peer relations, physical or emotional problems, for example, must be individually treated. The rule was "treat the child, not the crime."

The progressives used the findings of the emerging social sciences of psychology and sociology to guide the juvenile court's activities. As Rothman states: "The juvenile court was to concern itself first not with the specific charge facing the delinquent, but with his character and life-style, his psychological strengths and weaknesses, the advantages and disadvantages of his home life. It was not his act, but . . . his soul that was at issue."

However, such reform efforts were not without their pitfalls. The relaxed atmosphere and promise of rehabilitation espoused by the first juvenile courts prompted police and district attorneys to make extensive use of their services. Children who in the past might have been given their release by police officers after a stern warning were now placed in the hands of juvenile court judges who used their own discretion in deciding their fate. District attorneys were happy to have children sent to the new court because it freed up their crowded court schedules for more important matters and because the informal nature of the juvenile court demanded little of their time or effort. Likewise, reformatory directors applauded the juvenile court, whose rehabilitation philosophy gave them greater credibility in the community. Now if a child were sent to a reformatory, the purpose was treatment and kindness rather than punishment. Reformatory directors were no longer "ogres."

Was the juvenile court an early success? One indication may be the incarceration rate. Though it was originally expected that the number of youths who would have to be incarcerated would decline after a separate juvenile court was created, admission rates to juvenile reformatories actually rose rapidly between 1923 and 1933 (from 15.5 per 100,000 to 20.2 per 100,000). In 1923, there were about 25,000 youths in juvenile reformatories, while in 1933, the number rose to over 30,000. The juvenile court was not a panacea for all juvenile offenders.

According to Rothman, it was the juvenile reformatories themselves that really exposed the false promises of progressive reform. Although they were dedicated to rehabilitation and treatment, many were merely warehouses that provided little or no education or training and invoked harsh disciplinary codes. Children were subjected to solitary confinement and fierce physical punishment. There was actually scant difference between the reformatory and the adult prison. What started as a movement to ease the conscience of liberal reformers had become a mechanism for conveniently dealing with troublesome youths.

Source: David Rothman, *Conscience and Convenience* (Boston: Little Brown, 1980), quotation from p. 215.

The Child Savers, critical thinker Anthony Platt painted a picture of the child savers as representative of the ruling class who were galvanized by the threat of newly arriving immigrants and the urban poor to take action to preserve their way of life.[42] He claims:

> The child savers should not be considered humanists: (1) their reforms did not herald a new system of justice but rather expedited traditional policies which had been informally developed during the nineteenth century; (2) they implicitly assumed the natural dependence of adolescents and created a special court to impose sanctions on premature independents and behavior unbecoming to youth; (3) their attitudes toward delinquent youth were largely paternalistic and romantic but their commands were backed up by force; (4) they promoted correctional programs requiring longer terms of imprisonment, longer hours of labor, and militaristic discipline, and the inculcation of middle-class values and lower-class skills.[43]

Other critical thinkers followed Platt in finding that child saving was motivated more by self-interest than benevolence.[44] For example, in a recent paper, Randall Shelden and Lynn Osborne have traced the early child-saving movement in Memphis, Tennessee, and found that its leaders were a small group of upper-class citizens who desired to control the behavior and life-styles of another class of citizens: lower-class youth. The outcome was ominous: most cases petitioned to the juvenile court (which opened in 1910) were for petty crimes, truancy, and other status-type offenses, yet 25 percent of the youths were committed to some form of incarceration. Of the females placed in incarceration, 96 percent were institutionalized for status offenses.[45] Sanford Fox, a respected legal scholar, has also been critical of the early child-saving reforms. According to Fox, the Illinois act restated the belief in the value of coercive prediction; continued nineteenth-century summary trials for children about whom the predictions were to be made; made no improvements in the long-condemned institutional care furnished these same children; codified the view that institutions should, even without badly needed financial help from the legislature, replicate family life; and reinforced sectarian interests whose role had long been decried by leading child-welfare reformers in the area of juvenile care.[46]

Thus, according to the revisionist approach, the reformers applied the concept of *parens patriae* for their own purposes, including the continuance of middle- and upper-class values, the control of political systems, and the furtherance of a child labor system consisting of marginal and lower-class skilled workers.

CASE IN POINT

It is the year 1898 and you have just become a member of the local child-saving organization.

The state is now willing to create a separate juvenile justice system. The governor has become sensitive to newspaper articles in which members of your organization have taken him to task for the maltreatment of youth. The state has tried young criminals in adult courts and sent the convicted ones to the state prison system to be housed with hardened adult criminals.

There is also concern about the fate of neglected and wayward youth who have been maintained in a series of orphanages, workhouses, and county

continued

jails. There have been rumors that these kids are being exploited by masters who sell their services to sweatshop owners and keep their earnings. There have also been charges that the county-run youth institutions use harsh physical punishments.

The child savers appoint you to head a committee charged with developing a plan for a new juvenile justice system. It is up to you to describe its goals, components, and jurisdiction. The state seems willing to go along with whatever you suggest, though you are suspicious that radical reform might cause a backlash by conservatives who can't see why young criminals should be spared the "pains of imprisonment."

What agencies should control the juvenile justice system?

Would you make the system police-oriented or treatment-oriented?

Would you maintain control over all cases involving at-risk youth, including custody, paternity, and family problems?

DEVELOPING THE JUVENILE JUSTICE SYSTEM

Following the passage of the Illinois Juvenile Court Act, similar legislation was enacted throughout the nation. The courts created by this legislation became known as special courts. Predelinquent children (neglected and dependent children) as well as delinquent children were brought before them. These juvenile courts segregated delinquents from adult criminals and attempted to use individual treatment programs to prevent further delinquency. Their jurisdiction during the twentieth century was based primarily on a child's actions and status, not strictly on the basis of violation of criminal law. Furthermore, because the *parens patriae* philosophy predominated, there developed a form of personalized justice characterized by a procedural laxity and informality that did not provide juvenile offenders with the full panoply of constitutional protections. The court's process was paternalistic rather than adversary in nature. For example, attorneys were not required. Hearsay evidence, inadmissible in criminal trials, was admissible in the adjudication of juvenile offenders. Verdicts were based on a "preponderance of the evidence" instead of "beyond a reasonable doubt," and children were often not granted any right to appeal their convictions. These characteristics allowed the juvenile court to function in a nonlegal manner and to provide various social services to children in need.

The major functions of the juvenile justice system were to prevent juvenile crime and to rehabilitate juvenile offenders. The functions of the two most important actors, the juvenile court judge and the probation staff, were to diagnose the child's condition and prescribe programs to alleviate it. Until 1967, consideration for children's constitutional rights were secondary.

By the 1920s, noncriminal behavior in the form of incorrigibility and truancy from school was added to the jurisdiction of many juvenile court systems. Programs of all kinds—including individualized counseling and institutional care—were used as methods to cure juvenile criminality. An entire group of new

workers—criminologists, sociologists, social workers, probation officers, and psychologists—began to emerge to deal with delinquency and noncriminal behavior. Much of their efforts were involved in seeking to rehabilitate children brought before the court.

By 1925, juvenile courts existed in virtually every jurisdiction in every state. Although the juvenile court concept expanded rapidly, it cannot be said that each state implemented the philosophy of the court thoroughly. Some jurisdictions established elaborate juvenile court systems, others passed legislation but provided no services. Some courts had trained juvenile court judges; others had nonlawyers sitting in juvenile cases. Some courts had extensive probation departments; others had untrained probation personnel.[47]

There was also great diversity in juvenile institutions. While some maintained a lenient, treatment-oriented schedule, others relied on harsh physical punishments, including beatings, restraining in straight jackets, immersion in cold water, and solitary confinement in dark cells with a diet of bread and water. In 1912, the U.S. Children's Bureau was formed as the first federal child welfare agency. By the 1930s, the bureau began to investigate the state of juvenile institutions and tried to expose some of the more repressive aspects of these programs with a series of federally sponsored books and research reports.[48]

A number of significant events occurred during the 1960s and affected the development of the juvenile justice system. In 1962, the state of New York passed legislation creating a family court system.[49] The new family court was to assume the responsibility for all matters involving family life. Its particular emphasis was to be on delinquent, dependent, and neglected children and paternity, adoption, and support proceedings involving parents. In addition, the legislation established a separate classification, Person in Need of Supervision (PINS). This category, covering noncriminal behavior, was the forerunner of such legislative categories as Children in Need of Supervision (CHINS), Minors in Need of Supervision (MINS), and Families in Need of Supervision (FINS). These labels covered such actions as truancy, running away, and incorrigibility. In using them to establish jurisdiction over children and their families, juvenile courts expanded their role as social agencies. Because noncriminal children were now involved in the juvenile court system to a greater degree, many juvenile courts had to improve their services as social agencies, and efforts were made to play down the authority of the court as a court of law and to increase the personalized system of justice for children.

History, philosophical ideals, legal decisions, and scientific theories all have influenced the shape of the contemporary juvenile justice system. The characteristics of this system—legal social courts, unclear goals and objectives, abuses of discretion by police and judges, ineffective programs, and unqualified personnel—will be examined in future chapters. Table 13.2 highlights events in the development of delinquency and juvenile justice.

SUMMARY

This chapter focused on the historical development of juvenile justice from the Middle Ages to the beginning of the twentieth century and the development of the modern juvenile court. First, the chapter described the care of children and the early concepts of family life in the fifteenth and sixteenth centuries. In addition, it explored some of the early concepts of family living, such as dower, primogeniture, and punishment, in an attempt to understand how children and families lived during that period.

As the seventeenth century began, there was greater recognition of the needs of children. In Great Britain, the chancery court movement, the Poor Laws, and the apprenticeship programs had a great impact on the lives of children. In colonial America, many of the characteristics of English family living were adopted.

In the nineteenth century, neglected, delinquent, and dependent or runaway children were treated no differently than criminal defendants. Often, children were charged and convicted of crimes through procedures used with adults. However, during this time, because of philosophical shifts in the areas of crime and delinquency as well as a change in the emphasis of the concept of *parens patriae*, steps were begun to reduce the responsibility of children under the criminal law in both Great Britain and the United States. Some issues that had a strong effect on the development of the juvenile court were the child-saving movement, the development of reform schools, and the problems of urbanization in America.

At the end of the chapter was a summary of the original Illinois Juvenile Court Act and its specific characteristics and goals. Thus, the chapter presented a history of the juvenile justice movement, highlighting the main ideas and factors that led to the creation of the juvenile court movement in the United States.

TABLE 13.2   Children's Rights

1787	Signing of the Constitution of the United States.
1791	Passage of the Bill of Rights.
1825	New York House of Refuge is founded.
1826	Boston House of Refuge is founded.
1838	*Ex Parte Crouse*—*Parens patriae* concept relied on. The right of the parent is not inalienable.
1841	John Augustus, first official probation officer in the United States, begins working in Boston.
1847	State institutions for juvenile delinquents open in Boston and New York.
1850	The House of Refuge in Philadelphia closes.
1851	The first adoption act in the United States is passed in Massachusetts.
1853	New York Juvenile Asylum started by the Children's Aid Society.
1866	Massachusetts establishes that the state has power over children under 16 whose parents are "unfit."
1868	Passage of the Fourteenth Amendment to the U.S. Constitution.
1870	Illinois Supreme Court reverses Dan O'Connell's vagrancy sentence to the Chicago Reform School due to lack of due process procedures in *People v. Turner*.
1881	Michigan begins child protection with the Michigan Public Acts of 1881.
1875–1900	Case law begins to deal with protective statutes.
1884	The state assumes the authority to take neglected children and place them in an institution. See *Reynolds v. Howe*, 51 Conn. 472, 478 (1884).
1886	First neglect case is heard in Massachusetts.
1889	Board of children's guardians is established in Indiana and given jurisdiction over neglected and dependent children.
1890	Children's Aid Society of Pennsylvania, a foster home for the juvenile delinquent used as an alternative to reform schools, is established.
1891	Supreme Court of Minnesota establishes the doctrine of parental immunity.
1897	*Ex Parte Becknell*, a California decision that reverses the sentence of a juvenile who has not been given a jury trial.
1899	Illinois Juvenile Court Act.
1903–1905	Many other states pass juvenile court acts.
1905	*Commonwealth v. Fisher*—Pennsylvania Supreme Court upholds the constitutionality of the Juvenile Court Act.
1906	Massachusetts passes an act to provide for the treatment of children not as criminals but as children in need of guidance and aid.
1908	*Ex Parte Sharpe* defines more clearly the role of the juvenile court to include *parens patriae*.
1910	Compulsory school acts.
1918	Chicago area studies are conducted by Shaw and McKay.
1924	Federal Probation Act.
1930	Children's Charter.
1954	*Brown v. Board of Education*, a major school desegregation decision.
1959	Standard Family Court Act of National Council on Crime and Delinquency establishes that juvenile hearings are to be informal.
1966	*Kent v. United States*—initial decision to establish due process protections for juveniles at transfer proceedings.
1967	President's Commission on Law Enforcement recognizes the problems of the juvenile justice system.
1967	*In re Gault*, a U.S. Supreme Court decision that establishes that juveniles have the right to counsel, notice, confrontation of witnesses, and the avoidance of self-incrimination. The decision also applies procedural due process to juveniles in the adjudicatory phase of a hearing and if loss of liberty is threatened. In general, the court holds that Fourteenth Amendment due process applies to the juvenile justice system, specifically in adjudicatory hearings.

TABLE 13.2 *continued*

1968	*Ginsberg v. New York* establishes that it is unlawful to sell pornography to a minor.
1969	*Tinker v. Des Moines School District* establishes that the First Amendment applies to juveniles and protects their constitutional right to free speech.
1969	Hirschi publishes *Causes of Delinquency.*
1970	*In re Winship* establishes that proof beyond a reasonable doubt is necessary in the adjudicatory phase of a juvenile hearing. A juvenile can appeal on the ground of insufficiency of the evidence if the offense alleged is an act that would be a crime in an adult court.
1970	White House Conference on Children.
1971	*McKeiver v. Pennsylvania* establishes that a jury trial is not constitutionally required in a juvenile hearing but states can permit one if they wish.
1971	The Twenty-Sixth Amendment to the Constitution is passed, granting the right to vote to 18-year-olds.
1972	*Wisconsin v. Yoder* gives parents the right to impose their religion on their children.
1972	Wolfgang publishes *Delinquency in a Birth Cohort.*
1973	*In re Snyder* gives minors the right to bring proceedings against their parents.
1973	*San Antonio Independent School District v. Rodriguez* establishes that differences in education based on wealth were not necessarily discriminatory.
1974	Federal Child Abuse Prevention Act.
1974	Buckley Amendment to the Education Act of 1974, the Family Education Rights and Privacy Act. Students have the right to see their own files with parental consent.
1974	Juvenile Justice and Delinquency Prevention Act.
1975	*Goss v. Lopez* establishes that a student facing suspension has the right to due process, prior notice, and an open hearing.
1977	Report of the Committee of the Judiciary, especially concerning the rights of the unborn and the right of 18-year-olds to vote.
1977	Juvenile Justice Amendment of 1977.
1977	*Ingraham v. Wright* establishes that corporal punishment is permissible in public schools and is not a violation of the Eighth Amendment.
1977	American Bar Association, Standards on Juvenile Justice.
1977	Washington State amends its sentencing policy.
1979	International Year of the Child.
1980	National concern over child abuse and neglect.
1981	*Fare v. Michael C.* defines *Miranda* rights of minors.
1982	Efforts to decarcerate status offenders escalate.
1983	The Federal Government focuses its attention on chronic offenders.
1984	*Schall v. Martin* allows states to use preventive detention with juvenile offenders.
1985	*New Jersey v. T.L.O.* allows teachers to search students without a warrant or probable cause.
1985	Wilson and Herrnstein publish *Crime and Human Nature*, focusing attention on biological causes of delinquency.
1986	Juvenile offenders waived to adult court are executed, focusing attention on the death penalty for children.
1987	Conservative trends result in 10,000 juvenile waivers to adult courts.
1988	Reemergence of nationwide gang problem.
1989	Supreme Court upholds death penalty for children over 16.
1990	*Maryland v. Craig* allows child abuse victims to testify on closed-circuit television.

The authors wish to express their appreciation to Dr. Lynn Sametz for preparing this table.

QUESTIONS FOR DISCUSSION

1. What is the relationship between the historical and philosophical approaches to caring for children in the fifteenth, sixteenth, and seventeenth centuries and the understanding of our present juvenile justice system?

2. What factors precipitated the development of the Illinois Juvenile Court Act of 1899? In Great Britain? In the United States?

3. Such terms as *apprenticeship, Poor Laws, chancery court*, and *parens patriae* exist in the early history of the juvenile court movement. What do these terms mean? Where did the term *delinquency* originate?

4. Throughout history, children have often been treated under the criminal law differently from adults. Prior to the twentieth century, were children held responsible for criminal actions? Are children responsible for crimes they commit today? Are they liable for civil wrong?

5. One of the most significant reforms in dealing with the juvenile offenders was the opening of the New York House of Refuge in 1825. What was the social and judicial impact of this reform on the juvenile justice system?

KEY TERMS

primogeniture

dower system

Poor Laws

apprenticeship

chancery court

Wellesley v. Wellesley

child savers

House of Refuge

Ex Parte Crouse

O'Connell v. Turner

Children's Aid Society

Society for the Prevention of Cruelty to Children (SPCC)

Illinois Juvenile Court Act

NOTES

1. See Sanford J. Fox, "Juvenile Justice Reform: A Historical Perspective," *Stanford Law Review* 22:1187 (1970).

2. See Lawrence Stone, *The Family, Sex, and Marriage in England: 1500–1800* (New York: Harper & Row, 1977).

3. See Philipe Fries, *Century of Childhood: A Social History of Family Life* (New York: Vintage, 1962).

4. See Douglas R. Rendleman, "Parens Patriae: From Chancery to the Juvenile Court," *South Carolina Law Review* 23:205 (1971).

5. See Stone, *The Family, Sex, and Marriage in England;* Lawrence Stone, ed., *Schooling and Society: Studies in the History of Education* (Baltimore: Johns Hopkins University Press, 1970).

6. *Ibid.*

7. See Wiley B. Sanders, *Some Early Beginnings of the Children's Court Movement in England*, National Probation Association Yearbook (New York: National Council on Crime and Delinquency, 1945).

8. Rendleman, "Parens Patriae," p. 205.

9. Douglas Besharov, *Juvenile Justice Advocacy—Practice in a Unique Court* (New York: Practicing Law Institute, 1974), p. 2.

10. *Wellesley v. Wellesley*, 4 Eng. Rep. 1078 (1827).

11. Rendleman, "Parens Patriae," p. 209.

12. See Anthony Platt, "The Rise of the Child Saving Movement: A Study in Social Policy and Correctional Reform," *Annals of the American Academy of Political and Social Science* 381:21–38 (1969).

13. Robert Bremmer, ed., and John Barnard, Hareven Tamara, and Robert Mennel, asst. eds., *Children and Youth in America* (Cambridge, Mass.: Harvard University Press, 1970), p. 64.

14. Elizabeth Pleck, "Criminal Approaches to Family Violence, 1640–1980," in *Family Violence*, ed. Lloyd Ohliln and Michael Tonry (Chicago: University of Chicago Press, 1989), pp. 19–58.

15. *Ibid.*, p. 29.

16. John R. Sutton, *Stubborn Children: Controlling Delinquency in the United States, 1640–1981* (Berkeley, Calif.: University of California Press, 1988).

17. Pleck, "Criminal Approaches to Family Violence, 1640–1980," p. 29.

18. John Demos, *Past, Present and Personal* (New York: Oxford University Press, 1986), pp. 80–88.

19. Elizabeth Pleck, *Domestic Tyranny: The Making of Social Policy against Family Violence from Colonial Times to the Present* (New York: Oxford University Press, 1987), p. 28–30.

20. Robert M. Mennel, "Origins of the Juvenile Court: Changing Perspectives on the Legal Rights of Juvenile Delinquents," *Crime and Delinquency* 18:68–78 (1972).

21. See, generally, Daniel Glaser, *The Effectiveness of a Prison and Parole System* (Indianapolis: Bobbs-Merrill, 1964); Charles Newman, ed., *Sourcebook on Probation, Parole, and Pardons*, 2nd ed. (Springfield, Ill.: Charles C. Thomas, 1964).

22. Anthony M. Platt, *The Child Savers: The Invention of Delinquency* (Chicago: University of Chicago Press, 1969).

23. *Ibid.*

24. Fox, "Juvenile Justice Reform," p. 1188.

25. See Robert S. Pickett, *House of Refuge—Origins of Juvenile Reform in New York State, 1815–1857* (Syracuse, N.Y.: Syracuse University Press, 1969).

26. Mennel, "Origins of the Juvenile Court," pp. 69–70.

27. *Ibid.*, pp. 70–71.

28. 4 Whart. 9 (1839).

29. *Ibid.*, p. 11.

30. 55 Ill. 280 (1870).

31. *Ibid.*, p. 283.

32. Fox, "Juvenile Justice Reform," p. 1217.

33. See U.S. Department of Justice, Juvenile Justice and Delinquency Prevention, *Two Hundred Years of American Criminal Justice: An LEAA Bicentennial Study* (Washington, D.C.: Law Enforcement Assistance Administration, 1976).

34. *Ibid.*, pp. 62–74.

35. Beverly Smith, "Female Admissions and Paroles of the Western House of Refuge in the 1880s: An Historical Example of Community Corrections," *Journal of Research in Crime and Delinquency* 26:36–66 (1989).

36. Fox, "Juvenile Justice Reform," p. 1229.

37. *Ibid.*, p. 1211.

38. Pleck, "Criminal Approaches to Family Violence, 1640–1980," p. 35.

39. Pleck, *Domestic–Tyranny*, p. 82.

40. Linda Gordon, *Family Violence and Social Control* (New York: Viking Press, 1988).

41. *In re Gault*, 387 U.S. 1, 87 S.Ct. 1428, 18 L.Ed. 2d 527 (1967).

42. Anthony Platt, *The Child Savers* (Chicago: University of Chicago Press, 1977).

43. Platt, *The Child Savers*, p. 116.

44. Herman Schwendinger and Julia Schwendinger, "Delinquency and the Collective Varieties of Youth," *Crime and Social Justice* 5:7–25 (1976).

45. Randall Shelden and Lynn Osborne, " 'For Their Own Good': Class Interests and the Child-Saving Movement in Memphis, Tennessee, 1900–1917," *Criminology* 27:747–67 (1989).

46. Fox, "Juvenile Justice Reform," p. 1229.

47. Katharine Lenroot and Emma Lundberg, *Juvenile Courts at Work*, U.S. Children's Bureau Publication No. 141 (Washington, D.C.: U.S. Government Printing Office, 1925).

48. Margueritte Rosenthal, "Reforming the Juvenile Correctional Institution: Efforts of the U.S. Children's Bureau in the 1930s," *Journal of Sociology and Social Welfare* 14:47–74 (1987).

49. See N.Y. Fam. Ct. Act, Article 7, Sec. 712 (Consol.1962).

14 An Overview of the Juvenile Justice System and Its Goals

This chapter is an overview of what juvenile justice means, how it is implemented, and the various processes, organizations, and legal constraints that dominate its operations. A distinction is made between the terms "system," which refers to the interrelationship among juvenile justice agencies, and "process," which takes a youthful offender through a series of steps beginning with arrest and concluding with reentry into society. What happens to young people who violate the law? Do they have legal rights? How are they helped? How are they punished? What is the jurisdiction of a juvenile court? The answers to these questions explain why the juvenile system exists in its present form.

Included in this chapter is a discussion of the similarities and differences between the adult and juvenile justice systems. This helps the student recognize the important principle that children are treated separately in our society. By establishing legislation to segregate delinquent children from adult offenders, society has placed greater importance on the delinquent as a "child" as opposed to being a "criminal." Consequently, rehabilitation rather than punishment has traditionally been the goal. Today, with children committing more serious and violent crimes, the juvenile justice system is having greater difficulties finding solutions to handling juvenile offenders.

What are the goals and strategies that are now being used as a blueprint for juvenile justice reform—from programs of crime prevention to innovative sentencing approaches?[1] Today, no single ideology or program dominates the system. This chapter also analyzes the role of the federal government in juvenile delinquency prevention and discusses the impact of the landmark Juvenile Justice and Delinquency Prevention Act of 1974.

The Chapter's final section reviews the organization and jurisdiction of the juvenile court. The juvenile court plays a pivotal role in the juvenile justice system. It does much more than merely find facts and try cases. It provides social services, evaluates family dynamics, prevents delinquency, and champions the *parens patriae* philosophy. For the first sixty years of its existence, legal rules and procedures were usually absent from the juvenile court, and its operations stressed social service functions. Hearings were informal, there were no attorneys, and the proceedings resembled activities of a social agency as much as a court of law. In the 1960s and 1970s, these procedures changed radically, however, when a series of U.S. Supreme Court decisions brought the juvenile justice system within the scope of the Constitution and fundamentally and permanently changed the face of the nation's juvenile courts.[2] This chapter explains how these decisions have influenced the day-to-day operations of the juvenile justice system.

THE DEVELOPMENT OF JUVENILE JUSTICE

The term **juvenile justice** refers to society's efforts to control juvenile crime through public and private crime prevention and social control agencies.[3] The term encompasses many areas of study, including the etiology of crime, institutional and agency controls, methods of prevention and community services, and the legal methods for dealing with young people who violate the law.

The contemporary American system of dealing with children in trouble began in 1899 with the establishment of the first juvenile court in the state of Illinois.[4] The principles motivating the Illinois reformers at that time were:

1. That children, because of their minority status, should not be held as accountable as adult transgressors;
2. That the objective of juvenile justice is to help the youngster, to treat and rehabilitate rather than punish;
3. That disposition should be predicated on analysis of the youth's special circumstances and needs; and
4. That the system should avoid the punitive, adversary, and formalized trappings of the adult criminal process, with all its confusing rules of evidence and tightly controlled procedures.[5]

The intention of the **Illinois Juvenile Court Act of 1899** was to create a statewide special court for predelinquent and delinquent youths. In such a setting, children were to be segregated from adults and individual treatment programs to prevent future delinquency were to be adopted. Programs were to be administered by a juvenile court judge and other staff, such as probation and social service personnel, utilizing individual and group rehabilitation techniques. This juvenile court was supposed to be a nonlegal social service agency providing care for delinquent and neglected children. In addition, the court and its personnel were to act under the concept of *parens patriae,* that is, in the child's best interest. The court's approach was to be paternalistic rather than adversarial in nature.

These concepts about juvenile justice spread rapidly across the nation during the early decades of the twentieth century. Statutes similar to the Illinois Juvenile Court Act were enacted in almost every state. In addition, juvenile courts came to be staffed by groups of probation officers, social workers, and treatment specialists. Thus, the goal of the early reform movement was to create a juvenile justice system geared to treatment, not to punishment. The purpose of the court was to keep children from criminal behavior by rehabilitating instead of punishing them.

From its origin, the juvenile court system denied children procedural rights normally available to adult offenders. Due process rights such as counsel, a jury trial, freedom from self-incrimination, and freedom from unreasonable search and seizure were not considered essential for the juvenile court system because the primary purpose of the system was not punishment but rehabilitation.[6] However, the dream of trying to rehabilitate children from a benign court setting was not achieved. Individual treatment approaches failed, and delinquency rates soared. In many instances, the courts deprived children of their liberty and treated them unfairly.

Conditions became so oppressive that in the early 1960s, the U.S. Supreme Court itself expressed a new and deep concern over the rights of minors and encouraged litigation to extend due process to juvenile offenders. As a result, the "due process revolution" of that era mandated procedural guarantees at virtually every stage of the juvenile justice system.

Today, the juvenile system is very much a legal system. The Supreme Court has played a significant, if not monumental, role in the formulation of juvenile law and procedure over the past twenty years. Notwithstanding this position, the courts have neither repudiated the goal of rehabilitating children nor subjected children totally to the procedures and philosophy of the adult criminal justice system.

THE JUVENILE JUSTICE SYSTEM

Today, the American **juvenile justice system** exists in all states by statute. Each jurisdiction has a juvenile code and a special court structure to deal with children in trouble.

On a nationwide basis, the juvenile justice system consists of thousands of public and private agencies, with a total budget amounting to hundreds of millions of dollars. Most of the nation's 20,000 police agencies have a juvenile component, and more than 3,000 juvenile courts and about 3,000 juvenile correctional facilities exist throughout the nation. There are thousands of juvenile police officers, more than 3,000 juvenile court judges, more than 6,500 juvenile probation officers, and thousands of juvenile correctional employees.[7]

Annually, there are about 1.5 million juvenile arrests, more than 1.3 million delinquency cases petitioned to the courts by police and others, and 500,000 children placed on formal or informal probation; approximately 90,000 youths are held in secure and nonsecure treatment centers.[8]

These figures do not take into account the great number of children who are referred to community diversion and mental health programs. There are thousands of these programs throughout the nation, and thousands of youth are being held in these community-based institutions. This multitude of agencies and people dealing with juvenile delinquency and status offenses has led to the development of what professionals in the field view as an incredibly expanded and complex juvenile justice system.

The "Systems" Approach

Before proceeding, it is important to clarify the meaning of the term *system.* It refers to groups or organizations with a formal structure and clearly stated goals. Often a system is considered the ideal kind of formal organization. The idea that all these agencies of juvenile justice are actually a coordinated system is popular among practitioners, academicians, and other professionals who deal with juvenile crime. It implies that interrelationships exist among the agencies concerned with juvenile delinquency prevention and control. The **systems approach,** as it is often called, sees a change in one part of the system affecting changes in other parts. It implies that a closely knit, coordinated structure of organizations exists among various agencies of juvenile justice.[9] For example, broadening the arrest power of the police officer regarding juvenile offenders adds to the burdens of the juvenile courts; changing dispositional procedures affects the juvenile correctional agencies; revising the juvenile code by eliminating status offenses decreases the number of children entering the system.

The systems approach exists more in theory than in practice. The various elements of the juvenile system are all related, but only to the degree that they influence each other's policies and practices. They are not so coordinated that they operate in unison. In fact, many juvenile justice agencies compete for budgetary support, espouse different philosophies, and have personnel standards that differ significantly. It would be useful for all the agencies concerned with juvenile justice to be in an integrated system. As one national commission pointed out, "Even in the most disjointed system, police, prosecution, courts, and corrections function in a roughly interdependent fashion, linked, as if they are parts of a single system."[10] However, most program decisions are made without proper planning information or objective data, and effective evaluation is a rarity in the juvenile justice field. Consequently, the vast majority of states operate fragmented and generally uncoordinated juvenile justice systems.

Police, courts, and juvenile correctional agencies comprise the major components of juvenile justice. This is the official government system that exists in each community. It is also the primary system for handling delinquent and noncriminal behavior. In most jurisdictions, however, other institutions also handle juvenile antisocial behavior—the mental health system, the schools, and extensive networks of private social service programs. Furthermore, the workload of the juvenile justice system is directly related to the ability of the family and the community to resolve and contain juvenile problems.[11] Which of the various institutional systems children are sent to depends on the community's ability to prevent juvenile misbehavior. Thus, a typical flowchart of a juvenile justice system often begins with the concept of prevention, followed by police, judicial, and correctional intervention. Figure 14.1 illustrates the system of juvenile justice.

THE JUVENILE JUSTICE PROCESS

How are children processed by the agencies and organizations of the juvenile justice system?[12] What are the sequential stages that juvenile offenders pass through? Most children initially came in contact with the police officer. When a juvenile commits a serious crime, the police are empowered to make an arrest. Less serious offenses may also require police action, but instead of being arrested, the child may be warned, the parents may be called, or a referral may be made to a juvenile social service program. Only about half of all children arrested by the police are actually referred to the juvenile court.

When a police officer decides to take a child into custody, the child may be brought to the station house lockup and then to a county detention program or intake program prior to a court appearance. At this point, further referral to a social service agency may occur. If the crime is a serious one, the juvenile court prosecutor may initiate a petition against the child. This begins the trial process. After a petition is filed, the child can be released to the custody of his or her parents until the court appearance, but sometimes the child may be detained. When the child appears before the court, the court can decide whether to **waive** the case (transfer it to an adult court) or to adjudicate it in juvenile court. If the

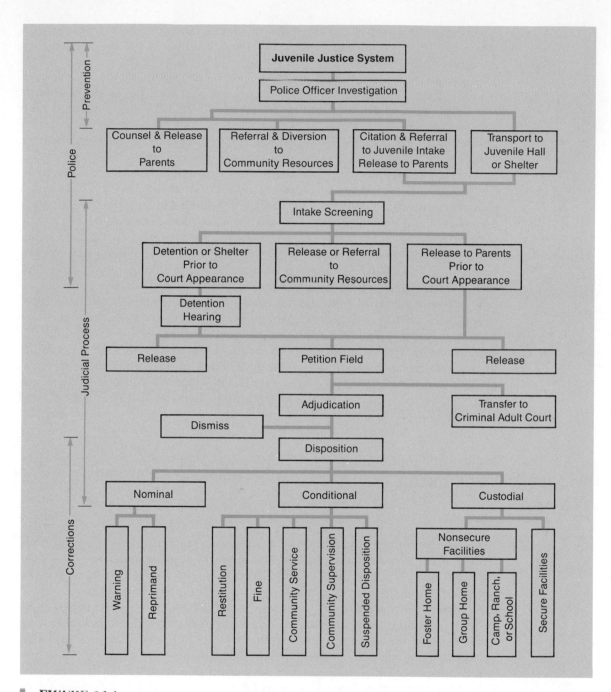

FIGURE 14.1

The juvenile justice system

adjudication or trial declares the child delinquent or in need of supervision, the court initiates a social study of the child's background. After this study, which is called a **predisposition report,** an appropriate disposition leading to a correctional and rehabilitation program is provided. A more detailed analysis of the stages in the process follows.

Police Investigation

When a juvenile commits a crime, police agencies have the authority to investigate the incident and then to decide whether to release the child or to detain and refer him or her to the juvenile court. This is often a discretionary decision based not only on the nature of the offense committed but also on the conditions existing at the time of the arrest. Such factors as the type and seriousness of the offense, the child's past contacts with the police, and whether or not the crime is denied determine whether a petition is filed. While juveniles are in the custody of the police, they have basic constitutional rights similar to those of adult offenders. Children are protected against unreasonable search and seizure under the Fourth and Fourteenth Amendments. Constitutional limitations are also placed on police interrogation procedures under the Fifth Amendment.

Intake Screening at the Court

If the police decide to file a petition, the child is referred to juvenile court. The primary issue at this point is whether the child should remain in the community or be placed in a detention or shelter home. Also, it is essential to determine whether referral services should be obtained before any further court action. In the past, too many children were routinely taken to court and held in detention facilities to await court appearances. Normally, there is a **detention hearing** that results in a decision either to remand the child to a shelter or to release the child. At this point, the child has a right to counsel and other procedural safeguards. A child who is not detained is usually released to his or her parent or guardian. Most state juvenile court acts provide for a child to return home to await further court action, except when it is necessary to protect the child, when the child presents a serious danger to the public, or when it is not certain that the child will return to court for further adjudication. In many cases, the police will refer the child to a community service program at intake instead of filing a formal charge.

Pretrial Procedures

In most juvenile court jurisdictions, the adjudication process begins with some sort of initial hearing. At this hearing, juvenile court rules of procedure normally require that the children be informed of their right to a trial, that the plea or admission be voluntary, and that they understand the charges and consequences of the plea. The case will often not be further adjudicated if a child admits to the crime at the initial hearing.

In some cases, a youth may be detained pending a trial. Many states permit detention or the removal of a child from the home where there is a likelihood of danger to himself or others. Juveniles who are detained are eligible for bail in a handful of jurisdictions. Plea bargaining may also occur in the juvenile process, particularly involving a reduction in the charges or the severity of the disposition. Such negotiations may be pursued at any stage of the proceedings.

If the child denies the allegation of delinquency, an **adjudicatory hearing** or trial is scheduled. Under extraordinary circumstances, a juvenile who commits a serious crime may be transferred to an adult court instead of being adjudicated. Today, most jurisdictions have laws providing for such transfers. Whether they occur depends on the type of offense, the child's prior record, the nature of past treatment efforts, the availability of treatment services, and the likelihood that the child will be rehabilitated in the juvenile court.

Adjudication

The adjudication is the trial stage of the juvenile court process. If the child does not admit to the charges at the initial hearing and is not transferred to an adult court, an adjudication hearing is held to determine the facts of the case. The court hears evidence on the allegations in the delinquency petition. This is a trial on the merits, and rules of evidence similar to criminal proceedings generally apply. At this stage of the proceeding, the juvenile offender is entitled to many of the procedural guarantees given adult offenders. These rights include the right to representation by counsel, freedom from self-incrimination, the right to confrontation and cross-examination of witnesses, and in certain instances the right to a jury trial. In addition, many states have their own procedures concerning rules of evidence, competence of witnesses, pleadings, and pretrial motions. At the end of the adjudicatory hearing, the court enters a judgment against the child.

Disposition

If the adjudication process finds the child delinquent, the court must then decide what should be done to treat the child. Most juvenile court acts require a separate dispositional hearing apart from the adjudication. This is often referred to as a *bifurcated process.* The dispositional hearing is less formal than adjudication. Here, the judge imposes a **disposition** on the juvenile offender in light of the offense, prior record, and family background. The judge has broad discretion and can prescribe a wide range of dispositions—from a simple warning or reprimand to community service or probation or more intense social control measures, such as institutional commitment, including group home, foster care, or secure facility care. In theory, the judge's decision serves the best interests of the child, the family, and the community. Many juvenile statutes require that the judge consider the least restrictive dispositional alternative before imposing any sentence. The disposition is one of the most important stages in the juvenile process because it may be the court's last opportunity to influence the child's behavior. Disposition is concerned primarily with treating the child and controlling antisocial behavior.

Postdisposition

Some jurisdictions allow for a program of juvenile aftercare or parole. They also may allow cases to be appealed. There may be a review of the statutory basis under which the child is to receive treatment from the state.

A child can be paroled from an institution and placed under the supervision of a parole officer. This means that the child will complete the period of confine-

Juvenile court disposition can be placement in a community-based counseling program.

ment in the community and receive assistance from the parole officer in the form of counseling, school referral, and vocational training. In some jurisdictions, adjudication of a delinquency petition can be appealed to a higher court. Provisions for such appeals vary greatly with each jurisdiction.

Finally, there is the question of whether juveniles who are committed to programs of treatment and control have a legal right to treatment. The right to treatment requires that states provide suitable rehabilitation programs for children that include counseling, education, and vocational services. Appellate courts have ruled that if such treatment is not provided, individuals must be released from confinement.

CRIMINAL JUSTICE VERSUS JUVENILE JUSTICE

The components of the adult and juvenile criminal processes are similar. Both include police investigation, arrest, administrative booking, preliminary hearings, bail, plea-bargaining and admission of a plea, grand jury indictment, formal arraignment, trial, verdict, sentence, and appeal. However, the juvenile system has a separate, complementary (almost parallel) organizational structure. In many communities, juvenile justice is administered by people who bring special skills to the task. Also, more facilities and services are available to juveniles than to adults.

The juvenile court, emphasizing individualized treatment, was originally conceived of as a social court, not a formalized court of law. This view met with much

TABLE 14.1   Comparison of Terms Used in Adult and Juvenile Justice Systems

	JUVENILE TERMS	ADULT TERMS
The person and the act	Delinquent child	Criminal
	Delinquent act	Crime
Pre-adjudicatory stage	Take into custody	Arrest
	Petition	Indictment
	Agree to a finding	Plead guilty
	Deny the petition	Plead not guilty
	Adjustment	Plea-bargain
	Detention facility, child-care shelter	Jail
Adjudicatory stage	Substitution	Reduction of charges
	Adjudicatory or fact-finding hearing	Trial
	Adjudication	Conviction
Post-adjudicatory stage	Dispositional hearing	Sentencing hearing
	Disposition	Sentence
	Commitment	Incarceration
	Youth development center, treatment center, training school	Prison
	Residential child-care facility	Halfway house
	After-care	Parole

criticism over the first sixty years of the twentieth century, resulting in the development of procedures and laws similar to those that protect adult offenders.[13] However, the purpose of the juvenile court is to treat and rehabilitate children, not to punish them. The juvenile justice system was designed not only to prevent juvenile crime and to rehabilitate juvenile offenders but also to provide for abused, neglected, and incorrigible children. In essence, it was to provide services to promote the normal growth and development of all adjudicated children.

One major concern of the juvenile court reform movement was to make certain that the stigma attached to a person who became a convicted criminal offender would not be affixed to children in juvenile proceedings. Thus, even the language used in the juvenile court differs from that used in the adult criminal court (see Table 14.1). Children are not formally indicted for a crime; they have a **petition** filed against them. Secure pretrial holding facilities are called detention centers rather than jails. Similarly, the criminal court trial is called a **hearing** in the juvenile justice system. The Focus on Delinquency entitled "Similarities and Differences between Adult and Juvenile Justice" compares the two systems.

THE GOALS AND STANDARDS OF JUVENILE JUSTICE

As we have seen, the juvenile justice system is entrusted with a multiplicity of often conflicting tasks: upholding the law; protecting the victim; meting out jus-

Similarities and Differences between Adult and Juvenile Justice

Since its creation, the juvenile justice system has sought to maintain its independence from the adult justice system. Yet there are a number of similarities that characterize the institutions, processes, and law of the two systems.

Similarities between Juvenile and Adult Justice Systems

■ Police officers, judges, and correctional personnel use discretion in decision making in both the adult and the juvenile systems.

■ The right to receive *Miranda* warnings applies to juveniles as well as to adults.

■ Juveniles and adults are protected from prejudicial lineups or other identification procedures.

■ Similar procedural safeguards protect juveniles and adults when they make an admission of guilt.

■ Prosecutors and defense attorneys play equally critical roles in juvenile and adult advocacy.

■ Juveniles and adults have the right to counsel at most key stages of the court process.

■ Pretrial motions are available in juvenile and criminal court proceedings.

■ Negotiations and the plea-bargain exist for children and adult offenders.

■ Children and adults have a right to a hearing and an appeal.

■ The standard of evidence in juvenile delinquency adjudications, as in adult criminal trials, is proof beyond a reasonable doubt.

■ Juveniles and adults can be placed on probation by the court.

■ Both juveniles and adults can be placed in pretrial detention facilities.

■ Juveniles and adults can be kept in detention without bail if they are considered dangerous.

■ After trial, both can be placed in community treatment programs.

Differences between Juvenile and Adult Justice Systems

■ The primary purpose of juvenile procedures is protection and treatment. With adults, the aim is to punish the guilty.

■ Age determines the jurisdiction of the juvenile court. The nature of the offense determines jurisdiction in the adult system.

■ Juveniles can be apprehended for acts that would not be criminal if they were committed by an adult (status offenses).

■ Juvenile proceedings are not considered criminal; adult proceedings are.

■ Juvenile court procedures are generally informal and private. Those of adult courts are more formal and are open to the public.

■ Courts cannot release identifying information about a juvenile to the press, but they must release information about an adult.

■ Parents are highly involved in the juvenile process but not in the adult process.

■ The standard of arrest is more stringent for adults than for juveniles.

■ Juveniles are released into parental custody. Adults are generally given the opportunity for bail.

■ Juveniles have no constitutional right to a jury trial. Adults have this right.

■ Juveniles can be searched in school without probable cause or a warrant.

■ A juvenile's record is sealed when the age of majority is reached. The record of an adult is permanent.

■ A juvenile court cannot sentence juveniles to county jails or state prisons; these are reserved for adults.

■ There is no death penalty in the juvenile justice system.

tice; evaluating the best interests of the child; rehabilitating wayward youth; acting as a conduit to social agencies, and so on. The multiplicity of goals and priorities and the interrelationship between juvenile justice and other institutional groups make it difficult to assess whether the system is meeting the needs of children in trouble.

What exactly are the goals of juvenile justice today? Experts continue to debate which goals should be given priority. Some claim that the most important goal is to protect potential and actual victims and deter children from committing antisocial acts. Others argue that social reform, legislative progress, and programs leading to education, recreation, and employment are the most practical methods of reducing the threat of youth crime. To some experts, the threat of stigma and labeling by the justice system is an overriding problem; these experts emphasize diverting children before the formal trial. Still others spend considerable time talking about how to respond to children with special needs—the uneducated, the mentally ill, and the mentally retarded.

Establishing Juvenile Justice Goals

Since the 1960s, four major efforts have been funded by the government and private sources to identify the goals of juvenile justice and delinquency reform. First, in 1967, the **President's Commission on Law Enforcement and the Administration of Justice**, a product of the Johnson administration's concern for social welfare, issued its well-thought out and documented report on juvenile delinquency and its control. Influenced by Cloward and Ohlin's then popular opportunity theory, the commission suggested that the juvenile justice system must provide underprivileged youth with the opportunities for success, including jobs and education. The commission also recognized the need to develop effective law enforcement procedures to control hard-core youthful offenders and at the same time grant them due process of law when they came before the courts. But the main thrust of the commission's report was that the juvenile justice system must develop sensitivity to the needs of young offenders:

> there should be a response to the special needs of youths with special problems. They may be delinquent, they may be law abiding but alienated and uncooperative, they may be behavior or academic problems in school or misfits among their peers or disruptive in recreation groups. For such youths, it is imperative to furnish help that is particularized enough to deal with their individual needs but not separate them from their peers and label them for life.[14]

During the 1960s, the concern was primarily for individual treatment and the rights of juvenile offenders. Child advocates and federal lawmakers were interested in merging the rehabilitation model with due process of law.

The presidential commission report of 1967 acted as a catalyst for the passage of federal legislature entitled the **Juvenile Delinquency Prevention and Control (JDP) Act of 1968.**[15] This law created a Youth Development and Delinquency Prevention Administration, which concentrated its efforts on helping states develop new juvenile justice programs, particularly involving diversion of youth, decriminalization and decarceration. In 1968, Congress also passed the **Omnibus Safe Streets and Crime Control Act.**[16] Title I of this law established the **Law Enforcement Assistance Administration,** known as **LEAA,** to provide federal funds to improve the adult and juvenile justice systems. In 1972, Congress amended the JDP Act of 1968 to allow LEAA to focus its funding on juvenile justice and delinquency prevention programs. State and local governments were required to develop and adopt comprehensive plans to obtain federal assistance.

Because crime continued to receive much publicity, a second effort called the **National Advisory Commission on Criminal Justice Standards and Goals** was established in 1973 by the more conservative Nixon Administration.[17] Its report on juvenile justice and delinquency prevention identified twelve major themes as central to the development of standards and goals for juvenile justice:

1. Increase family stability.
2. Develop programs for families needing service, including families with children who are truant or who run away, families with children who disregard parental authority, and families with children who use intoxicating beverages or who are under 10 years of age and commit delinquent acts.
3. Develop programs for children who are neglected or physically abused.
4. Develop programs for young people to prevent delinquent behavior before it occurs.
5. Develop diversion activities whereby youths are processed out of the juvenile justice system.
6. Develop dispositional alternatives so that institutionalization can be used only as a last resort.
7. Extend due process to all juveniles.
8. Control the violent and the chronic delinquent.
9. Reduce the proportion of minorities who are victims of delinquent acts and who are clients in the juvenile justice system. Increase the proportion of minority policymakers and operators in the juvenile system.
10. Increase the coordination among agencies to improve the operation of the juvenile justice system and to increase resources and knowledge about how to deal with juvenile offenders.
11. Improve research.
12. Allocate resources, especially to the many states that do not have their own resources to deal with juvenile programs.[18]

The National Advisory Commission recommendations formed the basis for additional legislation entitled the **Juvenile Justice and Delinquency Prevention Act of 1974.**[19] This important act eliminated the old Youth Development and Delinquency Prevention Administration and replaced it with the Office of Juvenile Justice and **Delinquency Prevention (OJJDP)** within LEAA. In 1980, LEAA was phased out and the **OJJDP** became an independent agency in the Department of Justice, Attorney General's Office. The role of the **OJJDP** was to develop and implement worthwhile programs that prevent and reduce juvenile crimes in America.

Throughout the 1970s, its two most important goals were: (1) removing juveniles from detention in adult jails and (2) eliminating the co-incarceration of juvenile and status offenders. During this period, the **OJJDP** stressed the creation of formal diversion and restitution programs around the United States. These goals reflected the influence of labeling theory during this period, a movement that sparked the federal agency's efforts to reduce stigma whenever possible.

In the 1980s, the OJJDP shifted its priorities from stigma reduction to the identification and control of chronic, violent juvenile offenders.[20] This goal was in line with the Reagan administration's more conservative views of justice. The federal government poured millions of dollars into research projects designed to study chronic offenders, predict their behavior, and evaluate programs designed to control their activities.

American Bar Association Standards

While the federal effort was proceeding, the **Institute of Judicial Administration (IJA)** and the **American Bar Association (ABA)** created a widely read set of standards (the **Juvenile Justice Standards Project**) designed to promote proportionality and rationale decision making in the juvenile justice system and to restrict the often unfair discretion that had marked its early existence.[21] The standards consist of twenty-three volumes covering every aspect of juvenile justice administration, from police handling of juveniles to dispositional procedures and the rights of minors. The IJA/ABA report reflects the ideas of equal and "just desert-"based sentencing reforms that were also popular in the adult system at that time.[22] "Just deserts" means that the distribution of penalties among convicted juveniles should be decided primarily by the seriousness of the offense, not by the number of prior convictions. The principles on which the major IJA/ABA recommendations for changes are based are:

1. Sanctions for juvenile offenders should be proportional.
2. Sentences or dispositions should be determinate.
3. Decision makers should choose the least restrictive alternative when intervening in the lives of juveniles and their families.
4. Noncriminal misbehavior (status offenses, private offenses, victimless crimes) should be removed from juvenile court jurisdiction.
5. Open proceedings and accountability should replace closed proceedings and unrestrained official discretion.
6. All affected persons should have the right to counsel at all stages of the proceedings.
7. Juveniles should have the right to decide on actions affecting their lives and freedom unless they are incapable of making reasonable decisions.
8. The role of parents in juvenile proceedings should be redefined, with particular attention to possible conflicts of interest between parent and child.
9. Detention, treatment, and other intervention prior to adjudication and disposition should be limited.
10. Strict criteria should be established for the waiver of juvenile court jurisdiction in order to regulate the transfer of juveniles to adult criminal courts.[23]

Not surprisingly, some of the goals suggested by the IJA/ABA standards are controversial. For example, the first three eliminate indeterminate commitments and discretion and recommend the criminal law approach of definiteness in sentencing. The fourth principle limits the jurisdiction of the court and eliminates status offenses from the court's responsibility. The sixth principle views hearings as adversarial rather than informal and requires representation by counsel at all critical points in the proceedings.

Nonetheless, the IJA/ABA standards are a comprehensive, well-researched set of guidelines used to govern the juvenile justice system. They are considered by experts to be the most universally accepted standards in the field, and many jurisdictions have adopted their key provisions.

The ALEC Report

The impact of the conservative crime-control outlook can be viewed in the more recent model of juvenile justice goals and procedures created by the Rose Foundation and the **American Legislative Exchange Council (ALEC)**, a project supported by a grant from the federal government in 1985.[24] This controversial model calls for a rethinking of the juvenile justice system along the lines of the adult system. Among other things, it suggests the creation of sentencing guidelines that limit judges' traditional discretion. All serious offenders would be subjected to at least thirty days of confinement. The guidelines could be circumvented if a judge concluded upon "clear and convincing evidence" that they would produce a "manifest injustice."

This model code also recommends required pretrial detention for any juvenile who is arrested for serious offenses, considered likely to miss court appearances, considered a threat to the community, a repeat offender, or considered likely to intimidate witnesses, upon showing of probable cause or an admission of guilt. Release can be obtained if the parent or guardian posts bail.

In addition, the **ALEC report** suggests that prosecutors should have the right to easily examine all evidence obtained by the police ("discovery"); juvenile court jurisdiction should extend to age 21 but a policy of transfer to criminal court should be maintained; juvenile records should be open to the public except in special cases; restitution should be imposed in almost all offenses in recognition of the right of victims; and juveniles and their parents should be responsible for fines, court costs, and restitution. Finally, the model maintains that there should be a greater accountability placed on parents for the cost of correcting their children and that prosecutors should have a greater role in charging delinquent offenders.

Adopting this model would change the overall goal of juvenile justice from one of treatment to **accountability.** This translates into the concept of punishing children for their misdeeds because they are deserving of social sanctions. Because this system mirrors the adult justice system, juveniles should be granted the same due process rights as adults.[25] The ALEC report has drawn much heated criticism because of its conservative outlook on juvenile justice.

While both the ABA standards and the ALEC report have a number of basic principles in common—determinate sentencing, proportionality, and procedural due process—how these principles are translated into practice is different. The ALEC report, for instance, does not extend right to counsel to children in all stages of the juvenile process, nor does it provide for the right to a jury trial under any conditions. Some experts, therefore, believe it has due process deficiencies.

A Liberal Agenda

Since the ALEC report was published, the conservative trend in juvenile justice has prompted a "liberal" response. Ira Schwartz, a noted juvenile justice profes-

According to the ALEC model, juveniles should be held accountable for their misdeeds. Some experts have called for the creation of boot-camps to correct delinquent youth. These offenders are undergoing correction at a "bootcamp" institution in Florida.

sional, has suggested that the juvenile justice system must adopt a more liberal goal orientation. Some of his most significant recommendations deal with changes in juvenile corrections, such as closing training schools, prohibiting the confinement of juveniles in jails, and restructuring detention services. Others are grouped around reforming the juvenile court and include raising the age of juvenile court jurisdiction to 18 and eliminating minor juvenile crime and status offenses from the court's responsibility. Guaranteeing due process rights to children, upgrading the judiciary and probation services, and replacing the *parens patriae* model with a "justice" model are also part of Schwartz's 1990 action agenda.[26]

In reviewing these proposed goals for the juvenile justice system—from both government and private sources—the ebb and flow of justice policy can be easily observed. Thirty years ago, the focus was on the treatment of unfortunate youths who had fallen into criminal behavior patterns through no fault of their own. Fifteen years ago, the main concern was avoiding criminal labels. Today, many experts are concerned with the control of serious juvenile offenders, the creation of firm but fair sentencing options in the juvenile court system, and the reform of juvenile correctional institutions. Whether the Bush administration will develop an agenda for juvenile justice reform remains uncertain at this writing.

IMPROVING THE JUVENILE JUSTICE SYSTEM

After reviewing the literature on juvenile justice and delinquency, a number of themes on what the juvenile justice system should be doing to help youth in trouble and protect society as a whole can be found. Today's experts seem to be saying that the system can be improved by concerted efforts directed at (1) the prevention of juvenile delinquency, (2) the diversion and removal of problem youths from the juvenile justice system, (3) the incapacitation of serious offenders, (4) fair and just treatment of all youthful offenders, (5) making the juvenile justice system efficient and effective, particularly the juvenile court, and (6) the application of new technology to the juvenile system.

Preventing Juvenile Crime

Prevention seeks to divert individual children from antisocial behavior during the early stages of their lives. Building stronger family units, providing counseling in schools, and improving living conditions are all examples of prevention. The proposed federal Early Childhood and Education Act of 1990 is an example of child-care legislation that will provide financial assistance for a variety of social programs—mainly for the poor—and in so doing help prevent juvenile crime. Prevention also involves developing a comprehensive delinquency plan, collecting data about delinquency in local communities, clarifying delinquency goals, and providing an inventory of community resources and programs. Once that is accomplished, programs of prevention involving health, family, education, employment, recreation, housing, religion, and even the media can play an important role in thwarting juvenile delinquency.

Diversion and Delinquency

Even the most conservative critic sees the value of diverting minor offenders from the formal justice process and treating them in a nonpunitive, treatment-oriented fashion. A child can be diverted at any stage of the process. Basically, diversion has focused on certain groups—youths committing minor, noncriminal acts, first offenders, and youths committing minor crimes who might be more appropriately handled by social agencies. Diversion programs can exist at the police department level, at the intake level of the court system, at the petition-filing level, and even at the time an adjudication occurs.

The goal of removing noncriminal misbehavior, such as status offenses, from juvenile court jurisdiction also should be seriously considered. In addition, whenever possible, delinquent offenders should be kept separate from contact with adult criminals. School programs, counseling centers, and other activities within the mental health and educational systems might be more appropriate for children involved in problems of truancy. Children who are incorrigible can be handled in mental health settings.

Controlling Chronic Offenders

Research has shown that a small group of youthful offenders may be responsible for a significant amount of serious delinquency and may later grow up to become adult offenders. A major national effort is being undertaken to study chronic offenders and develop mechanisms to identify them early in their careers. The

Shindan Juvenile Prison, Illinois.

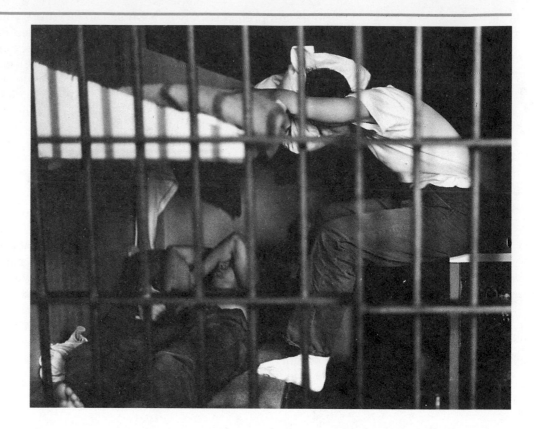

juvenile justice system must also develop treatment facilities to deal effectively with the needs of these special offenders, such as serious drug offenders, while protecting the community from their activities. At first glance, incarceration in secure juvenile facilities may seem to be an inappropriate goal for juvenile justice, but it is actually more humane than the current practice of transferring these youths to the adult system so that they can be held in state prisons.

Fairness and Justice

All children processed through the juvenile justice system should be treated fairly and humanely. No distinction should be made between white and minority juvenile offenders or between those in the lower classes and those in the middle and upper strata of society. Nonetheless, research indicates that these distinctions are still being made.[27]

Procedures to ensure due process should be present in all areas of the juvenile justice system. Investigation, arrest, diversion, detention, arraignment, adjudication, sentencing, and institutionalization must be consistent with our democratic system. Recent U.S. Supreme Court decisions have made it clear that youths charged with delinquent acts and others brought into the juvenile justice system are entitled to virtually all of the due process rights accorded adults.

Increasing Effectiveness

Juvenile justice agencies should be well organized and well managed. The efficient operation of juvenile services requires qualified personnel, adequate organizational structure, sound fiscal planning, and development of successful programs. The general public has for the most part been unenthusiastic about providing money for the care and protection of children in the juvenile justice system. Often, facilities for juveniles are crowded, courts lack personnel, probation services are not sufficiently extensive, and educational and recreational programs are underfinanced and inadequate. Thus, resources must be developed to provide an efficient, effective juvenile justice program. The federal government needs to provide national leadership for the adaptation of such programs on the state level.

Technology Exchange

New technology, such as computerized information retrieval services, must be used for disseminating information about juvenile justice. The juvenile justice system still operates on scant information about the success or failure of treatment or prevention programs. There is an urgent need to develop, support, and stimulate juvenile justice research. What is going on in California may take years to filter back to Connecticut. Since there have been major cutbacks in federal funding for justice-related programs and a concomitant reduction in resources, effective evaluation and dissemination becomes an even more important goal if positive change in the system is to be achieved.

THE JUVENILE COURT AND ITS OPERATIONS

Regardless of what goals or strategies for reform are adopted, the juvenile court is the centerpiece of the justice system. It plays a major role in controlling juvenile behavior and delivering social services to children in need. How it is organized and what laws apply to those who appear before it is critical to any meaningful reform effort.

Today's juvenile court is a specialized court for children. Its organizational structure varies within each state. A juvenile court can be (1) part of a high court of general trial jurisdiction, (2) a special session of a lower court of trial jurisdiction, (3) an independent statewide court, or even (4) part of a broader family court. The juvenile court includes a judge, probation staff, government prosecutors and defense attorneys, and a variety of social service programs. It functions in a socio-legal manner and seeks to promote rehabilitation within a framework of procedural due process. It is concerned with acting "in the best interest of the child" and public protection, often incompatible goals.

Most juvenile courts in the United States are established as *lower courts of limited jurisdiction*, where juvenile jurisdiction is part of a district court, city court, or recorder's court and where the jurisdiction is limited solely to juvenile delinquency matters. Salaries, physical facilities, and even the prestige of the court can all be directly affected by its jurisdictional location. These factors tend to limit the ability of the court to attract competent people, including judges, and to obtain necessary resources from the state legislature. It is unclear why juvenile courts have been structured in lower trial courts in many states. Quite possibly it was to provide local attention to juvenile matters, since some experts believe that a lower court relates more efficiently and effectively to the concerns of parents and young people in the local area. In addition, legislators may have seen the juvenile court as an inferior court, relegated to the lowest level because of its jurisdiction over children. Massachusetts is an example of a state whose juvenile courts are placed in a special session of lower court of limited trial jurisdiction. The state allows juvenile sessions to be heard in its district courts, and it has established special juvenile courts in major urban areas.

On the other hand, an increasing number of states—including Alaska, California, Colorado, Florida, Illinois, and Wisconsin—place juvenile matters at the *highest court of general trial jurisdiction*.[28] Here juvenile cases are tried in the more prestigious courts of general jurisdiction. States that deal with juvenile matters at the highest trial court level have an integrated organizational structure that results in more efficient and effective court administration. Such courts are better able to secure the funding they need to improve physical facilities and hire competent judicial and probation personnel.

Some states have *independent juvenile court systems*. Such systems may be referred to as statewide juvenile courts. Separately organized and independent juvenile courts exist in such states as Connecticut and Utah and in parts of other states, such as Georgia and Kansas. New York and Hawaii have also organized their juvenile courts on a statewide basis, although the New York system is called a family court system.[29] The major advantages to the statewide independent system are that it can service sparsely populated areas within a given jurisdiction, that it permits judicial personnel and others to deal exclusively with children's matters, and that it can obtain legislative funding better than other court systems. On the other hand, the very reason for its form—obtaining legislative funding—can also act to its detriment. Separately organized juvenile courts encounter resistance from legislative funding groups concerned with duplication of effort and unwilling to provide resources for the control and prevention of juvenile delinquency.

The major disadvantage of implementing a *family court* structure is that it requires major reorganization of the existing court system by the legislature. The costs are substantial, especially in the first few years of the court's existence. Where family court structures do exist, there is little statistical data to indicate that they have reduced delinquency or improved family programs.

However, it has become apparent to some experts that to treat the related problems of intrafamily crime, divorce, adoption, and neglect in separate courts is to encourage inconsistency in court administration and decision making and to foster ineffective case-flow management. Thus, it would be preferable to deal with juvenile matters in a family court system.

JUVENILE COURT JURISDICTION

Juvenile court jurisdiction is defined by state statutes, constitutional amendments, or state legislation. The New York family court, for example, is part of the

New York State constitution. Legislation is passed to implement the constitutional mandate and to specify the actual details of the state court. More often, however, the juvenile courts are created by the authority of the legislature. Thus, the jurisdiction itself is generally controlled by legislative enactment.

Age

The states differ over the age that brings children under the jurisdiction of the juvenile court.[30] Most (for example, Alaska, California, Minnesota, and Wyoming) include all children under 18. Others, including Louisiana, Massachusetts, and Michigan, set the upper limit at under 17. Still other jurisdictions (for example, North Carolina and Connecticut) have established the juvenile age as 16 or under (see Table 14.2).

At one time, some jurisdictions established age ranges that varied according to the sex or geographic location of the juvenile, but statutes employing these distinctions have been held to be in violation of the equal protection clause or due process clause of the Constitution. For example, in the case of *Lamb v. Brown*, an Oklahoma statute that allowed females under the age of 18 the benefits of juvenile court proceedings while limiting the same benefits to males under 16 was held to be unconstitutional.[31]

A few state statutes describe juvenile court jurisdiction in terms of minimum age. Massachusetts, for example, defines a child as a person who is under 17 but over 7 years of age.[32] Normally, what operates is the common-law understanding

TABLE 14.2 Age at Which Criminal Courts Gain Jurisdiction of Young Offenders—Ranges from 16 to 19

AGE OF OFFENDER WHEN UNDER CRIMINAL COURT JURISDICTION	STATES
16 years	Connecticut, New York, North Carolina
17	Georgia, Illinois, Louisiana, Massachusetts, Missouri, South Carolina, Texas
18	Alabama, Alaska, Arizona, Arkansas, California, Colorado, Delaware, District of Columbia, Florida, Hawaii, Idaho, Indiana, Iowa, Kansas, Kentucky, Maine, Maryland, Michigan, Minnesota, Mississippi, Montana, Nebraska, Nevada, New Hampshire, New Jersey, New Mexico, North Dakota, Ohio, Oklahoma, Oregon, Pennsylvania, Rhode Island, South Dakota, Tennessee, Utah, Vermont, Virginia, Washington, West Virginia, Wisconsin, federal districts
19	Wyoming

Source: Linda A. Szymanski, *Upper Age of Juvenile Court Jurisdiction Statutes Analysis.* (Pittsburgh: National Center for Juvenile Justice, March 1987).

of the responsibility of children. Under the age of 7, children are deemed incapable of committing crimes. There is a rebuttable presumption that children between 7 and 14 do not have the capacity for criminal behavior. Over the age of 14, children are believed to be responsible for their actions.

The Nature of the Offense—Delinquency

Juvenile court jurisdiction is also based on the nature of the child's actions. If a child commits a crime, this conduct normally falls in the category of juvenile delinquency. Definitions of delinquency vary from state to state, but most are based on the common element of a maximum age as well as on the fact that delinquency is an intentional violation of the criminal law.

In recent years, state legislatures concerned about serious juvenile crime have passed laws automatically excluding serious offenses from the jurisdiction of the juvenile court. For example, Maryland excludes crimes punishable by death or life in prison allegedly committed by children over 14 years of age and robbery committed with a dangerous weapon if the accused is over 16 (however, the case can be transferred back to juvenile court from the adult court).[33]

Another approach has been to give prosecutors the choice of bringing the case either to juvenile court or to adult court. For example, Florida gives the prosecutor the right to decide where to bring a case if a child is accused of committing a crime punishable by death or life in prison or if the child is 16 or over and has committed two prior delinquent offenses.[34] (These issues will be discussed more fully in Chapters 16 and 17.)

Such trends reflect a "toughening up" of juvenile justice policy—removing young offenders from the jurisdiction of the juvenile court so that they can be tried and punished as adults and eventually be sentenced to adult prisons. However, this does not mean that the juvenile court has totally abandoned its rehabilitative ideals. Some states still require that juveniles manifest a "need for treatment" or supervision before they can be declared delinquents or status offenders; committing an illegal act is not enough for the state to take control of a child.[35] So there is still recognition that the juvenile court's mandate is something other than control and punishment.

The Nature of the Offense—Status Offenders

Juvenile courts also have jurisdiction over **status offenders,** children whose offenses are not the type of activities for which adults are normally prosecuted. Some juvenile delinquency statutes still include status offenses within their definition, but most now separate the PINS and CHINS (Persons or Children in Need of Supervision) statutes so that separate proceedings can be held for children who are runaways, unmanageable, truant, and incorrigible.

The position of the status offenders within the juvenile justice system remains controversial today. One of the most difficult problems with such jurisdiction is the statutes themselves. For example, the behaviors commonly included in these statutes—for example, "unmanageable," "unruly," and "in danger of leading an idle, dissolute, lewd, or immoral life"—have been challenged in court for being unconstitutionally vague and indefinite. However, most courts that have addressed this issue have upheld the breadth of the statutes in view of their overall concern for the welfare of the child.[36]

The removal of status offenders from secure lockups with delinquent youths has been one of the more successful justice-related policy initiatives in the United States. Almost all states have legally prohibited incarcerating status offenders with delinquents. For example, a West Virginia court prohibited the housing of status offenders in "secure, prison-like facilities which also house children guilty of criminal conduct or needlessly subject status offenders to the degradation and physical abuse of incarceration."[37] However, it is not uncommon for judges to get around these prohibitions by holding status offenders in contempt of court if they refuse to honor judicial decrees; a number of states have permitted these youths to then be held in secure detention facilities.[38]

The status offense category often becomes a catchall for offenders who do not fit anywhere else. If there is not enough evidence to support a finding of delinquency, prosecutors sometimes charge youths with being status offenders on the grounds that their behavior endangered their morals, health, or general welfare.[39] Defense attorneys may welcome the substitution since it means that their clients will not be subject to the same degree of confinement and control as they would be if they had been found delinquent. Because youths originally charged as delinquents can wind up as status offenders, the line between status offenders and delinquency is often vague and ill-defined. In light of such overlap, the primary role of the juvenile court is to clarify the needs of the child, as in the following "Case in Point."

CASE IN POINT

You are an experienced juvenile court social worker responsible for making decisions about screening children from the stigma of juvenile court jurisdiction.

Joann, 15, is charged with assault with a dangerous weapon, her first offense. She lives with two siblings and her 50-year-old mother, who is on welfare. Joann has had serious learning problems in school and views herself as intellectually limited. She began having problems when she entered junior high school and started using drugs and "fooling around with boys." In the last year, she has been absent from school for weeks at a time, and school counselors were preparing a petition for truancy to the juvenile court at the time of this offense.

In addition to school problems, Joann's behavior has become aggressive at home. She has taken to running away from home, staying out nights, and adopting what amounts to an incorrigible life-style.

As a multiple-problem youngster on the verge of delinquency (the assault case involved a fight with another juvenile), Joann exhibits behavioral characteristics indicating delinquency and a person in need of supervision (PINS). She has educational, family, and personal needs.

What role should the juvenile court play in this case? Develop a set of criteria which would guide you in deciding Joann's case.

LEGAL RIGHTS FOR THE JUVENILE OFFENDER

No overview of the juvenile court and its control over juvenile justice is complete without discussing the legal rights of juvenile offenders and the role of the U.S. Supreme Court in recognizing these rights. Throughout the 1960s and 1970s, the Supreme Court significantly increased procedural safeguards for the adult criminal offender. Nearly all the provisions of the Bill of Rights dealing with the criminal process were made applicable to the states through the due process clause of the Fourteenth Amendment. The most significant of these decisions include the following:

- *Mapp v. Ohio* extended the exclusionary rule (preventing admission of illegally obtained evidence at trial) to state court proceedings.[40]
- *Escobedo v. Illinois* held that a state must afford the accused the right to counsel in a police station.[41]
- *Terry v. Ohio* upheld the right of the police to conduct threshold inquiries of suspicious persons when there is reason to believe that such persons may be armed and dangerous to the police or others.[42]
- *Miranda v. Arizona* defined the defendant's Fifth Amendment privilege against self-incrimination when taken into custody.[43]
- *Gideon v. Wainwright* established the right of the defendant in a felony trial to have counsel in a state prosecution.[44]
- *Argersinger v. Hamlin* extended the indigent defendant's right to counsel in all criminal cases where prison sentence could be imposed.[45]
- *Barker v. Wingo* set out the criteria for judging whether the Sixth Amendment right to a speedy trial is being violated.[46]

As a result of these decisions and others affecting the adult process, children have been granted similar protections throughout the juvenile justice process.

Significant Supreme Court Decisions in Juvenile Law

The constitutional due process revolution in the adult system described above had a significant impact on the development of rights in the juvenile justice system. Within one decade—1966 to 1975—the Supreme Court handed down five major decisions affecting the equal rights of children within the jurisdiction of the juvenile court. A brief statement regarding each of these cases follows:

- *Kent v. United States (1966)* established that procedures concerning waiver (whether the juvenile court would hear a case or waive it to an adult court for trial) must measure up to the essentials of due process of law. A hearing, a right to counsel, and access to social records were required. This case was an important forerunner to the most significant juvenile decision by the Supreme Court, In re Gault.[47]
- *In re Gault (1967)* held that juveniles at trial, faced with incarceration, were entitled to many of the rights granted adult offenders. These included counsel, notice of the charges, cross-examination of witnesses, and protection against self-incrimination. Gault mandated a more formalized juvenile court system.[48]

- *In re Winship (1970)* ruled that the standard of proof in a delinquency proceeding that could result in a child's commitment must be "proof beyond a reasonable doubt" and not a "preponderance of the evidence." According to the Court, civil labels and good intentions do not obviate the need for criminal due process safeguards in juvenile courts.[49]
- *McKeiver v. Pennsylvania (1971)* held that juveniles were not to be afforded the constitutional right to a jury trial in a delinquency proceeding. The Court felt that this aspect of the adversarial process was not appropriate for the juvenile justice system.[50]
- *Breed v. Jones (1975)* established that the double jeopardy clause of the Fifth Amendment of the Constitution extends to juvenile offenders through the Fourteenth Amendment due process clause. Juveniles, henceforth, could not be tried in a juvenile court and transferred to an adult court for a similar action.[51]

Since 1975, the Supreme Court has decided a number of other cases dealing with juvenile offenders:

- *Fare v. Michael C. (1979)* held that a child's request to see his probation officer at the time of interrogation did not operate to invoke his Fifth Amendment right to remain silent. According to the Court, the probation officer cannot be expected to offer the type of advice that an accused would expect from an attorney.[52]
- *Schall v. Martin (1984)* upheld a state statute allowing for the placement of children in preventive detention before their trial. The Court concluded that it was not unreasonable to detain juveniles for their own protection.[53]
- *New Jersey v. T.L.O. (1985)* determined that the Fourth Amendment applies to school searches. The Court adopted a "reasonable suspicion" standard as opposed to "probable cause" to evaluate the legality of searches and seizures in a school setting.[54]
- *Stanford v. Kentucky* and *Wilkens v. Missouri* (*1989*) concluded that the imposition of the death penalty on a juvenile who committed a crime between the ages of 16 and 18 was not unconstitutional and that the Eighth Amendment's cruel and unusual punishment clause did not prohibit capital punishment.[55]

In the hundred or so years that the juvenile court system has been in operation, the Supreme Court has heard very few cases dealing with juvenile delinquency proceedings. The most far-reaching was the *In re Gault* case of 1967, which extended the essentials of due process and fair treatment throughout the juvenile justice system.

Each of the above decisions is discussed in detail in subsequent chapters.

The Due Process Revolution in Retrospect

Although the *Gault* decision heralded the due process revolution, the movement toward broader procedural protections for juveniles was slowed by a more conservative Supreme Court in the 1970s. Chief Justice Warren Burger believed that the answer to the problems of the juvenile justice system was a return to the informality of the past. This view was operationalized in 1971, for example, in the case of *McKeiver v. Pennsylvania*.[56] The Court expressed its concern that juries in juvenile courts would impinge on the interests of the state and the public in conducting juvenile court proceedings in an efficient, reasonably informal, and flexible manner. What the Court was saying was that a jury trial for juveniles was not essential to a fair and accurate fact-finding process in the juvenile court system.

In the 1980s, the Court continued to limit the expansion of juvenile rights with rulings that recognize the special needs of children. In the *Schall* case, the Court distinguished between adults and juveniles with respect to detaining them before trial, holding that juveniles could be denied bail and held for their own protection and the protection of society.[57] *Schall* played an important role because it dealt with the issue of preventive detention before trial, a process that affects all juvenile court systems. Similarly, in the *New Jersey v. T.L.O.* case, the Court limited the right of juveniles to be secure from search and seizures.[58] In this case, the Court held that teachers had the right to search students if they violated school rules, though they were not suspected of a criminal law violation; adults would be legally immune from this type of search. The *T.L.O.* case concluded that school officials as representatives of the state may lawfully conduct searches without a warrant or probable cause.

The future course of constitutional decisions affecting the rights of juveniles now that William Rhenquist is chief justice and other legal conservatives, such as Antonin Scalia and Anthony Kennedy, have been placed on the bench is difficult to ascertain. Certainly the thrust of the Supreme Court has been clear over the past decade. Due process and fair treatment must be accorded juveniles throughout the entire juvenile justice process. However, the Court seems to be saying that the special status of minors gives the state the right to exercise legal controls from which an adult would be exempted. The *McKeiver, Schall,* and *T.L.O.* decisions appear to reflect a shift back to the informality and paternal protection of the juvenile court in preference to further formalizing court proceedings. Whether this trend will continue remains to be seen. However, as Justice Harry A. Blackmun stated in the *McKeiver* case, "If the formalities of the criminal adjudicative process are to be superimposed upon the juvenile court system, there is little need for its separate existence. Perhaps that ultimate disillusionment will come one day, but for the moment we are disinclined to give impetus to it."[59] Considering the makeup and directions of today's Court, we would expect to see Justice Blackmun's views taken quite seriously.[60]

The death penalty cases, on the other hand, seem to be a strong conservative reaction to liberal and ineffective crime-control programs.[61]

Given the more conservative mood of the nation and its legal system, it is unlikely that any liberalization of the legal rights of juveniles will take place in the near future. If anything, the Supreme Court will give states more opportunities to control minors. According to Samuel Davis, a leading expert on juvenile law, the Court will most likely decide juvenile cases individually and apply the theory of due process under the Fourteenth Amendment to establish the child's constitutional rights in the future.[62]

For the time being, these cases affirm the Supreme Court's interest in applying constitutional principles of due process to juvenile justice while maintaining the *parens patriae* philosophy. In so doing, all the states are required to create juvenile court statutes that conform to the dictates of the Court.

SUMMARY

The study of juvenile justice is concerned with juvenile delinquency and antisocial behavior and the agencies involved in its prevention, control, and treatment. The juvenile justice system is also a process consisting of the steps that a child takes from the initial investigation of a crime through the appeal of a case. These steps are the police investigation, the intake procedure in the juvenile court, the pretrial procedures used for juvenile offenders, adjudication, disposition, and the postdispositional procedures.

The juvenile system can be compared with the adult criminal justice system to show their similarities and differences in processing and terminology. The juvenile court is the heart of the juvenile process. Each jurisdiction organizes its court differently and has varying criteria. The most important factors determining jurisdiction are the age of the offender and the nature of his or her offense.

Over the past two decades, the courts have moved in to eliminate the traditional view that a child brought into the juvenile justice system has no rights. Both the U.S. Supreme Court and the lower courts have granted children procedural safeguards and the protection of due process in the juvenile courts. Major Supreme Court and lower court decisions pertaining to the entire juvenile process have laid down the constitutional requirements for juvenile proceedings.[63] It is important to recognize that in years past, the protections currently afforded both adults and children were not available to children.[64]

How the juvenile justice system deals with the child is also determined by the multiple goals of the system and its individual agencies. There are a number of goals of juvenile justice, as stated by the National Advisory Commission on Criminal Justice Standards and Goals and the American Bar Association. The following are considered realistic strategies for juvenile justice: (1) delinquency prevention, (2) diversion, (3) incapacitation, (4) fairness and justice for children, (5) efficiency and effectiveness, and (6) technology exchange.

Juvenile justice is a very complex system and process whose many goals and strategies are often translated into day-to-day operations and programs. If professionals responsible for the administration of juvenile justice are to make progress against delinquency, the quest for knowledge and success must be based on clearly defined goals for the system. In addition, certain key agencies, such as the juvenile court and correctional institutions, must explore how they can deal with youth more comprehensively and effectively.

KEY TERMS

juvenile justice

Illinois Juvenile Court Act of 1899

parens patriae

juvenile justice system

systems approach

waive

predisposition report

detention hearing

adjudicatory hearing

disposition

petition

hearing

President's Commission on Law Enforcement and the Administration of Justice

National Advisory Commission on Criminal Justice Standards and Goals

Institute of Judicial Administration (IJA)

American Bar Association (ABA)

American Legislative Exchange Council (ALEC)

accountability

status offenders

Kent v. United States (1966)

In re Gault (1967)

In re Winship (1971)

McKeiver v. Pennsylvania (1971)

Breed v. Jones (1975)

Fare v. Michael C. (1979)

Schall v. Martin (1984)

New Jersey v. T.L.O. (1985)

Stanford v. Kentucky and *Wilkens v. Missouri* (1989)

QUESTIONS FOR DISCUSSION

1. The terms *juvenile justice system* and *juvenile justice process* are often used synonymously. What is meant by each term, and how do they differ from each other?

2. The formal components of the criminal justice system are often considered to be the police, the court, and the correctional agency. How do these components compare with the major areas of the juvenile justice system? Is the operation of justice similar in the juvenile and the adult system?

3. Which philosophy of juvenile justice do you hold? What do you believe is wrong with the other philosophies?

4. Should there be a juvenile justice system, or should juveniles who commit serious crimes be treated as adults and the others be handled by social welfare agencies?

5. The Supreme Court has made a number of major decisions in the area of juvenile justice. What are these decisions? What is their impact on the juvenile justice system?

6. What is the meaning of the term *procedural due process of law*? Explain why and how procedural due process has had an impact on juvenile justice.

7. The juvenile court is considered a specialized court for children. How is it organized and why?

NOTES

1. See *Report of the Task Force on Juvenile Justice and Delinquency Prevention, Juvenile Justice and Delinquency Prevention* (Washington, D.C.: U.S. Government Printing Office, 1976).

2. See, generally, Paul Kfoury, *Children before the Court: Reflections on Legal Issues Effecting Minors* (Boston: Butterworth's Legal Group, 1987); also Francis Allen, *The Decline of the Rehabilitative Ideal* (New Haven: Yale University Press, 1981).

3. See, generally, President's Commission on Law Enforcement and the Administration of Justice, *The Challenge of Crime in a Free Society* (Washington, D.C.: U.S. Government Printing Office, 1967); National Advisory Commission on Criminal Justice Standards and Goals, *Report of the Task Force on Juvenile Justice and Delinquency Prevention* (Washington, D.C.: Law Enforcement Assistance Administration, 1976); American Bar Association and Institute of Judicial Administration, *Standards for Juvenile Justice: A Summary and Analysis* (Cambridge, Mass.: Ballinger Press, 1977).

4. See Herbert Lou, *Juvenile Courts in the United States* (Charlotte: University of North Carolina Press, 1927); also *Commonwealth v. Fisher*, 213 Pennsylvania 48 (1905).

5. National Advisory Commission on Criminal Justice Standards and Goals, *Report of the Task Force on Juvenile Justice and Delinquency Prevention*, p. 6.

6. See, for example, *Ex Parte Sharp*, Idaho 126, 96 P.563 (1908).

7. Katherine M. Jamieson and Timothy J. Flanagan, eds., *Sourcebook of Criminal Justice Statistics, 1988* (Washington, D.C.: U.S. Government Printing Office, 1989); National Institute of Juvenile Justice and Delinquency Prevention, *Annual Report 1988* (Washington, D.C.: U.S. Department of Justice, 1989).

8. Information in this section comes from a variety of sources, including Jamieson and Flanagan, *Sourcebook of Criminal Justice Statistics, 1988; Uniform Crime Reports, 1988* (Washington, D.C.: U.S. Government Printing Office, 1989; National Institute of Juvenile Justice and Delinquency Prevention, *Annual Report 1988.*

9. See, generally, Herbert Packer, *The Limits of the Criminal Sanction.* (Palo Alto, Calif.: Stanford University Press, 1968).

10. *Report of the Task Force on Juvenile Justice and Delinquency Prevention*, p. 730.

11. *Ibid.*, p. 720.

12. For an excellent review of the juvenile process, see Adrienne Volenik, *Checklists for Use in Juvenile Delinquency Proceedings* (Washington, D.C.: American Bar Association, 1985).

13. Daniel Besharov, *Juvenile Justice Advocacy-Practice in a Unique Court* (New York: Practicing Law Institute, 1974); also Volenik, *Practice Paper Series: Checklists for Use in Juvenile Delinquency Proceedings.*

14. President's Commission on Law Enforcement and the Administration of Justice, *The Challenge of Crime in a Free Society*, p. 88.

15. Juvenile Delinquency Prevention and Control Act of 1968.

16. Public Law 90–351, Title I-Omnibus Safe Streets and Crime Control Act of 1968, 90th Congress, 19 June 1968.

17. National Advisory Commission on Criminal Justice Standards and Goals, *A National Strategy to Reduce Crime* (Washington, D.C.: U.S. Government Printing Office, 1973).

18. *Report of the Task Force on Juvenile Justice and Delinquency Prevention*, pp. 11–14.

19. Juvenile Justice and Delinquency Prevention Act of 1974, Public Law 93–415 (1974). Funding under this act has declined from $100 million in 1979 to $70 million in 1981 and to $66 million in 1989.

20. Juvenile Justice and Delinquency Prevention Act of 1974, 42 U.S.C. 5601; for a discussion of federal delinquency prevention efforts, see Gayle Olson-Raymer, "The Role of the Federal Government in Juvenile Delinquency Prevention: Historical and Contemporary Perspective," *Journal of Criminal Law and Criminology* 74:578–600 (1983).

21. See American Bar Association and Institute of Justice Administration.

22. Andrew von Hirsch, *Doing Justice* (New York: Hill and Wang, 1976).

23. David Gilman, "IJA-ABA Juvenile Justice Standards Project: An Introduction," *Boston University Law Review* 57:622–23 (1977).

24. *Juvenile Justice Reform: A Model for the States* (Ann Arbor, Michigan: Rose Institute and American Legislative Exchange Council, March 1987). Also see "Draft of New Juvenile Justice Code Introduced," *Juvenile Justice Digest* 14:9–10 (May 1986); "Federal Study on Youth Urges Fixed Sentences," *New York Times*, 29 August 1986, p. 33.

25. Pat McAnany, "Commentary of the American Probation and Parole Association on the Model Juvenile Justice Code," *Justice for Children* 2:5–6 (1987); also see Alan Breed and Robert Smith, "Reforming Juvenile Justice: A Model or Ideology," *Juvenile Justice Digest* 15:6–12 (6 April 1987).

26. Ira M. Schwartz, (*In Justice for Juveniles—Rethinking the Best Interests of the Child* (Lexington, Mass.: D.C. Heath & Co., 1989), p. 164.

27. Robert Smith, "The Elephant in My Living Room," *Crime and Delinquency* 33:317–24 (1987).

28. National Advisory Commission on Criminal Justice Standards and Goals, *Report of the Task Force on Juvenile Justice and Delinquency Prevention*, p. 277.

29. See N.Y.Fam.Ct.Act 712 (1982).

30. See Samuel Davis, *The Rights of Juveniles*, 2nd ed. (New York: Clark Boardman, 1984) update 1989; also Mark Soler, James Bell, Elizabeth Jameson, Carole Shauffer, Alice Shotton, and Loren Warboys, *Representing the Child Client*, (New York: Matthew Bender & Co., 1988).

31. *Lamb v. Brown*, 456 F.2d 18 (1972).

32. Mass.Gen.Laws Ann. ch. 119, 53 (1979).

33. Md.Cts. & Jud.Proc.Code Ann. 3-804(d)(1)(4) (1980).

34. Fla.Stat.Ann. 39.02(5)(c)(Supp.1982); Fla.Stat.Ann. 39.04 (2)(E)(4) (Supp.1981).

35. N.Y.Fam.Ct.Act 73(1)(C) and 732(c) (McKinney Supp. 1979).

36. 359 Mass. 550 (1971); 322 A.2d 58 (1975).

37. State ex rel. *Harris v. Calendine*, 333 S.E.2d 318 (1977).

38. *O.W. v. Bird*, 461 So.2d 967 (Fla.Dist.Ct.App.1984); *In re Michael G.*, 214 Cal.Rptr. 755 App.Ct.1 (1985).

39. *In re A*, 130 N.J.Super.Ct. 138, 325 A.2d 837 (1974).

40. 367 U.S. 643, 81 S.Ct. 1684 (1961).

41. 378 U.S. 478, 84 S.Ct. 1758 (1964).

42. 392 U.S. 1, 88 S.Ct. 1868 (1968).

43. 384 U.S. 436, 86 S.Ct. 1602 (1966).

44. 372 U.S. 335, 83 S.Ct. 792 (1963).

45. 407 U.S. 25, 92 S.Ct. 2006 (1972).

46. 407 U.S. 514, 92 S.Ct. 2182 (1972).

47. 383 U.S. 541 (1966).

48. 387 U.S. 1, 19 (1967).

49. 397 U.S. 358, 90 S.Ct. 1068 (1970).

50. 403 U.S. 528, 91 S.Ct. 1976 (1971).

51. 421 U.S. 519 (1975).

52. 442 U.S. 707 (1979).

53. 467 U.S. 253 (1984).

54. 469 U.S. 325 (1985).

55. 492 U.S.-(1989), 109 S.Ct. 2969 (1989); for an interesting article about whether victims of child and emotional abuse will victimize others, see Katharine Bishop, "Man-Made Disasters on Death Row," *New York Times*, 8 April 1990, Sec. 4, p. 4.

56. McKeiver v. Pennsylvania, 403 U.S. 528 at 538 (1971).

57. Schall v. Martin.

58. New Jersey v. T.L.O.

59. *Ibid.,* p. 538.

60. For differing views of juvenile justice legal policy, see H. Ted Rubin, *Behind the Black Robe—Juvenile Court Judges and the Court* (Beverly Hills, Calif.: Sage, 1985).

61. Sandra Evans Skouron, Joseph Scott, and Francis Cullen, "The Death Penalty for Juveniles: An Assessment of Public Support," *Crime and Delinquency* 45:562–576 (1989).

62. Davis, *The Rights of Juveniles*, pp. 7–12.

63. See Barry Feld, "The Juvenile Court Meets the Principle of the Offense: Legislative Changes in Juvenile Waiver Statutes," *Journal of Criminal Law and Criminology* 78:471 (1987).

64. Patricia Harris, "Is the Juvenile Justice System Lenient," *Criminal Justice Abstracts*, March:104–118 (1986).

Controlling Juvenile Offenders

Controlling juvenile delinquency is a complex task. While adults who violate the law are subject to clearly defined sanctions, the *parens patriae* philosophy demands that the state always consider the best interests of the child when controlling juvenile behavior. However, the line between treatment and punishment is often a narrow one. When do the efforts of people truly desiring to help a troubled youngster actually become a crushing burden on them? Is it possible that the doctrine of *parens patriae* goes too far? These are questions that constantly perplex juvenile justice policy-makers. Is it possible to create a system in which troubled juveniles are helped using the least restrictive alternatives possible, while at the same time serious juvenile offenders are restrained? Should we be more punitive than we have been, or should we employ even greater compassion and understanding? Or does the answer lie somewhere in between?

Part 5 contains three chapters devoted to the process and policies used to control juvenile offenders. Chapter 15 deals with police handling of delinquent and status offenders. It contains information on the police role, organization, and prevention efforts. It explores the power of a police officer to take a child into custody and the rights of the child when arrested and outlines the applicability of *Miranda v. Arizona* to the juvenile process. This chapter also points out how the U.S. Supreme Court has expressly found that juveniles fall within the protection of the Fourth Amendment. Chapter 16 is concerned with the important topic of early court processing. It describes such current issues as diversion programs, removal of minor offenders from secure detention facilities, and the transfer of youths to adult courts. The "transfer of jurisdiction" issue, often called waiver, remand, or removal to the criminal court, is a unique statutory process. Chapter 17 discusses the equally important topic of juvenile trial and disposition. It discusses the role of the prosecutor, the juvenile court judge, and the defense attorney at adjudication and disposition. Since juveniles, as well as adults, are entitled to fair trials, this chapter concerns itself with a detailed analysis of the landmark constitutional decisions on juvenile justice. Next, it deals with disposition and sentencing—the key element in the juvenile process.

After reading these chapters, you should have an understanding of how society has attempted to control juvenile offenders, beginning with the pre-judicial process and concluding with the disposition.

15 Police Work with Juveniles

The modern juvenile justice system is the primary source of efforts to control juvenile crime. Other segments of society—the political system, the schools, and religious institutions—play a role, but social control rests mainly with the juvenile justice system. As its law enforcement and social control arm, the police, therefore, become the frontline agency that deals with the prevention and control of juvenile delinquency.

Traditionally, the primary responsibility of the police has been to protect the public. In the minds of most citizens, that is still their most important responsibility. From the vast array of films, books, and TV shows that depict the derring-do of police officers in the field, the public has obtained an image of "crime fighters" who "always get their man." Since the tumultuous 1960s, the public has become increasingly more aware that the reality of police work is quite a bit different from its fictional glorification. When police departments failed to bring the crime rate down despite massive government subsidies, when citizens complained of civil rights violations, and when tales of corruption became widespread, it was evident that there was a crisis imminent in American policing.

During the 1980s, a new view of policing emerged around the nation. Rather than foster the view of the police officer as a hell-bent-for-leather crime fighter who only tracks down serious criminals or stops armed robberies in progress, police departments adopted the concept that the police role should be to maintain order in the community, to interact with citizens, and to be a visible and accessible component of the community. The argument is that police efforts can only be successful if they are conducted in partnership with concerned and active citizens. This movement is referred to as **community policing.**[1]

Interest in the community policing concept does not mean that the crime-control model of law enforcement is past history. An ongoing effort is being made to improve the crime-fighting capability of police agencies, and there are some indications that the effort is being rewarded. Recent research indicates that aggressive, formal action by the police can help reduce the incidence of repeat offending.[2] And technological innovation, such as fingerprint-reading computers, may bring about greater police efficiency. Nonetheless, after twenty-five years of attempting to improve police effectiveness through a combination of policy and technical advancement, there is little evidence that adding police or improving their skills has a major impact on their crime-fighting success.[3]

During this era in which experts are rethinking the basic police role, the relationship between police and juvenile offenders has become quite critical. Because police officers represent the authority of the community, even the most casual meeting between a police officer and a child can have a profound effect on the youth's future. How the child reacts to this authority may depend on the police officer's response to the child's behavior. This more often than not depends on the officer's personal biases and values, as well as his or her role orientation and attitudes toward police work. Working with juvenile offenders may be especially perplexing for police officers since the need to help young people and guide them away from a criminal career may seem to be in conflict with the traditional police duties of crime prevention and order maintenance.

This chapter focuses on police work in juvenile justice and delinquency prevention. It covers the role and responsibilities of the police; the organization and management of police-juvenile operations; the legal aspects of police work, including custodial interrogation, search and seizure, and lineups; the concept of police discretion; and the relationship between the police and community efforts to prevent crime.

THE ROLE OF THE POLICE IN HANDLING JUVENILE OFFENDERS

How do **juvenile officers** spend their time and what roles do they perform in the overall police and criminal justice system? Juvenile officers either operate alone as specialists within a police department or as part of the juvenile unit of a police department. Their role is similar to that of officers working with adult offenders— to intervene if the actions of a citizen produce public danger or disorder. Most officers regard the violations of juveniles as nonserious unless they are committed by a chronic troublemaker or involve significant damage to persons or property. Juveniles who misbehave are often ignored or treated informally. Police encounters with juveniles are generally the result of reports made by citizens, and the bulk of such encounters pertain to matters of minor legal consequence.[4]

Of course, police must also deal with serious juvenile offenders whose criminal acts are similar to those of adults, but these are only a small minority of the offender population. Thus police who deal with delinquency must concentrate on being peacekeepers and crime preventers.[5]

Handling juvenile offenders can produce major **role conflicts** for the police. They may find what they consider their primary duty, **law enforcement**, undercut by the need to aid in the rehabilitation of youthful offenders. A police officer's actions in cases involving adults are usually controlled by the rule of criminal law and his or her own personal judgment, or **discretion.** In contrast, a case involving a juvenile often demands that the officer consider the "best interests of the child" and how the officer's actions will influence the child's future life and well-being. Consequently, police are much more likely to use informal procedures with juvenile offenders than with adults. It is estimated that anywhere between 40 and 50 percent of all juveniles arrested by police are handled informally within the police department or referred to a community service agency. These informal dispositions are the result of the police officer's discretionary authority.[6]

Many officers dislike getting involved in juvenile matters, probably because most juvenile crimes are held in low regard by fellow police officers.[7] Juvenile detectives are sometimes referred to as the "Lollipop Squad" or "Diaper Dicks." Arresting a 12-year-old girl for shoplifting and bringing her in tears to the police station is not considered the way to win respect from one's peers.

Police who deal with juvenile offenders also find themselves caught in the dilemma of enforcing laws that conflict with the basic life-style of youths: clearing the corner hangout, putting a stop to drag racing or car cruising, enforcing liquor laws. As police expert Samuel Walker states:

> Police intervention in these disorder situations is difficult and frustrating. The officer often encounters hostile or belligerent behavior. Overreaction by the officer creates the possibility of a major violent incident. Even if the officer succeeds in quieting or dispersing the crowd, the problem will probably reappear the next day, often in the same place.[8]

Role conflicts are often exacerbated because most police-juvenile encounters involve confrontations brought about by loitering, disturbing the peace, and rowdiness, rather than by serious law violations. Dealing with youth problems brings little of the rewards or job satisfaction desired by police officers.

What role should the police take in mediating problems with youths—hardline law enforcement or social service-oriented delinquency prevention? The International Association of Chiefs of Police sees the solution as lying somewhere

in between: "Most police departments operate juvenile programs that combine the law enforcement and delinquency prevention roles, and the police should work with the juvenile court to determine a role that is most suitable for the community."[9] In fact, police officers may also act as juvenile prosecutors in some rural courts when attorneys are not available. Thus, the police-juvenile role extends from the on-street encounter to the station house to the juvenile court. It seems that for juvenile matters involving minor criminal conduct or incorrigible behavior, the police ordinarily select the "least restrictive alternative" course of action. Such courses include nonintervention, temporary assistance, and referral to community agencies. Serious juvenile crime, on the other hand, requires that the police investigate, arrest, and even detain youths while providing constitutional safeguards similar to those available to adult offenders.

ORGANIZATION OF POLICE SERVICES FOR JUVENILES

The problem of juvenile delinquency and youth crime used to receive little attention from most municipal police departments. Even when juvenile crime continued to increase during the 1960s and 1970s, police resources were generally geared to adult offenders. However, the alarming increase in serious juvenile crime in the past few years has made it obvious that the police can no longer neglect youthful antisocial behavior. They need to assign resources to the problem and have the proper organization for coping with it. The theory and practice of police organization has recently undergone many changes, and as a result, police departments are giving greater emphasis to the juvenile function.

The organization of juvenile work depends on the size of the police department, the kind of community in which the department is located, and the amount and quality of resources available in the community. Today, most police agencies recognize that juvenile crime requires special attention. Specialized police work with children goes back to the first juvenile court in 1899 in Illinois, and its importance has been recognized for many years.[10]

The police who work with juvenile offenders usually have special skills and talents that go beyond those generally associated with regular police work. In large urban police departments, juvenile services are often established through a special unit. Ordinarily this unit is the responsibility of a command-level police officer. The unit commander assigns officers to deal with juvenile problems throughout the police department's jurisdiction. Police departments with very few officers have little need for an internal division with special functions. Most small departments make one officer responsible for handling juvenile matters for the entire community.

In either large or small departments, it cannot be assumed that only police officers assigned to work with juveniles will be involved in juvenile offenses. When officers on patrol encounter a youngster committing a crime, they are responsible for dealing with the problem initially. However, they generally refer the case to the juvenile unit or the juvenile police officer to follow up. In working with adult offenders, most police officers are concerned primarily about the type of offense the suspect has committed. When working with young people, the juvenile officer is concerned with what to do in cases that cannot be handled with on-the-scene referrals to families or social agencies.[11]

The number of police officers assigned to juvenile work has increased in recent years. The International Association of Chiefs of Police found that approximately 500 departments of the 1,400 surveyed in 1960 had juvenile units. By 1970, the number of police departments with a juvenile specialist had doubled. Today, even relatively small departments have a juvenile specialist.[12] The number of personnel allocated for juvenile work varies widely—between 2.5 and 7.5 percent of departmental personnel.[13]

Most juvenile officers are appointed after they have had some general patrol experience. A desire to work with juveniles and a basic understanding of human behavior are generally considered essential.[14] Sometimes juvenile officers are assigned on the basis of written and oral examinations, as well as general experience. Of course, juvenile officers should have an aptitude for working with young people.[15]

POLICE AND THE RULE OF LAW

While serving as a primary source of referral and diversion of youth from juvenile court, the police are simultaneously required to investigate criminal activity and take children into custody in appropriate cases. Their actions are controlled by statute, constitutional case law, and judicial review. The following methods of police investigation and control in dealing with juvenile offenders are discussed below: (1) the arrest procedure; (2) search and seizure; (3) custodial interrogation; and (4) juvenile lineups.

The Arrest Procedure

Judicial limitations on police discretion in the investigation of offenses involving juveniles are similar to the limitations applied to adult offenders. When a juvenile is apprehended, the police must decide whether to release the chid or refer him or her to the juvenile court. Cases involving serious crimes against property or persons are often referred to court. On the other hand, minor disputes between juveniles, school and neighborhood complaints, petty shoplifting cases, runaways, and assaults and batteries of minors are often diverted from court action.

Most states require that the law of **arrest** is the same for both adults and juveniles. To make a legal arrest, an officer must have **probable cause** to believe that an offense took place and that the suspect is the guilty party. Probable cause is usually defined as falling somewhere between a mere suspicion and absolute certainty. In misdemeanor cases, the police officer must personally observe the crime in order to place a suspect in custody. For a felony, police officers may arrest if they have probable cause to believe the crime has occurred and the person has committed it, as well as if they observe the offense.

The main difference between arrests of adult and juvenile offenders is the broader latitude police have to control youthful behavior. Police can arrest youths for status offenses, such as truancy, running away, and possession of alcohol; adults would be immune to arrest for such acts. Most existing juvenile codes for instance provide broad authority for the police to take juveniles into custody.[16] Such statutes are designed to give the police the authority to act "in loco parentis." According to Samuel Davis, the broad power granted to police is consistent with the notion that a juvenile is not arrested but "taken into custody," which implies a protective and not a punitive form of detention.[17] Once a juvenile is formally arrested, however, the constitutional safeguards of the Fourth and Fifth Amendments available to adults are applicable to the juvenile as well.

Section 13 of the Uniform Juvenile Court Act, created by the National Conference of Commissioners on Uniform State Laws, is an excellent example of the statutory provisions typically utilized in state codes regarding juvenile arrest procedures.

> Section 13. [taking into custody.]
> (a) A child may be taken into custody:
> (1) pursuant to an order of the court under this Act;
> (2) pursuant to the laws of arrest;
> (3) by a law enforcement officer [or duly authorized officer of the court] if there are reasonable grounds to believe that the child is suffering from illness or injury or is in immediate danger from his surroundings, and that his removal is necessary; or
> (4) by a law enforcement officer [or duly authorized officer of the court] if there are reasonable grounds to believe that the child has run away from his parents, guardian, or other custodian.
> (b) The taking of a child into custody is not an arrest, except for the purpose of determining its validity under the constitution of this State or of the United States.[18]

Police have broad latitude to control youthful behavior through their powers of arrest.

Search and Seizure

Do juveniles have the same constitutional right to be free from unreasonable **search and seizure** as adults? In general, a citizen's privacy is protected by the Constitution's Fourth Amendment, which states:

> The right of the people to be secure in their persons, houses, papers, and effects, against unreasonable searches and seizures, shall not be violated, and no warrants shall issue, but upon probable cause, supported by oaths or affirmation, and particularly describing the place to be searched, and the persons or things to be seized.

Most courts have held in state jurisdictions that the Fourth Amendment ban against unreasonable search and seizure applies to juveniles in delinquency proceedings and that illegally seized evidence is inadmissable in a juvenile trial. To exclude incriminating evidence, a child's attorney makes a pretrial motion to suppress the evidence—the same procedure that is used in the adult criminal process. Virtually all lower court decisions that have considered this issue have mentioned this view. In *State v. Lowry*, the Court stated:

> Is it not more outrageous for the police to treat children more harshly than adult offenders, especially when such is violative of due process and fair treatment? Can a court countenance a system, where, as here, an adult may suppress evidence with the usual effect of having the charges dropped for lack of proof, and on the other hand a juvenile can be institutionalized—lose the most sacred possession a human being has, his freedom—for "rehabilitative" purposes because the Fourth Amendment right is unavailable to him?[19]

A full discussion of search and seizure is beyond the scope of this text, but it is important to note that the Supreme Court has ruled that police may stop a

New Jersey v. T.L.O.

Facts

On March 7, 1980, a teacher at Piscataway High in Middlesex County, New Jersey, discovered two girls smoking in a lavatory. Because this was in violation of school rules, he reported the incident to the principal's office, and the girls were summoned to meet with assistant vice principal Theodore Choplick, who questioned them about their behavior. When one of the girls, T.L.O., claimed she had done nothing wrong, the assistant vice principal demanded to see her purse. When he examined it, he found a pack of cigarettes and also noticed a package of cigarette rolling papers, which are generally associated with the use of marijuana. He then searched the purse thoroughly and found some marijuana, a pipe, a substantial amount of money, a list of students who owed T.L.O. money, and letters implicating her in marijuana dealing. Mr. Choplick then informed both T.L.O.'s mother and the police about the evidence he uncovered. Later at the police station, T.L.O. confessed to dealing drugs on campus.

Based on her confession and the evidence recovered from her purse, the state proceeded against T.L.O. in the juvenile court. Her motion to suppress the evidence taken during the school search was rejected by the trial court on the grounds that school officials could search students if they had reasonable cause to believe that the search was necessary to maintain school discipline or enforce school policies; consequently, T.L.O. was found delinquent and sentenced to a year's probation. T.L.O.'s subsequent appeal of the decision was eventually upheld by the New Jersey Supreme Court on the grounds that Mr. Choplick's search of T.L.O.'s purse was not justified under the circumstances of the case. The state appealed to the U.S. Supreme Court.

Decision

The Supreme Court held that the prohibitions against illegal search and seizure apply to school as well as law enforcement officials. Teachers are
continued

suspect and search for and seize evidence without a search warrant under certain circumstances. A person may be searched after a legal arrest, but then only in the immediate area of the suspect's control, for example, after an arrest for possession of drugs, the pockets of a suspect's jacket may be searched;[20] an automobile may be searched if there is probable cause to believe a crime has taken place;[21] a suspect's outer garments may be frisked if police are suspicious of his or her activities;[22] a search may be conducted if a person volunteers for the search.[23] These rules are usually applied to juveniles as well as to adults. However, there are two differences between adult and juvenile law that make it somewhat easier for police to conduct searches of suspected delinquent offenders. First, juveniles can be arrested for status offenses, such as curfew violations or truancy, and police can legally search them after such an arrest is made. Furthermore, most courts have upheld the right of parents to give police permission or the right to search the rooms and possessions of their minor children.[24]

not merely substitute parents but agents of the state who are required to carry out state policy and law. Students do not give up their constitutional rights when they walk on school property. However, school officials also have to maintain an atmosphere that is conducive to learning. A balance must be achieved between a student's right to privacy and the school's need to provide a safe, secure environment. Therefore, the Court ruled that teachers do not need to obtain a warrant before searching a student who is under their authority. In addition, the search need not be based on probable cause to believe that a crime has taken place; rather the legality of the search of a student should depend simply on its reasonableness, considering the scope of the search, the age and sex of the student, and the behavior that prompted it to be made. Of considerable importance is the fact that school searches were found justified if a student was suspected of violating the law or suspected of violating school rules. Considering this standard, the search of T.L.O. was found to be justified, since the report of her smoking created a reasonable suspicion that she had cigarettes in her purse and the discovery of the rolling papers then gave rise to a reasonable suspicion that the girl was in possession of marijuana.

Significance of the Case

By giving teachers and other school officials the right to search students if they are suspected of being in violation of school rules, the Court established a significant difference between the due process rights of adults and juveniles. An adult could not be legally searched by an agent of the government under the same circumstances under which T.L.O. was searched. Thus, the *T.L.O.* decision is in keeping with the judicial philosophy espoused in cases such as *Schall v. Martin* and *McKeiver v. Pennsylvania*, which find that juveniles, for their own protection, may be denied certain constitutional safeguards available to adults.

As a practical matter, *New Jersey v. T.L.O.* opens the door for greater security measures being taken on school grounds. It represents the Court's recognition that the nation's educational system is under siege and that educators need greater freedom to maintain school security. Underlying the decision is a recognition of the inherent rights of the mass of law-abiding students to receive an education unimpeded by the disruptive activities of a few troublemakers.

Source: New Jersey v. T.L.O., *105 S.Ct. 733 (1985).*

Search and Seizure in Schools

One major issue of search and seizure in juvenile law is the right of school officials to search students and their possessions on school grounds and turn over evidence to the police. Searches of students' persons or lockers become necessary when it is believed that students are in the process of violating the law. Drug abuse, theft, assault and battery, and racial conflicts in schools have increased the need to take action against troublemakers. School administrators have questioned students about their illegal activities, conducted searches of students' persons and possessions, and reported suspicious behavior to the police.

In the 1985 landmark decision, *New Jersey v. T.L.O.,* the Supreme Court helped clarify one of the most vexing problems of school searches: whether the Fourth Amendment's prohibition against unreasonable searches and seizures applies to school officials as well as police officers.[25] In this important case, set out in the accompanying Focus on Delinquency, the Court found that students are in fact constitutionally protected from illegal searches but that school officials are not bound by the same restrictions as law enforcement agents. While police need "probable cause" before a search can be undertaken, educators can legally search students when there are reasonable grounds that the students have violated the law or broken school rules. In creating this distinction, the Court recognized the needs of school officials to preserve an environment conducive to education and to secure the safety of their students.

One of the most significant questions left unanswered by *New Jersey v. T.L.O.* is whether teachers and other school officials can search school lockers and desks. Here the law has been controlled by state decisions, and each jurisdiction may create its own standards. Some allow teachers a free hand in opening lockers and desks.[26] However, not all school districts allow warrantless searches, holding as New Jersey did in *State v. Engerud:*

> [W]e are satisfied that in the context of this case the student had an expectation of privacy in the contents of his locker. . . . For the four years of high school, the school locker is a home away from home. In it the student stores the kind of personal "effects" protected by the Fourth Amendment.[27]

These and other lower court decisions have helped establish, limit, and define the scope of the school's authority to search lockers and desks.[28]

However, faced with increased crime by students in public schools, particularly illicit drug use, school administrators today are inclined to enforce drug control statutes and administrative rules.[29] Some urban schools are using breathalyzers, drug-sniffing dogs, hidden video cameras, and routine searches of students' pockets, purses, lockers, and cars.[30] In general, courts consider such searches permissible when they are not overly offensive and where there are reasonable grounds to suspect that the student may have violated the law.[31] School administrators are walking a tightrope between students' constitutional right to privacy and school safety.[32]

In summary, the critical issue with regard to the rights of the child and school searches is the extent of the student's Fourth Amendment protection against unreasonable search and seizure as compared with the extent of the school's authority to conduct searches and the duty of educators to protect other students.

Custodial Interrogation of Juveniles

Parents are usually contacted immediately after a child is taken into custody. In years past, the police often questioned juveniles without their parents or even an attorney present. Any incriminatory statements or confessions that the juveniles made could be used in evidence at their trials. However, in 1966, the landmark Supreme Court case *Miranda v. Arizona* placed constitutional limitations on police interrogation procedures used with adult offenders. *Miranda* held that persons in police custody must be told that:

■ They have the right to remain silent.

■ Any statements they make can be used against them.

■ They have the right to counsel.

■ If they cannot afford counsel, it will be furnished at public expense.[33]

These "Miranda warnings," which secure the adult defendant's Fifth Amendment privilege against self-incrimination, have been made applicable to children taken into custody. The Supreme Court case of *In re Gault* stated that constitutional privileges against self-incrimination are applicable in juvenile cases as well as in adult cases. Because *In re Gault* implies that *Miranda v. Arizona* applies to **custodial interrogation** of juvenile offenders in the pre-judicial stage of the juvenile process, state court jurisdictions apply the requirements of *Miranda* to juvenile proceedings as well. Since *Gault* in 1967, virtually all of the courts that have ruled on the question of the *Miranda* warning have concluded that the warning does apply to the juvenile process.

One difficult problem associated with the custodial interrogation of children has to do with their waiver of *Miranda* rights: under what circumstances can juveniles knowingly and willingly waive the rights given them by *Miranda v. Arizona* and discuss their actions with police without benefit of lawyer? Is it possible for a youngster, acting alone, to be mature enough to appreciate the right to remain silent?

Most courts have concluded that parents or attorneys need not be present for children to effectively waive their rights.[34] In a frequently cited California case, *People v. Lara*, the court said that the question of a child's waiver is to be determined by the **totality of the circumstances doctrine.**[35] This means that the validity of a waiver rests not only on the age of the child but also on a combination of other factors, including: the education of the accused; the accused's knowledge of the charge and of the right to remain silent and have an attorney present; whether the youth was allowed to consult with family or friends; whether the interrogation took place before or after charges were placed; the method of interrogation; whether the accused refused to give statements on prior occasions.[36]

The general rule is that juveniles can intentionally waive their rights to protection from self-incrimination, but the validity of this waiver is determined by the circumstances of each case. For example, in *New Hampshire v. Benoit*, a child's custodial statements were considered inadmissible because the child had not been told of the possibility that the statements could be used against him if he were tried as an adult.[37]

In addition, a number of states, recognizing the inability of children to comprehend their legal rights, have demanded by law that a parent or attorney be present when a juvenile is questioned by police; this is referred to as the "interested adult rule."[38]

This doctrine requires that the police explain the *Miranda* warning to the juvenile in the presence of a parent or someone acting in loco parentis for the child. Then, the adult must have the opportunity to consult with the child so that the child understands the rights and their significance. Most courts using this rule require that the adult present during the interrogation must be acting in the child's interest and not in any official capacity, such as a youth service employee, court social worker, or probation officer.

In a recent Massachusetts case dealing with this problem, the court acted to protect the rights of the juvenile by holding that no other minor, not even a relative, can act as an interested adult. In *Commonwealth v. Guyton*, Guyton's sister, who was three weeks short of her eighteenth birthday, was acting in loco

Fare v. Michael C.

Facts

Michael C. was implicated in the murder of Robert Yeager, which occurred during a robbery of Yeager's home. A small truck registered in the name of Michael's mother was identified as having been near the Yeager home at the time of the killing, and a young man answering Michael's description was seen by witnesses near the truck and near the home shortly before Yeager was murdered.

On the basis of this information, the police of Van Nuys, California, arrested Michael at approximately 6:30 p.m. on February 4. He was then 16½ years old and on probation to the juvenile court. He had been on probation since the age of 12. Approximately one year earlier, he had served a term in a youth corrections camp under the supervision of the juvenile court. He had a record of several previous offenses, including burglary of guns and purse snatching, stretching back over several years.

When Michael arrived at the Van Nuys station house, two police officers began to interrogate him. No one else was present during the interrogation. The conversation was tape-recorded. One of the officers initiated the interview by informing Michael that he had been brought in for questioning in relation to a murder. The officer fully advised him of his *Miranda* rights. The following exchange then occurred:

Q: Do you understand all of these rights as I have explained them to you?
A: Yeah.

Q: Okay, do you wish to give up your right to remain silent and talk to us about this murder?
A: What murder? I don't know about no murder.
Q: Do you want to give up your right to have an attorney present here while we talk about it?
A: Can I have my probation officer here?
Q: Well, I can't get a hold of your probation officer right now. You have a right to an attorney.
A: How do I know you guys won't pull no police officer in and tell me he's an attorney?
Q: Your probation officer is Mr. Christiansen.
A: Yeah.
Q: Well I'm not going to call Mr. Christiansen tonight. There's a good chance we can talk to him later, but I'm not going to call him right now. If you want to talk to us without an attorney present, you can. If you don't want to, you don't have to. But if you want to say something, you can, and if you don't want to say something, you don't have to. That's your right. You understand that right?
A: Yeah.
Q: Okay, will you talk to us without an attorney present?
A: Yeah, I want to talk to you.

Michael thereupon proceeded to answer questions. He made statements and drew sketches that incriminated him in the Yeager murder.

Largely on the basis of Michael's incriminating statements, probation authorities filed a petition in juvenile court alleging that he had murdered Robert Yeager and that he should be made a ward of the juvenile court.

continued

parentis for the brother while their mother was away, and the Court ruled that she could not act as an interested adult.[39] On the other hand, some courts have recognized that the interested adult need not be a parent but may be a relative, such as the juvenile's grandfather.[40] Usually, the one exception to the application of the interested adult rule is when the child is over age 14 and the circumstances demonstrate a high degree of intelligence, experience, and knowledge on the part of the child. Only then may child act alone.

The waiver of Miranda rights by a juvenile is probably one of the most controversial legal issues often addressed in the state courts. It has also been the subject of federal constitutional review, discussed above.

The California Supreme Court reversed the conviction, holding that Michael's request to see his probation officer negated any possible willingness on his part to discuss his case with the police and thereby invoked his Fifth Amendment privilege.

Decision

Michael alleged that statements had been obtained from him in violation of *Miranda* because his request to see his probation officer at the outset of the questioning invoked his Fifth Amendment right to remain silent, just as if he had requested the assistance of an attorney. Accordingly, Michael argued that since the interrogation did not cease until he had a chance to confer with his probation officer, the statements and sketches could not be admitted against him in the juvenile court proceedings.

The Supreme Court reversed and remanded in an opinion by Justice Harry Blackmun. The *Miranda* rule that prior to interrogation the state must warn the accused of the right to an attorney and of the right to remain silent unless an attorney is present "has the virtue of informing police and prosecutors with specificity as to what they may do in conducting custodial interrogation, and of informing courts under what circumstances statements obtained during such interrogation are not admissible," the Court said. In this case, the California court had significantly extended the rule, it continued, and had ignored the basis of the *Miranda* rule, which is the "critical position" lawyers occupy in our legal system. Probation officers frequently are not trained in the law, and moreover they are employees of the state, duty bound to report wrongdoing by the juvenile. "In these circumstances," the Court said, "it cannot be said that the probation officer is able to offer the type of independent advice that an accused would expect from a lawyer retained or assigned to assist him during questioning."

The Court also rejected the contention that the youth's request constituted a request to remain silent. On the basis of the record, his replies show that he "voluntarily and knowingly waived his Fifth Amendment rights."

Significance of Case

The *Fare v. Michael C.* case applied the "totality of the circumstances" approach to the interrogation of juveniles. The question of whether the accused waived his rights is one of substance, not form. Did the defendant knowingly and voluntarily waive the rights delineated in *Miranda*? The juvenile court was originally correct. The transcript of the interrogation took care to ensure that Michael understood his rights. The police fully explained that he was being questioned in connection with a murder. They informed him of all the rights delineated in *Miranda* and ascertained that he understood them. Nothing indicates that Michael failed to understand what the officers told him. Moreover, after his request to see his probation officer had been denied and after the police officer once more had explained his rights to him, he clearly expressed his willingness to waive his rights and continue the interrogation.

In addition, the Court held that the *Miranda* rule should not be extended to include a juvenile's request to see his or her probation officer. Such a request does not have the same effect as the request to see a lawyer.

Source: Fare v. Michael C., 442 U.S. 23, 99 S.Ct. 2560 (1979).

Supreme Court Interpretations of *Miranda* to Juvenile Proceedings

The Supreme Court has attempted to clarify children's rights when they are interrogated by the police in two cases, *Fare v. Michael C.* and *California v. Prysock*. In *Fare v. Michael C.*, the Court ruled that a child's asking to speak to his probation officer was not the equivalent of asking for an attorney; consequently, admissions he made to the police absent legal counsel were held to be admissible in court.[41] (Because of the importance of this case, it is set out in the Focus on Delinquency entitled "*Fare v. Michael C.*") And in *California v. Prysock*, the Court was asked to rule on the adequacy of a *Miranda* warning given Randall Prysock, a youthful murder suspect.[42] After reviewing the taped exchange between the police interrogator and the boy, the Court upheld Prysock's conviction when it ruled that even though the *Miranda* warning was given in slightly different language and out of exact context, its meaning was plain and easily understandable, even to a juvenile.

Taken together, *Fare* and *Prysock* make it seem indisputable that juveniles are at least entitled to receive the same *Miranda* rights as adults and ought to be entitled to even greater consideration to ensure that they understand their legal rights.

Miranda v. Arizona is an historic and often symbolic decision that continues to effect the rights of all suspects, adults and children, placed in custody.[43] The following "Case in Point" exemplifies the extent to which *Miranda* can be applied in the juvenile justice system.

CASE IN POINT

You are a juvenile court prosecutor faced with the responsibility of assessing the admissibility of evidence in juvenile cases. Defendant Kevin W., age 16 years and 9 months, was convicted of attempted second-degree murder and burglary of a convenience food store. After shooting the clerk, he fled the scene, leaving behind a friend who had accompanied Kevin but refused to enter the store.

One of the police officers who arrived at the scene was Kevin's father, Sergeant W. Knowing his son was supposed to be with the friend, Sergeant W. went home, found his son, and questioned him in the presence of the defendant's mother and brother. At this time, Sergeant W. did not advise his son of his *Miranda* rights. Kevin admitted that he had shot the victim and told his father where the gun was hidden.

Later at the police station, Kevin, while in the process of confessing to other police officers and having been informed of his rights, was interrupted by his father, who recommended that the boy say nothing further without speaking with an attorney. The defendant then invoked his right to remain silent.

On appeal, Kevin contends that the statements made to his policeman father should have been suppressed as the product of a custodial interrogation without the benefit of *Miranda* warnings. He argues that his confession was involuntary by reason of the fact that the officer was his father and further that his home was a custodial setting requiring the application of *Miranda* protection.

On the other hand, the state pointed out that the physical setting in which the statements were made was not coercive and the questioning very brief. In addition, the fact that the father was in uniform when he questioned his son did not necessarily constitute custodial activity. Although Sergeant W.'s investigation focused on his son, *Miranda* warnings are not required merely because the questioned person is a suspect. Only when the

continued

accused is "in custody" and deprived of his freedom in a significant way does *Miranda* apply.

Do you believe that Kevin's confession to his policeman father was voluntary, and, therefore, not of a custodial nature requiring the application of *Miranda v. Arizona?*

Identification from Lineups

Another important issue arises in the early police processing of juvenile offenders. Should the constitutional safeguards established for adult offenders to protect them during lineups and other forms of identification be applied to juvenile proceedings? In *United States v. Wade*, the Supreme Court held that the accused has a right to have counsel present at post-indictment lineup procedures and that pretrial identification is inadmissible when the right to counsel is violated.[44] The Court further clarified this issue in *Kirby v. Illinois*, holding that the defendant's right to counsel at pretrial identification proceedings goes into effect only after the complaint or the indictment has been issued.[45] Based on these decisions, courts have ruled that juveniles also have constitutional protection during lineup and identification procedures. They have a right to counsel at a police lineup once they are charged with a delinquent act, and if this right is violated, the pretrial identification is excluded. For example, in the case of *In re Holley*, a juvenile accused of rape did not have counsel during the lineup identification procedure. In reversing Holley's conviction, the appellate court said the absence of counsel during Holley's lineup precluded a fair trial.[46] State courts have generally followed the mandate of the Supreme Court and applied its holdings to juvenile delinquency proceedings.

Today, almost as much procedural protection is given to children in the juvenile justice courts as to adults brought to the criminal courts. However, the authority of the police to deal with juvenile misconduct under most juvenile codes is ordinarily broader than with adults. Therefore, no aspect of the police role is more important than its reliance on granting juvenile officers a reasonable amount of discretion in the handling of juvenile problems. When should a police officer act to assist a juvenile in need against his or her will? Should a summons be used in lieu of arrest? Under what conditions should a juvenile be taken into protective custody? The following sections describe the factors that influence police discretion and review the policies and programs for its control.

POLICE WORK WITH JUVENILES: DISCRETIONARY JUSTICE

When police officers get embroiled in a case involving a juvenile offender, they are forced to use their personal discretion to choose an appropriate course of action. Police discretion is defined as selective enforcement of the law by duly authorized police agents. Roscoe Pound defined discretion as the authority conferred by law to act in certain conditions or situations in accordance with an official's or agency's own considered conscience or judgment.[47] Discretion operates in the twilight zone between law and morals. According to Kenneth Davis, discretion gives officers a choice among possible courses of action within the effective limits on their power.[48] Joseph Goldstein has termed the exercise of police discretion a prime example of **low-visibility decision making** in the criminal justice system.[49] Low-visibility decision making refers to decisions made by public officials in the criminal or juvenile justice systems that the public is not in a position to understand, regulate, or criticize.

Police discretion is probably one of the most controversial and important of all police practices. It exists not only in the police area but also in prosecutorial decision making, judicial judgments, and corrections. Discretion results in the law being applied differently in similar situations. For example, two teenagers are caught in a stolen automobile; one is arrested, the other is released. Two youths are drunk and disorderly; one is sent home, the other is booked and sent to juvenile court. A group of youngsters are involved in a gang fight; only a few are arrested, the others are released.

Regardless of what enforcement style they employ, police officers in both the adult and juvenile systems use a high degree of personal discretion in carrying out their daily tasks. In particular, much discretion is exercised in juvenile work because of the informality that has been built into the system to individualize justice. According to Victor Streib, arbitrary discretion is a characteristic of the informal juvenile system.[50] Furthermore, Streib says, police intake officials, prosecutors, judges, and correctional administrators make final, largely unreviewed decisions about children that are almost totally unsupervised in any meaningful way.

The daily procedures of juvenile personnel are not subjected to administrative scrutiny or judicial review, except when they clearly violate a child's constitutional rights. As a result, discretion sometimes deteriorates into discrimination, violence, and other abusive practices on the part of the police. As Herbert Packer has stated, the real danger in discretion is that it allows the law to discriminate against precisely those elements in the population—the poor, the ignorant, the unpopular—who are the least able to draw attention to their plight and to whose sufferings the vast majority of the population is not responsive.[51]

The problem of discretion of juvenile justice is one of two extremes. Too little discretion ties the hands of decision makers and does not provide flexibility in dealing with individual juvenile offenders. Guidelines and controls are needed to structure the use of discretion.

The first contact a child usually has with the juvenile justice system is with the police, and studies indicate that a large majority of police decisions at this initial contact involve discretion. Paul Strasburg found that only about 50 percent of all children who come in contact with the police ever get past this initial stage of the juvenile justice process.[52]

In a classic study, Nathan Goldman examined the arrest records for over 1,000 juveniles from four communities in Pennsylvania to determine what factors operated in police referrals of juveniles to the court.[53] He concluded that over 64 percent of police contacts with juveniles were handled informally without court referral. In another early effort, Irving Piliavin and Scott Briar observed the behavior of thirty officers in the juvenile bureau of a large industrial city. Their study documented further the informality of police discretion in the initial arrest decision.[54] In 1966, Donald Black and Albert Reiss recorded descriptions of 280 encounters between juveniles and the police in efforts to discover discriminatory decision making. They found an unusually low arrest rate.[55] The FBI estimates that about one-third of all juvenile arrests involve interdepartmental handling of the case rather than juvenile court referral.[56]

These studies indicate that the police use a large amount of discretion in their decisions regarding juvenile offenders. Research generally shows that differential decision making goes on without clear guidance and uniformity.

Factors Affecting Police Discretion

How does a juvenile officer decide what to do about a child who is apprehended? As might be expected, the seriousness of the crime, the situation in which it occurred, and the legal record of the juvenile have been found to significantly effect decision making. Police are much more likely to take formal action if the crime is serious and has been reported by a victim who is a respected member of the community and if the offender is well known to them.[57] However, these factors are not the only ones that have been found to influence discretion. Some other important influences are discussed below.

The general environment in which the officer works effects the decision. For instance, some officers work in communities that tolerate a fair amount of personal freedom. In liberal environments, the police may be inclined to release children into the community rather than arrest them. Other officers may work in extremely conservative communities that expect a no-nonsense approach to police behavior. Here police may be more inclined to arrest a child.

The policies, practices, and customs of the local police department also provide a source of environmental influence. Juvenile officers may be pressured to make more arrests or to refrain from making arrests under certain circumstances. Directives and orders instruct officers to be alert to certain types of violations on the part of juveniles. The chief of police and political officials of a community might initiate policies governing the arrest practices of the juvenile department. For example, local merchants may complain that youths congregating in a shopping center's parking lot are inhibiting business. Police may be called on to make arrests in order to get the point across that loitering will not be tolerated. Under other circumstances, a more informal warning might be given. Similarly, a rash of deaths caused by teenage drunk driving may galvanize the local media to demand police action. The mayor and police chief, sensitive to possible voter dissatisfaction, may therefore demand that formal police action be taken in cases of drunk driving.

Another source of influence is the pressure that individual superiors, such as police supervisors, exert. The sergeant, for example, may initiate formal or informal directives regarding the handling of youths in a given community. Some supervising officers may believe that it is important to curtail disorderly conduct, drinking, or drug use. In addition, certain officers are influenced by the way their peers handle discretionary decision making.

A final environmental factor affecting the performance of officers is their perception of community alternatives to police intervention. Police officers may use arrest because they believe that nothing else can be done and that arrest is the best possible example of good police work. On the other hand, juvenile officers

may be apt to refer a large number of juveniles to social service agencies, particularly if they believe that a community has a variety of good resources.

Situational Influences

In addition to the environment, a variety of situational factors effect a police officer's decisions. Situational influences are those attached to a particular crime. It is difficult to identify every factor influencing police discretion, but a few stand out as having major significance. Studies show that police officers rely heavily on the demeanor of a child in making decisions. In other words, the child's attitude and appearance play a serious role in the decision-making process. Goldman discovered that community attitudes, political pressures, and the bias of the individual police officer may also influence whether an offender is arrested, taken into custody, or released.[58] Aaron Cicourel found that the decision to arrest is often based on information regarding the offender's overall demeanor, including dress, attitude, speech, and level of hostility toward the police.[59] Piliavin and Briar found that police perceptions of the attitudes of offenders toward the police, the law, and their own behavior were the most important factors in the decision to process or release an offender.[60]

Whether the decisions involve juvenile or adult offenders, most studies conclude that the following variables are important to decisions made by police officers:

- The attitude of the complainant
- The type and seriousness of the offense
- The race and sex of the offender
- The age of the offender

- The attitude of the offender
- The history of the offender's prior contacts with the police
- In the case of a child, the perceived willingness of the parents to assist in disciplining the child and solving the problem
- The setting or location in which the incident occurs
- In the case of a child, whether the child denies the actions or insists on a court hearing
- The likelihood that a child can be serviced by a referral agency in the community

Extralegal Factors Affecting Police Discretion: Race and Gender

Do police allow racial, gender, or class bias to affect their decisions on whether to arrest youths? There has actually been a great deal of debate over this very critical issue. Some experts believe that police decision making is deeply influenced by the offender's personal characteristics, while others maintain that crime-related variables are actually more significant.

One suspected source of police bias is racial discrimination. It has long been charged that police are more likely to act formally with black suspects and use their discretion to benefit whites.[61] However, clear-cut proof that police officers act in a generally biased fashion has not been established. A number of well-respected studies by Robert Terry, Donald Black, and Albert Reiss and by Richard Lundman found that police are more likely to take offense and demeanor into account than race.[62] Polite, respectful youths were more likely to get the benefit of police discretion, whether they were black or white, than youths who displayed a "bad attitude." These findings are supported by T. Edwin Black and Charles Smith's national assessment of juvenile justice processing, which found that there was no difference in the proportion of blacks and whites arrested and referred to court, regardless of the nature of the offense.[63] However, it should be noted that Black and Smith found that Hispanics and other racial or ethnic minority groups had a greater chance for court referral than either black or white youths.

Some research efforts do show that police discriminate against black youths, most notably studies conducted by Terence Thornberry, Dale Dannefer, and Russel Schutt and by Jeffrey Fagan and his associates.[64] However, even research supportive of police discrimination does not indicate that it is overt and unidimensional. For example, Fagan and his associates found that police are more likely to formally process minorities except for crimes of violence, where the pattern is reversed and Anglo offenders are referred to juvenile court at a higher rate.[65]

David Griswold states: "The preponderance, as well as the strength, of the evidence leans toward a view that the police do not discriminate against minorities and that factors other than race weigh most heavily in the police decision-making process."[66]

On the other hand, Donna Bishop and Charles Frazier find that race has a direct effect on decisions made at several processing junctures on the juvenile justice process.[67] Their recent research examines the effect of a juvenile's race in a cohort group of over 50,000 youths in a large southern city where decisions were made from intake to disposition. According to Bishop and Frazier, blacks are more likely to be recommended for formal processing, referred to court, adjudicated delinquent, and given harsher dispositions than comparable white youths. In the arrest category, specifically, being black increases the probability of formal police action by 11 percent.[68]

One of the most significant recent research efforts on differential processing of minorities is a report from the National Coalition of State Juvenile Justice Advisory Groups.[69] The report points out that minority youth, particularly blacks and Hispanics, are overrepresented at various stages of the juvenile justice system. The National Coalition suggests two possible explanations for this disparity; (1) differential rates in arrest, incarceration, and even release are the result of a racist system, and (2) the differential rates are the result of greater involvement by minorities in juvenile crime.[70] In either case, according to the report, in order to rectify this imbalance, there is an urgent need to alter the social structure of society by improving the educational system, creating more job opportunities, and providing more services for families. The report also recommends that the Office of Juvenile Justice and Delinquency Prevention examine police surveillance and apprehension procedures to determine why minority youths are at a greater risk of being handled differently and to reduce or eliminate any subtle discrimination that may exist in the early stages of the juvenile process.[71]

Obviously, some studies report evidence of race bias in police arrest and referral decisions while others do not. Further research is needed to document what appear to be findings of disproportional arrests of minority juvenile offenders.

There is also disagreement over police handling of female offenders. Some experts favor the **chivalry hypothesis,** which holds that police are more likely to act paternally toward young girls. Others believe that police may be *more* likely to arrest female offenders because their actions violate the police officer's cherished stereotypes of the female.

Research by Christy Visher shows that police take race and age into account when arresting females but that these factors are less important for male arrests.[72] Visher finds that chivalry does indeed play a role in female arrests: younger girls who do not meet police officers' role expectations are more likely to be arrested than their older, more contrite sisters. Meda Chesney-Lind has found that female status offenders may be the victims of police discrimination; she concluded that adolescent girls are often arrested for less serious offenses than boys.[73] Again, there is disagreement over the extent of police gender bias. Merry Morash found that young boys who engage in "typical" male delinquent activities are much more likely to develop police records than females.[74] And Black and Smith's national assessment study found that "the sex of the offender alone appears to have no influence on whether an offender, after being arrested, is referred to the court."[75] To a large degree, the current research findings seem to be inconclusive regarding the degree of differential treatment of females by the police in the juvenile justice system.

Organizational Bias

Even when police officers may not be discriminating on an individual level, the policies being used in some departments may result in biased law enforcement practices. Research conducted by a number of police experts, including Douglas Smith, has found that police departments can be characterized by their professionalism and degree of bureaucratization.[76] Departments that are highly bureaucratized and at the same time unprofessional are the ones most likely to be insulated from the community they serve (Smith labels these departments "militaristic"). According to Smith, isolation can result in the introduction into the social control process of bias toward minorities and the socially disadvantaged.

The direction of organizational policy may be fueled by the perceptions of police decision makers. A number of experts have found that law enforcement administrators have a stereotyped view of the urban poor as troublemakers who must be kept under control.[77] Consequently, lower-class neighborhoods experience much greater police scrutiny than middle-class areas, and their residents stand a proportionately greater chance of arrest and official processing.[78] Merry Morash concludes that if they fit the "common image"—for example, males, who hang with a tough crowd—youths significantly increase their chance of arrest and being officially labeled.[79]

This relationship has been explored in some important recent research. Robert Sampson, making use of both self-reports and official data, found that teenage residents of neighborhoods with low socioeconomic status had a significantly greater chance of acquiring police records than youths living in higher socioeconomic-status areas, regardless of the actual crime rates in these areas. Furthermore, Sampson found that this relationship held up after sex, individual income, race, gang membership, and delinquent peers were controlled.[80] When it came time to officially process arrested youth to the juvenile court, Sampson found that the decision was significantly related to the individuals' socioeconomic status.

This research indicates that while police officers may not discriminate on an individual level, departmental policy that focuses attention on lower-class areas may result in class and racial bias in the police processing of delinquent youth.

Considerations of race, economic status, or gender should not determine how the police exercise their authority.[81] Because the police retain a large degree of discretionary power, the ideal goal of nondiscrimination is often difficult to achieve in actual practice. However, the formulation and implementation of policy guidelines in the juvenile area eliminating bias and unfettered police discretion are not beyond our control.

Controlling Police Discretion

A number of leading organizations have suggested the use of guidelines to control police discretion. The American Bar Association (ABA) states, "Since individual police officers may make important decisions affecting police operations without direction, with limited accountability and without any uniformity within a department, police discretion should be structured and controlled."[82] The ABA noted further, "There is almost a unanimous opinion that steps must be taken to provide better control and guidance over police discretion in street and station house adjustments of juvenile cases."[83]

One of the leading exponents of police discretion is Kenneth Culp Davis, who has done much to raise the consciousness of criminal justice practitioners about discretionary decision making. Davis recommends controlling administrative discretion through (1) the use of statutorial definition, (2) the development of written policies, and (3) the recording of decisions by criminal justice personnel.[84] Narrowing the scope of juvenile codes, for example, would limit and redefine the broad authority police officers currently have to take children into custody for criminal and noncriminal behavior. Such practices would provide fair criteria for arrests, adjustment, and police referral of juvenile offenders and would help eliminate largely personal judgments based on the race, attitude, or demeanor of the juvenile. Discretionary decision making in juvenile police work can be understood by analysis of the following "Case in Point."

CASE IN POINT

You are a newly appointed police officer assigned to a juvenile unit of a medium size urban police department.

Wayne W. is a 14-year-old white boy who was caught shoplifting with two friends of the same age and sex. Wayne attempted to leave a large department store with a twelve-dollar shirt and was apprehended by a police officer in front of the store.

Wayne seemed quite remorseful about the offense. He said several times that he did not know why he did it and that he had not planned the act. He seemed upset and scared and, while admitting the offense, did not want to go to court.

Wayne had three previous contacts with the police: one for malicious mischief when he destroyed some property, another involving a minor assault of a boy, and a third involving another shoplifting charge. In all three cases, Wayne promised to refrain from ever committing such acts again, and as a result, he was not required to go to court. The other shoplifting involved a small baseball worth only three dollars.

Wayne appeared at the police department with his mother because his parents are divorced. She did not seem overly concerned about the case and felt that her son was not really to blame. She argued that he was always getting in trouble and she was not sure how to control him. She blamed most of his troubles with the law on his being in the wrong crowd.

The store had left matters in the hands of the police and would support their decision.

The other two boys did not steal anything and claimed that they had no idea that Wayne was planning anything when they entered the store. Neither had any criminal record.

Should Wayne be sent to court for trial? What other remedy might be appropriate?

POLICE WORK AND DELINQUENCY PREVENTION

If the police are to effectively provide services to children and enforce the law, they need to develop programs and relationships with social service systems. Then they can play an important role in implementing policies to control and prevent delinquency. Since the police decide what happens to a juvenile taken into custody, it is essential that they work closely with social service groups on a day-to-day basis. In addition the police need to assume a leadership role in identifying the needs of children in the community and helping the community provide for such needs. In helping develop **delinquency prevention** programs, the police need to work closely with such organizations as youth service bureaus, the schools, recreational facilities, welfare agencies, and employment programs.[85]

Using **community services** to deal with delinquent and nondelinquent children has many advantages. Such services allow children to avoid the stigma of being processed by a police agency. They also improve the community's awareness of the need to help children, and through involvement of local residents, they give a greater recognition to the complexity of the delinquent's problem, thus developing a sense of public responsibility and support for such programs. Another advantage of using community services is that they make it possible to restrict court referral by the police to cases involving serious crime.

One of the most important institutions playing a role in delinquency prevention is the school. Linking the school with the police in the community is one way to help prevent delinquency. Liaison programs between the police and the schools have been implemented in many communities throughout the United States. Liaison officers from schools and police departments have played a leadership role in developing recreational programs for juveniles. In some instances, they have actually operated such programs. In others, they have encouraged community support for recreational activities, including Little League baseball, athletic clubs, camping programs, police athletic programs, and scouting programs.

One prominent example of a successful police-community prevention effort is the privately funded **TOP program** in Rochester, New York. **TOP** stands for Teens on Patrol. Each summer, about one hundred youths are hired to patrol the city's parks and recreational areas. The young people help keep the parks "cool" and also learn a lot about police officers. A number of TOP graduates have gone on to become police officers.[86] As previously mentioned in chapter 12, the Focus on Delinquency entitled "Project DARE" describes a well-respected and effective effort by a local police department to prevent teenage drug abuse. DARE projects have been adopted by hundreds of police departments throughout the country.

COMMUNITY POLICING

One of the most important changes in American law enforcement is the emergence of the community policing model of crime prevention. This concept is based on the premise that police departments do not make efficient crime-fighting organizations when they operate independently. However, if they gain the trust and assistance of concerned citizens, they can carry out their duties more effectively. Therefore, the main police role should be to increase feelings of community safety and encourage area residents to cooperate with their local police agencies.[87]

Project DARE

Police departments around the country have been allocating resources to delinquency prevention programs. One of the most well known is **Project DARE** in Los Angeles. DARE, an acronym for Drug Abuse Resistance Education, is a joint project of the Los Angeles Police Department and the Los Angeles Unified School District. It is designed to equip elementary school children with the skill to resist peer pressure to take drugs. The program is carried out by experienced officers who bring their "street smarts" into the classroom. The curriculum they teach is organized into seventeen classroom sessions that are summarized below:

1. **Practices for personal safety.** The DARE officer reviews common safety practices to protect students from harm at home, on the way to and from school, and in the neighborhood.

2. **Drug use and misuse.** Students learn the harmful effects of misused drugs as depicted in a film, "Drugs and Your Amazing Mind."

3. **Consequences.** The focus is on the consequences of using or choosing not to use alcohol, marijuana, and other drugs. If students are aware of those consequences, they can make better informed decisions regarding their own behavior.

4. **Resisting pressures to use drugs.** The DARE officer explains different types of pressure that friends and others exert on students to get them to try alcohol or drugs, ranging from friendly persuasion and teasing to threats.

5. **Resistance techniques: ways to say no.** Students rehearse the many ways of refusing offers to try alcohol or drugs—simply saying "no" and repeating it as often as necessary; changing the subject; walking away or ignoring the person. They learn that they can avoid situations where they might be subjected to such pressure and can "hang around" with nonusers.

continued

The community policing model has been translated into a number of different policy initiatives. It has encouraged police departments around the country to get patrol officers out of patrol cars, where they were viewed as faceless strangers insulated from the community, and into the streets via **foot patrol.** Hundreds of experimental programs have been implemented around the country, and evaluation by the National Neighborhood Foot Patrol Center at Michigan State University indicates they are highly successful.[88]

In addition, the police have encouraged and worked with citizen groups to create neighborhood watch and crime prevention organizations. The Police Foundation, a nonprofit organization that conducts research on police issues, has reviewed such efforts in Houston and Newark and found them to be effective methods of increasing citizen cooperation.[89] One of the most well-known programs is the Philadelphia block watch program, which cooperates with the police in a number of different delinquency control and victim aid projects.[90]

In sum, there have been important efforts made by local police departments to involve citizens in the process of delinquency control. And while there is little clear-cut evidence that these efforts can lower crime rates, they seem to be effective methods of improving perceptions of community safety and the quality of community life while involving citizens in the wider juvenile justice network.[91]

6. **Building self-esteem.** Poor self-esteem is one of the factors associated with drug misuse. How the students feel about themselves results from positive and negative feelings and experiences. They learn to see their own positive qualities and discover ways to compliment others.

7. **Assertiveness: a response style.** Students have certain rights—to be themselves, to say what they think, to say no to offers of drugs. They must assert those rights confidently without also interfering with others' rights.

8. **Managing stress without taking drugs.** Students learn to recognize sources of stress in their lives and to develop techniques for avoiding or relieving it, including exercise, deep breathing, and talking to others. Using drugs or alcohol to relieve stress causes new problems.

9. **Media influences on drug use.** The DARE officer reviews strategies used in the media to encourage tobacco and alcohol use, including testimonials from celebrities and pressure to conform.

10. **Decision making and risk taking.** Students learn the difference between bad risks and reasonable risks, how to recognize the choices they have, and how to make a decision that promotes their self-interest.

11. **Alternatives to drug abuse.** Drug and alcohol use are not the only way to have fun, to be accepted by peers, or to deal with feelings of anger or hurt.

12. **Alternative activities.** Sports or other physical fitness activities are good alternatives. Exercise improves health and relieves emotional distress.

13. **Officer-planned lessons.** The class is spent on a special lesson devised by the DARE officer.

14. **Role modeling.** A high school student selected by the DARE officer visits the class, providing students with a positive role model. Students learn that drug users are in the minority.

15. **Project DARE summary.** Students summarize and assess what they have learned.

16. **Taking a stand.** Students compose and read aloud essays on how they can respond when they are pressured to use drugs and alcohol. The essay represents each student's "DARE Pledge."

17. **Assembly.** In a schoolwide assembly, planned in concert with school administrators, all students who participated in Project DARE receive certificates of achievement.

Source: William DeJong, "Project DARE: Teaching Kids to Say 'No' to Drugs and Alcohol," National Institute of Justice Reporter, *March 1986, pp. 1–5.*

SUMMARY

As society has become more complex and rates of delinquency and noncriminal behavior have soared, the police have become more important than ever to the juvenile justice system. It is almost always the police officer who has the initial contact with the large number of young people committing antisocial acts, so the importance of the juvenile police officer cannot be overemphasized.

Numerous factors influence the decisions that the police make about juvenile offenders. They include the seriousness of the offense, the harm inflicted on the victim, and the likelihood that the child will break the law again.

The recruitment, selection, and training of juvenile police officers is essential to good police organizations. Police work with children includes the legal aspects of arrest, custodial interrogation, and lineups. Through the *Miranda v. Arizona* decision, the U.S. Supreme Court established an affirmative procedure for custodial interrogation and police investigations. Such practices are applicable to juvenile suspects. Search and seizure procedures, lineups, and other police procedures are also subject to court review.

One important issue is police discretion in dealing with juvenile offenders. Discretion is a low-visibility decision made in the administration of adult and juvenile justice. Discretionary decisions are made without guidelines or policy statements from the police administrator. Discretion is essential in providing individualized justice, but such problems as discrimination, unfairness, and bias toward particular groups of children must be controlled.

KEY TERMS

community policing

juvenile officers

role conflicts

law enforcement

discretion

arrest

probable cause

search and seizure

New Jersey v. T.L.O.

Miranda v. Arizona

custodial interrogations

totality of the circumstances doctrine

Fare v. Michael C.

low-visibility decision making

chivalry hypothesis

delinquency prevention

community services

TOP program

Project "DARE"

foot patrol

QUESTIONS FOR DISCUSSION

1. The term *discretion* is often defined as selective decision making by police and others in the juvenile justice system who are faced with alternative modes of action. Discuss some of the factors affecting the discretion of the police when dealing with juvenile offenders.

2. What role should police organizations play in delinquency prevention and control? Is it feasible to expect police departments to provide social services to children and families? How should police departments be better organized to provide for the control of juvenile delinquency?

3. What qualities should a police juvenile officer have? Should a college education be a requirement?

4. In *New Jersey v. T.L.O.*, the Supreme Court held that prohibitions against illegal search and seizure apply to school as well as law enforcement officials. As a practical matter, will this decision give rise to overused safety and security measures in our school systems?

5. In light of the traditional and protective role assumed by law enforcement personnel in juvenile justice, is there any reason to have a *Miranda* warning for children taken into custody?

6. Can the police and community be truly effective in forming a partnership to reduce juvenile delinquency? Discuss the role of the juvenile police officer in preventing and investigating juvenile crime.

NOTES

1. Herman Goldstein, "Toward Community-Oriented Policing: Potential Basic Requirements and Threshold Questions," *Crime and Delinquency* 33:630 (1987).

2. Lawrence Sherman and Richard Berk, "The Specific Deterrent Effects of Arrest for Domestic Assault," *American Sociological Review* 49:261–72 (1984).

3. Craig Uchida and Robert Goldberg, *Police Employment and Expenditure Trends* (Washington, D.C.: Bureau of Government Statistics, 1986).

4. Donald Black and Albert J. Reiss, Jr., "Police Control of Juveniles," *American Sociological Review* 35:63 (1970); Richard Lundman, Richard Sykes, and John Clark, "Police Control of Juveniles: A Replication," *Journal of Research on Crime and Delinquency* 15:74 (1978).

5. American Bar Association, *Standards Relating to Police Handling of Juvenile Problems* (Cambridge, Mass. Ballinger, 1977), p. 1.

6. FBI,: *Uniform Crime Reports* 1989 (Washington, D.C.: U.S. Government Printing Office, 1988). Over 50 percent of police-juvenile contacts are referred to juvenile court.

7. For a discussion of police values and roles, see Michael Brown, *Working the Street: Police Discretion and the Dilemmas of Reform* (New York: Russell Sage, 1981).

8. Samuel Walker, *The Police in America* (New York: McGraw-Hill, 1983), p. 133.

9. R. Kobetz and B. Borsage, *Juvenile Justice Administration* (Gaithersburg, MD: IACO, 1973), p. 112.

10. See August Vollmer, *The Police and Modern Society* (Berkeley: University of California Press, 1936); O. W. Wilson, *Police Administration*, 2nd ed. (New York: McGraw-Hill, 1963).

11. National Advisory Commission on Criminal Justice Standards and Goals, *Task Force Report on Juvenile Justice and Delinquency Prevention* (Washington, D.C.: Law Enforcement Assistance Administration, 1976), p. 245.

12. *Ibid.*

13. Bernard Greenblatt, *Staff and Training for Juvenile Law Enforcement in Urban Police Departments*, Children's Bureau Publication 13 (Washington, D.C.: U.S. Government Printing Office, 1960).

14. National Advisory Commission on Criminal Justice Standards and Goals, *Task Force Report on Juvenile Justice and Delinquency Prevention*, p. 258.

15. American Bar Association, *Standards Relating to Police Handling of Juvenile Problems*, p. 109.

16. Linda Szymanski, *Summary of Juvenile Code Purpose Clauses* (Pittsburgh: National Center for Juvenile Justice, 1988); see also, for example, GA Code Ann. 15; Iowa Code Ann. 232.2; Mass. Gen. Laws, ch. 119, 56.

17. Samuel M. Davis, *Rights of Juveniles—The Juvenile Justice System* (New York: Clark-Boardmen Co. Ltd., revised June 1989), Sec. 3.3.

18. National Conference of Commissioners on Uniform State Laws, *Uniform Juvenile Court Act* (Chicago: National Conference on Uniform State Laws, 1968), Sec. 13.

19. *State v. Lowry,* 230 A.2d 907 (1967).

20. *Chimel v. Cal.,* 395 U.S. 752, 89 S.Ct. 2034 (1969).

21. *United States v. Ross,* 456 U.S. 798, 102 S.Ct. 2157 (1982).

22. *Terry v. Ohio,* 392 U.S.1, 88 S. Ct. 1868 (1968).

23. *Bumper v. North Carolina*, 391 U.S. 543, 88 S.Ct. 1788 (1968).

24. See, for example, *Vandenberg v. Superior Court,* 8 Cal.App.3d 1048, 87 Cal.Rptr. 876 (1970).

25. 469 U.S. 325 (1985).

26. *People v. Overton,* 24 N.Y.2d 522, 301 N.Y.S.2d 479, 249 N.E.2d 366 (1969).

27. 94 N.J. 331(1983).

28. *In re Donaldson,* 75 Cal.Rptr. 220 (1969); *People v. Bowers,* 77 Misc.2d 697, 356 N.Y.S.2d 432 (1974); *In re W.,* 29 Cal.App.3d 777, 105 Cal.Rptr. 775 (1973); *Comm. of Pa. v. Dingfelt,* 227 Pa.Supr.380, 323 A.2d 145 (1974).

29. See D. A. Walls, "New Jersey v. T.L.O.: The Fourth Amendment Applied to School Searches," *Oklahoma University Law Review 11* (1986):225–41; also Robert Shepherd, Jr., "Juvenile Justice—Search and Seizures Involving Juveniles," *American Bar Association Journal on Criminal Justice* 5:27–29 (1990).

30. K. A. Bucker, "School Drug Tests: A Fourth Amendment Perspective," *University of Illinois Law Review* 5 (1987):275.

31. See J. Hogan and M. Schwartz, "Search and Seizure in the Public Schools," *Case and Comment* 90 (1985): 28–32; see also M. Meyers, "T.L.O. v. New Jersey—Officially Conducted School Searches and a New Balancing Test," *Juvenile Family Journal* 37:27–37 (1986).

32. For an interesting article suggesting that school officials should not be permitted to search students without suspicion that each student searched has violated the drug or weapons law, see J. Braverman, "Public School Drug Searches," *Fordham Urban Law Journal* 14:629–84 (1986).

33. 384 U.S. 436, 86 S.Ct. 1602 (1966).

34. *Commonwealth v. Gaskins*, 471 Pa. 238, 369 A.2d 1285(1977); *In re E.T.C.*, 141 Vt. 375, 449 A.2d 937 (1982).

35. 67 Cal.2d 365, 62 Cal.Rptr. 586, 432 P.2d 202 (1967).

36. 399 F.2d 467 (5th Cir.1968).

37. 490 A.2d 295 (N.H.1985).

38. See, for example, *In re E.T.C.*, 141 Vt. 375, 449 A.2d 937 (1982).

39. 405 Mass. 497 (1989).

40. *Commonwealth v. McNeil*, 399 Mass. 71 (1987).

41. 442 U.S. 23, 99 S.Ct. 2560 (1979).

42. 453 U.S. 355, 101 S.Ct. 2806 (1981).

43. See, for example, Larry Holtz, "Miranda in A Juvenile Setting—A Child's Right to Silence," *Journal of Criminal Law and Criminology* 79:534–556 (1987).

44. 388 U.S. 218, 87 S.Ct. 1926 (1967).

45. 406 U.S. 682, 92 S.Ct. 1877 (1972).

46. 107 R.I. 615, 268 A.2d 723 (1970).

47. See Roscoe Pound, "Discretion, Dispensation, and Mitigation: The Problem of the Individual Special Case," *New York University Law Review* 35:936 (1960).

48. Kenneth C. Davis, *Discretionary Justice: A Preliminary Inquiry* (Baton Rouge: Louisiana State University Press, 1969); see also M. Ted Rubin, *Juvenile Justice: Police, Practice and Law* (Santa Monica, Calif.: Goodyear Publishing Co., 1979).

49. Joseph Goldstein, "Police Discretion Not to Invoke the Criminal Process: Low-Visibility Decisions in the Administration of Justice," *Yale Law Journal* 69:544 (1960).

50. Victor Streib, *Juvenile Justice in America* (Port Washington, N.Y.: Kennikat, 1978).

51. Herbert Packer, *The Limits of the Criminal Sanction* (Palo Alto, Calif.: Stanford University Press, 1968).

52. See Paul Strasburg, *Violent Delinquents: Report to Ford Foundation from Vera Institute of Justice* (New York: Monarch, 1978), p. 11; see also Robert Terry, "The Screening of Juvenile Offenders," *Journal of Criminal Law, Criminology, and Police Science* 58:173–81 (1967).

53. Nathan Goldman, *The Differential Selection of Juvenile Offenders for Court Appearance* (Washington, D.C.: National Council on Crime and Delinquency, 1963).

54. Irving Piliavin and Scott Briar, "Police Encounters with Juveniles," *American Journal of Sociology* 70:206–14 (1964); Theodore Ferdinand and Elmer Luchterhand, "Inner-City Youth, the Police, Juvenile Court, and Justice," *Social Problems* 8:510–26 (1970).

55. Black and Reiss, "Police Control of Juveniles"; see also Richard J. Lundman, "Routine Police Arrest Practices," *Social Problems* 22:127–41 (1974).

56. FBI, *Uniform Crime Reports, 1989*, p. 240.

57. Douglas Smith and Christy Visher, "Street-Level Justice: Situational Determinants of Police Arrest Decisions," *Social Problems* 29:167–78 (1981).

58. Goldman, *The Differential Selection of Juvenile Offenders*, p. 25; Norman Werner and Charles Willie, "Decisions of Juvenile Officers," *American Journal of Sociology* 77:199–214 (1971).

59. See Aaron Cicourel, *The Social Organization of Juvenile Justice* (New York: Wiley, 1968).

60. Piliavin and Briar, "Police Encounters with Juveniles," p. 215.

61. Dale Dannefer and Russel Schutt, "Race and Juvenile Justice Processing in Police and Court Agencies," *American Journal of Sociology* 87:1113–32 (1982); Smith and Visher, "Street-Level Justice: Situational Determinants of Police Arrest Decisions."

62. Terry, "The Screening of Juvenile Offenders;" Black and Reiss, "Police Control of Juveniles;" Lundman, "Routine Police Arrest Practices."

63. T. Edwin Black and Charles Smith, *A Preliminary National Assessment of the Numbers and Characteristics of Juveniles Processed in the Juvenile Justice System* (Washington, D.C.: U.S. Government Printing Office, 1980), p. 39.

64. Terence Thornberry, "Race, Socioeconomic Status, and Sentencing in the Juvenile Justice System," *Journal of Criminal Law and Criminology* 70:164–71 (1979); Dannefer and Schutt, "Race and Juvenile Justice Processing in Court and Police Agencies"; Jeffrey Fagan, Ellen Slaughter, and Eliot Hartstane, "Blind Justice? The Impact of Race on the Juvenile Justice Process," *Crime and Delinquency* 33:224–58 (1987).

65. Fagan, Slaughter, and Hartstane, "Blind Justice? The Impact of Race on the Juvenile Justice Process," pp. 237–38.

66. David Griswold, "Police Discrimination: An Elusive Question," *Journal of Police Science and Administration* 6:65–66 (1978).

67. Donna M. Bishop and Charles E. Frazier, "The Influence of Race in Juvenile Justice Processing," *Journal of Research in Crime and Delinquency* 25:242–261 (1988).

68. *Ibid.*, p. 258.

69. National Coalition of State Juvenile Justice Advisory Groups, *A Delicate Balance* (Bethesda, Md.: National Coalition of State Juvenile Justice Advisory Groups, 1989).

70. *Ibid.*, p. 4.

71. *Ibid.*, p. 2. While not specifically dealing with juveniles, the issue of differential processing for young black males is addressed in the following recent study that found that nearly one of every four black men in their

twenties is caught up in the criminal justice system: Marc Mauer, *Young Black Men and the Criminal Justice System* (Washington, D.C.: The Sentencing Project, 1990).

72. Christy Visher, "Arrest Decisions and Notions of Chivalry," *Criminology* 21:5–28 (1983).

73. Meda Chesney-Lund, "Judicial Enforcement of the Female Sex Role: The Family Court and Female Delinquency Issues" *Criminology* 8:51–71 (1973); Chesney-Lund, "Young Women in the Arms of Law," in L. Bowker, *Women, Crime and the Criminal Justice System*, 2nd ed. (Lexington, Mass.: Lexington Books, 1978).

74. Merry Morash, "Establishment of a Juvenile Record The Influence of Individual and Peer Group Characteristics," *Criminology* 22:97–112 (1984).

75. Black and Smith, *Juveniles Processed in the Juvenile Justice System*, p. 37.

76. Douglas Smith, "The Organizational Context of Legal Control," *Criminology* 22:19–38 (1984); see also Charles Swanson, "The Influence of Organization and Environment on Arrest Practices in Major U.S. Cities," *Policy Studies* 7:390–98 (1978).

77. John Irwin, *The Jail: Managing the Underclass in American Society* (Berkeley: University of California Press, 1985).

78. Merry Morash, "Establishment of a Juvenile Record: The Influence of Individual and Peer Group Characteristics," *Criminology* 22:97–112 (1984).

79. *Ibid.*

80. Robert Sampson, "Effects of Socioeconomic Context of Official Reaction to Juvenile Delinquency," *American Sociological Review* 51:876–85 (1986).

81. Institute of Judicial Administration and American Bar Association, Juvenile Justice Standards Project, *Standards Relating to Police Handling of Juvenile Problems*, (Cambridge, Mass.: Ballinger Publishing Co., 1977), Standard 2.1.

82. American Bar Association, *Standards of Criminal Justice: Standards Relating to Urban Police Function* (New York: Institute of Judicial Administration, 1972), Standard 4.2, p. 121.

83. *Ibid.*, p. 45.

84. Kenneth C. Davis, *Police Discretion* (St. Paul: West Publishing Co., 1975).

85. Sherwood Norman, *The Youth Service Bureau—A Key to Delinquency Prevention* (Hackensack, N.J.: National Council on Crime and Delinquency, 1972), p. 8.

86. Karin Lipson, "Cops and TOPS: A Program for Police and Teens That Works," *Police Chief* 49:45–46 (1982).

87. For an analysis of this position, see George Kelling and James Q. Wilson, "Broken Windows: The Police and Neighborhood Safety," *Atlantic Monthly* 249:29–38 (1982).

88. Robert Trojanowicz and Hazel Harden, *The Status of Contemporary Community Policing Programs* (East Lansing, Mich.: Michigan State University Neighborhood Foot Patrol Center, 1985).

89. Police Foundation, *The Effects of Police Fear Reduction Strategies: A Summary of Findings from Houston and Newark* (Washington, D.C.: Police Foundation, 1986).

90. Peter Finn, "Block Watches Help Crime Victims in Philadelphia," *NIJ Reports*, December 1986, pp. 2–10.

91. U.S. Department of Justice, Office of Juvenile Justice and Delinquency Prevention and NCCD, *The Impact of Juvenile Court Intervention* (San Francisco: NCCD, 1987).

16 Pretrial Procedures

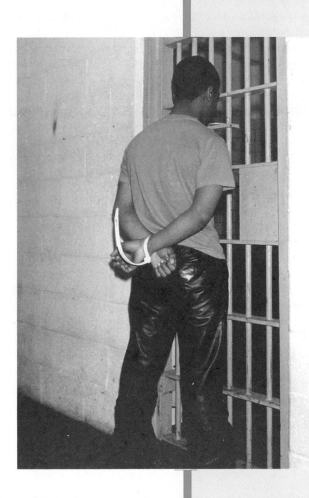

One of the most important stages in the juvenile process is the time between the child's arrest and adjudicatory hearing. After the juvenile has been taken into police custody, decisions as to the disposition of the case need to be made under police and judicial discretionary authority. By this point, the child has been informed of his or her right to counsel and right to remain silent during questioning. In addition, the child's parents have probably been notified. At this time, the child may be faced with involuntary placement in a detention or shelter care facility. Detention, even if only for a short period, may have a serious effect on the child. For children who are confined unnecessarily, it may contribute to future antisocial and delinquent behavior.

During this period, the child either retains an attorney or is assigned counsel by the court. In addition to detention, the juvenile, the family, and the attorney must also consider diversion, bail, plea bargaining, and, in serious cases, transfer of the child to adult court. The family may seek to work with the police department and the courts to avoid formal judicial proceedings and to get help through a diversion program. Or after an interview, the intake probation officer in the court may recommend that no further action be taken against the juvenile. Alternatively, the juvenile might be supervised by the intake section of the court without a judicial determination.

If the decision is to file a petition initiating formal judicial action against the juvenile, the child's attorney will seek pretrial release through bail or some other release measure and possibly enter into plea-bargaining discussions.

Thus, the period between arrest and adjudication is one of the most critical points in the juvenile justice system. Because the steps in this process are so important, this chapter will examine how the child is handled during this period. First, we will look at the detention system, which takes children out of the community before either their adjudication, disposition, or treatment. Then we discuss intake in the juvenile court. Intake procedures serve as a means of screening and diverting certain juvenile offenders from juvenile proceedings. Lastly, the chapter will examine bail and plea bargaining for children, diversion, and waiver to the adult court.

THE CONCEPT OF DETENTION

Detention is the temporary care of children in physically restricted facilities pending court disposition or transfer to another agency.[1] Traditional detention facilities for children are designed as secure environments. The approximately five hundred secure detention facilities operating around the United States have locked doors, high fences or walls, screen or bars, and other obstructions designed to prevent detainees from leaving the facility at will.

Detention facilities of this kind normally handle juveniles at different stages of the juvenile justice process. Some juveniles are kept in detention to await their court hearings. Others have had a trial but have not been sentenced or are awaiting the imposition of their sentences. A third group of children are those whose sentences have been imposed but who are awaiting admittance to a correctional training school. Thus, as the American Bar Association states, "the term 'pre-trial detainee' is inaccurate to describe the many juveniles in detention whose cases have already been adjudicated but whose disposition remains unimplemented."[2]

There are other types of residential care programs that should be distinguished from detention. **Shelter care,** for example, is the temporary care of children in physically unrestricting facilities. The secure detention facility is normally used for children who have been charged with delinquent acts. Shelter care programs, including receiving homes, group homes, foster care homes, and temporary care facilities, are normally used for dependent and neglected children and status offenders who may be runaways or truants or who are often the victims of sexual and physical abuse.[3]

Regardless of its form, detention should not be viewed as a form of punishment. A juvenile is normally not a sentenced offender when placed in detention. In other words, a detention facility is not to be used as a permanent correctional facility. It provides temporary care for children who require secure custody.

Most experts in juvenile justice advocate that detention be limited to alleged delinquent offenders who require secure custody for the protection of themselves and others. In the past, however, children who were neglected and dependent, as well as status offenders, were placed in secure detention facilities. To remedy this situation, there has been an ongoing national effort to remove status offenders and neglected children from detention facilities that also house juvenile delinquents. In addition, alternatives to detention centers—for example, temporary foster homes, detention boarding homes, and programs of neighborhood supervision—have been developed in numerous jurisdictions. They enable youths to live in private homes while the courts dispose of their cases. New types of residential facilities also are being created. Young persons who cannot return home are being held in dormitories and multiple-resident dwellings.[4] Efforts have also been made to improve services in existing secure detention facilities. Such programs as reception and diagnosis, community contact involving legal services and family visiting, and counseling, recreational, and educational services are important aspects of secure detention in some jurisdictions.

In 1975, about 11,000 youths were housed in detention centers on a given day. Despite ten years of effort to curb the use of detention, about 15,000 youths were in detention centers on a given day in 1985. There were also about 400,000 admissions to detention facilities during that year.

Since 1985, the number of youth held in short-term detention facilities has *increased* by about 15 percent, or over 17,000 children! In addition, there has been more than a 30-percent increase in the number of minority children (blacks and Hispanics) held in detention facilities, and this has caused considerable concern to juvenile justice practitioners.[5] (See Figure 16.1.)

Today about one-third of all young arrestees are held in a secure detention facility at some point between referral to court intake and case disposition. While 38 percent of the youth committing person, drug, and public order crimes were held in a secure facility, only 30 percent of property offenders were securely detained. Juveniles charged with property offenses, therefore, were the least likely to be detained.[6] (See Figure 16.2.) Disturbingly, 18 percent of all status offenders were held in secure detention. Runaways were the most likely group to be detained (34 percent), while only 20 percent of children charged with ungovernability and 10 percent of those charged with truancy required secure detention.[7] (See Figure 16.3.)

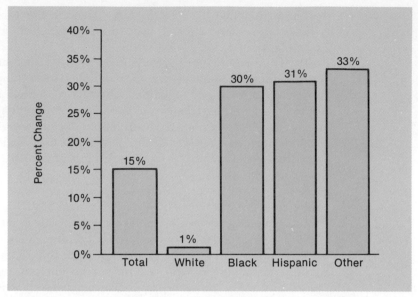

Source: "Growth in Minority Detentions Attributed to Drug Law Violators," *Juvenile and Family Court Newsletter,* vol. 20 (Reno, Nev.: National Court of Juvenile and Family Court Judges, 1990).

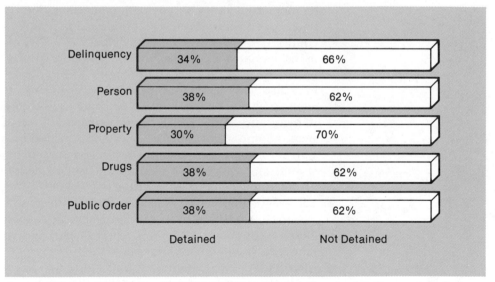

Source: H. Snyder, T. Finnegan, E. Nimick, M. Sickmund, D. Sullivan, and N. Tierney, *Juvenile Court Statistics, 1985* (Pittsburgh: National Center for Juvenile Justice, 1989).

These national and local increases are occurring at a time when the population of juvenile offenders is decreasing. Experts believe the steady increase in detention use may result from (1) a rise in serious crime by juveniles; (2) a growing link to drug-related crimes; and (3) the involvement of younger children in the juvenile justice system.[8]

Thus, detention of youth continues to be a major issue in the juvenile justice system and reducing its use has not been an easy task.

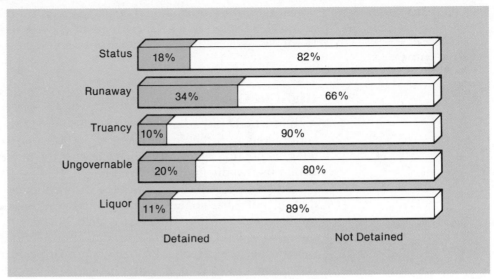

Status	18%	82%
Runaway	34%	66%
Truancy	10%	90%
Ungovernable	20%	80%
Liquor	11%	89%
	Detained	Not Detained

Source: H. Snyder, T. Finnegan, E. Nimick, M. Sickmund, D. Sullivan, and N. Tierney, *Juvenile Court Statistics, 1985*, (Pittsburgh: National Center for Juvenile Justice, 1989).

Preadjudication Detention

The majority of children taken into custody by the police are released to their parents or guardians. Some are detained overnight in a detention facility until their parents can be notified of the arrest. Police officers normally take a child to a place of detention only after other alternatives have been tried. Many juvenile courts in large urban areas have staff members, such as intake probation officers, on duty twenty-four hours a day to screen detention admissions.

Ordinarily, children who are apprehended for juvenile delinquency are detained if they are inclined to run away while awaiting their trials, if it appears that they will commit an offense dangerous to themselves or the community, or if they are violators from other jurisdictions. For example, in an analysis of detention decisions in a single county in Alabama, Belinda McCarthy found that juveniles were indeed being detained because they were a threat to the community, because their own safety was endangered, and because they tended to commit more serious crimes; offender race, class, and gender did not play a role in detention decision making.[9]

However, the criteria used in deciding whether a child should be placed in detention are far from clear; each jurisdiction handles detention decisions differently. In fact, a recent study by Charles Frazier and Donna Bishop employing data on all juveniles processed in a single state over a two-year period failed to uncover any pattern that could help explain how detention decisions were made.[10] Frazier and Bishop concluded that detention decisions were based solely on judicial discretion. Similarly, a recent study of New York State's Juvenile Offender Law in Westchester County, New York, also concluded that detention decisions lack the clearly defined statutory criteria needed to reduce the number of youths admitted to secure detention facilities.[11]

Today, many courts are striving to implement the recommendations of the National Council on Crime and Delinquency and other standard-setting groups that suggest that youth should be detained only if they are (1) likely to commit a new offense, (2) present a danger to themselves or the community, or (3) are likely to run away or fail to appear at subsequent court hearings.[12]

Right to Detention Hearings

A child who is placed in a detention facility or shelter care unit should not be kept there longer than twenty-four hours. Most jurisdictions require the filing of a formal petition against the child invoking the jurisdiction of the juvenile court within the twenty-four-hour period.

To detain a juvenile, there must be clear evidence of probable cause to believe that the child has committed the offense and that he or she will flee the area if not detained. Furthermore, once a child has been detained and a petition filed, the child should not continue in detention without a **detention hearing**.[13] Although the requirements for detention hearings vary considerably among the states, most jurisdictions require that they occur almost immediately after the child's admission to a detention facility and provide the youth with notice and counsel.[14]

The probation department of the juvenile court may help the judge decide whether or not to keep a child in detention when the police file a petition. Usually a probation officer in the intake department assists the court in making a decision about the child's release.

In sum, the ultimate decision to detain or release depends on the nature of the children's actions, whether they are a danger to themselves or others, and whether their parents or lawful guardians can be reached quickly to take them home. If children are to be kept longer than twenty-four hours, a formal petition must be filed against them and their parents must be notified so the children can possibly be released in their custody.

Detention Problems

Detention has long been criticized because it entails placing children who have not yet been found to be delinquent in an often harsh environment that is more often than not lacking in any rehabilitative services. As one national survey of detention conditions put it: "the custody was a matter of lock and key, and the instructive experience was more the exception than the rule. . . . Repeatedly, detention emerged as a form of punishment without conviction—and often without crime."[15]

In addition, critics charge that the discretion used when selecting youths for detention often works against the poor and minorities. A recent study by the Humphrey Institute of Public Affairs found that minority youths are placed in secure detention facilities at a rate three to four times higher than white youths; during the three-year period studied (1979 to 1982), the overrepresentation became increasingly more pronounced.[16] Other researchers also report that differential detention rates are produced by economic, family, and community forces. For example, of almost 2,500 cases taken from the juvenile court records of six New Jersey counties, researchers Russell Schutt and Dale Dannefer found that detention decisions favor protecting some classes of juveniles rather than ensuring them due process.[17] For example, black and Hispanic juveniles were quite likely to be detained even if they lived with two parents, white juveniles were subject to detention if they lived with one parent only.

New Approaches to Detention

There have been ongoing efforts to improve the process of detention and to better detention conditions. The Juvenile Detention Committee of the American Correctional Association has developed standards for detention that establish fair and uniform positive expectations for its use. These standards state that:

> "Juvenile detention is the temporary and secure custody of children accused or adjudicated of conduct subject to the jurisdiction of the family/juvenile court who require a physically restricting environment for their own or the community's protection while pending legal action. Further, juvenile detention should provide and maintain a wide range of helpful services that include, but are not limited to, the following: education, visitation, private communications, counseling, continuous supervision, medical and health care, nutrition, recreation, and reading. To advise the court on the proper course of action required to restore the child to a productive role in the community, detention should also include or provide a system for clinical observation and diagnosis that compliments the wide range of helpful services.[18]

Some evidence indicates that preadjudicatory facilities are meeting this goal. The consensus of professional opinion today is that juvenile detention centers should be reserved for those youth who present a clear and substantial threat to the community. As a result, attention is being focused on the development of new approaches to detention care, such as day resource centers, detention alternative programs, and family shelters.[19] In Tennessee and Michigan, for example, nonsecure holdover facilities are being used to service juveniles for a limited period. In Utah, special intake programs are used to screen children to locate more secure housing whenever possible.

In addition, many pretrial detention centers are providing extensive education programs. The Spofford Juvenile Center in the Bronx, New York, is the only

There have been attempts to improve detention. This is an artist's rendering of the recently constructed Judge Enrique H. Peña Juvenile Justice Center in El Paso, Texas designed by architect Mervin Moore. The facility houses administrative offices, 64 private rooms, a gymnasium, a library, a processing evaluation center, and a halfway house.

MERVIN MOORE ARCHITECT

EL PASO COUNTY JUVENILE JUSTICE CENTER

pretrial detention center in New York with an educational program approved by the state.[20] The center's instructional program includes a five-and-a-half-hour day, with a curriculum of reading and language arts, math, social studies, science, health and safety education, library skills, physical education, art, and music. Because students remain in detention for varying lengths of stay, the curriculum is organized in short modules so that students whose stays are brief can still complete a body of work. The Los Patrinos Juvenile Hall School in Downey, California, also operates with a highly transient population. Yet, it has been successful in offering comprehensive instruction in basic academic subjects and technological and functional living skills. It emphasizes helping students to develop positive self-concepts and improved relationships with others.[21] In New Hampshire, young people spend an average of twenty-one days in the ADC (Awaiting Disposition of the Court) Unit. The unit's on-site educational program employs a nontraditional, holistic learning approach designed to generate student opinions, cultivate discussions, and stimulate responses. The prime curriculum variable is the "Weekly Theme." Several educational themes or modules have been designed both to provide factual information and to promote student discussions on a variety of topics, including U.S. history, basic psychology, and family problems.[22]

Undoubtedly, juveniles pose special detention problems. But some efforts are being made to improve programs and reduce pretrial detention use, especially in secure settings. Of all the problems associated with detention, however, none is as critical as the issue of placing youths in adult jails, a practice that is addressed in the following section.

Detention in Adult Jails

One of the most significant problems with detention is placing youngsters under 18 in adult jails. This is usually done in rural areas where no other facility exists. Almost all experts in the field of juvenile justice agree that placing children under the age of 18 in any type of jail facility should be prohibited. Juveniles in adult jails can become the victims of other inmates, of the staff, and of their own hands.[23]

The placement of juveniles in jails is also particularly distressing when the sorry state of the nation's jails is considered. Juveniles detained in adult jails often live in squalid conditions and are subjected to physical and sexual abuse. A federally sponsored study found that children confined in adult institutions were eight times as likely to commit suicide as those placed in detention centers exclusively for juveniles and have a 4.5 percent higher rate of suicide than children in the general population.[24] Over the years, jails have been the least progressive of all correctional institutions in the United States. Most jails were constructed in the nineteenth century; few have been substantially improved in the twentieth century, and many are in poor physical condition. Many jails throughout the nation are overcrowded, have no rehabilitation programs, provide little or no medical attention, and make no effort to provide adequate plumbing, ventilation, or heating. Many are fire hazards. Courts throughout the nation have ruled that conditions in certain jails make incarceration there a cruel and unusual punishment, a violation of the Eighth and Fourteenth Amendments to the U.S. Constitution. Regardless of the conditions, the argument can be made that jailing juveniles with adults must be viewed as cruel and unusual punishment, considering their status.

Until recently, the placement of juveniles in adult facilities was common. According to a study by the Community Research Center at the University of Illinois, 479,000 juveniles were admitted to adult jails in 1979. Of these, 20 percent were status offenders whose "crimes" included running away or underage drinking. Some 4 percent (over 19,000 youths) were jailed without having committed an offense of any sort; 9 percent were 13 years old or less.[25]

REMOVING YOUTHS FROM ADULT JAILS. The impetus for removing juveniles from adult jails comes from the Office of Juvenile Justice and Delinquency Prevention (OJJDP).[26] According to federal guidelines, all juveniles in state custody must be separated from adult offenders or the state will face a cutoff of federal juvenile justice funds. The OJJDP defines separation as the condition in which juvenile detainees have either totally independent facilities or shared facilities that are designed so that juveniles and adults neither have accidental contact nor share programs or treatment staff.[27]

There has been much debate about whether the initiative to remove juveniles from adult jails has succeeded. It is still not known how many youths are being held in adult facilities. Some indications are that the numbers have declined significantly from the almost half a million a year recorded in 1979. Today, federal agencies estimate that about 1,500 juveniles are being held in adult jails on any given day and about 50,000 are held in adult jails or lockups some time during the year; about 30 states are in substantial (75 percent) compliance with federal guidelines.[28]

Despite such assurances, these figures do not include youths held in urban jails for under six hours or in rural ones for under twenty-four hours, youths transferred to the criminal court, youths in four states that do not cooperate with the federal jail removal initiative, or youths in states that consider anyone over 16 or 17 to be an adult. The Community Research Center in Champaign, Illinois, which monitors the jailing of delinquent youths, believes that a more accurate estimate is that about 200,000 youths are still being jailed with adults each year.[29] Other researchers, on the other hand, still believe that close to half a million youths are detained in adult preadjudicatory facilities (jails or lockups) each year.[30] National trends in juvenile detention rates suggests that the actual number of detainees may have occasionally decreased over the last decade, but the length of time juveniles are held in jails and other secure facilities has increased.

Eliminating the confinement of juveniles in adult institutions continues to be a difficult and ongoing task. In a recent comprehensive study of the jailing of juveniles in Minnesota, Ira Schwartz found that even in a state recognized nationally for juvenile justice reform, the rate of admission of juveniles to adult jails remains unacceptably high.[31] His research also revealed that while the rate of admission was not related to the *seriousness* of the offense, minority youth spent greater amounts of time in jail for the same offenses than white offenders.[32]

In his report, Schwartz suggests: (1) that government enact legislation prohibiting the confinement of juveniles in jail; (2) that appropriate juvenile detention facilities be established; (3) that funds be allocated for such programs; (4) that racial disparity in detention be examined; and (5) that responsibility for monitoring conditions of confinement be fixed by statutes and court decisions.[33]

There are some promising trends. California, for example, passed legislation ensuring that no minor under juvenile court jurisdiction can be incarcerated in any jail after July 1, 1989.[34] And in the recent landmark federal court case, *Hendrickson v. Griggs*, the court found that the state of Iowa had not complied with the juvenile jail removal mandate of the Juvenile Justice and Delinquency Prevention Act and ordered local officials to develop a plan for bringing the state into conformity with the law.[35] As a result, states will face increasing legal pressure to meet jail removal requirements in the future.

Because the actual number of juvenile detainees in adult jails is uncertain, it remains a difficult job to monitor progress in this area. With federal help, however, there appears to be some progress in removing juveniles from adult facilities, but thousands each year continue to be held in close contact with adults, and thousands more are held in facilities that, though physically separate, put them in close proximity to adults. To the youths held within their walls, there may appear to be little difference between the juvenile detention facilities and the adult jail.

DEINSTITUTIONALIZATION OF STATUS OFFENDERS

One of the most important juvenile justice policy initiatives of the past two decades has been the removal of status offenders from secure detention facilities that also house delinquents. Along with removing all juveniles from adult jails, the OJJDP has made deinstitutionalization of status offenders a cornerstone of its policy.

The purpose of removing status offenders from secure detention facilities is both to reduce their interface and personal relationships with serious delinquent offenders and to insulate them from the stigma and negative labels associated with being a detainee in a locked facility. **Deinstitutionalization** has its roots in labeling theory, which views the experience of being labeled a delinquent as a primary cause of delinquent careers, and the conflict perspective, which holds that those chosen for sanctions will most likely be social and political outcasts. To counteract the effects of labeling, stigma, and delinquent learning opportunities, nonsecure alternatives—counseling, after-school programs, shelter care, and foster care—have been developed for nondelinquent youths.

The national effort seems to be paying some important dividends. In 1977, 4,916 status offenders were in some sort of public secure confinement; in 1979, this number dropped to 2,789. Since then, the number of status offenders still being held in some sort of secure confinement has remained stable at approximately 2,500.

Evaluating Deinstitutionalization

Over a decade ago, the OJJDP funded a national **Deinstitutionalization of Status Offenders Project (DSO)** to demonstrate the feasibility of removing status offenders from secure lockups and to evaluate the effects of deinstitutionalization. Eight sites were tested: Spokane and Clark Counties in Washington, Alameda County in California, Pima County in Arizona, and the states of Delaware, Connecticut, Illinois, and South Carolina. In addition to local evaluation, a comprehensive national evaluation was conducted by Solomon Kobrin and Malcolm Klein.[36]

Since their inception, the DSO programs netted mixed results. One problem was the definition of status offenders. Some areas limited their programs to "pure" status offenders, who had no record of prior delinquency involvement, while others included "mixed offenders," those with a record of prior delinquency. The evaluation found that the pure status offender was relatively rare; most current status offenders had prior delinquent experiences. Another problem was "net widening." Because a new program was available, police were more willing to send youths to the juvenile court rather than handle the case themselves. Thus, the number of youths processed to court *increased* in a number of cities, impeding the antilabeling, antistigma aspects of the program.

Another problem was uncovered by M. A. Bortner, Mary Sutherland, and Russ Winn, who examined a midwestern community before and after it attempted to comply with deinstitutionalization of status offenders. One disappointing finding was that there was very little overall change in the processing of status offenders. Of greater concern was the fact that black status offenders were detained more often that whites and that their detention rates actually increased after the DSO effort had been implemented. On a more positive note, the researchers found that after the deinstitutionalization effort was undertaken, the use of formal hearings and severe dispositions for both black and white youths dropped substantially.[37]

Anne Schneider has conducted the most comprehensive evaluation of DSO programs on a national level. She found that the DSO programs were successful overall in significantly reducing—but not eliminating—the number of status offenders held in secure detention and the number of status offenders institutionalized after trial. However, the recidivism rate was unaffected by the DSO project, and in some sites, it actually increased. That is, status offenders placed in nonsecure facilities, separate from delinquents, were sometimes more likely to commit repeat offenses than those held in secure detention centers.[38]

This finding suggests that removing status offenders from detention is not a panacea for preventing juvenile crime. While removal did not reduce crime, however, it was as effective as secure detention. Because shelter and foster care is much less expensive than maintaining a secure detention facility, removal at least can be a more cost-effective juvenile justice policy.

THE INTAKE PROCESS

When the police believe a child needs a court referral, they become involved in the intake division of the court. The term **intake** refers to the screening of cases by the juvenile court system. The child and his or her family are screened by intake officers, who are often probation staff members, to determine whether the child needs the services of the juvenile court. Intake officers may (1) send the youth home with no further action, (2) divert the child to a social agency, (3) petition him or her to the juvenile court, (4) file a petition and hold the child in detention.[39] The intake process reduces demands on limited court resources, screens out cases that are not within the court's jurisdiction, and obtains assistance from community agencies when court authority is not necessary for referral.[40]

Juvenile court intake is now provided for by statute in the majority of states.[41] Also, most of the model acts and standards in juvenile justice suggest the development of juvenile court intake proceedings.[42]

Intake procedures are desirable for the following reasons:

■ Filing complaints against children in a court may do more harm than good, because rehabilitation often fails in the juvenile court system.

■ Processing children in the juvenile court labels them delinquent, stigmatizes them, and thus reinforces their antisocial behavior.

■ Nonjudicial handling of children gives them and their families an opportunity to work with a voluntary social service agency.

■ Intake screening of children helps conserve already overburdened resources in the juvenile court system.

■ Intake screening allows juvenile courts to enter into consent decrees with juveniles without filing petitions and without formal adjudication. (The consent decree is basically a court order authorizing disposition of the case without a formal finding of delinquency. It is based on an agreement between the intake department of the court and the juvenile who is the subject of the complaint.)[43]

Notwithstanding all of its advantages, intake also has some problems. First, because half of all juveniles who are arrested and brought to court are handled nonjudicially, intake sections are constantly pressured to provide available services for a large group of children. Intake programs also need to be provided twenty-four hours a day in many urban courts so dispositions can be resolved quickly on the day the child is referred to court. Second, poorly qualified employees in intake are a serious flaw in many court systems.

A third problem is that although almost three-quarters of all state juvenile court systems provide intake and diversion programs, the criteria and procedures for selecting children for such nonjudicial alternatives have not been established. Normally, the intake probation officer undertakes a preliminary investigation to obtain information about the child and the family prior to making a decision. Written guidelines are needed to assist intake personnel in their duties and to alert juveniles and their families to their procedural rights. Some jurisdictions have attempted to provide guidelines for intake decision-making. Those used in New York to determine whether a juvenile case is suitable for adjustment or whether court jurisdiction should be invoked include: (1) age of the child; (2) conduct; (3) prior or pending juvenile complaints; (4) the substantial likelihood that the child will cooperate with the adjustment process; (5) and the substantial likelihood that the child can receive and is in need of appropriate services without court intervention.[44]

Finally, a number of legal problems are associated with the intake process. Among them are whether the child has a right to counsel at this stage, whether the child is protected against self-incrimination at intake, and to what degree the child needs to consent to nonjudicial disposition as recommended by the intake probation officer.

Changing the Intake Process

Since the intake process is so critical, it has been undergoing changes in various jurisdictions. One important trend in the intake process has been the influence of prosecutors on decision making. The traditional intake process was controlled by probation personnel whose decisions influenced heavily the presiding juvenile court judge's concept of which cases should be handled formally and which should be settled without court action.

The traditional role of intake, which has been to dispense the least incursive amount of rehabilitative justice, is being replaced in some jurisdictions by a prosecutor who may be more concerned with protecting the public and controlling offenders. Some states, such as Florida, now require that the intake officers get approval from the prosecutor before either accepting or rejecting a delinquency petition. Other states, such as Maryland and California, allow the complaining party to appeal petitions rejected by intake officers to the prosecutor, while in Colorado and Washington, prosecutorial screening of cases eliminates any significant probation intake role.[45]

The county's chief legal officer, the district attorney, is now playing a greater role in the juvenile court process. There is evidence of a shift from the rehabilitation model to the due process approach in juvenile justice. As Ted Rubin puts it: "The prosecutor's authority in the juvenile intake process is likely to develop into a controlling one, stimulated by the prosecutor's public protection image, the increased interest in handling juveniles according to offense and prior record, and diminished confidence in the ideal of rehabilitation."[46]

DIVERSION

One of the most important alternatives chosen at intake is nonjudicial disposition, or, as it is variously called, nonjudicial adjustment, handling or processing, informal disposition, adjustment, or diversion. **Diversion** is the most common term used to refer to screening out children from the juvenile court without judicial determination.

Numerous national groups, commentators, lawyers, and criminal justice experts have sought to define the concept of diversion since its inception in the mid-1960s. We suggest that juvenile diversion is the process of placing youths suspected of law-violating behavior into treatment-oriented programs prior to formal trial and disposition in order to minimize their penetration into the justice system and thereby avoid any potential stigma and labeling.

Diversion implies more than simply screening out cases that are trivial or unimportant and for which no additional treatment is needed. *Screening* involves abandoning efforts to apply any coercive measures to a defendant.[47] In contrasts, *diversion* encourages an individual to participate in some specific program or activity by express or implied threat of further prosecution. Consequently, juvenile justice experts such as Paul Nejelski define diversion as "the channeling of cases to noncourt institutions in instances where these cases would ordinarily have received an adjudicatory hearing by a court."[48] Whatever definition is used, diversion generally refers to formally acknowledged and organized efforts to process juvenile and adult offenders outside the justice system.[49]

Diversion has become one of the most popular reforms in juvenile justice since it was recommended by the President's Crime Commission in 1967. Arguments for the use of diversion programs contend that:

1. It keeps the juvenile justice system operating; without it, the system would collapse from voluminous caseloads;
2. It is preferable to dealing with the inadequate juvenile justice treatment system;
3. It gives legislators and other government leaders the opportunity to reallocate resources to programs that may be more successful in the treatment of juvenile offenders;
4. Its costs are significantly less than the per capita cost of institutionalization; and
5. It helps youths avoid the stigma of being labeled a delinquent, which is believed to be an important factor in developing a delinquent career.

There are police-based diversion models that include family crisis intervention projects, referral programs, and youth service bureaus. In addition, there are court-based diversion models that have been used extensively for status offenders, minor first offenders, children involved in family disturbances, and children involved in such offenses as shoplifting or minor assault and battery. Court-based diversion programs include intervention projects involving employment, referral for educational programs, and placement of juveniles who are involved with drugs in drug-related programs.

Most court-based diversion programs employ a particular formula for choosing youths for diversion. Such criteria as first offender, nonviolent, or status offender, and drug or alcohol dependent are used to select clients. In some instances, youths will be asked to partake of services voluntarily in lieu of a court appearance. In other programs, prosecutors will agree to defer a case until a youth has successfully completed a treatment program and to then dismiss all charges. Finally, some programs can be initiated by the juvenile court judge after the case has been brought to his or her attention at an initial hearing.[50]

In summary, diversion programs have been created to remove nonserious offenders from the formal justice system in order to provide them with nonpunitive treatment services and help them avoid the stigma of a delinquent label.

ISSUES IN DIVERSION: WIDENING THE NET

Diversion has been viewed as a promising alternative to official procedures, but over the years its basic premises have been questioned by a number of experts.[51] The most damaging criticism has been that diversion programs, rather than limiting stigma and system penetration, actually involve children in the justice system who previously would have been released without official notice. This phenomenon is referred to as **widening the net**. Various studies indicate that police and court personnel are likely to use diversion program services for youths who ordinarily would have been turned loose at the intake or arrest stage.[52] For example, in an analysis of diversion programs in Florida, Charles Frazier and John Cochran found that after controlling for such social and legal variables as race, sex, age, offense severity, and prior record, diverted youths experienced at least as much involvement with the juvenile justice system as did youths who were not selected for diversion.[53] Similarly, after reviewing existing research on the effectiveness of employing diversion with status offenders, Dennis Anderson and Donald Schoen found little evidence that diversion programs have met their stated goals. They conclude that while diversion should not be dismissed as an "unrealistic or harmful fad," neither should it be judged as a "satisfactory approach to juvenile delinquency."[54] Thus, the youths in diversion programs may not be "saved" from a more serious delinquency label, nor are they freed from significant intrusion in their lives.

Why does net widening occur? One explanation is that police and prosecutors find diversion a more attractive alternative to both official processing and outright release—diversion helps them resolve the conflict between doing too much or too little. Second, many local diversion programs have been funded by outside money (federal, state, or private). Local officials, worried that support will be dropped if client quotas are not maintained, beg police and court officials for a few "warm bodies." Police and judges who are reluctant to give up control of offenders they feel need more formal treatment, refer youths whom they might have released with a warning in the past. As Sharla Rausch and Charles Logan put it:

> In essence, the diverted population was drawn from a pool of offenders who, prior to the implementation of diversion programs, would probably have been released or left alone. The effect of such a policy has been to expand control over a larger, less seriously involved sector of the juvenile population.[55]

Similarly, Frazier and Cochran found that net widening may actually have a benign origin, since diversion staff members often have social service backgrounds: "Most staff believed that the more attention given a youth and the longer the period of time over which the attention was given, the better the prospects for a successful outcome."[56]

Diversion has also been criticized as ineffective and unproductive. That is, youths being diverted make no better adjustment in the community than those who go through official channels. However, not all delinquency experts are critical of diversion. Arnold Binder and Gilbert Geis claim that there are many benefits to diversion that more than balance its negative qualities.[57] They challenge the net-widening concept as being naive—how do we know that diverted youths would have had less interface with the justice system if diversion didn't exist? They suggest that even if juveniles had escaped official labels for their current offense, it may be inevitable that they would eventually fall into the hands of the police and juvenile court. They also point out that the rehabilitative potential of diversion should not be overlooked.

Although diversion programs are not the panacea their originators believed them to be, at least they offer an alternative to official processing. They can help the justice system devote its energies to more serious offenders while providing counseling and other rehabilitative services to needy youths.

Providing treatment services for nonserious young offenders who voluntarily enter a diversion program is exemplified by the following "Case in Point":

You are the intake worker assigned to the local juvenile court.

Charles is a 13 year old who was arrested for shoplifting in a department store. He was before the juvenile court for trial and disposition on his first delinquency offense. Charles comes from a broken home. He lives with his mother and three younger siblings in a public housing project. His parents are separated, and Charles hasn't seen his father in over a year. Charles is in the eighth grade, seems bright, but frequently fights in school. The school report indicates that Charles is a sad, lonely child with a hot temper.

The intake worker and defense attorney indicate that Charles wants to remain at home, and both recommend closing the delinquency case. The prosecutor and arresting police officer feel that Charles is an aggressive, acting-out youth whose behavior is unpredictable and who is in need of juvenile court supervision.

Do you believe that Charles would benefit from a diversion program? How would you assess the juvenile court's role in this type of case?

THE PETITION

A **complaint** is the report that the police or some other agency makes to the court to initiate the intake process. Once the agency makes a decision in intake that judicial disposition is required, a formal petition is filed. The **petition** is the formal legal complaint that initiates judicial action against a juvenile charged with actions alleging juvenile delinquency or noncriminal behavior. The petition also includes such basic information as the name, age, and residence of the child, the parents' names, and the facts alleging the child's delinquency. The police officer, a family member, or a social service agency can bring a petition. If, after being given the right to counsel, the child admits the allegation in the petition, an initial hearing is immediately scheduled for the child to make the admission before the court, and information is gathered to develop a treatment plan.

If the child does not admit to any of the facts in the petition, a date for a scheduled hearing on the petition is set. This hearing, whose purpose is to determine the merits of the petition, is similar to the adult trial. Once a hearing or adjudication date has been set, the probation department, which is the agency providing social services to the court, is normally asked to prepare a social study report. This report, often known as the predisposition report, collects relevant information about the child and recommends treatment and service.

When a date has been set for the hearing on the petition, parents or guardians and other persons associated with the petition, such as witnesss, the arresting police officer, and victims, are notified of the hearing. On occasion, the court may issue a summons—a court order requiring the juvenile or others involved in the case to appear for the hearing. The statutes or the juvenile code in a given jurisdiction govern the contents of the petition. Some jurisdictions, for instance, require that a petition be filed on information and belief of the complainant alone. Others require that the petition be filed under oath or that an affidavit accompany the petition. Some jurisdictions authorize only one official, such as a probation officer or prosecutor, to file the petition. Others allow numerous officials, including family and social service agencies, to set forth facts in the petition.

BAIL FOR CHILDREN

Bail is money or some other security provided to the court to ensure the appearance of a defendant at every subsequent stage of the justice process. Its purpose is to obtain the release from custody of the person charged with the crime. Once the amount of bail is set by the court, the defendant is required to pay a percentage of the entire amount in cash or securities or to pay a professional bail bonding agency to submit a bond as a guarantee for returning to court. If a person is released on bail but fails to appear in court at the stipulated time, the bail deposit is forfeited. The person, if apprehended, is then confined in a detention facility until the court appearance.

With a few exceptions, persons other than those accused of murder are entitled to reasonable bail, as stated in the Eighth Amendment of the U.S. Constitution. There is some controversy today about whether a constitutional right to bail exists or whether the court can impose excessive bail resulting in a person's confinement. In most cases, a defendant has the right to be released on reasonable bail. Many jurisdictions require a bail review hearing by a higher court when a person is detained because the initial judge sets excessive bail.

Whether a defendant will appear at the next stage of the juvenile or criminal proceeding is a key issue in determining bail. Bail cannot be used to punish an accused, nor can it be denied or revoked simply at the discretion of the court. Many experts believe that money bail is one of the worst aspects of the criminal justice system. It has plagued the system for decades. It is discriminatory because it works against the poor. It is costly because the government must pay to detain offenders who are unable to pay bail and who could otherwise be in the community. It is believed that people who await trial in jail have a higher proportion of subsequent convictions than people who are released on bail. The detention of individuals who cannot pay has a dehumanizing effect on them.

Over the years, few people have realized that the same issues are involved in the detention of juveniles. Juvenile detention prior to adjudication is one of the most serious problems facing the juvenile justice system. Large numbers of juveniles are incarcerated at this critical stage. Poor conditions exist in the detention facilities where they are held, and there are harmful aftereffects of the detention process.

Despite these facts, many states refuse juveniles the right to bail. They argue that juvenile proceedings are civil, not criminal, and that detention is rehabilitative, not punitive. In addition, juveniles do not need a constitutional right to bail because statutory provisions allow children to be released in parental custody. Furthermore, it is suggested that detention facilities and the number of children in them should be reduced instead of developing a bail program.[58]

In view of the recognized deficiency of the adult bail system, some experts believe that alternative release programs should be developed for the juvenile justice system. These programs include release on recognizance, release to a third party, and the use of station-house summonses or citation programs in lieu of arrest.

Some states do provide bail programs for children. Massachusetts, for example, applies the same standard in deciding bail for children and adults.[59] Bail is used only to assure the presence of the accused at trial. A presumption exists that the accused should be released solely on this promise. Mark Solar points out that state juvenile bail statutes are divided into three categories: (1) those guaranteeing the right to bail; (2) those which grant the court discretion to give bail; and (3) those that deny a juvenile the right to bail.[60] The consensus generally exists that allowing bail for juveniles is in conflict with the *parens patriae* concept and rehabilitation goals of the juvenile justice system.

There is no agreement among jurisdictions, however, on whether a child has the constitutional right to be released on bail. The U.S. Supreme Court has never decided the issue of whether juveniles have a constitutional right to bail. Some courts have stated that bail provisions do not apply to juveniles. Others rely on the Eighth Amendment or on state constitutional provisions or statutes and conclude that juveniles do have a right to bail.

In a bail hearing for a child, the court reviews such factors as the charge, the history of the parents' ability to control the child's behavior, the child's school participation, psychological and psychiatric evaluations, the child's desire to go home, and the parents' interest in continuing to take care of the child while awaiting the trial.

Preventive Detention

An issue closely related to bail is **preventive detention.** This refers to the practice of keeping a person in custody before trial because of his or her suspected danger to the community. Proponents argue that preventive detention can save the victim of crime from any additional trouble from an offender released on bail and also protect potential new victims from harm. Opponents hold that preventive detention statutes deprive offenders of their freedom since guilt has not been proven in the case at hand. It is also unfair, they claim, to punish people for what judicial authorities believe they may do in the future, since it is impossible to predict accurately who will be dangerous. Moreover, because judges are able to use unchecked discretion in their detention decisions, an offender could unfairly be deprived of freedom without legal recourse.

Though the Supreme Court has upheld preventive detention of adults, most state jurisdictions allow judges to deny bail to adult offenders only in cases involving murder (capital crimes), when the offenders have jumped bail in the past, or when they have committed another crime while on bail. However, every state allows preventive detention of juveniles. The reason for this discrepancy hinges on the legal principle that while adults have the right to liberty, juveniles have a right to custody. Therefore, it is not unreasonable to detain youths for their own protection. On June 4, 1984, the Supreme Court dealt with this issue in *Schall v. Martin,* when it upheld New York State's preventive detention statute. The Court concluded that there was no indication in the statute that preventive detention was used as punishment.[61] Because of the importance of this case, it is set out in the Focus on Delinquency entitled "*Schall v. Martin.*"

Schall v. Martin

Facts

Gregory Martin was arrested in New York City on December 13, 1977, on charges of robbery, assault, and criminal possession of a weapon. Since he was arrested at 11:30 P.M. and lied about his residence, Martin was kept overnight in detention and brought to juvenile court the next day for an "initial appearance" accompanied by his grandmother. The family court judge, citing possession of the loaded weapon, the false address given to police, and the lateness of the hour the crime occurred (as evidence of a lack of supervision), ordered him detained before trial under section 320.5(3)(6) of the New York State code. Section 320.5 authorizes pretrial detention of an accused juvenile delinquent if "there is a substantial probability that he will not appear in court on the return date or there is a serious risk that he may before the return date commit an act which if committed by an adult would constitute a crime." Later at trial, Martin was found to be a delinquent and sentenced to two years' probation.

Martin's attorneys filed a habeas corpus petition (demanding his release from custody) while he was in pretrial detention. Their petition charged that his detention denied him due process rights under the Fifth and Fourteenth Amendments. Their suit was a class action in behalf of all youths subject to preventive detention in New York. The New York appellate courts upheld Martin's claim on the grounds that because most delinquents are released or placed on probation, it was unfair to incarcerate them before trial. The prosecution brought the case to the U.S. Supreme Court for final judgment.

Decision

The Supreme Court upheld the state's right to place juveniles in preventive detention. It held that preventive detention serves the legitimate objective of protecting both the juvenile and society from pretrial crime. Pretrial detention need not be considered punishment merely because the juvenile is eventually released or put on probation. And after all, there are procedural safeguards, such as notice and a hearing, and a statement of facts that must be given to juveniles before they are placed in detention. The Court also found that detention based on prediction of future behavior was not a violation of due process. There are many decisions made in the justice system, such as the decision to sentence or grant parole, which are based in part on a prediction of future behavior, and these have all been accepted by the court as legitimate exercises of state power.

Significance of the Case

Schall v. Martin establishes the right of juvenile court judges to deny youths pretrial release if they perceive them to be "dangerous." However, the case establishes a due process standard for detention hearings that includes notice and a statement of substantial reasons for the detention.

Source: Schall v. Martin, *104 S.Ct. 2403 (1984).*

In a recent study of the effect of *Schall,* the American Bar Association concluded that continued refinement of the detention screening process is needed to achieve the twin goals of public safety and protection of the juvenile offenders' constitutional rights.[62] Because preventive detention may attach a stigma of guilt to a child presumed innocent, the practice remains a highly controversial one.

THE PLEA AND PLEA BARGAINING

In the adult criminal justice system, the defendant normally enters a plea of guilty or not guilty. More than 90 percent of all adult defendants plead guilty before the trial stage. A large proportion of those pleas involve what is known as plea bargaining. **Plea bargaining** is the exchange of prosecutorial and judicial concessions for guilty pleas.[63] It permits a defendant to plead guilty in exchange for a less serious charge on an agreement by the prosecutor to recommend a reduced sentence to the court.

Few juvenile codes require a guilty or not guilty plea when a petition is filed against a child in juvenile court. In most jurisdictions, an initial hearing is held at which the child either submits to a finding of the facts or denies the petition.[64] When the child admits to the facts, the court determines an appropriate disposition and treatment plan for the child. If the allegations in the petition are denied, the case normally proceeds to the trial or adjudication stage of the juvenile process. When a child enters no plea, the court imposes a denial of the charges for the child.

A high percentage of juvenile offenders enter guilty pleas or admissions in the juvenile court. How many of these pleas involve plea bargaining between the prosecutor or probation officer and the child's attorney is unknown. In the past, it was believed that plea bargaining was unnecessary in the juvenile justice system because there was little incentive for either the prosecution or defense to bargain in a system that does not have jury trials, criminal labels, or long sentences. In addition, since the court must dispose of cases in the best interests of the child, plea negotiation seemed unnecessary. Consequently, there has long been a debate among experts over the appropriateness of plea bargaining in the juvenile justice system. The arguments in favor of plea bargaining include lower court costs and efficiency. Others believe that it is an invisible, unfair, unregulated, and unethical process. When used, experts believe the process requires the highest standards of good faith by the prosecutor in the juvenile and adult system.[65]

In recent years, however, with concern about violent juvenile crime, attorneys have begun to see advantages to negotiating a plea rather than accepting the so-called good interests of the court regarding the child's offense. The extension of the adversary process for children has led to an increase in plea bargaining, creating an informal trial process that parallels the adult system. Other factors in the trend toward juvenile plea bargaining include the use of prosecutors rather than probation personnel and police officers in juvenile courts and the ever-increasing caseloads in such courts.

Plea-bargaining negotiations generally involve the reduction of a charge, the changing of the proceedings from delinquency to a status offense, the elimination of possible waiver proceedings to the criminal court, and suggested agreements between the government and defense regarding dispositional programs for the child. In states where youths are subject to long, mandatory sentences, reduction of the charges may have a significant impact on the outcome of the case. And in states where youths may be waived to the adult court for committing certain serious crimes, a plea reduction may result in the juvenile court maintaining jurisdiction.

Although there is little clear evidence of how much plea bargaining there is in the juvenile justice system, it is apparent that such negotiations do exist and seem to be increasing. In one of the most comprehensive studies of juvenile plea negotiation in juvenile court, Joseph Sanborn found that about 20 percent of the cases processed in Philadelphia resulted in a negotiated plea. Most were for reduced sentences, most typically probation in lieu of incarceration, or if an institutional sentence could not be avoided, the juvenile was assigned to a less restrictive environment. Sanborn found that plea bargaining was a very complex process in juvenile court, depending in large measure on the philosophy of the judge and court staff; in general, he found it to be a device that has greater benefit for the defendants than for the court itself.[66]

In summary, the majority of juvenile court cases that are not adjudicated seem to be the result of open admissions rather than actual plea bargaining. Unlike the adult system, where almost 90 percent of all charged offenders are involved in some plea bargaining, there is less plea bargaining in the juvenile court since such common incentives as dropping multiple charges or substituting a misdemeanor for a felony are unlikely. Nonetheless, plea bargaining is firmly entrenched in the juvenile process. Any plea bargain, however, must be entered into voluntarily and knowingly; otherwise, the conviction may be overturned on appeal.

TRANSFER TO THE ADULT COURT

One of the most significant actions that occurs in the early court processing of a juvenile offender is the **transfer** process. Otherwise known as **waiver, bindover** or **removal,** this process involves transferring a juvenile from the juvenile court to the criminal court. Most state statutes allow for this kind of transfer.

Historically, the American justice system has made a fundamental distinction between children and adults. The juvenile justice system emphasizes rehabilitation, and the criminal justice system emphasizes deterrence, punishment, and social control. Proponents of the transfer process claim that children who commit serious, chronic offenses and who may be hardened offenders should be handled by the criminal court system. In fact, so the argument goes, these children cannot be rehabilitated. Even such well-regarded institutions as the National Council of Juvenile and Family Court Judges have made it their stated policy to favor transfer.[67] Unless a waiver policy exists, children may feel immune from "real" punishment as the accompanying cartoon suggests.

Opponents suggest that the transfer process is applied to children unfairly and is a halfhearted effort at implementing the treatment philosophy of the juvenile court. Furthermore, some children tried in the adult criminal court may be incarcerated under conditions so extreme that the children will be permanently damaged. Another serious disadvantage of transferring a child is the stigma that may be attached to a conviction in the criminal court. Labeling children as adult offenders early in life may seriously impair their further educational, employment, and other opportunities.

In reality, however, some juveniles take advantage of decisions to transfer them to the adult court. Often, although the charge against a child may be considered

"Pepper . . . and Salt"
From the *Wall Street Journal*, November 9, 1989.
Permission, Cartoon Features Syndicate.

"I reckon I can make a couple of million before they can try me as an adult."

serious in the juvenile court, the adult criminal court will not find it so, and a child will have a better chance for dismissal of the charges or acquittal after a jury trial.

Statutory Criteria in Transfer

In the forty-eight states that use waiver to adult courts, statutes set the standards for transfer procedures. Age is of particular importance. Some jurisdictions allow for transfer between the ages of 14 and 17. Others restrict waiver proceedings to mature juveniles and specify particular offenses. In a few jurisdictions, any child can be sentenced to the criminal court system, regardless of age. For example, Massachusetts law states that only juveniles between the ages of 14 and 17 are eligible for transfer and that a child can be transferred only if he or she has (1) previously been committed to the Department of Youth Services and the present offense is punishable by imprisonment or (2) has committed an offense invoking infliction or threat of serious bodily harm.[68] If the above conditions are met, a transfer hearing must be held to determine whether it is in the public interest to transfer the child. The court must consider the seriousness of the alleged offense; the child's family, school, and social history; the general protection of the public;

the nature of past treatment efforts for the child; and the likelihood of the child's rehabilitation in the juvenile court.

More than thirty states have amended their waiver policies to automatically exclude certain offenses from juvenile court jurisdiction. For example, Indiana excludes cases involving 16- and 17-year-olds charged with kidnapping, rape, and robbery (if a weapon was used or bodily injury occurred); in Illinois, youths 15 to 16 who are charged with murder, aggravated or sexual assault, or armed robbery with a firearm are automatically sent to criminal court; in Pennsylvania, any child accused of murder, regardless of age, is tried before the criminal court.[69] While about half of these jurisdictions automatically exclude serious crimes, such as murder or rape, from the juvenile court, the rest use exclusion to remove minor traffic offenses and public ordinance violations, which are then handled by lower criminal courts. Nonetheless, the trend has been to exclude serious violent offenses from juvenile court jurisdictions, a response to the growing recognition of the chronic offender problem.

In eight states, statutes allow prosecutors to file particularly serious cases either in the juvenile court or the adult court at their own discretion; this is called **concurrent jurisdiction**.[70]

A few states do not waive juveniles to the adult court. Nebraska has concurrent jurisdiction for all felonies. It allows the prosecuting attorney to choose between bringing the case to either juvenile court or adult court. New York gives original jurisdiction for serious cases to the adult court and allows waiver to the juvenile court at the judge's discretion. Vermont uses concurrent jurisdiction statutes for serious but not all offenses.[71] Most statutes consider age and/or seriousness of the offense as the basis for removing the child from the juvenile court (see Table 16.1).[72]

Thus, the waiver process is a statutory one, and the criteria that effect the decision to transfer the child to the criminal court are found in each of the state juvenile court acts. Many states, however, favor keeping children in juvenile court rather than transferring them to criminal court. The ineffectiveness of the criminal justice system is itself an adequate argument for keeping children in juvenile court.

PROSECUTING JUVENILES IN ADULT COURTS: THE FLORIDA EXPERIENCE. The way the state of Florida handles transfers to the adult court provides a relevant example of how the waiver decision is currently being made.[73]

A juvenile can get to adult court in Florida in a number of different ways. First, juveniles who have committed a delinquent act have the right to request their own transfer to the adult system if they believe it may benefit them; for example, if they feel that having a jury trial will benefit their case.[74] In addition, a child of any age may be tried as an adult if he or she has committed a crime punishable by death or life in prison and has been indicted on the charge by a grand jury.[75] Florida law also allows prosecutors the right to request a waiver hearing before the juvenile court if the youth is between 14 and 16 years old and the prosecutor believes the case warrants the attention of the adult court.[76] The prosecutor *must* request a waiver in a case involving a child aged 14 to 16 who has a previous record of a violent juvenile crime, such as murder, sexual battery, armed robbery, or aggravated assault, and is again being charged with the same type of crime. And though the age of majority remains 18 in Florida, a prosecutor *must* send to

TABLE 16.1   Age for Waiver to the Adult Court

FORTY-EIGHT STATES, THE DISTRICT OF COLUMBIA, AND THE FEDERAL
GOVERNMENT HAVE JUDICIAL WAIVER PROVISIONS

Youngest Age at which Juvenile May Be Transferred to Criminal Court by Judicial Waiver	States
No specific age	Alaska, Arizona, Arkansas, Delaware, Florida, Indiana, Kentucky, Maine, Maryland, New Hampshire, New Jersey, Oklahoma, South Dakota, West Virginia, Wyoming, federal districts
10 Years	Vermont
12	Montana
13	Georgia, Illinois, Mississippi
14	Alabama, Colorado, Connecticut, Idaho, Iowa, Massachusetts, Minnesota, Missouri, North Carolina, North Dakota, Pennsylvania, South Carolina, Tennessee, Utah
15	District of Columbia, Louisiana, Michigan, New Mexico, Ohio, Oregon, Texas, Virginia
16	California, Hawaii, Kansas, Nevada, Rhode Island, Washington, Wisconsin

Note: Many judicial waiver statutes also specify offenses that are waivable. This chart lists the states by the youngest age for which judicial waiver may be sought without regard to offense.

Source: Linda A. Szymanski, *Waiver/Transfer/Certification of Juveniles to Criminal Court: Age Restrictions: Crime Restrictions*, (Pittsburgh: National Center for Juvenile Justice, February 1987).

the adult court any juvenile 16 or 17 who is being charged with a second violent personal crime.[77] Finally, the juvenile prosecutor retains the right to petition to the adult court any juvenile between 16 and 18 "when in his judgment and discretion, the public interest requires that adult sanctions be considered or imposed."[78] Clearly, these last provisions reflect the desire of Florida legislators to crack down on serious juvenile offenders and embrace a crime-control model of juvenile justice.

Charles Thomas and Shay Bilchik studied the implementation of Florida's transfer policy. They found that over a one-year period (1981), 693 juveniles were bound over to the adult court after a waiver proceeding, and 1,614 juveniles had their cases directly filed as a result of prosecutorial initiative. Looking at data from Dade County, Thomas and Bilchik concluded that the adult criminal system treats juvenile cases quite seriously. A greater proportion of cases involving juveniles reached the trial stage (73 percent) than might be expected, considering the usual attrition of criminal cases (estimated to be 50 percent) in the adult justice system. Similarly, in about 67 percent of the cases involving juvenile offenders, those found guilty received some sort of prison sentence.

While only a small percentage of juvenile cases wound up in adult court, this dual system of justice seems needed. The reality of the situation is that some offenders are not amenable to the treatment afforded by the juvenile justice system, and placing them with the adult authorities opens ups sentencing and treatment provisions not available in the juvenile court. Consequently, transfer provisions should not be dismissed out of hand by juvenile court proponents as reactionary ways of treating troubled youths.

DUE PROCESS IN TRANSFER PROCEEDINGS

Since 1966, the U.S. Supreme Court and other federal and state courts have attempted to ensure fairness in the waiver process by handing down decisions that spell out the need for due process. Two Supreme Court decisions, *Kent v. United States* (1966) and *Breed v. Jones* (1975), are set out in the Focus on Delinquency entitled "Due Process and the Waiver Decision" because of their significance.[79] The *Kent* case declared a District of Columbia transfer statute unconstitutional and attacked the subsequent conviction of the child by granting him specific due process rights. In *Breed v. Jones*, the Supreme Court declared that the child was granted the protection of the double-jeopardy clause of the Fifth Amendment after he was tried as a delinquent in the juvenile court.

Today, as a result of *Kent* and *Breed*, states what have transfer hearings provide specific requirements for transfer proceedings in their juvenile code. For the most part, when a transfer hearing is conducted today, due process of law requires there be: (1) a legitimate transfer hearing, (2) sufficient notice to the child's family and defense attorney, (3) the right to counsel, and (4) a statement of the reason for the court order regarding transfer. These rights recognize what *Kent v. United States* indicated: namely, that the transfer proceeding is a critically important action in determining the statutory rights of the juvenile offender.

YOUTHS IN ADULT COURT

The issue of waiver is an important one. Waiver is attractive to conservatives because it jibes with the get-tough policy currently popular in the juvenile justice system. Liberals oppose its use because it is in contradistinction to the rehabilitative ideal. Some conservative thinkers have argued that the increased use of waiver can help get violent, chronic offenders off the streets. Barry Feld suggests that waiver to adult court should be mandatory for juveniles committing serious, violent crimes.[80] He argues that mandatory waiver would coincide with the currently popular just-deserts sentencing policy and eliminate potential bias and disparity in judicial decision making. A recent detailed analysis by Feld of legislative changes in juvenile waiver statutes indicates that the nature of the offense dominates the waiver decision, rather than the real needs of the offender. According to Feld, the waiver of a serious juvenile offender into the adult system on the basis of his offense, rather than an individualized evaluation of the youth's amenability to treatment or dangerousness, is both an indication of and a contributor to the substantive and procedural criminalization of the juvenile court.[81]

Due Process and the Waiver Decision

Kent v. United States

Facts

Morris Kent was arrested at the age of 16 in connection with charges of housebreaking, robbery, and rape. As a juvenile, he was subject to the exclusive jurisdiction of the District of Columbia Juvenile Court. The District of Columbia statute declared that the court could transfer the petitioner "after full investigation" and remit him to trial in the U.S. District Court. Kent admitted his involvement in the offenses and was placed in a receiving home for children. Subsequently, his mother obtained counsel, and they discussed with the social service director the possibility that the juvenile court might waive its jurisdiction. Kent was detained at the receiving home for almost one week. There was no arraignment, no hearing, and no hearing for petitioner's apprehension. Kent's counsel arranged for a psychiatric examination, and a motion requesting a hearing on the waiver was filed. The juvenile court judge did not rule on the motion and entered an order stating, "After full investigation, the court waives its jurisdiction and directs that a trial be held under the regular proceedings of the criminal court." The judge made no finding and gave no reasons for his waiver decision. It appeared that the judge denied motions for a hearing, recommendations for hospitalization for psychiatric observation, requests for access to the social service file, and offers to prove that the petitioner was a fit subject for rehabilitation under the juvenile court.

After the juvenile court waived its jurisdiction, Kent was indicted by the grand jury and was subsequently found guilty of housebreaking and robbery and not guilty by reason of insanity on the charge of rape. Kent was sentenced to serve a period of thirty to ninety years on his conviction.

Decision

The petitioner's lawyer appealed the decision on the basis of the infirmity of the proceedings by which the juvenile court waived its jurisdiction. He further attacked the waiver on statutory and constitutional grounds, stating: "(1) no hearing occurred, (2) no findings were made, (3) no reasons were stated before the waiver, and (4) counsel was denied access to the social service file." The U.S. Supreme Court found that the juvenile court order waiving jurisdiction and remitting the child to trial in the district court was invalid. Its arguments were based on the following:

- The theory of the juvenile court act is rooted in social welfare procedures and treatments.
- The philosophy of the juvenile court, namely *parens patriae*, is not supposed to allow procedural unfairness.
- Waiver proceedings are critically important actions in the juvenile court.
- The juvenile court act requiring full investigation in the District of Columbia should be read in the context of constitutional principles relating to due process of law. These principles require at a minimum that the petitioner be entitled to a hearing, access to counsel, access by counsel to social service records, and a statement of the reason for the juvenile court decision.

Significance of the Case

This case examined for the first time the substantial degree of discretion associated with a transfer
continued

proceeding in the District of Columbia. Thus, the Supreme Court significantly limited its holding to the statute involved but justified its reference to constitutional principles relating to due process and the assistance of counsel. In addition, it said that the juvenile court waiver hearings need to measure up to the essentials of due process and fair treatment. Furthermore, in an appendix to its opinion, the Court set up criteria concerning waiver of the jurisdictions. These are:

- The seriousness of the alleged offense to the community
- Whether the alleged offense was committed in an aggressive, violent, or willful manner
- Whether the alleged offense was committed against persons or against property
- The prosecutive merit of the complaint
- The desirability of trial and disposition
- The sophistication and maturity of the juvenile
- The record and previous history of the juvenile
- Prospects for adequate protection of the public and the likelihood of reasonable rehabilitation

Breed v. Jones

Facts

In 1971, a petition in the juvenile court in the state of California was filed against Jones, who was then 17, alleging that he had committed an offense that, if committed by an adult, would constitute robbery. The petitioner was detained pending a hearing. At the hearing, the juvenile court took testimony and found that the allegations were true and sustained the petition. The proceedings were continued for a disposition hearing, at which point Jones was found unfit for treatment in the juvenile court. It was ordered that he be prosecuted as an adult offender. At a subsequent preliminary hearing, the petitioner was held for criminal trial, an information was filed against him for robbery, and he was tried and found guilty. He was committed to the California Youth Authority, over objections that he was being subjected to double jeopardy.

Petitioner Jones sought an appeal in the federal district court on the basis of the double-jeopardy argument that jeopardy attaches at the juvenile delinquency proceedings. The writ of habeas corpus was denied.

Decision

The U.S. Supreme Court held that the prosecution of Jones as an adult in the California Superior Court, after an adjudicatory finding in the juvenile court that he had violated a criminal statute and a subsequent finding that he was unfit for treatment as a juvenile, violated the double-jeopardy clause of the Fifth Amendment of the U.S. Constitution as applied to the states through the Fourteenth Amendment. Thus, Jones's trial in Superior Court for the same offense as that for which he was tried in the juvenile court violated the policy of the double-jeopardy clause, even if he never faced the risk of more than one punishment, since double jeopard refers to the risk or potential risk of trial and conviction, not punishment.

Significance of the Case

The *Breed* case provided answers on several important transfer issues: (1) *Breed* prohibits trying a child in an adult court when there has been a prior adjudicatory juvenile proceeding; (2) probable cause may exist at a transfer hearing, and this does not violate subsequent jeopardy if the child is transferred to the adult court; (3) because the same evidence is often used in both the transfer hearing and subsequent trial in either the juvenile or adult court, a different judge is often required for the different hearing.

Sources: Kent v. United States, 383 U.S. 541, 86 S.Ct. 1045, 16 L.Ed.2d 84 (1966); Breed v. Jones, 421 U.S. 519, 95 S.Ct. 1779 (1975).

In a widely publicized 1986 case, 14-year-old Rod Matthews, left, lured ten-year-old Shaun Ouillette into the woods and killed him with a baseball bat. Tried as an adult, Matthews is currently serving a life sentence in the Massachusetts correctional system.

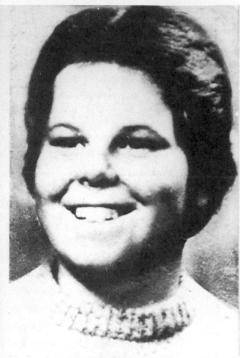

In a similar fashion, there has been a trend toward giving original jurisdiction for serious juvenile crimes to the adult courts and then allowing judges the power to waive deserving cases back to the juvenile court. These are known as concurrent jurisdiction statutes. The most well-known statute is New York's 1978 Omnibus Crime Act, which gives adult courts jurisdiction over 13-year-olds accused of murder, rape, and robbery.[82] The adult court judge is entitled to transfer these youths to juvenile court, and not vice versa. However, youths cannot be placed in adult correctional facilities until they reach their sixteenth birthday.

Because of its popularity, the number of youths processed in adult courts has become significant. A federally sponsored survey found that in a single year, 9,000 juveniles were waived to adult courts, 2,000 were prosecuted as adults because of concurrent jurisdiction, and 1,300 were prosecuted as adults because the offenses they committed were excluded from juvenile court jurisdiction.[83] In addition, since twelve states use low juvenile court maximum age limits, about 250,000 16- and 17-year-olds are handled by adult court each year. The study also found that (1) most waived youths were charged not with violent crimes but with property and public order (drug, alcohol) crimes; (2) most of the youths tried in adult courts are convicted or plead guilty; (3) youths are more likely to receive a probation sentence than confinement (but 46 percent of youths judicially waived were sent to adult correctional facilities); and (4) youths convicted as adults and sentenced to confinement do more time than they would have under juvenile court disposition. While the report does not recommend abolition of waiver, it suggests that juveniles should always be kept out of adult correctional facilities and be treated as juveniles as long as possible.

CRITICISMS OF THE WAIVER CONCEPT

Despite the increased use of waiver, the efficacy of transferring youths to the adult court has been questioned. One alleged shortcoming is that the actual treatment of delinquents in adult court is quite similar to what they might have received had they remained in the custody of juvenile authorities; therefore, why transfer them? For example, New York's law has been criticized on the grounds that 70 percent of children arraigned in adult courts are waived to juvenile court, wasting both time and money; 40 percent of juveniles tried in adult court are sentenced to probation; and only 3 percent of the juvenile offenders tried in adult court received longer sentences than they could have been given in juvenile court.[84]

Other critics view transfer as adding undue burdens to youthful offenders. Research conducted by Cary Rudman, Eliot Hartstone, Jeffrey Fagan, and Melinda Moore compared case outcomes of a group of waived violent juvenile offenders to a control group of offenders with similar case characteristics retained in juvenile court. Using data from four jurisdictions, the researchers found that it took two and a half times as long (246 days verses 98 days) to process a waiver case than one that was retained in juvenile court.[85] During most of this added time, the juvenile was held in a detention center. The study also found that waived youths were treated quite harshly by the adult justice system: 90 percent were convicted; all convictions were to the top offense charged, indicating they engaged in relatively little plea negotiation; 90 percent of convicted youth were incarcerated (73 percent in prison and 18 percent in jail); and youths convicted in adult court received sentences five times longer than those retained in the juvenile court. With regard to the latter issue, youths convicted in adult courts received sentences averaging 247 months for murder and 171 months for rape; in comparison, juvenile courts sentenced offenders to 55 months for murder and 16 for rape. The research effort concluded that transferring youths to the adult court did indeed fulfill the get-tough role for which it was designed. However, it also found that program services for waived youths were lacking and that delinquencies will eventually come back to haunt society when waived youngsters are eventually released from prison without receiving adequate treatment.

The severe sentences given to waived youth have been substantiated by a recent federally sponsored survey of waiver in twelve urban jurisdictions, including Seattle, Miami, Chicago, and Denver. Of the 344 cases sent to criminal court, 66 percent resulted in a finding of guilt and 77 percent of the convicted juveniles were sentenced to jail or prison for an average of 6.8 years. These figures indicate that juveniles are receiving somewhat longer prison sentences than adults get for comparable crimes.[86]

More serious are the objections raised by M. A. Bortner, whose research led to the conclusion that the transfer decision may be motivated by administrative and political considerations.[87] Bortner studied the records of 214 youths remanded to adult court in a western county. There was little evidence that the waived youths were any more dangerous or unruly than youths treated by the juvenile court. Nor was there any evidence that their transfer enhanced public safety. By turning a small portion of their clientele over to the adult court and by portraying these youths as the most dangerous, the juvenile court authorities were able to show that they were concenred for public safety while at the same time keeping control over the vast majority of youths in their jurisdiction and deflecting criticism of their entire juvenile justice operations. Critics see the new methods of dealing with offenders as inefficient and ineffective. Supporters view them as a means of getting the most serious, chronic juvenile offenders off the streets for long periods of time.

Another question raised by critics is whether or not transfers to the adult court are carried out in a fair and equal manner. One warning sign is the fact that minorities are waived at a rate that is greater than their representation in the population. Jeffery Fagan and his associates have identified the existence of such racial disparity in decision making from apprehension through the commitment stage.[88]

Using prosecutorial discretion to determine whether to proceed in the juvenile or the criminal justice system is also a much maligned practice. While most states decide to waive a child by a judicial hearing, a few jurisdictions allow the prosecutor to determine jurisdiction by filing a complaint in the juvenile or adult court. In other jurisdictions, where the juvenile court may have no jurisdiction over certain crimes, the prosecutor can control the jurisdiction by the charge filed against the child. Such an approach eliminates the requirement of a waiver hearing but leaves a great deal of discretion in the hands of the prosecutor.[89]

In sum, there has been a trend to increase the flow of juvenile cases to adult courts and hold others in the criminal courts. This policy change can be attributed to the get-tough attitude toward the serious, chronic juvenile offender. A number of important questions have been raised about the fairness and propriety of this method of handling serious juvenile cases.

CASE IN POINT

You are a newly appointed judge whose jurisdiction embraces criminal cases heard in the lower criminal court.

One week after his twelfth birthday, Dexter G., an honor student with a strict religious eduction, had his first contact with the justice system.

Dexter was arrested and charged with criminal homicide after he allegedly took his father's rifle, aimed from a third floor bedroom window, and shot 8-year-old James once in the head as he rode along on his bicycle. The boy died instantly. Dexter was subsequently released to the custody of his parents.

The law of this jurisdiction requires that all persons charged with murder, regardless of age, stand trial as an adult in criminal court. If convicted of murder, Dexter could be sentenced to life imprisonment without parole. The state's Juvenile Court Act has a waiver provision that permits the criminal court judge to transfer the case to juvenile court if the child is under 17 and if the accused demonstrates that he is amenable to treatment and rehabilitation.

Dexter is a healthy youth with above-average intelligence and no apparent psychological problems. He has shown no emotion or remorse regarding the killing. Psychiatrists who examined Dexter indicate that the boy said he was "playing hunter" when the rifle accidently discharged.

If you were the judge, would you transfer the case to the juvenile court for jurisdiction? What criteria would you use?

The issue of waiver has become critical in recent years because transfer to the adult court is viewed as an efficient means of dealing with the violent and chronic juvenile offender. Seriousness of the offense plays a significant role in determining juvenile waiver, as does the number and nature of prior offenses and prior treatment.[90] Waiver is also a refutation of the child's right to be treated in the juvenile justice system.[91]

SUMMARY

Many important decisions about what happens to a child may occur prior to adjudication. Detention in secure facilities for those charged with juvenile delinquency and involuntary placement in shelter care for those involved in noncriminal behavior place a severe limitation on the rights of the child and the parents. There has been a major effort in the past few years to remove juveniles from detention in adult jails and to make sure that status offenders are not placed in secure pretrial detention facilities.

Most statutes ordinarily require a hearing on detention if the initial decision is to keep the child in custody. At a detention hearing, the child has a right to counsel and is generally given other procedural due process safeguards, notably the privilege against self-incrimination and the right to confront and cross-examine witnesses. In addition, most state juvenile court procedures provide criteria to be used in deciding whether to detain a child. These include (1) the need to protect the child, (2) the likelihood that the child presents a serious danger to the public, and (3) the likelihood that the child will return to court for adjudication.

The intake stage is essentially a screening process to decide what action should be taken regarding matters referred to the court. The law enforcement officer is required to make hard decisions about court action or referral to social agencies. In addition, it is important for law enforcement agencies and the juvenile courts to have sound working relationships. Their objective is basically similar: the protection of the child and the community.

Throughout the early court stage of the juvenile process, the issue of discretion plays a major role. In the last decade, juvenile justice practitioners have made efforts to divert as many children as possible from the juvenile courts and place them in nonsecure treatment programs. Critics charge that diversion programs actually involve more youths in the justice system than would be the case had the programs not been in operation, a concept referred to as widening the net. Moreover, the effectiveness of diversion as a crime-reducing policy has been questioned.

Those who are held for trial are generally released to their parents, released on bail, or released through other alternatives, such as on recognizance. Since the juvenile justice system, like the adult system, is not able to try every child accused of a crime or a status offense due to personnel limitations, diversion programs seem to hold a better hope for the prevention and control of delinquency. As a result, such subsystems as diversion, statutory intake proceedings, some amount of plea bargaining, and other informal adjustments are essential ingredients in the administration of the juvenile justice system.

An issue related to bail is preventive detention, which refers to the right of a judge to deny persons release before trial on the grounds that they may be dangerous to themselves or others. Advocates of preventive detention argue that dangerous juvenile offenders should not be granted bail and pretrial release since they would then have an opportunity to intimidate witnesses and commit further crimes. Opponents retaliate that defendants are "innocent until proven guilty" and therefore should be allowed freedom before trial.

In addition to normal juvenile justice processing, thousands of other youngsters are transferred to the adult court because of the serious nature of their crimes. This process, known as waiver, is an effort to remove serious offenders from the juvenile process and into the more punitive adult system. Recent research indicates that waived youth are quite likely to receive incarceration sentences.

Prior to the first modern juvenile court in Illinois in 1899, juveniles were tried in adult criminal courts.

However, the juvenile court system did recognize that certain crimes required that children be tried as adults. Today, virtually all jurisdictions provide by statute for waiver or transfer of juvenile offenders to the criminal courts.

KEY TERMS

detention

shelter care

detention hearing

deinstitutionalization

Deinstitutionalization of Status Offenders
    Project (DSO)

intake

diversion

widening the net

complaint

petition

bail

preventive detention

Schall v. Martin

plea bargaining

transfer

waiver

bindover

removal

concurrent jurisdiction

Kent v. United States

Breed v. Jones

QUESTIONS FOR DISCUSSION

1. Why has the use of jails and detention facilities for children been considered one of the greatest tragedies in the juvenile justice system?

2. Processing juvenile cases in an informal manner—that is, without filing a formal petition—is common in the juvenile court system. Describe some methods of informally handling cases in the juvenile court.

3. The use of diversion programs in the juvenile justice system has become common as an effort to channel cases to noncourt institutions. Discuss the advantages and disadvantages of diversion. Describe diversion programs and their common characteristics.

4. What is the purpose of bail? Do children as well as adults have a constitutional or statutory right to

bail? What factors are considered in the release of a child prior to formal adjudication?

5. Under extraordinary circumstances, once juvenile proceedings have begun, the juvenile court may seek to transfer a juvenile to the adult court. This is often referred to as a transfer proceeding. Is such a proceeding justified? Under what conditions? Does the juvenile court afford the public sufficient protection against serious juvenile offenders?

6. Explain the meaning of preventive detention. Is such a concept in conflict with the fundamental principle of presumption of innocence?

NOTES

1. National Council on Crime and Delinquency, *Standards and Guides for the Detention of Children and Youth* (New York: NCCD, 1961), p. 1.

2. American Bar Association, *Standards Relating to Interim Status of Juveniles* (Cambridge, Mass.: Ballinger Publishing Co., 1977), p. 4.

3. National Council on Crime and Delinquency, *Standards and Guides for the Detention of Children and Youth*, p. 12.

4. See Donnell Pappenfort, Dee Morgan Kilpatrick, and Robin Roberts, eds., *Detention Facilities and Temporary Shelters in Child Caring: Social Policy and the Institution* (Chicago: Aldine, 1978). Also for a report that provides alternatives to jail and secure detention, see Community Research Associates, *Michigan Holdover Newtork—Short-term Detention Strategies* (Washington, D.C.: U.S. Department of Justice, 1986).

5. Melissa Sickmund and Phyllis Jo Baunach, *Children in Custody, 1985* (Washington, D.C.: Bureau of Justice Statistics, 1986); also "Growth in Minority Detentions Attributed to Drug Law Violators," *Juvenile and Family Court Newsletter*, vol. 20 (Reno, Nev.: National Council of Juvenile and Family Court Judges, 1990), p. 3. See also NCCD, *Recommendations on Juvenile Detention* (San Francisco: NCCD Council of Judges, March 1, 1989).

6. Howard Snyder, Terrence Finnegan, Ellen Nimick, Melissa Sickmund, Dennis Sullivan, and Nancy Tierney, *Juvenile Court Statistics–1985* (Pittsburgh: National Center for Juvenile Justice, 1989), p. 6.

7. *Ibid.*, p. 27.

8. Edward J. Loughran, "How to Stop Our Kids from Going Bad," *Boston Globe*, 11 February 1990.

9. Belinda McCarthy, "An Anlaysis of Detention," *Juvenile and Family Court Journal* 36:49–50 (1985).

10. Charles Frazier and Donna Bishop, "The Pretrial Detention of Juveniles and Its Impact on Case Dispositions," *Journal of Criminal Law and Criminology* 76:1132–52 (1986).

11. L. Rosner, "Juvenile Secure Detention," *Journal of Offender Counseling Services and Rehabilitation* 12:57–76 1988.

12. National Council on Crime and Delinquency, *Standards and Guides for Detention for Children and Youth*, p. 1; also Michael McMillan, "Bringing Flexibility to Juvenile Detention: The Minimum Security Approach," *Corrections Today* 49: 44–48 (1987).

13. American Bar Association, *Standards Relating to Interim Status of Juveniles*, p. 86; see also Claudia Worrell, "Pretrial Detention of Juveniles: Denial of Equal Protection Marked by the *Parens Patriae* Doctrine," *Yale Law Review* 95:174–93 (1985).

14. National Council on Crime and Delinquency, *Standard Juvenile and Family Court Act* (New York: NCCD, 1965); National Advisory Commissions on Criminal Justice Standards and Goals, *Corrections* (Washington, D.C.: U.S. Department of Justice, 1976); William Sheridan, *Model Acts for Juvenile and Family Courts* (Washington, D.C.: Department of Health, Education, and Welfare, Office of Human Development, 1975). All of these sources state that children should receive a detention hearing within a short period after admission.

15. Edward Wakin, *Children without Justice—A Report by the National Council of Jewish Women* (New York: National Council of Jewish Women, 1975), p. 43.

16. Hubert H. Humphrey Institute of Public Affairs, *The Incarceration of Minority Youth* (Minneapolis: Humphrey Institute, 1986).

17. Russell Schutt and Dale Dannefer, "Detention Decisions in Juvenile Cases: JINS, JDs and Genders," *Law and Society Review* 22:509–20 (1988).

18. S. Smith and D. Roush, "Defining Juvenile Detention Goals: ACA Committee Takes the Lead," *Corrections Today* 51:220–221 (1989).

19. I. Schwartz, G. Fishman, R. Hatfield, B. A. Krisberg, and Z. Eisikovitz, "Juvenile Detention: The Hidden Closets Revisited," *Justice Quarterly* 4:219–35 (1987); John Criswell, "Juvenile Detention Resource Centers: Florida's Experience Provides a Model for Nation in Juvenile Detention," *Corrections Today* 49:22–26 (1987).

20. *Learning behind Bars: Selected Educational Programs from Juvenile Jail and Prison Facilities* (Laurel, Ind.: Correctional Education Association, 1989), p. 5.

21. *Ibid.*, p. 10.

22. *Ibid.*, p. 13.

23. National Council on Crime and Delinquency, *Standards and Guides for the Detention of Children and Youth*, p. 3.

24. Office of Juvenile Justice and Delinquency Prevention News Release, 4 January 1981.

25. Reported in "Juveniles in Our Nation's Jails," *Criminal Justice Newsletter*, 14 February 1983, p. 8. These youths could have been held separately from adult offenders, although in the same facility.

26. "$3.8 Million Awarded to Remove Juveniles from Adult Jails, Lockups," *Justice Assistance News* 3:5 (May 1982).

27. Reported in the *Federal Register*, 14 January 1984, p. 2054.

28. "Qualities of Best Plans for Rural 'Jail Removal' Described," *Criminal Justice Newsletter*, 15 April 1987.

29. Personal communication, Community Research Center, 19 February 1987.

30. Charles Frazier, *Preadjudicatory Detention—From Juvenile Justice: Policies, Programs and Services* (Chicago: Dorsey Press, 1989), pp. 143–68.

31. Ira Schwartz, Linda Harris, and Lauri Levi, "The Jailing of Juveniles in Minnesota," *Crime and Delinquency* 34:131 (1988).

32. See, generally, Ira Schwartz, ed., "Children in Jails," *Crime and Delinquency* 34:131–228 (1988).

33. See Schwartz, Harris, and Levi, "The Jailing of Juveniles in Minnesota," p. 134.

34. David Steinhart, "California Legislation Ends Jailing of Children—the Story of a Policy Reversal," *Crime and Delinquency* 34:150 (1988).

35. See Henry Swanger, "*Hendrickson v. Griggs*—a Review of Legal and Policy Implications for Juvenile Justice Policymakers," *Crime and Delinquency* 34:209 (1988); *Hendrickson v. Griggs*, 672 F.Supp. 1126 (N.D. Iowa 1987).

36. Solomon Kobrin and Malcolm Klein, *National Evaluation of the Deinstitutionalization of Status Offender Programs, Executive Summary* (Washington, D.C.: U.S. Department of Justice, 1982); see also I. Spergel, F. Reamer, and J. Lynch, "Deinstitutionalization of Status Offenders: Individual Outcome and System Effects," *Journal of Research in Crime and Delinquency* 4:32 (1981).

37. M. A. Bortner, Mary Sutherland, and Russ Winn, "Race and the Impact of Juvenile Institutionalization," *Crime and Delinquency* 31:35–46 (1985).

38. Anne L. Schneider, *The Impact of Deinstitutionalization on Recidivism and Secure Confinement of Status Offenders* (Washington, D.C.: U.S. Department of Justice, 1985). For a similar view, see Susan Datesman and Mikel Aickin, "Offense Specialization and Escalation among Status Offenders," *Journal of Criminal Law and Criminology* 75:1246–75 (1984).

39. Duran Bell and Kevin Lang, "The Intake Dispositions of Juvenile Offenders," *Journal of Research in Crime and Delinquency* 22:309–28 (1985).

40. President's Commission on Law Enforcement and the Administration of Justice, *Task Force Report: Juvenile Delinquency and Youth Crime* (Washington, D.C.: U.S. Government Printing Office, 1967), p. 147.

41. American Bar Association, *Standards Relating to Juvenile Probation Function* (Cambridge, Mass.: Ballinger Publishing Co., 1977), p. 25.

42. National Council on Crime and Delinquency, *Standard Family Court Act*, 12; William Sheridan, *Model Acts for Juvenile and Family Courts*, 13; National Conference on Commissioners on Uniform State Laws, *Uniform Juvenile Court Act*, 9.

43. American Bar Association, *Standards Relating to Juvenile Probation Function*, p. 53.

44. *Uniform Family Court Rules of the State of New York*, Section 2507.3.

45. Ted Rubin, "The Emerging Prosecutor Dominance of the Juvenile Court Intake Process," *Crime and Delinquency* 26:299–318 (1980).

46. *Ibid.*, p. 318.

47. National Advisory Commission on Criminal Justice Standards and Goals, *Courts* (Washington, D.C.: U.S. Government Printing Office, 1967), p. 20.

48. Paul Nejelski, "Diversion: The Promise and the Danger," *Crime and Delinquency Journal* 22:393–410 (1976); Kenneth Polk, "Juvenile Diversion: A Look at the Record," *Crime and Delinquency* 30:648–59 (1984).

49. LaMar T. Empey, *American Delinquency—Its Meaning and Construction* (Homewood, Ill.: Dorsey, 1978), p. 532.

50. See Raymond T. Nimmer, *Diversion—The Search for Alternative Forms of Prosecution* (Chicago: American Bar Foundation, 1974).

51. Edwin E. Lemert, "Diversion in Juvenile Justice: What Hath Been Wrought," *Journal of Research in Crime and Delinquency* 18:34–46 (1981).

52. Don C. Gibbons and Gerald F. Blake, "Evaluating the Impact of Juvenile Diversion Programs," *Crime and Delinquency Journal* 22:411–19 (1976); Richard J. Lundman, "Will Diversion Reduce Recidivism?" *Crime and Delinquency Journal* 22:428–37 (1976); B. Bullington, J. Sprowls, D. Katkin, and M. Phillips, "A Critique of Diversionary Juvenile Justice," *Crime and Delinquency* 24:59–71 (1978); Thomas Blomberg, "Diversion and Accelerated Social Control," *Journal of Criminal Law and Criminology* 68:274–82 (1977); Sharla Rausch and Charles Logan, "Diversion from Juvenile Court, Panacea or Pandora's Box," in *Evaluating Juvenile Justice*, ed. J. Klugel (Beverly Hills, Calif.: Sage, 1983), pp. 19–30.

53. Charles Frazier and John Cochran, "Official Intervention, Diversion from the Juvenile Justice System, and Dynamics of Human Services Work: Effects of a Reform Goal Based on Labeling Theory," *Crime and Delinquency* 32:157–76 (1986).

54. Dennis Anderson and Donald Schoen, "Diversion Programs: Effect of Stigmatization on Juvenile/Status Offender," *Juvenile and Family Court Journal* 36:13–25 (1985).

55. Rausch and Logan, "Diversion from Juvenile Court," p. 20.

56. Frazier and Cochran, "Official Intervention," p. 171.

57. Arnold Binder and Gilbert Geis, "Ad Populum Argumentation in Criminology: Juvenile Diversion as Rhetoric," *Criminology* 30:309–33 (1984).

58. Paul Piersma, et al., *Law and Tactics in Juvenile Cases* (Philadelphia: American Law Institute - American Bar Association Committee on Continuing Education, 1977), pp. 195–99.

59. Mass.Gen.Laws Ann. ch. 276 (1979).

60. Mark Soler, James Bell, Elizabeth Jameson, Carole Shauffer, Alice Shotton, and Loren Warboys, *Representing the Child Client* (New York: Matthew Bender Co., 1989), Sec. 5.03b.

61. 467 U.S. 253, 104 S.Ct. 2403 (1984).

62. James Brown, Robert Shepherd, and Andrew Shookhoff, *Preventive Detention after Schall v. Martin,* (Washington, D.C.: American Bar Association, 1985).

63. Albert W. Alschuler, "The Prosecutor's Role in Plea Bargaining," *University of Chicago Law Review* 36:50–112 (1968); see also Joyce Dougherty, "A Comparison of Adult Plea Bargaining and Juvenile Intake," *Federal Probation* (June 1988): 72–79.

64. Sanford Fox, *Juvenile Courts in a Nutshell* (St. Paul: West Publishing Co., 1984–1985), pp. 154–56.

65. See Darlene Ewing, "Juvenile Plea Bargaining: A Case Study," *American Journal of Criminal Law* 6:167 (1978); Adrienne Volenik, *Checklists for Use in Juvenile Delinquency Proceedings* (Chicago: American Bar Association, 1985); Bruce Green, "Package Plea Bargaining and the Prosecutor's Duty of Good Faith," *Criminal Law Bulletin* 25:507–50 (1989).

66. Joseph Sanborn, "Plea Negotiations in Juvenile Court" (Ph.D. diss., State University of New York at Albany, 1984); see also Douglas J. Besharov, *Juvenile Justice Advocacy-Practice in a Unique Court* (New York: Practicing Law Institute, 1974), p. 311.

67. The National Council of Juvenile and Family Court Judges, "The Juvenile Court and Serious Offenders," *Juvenile and Family Court Journal* 35:13 (1984).

68. Mass.Gen.Laws Ann. ch. C.119, 61 (1979).

69. Ind. Code Ann. 31–6–2(d)1987; Ill. Ann. Stat. Ch. 37 Sec. 805 (1988); Penn. Stat. Ann. Title 42 6355(a) (1982).

70. Joseph White, "The Waiver Decision: A Judicial, Prosecutorial or Legislative Responsibility," *Justice for Children* 2:28–30 (1987).

71. Donna Hamparian, et al., *Major Issues in Juvenile Justice Information and Training, Youth in Adult Court: Between Two Worlds* (Washington, D.C.: U.S. Department of Justice, 1982), pp. 18–21; see also Ver. Code Ann. Sec. 33–635.

72. Linda A. Szymanski, *Statutory Waiver Criteria* (Pittsburgh: National Center For Juvenile Justice, October 1989).

73. Material in this section comes from Charles Thomas and Shay Bilchik, "Prosecuting Juveniles in Criminal Courts: A Legal and Empirical Analysis," *Journal of Criminal Law and Criminology* 76:439–79 (1985).

74. Florida Statutes Ann. 39.02(5)(b) (West Supp. 1985).

75. Florida Statutes Ann. 39.02(2)(c)(1).

76. Florida Statutes Ann. 39.02(2)(c)(1–8).

77. Florida Statutes Ann. 39.02(2)(a).

78. Florida Statutes Ann. 39.04(2)(e)(4).

79. 383 U.S. 541, 86 S.Ct. 1045, 16 L.Ed.2d 84 (1966); 421 U.S. 519, 95 S.Ct. 1179, 44 L.Ed.2d 346 (1975).

80. Barry Feld, "Delinquent Careers and Criminal Policy," *Criminology* 21:195–212 (1983).

81. Barry Feld, "The Juvenile Court Meets the Principle of the Offense: Legislative Changes in Juvenile Waiver Statutes," *Journal of Criminal Law and Criminology* 78:471–534 (1987); see also Paul Marcotte, "Criminal Kids," *American Bar Association Journal* 76:60–66 (1990).

82. *Laws of the State of New York, Juvenile Justice Reform Act of 1976*, ch. 878.

83. Hamparian, et al., "Major Issues," pp. 18–21.

84. Richard Allinson and Joan Potter, "Is New York's Tough Juvenile Law a Charade?" *Corrections* 9:40–45 (February 1983).

85. Cary Rudman, Eliot Hartstone, Jeffrey Fagan, and Melinda Moore, "Violent Youth in Adult Court: Process and Punishment," *Crime and Delinquency* 32:75–96 (1986).

86. "Study Finds Strict Handling of Youths Sent to Adult Court," *Criminal Justice Newsletter,* 15 May 1987.

87. M. A. Bortner, "Traditional Rhetoric, Organizational Realities: Remand of Juveniles to Adult Court," *Crime and Delinquency* 32:53–73 (1986).

88. Jeffrey Fagan, Martin Forst, and T. Scott Vivona, "Racial Determinants of the Judicial Transfer Decision: Prosecuting Violent Youth in Criminal Court," *Crime and Delinquency* 33:359–86 (1987); also J. Fagan, E. Slaughter, and E. Hartstone, "Blind Justice: The Impact of Race on the Juvenile Justice Process," *Crime and Delinquency* 53: 224–58 (1987).

89. Soler, et al., *Representing the Child Client.*

90. F. W. Barnes and R. S. Franz, "Questionably Adult: Determinants and Effects of the Juvenile Waiver Decision," *Justice Quarterly* 6:117–35 (1989).

91. See the interesting case of *Toomey v. Clark*, 876 F.2d 1433 (9th Cir., 1989), where the juvenile court's consideration of criteria involving petitioner's pregnancy in its decision to decline jurisdiction was not sex discrimination and a violation of the equal protection law.

17 The Juvenile Trial and Disposition

The development of the juvenile court and the separate process for handling children resulted from reform movements of the nineteenth and early twentieth centuries. The strategic role played by the juvenile court in setting juvenile justice policy has already been described. Throughout its history, the juvenile court has played a major role in helping to care for troubled youths who come before its tribunals. In fact, its influence is probably greater than that of the adult court because it is also charged with the care and treatment of offenders and not merely their punishment and control.[1] Therefore, the court and its representatives must consider their actions carefully, because a wrong decision can have long-term consequences for young offenders.

Compounding the problem is the magnitude of cases handled by the nation's juvenile courts each year. The latest study found that the nation's juvenile courts petitioned and formally processed an estimated 535,000 delinquency offense cases and 90,000 status offense cases (see Figure 17.1). This estimate does not take into account the hundreds of thousands of informally handled or nonpetitioned

FIGURE 17.1

Dispositions by juvenile courts

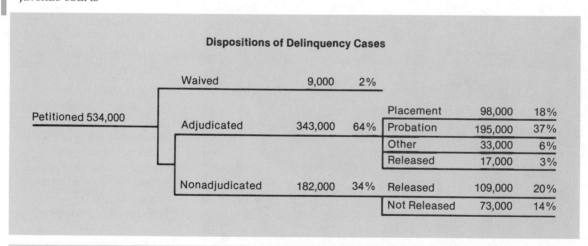

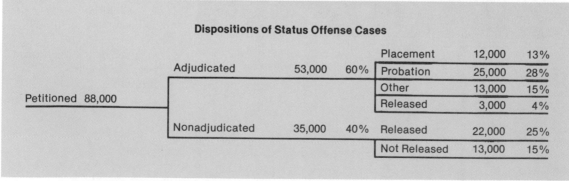

Source: H. Snyder, T. Finnegan, E. Nimick, M. Sickmund, D. Sullivan, and N. Tierney, *Juvenile Court Statistics, 1985* (Pittsburgh: National Center for Juvenile Justice, 1989), pp. 14–34.

cases adjusted or diverted by the courts. Thus, the nation's juvenile court system is faced with dealing with an enormous number of youths who need care, protection, treatment, and control.

This chapter describes the adjudication stage of the juvenile justice process. The term *adjudication* refers to the trial stage of the juvenile court proceedings. It initially explores the role of the important legal actors in the trial and disposition—the juvenile court prosecutor, judge, defense attorney and probation officer. In addition, it looks at the constitutional and due process rights of the child at the trial—particularly those rights dealing with counsel and trial by jury—through a detailed analysis of landmark U.S. Supreme Court decisions. Various procedural rules that govern the adjudicatory and dispositional hearings are also reviewed. The chapter concludes with a discussion of dispositional alternatives and trends in sentencing that effect juvenile dispositions.

THE PROSECUTOR IN THE JUVENILE COURT

The **juvenile prosecutor** is the government attorney responsible for representing the interests of the state and who brings the state's case against the accused child. Depending on the level of government and the jurisdiction, the prosecutor can be called a district attorney, a county attorney, a state attorney, or a United States attorney. He or she is a member of the bar and becomes a public prosecutor through political appointment or popular election.

Ordinarily, the juvenile prosecutor is a staff member of the local prosecuting attorney's office. If the office of the district attorney is in an urban area and of sufficient size, the juvenile prosecutor may work exclusively on juvenile and other family law matters. If the caseload of juvenile offenders is small, the juvenile prosecutor also has criminal prosecution responsibilities.

For the first sixty years of its existence, the juvenile court did not include a prosecutor as a representative of the state in court proceedings.[2] The concept of advocacy and the adversary process were seen as inconsistent with the philosophy of diagnosis and treatment in the juvenile court system. The court followed a social service helping model with informal and noncriminal proceedings believed to be in the best interests of the child.

As we know, these views changed dramatically with the Supreme Court decisions of *Kent v. United States*, *In re Gault* and *In re Winship*, which ushered in an era of greater formality and due process rights for children in the juvenile court system.[3] Today, almost all jurisdictions require by law that a prosecutor be present in the juvenile court.

The prosecutor's role in juvenile court is expanding. A number of states have passed legislation giving prosecutors control over intake and waiver decisions. Some have passed concurrent jurisdiction laws, which allow prosecutors to decide where to bring serious juvenile cases. In some jurisdictions, it is the prosecutor and not the juvenile court judge who is entrusted with making the critical decision of whether to transfer the case to adult court. Consequently, the role of juvenile court prosecutor has become a critical element of the juvenile justice process.

In the words of the American Bar Association, "An attorney for the state, hereinafter referred to as the juvenile prosecutor, should participate in every proceeding of every stage of every case subject to the jurisdiction of the family court in which the state has an interest."[4] Including a prosecutor in juvenile court balances the interests of the state, the defense attorney, the child, and the judge in their respective roles. The independence of their respective functions and responsibilities is preserved.

The Responsibilities of the Juvenile Prosecutor

A prosecutor enforces the law, represents the government, maintains proper standards of ethical conduct as an attorney and court officer, participates in programs and legislation involving legal changes in the juvenile justice system, acts as a spokesperson for the field of law, and takes an active role in the community in preventing delinquency and protecting the rights of juveniles. Of these responsibilities, representing the government while presenting the state's case to the court is the prosecutor's most frequent task. In this regard, the prosecutor has many of the following duties:

- Investigates possible violations of the law
- Cooperates with the police, intake officer, and probation officer regarding the facts alleged in the petition
- Authorizes, reviews, and prepares petitions for court
- Plays a role in the initial detention decision
- Represents the case in all pretrial motions, probable cause hearings, and consent decrees
- Represents the state at transfer hearings
- If necessary, recommends physical or mental examinations for children brought before the court
- Seeks amendments or dismissals of filed petitions if appropriate
- Represents the state at the adjudication of the case
- Represents the state at the disposition of the case
- Enters into plea-bargaining discussions with the defense attorney
- Represents the government on appeal and in habeas corpus proceedings
- Is involved in hearings dealing with violation of probation

The power to initiate formal petitions against a child is key to prosecutorial responsibility. The ability either to initiate or to discontinue delinquency or status offense allegations represents the control and power a juvenile prosecutor has over a child. Prosecutors have broad discretion in the exercise of their duties. Because due process rights have been extended to juveniles, the prosecutor's role in the juvenile court has in some ways become similar to the role of the attorney in the adult court. In the case of *State v. Grayer*, for example, a Nebraska court upheld the validity of the discretionary power of the juvenile prosecutor to decide whether to prosecute the child as a juvenile or as an adult.[5]

Such an approach demonstrates the judicial movement toward developing procedures for juveniles that are similar to those for adult offenders. However, it is important for the juvenile prosecutor not only to represent the government but also to remain cognizant of the philosophy and purpose of the juvenile court.

The Real World of Juvenile Prosecution

While it seems evident that prosecutors are beginning to play an ever-expanding role in juvenile courts, the actual impact of their presence may be open to debate. Research by John Laub and Bruce MacMurray conducted in the juvenile court in Boston indicates that prosecutors may find their roles to be rather limited in controlling juvenile court policies.[6] Laub and MacMurray found that prosecutors are considered "outsiders" whose adversarial ideas are not appreciated by juvenile court personnel. Some judges believe that the voice of law and order has a limited role in the juvenile court and that if district attorneys actively pursue such conservative policies as binding children over to the adult court, they will be committing "political suicide." Similarly, the researchers found that these district attorneys do not relish their juvenile court assignments and consider juvenile cases to be "garbage cases."[7]

Laub and MacMurray found that juvenile court personnel are not open to the idea of having the prosecutor play an important role in the processing of cases or introducing an adversarial system within its confines. They suggest that the prosecutor has to be perceived as being an insider or part of the team before he or she can begin to have an important influence on juvenile court operations.

To control the role played by the prosecutor in juvenile court, some states have attempted to draw up general policy guidelines or principles for juvenile prosecution. In a report entitled "Principles of Juvenile Court Prosecution," the guidelines for the state of Massachusetts declare that the prosecutor is an advocate of the state's interest in juvenile court. This means that the state's interest includes: (1) The protection of the community from the danger of harmful conduct by the restraint and rehabilitation of juvenile offenders and (2) the concern shared by all juvenile justice system personnel, as *parens patriae*, with promoting the best interests of the child. The prosecutor also has a duty to seek justice in juvenile court by insisting upon fair and lawful procedures. This entails the responsibility to ensure, for example, that baseless prosecutions are not brought, that all juveniles receive fair and equal treatment, that liberal discovery of the state's case is available to defense counsel, that exculpatory evidence is made available to the defense counsel, and that excessively harsh dispositions are not sought. It also entails the responsibility to oversee police investigative behavior to ensure its compliance with the law.[8]

Because children are committing more serious crimes today and the courts have granted juveniles constitutional safeguards, the prosecutor is likely to play a more significant role in the juvenile court system than in the past.

THE JUVENILE COURT JUDGE

The **judge** is the central character in a court of juvenile or family law. His or her responsibilities are quite varied and have become far more extensive and complex in recent years. Following *Kent* and *Gault*, new legal rulings have probed the basic legal aspects of the juvenile justice system. In addition, juvenile cases are far more complex today and represent issues involving social change, such as truancy, alcoholism, the use of drugs by children, juvenile prostitution, and violent juvenile crime. Such cases involve problems of both public safety and individualized treatment for children.

Juvenile or family court judges perform the following functions:

- Rule on pretrial motions involving such legal issues as arrest, search and seizure, interrogation, and lineup identification
- Make decisions about the continued detention of children prior to trial
- Make decisions about plea-bargaining agreements and the informal adjustment of juvenile cases
- Handle bench and jury trials, rule on the appropriateness of conduct, settle questions of evidence and procedure, and guide the questioning of witnesses
- Assume responsibility for holding dispositional hearings and deciding on the treatment accorded the child
- Handle waiver proceedings
- Handle appeals where allowed by statute and where no prior contact has been made with the case[9]

In addition, judges often have extensive control and influence over other service agencies of the court: probation, the court clerk, the law enforcement officer, and the office of the juvenile prosecutor. Of course, courts differ organizationally and procedurally. Larger courts have more resources to handle the volume of juvenile cases. They may have unique approaches to juvenile problems, including specialized offender caseloads, such as drug users, diversion programs, and a whole host of special social services. Smaller courts have no more than a judge, a clerk, and a probation staff.

Juvenile court judges exercise considerable leadership in developing services and solutions to juvenile justice problems. In this role, juvenile court judges must respond to the external pressures the community places on juvenile court resources. In fact, research indicates that juvenile court decision making may be influenced more by the needs of the outside community than by the particular philosophy or views of the presiding judge.[10]

Despite the political realities of their position, juvenile court judges can have enormous personal influence over the outcome of delinquency proceedings. Judges who believe that the juvenile court should remain an informal forum controlled by their personal views of justice can use their power to control the trial process. The judge has the power to control the appointment of attorneys in most cases, and it is possible for them to strike the names of overly zealous advocates from law guardian lists. The judge often controls the appointment and subsequent careers of court personnel, such as clerks and probation officers; those who do not sympathize with the judge's position on juvenile justice can find their careers in jeopardy. In his observations of juvenile court, Joseph Sanborn observed at least one judge who told lawyers not to win cases and viewed himself as the guardian and the lawyer as the enemy of the child being tried.[11]

Selection and Qualifications of Juvenile Court Judges

A variety of methods are used to select juvenile court judges.[12] In some jurisdictions, the governor simply appoints candidates chosen by a screening board. In other states, judges are chosen by popular partisan elections, while in others,

Judge Benjamin Lindsey, left, and others of the juvenile court talk to a juvenile offender in the judge's chambers. Lindsey was a judge in the juvenile court of Denver from 1900 until 1927.

judges run for office without party affiliation. In three states—Connecticut, Virginia, and South Carolina—the state legislature appoints judges. About a dozen states have adopted the **Missouri Plan,** which involves (1) a commission to nominate candidates for the bench; (2) an elected official, usually the governor, to make appointments from the list submitted by the commission; and (3) subsequent nonpartisan and noncontested elections in which incumbent judges run on their records (usually every three years).

In some jurisdictions, juvenile court judges handle family-related cases exclusively. In others, they handle criminal and civil cases as well. Traditionally, juvenile court judges have been relegated to a lower status than other judges, with less prestige, responsibility, and salary. Judges assigned to juvenile courts have not ordinarily been chosen from the highest levels of the legal profession. Such groups as the American Judicature Society have noted that the field of juvenile justice has often been shortchanged by the appointment of unqualified judges and staff. In some jurisdictions, particularly major urban areas, juvenile court judges may be of the highest caliber, but many courts throughout the nation continue to function with mediocre judges. As the Advisory Council of Judges of the National Council on Crime and Delinquency states, "Juvenile court has been brilliantly conceived; its legal and social facets are not antithetical, but the preservation of equilibrium between them, which is the key to their successful fusion, depends upon the legal knowledge, social perspective, and eternal vigilance of one person, the judge."[13]

Inducing the best legally trained individuals to accept juvenile court judgeships is a very important goal. Where the juvenile court is part of the highest general court of trial jurisdiction, the problem of securing qualified personnel is not as great. However, if the juvenile court is of limited or specialized jurisdiction and has the authority to try only minor cases, it may attract only poorly trained and poorly qualified personnel. The juvenile court has a negative image to overcome, because even though what it does is of great importance to parents, children, and society in general, it has been placed at the lowest level of the judicial hierarchy. One group that has struggled to upgrade the juvenile court judiciary is the **National Council of Juvenile and Family Court Judges.** Located in Reno, Nevada, this organization sponsors research and continuing legal education efforts designed to help local judges master their field of expertise. Its research arm, the National Center for Juvenile Justice in Pittsburgh, also offers assistance to courts in developing information processing, methods to develop statute analysis, and legal consultation to judicial groups.[14]

THE DEFENSE ATTORNEY

Through a series of leading Supreme Court decisions, the right of a criminal defendant to have counsel at state trials has become a fundamental right in the criminal justice system.[15] Today, state courts must provide counsel to indigent defendants who face the possibility of incarceration.

The American Bar Association (ABA) has described the responsibility of the legal profession to the juvenile court in Standard 2.3 of *Standards Relating to Counsel for Private Parties.* The ABA states that legal representation should be provided in all proceedings arising from or related to a delinquency or in-need-of-supervision action — including mental competency, transfer, postdisposition, probation revocation and classification, institutional transfer, and disciplinary or other administrative proceedings related to the treatment process — that may substantially effect the juvenile's custody, status, or course of treatment.[16]

Over the past two decades, the rules and procedures of criminal and juvenile justice administration have become extremely complex. Specialized knowledge is essential for the adversary process to operate effectively. Today, preparation of a case for juvenile court often involves detailed investigation of a crime, knowledge of court procedures, use of rules of evidence, and skills in trial advocacy. Prosecuting and defense attorneys must both have this expertise, particularly when a child's freedom is at stake. The right to counsel in the juvenile justice system is essential if children are to have a fair chance of presenting their cases in court.

In many respects, the role of **defense attorneys** in the juvenile process is similar to the one they play in the criminal and civil areas. Defense attorneys representing children in the juvenile court play an active and important part in virtually all stages of juvenile proceedings. For example, the lawyer helps to clarify jurisdictional problems and to decide whether there is sufficient evidence to warrant filing a formal petition at intake. The defense attorney also helps outline the child's position regarding detention hearings and bail and explores the opportunities for informal adjustment of the case. If no adjustment or diversion occurs, the attorney represents the child at adjudication, presenting evidence and cross-examining witnesses to see that the child's position is made clear to the court. Defense attorneys also play a critically important role in the dispositional hearing. They present evidence bearing on the treatment decision and help the court formulate alternative plans for the child's care. Finally, defense attorneys pursue any appeals from the trial, represent the child in probation revocation proceedings, and generally protect the child's right to treatment.

In some cases, a **guardian** *ad litem* may be appointed by the court. The guardian *ad litem* is an attorney appointed by the court "to promote and protect the interests of a child involved in a judicial proceeding, through assuring representation of those interests in the courts and throughout the social services and ancillary service systems."[17] While nominally used in abuse, neglect, and dependency cases, the guardian ad litem may be appointed in delinquency cases where there is a question of a need for a particular treatment (for example, placement in a mental health center) and the offender and his or her attorney resist placement. The guardian *ad litem* may advocate for the commitment on the grounds that it is in the child's "best interests."[18]

Public Defender Services for Children

To satisfy the requirement that indigent children and their families be provided with counsel at the various stages of the juvenile justice process, the federal government and the states have had to expand **public defender** services. Three primary alternatives exist for providing children with legal counsel in the juvenile court today: (1) an all-public defender program, (2) an appointed private counsel system, and (3) a combination system of public defenders and appointed private attorneys.

The public defender program is a statewide program organized by legislation and funded by the government to provide counsel to children at public expense. This approach brings to juvenile proceedings the expertise of lawyers who spend a considerable amount of time representing juvenile offenders every day. Defender programs generally provide separate office space for juvenile court personnel as well as support staff and training programs for new lawyers.

In many rural areas, individual public defender programs are not available, and defense services are offered through appointed private counsel. Private lawyers are assigned to individual juvenile court cases and receive compensation for the time and services they provide to the child and the family. When private attorneys are used in large urban areas, they are generally selected from a list established by the court, and they often operate in conjunction with a public defender program. A system of assigned counsel used by itself suffers from such problems as unequal case assignments, inadequate legal fees, and lack of supportive or supervisory services.

Even though public defense services for children have grown in recent years, a major concern is continued provision of quality representation to the child and the family at all stages of the juvenile process. In some jurisdictions today, counsel is available to children in only part of the juvenile proceedings. In other jurisdictions, children are not represented in persons-in-need-of-supervision or neglect cases. Often public defender agencies and the assigned counsel system are understaffed and lack adequate support services. Representation should be upgraded in all areas of the juvenile court system.

Although juvenile court practice has not traditionally been viewed by the bar with the same esteem as a lucrative corporate practice or adult trial work, defense attorneys must meet the same high standards for competency and professional responsibility when representing a child in the juvenile justice system.

Do Lawyers Make a Difference in Juvenile Court?

A number of studies have found that having an attorney either makes no difference in juvenile cases or actually results in more damaging dispositions for clients.[19] Juveniles represented by an attorney are more likely to receive institutional sentences than those who waive their right to counsel. While not all research efforts arrive at this conclusion, there is sufficient evidence that at least in some jurisdictions, legal representation may not be in a juvenile's best interests.

One possible reason for this surprising finding is that only the most serious juvenile offenders request counsel, and these youths also have the greatest likelihood of receiving an institutional sentence. Another view is that counsel in juvenile court functions in a nonadversarial capacity, furthering the interests of the juvenile court rather than those of the client. **Joseph Sanborn** found quite a bit of role confusion in the three juvenile courts he studied. He found that some juvenile court personnel believed that the lawyer's role should be one of a fighting advocate for their client, while others viewed them as guardians who helped guide the juvenile through the treatment process.[20] Some of those Sanborn interviewed felt that attorneys should fight to prove their clients innocent during the trial stage, but that once delinquency was established, they should revert to the guardian role in order to obtain the best treatment possible for their clients. In a case in which the judge believes that a child needs placement in a secure facility, the attorney may help convince the client that placement is in his or her best interest, rather than use all means to block the incarceration.[21] Still another explanation is that because juvenile defense work is generally a low-paid, low-prestige aspect of the law, the services children receive are less than adequate.

The Problems of Juvenile Defense Work

The problem of legal counsel in juvenile court has been confirmed by a New York study of juvenile defense work. The study, sponsored by the New York State Bar Association, found significant deficiencies in the quality of legal care given youths by their court-appointed lawyers. In 45 percent of the almost two hundred cases studied, the representation was considered inadequate, and in another 47 percent, it appeared that the lawyer had done little or no preparation on the case.

The study also found that lawyer representing children had little knowledge of the statutes governing juvenile law and were also unfamiliar with social services available to children. There were frequent instances of insensitivity to the client's feelings, particularly in cases involving sexual issues or abuse.[22] Based on such information, improved legal services for indigent juveniles may be a tough goal to achieve.

On the other hand, Sanford Fox claims: "Few of the rights granted children in the juvenile justice system would have much real meaning without an attorney to assert them or to advise the child when it is in his best interests to waive them."[23] However, Fox's statement has relevance only when counsel uses the full power of the law to protect the client's best interests. With the increase in serious crimes by juveniles and harsher sentences, appropriate procedural safeguards, such as the right to counsel, are essential elements of the juvenile justice system.

In one of the most comprehensive empirical examinations to date on right to counsel, Barry Feld analyzed variations in the rates of representation and the impact of counsel on juvenile delinquency and status proceedings in Minnesota in 1986.[24] Feld reported that overall, only 45.3 percent of juveniles in Minnesota received the assistance of counsel. In counties with high rates of representation, 94.5 percent of juveniles had counsel; in counties with medium rates, 46.8 percent had counsel; and in counties with low rates, only 19.3 percent had counsel.[25] The seriousness of the offense increases the likelihood of representation, while many juveniles who commit petty offenses go unrepresented because they waive their right to counsel.

Feld's findings confirm previous research in this area: youths with lawyers receive more serious sentencing dispositions. Almost twice as many youths were removed from their homes and institutionalized in the high representation counties as in areas where there is low representation. Feld's study provides support for the existence of "varieties of juvenile justice" and suggests that administrative criteria and sentencing guidelines should be used to structure dispositional practices in the juvenile court.[26] Feld acknowledges the punitive nature of today's juvenile court and argues that the state must provide appropriate due process protection in this more formal legalistic system.[27]

ADJUDICATION

At the **adjudication** stage of the juvenile process, a hearing is held to determine the merits of the petition claiming that a child is either a delinquent youth or in need of court supervision. The judge is required to make a finding on the evidence in the case and arrive at a judgment. Adjudication is comparable to an adult trial. Rules of evidence in adult criminal proceedings are generally applicable, and the standard of proof used — "beyond a reasonable doubt" — is similar to that in adult trials. The majority of juvenile cases do not reach the adjudicatory state, but serious delinquency cases based on violations of the criminal law, situations where children deny any guilt, cases of repeat offenders, and cases where children are a threat to themselves or the community often do reach this stage.

Much of the controversy over the adjudication process has centered on whether juveniles have been accorded fair procedures. State juvenile codes vary with regard to the basic requirements of due process and fairness. Most juvenile courts have bifurcated hearings — that is, separate hearings for adjudication and disposition. At disposition hearings, evidence can be submitted that reflects non-legal factors, such as the child's home life, relationships, and background. While there has not been sufficient research on hearing fairness, there are some indications that minorities may be handled with disproportionate harshness at disposition.[28] However, what sometimes seems to be racial or ethnic bias is actually a result of legal or socially relevant factors, such as the willingness to plea-bargain, the seriousness of the crime, school performance, and so on.

At present, most state juvenile codes provide for specific rules of procedure and a finding at adjudication. These rules require that a written petition be submitted to the court, assure the right of a child to have an attorney, provide that the adjudication proceedings be recorded, allow the petition to be amended, and provide that a child's plea be accepted. Where the child admits to the facts of the petition, the courts generally seek assurance that the plea is voluntary. If plea

bargaining is used, prosecutors, defense counsel, and trial judges take steps to assure the fairness of such negotiations.

At the end of the adjudication hearing, most juvenile court statutes require the judge to make a factual finding on the legal issues and evidence reviewed in the child's hearing. In the criminal court, this finding is normally an entry of judgment involving a verdict. In the juvenile court, the juvenile court judge normally (1) makes a finding of fact that the child or juvenile is not delinquent or in need of supervision, (2) makes a finding of fact that the juvenile is delinquent or in need of supervision, or (3) dismisses the case because of insufficient or faulty evidence. In some jurisdictions, informal alternatives are used, such as filing the case with no further consequences or continuing the case without a finding. These alternatives involve no determination of delinquency or noncriminal behavior. Because of the philosophy of the juvenile court of treatment and rehabilitation, a delinquency finding is not the same thing as a criminal conviction. The disabilities associated with conviction, such as disqualifications for employment, entrance into the military service, or involvement in politics, are not created by an adjudication of delinquency.

Consequently, there are still some significant differences between adult and juvenile proceedings. For instance, only a small proportion of states entitle juveniles to jury trials. And in almost all jurisdictions, juvenile trials remain closed to the public.[29]

Constitutional Rights at Trial

In addition to state juvenile code requirements, the U.S. Supreme Court has mandated the application of constitutional due process standards to the juvenile trial. The term *due process* is mentioned in the Fifth and Fourteenth Amendments to the U.S. Constitution. It refers to the need in our legal system for rules and procedures that protect individual rights. Having the right to due process means that no person can be deprived of life, liberty, or property without such protections as legal counsel, an open and fair hearing, an opportunity to confront those making accusations against them, and so on. Basically, due process is intended to guarantee that fundamental fairness is available to every citizen.

For many years, children were deprived of their due process rights because the *parens patriae* philosophy governed their relationship to the juvenile justice system. Such rights as having counsel and confronting one's accusers were forbidden. Why should children need protection from the state when the only issue was their treatment, care, and protection? This view changed in the 1960s when, under the leadership of Chief Justice Earl Warren, the U.S. Supreme Court recognized the problems inherent in the juvenile justice system and began to grant due process rights and procedures to minors. As a result of Supreme Court activism, a child is now entitled to many of the same due process rights as an adult. As Justice Hugo Black stated in the landmark 1967 case *In re Gault:*

> When a person, infant or adult, can be seized by the state, charged and convicted, for violating a state criminal law, and then ordered by the state to be confined for six years, I think the Constitution requires that he be tried in accordance with the guarantees of all the provisions of the Bill of Rights, made applicable to the states by the Fourteenth Amendment. Appellants are entitled to these rights not because fairness, impartiality and orderliness, in short, the essentials of due process, require them, and not because they are the procedural rules which have been fashioned from the generality of due process, but because they are specifically and unequivocally granted by provisions of the Fifth and Sixth Amendments which the Fourteenth Amendment makes applicable to the states.[30]

The Warren Court set forth the role of due process in juvenile justice through major decisions made during the 1960s, beginning with *Kent v. United States*, decided in 1966.[31] In *Kent*, the court held that a transfer proceedings was a critically important stage in the juvenile process and must hold to at least minimal due process and fair treatment standards as required by the Fourteenth Amendment. This case was detailed in Chapter 15.

In the landmark case of *In re Gault*, the Supreme Court further articulated the basic requirements of due process that must be satisfied in juvenile court proceedings. It held that in an adjudicatory hearing:

■ The child must be given adequate notice of the charges.
■ The child and the parent must be advised of the right to be represented by counsel.
■ The child has a constitutional privilege against self-incrimination.
■ The child has the right of confrontation and sworn testimony of witnesses available for cross-examination.[32]

Because of the importance of the *Gault* case, it is set out in the Focus on Delinquency entitled "*In re Gault.*"

The *Gault* decision reshaped the constitutional and philosophical nature of the juvenile court system. As a result, those working in the system — judges, social workers, attorneys, and so on — were faced with the problem of reaffirming the rehabilitative ideal of the juvenile court while ensuring that juveniles received proper procedural due process rights. Prior to the *Gault* decision, only a few

In re Gault

Facts

Gerald Gault, 15 years of age, was taken into custody by the sheriff of Gila County, Arizona, because a woman complained that he and another boy had made an obscene telephone call to her. At the time, Gerald was under a six-month probation as a result of being found delinquent for stealing a wallet. Because of the verbal complaint, Gerald was taken to the children's home. His parents were not informed that he was being taken into custody. His mother appeared in the evening and was told by the superintendent of detention that a hearing would be held in the juvenile court the following day. On the day in question, the police officer who had taken Gerald into custody filed a petition alleging his delinquency. Gerald, his mother, and the police officer appeared before the judge in his chambers. Mrs. Cook, the complainant, was not at the hearing. Gerald was questioned about the telephone calls and was sent back to the detention home and then subsequently released a few days later.

On the day of Gerald's release, Mrs. Gault received a letter indicating that a hearing would be held on Gerald's delinquency a few days later. A hearing was held, and the complainant again was not present. There was no transcript or recording of the proceedings, and the juvenile officer stated that Gerald had admitted making the lewd telephone calls. Neither the boy nor his parents were advised of any right to remain silent, the right to be represented by counsel, or any other constitutional rights. At the conclusion of the hearing, the juvenile court committed Gerald as a juvenile delinquent to the state industrial school in Arizona for the period of his minority.

This meant that, at the age of 15, Gerald was sent to the state school until he reached the age of 21 unless discharged sooner. An adult charged with the same crime would have received a maximum punishment of no more than a $50 fine or two months in prison.

continued

states required that juveniles have assistance of counsel. Now, according to Linda Szymanski of the National Center for Juvenile Justice, virtually all states provide counsel in one form or another at various stages of the juvenile proceedings.[33]

Following the *Gault* case, the Supreme Court decided *In re Winship* in 1970. This case considered the problem of the quantum of proof required in juvenile delinquency adjudications.[34] Prior to *Winship*, most juvenile courts judged the sufficiency of evidence in juvenile matters by applying a preponderance of the evidence, or clear and convincing evidence, test. In *Winship*, the Court rejected the idea that the juvenile system was a civil system and held that the Fourteenth Amendment due process clause required that delinquency charges in juvenile court be proved beyond a reasonable doubt.

Although the traditional juvenile court was severely altered by *Kent*, *Gault*, and *Winship*, the trend for increased rights for juveniles was somewhat curtailed by the Supreme Court's decision in *McKeiver v. Pennsylvania* (1971). In *McKeiver*, the

Decision

Gerald's attorneys filed a writ of habeas corpus, which was denied by the Superior Court of the state of Arizona. That decision was subsequently affirmed by the Arizona Supreme Court. On appeal to the U.S. Supreme Court, Gerald's counsel argued that the juvenile code of Arizona under which Gerald was found delinquent was invalid because it was contrary to the due process clause of the Fourteenth Amendment. In addition, Gerald was denied the following basic due process rights: (1) notice of the charges with regard to their timeliness and specificity, (2) right to counsel, (3) right to confrontation and cross-examination, (4) privilege against self-incrimination, (5) right to a transcript of the trial record, and (6) right to appellate review. In deciding the case, the Supreme Court had to determine whether procedural due process of law within the context of fundamental fairness under the Fourteenth Amendment applied to juvenile delinquency proceedings in which a child is committed to a state industrial school.

The Court, in a far-reaching opinion written by Justice Abe Fortas, agreed that Gerald's constitutional rights had been violated. Notice of charges was an essential ingredient of due process of law, as was the right to counsel, the right to cross-examine and to confront witnesses, and the privilege against self-incrimination. The questions of appellate review and a right to a transcript were not answered by the Court in this case.

Significance of the Case

The *Gault* case established that a child had the procedural due process constitutional rights listed above in delinquency adjudication proceedings where the consequences were that the child could be committed to a state institution. It was confined to rulings at the adjudication stage of the juvenile process.

However, this decision was significant not only because of the procedural reforms it initiated but also because of its far-reaching impact throughout the entire juvenile justice system. *Gault* instilled in juvenile proceedings the development of due process standards at the pretrial, trial, and post-trial stages of the juvenile process. While recognizing the history and development of the juvenile court, it sought to accommodate the motives of rehabilitation and treatment with children's rights. It recognized the principle of fundamental fairness ofthe law for children as well as for adults. Judged in the context of today's juvenile justice system, *Gault* redefined the relationships between juveniles, their parents, and the state. It remains the single most significant constitutional case in the area of juvenile justice.

Source: In re Gault, 387 U.S. 1; 87 S.Ct. 1248 (1967).

Court held that trial by jury in a juvenile court's adjudicative stage is not a constitutional requirement.[35] This decision, however, does not prevent states from giving the juvenile a trial by jury as a state constitutional right or by state statute. In the majority of states, a child has no such right, while a small number of jurisdictions do grant it.

In re Winship and *McKeiver v. Pennsylvania,* major decisions signaling the Supreme Court's determination to evaluate the adjudicatory rights of juvenile offenders, are highlighted in a following Focus on Delinquency.

Once an adjudicatory hearing has been completed, the court is normally required to enter a judgment against the child. This may take the form of declaring the child delinquent, adjudging the child to be a ward of the court, or possibly even suspending judgment so as to avoid the stigma of a juvenile record. After a judgment has been entered in accordance with the appropriate state statute, the court can begin its determination of possible dispositions for the child.

In re Winship and McKeiver v. Pennsylvania

Standard of Proof: In re Winship

Following the *Gault* case came *In re Winship*. This case expressly held that a juvenile in a delinquency adjudication must be proven guilty beyond a reasonable doubt.

Facts

Winship, a 12-year-old boy in New York, stole $112 from a woman's pocketbook. The petition that charged Winship with delinquency alleged that this act, if done by an adult, would constitute larceny. Winship was adjudicated a delinquent on the basis of a preponderance of the evidence submitted at the court hearing. During a subsequent dispositional hearing, Winship was ordered placed in a training school in New York State for an initial period of eighteen months, subject to extensions of his commitment until his eighteenth birthday—six years in total. The New York State Supreme Court and the New York Court of Appeals affirmed the lower court decision, sustaining the conviction.

Decision

The problem in the case was whether Section 744(b) of the New York State Family Court Act was constitutional. This section provided that any determination at the conclusion of an adjudicatory hearing must be based on a preponderance of the evidence. The judge decided Winship's guilt on the basis of this standard and not on the basis of proof beyond a reasonable doubt, which is the standard in the adult criminal justice system. The issue in the case was whether proof beyond a reasonable doubt was essential to due process and fair treatment for juveniles charged with an act that would constitute a crime if committed by an adult.

Significance of the Case

Although the standard of proof beyond a reasonable doubt is not stated in the Constitution, the U.S. Supreme Court said that *Gault* had established that due process required the essentials of fair treatment, although it did not require that the adjudication conform to all the requirements of the criminal trial. The Court further said that the due process clause recognized proof beyond a reasonable doubt as being among the essentials of fairness required when a child is charged with a delinquent act. The state of New York argued that juvenile delinquency proceedings were civil in nature, not criminal, and that the preponderance of evidence standard was therefore valid. The U.S. Supreme Court indicated that the standard of proof beyond a reasonable doubt plays a vital role in the American criminal justice system and ensures a greater degree of safety for the presumption of innocence of those accused of a crime.

Thus, the *Winship* case required proof beyond a reasonable doubt as a standard for juvenile adjudication proceedings and eliminated the use of lesser standards such as a preponderance of the evidence, clear and convincing proof, and reasonable proof.

Right to a Jury Trial: McKeiver v. Pennsylvania

One of the most controversial issues in the areas of children's rights at adjudication involves the jury trial. Although the Sixth Amendment guarantees to the adult criminal defendant the right to a jury

continued

trial, the Supreme Court had not seen fit to grant this right to juvenile offenders. In fact, the U.S. Constitution is silent on whether all defendants, including those charged with misdemeanors, have a right to a trial by jury. In the case of *Duncan v. Louisiana*, the Supreme Court held that the Sixth Amendment right to a jury trial applied to all adult defendants accused of serious crimes. However, no mention was made of the juvenile offender.

The case of *McKeiver v. Pennsylvania* deals with the right of the juvenile defendant to a jury trial.

Facts

Joseph McKeiver, age 16, was charged with robbery, larceny, and receiving stolen goods, all of which were felonies under Pennsylvania law. McKeiver was subsequently declared delinquent at an adjudication hearing and placed on probation after his request for a jury trial was denied.

In another case, Edward Terry, age 15, was charged with assault and battery on a police officer, misdemeanors under Pennsylvania law. He was declared a juvenile delinquent after an adjudication following a denial of his request for trial by jury.

In an unrelated case in North Carolina, a group of juveniles were charged with willful, riotous, and disorderly conduct, declared delinquent, and placed on probation. Their request for a jury trial was denied.

The Supreme Court heard all three cases together on the single issue of whether a juvenile has a constitutional right to a jury trial in the juvenile court system.

Decision

The Court was required to decide whether the due process clause of the Fourteenth Amendment guarantees the right to a jury trial in the adjudication of a juvenile court delinquency case. It answered in the negative, stating that the right to a jury trial guaranteed by the Sixth Amendment and incorporated in the Fourteenth Amendment is not among the constitutional safeguards that the due process clause requires at delinquency adjudication hearings. The Court's reasons were as follows:

- A jury trial is not a necessary component of accurate fact-finding, as are the procedural requirements stated in the *Gault* case.
- Not all the rights constitutionally assured to an adult are to be given to a juvenile.
- Insisting on a jury trial for juvenile offenders could fully turn the adjudication into an adversary process.
- Insisting on a jury trial would not remedy the problems associated with the lack of rehabilitation in the juvenile court.
- The preferable approach would be to allow states to experiment and adopt for themselves a jury trial concept in their individual jurisdictions.
- The jury trial, if imposed in the juvenile court, would certainly result in a delay, formality, and the possibility of a public trial, which at this point is not provided in most jurisdictions.

Significance of the Case

The *McKeiver* case temporarily stopped the march toward procedural constitutional due process for juvenile offenders in the juvenile justice system. The majority of the Court believed that juvenile proceedings were different from adult criminal prosecutions. The case also emphasized the fact that, as Justice Blackmun said, jurisdictions are free to adopt their own jury trial position in juvenile proceedings. The Court further noted that the majority of states denied a juvenile the right to a jury trial by statute. Thus, the Court believed that granting the juvenile offender the right to a jury trial would hinder rather than advance the system of juvenile justice in the United States.

Source: In re Winship, 397 U.S. 358, 90 S.Ct. 1068 (1970); McKeiver v. Pennsylvania, 403 U.S. 528, 91 S.Ct. 1976 (1971).

DISPOSITION

The stage of the juvenile justice process after adjudication is called **disposition**. It is the sentencing step of the juvenile proceedings. At this point, the juvenile court orders treatment for the juvenile in order to prevent further delinquency. Adrienne Volenik claims that it is here where the original child-saving philosophy of the juvenile court can come into play.[36]

Disposition is the most important phase of juvenile proceedings.[37] Paul Piersma and his associates describe the disposition as the heart of the juvenile process.[38] Lindsay G. Arthur, who has spent many years working on behalf of the National Council of Juvenile and Family Court Judges, speaks about the importance and the philosophy of disposition:

> A disposition is not simply a sentencing. It is far broader in concept and in application. It should be in the best interest of the child, which in this context means effectively to provide the help necessary to resolve or mee tthe individual's definable needs, while, at the same time, meeting society's needs for protection.[39]

The dispositional process has not received much attention from the courts. None of the Supreme Court decisions dealing with juvenile justice refers to its significance. Consequently, according to most legal documents, one of the most important issues in the disposition is the lack of proper procedure and due process for the child. In most jurisdictions today, adjudication and disposition hearings are separated, or bifurcated. In addition to a separate dispositional hearing, a child is generally accorded the right to counsel.

The Supreme Court has not ruled on the right to counsel at disposition, but counsel's participation is generally allowed either by a state statute or by general practice. Defense counsel often represents the child, helps the parents understand the court's decision, and influences the direction of the disposition. Others involved at the dispositional stage include representatives of social service agencies, psychologists, social workers, and probation personnel. Their information about the child's background often may be disputed at the disposition, and many states now allow cross-examination at this stage of the juvenile process.

Another important issue at the dispositional hearing is the need to obtain information about the child in order to formulate the treatment plan. In determining the type of disposition to be imposed on the child, juvenile court statutes often require the completion of a **predispositional investigation.** Fox describes the needs and purposes of this report:

> Individualized justice is often taken to be the most salient characteristic of juvenile court dispositions. In order to have the disposition conform to this ideal, the juvenile court judge requires information about each particular child. This is usually provided by an investigation, usually performed by a member of the probation staff, and report, known as the social study or disposition report.[40]

The predisposition report in the juvenile court is similar to the presentence report in the adult criminal justice system. Its use at the adjudication may result in prejudicial error against the child and often results in a mistrial. However, social service information is often used at the intake phase of the juvenile process as well as at the disposition. In some jurisdictions, statutes mandate completion of a predisposition report, particularly before a child can be placed in a youth program.

The Predisposition Report

After the child has admitted to the allegations in the petition or after the allegations have been proved in a juvenile trial, the judge normally orders the probation department to complete a predisposition report. Investigating and evaluating the child coming before the court for juvenile disposition is one of the most important tasks of juvenile probation officers. The predisposition report has a number of purposes:

- It helps the judge decide which disposition is best for the child.
- It aids the juvenile probation officer in developing treatment programs where the child is in need of counseling or community supervision.
- It helps the court develop a body of knowledge about the child that can aid others in treating the child.
- It serves as a source of basic information for systematic research in juvenile justice.

The style and content of predisposition reports vary among jurisdictions and also among juvenile probation officers within the same jurisdiction. The requirements for the use of the report, the sources of dispositional information, the techniques for obtaining it, and the conditions of its distribution vary among jurisdictions and are based on rules of law and procedure.

Some juvenile court probation departments require voluminous reports covering every aspect of the child's life. Other jurisdictions require information about the basic facts of the case and only limited information about the child's background. Individual officers bring their personal styles and educational backgrounds to bear on the development of the report. The probation officer who is a trained social worker, for example, might stress the use of psychological data, while the probation officer who is a lawyer might concentrate on the child's prior record and how dangerous the child is to him- or herself and to the community.

Sources of dispositional data include questioning the juvenile as well as collecting information about the child from family and school officials. In addition, the results of psychological testing, psychiatric evaluations, and intelligence testing may be relevant to the predispositional report. Furthermore, the probation officer might include information about the juvenile's feelings and attitudes regarding the present situation.

Some state statutes make the predisposition report mandatory. Other jurisdictions require the report only when there is a probability that the child will be institutionalized. In Massachusetts, for example, the law reads that "in every case of a delinquent child, a probation officer shall make a report regarding the character of such child, his school record, home surroundings, and previous complaint, if any."[41] Some appellate courts have reversed orders institutionalizing children where the juvenile court did not use a predisposition report in reaching its decision.

Access to predisposition reports is an important legal issue. The Supreme Court ruled in the case of *Kent v. United States* that the child and counsel must be given access to the social service report at transfer proceedings.[42] The National Advisory Commission on Criminal Justice Standards and Goals recommends that no dispositional decision be made on the basis of facts or information in a report if they have not previously been disclosed to the defense attorney for the child and to the prosecutor representing the state.[43]

In the final section of the predisposition report, the probation department recommends a disposition to the presiding judge. This is a very critical aspect of the report, since it has been estimated that the court follows more than 90 percent of all probation department recommendations. Thus, it is essential that the purpose of the report, which is to determine the care or treatment plan the child needs and not to prove or disprove the child's innocence or guilt, be accomplished.

Types of Dispositions

Historically, the juvenile court has had broad discretionary power to make dispositional decisions after adjudication. The major categories of dispositional choices include: (1) community release, (2) out-of-home placements, (3) fines or restitution, (4) community service, and (5) institutionalization. A more detailed list of the numerous possible dispositions open to the juvenile court judge follows:[44]

- *Informal consent decree.* In minor or first offenses, an informal hearing is held, and the judge will ask the youth and his or her guardian to agree to a treatment program, such as counseling. No formal trial or disposition hearing is held.
- *Probation.* A youth is placed under the control of the county probation department and asked to obey a set of probation rules and participate in a treatment program.
- *Home detention.* A child is restricted to his or her home in lieu of a secure placement. Rules include regular school attendance, curfew observance, avoidance of alcohol and drugs, and notification of parents and the youth worker of the child's whereabouts.
- *Court-ordered school attendance.* If truancy was the problem that brought the youth to court, a judge may order mandatory school attendance. Some courts have established court-operated day schools and court-based tutorial programs staffed by community volunteers.
- *Financial restitution.* A judge can order the juvenile offender to make financial restitution to the victim. In most jurisdictions, restitution is part of probation (see Chapter 18), but in a few states, such as Maryland, restitution can be a sole order.
- *Fines.* Some states allow fines to be levied against juveniles age 16 and over.
- *Community service.* Courts in many jurisdictions require juveniles to spend time in the community working off their debt to society. Community service orders are usually reserved for victimless crimes, such as possession of drugs, or crimes against public order, such as vandalism of school property. Community service orders are usually carried out in schools, hospitals, nursing homes, and so on.
- *Outpatient psychotherapy.* Youths whose behavior is bizarre and disorganized may be required to undergo therapy at a local mental health clinic.
- *Drug and alcohol treatment.* Youths with drug- or alcohol-related problems may be allowed to remain in the community if they agree to undergo drug or alcohol therapy.
- *Commitment to secure treatment.* In the most serious cases, a judge may order an offender put in a long-term treatment center, referred to as training

schools, camps, ranches, homes, and so on. These may be either state- or privately run institutions, usually located in remote regions of the state. Training schools provide educational, vocational, and rehabilitation programs in a secure environment (see Chapter 19).

■ *Commitment to a residential community program.* Youths who commit crimes of a less serious nature but still need to be removed from their homes can be placed in community-based group homes or halfway houses. They attend school or work during the day and live in a controlled, therapeutic environment at night.

■ *Foster home placement.* Foster homes are usually used for dependent or neglected children and status offenders. Judges are today placing delinquents with insurmountable problems at home in state-licensed foster care homes.

The authority to order dispositional alternatives generally stems from the juvenile code. Most state statutes allow the juvenile court judge to select whatever disposition is best suited to the child's needs. In addition to the above dispositions, some states go so far as to grant the juvenile court the power to order parents into treatment, suspend a youth's driver's license, or compel a child to do community service.

On the other hand, state juvenile codes can have specific prohibitions that limit the judge's discretionary power. For instance, twenty-one states prohibit confining children in adult institutions.[45] Some states use a minimum age as a criteria for institutional placement, while others limit placement in such facilities to felony offenders only. In certain states, the juvenile court determines commitment in a specific institution while in others, the youth corrections agency determines where the child will be placed. In other words, there is almost an infinite number of statutory variations to the dispositional process. (See the following "Case in Point.")

You are a family court judge at a dispositional hearing faced with making a difficult sentencing decision.

John M. was arrested at the age of 16 for robbery and rape. As a juvenile offender, he was subject to the jurisdiction of the juvenile division of the state family court. After a thorough investigation by the police department, the prosecutor formally filed a petition against John for the alleged offenses. Subsequently, John's mother obtained counsel for him. When the prosecutor suggested that the court might consider transferring the case to the adult court, John admitted his involvement in the offenses and was sent home pending plans for disposition.

At the dispositional hearing, the probation officer reported that John was the oldest of three siblings living in a single-parent home. He has had no contact with his father for over ten years. Psychological evaluation showed hostility, anger toward females, and great feelings of frustration. His intelligence was below average, and his behavioral and academic records were poor. In addition, John seemed to be involved with a local youth gang, although he denied any formal association with the group. This is John's first formal petition in the family court. Previous contact was limited to an informal complaint for disorderly conduct at the age of 13, which was dismissed by the court's intake department. John verbalizes superficial remorse for his offenses.

To the prosecutor, John seems to be a youth with poor controls who is likely to commit future crimes. The defense attorney and court staff see the need for program planning to meet John's needs. The judge recognizes the seriousness of the crimes committed by John and has at his disposal a wide range of court services that might help in John's rehabilitation. No one can predict or assess John's future behavior and potential dangerousness.

What disposition would you order? The Family Court Act lists ten dispositional alternatives for juvenile delinquents: the most severe is commitment to training school; the others are community-level alternatives.

THE CHILD'S RIGHT TO APPEAL

Juvenile court statutes normally restrict appeals to cases where the juvenile seeks review of a "final order" or a final judgment.[46] Paul Piersma and his associates define a final order as one that ends the litigation between two parties by determining all their rights and disposing of all the issues.[47] The **appellate process** gives the juvenile the opportunity to have the case brought before a reviewing court after it has been heard in the juvenile or family court. Today, the law does not recognize a federal constitutional right of appeal in juvenile or adult criminal cases. In other words, the U.S. Constitution does not require any state to furnish an appeal to a juvenile charged and found to be delinquent in a juvenile or family court setting. Consequently, appellate review of a juvenile case is a matter of statutory right in each jurisdiction. However, the majority of states do provide juveniles with some method of statutory appeal.

The appeal process was not always part of the juvenile law system. For example, J. Addison Bowman found that in 1965, few states extended the right of appeal to juveniles.[48] According to the President's Commission on Law Enforcement and Administration of Justice, appellate review was equally limited in 1967:

> By and large, the juvenile court system has operated without appellate surveillance . . . . Two factors contribute substantially to the lack of review. The absence of counsel in the great majority of cases in the first . . . . The other important factor is the general absence of transcripts of juvenile proceedings.[49]

Even in the *Gault* case in 1967, the Supreme Court refused to review the Arizona juvenile code, which provided no appellate review in juvenile matters. It further rejected the right of a juvenile to a transcript.[50]

Today, however, most jurisdictions that provide a child with some form of appeal also provide for counsel and for the securing of a record and transcript, which are crucial to the success of any appeal. Since adult criminal defendants have both a right to counsel at their initial appeal and a right to a stenographic transcript of trial proceedings, it would violate equal protection if juveniles were denied the same rights.

Since juvenile appellate review is a matter of statutory right, each jurisdiction determines for itself what method or scope of review will be used. There are two basic methods of appeal: the direct appeal and the collateral attack. The direct appeal normally involves an appellate court review to determine whether the rulings of law and the judgment of the court based on the evidence presented at the trial were correct. This approach is laid out in Section 59 of the Uniform Juvenile Court Act of the National Conference of Commissioners on Uniform State Law: "The appeal of the finding should be heard upon the files, records, and minutes or transcripts of the evidence of the juvenile court, giving appreciable weight to the findings of the juvenile court."[51] A similar approach is suggested by the National Advisory Commission on Criminal Justice Standards and Goals: "The appeal should be heard upon the files, records, and transcript of the evidence of the family court."[52]

A broader review procedure, which is a form of direct review, is the *de novo* review. A **trial *de novo*** is a complete retrial of the original case based on the original petition. All evidence produced at the first trial can be resubmitted, as can additional evidence. The trial *de novo* appeal is limited to only a few jurisdictions in the nation. It is usually encountered when a juvenile is originally tried in a court of very limited jurisdiction and in some administrative proceedings before masters or referees.

The second major area of review involves the collateral attack of a case. The term *collateral* refers to a secondary or indirect method of attacking a final judgment or order of the court. Instead of appealing the original juvenile trial because of errors, prejudice, or lack of evidence, collateral review uses extraordinary legal writs to challenge the lower court position. Two such procedural devices include the **writ of habeas corpus** and the **writ of certiorari**. The habeas corpus writ, known as the "Great Writ," refers to a procedure for determining the validity of a person's custody. In the context of the juvenile court, it is used to challenge the custody of a child in detention or in an institution. The writ of certiorari is an order from a higher to a lower court commanding that the case be brought forward for review. This writ is often the method by which the Supreme Court exercises its discretionary authority to hear cases regarding constitutional issues. Even though there is no constitutional right to appeal a juvenile case and each jurisdiction provides for appeals differently, juveniles have a far greater opportunity for appellate review today than in years past.

TRENDS IN JUVENILE SENTENCING

For most of the juvenile court's history, disposition was based on the presumed needs of the child. Although such critics as David Rothman and Anthony Platt have challenged the motivations of early reformers, there is little question that the rhetoric of the juvenile court has promoted the rehabilitation ideal.[53] For example, Joseph Goldstein, Anna Freud, and Albert Solnit, in their classic work, *Beyond the Best Interest of the Child,* say that placement of children should be based on the **least detrimental alternative** available in order to foster the child's growth and development.[54] This should be the goal whether the children are delinquents or status offenders or whether they are neglected, abandoned, or abused.

These views have changed in the late 1980s. In Chapter 16, we discussed the changes in transfer policy that make it easier to waive children to the adult court. These changes are evidence of concern about how to handle the chronic juvenile offender. On the other hand, we have also noted a trend to deinstitutionalize status offenders and prohibit their incarceration with delinquent youths. Yet, as we shall see below, many states have imposed requirements for greater proportionality and determinacy in juvenile disposition.

Sentencing Today

Traditionally, states have used the **indeterminate sentence** in juvenile court. In about thirty states, this means having the judge simply place the offender with the state department of juvenile corrections until correctional authorities consider him or her ready to return to society or until the youth reaches his or her legal majority. The majority of states, including Missouri, Texas, and West Virginia, consider 18 to be the age of release; others, such as Michigan and Tennessee, peg the termination age at 19; a few, including Kansas, Montana, Ohio, South Carolina, South Dakota, Utah, Virginia, and Wyoming, can retain youths until their twenty-first birthday.[55] In practice, few youths remain in custody for the entire statutory period; children are usually released if their rehabilitation has been judged by the youth corrections department, judge, or parole board to have progressed satisfactorily. This practice is referred to as the **individualized treatment model** — each sentence must be tailored to the individual needs of the child.

Another form of the indeterminate sentence allows judges to specify a maximum term that can be served. For example, in Alabama, Alaska, North Dakota, and Colorado, youths can be sentenced to a maximum of not more than two years in an institution; in Maryland, New Jersey, and Pennsylvania, the maximum sentence is three years.[56] Youths may also be released from incarceration in these jurisdictions if the corrections department considers them to be rehabilitated or they reach the automatic age of termination (usually 18 or 21). In most of the twelve states that signify a maximum sentence, the court may extend the sentence for a one- or two-year period, depending on the youth's progress in the institutional facility.[57]

A number of states have changed their sentencing policies in an effort to toughen up on juvenile offenders. Some, including Arizona, Georgia, Minnesota, and California, have changed from indeterminate to determinate sentencing in juvenile court. This means sentencing juvenile offenders to a fixed term of years which must be served in their entirety. Virginia and Tennessee have enacted provisions allowing determinate commitments of youth adjudicated for certain serious offenses. Arizona, for example, allows the state juvenile corrections agency to set standards for release by creating guidelines based on offense conditions which are applied during the intake process.[58] California, Colorado, Delaware, Georgia, Connecticut, and Pennsylvania are among the states that have passed laws creating **mandatory sentences** for serious juvenile offenders. For example, Delaware law provides a one-year mandatory sentence for a juvenile who commits any two felony acts during a one-year period; if a previously adjudicated delinquent commits three felonies within a three-year period, he or she receives a mandatory three-year sentence.[59] Juveniles receiving mandatory sentences are usually institutionalized for the full sentence and not eligible for early parole. Pennsylvania passed legislation in 1986 that sets up a statewide depository for fingerprints and photographs of dangerous juvenile offenders and youths aged 15 to 17 who are repeat violent offenders.[60]

New York's juvenile code gives the adult court original jurisdiction over cases involving 14- and 15-year-olds who commit serious violent felonies and over cases of 13-year-olds who commit murder.[61] If there are mitigating circumstances — for example, if the offender had a small role in the crime — the adult court judge can waive the case back to the juvenile court. Known as New York's Juvenile Offender Law, this controversial statute reduced the age of criminal responsibility provided for direct prosecution of youths committing certain offenses in the adult courts and authorized lengthy periods of incarceration. In addition, New York's Designated Felony Act allows the juvenile court judge to sentence children who commit murder, arson, or kidnapping to a sentence of five years in a juvenile institution.[62] The sentence can be renewed annually until the offender reaches 21. For less serious felony offenses, the judge can impose a three-year sentence, annually renewable.

Probably the best-known effort to reform sentencing in the juvenile court is the state of Washington's **Juvenile Justice Reform Act of 1977.** This act created a mandatory sentencing policy requiring juveniles ages 8 to 17 who are adjudicated delinquent to be confined in an institution for a minimum time.[63] The legislative intent of the act was to make juveniles accountable for criminal behavior and to provide for punishment commensurate with the (1) age, (2) crime, and (3) prior history of the offender. Washington's tough approach to juvenile sentencing is based on the principle of "proportionality." How much time a youth must spend in confinement is established by the Juvenile Dispositions Standards Commission based on the above three criteria. The introduction of such mandatory sentencing procedures standardizes juvenile dispositions and reduces disparity in the length of sentences, according to advocates of a "get-tough" juvenile justice system.

The Future of Juvenile Sentencing

During the past decade, the treatment-oriented philosophy has taken a back seat to the development of more formal and punitive laws toward juveniles charged with serious crimes. This pattern can be observed most clearly in studying statutory sentencing charges regarding the placement of children in secure settings. Although more than half the states still use indefinite sentencing, the trend is toward more determinate and fixed sentences.

A number of prominent national organizations have recommended the use of tougher mandatory sentences. For example, the American Bar Association has developed standards that affect the disposition process. Stanley Fisher points out that these standards point to a shift in juvenile court philosophy from traditional rehabilitation to the concept of just deserts.[64] The standards recommend that juveniles receive determinate or flat sentences without the possibility of parole, rather than the indeterminate sentences that most of them now receive.

The standards further recommend that punishment be classified into three major categories: nominal, conditional, and custodial. *Nominal sanctions* consist of reprimands, warnings, or other minor actions that do not affect the child's personal liberty. *Conditional sanctions* deal with such regulations as probation, restitution, and counseling programs. *Custodial sanctions*, which are the most extreme, remove the juvenile from the community into a nonsecure or secure institution. Other juvenile justice standards projects, such as the controversial model developed by the Rose Foundation, also recommend toughening juvenile sentences.[65] According to the National Conference of State Legislatures, nine states have already adapted the minimum/maximum sentencing pattern often used in the adult criminal justice system.[66] Also, more than half the states provide dispositional guidelines to assist in determining the juvenile's length of confinement.

Can such statutory changes in juvenile sentencing statutes have positive outcomes for the operation of the juvenile justice system? One reason for optimism has been the rather dramatic changes brought about in the state of Washington by the passage of the Juvenile Justice Reform Act of 1977. Research by Tom Castellano found that within two years of its passage, there was a high degree of compliance with its provisions.[67] The law has moved Washington's juvenile justice system away from informality and disparity toward the procedural regularity found in the adult system.

Castellano concludes that liberals should be able to cheer the due process rights afforded offenders, the proportionality that now exists in sentencing, and the fact that under the new code, status offenders no longer can be incarcerated with delinquents. In fact, he disputes the charge that the reform act is a get-tough approach.

Conservatives can be equally satisfied that under the new law serious offenders are given sterner sentences than they may have received earlier; over 90 percent of the serious juvenile offenders who come before the court are removed from the community, and many receive sentences ranging from two to four years.

On the other hand, not all statutory changes have the desired effect. For instance, while New York's Juvenile Offender Law requires that juveniles accused of violent offenses be tried in criminal court and provides serious penalties comparable to those for adults, Simon Singer and David McDowall conclude that the deterrent effect of the Juvenile Offender Law has not been achieved in reducing juvenile crime.[69] Since the law lowered the age of criminal responsibility and included family court jurisdiction, many youths ended up receiving lighter sentences under the Juvenile Offender Law than they would have received in the family court.

The growing realization that the juvenile crime rate has stabilized may slow the tide of legislative change in juvenile justice. What is more likely is that states will continue to pass legislation making it easier to transfer youths to the adult court or giving the adult court original jurisdiction over serious cases. Thus, rather than toughening juvenile law for everyone, society may exempt the few more serious cases from its advantages. As Lloyd Ohlin suggests: "Our society is unwilling to sustain the levels of repression and incarceration needed to make more limited incremental gains in crime control."[70] Thus, juvenile sentencing will probably remain wedded to the *parens patriae* philosophy, even if states pass legislation to incarcerate some very serious offenders.

Capital Punishment for Children

The most controversial of all sentences, adult or juvenile, continues to be the death penalty. The execution of minor children has not been uncommon in our nation's history. Victor Streib, a law professor and leading expert on the death penalty for children, claims that 281 youths have been executed since 1642.[71] Consequently, it is not so shocking that there are about thirty people (1990) on death row who committed their crimes while still teenagers but were waived to adult court for trial and sentencing.

Of the thirty-seven states that have laws authorizing **capital punishment**, twenty-two allow the death penalty for crimes committed by people under 18. The U.S. Supreme Court had a chance to resolve this issue in the 1982 case of *Eddings v. Oklahoma*, but it refused to do so.[72] The case involved a 16-year-old who killed a highway patrol officer. While the Court overturned his sentence, it did so on the grounds that the trial court had failed to consider his emotional state and troubled childhood when dispensing the death penalty. The Court did not deal with the issue of whether age alone could prohibit a person from being executed. In 1988, however, the Court prohibited the execution of persons below age 16 in the narrowly interpreted case of *Thompson v. Oklahoma*. Some justices endorsed the idea that less responsibility should exist when a child commits a criminal homicide. This decision left unanswered the issue of whether the Constitution prohibits the use of the death penalty for juveniles who were 16 or 17 years old when they committed their crimes.[73]

The Supreme Court finally confronted the highly emotional question in 1989 in the case of *Wilkins v. Missouri* and *Stanford v. Kentucky*.[74] Wilkins was 16 when he committed murder, while Standford was 17. The constitutional question raised by these two cases is basically the same as in the *Thompson* case: at what age does the Eighth Amendment ban the death penalty as punishment no matter what the crime? Critics of the death penalty believed that there was a consensus against executing young people in the United States. Supporters of capital punishment argued that juveniles after age 16 should be held fully responsible for murder. The Supreme Court concluded that states were free to impose the death penalty for murderers who committed their crimes while age 16 or 17. According to the majority opinion written by Justice Scalia, society had not formed a consensus that the execution of such minors constitutes a cruel and unusual punishment in violation of the Eighth Amendment.

Today, the death penalty stands for people who have committed capital crimes while still in their minority, and a number of executions of such offenders have already taken place. (However, it should be noted that by the time of their execution, the offenders had passed through their teens, since the trial and appeal process consumed many years.)

Those who oppose the death penalty for children, led by Streib, find that it has little deterrent effect on youngsters who are impulsive and do not have a realistic view of the destructiveness of the misdeeds or their consequences. Streib and his associates maintain the execution of a person who is a child at the time of the crime is cruel and unusual punishment because (1) the condemnation of children makes no measurable contribution to the legitimate goals of punishment, (2) condemning any minor to death violates contemporary standards of decency, (3) the capacity of the young for change, growth, and rehabilitation makes the death penalty particularly harsh and inappropriate, and (4) both legislative attitudes and public opinion reject juvenile executions. Supporters of the death penalty hold that people, regardless of their age, can form criminal intent and therefore should be responsible for their actions. If the death penalty is legal for adults, they argue, then it can be used for children who commit serious crimes also.

CONFIDENTIALITY IN JUVENILE PROCEEDINGS

In addition to examining the rights of juveniles at adjudication and disposition, the issue of **confidentiality** in juvenile proceedings has also received attention in recent years. The debate centers around whether the traditional approach of privacy for juveniles in the interest of their rehabilitation is preferred over the current cry for open proceedings that might increase public protection.[75] Confidentiality in the juvenile court deals with two areas: (1) open versus closed hearings, and (2) privacy of juvenile records. Considered by many to be a basic tenant of juvenile justice philosophy, the issue of complete confidentiality has lost some of its credibility, as many legislatures have broadened access to juvenile records.

Open versus Closed Hearings

Generally, juvenile trials are closed to the public and press, and the names of the offenders kept secret. The Supreme Court has ruled on the issue of privacy in three important decisions. In *Davis v. Alaska*, the Court concluded that any injury resulting from the disclosure of a juvenile's record is outweighed by the right to completely cross examine an adverse witness.[76] The *Davis* case involved an effort to obtain testimony from a juvenile probationer who was a witness in a criminal trial. After the prosecutor was granted a court order preventing the defense from making any reference to the juvenile's record, the Supreme Court reversed the state court, claiming that a juvenile's interest in confidentiality was secondary to the constitutional right to confront adverse witnesses.

The *Davis* case was a decision of evidentiary significance, whereas the subsequent two cases, **Oklahoma Publishing Co. v. District Court** and **Smith v. Daily Mail Publishing Co.** were cases balancing juvenile privacy with freedom of the press. In the *Oklahoma* case, the Supreme Court ruled that a state court was not allowed to prohibit the publication of information obtained in an open juvenile proceeding.[77] The case involved an 11-year-old boy suspected of homicide who appeared at a detention hearing and of whom photographs were taken and published in local newspapers. When the local district court prohibited further disclosure, the publishing company claimed that the court order was a restraint in violation of the First Amendment, and the Supreme Court agreed. The *Smith v. Daily Mail* case involved the discovery and subsequent publication by news reporters of the identity of a juvenile suspect in violation of a state statute prohibiting publication. The Supreme Court, however, declared the statute unconstitutional because it believed that the state's interest in protecting the child's identity was not of such a magnitude as to justify the use of such a statute.[78] Therefore, if newspapers lawfully obtain pictures or names of juveniles, they may publish them. Based on these decisions, it appears that the Supreme Court favors the constitutional rights of the press over the right to privacy of the juvenile offender.

None of the decisions, however, gave the press complete access to juvenile trials. Today, some jurisdictions still bar the press from juvenile proceedings unless they show at a hearing that their presence will not harm the youth. In other words, when states follow a *parens patriae* philosophy, ordinarily the public and press are generally excluded, but the court has discretion to permit interested parties to observe the hearings.

Privacy of Records

For most of the twentieth century, juvenile records were kept confidential by case, law or statute. The general rule has been that juvenile court records — both legal and social — are confidential information.[79] However, today, the record itself or information contained in it, can be opened by court order in many jurisdictions by statutory exception. The following groups can ordinarily gain access to juvenile records: (1) law enforcement personnel; (2) the child's attorney; (3) the parents or guardians; (4) military personnel; (5) and other public agencies, such as schools, court organizations, and correctional institutions.[80]

Some states also allow a juvenile adjudication for a criminal act such as rape to be used as evidence in a subsequent adult criminal proceeding for the same act, in order to show predisposition or criminal nature.[81] In addition, some states allow a juvenile's records to be used during the disposition or sentencing stage of an adult criminal trial.[82] According to such experts as Ira Schwartz, there is far less need for confidentiality to protect juveniles than for opening up the courts to public scrutiny and accountability.[83] The problem of confidentiality of juvenile records will become more acute in the future as computerization makes them both more durable and accessible to interested parties.[84]

SUMMARY

The purpose of this chapter has been to describe two major aspects of the juvenile justice system, adjudication and disposition. Most jurisdictions have a bifurcated juvenile code system that separates the adjudication hearing from the dispositional hearing. Juveniles alleged to be delinquent, as well as children in need of supervision, have virtually all the rights given a criminal defendant at trial — except possibly the right to a trial by jury. In addition, juvenile proceedings are generally closed to the public.

The types of dispositional orders that the juvenile court gives include dismissal, fine, probation, and institutionalization. The use of such disposition has not curtailed the rising rate of juvenile crime, however. As a result, legislatures and national commissions have begun to take a tougher position with regard to the sentencing of some juvenile offenders. The traditional notion of rehabilitation and treatment as the proper goals for disposition is now being questioned, and some jurisdictions have replaced it with proportionality in sentencing procedures. Many juvenile codes do require that the court con-

sider the "least restrictive" alternative before removing a juvenile from the home.

The predisposition report is the primary informational source for assisting the court in making a judgment about a child's care and treatment.

Once a juvenile is found delinquent or in need of supervision, the juvenile court is empowered through the dispositional process to make fundamental changes in the child's life. In recent years, a number of states have made drastic changes in juvenile sentencing law, moving away from the pure indeterminate sentence and embracing more structured, determinate forms of disposition. If there is any chance for juvenile crime to be reduced in the future, it may well depend on fair, just, and effective disposition.

Lastly, many state statutes require closed hearings and privacy of juvenile records in juvenile proceedings in order to protect the child from public scrutiny and provide a greater opportunity for rehabilitation. But this approach may be inconsistent with the public's recent interest in taking a closer look at the juvenile justice system.

KEY TERMS

juvenile prosecutor

judge

Missouri Plan

National Council of Juvenile and Family Court Judges

defense attorneys

guardian ad litem

public defender

adjudication

disposition

predispositional investigation

appellate process

trial *de novo*

writ of habeus corpus

writ of certiorari

least detrimental alternative

indeterminate sentence

individualized treatment model

mandatory sentences

Juvenile Justice Reform Act of 1977

capital punishment

Wilkins v. Missouri

Stanford v. Kentucky

confidentiality

Oklahoma Publishing v. District Court

Smith v. Daily Mail Publishing Co.

QUESTIONS FOR DISCUSSION

1. Discuss and identify the major participants in the conduct of a juvenile adjudication. What does each person do in the course of the juvenile trial?

2. The criminal justice system in the United States is based on the adversarial process. Does the same adversary principle apply in the juvenile justice system?

3. Children have certain constitutional rights at adjudication, such as the right to an attorney and the right to confront and cross-examine witnesses. But they do not have the right to trial by jury. Should juvenile offenders have a constitutional right to a jury trial? Should each state make that determination?

4. What is the point of obtaining a predisposition report in the juvenile court? Is it of any value in cases where the child is released to the community? Does it have a significant value in serious juvenile crime cases?

5. The standard of proof in juvenile adjudication is to show that the child is guilty beyond a reasonable doubt. Explain the meaning of this standard of proof in the American judicial system.

6. Should states adopt get-tough sentences in juvenile justice or adhere to the individualized treatment model?

7. Do you agree with the principle of a death penalty for children?

NOTES

1. Barry Krisberg, *The Juvenile Court: Reclaiming the Vision* (San Francisco: National Council on Crime and Delinquency, 1988).

2. U.S. Department of Justice, *Prosecution in the Juvenile Courts* (Washington, D.C.: U.S. Government Printing Office, 1973), p. 9.

3. 383 U.S. 541, 86 S.Ct. 1045, 16 L.Ed.2d 84 (1966); 387 U.S. 1, 87S.Ct. 1428, 18 L.Ed.2d 527 (1967); and 397 U.S. 358, 90 S.Ct. 1068, 25 L.Ed.2d 368 (1970).

4. American Bar Association, *Standards Relating to Juvenile Prosecution* (Cambridge, Mass.: Ballinger Publishing Co., 1977), p. 13.

5. 191 Neb. 5231 (1974).

6. John Laub and Bruce MacMurray, *Increasing the Prosecutor's Role in Juvenile Court: Exceptions and Realities* (Boston: Northeastern University, unpublished research report, 1987).

7. Ibid., p. 11.

8. U.S. Department of Justice, *Prosecution in the Juvenile Court: Guidelines for the Future* (Washington, D.C.: National Institute of Law Enforcement and Criminal Justice, 1973), p. 89.

9. F. Eastman, "Procedures and Due Process," *Juvenile and Family Court Journal* 35:36 (1983).

10. Yeheskel Hasenfeld and Paul Cheung, "The Juvenile Court and a People-Processing Organization: A Political Economy Perspective," *American Journal of Sociology* 90:801-24 (1985).

11. Joseph Sanborn, "The Defense Attorney's Role in Juvenile Court: Must Justice or Treatment (or Both) Be Compromised?" (Paper presented at the Academy of Criminal Justice Sciences, St. Louis, Missouri, 15–19 March 1987), p. 32.

12. See Sari Escovitz with Fred Kurland and Nan Gold, *Judicial Selection and Tenure* (Chicago: American Judicature Society, 1974), pp. 3–16.

13. Advisory Council of Judges of the National Council on Crime and Delinquency, *Procedure and Evidence in the Juvenile Court—A Guidebook for Judges* (New York: NCCD, 1962), p. 2; see also H. Ted Rubin, *Behind the Black Robes: Juvenile Court Judges and the Court* (Beverly Hills, Calif.: Sage, 1985).

14. *Annual Report, 1989* (Pittsburgh: National Center for Juvenile Justice, 1989).

15. 287 U.S. 45, 53 S.Ct. 55, 77, L.Ed.2d 158 (1932); 372 U.S. 335, 83 S.Ct. 792, 9 L.Ed.2d 799 (1963); and 407 U.S. 25, 92 S.Ct. 2006, 32 L.Ed.2d 530 (1972).

16. American Bar Association, *Standards Relating to Counsel for Private Parties* (Cambridge, Mass.: Ballinger Publishing Co., 1977).

17. Howard Davidson, "The Guardian at Litem: An Important Approach to the Protection of Children," *Children Today* 10:23 (1981).

18. Eastman, "Procedures and Due Process," p. 32.

19. S. H. Clarke and G. G. Koch, "Juvenile Court: Therapy or Crime Control and Do Lawyers Make a Difference?" *Law and Society Review* 14:263–308 (1980); Charles Thomas and Ineke Marshall, "The Effect of Legal Representation on Juvenile Court Dispositions," (Paper presented at the Southern Sociological Society, 1981); David Duffee and Larry Siegel, "The Organization Man: Legal Counsel in Juvenile Court," *Criminal Law Bulletin* 7:544–53 (1971).

20. Sanborn, "The Defense Attorney's Role in Juvenile Court," p. 8.

21. D. L. Horowitz, *The Courts and Social Policy* (Washington, D.C.: Brookings Institute, 1977).

22. Jane Knitzer, *Law Guardians in New York State* (New York: New York State Bar Association, 1985); David Hechler, "Lawyers for Children: No Experience Necessary," *Justice for Children* 1:14–15 (1985).

23. Sanford Fox, *Juvenile Courts* (St. Paul: West Publishing Co., 1984), p. 162.

24. Barry C. Feld, "The Right to Counsel in Juvenile Court: An Empirical Study of When Lawyers Appeal and the Difference They Make," *Journal of Criminal Law and Criminology* 79:1187–1346 (1989).

25. *Ibid.*, pp. 1217–18; for concern about the availability of counsel in the adult courts, see also Stephen Bright, Stephen Kinnard, and David Webster, "Keeping Gideon from Being Blown Away," *Criminal Justice Journal of the American Bar Association* 4:10–14 (1990).

26. *Ibid.*, p. 1318.

27. *Ibid.*, p. 1346.

28. Jeffery Fagan, Ellen Slaughter, and Eliot Hartstone, "Blind Justice? The Impact of Race on the Juvenile Justice Process," *Criminal Delinquency* 33:224–58 (1987).

29. See Institute of Judicial Administration, American Bar Association Joint Commission on Juvenile Justice Standards, *Standards Relating to Adjudication* (Cambridge, Mass.: Ballinger Publishing Co., 1980).

30. 387 U.S. 1 (1967), 19.

31. 383 U.S. 541 (1966).

32. 387 U.S. 1 (1967).

33. Linda Szymanski, *Juvenile Delinquents' Right to Counsel* (Pittsburgh: National Center for Juvenile Justice, 1988).

34. 397 U.S 358, 90 S.Ct. 1068 (1970).

35. 403 U.S. 528 (1971).

36. Adrienne E. Volenik, *Checklist for Use in Juvenile Delinquency Proceedings* (Washington, D.C.: American Bar Association, 1985), p. 42.

37. See, generally, R. T. Powell, "Disposition Concepts," *Juvenile and Family Court Journal* 34:7–18 (1983).

38. Paul Piersma, Jeanette Ganousis, and Prudence Kramer, "The Juvenile Court: Current Problems, Legislative Proposals, and a Model Act," *St. Louis University Law Review* 20:43 (1976).

39. See Lindsay Arthur, "Status Offenders Need a Court of Last Resort," *Boston University Law Review* 57:63–64 (1977).

40. Sanford Fox, *Juvenile Courts in a Nutshell* (St. Paul: West Publishing Co., 1984), p. 221.

41. Mass.Gen.Laws chap. 119, 57.

42. *Kent v. United States*, 383 U.S. 541, 86 S. Ct. 1045 (1966).

43. National Advisory Commission on Criminal Justice Standards and Goals, *Report of the Task Force on Juvenile Justice and Delinquency Prevention* (Washington, D.C.: U.S. Government Printing Office, 1976), p. 445.

44. This section is adapted from Jack Haynes and Eugene Moore, "Particular Dispositions," *Juvenile and Family Court Journal* 34:41–48 (1983).

45. Criminal Justice Program of National Conference of State Legislatures, *Legal Dispositions and Confinement Policies for Delinquent Youth* (Denver: National Conference of State Legislatures, July 1988), p. 3.

46. Fox, *Juvenile Courts in a Nutshell*, pp. 254–55.

47. Paul Piersma, et al., *Law and Tactics in Juvenile Cases* (Philadelphia: American Law Institute American Bar Association, Committee on Continuing Education, 1977), p. 397.

48. See J. Addison Bowman, "Appeals from Juvenile Courts," *Crime and Delinquency Journal* 11:63–77 (1965).

49. President's Commission on Law Enforcement and Administration of Justice, Task Force Report, *Juvenile Delinquency and Youth Crime* (Washington, D.C.: U.S. Government Printing Office, 1967), p. 115.

50. 387 U.S. 1 (1967).

51. National Conference of Commissioners on Uniform State Laws, *Uniform Juvenile Court Act*, 59 (1968).

52. National Advisory Commission on Criminal Justice Standards and Goals, *Report of the Task Force on Juvenile Justice and Delinquency Prevention*, p. 428.

53. See Anthony Platt, *The Child Savers: The Invention of Delinquency* (Chicago: University of Chicago Press, 1969); David Rothman, *Conscience and Convenience: The Asylum and the Alternative in Progressive America* (Boston: Little, Brown, 1980).

54. See Joseph Goldstein, Anna Freud, and Albert Solnit, *Beyond the Best Interests of the Child* (New York: Free Press, 1973).

55. Martin Forst, Bruce Fisher, and Robert Coates, "Indeterminate and Determinate Sentencing of Juvenile Delinquents: A National Survey of Approaches to Commitment and Release Decision Making," *Juvenile and Family Court Journal* 36:1–12 (1985).

56. *Ibid.,* p. 7.

57. *Ibid.,* p. 9.

58. *Ibid.*

59. Del.Code Ann. Title 10, 937(c) (1977).

60. "Pennsylvania to Build Central Data Base of Juvenile Records," *Criminal Justice Newsletter,* 16 January 1987, p. 1.

61. N.Y. Fam.Ct.Act 753 (1978); also see New York State Laws of 1976, Chap. 878.

62. Ibid., 753a (1978).

63. See Washington Juvenile Justice Act of 1977, Chap. 291. (Wash. Rev.Code Ann. Title 9A, Sec. 1–91) (1977).

64. Stanley Fisher, "The Dispositional Process under the Juvenile Justice Standards Project," *Boston University Law Review* 57:732 (1977).

65. Alan Breed, "Reforming Juvenile Justice: A Model or Ideology?" *Juvenile Justice Digest,* Vol. 15, April 6, 1987.

66. See Criminal Justice Program of National Conference of State Legislatures, *Legal Dispositions and Confinement Policies for Delinquent Youth,* p. 5.

67. Thomas Castellano, "The Justice Model in the Juvenile Justice System: Washington State's Experience" (Paper presented at the Academy of Criminal Justice Sciences, St. Louis, Missouri, 15–18 March 1987).

68. For an opposing view, see Anne Schneider, "Sentencing Guidelines and Recidivism Rates of Juvenile Offenders," *Justice Quarterly* 1:107–24 (1984).

69. Simon Singer and David McDowall, "Criminalizing Delinquency: The Deterrent Effects of NYJO Law," *Law and Society Review* 22:Sections 21–37 (1988).

70. Lloyd Ohlin, "The Future of Juvenile Justice," *Crime and Delinquency* 29:467 (1983).

71. Victor Streib, *Death Penalty for Juveniles* (Bloomington, Ind.: Indiana University Press, 1987); see also Paul Reidinger, "The Death Row Kids," *American Bar Association Journal* (April, 1989):78

72. 455 U.S. 104 (1982).

73. Steven Gerstein, "The Constitutionality of Executing Juvenile Offenders, *Thompson v. Oklahoma, Criminal Law Bulletin,* 24:91–98 (1988); also 108 S.Ct. 2687 (1988).

74. 109 S.Ct. 2969 (1989); for a recent analysis of the *Wilkins* and *Stanford* cases, see Note, "*Stanford v. Kentucky* and *Wilkins v. Missouri* — Juveniles, Capital Crime, and Death Penalty," *Criminal Justice Journal* 11:240–266 (1989).

75. Paul R. Kfoury, *Children before the Court: Reflection on Legal Issues Affecting Minors* (Boston: Butterworth Legal Publishers, 1987), p. 55.

76. 415 U.S. 308 (1974).

77. *Oklahoma Publishing Co. v. District Court,* 430 U.S. 97 (1977).

78. *Smith v. Daily Mail Publishing Co.,* 443 U.S. 97 (1977).

79. Linda Szymanski, *Confidentiality of Juvenile Court Records* (Pittsburgh: National Center for Juvenile Justice, 1989).

80. *Ibid.*

81. *Houser v. Georgia,* 326 S.E. 2d 513 (1985).

82. *Hayden v. South Carolina,* 322 S.E.2d 14 (1984).

83. Ira M. Schwartz, (In) *Justice for Juveniles: Rethinking the Best Interests of the Child* (Lexington, Mass.: D.C. Heath & Co., 1989), p. 172.

84. See the case of *Alonzo M. v. City Dept. of Probation,* 532 N.E.2d 1254 (1988), where a New York State statute forbade any reference, even to the family court, of changes that were not proven or were dismissed.

Juvenile Corrections

Despite efforts to decarcerate as many juveniles as possible, it sometimes becomes necessary to institutionalize youths who need care, custody, and control. A variety of methods have been developed to meet these goals, including community-based and secure treatment programs. Over the years there has been a massive effort to remove nonserious offenders from secure institutions and place them in small, community-based facilities. Yet thousands of youngsters are sent to secure, prison-like facilities each year. Compliance with the deinstitutionalization mandate of the Juvenile Justice and Delinquency Prevention Act of 1974 has not been successful.

Children in custody have become an American dilemma. Many incarcerated adult felons report that they were institutionalized as youths. Severe punishment seems to have little deterrent effect on teenagers—if anything, it may prepare them for a life of adult criminality. The juvenile justice system is caught between the futility of punishing juveniles and the public's demand that something be done about serious juvenile crime. Even though the nation seems to be in the midst of a punishment cycle, juvenile justice experts continue to press for judicial fairness, rehabilitation, and innovative programs for juvenile offenders.

The two chapters in Part VI describe the correctional treatment of juveniles in the community and in custody. Both approaches seek "the best interest of the child" and "the protection of the community." Although sometimes contradictory, these two major positions dominate the dispositional process.

Chapter 18 discusses efforts to treat juveniles while they remain in society. The most common community disposition employed by the juvenile court is probation. Theoretically, its goal is to rehabilitate the general offender by treatment, guidance and supplementary programs while the child remains in the community. In many jurisdictions, the juvenile court is required to give precedence to the "least restrictive" dispositional alternatives, of which probation is one example.

Chapter 19 reviews the history and practices of the juvenile institution and discusses efforts to rehabilitate youths in custody. Preadjudicatory facilities are often referred to as training schools, reform schools, or as in years past, industrial schools. They are institutions considered as a last resort for delinquents. Often status offenders are also sent to training schools, despite prohibitions against such placements. Most secure institutions are not equipped to provide successful treatment for serious juvenile offenders. They often have limited treatment and educational services, as well as antiquated physical plants. One can understand why the training school is under constant judicial scrutiny.

By reading these chapters you should be able to develop an understanding of how the juvenile justice system deals with children who need treatment and present a danger to themselves and others.

18

Community Treatment of the Juvenile Offender

After adjudication, the treatment needs of children found to be either delinquents or status offenders are evaluated by court personnel. Since prevailing juvenile court philosophy demands that children be subject to the least restrictive disposition alternative possible, this usually means a period of community-based corrections.

Community treatment refers to a wide variety of efforts to provide care, protection, and treatment for children in need. These efforts include probation, a variety of treatment services such as social casework, group work, the use of volunteers in probation, as well as **restitution** and other appropriate programs. The term *community treatment* also refers generally to the use of nonsecure and noninstitutional residences, such as foster homes, small group homes, boarding schools or semi-institutional cottage living programs, forestry camps or outdoor camps, and nonresidential programs where youths remain in their own homes and receive counseling, education, family assistance, diagnostic services, casework services, or vocational training. Parole (aftercare) is often considered an extension of community treatment, but this will be discussed in the following chapter. In a broader sense, community treatment includes preventive programs, such as street work with antisocial gangs or early identification and treatment of predelinquents. Such programs are discussed in Chapters 10, 11, and 15.

This chapter discusses the concept of community treatment as a dispositional alternative for juveniles who have violated the law and who have been found delinquent by the juvenile court. Their hope for rehabilitation and the hope of society for resolving the problems of juvenile crime lie in the use of community treatment programs. Such programs are generally preferable to training schools because they are smaller, operate in a community setting, and offer creative approaches to treating the juvenile offender. Traditional institutions, on the other hand, are costly to operate and offer limited services.

First, this chapter discusses probation in detail. It examines new and important approaches for providing effective probation services to juvenile offenders. Next, it reviews restitution, which is being used in many jurisdictions to supplement probation supervision. It then traces the development of alternatives to incarceration, including community-based, nonsecure treatment programs. Juvenile court judges generally have considerable latitude regarding the use of the various community-based dispositional alternatives, and this chapter focuses on these programs.

JUVENILE PROBATION

Probation is the primary form of community treatment in the juvenile justice system. It ordinarily refers to a disposition. The child is placed and maintained in the community under the supervision of a duly authorized officer of the court. The term also denotes a status or process whereby the child on probation is subject to rules that must be followed and conditions that must be met in order for the child to remain in the community. *Probation* often refers to an organizational structure—a probation department (either an independent agency or one attached to a court) that manages, supervises, and treats children and carries out investigations for the court. Although the term has many other meanings too, *probation* usually refers to a legal disposition of a nonpunitive type for delinquent youths and those in need of supervision, emphasizing maintenance in the community and treatment without incarceration.

Juvenile probation is based on the idea that the juvenile offender is not generally dangerous to the community and has a better chance of being rehabilitated within the community. Advocates of probation and community treatment suggest that the institutional experience can force juveniles to become further involved in antisocial behavior. Probation provides the child with the opportunity to be closely supervised by trained personnel who can help him or her reestablish forms of acceptable behavior in a community setting:

> Probation is a desirable disposition in appropriate cases because (1) it maximizes the liberty of the individual while at the same time vindicating the authority of the law and effectively protecting the public from further violations of law; (2) it affirmatively promotes the rehabilitation of the offender by continuing normal community contacts; (3) it avoids negative and frequently stultifying effects of confinement, which often severely and unnecessarily complicate the reintegration of the offender into the community; (4) it greatly reduces the financial cost to the public of an effective correctional system.[1]

In practice, probation is a legal disposition, and only a judge can place a juvenile under an order of probation. Two methods are generally used. One is a straight order of probation for such a time and under such conditions as the judge deems proper. The other method involves ordering a child to be committed to an institution or department of youth services and then suspending the order and placing the child on probation. In the majority of jurisdictions, probation is a direct order and is exercised under wide statutory discretion. In particular, the conditions to be followed during the probationary period are subject to the court's discretion.

The Nature of Probation

A probation sentence involves a contract between the court and the juvenile. The court promises to hold a period of institutionalization in abeyance; the juvenile promises to adhere to a set of rules or conditions mandated by the court. If the rules are violated, and especially if the child commits another offense, the probation may be revoked. In that case, the contact between the court and the child is over, and the original commitment order may be enforced. The rules of probation vary, but they most typically involve such conditions as attending school or work, keeping regular hours, remaining in the jurisdiction, and staying out of trouble.

In the juvenile court, probation is often ordered for an indefinite period of time. Depending on the statutes of the jurisdiction, the seriousness of the offense, and the juvenile's adjustment on probation, children can remain under the court's supervision until the court no longer has jurisdiction over them, that is, when they reach their majority. New York limits probation to two years for a delinquent and one year for a status offender, extendable under exceptional circumstances. Florida mandates that probation last no longer than could a term of commitment to an institution.[2] State statutes determine if a judge can specify how long a juvenile can be placed under an order of probation.

In most jurisdictions, the status of probation is reviewed regularly to assure that a child is not kept on probation needlessly. Generally, discretion lies with the probation officer to discharge the child if the child is adjusting to the supervision and treatment plan.

Since virtually all the states have adopted the Uniform Interstate Compact on Juveniles, the supervision of a juvenile probationer can be transferred from one state to another when it is necessary for a child to move from the original jurisdiction.[3] The compact provides jurisdiction over all nonresident children by allowing for the return of runaway children to their home state and for supervision of out-of-state children.

Historical Development

Although the major developments in juvenile probation have occurred in the present century, its roots go back much farther. In England, specialized procedures for dealing with youthful offenders can be found as early as 1820, when the magistrates of the Warwickshire quarter sessions adopted the practice of sentencing youthful criminals to prison terms of one day, then releasing them conditionally under the supervision of their parents or masters. This practice was developed further in Middlesex, Birmingham, and London, where probation supervision was first supplied by police officers, then by volunteer philanthropic organizations, and finally by public departments.[4]

In the United States, juvenile probation developed as part of the wave of social reform characterizing the latter half of the nineteenth century. Massachusetts took the first step toward development of a juvenile probation service. Under an act passed in 1869, an agent of the state board of charities was authorized to appear in criminal trials involving juveniles, to find them suitable homes, and to visit them periodically. These services were soon broadened and strengthened so that by 1890, probation had become a mandatory part of the court structure throughout the state.[5]

Probation made a central contribution to the development of the concept of the juvenile court. In fact, in some states the early supporters of the juvenile court movement accepted probation legislation as the first step toward achieving the benefits that the new court was intended to provide. The rapid spread of the juvenile court during the first decades of the present century encouraged the development of probation. The two closely related and to a large degree interdependent institutions sprang from the same dedicated conviction that the young could be rehabilitated and that the public was responsible for protecting them.

By the mid-1960s, juvenile probation had become a major social institution, large, complex, and touching the lives of an enormous number of children in the United States. Today, about 400,000 youths are being supervised on juvenile probation.[6] Probation departments have the main responsibility for processing and servicing the majority of cases referred to the juvenile court.

Organization and Administration

Juvenile probation systems are organized according to two main patterns. Most commonly, the juvenile court or a group of courts administers probation services. In the other, an administrative agency, such as a state correctional agency, public welfare department, or a combination of such agencies, provides probation services to the court. The relationship between the court (especially the judge) and the probation staff, whether it is under the court or in a separate administrative agency, is an extremely close one.

In the typical juvenile probation department, the leadership role of the chief probation officer is central to its effective operation.

Large probation departments also include one or more assistant chiefs. Each of these middle managers is responsible for one aspect of probation service. One assistant chief might oversee training, while another might supervise and treat special offender groups, and still another might act as liaison with juvenile, police, or community service agencies. The probation officers who investigate and supervise juvenile cases are in direct and personal contact with the supervisory staff.

Each state has its own approach to juvenile probation organization. In some states—Massachusetts, for example—a statewide probation service exists, but actual control over departments is localized within each district court. New York, on the other hand, has in each of its counties a family court with exclusive original jurisdiction over children aged 16 or under; a single department handles probation for the five boroughs of the city of New York. In Maryland, the State Department of Juvenile Services provides probation services to the juvenile courts in each county.[7] On the other hand, Wisconsin's probation program is administered by a county executive department, while in New Jersey, juvenile probation services are managed by judges. Thus, the administration of probation varies from one jurisdiction to another, and there is a considerable lack of uniformity in the roles, organization, and procedures of probation across the states.

As of 1989, the National Center for Juvenile Justice found that probation services are organized and administered exclusively by the local juvenile court or by the state administrative office of courts in twenty-four states and the District of Columbia. In another eleven states, probation administration is split between judicial and executive branch departments, while in ten sates, it is handled exclusively at the state level by a state agency. In two states, county governments administer probation, and in three other states, the responsibility for probation is shared by county and state agencies.[8]

While it appears that juvenile probation services continue to be predominantly organized under the judiciary, recent legislative activity has been in the direction of transferring those services from the local juvenile court judge to a state court administrative office.[9] Whether juvenile courts or state level agencies should administer juvenile probation services is debatable. In years past, the organization of probation depended primarily on the size of the program and the number of children under its supervision. Today, the judicial-executive controversy is often guided by the amount of money available for these services. Because of this momentum to develop unified court systems, juvenile court services, including probation, are now being consolidated into state court systems.

Duties and Responsibilities of Juvenile Probation Officers

The juvenile probation officer is responsible for the initial contact with the child, for continuing to process the case, and for providing services for the child while he or she is under court supervision.

According to the American Bar Association's standards for juvenile justice, juvenile probation officers are involved at four stages of the court process. At intake, they screen complaints by deciding to adjust the matter, refer to an agency for service, or refer to the court for judicial action. During the interim status or predisposition stage, they participate in release or detention decisions. At the postadjudication stage, they assist the court in reaching its dispositional decision. During postdisposition, they supervise juveniles placed on probation.[10]

At intake, the probation staff engages in preliminary explorations with the child and the family to determine whether court intervention is necessary or whether the matter can be better resolved by some other community service. If the child is placed in a detention facility, the probation officer helps the court decide whether the child should continue to be held or released pending the adjudication and disposition of the case.

The juvenile probation officer exercises tremendous influence over the child and the family by developing a **social investigation report** and submitting it to the court. This report is a clinical diagnosis of the child's problems and of his or her need for court assistance based on the child's social functioning. The report evaluates the child's personality and relationship to family, peers, and community in order to provide a future treatment plan.[11] A professional investigative report includes analyses of children's perceptions of and feelings about their violations, their problems, and their life situations. They should shed light on the value systems that influence behavior. They will consider the degree of motivation to solve the problems that cause deviant behavior as well as the youths' physical, intellectual, and emotional capacity to change. These reports must examine the influence of family members and other significant persons in producing and possibly solving problems. Neighborhood and peer group determinants of attitudes and behavior also must be analyzed. All of this information must be brought together into a meaningful picture of a complex whole composed of the personality, the problem, and the environmental situation. This relationship must be considered in relation to the various possible alternative dispositions available to the court. Out of this, a constructive treatment plan must be developed.[12]

Another important function of the juvenile probation officer is to provide the child with supervision and treatment in the community. The treatment plan is a product of the intake, diagnostic, and investigative aspects of probation. Treatment plans vary. Some children simply report to the probation officer and follow the conditions of probation. In other cases, the probation officer may need to counsel the child and family extensively or, more typically, refer them to other social service agencies, such as local mental health clinics and detoxification centers.

In sum, the juvenile probation officer's role requires a diversity of skills:

■ Providing direct counseling and casework services
■ Interviewing and collecting social service data
■ Making diagnostic recommendations
■ Maintaining working relationships with law enforcement agencies
■ Using community resources and services
■ Using volunteer case aides and probation officers
■ Writing predisposition reports
■ Working with families of children under supervision

- Providing specialized services, such as group work, behavior modification counseling, or reality therapy counseling
- Supervising specialized caseloads involving children on drugs or with special psychological or emotional problems
- Making decisions about the revocation of probation and its termination

Performance of all these functions requires a high-quality probation staff. Today, juvenile probation officers have legal or social work backgrounds or special counseling skills. Most jurisdictions require juvenile probation officers to have a background in the social sciences and a bachelor's degree. The probation officer's job is not an easy one. High caseloads often make the therapeutic goal difficult to achieve. Overseeing the probationer's compliance with the legal requirements of probation often becomes the short-term goal.

Conditions and Revocation of Juvenile Probation

Conditions of probation are rules and regulations mandating that a juvenile on probation behave in a particular way. They are important ingredients in the treatment plan devised for the child. Conditions can include restitution or reparation, intensive supervision, intensive probation counseling, participation in a therapeutic program, or participation in an educational or vocational training program. In addition to these specific conditions, state statutes generally allow courts to insist that probationers lead law-abiding lives during the period of probation, that they maintain a residence in a family setting, that they refrain from associating with certain types of people, and that they remain in a particular geographic area unless they have permission to leave.

Probation conditions vary, but they are never supposed to be capricious, cruel, or beyond the capacity of the juvenile to accomplish. Furthermore, conditions of probation should relate to the crime that was committed and to the conduct of the child.

In recent years, appellate courts have invalidated probation conditions that were harmful and that violated the child's basic due process rights. Restricting a child's movement, insisting on a mandatory program of treatment, ordering indefinite terms of probation, and demanding financial reparation where this is impossible are all grounds for an appellate court review.[13]

If a child violates the conditions of probation or breaks the law again, the court can **revoke** probation. The juvenile court ordinarily handles a decision to revoke probation upon recommendations of the probation officer. Today, as a result of Supreme Court decisions dealing with the rights of adult probationers, a juvenile is normally entitled to legal representation and a hearing when a violation of probation occurs.[14] This means that juveniles are virtually entitled to the same due process protections as adult probationers.

PROBATION INNOVATIONS

There have been a number of recent innovations in probation services that have or may soon impact services for juvenile offenders. Although probation programs have varying rates of recidivism, experts claim they are generally more successful than placement in an institution. As a result, there has been a great deal of experimentation over the years with different probation techniques. Rule enforcement plus guidance and the use of community services remain the common ingredients for delinquency-reducing programs in probation.

Intensive Probation Supervision

One approach that has generated a great deal of enthusiasm is the **intensive supervision** model. This involves treating offenders who would normally have been sent to a secure treatment facility in very small caseloads that are given almost daily scrutiny.[15]

Numerous jurisdictions have adopted programs of intensive community supervision that have proven more successful than limited probation supervision.[16] For example, Georgia, Oregon, and New Jersey are experimenting with and adopting programs of intensive supervision, and the results seem encouraging.[17] It seems evident that intensive probation will continue to grow as a mechanism for removing both children and adults from confinement. Even if intensive supervision is found to be no more effective in reducing recidivism than more restrictive correctional interventions, its demonstrated cost benefits (it costs about one-third that of confinement) make it an attractive alternative to traditional forms of treatment, such as confinement.[18]

In the last few years, the results of certain Juvenile Intensive Probation Supervision Programs (JIPS) in different jurisdictions also conclude that such programs may cause fewer youths to reenter the juvenile justice system.[19] Today, JIPS components can be found in most metropolitan juvenile probation departments representing all major regions of the country and are used as a true alternative to incarceration or other forms of out-of-home placement.[20]

Use of Volunteers

The utilization of civilian volunteers to assist probation officers is another practice that has proliferated. For example, the juvenile court of Boulder County, Colorado, has provided an extensive volunteer program of delinquency prevention and treatment.[21] Local volunteers work with juvenile offenders, providing tutoring, group counseling, and job training. The variety of community treatment programs available today allows the court greater flexibility in disposing of children's cases.

Electronic Monitoring

Another program that has been used with adult offenders and is finding its way into the juvenile justice system is **house arrest**, which is often coupled with **electronic monitoring**. This program allows offenders sentenced to probation to remain in the community on the condition that they stay in their home during specific periods of time—for example, after school or work, on weekends, during evenings. These offenders may be monitored through random phone calls or

Lois Lee, right, founder of Children of the Night, a non-profit volunteer group helping people escape the streets, consoles a young woman at the Hollywood clinic. Her volunteers help about 100 children a month—almost all who have fallen into prostitution which is job security for those on the streets.

visits, but some jurisdictions are experimenting with the use of computer-monitored electronic devices to keep track of their clients. Probationers are fitted with a nonremovable monitoring device that alerts the probation department's computers if they leave their place of confinement.[22] While house arrest has not been extensively evaluated in terms of reducing recidivism, its cost, even with active electronic monitoring, is often less than half of what a stay in a detention would involve. Two well-known programs, one in Indiana and the other in North Carolina, for instance, appear to operate safely and effectively as alternatives to institutionalization and have become a formal part of probation programming in these jurisdictions.

Joseph B. Vaughn conducted the most recent intensive and descriptive survey of juvenile electronic monitoring in 1989, involving eight programs in five different probation departments.[23] Vaughn found that all the programs adopted electronic monitoring to reduce institutional overcrowdedness and that most agencies reported success in reducing the number of days children spent in detention. In addition, the programs allowed the children who would otherwise be detained to remain in the home and participate in counseling, educational, or vocational activities under reasonable security. Of particular benefit to pretrial detainees was the opportunity to be placed in a natural environment with supervision. This provided the court with a much clearer picture of how the juvenile would eventually perform if given probation. On the other hand, Vaughn found that none of the benefits of the treatment objective in the programs had been empirically validated. The potential for modification in behavior and the duration of any personal changes remain unknown. Overall, the use of electronic monitoring is a new phenomena, and Vaughn reports that it is too early to assess the impact of such programs on the juvenile justice system.

Wilderness Probation

Another technique that seems to be growing in popularity with probation departments is **wilderness probation.** These programs, staffed by probation officers and lay volunteers, involve youngsters in outdoor expeditions to give them a sense of confidence and purpose.[24] Such programs are used as alternatives to standard dispositions for children being supervised in the juvenile court. They provide an opportunity for certain youth to confront the difficulties in their lives while achieving positive personal satisfaction. Probation counseling and group therapy are all part of a structured program that is significantly different than a purely recreational field trip. The wilderness program in Douglas County, Nevada, for instance, services between thirty and fifty youths in three different types of wilderness excursions every month.[25] These programs seem to be proving effective with both probationers and institutionalized youth (see Chapter 19 for a discussion of the Outward Bound programs).[26]

As part of the Douglas County, Nevada Juvenile Probation Wilderness Program, local probationers can be taken on day hikes of the neighboring Sierra Nevada Mountains, or they can experience a wilderness underwater program. (See chapter opening photo.)

Balanced Probation

In recent years, some jurisdictions have turned to a **balanced probation** approach in an effort to enhance the success of probation.[27] Probation systems that integrate community protection, the accountability of the juvenile offender, competency, and individualized attention to the offender incorporate the treatment values of this balanced approach. Some of these juvenile protection programs offer renewed promise for community treatment. This approach has been implemented with some success in Deschutes County, Oregon, and Travis County, Texas.[28] These programs are based on the view that children incur an obligation whenever they commit an offense and are responsible for their actions. The probation officer establishes a program tailored to the special needs of the offender, while helping the youth accept responsibility for his or her own actions.

While these approaches are still in their infancy and their effectiveness remains to be tested, they have caused immense interest because of their potential for relieving overcrowded correctional facilities and reducing the pain and stigma of incarceration. There seems to be little question that the use of these innovations and probation in general will increase in the years ahead, particularly since the juvenile court is uniquely organized to provide these programs. Not only can the probation officer do the individual therapy, but he or she can also make the above possibilities available to the juvenile offender.

RESTITUTION

Victim restitution is another widely used method of community treatment. In most jurisdictions, restitution is part of a probationary sentence and is administered by the county probation staff. In some jurisdictions, such as Oklahoma City and Prince George's County, Maryland, independent restitution programs have been set up by local governments, while in others, such as Covington, Louisiana, and Charleston, South Carolina, restitution is administered by a private nonprofit organization.[29]

Restitution itself can take several forms. A child can reimburse the victim of the crime or pay money to a worthy charity or public cause; this is referred to as **monetary restitution**. In other instances, a juvenile can be required to provide some service directly to the victim (**victim service**) or to assist a worthwhile community organization (**community service restitution**).

Requiring children to pay the victims of their crimes is the most widely used method of restitution in the United States. Less widely used but more common in Europe is restitution to a community charity. In the past few years, numerous programs have been set up to enable the juvenile offender to provide service to the victim or to participate in community programs—for example, working in schools for retarded children and fixing up neighborhoods. In some cases, children are required to contribute both money and community service.

Restitution programs can be employed at various stages of the juvenile justice process. They can be part of a diversion program prior to conviction, they can be a method of informal adjustment at intake, or they can be a condition of probation.

Restitution has a number of justifications.[30] It provides the court with alternative sentencing options. It offers direct monetary compensation or service to the victims of a crime. It is rehabilitative, because it gives the juvenile the opportunity to compensate the victim and take a step toward becoming a productive member of society. It also relieves overcrowded juvenile courts, probation caseloads, and detention facilities. Finally, it has the potential for allowing vast savings in the operation of the juvenile justice system. Institutional placement costs currently are about $25,000–$30,000 annually per child, but restitution programs cost far less. Monetary restitution programs in particular may improve the public's attitude toward juvenile justice by offering equity to the victims of crime and ensuring that offenders assume the obligations of their actions.

Despite what seem to be its many advantages, some believe that restitution contributes to retribution rather than rehabilitation because it emphasizes justice for the victim and criminal responsibility for illegal acts. There is some concern that restitution creates penalties for juvenile offenders where none existed before.

The use of restitution is increasing around the nation. Many states—among them, Minnesota, Massachusetts, Arizona, and Oklahoma—have developed novel approaches to restitution. Legislation authorizing restitution programs has been passed in virtually all jurisdictions in the United States. In 1977, there were fewer than fifteen formal restitution programs around the United States; by 1985, formal programs existed in 400 jurisdictions, and thirty-five states had statutory provisions that gave courts the authority to order juvenile restitution.[31] In 1990, all fifty states, as well as the District of Columbia, have statutory restitution programs in one form or another.[32]

A sample statute from the State Juvenile Code of North Carolina indicates the type of statutory language used for restitution programs, and the latitude given the juvenile court judge regarding this disposition.

North Carolina Restitution Statute
In the case of any juvenile who is delinquent, the judge may:
(2) Require restitution, full or partial, payable within a twelve-month period to any person who has suffered loss or damage as a result of the offense committed by the juvenile. The judge may determine the amount, terms, and conditions of the restitution. If the juvenile participated with another person or persons, all participants should be jointly and severally responsible for the payment of restitution; however, the judge shall not require the juvenile to make restitution if the juvenile satisfies the court that he does not have, and could not reasonably acquire, the means to make restitution;
(4) Order the juvenile to perform supervised community service consistent with the juvenile's age, skill, and ability, specifying the nature of the work and the number of hours required. The work shall be related to the seriousness of the juvenile's offense and in no event may the obligation to work exceed twelve months.[33]

An example of a successful restitution program is that developed in the Quincy, Massachusetts, district court. The **Alternative Work Sentencing Program,** or **Earn-It,** handles juveniles referred by the court, the county probation department, and the district attorney's office. The program brings the child together with the victim of the crime in order to develop an equitable work program. Program staff members determine the extent of the victim's loss and place the child in a paying job to earn the required restitution. Some children are placed in nonpaying community service jobs to work off court orders. By all indications, Earn-It has been a success. During its first year of operation, in 1975, the program returned $36,000 in restitution payments. Today, well over $100,000 is returned to victims, the courts, and the community each year.[34]

While it is difficult to assess the impact of programs like Earn-It on a national level, a federal government evaluation of eighty-five projects over a two-year period found that they had collected $2,593,581 in monetary restitution and had assigned 355,408 community service hours and 6,052 victim service hours.[35]

Does Restitution Work?

How successful is restitution with juvenile offenders? Most attempts at evaluation have shown that it is a reasonably effective treatment alternative. For example, in an analysis of federally sponsored restitution programs, Peter Schneider and his associates found that about 95 percent of youths who received restitution as a condition of probation successfully completed their orders.[36] Factors that related to success were: family incomes, good school attendance, few prior offenses, minor current offense, and size of restitution order. Schneider found that the youths who received restitution as a sole sanction (without probation) were those originally viewed by juvenile court judges as the better risks, and consequently, they actually had lower failure and recidivism rates than youths ordered to make restitution after being placed on probation.

In another more recent attempt to evaluate restitution, Anne Schneider conducted an in-depth analysis of our programs in Georgia, Oklahoma, Washington, D.C., and Idaho.[37] Schneider found that the program participants had lower recidivism rates than youths placed in control groups, such as regular probation caseloads. While Schneider's data indicate that restitution may reduce recidivism, the number of youths who had subsequent involvement in the justice system still seems high. For example, 49 percent of the restitutioners in the Clayton County, Georgia, program were petitioned to juvenile court within three years of completing the program, as compared to 60 percent of the probation group; in Washington, D.C., 53 percent of the restitutioners and 63 percent of the probationers recidivated.

In sum, the evidence indicates that most restitution orders are successfully completed and that youths who make restitution are less likely to recidivate. Existing programs meet the important twin goals of retribution and rehabilitation.[38] However, the number of repeat offenses committed by restitutioners suggests that by itself restitution is not an answer to the delinquency problem.

Critique of Restitution

The success of Earn-It and similar programs has encouraged the development of restitution programs in other communities. However, certain problems remain. Offenders often find it difficult to make monetary restitution without securing new or additional employment. This need, charges William Staples, makes restitution seem almost absurd at a time when unemployment rates for youth are "tragically high."[39] Since most members of such programs have been convicted of a crime, many employers are reluctant to hire them. Problems also arise when offenders who need jobs suffer from drinking, drug, or emotional problems. Public and private agencies are likely sites for community service restitution, but their directors are sometimes reluctant to allow delinquent youths access to their organizations.

Thus, even voluntary charitable work is difficult to obtain. To compensate for this problem, some programs find job opportunities for clients. However, Staples claims that this can cause some youths to view restitution programs as an employment office: "committing a crime can become, for some, the only means of obtaining a job."[40]

Another criticism directed at restitution programs is that they involve **widening the net** of social control. Some critics claim that those given restitution orders would not have received more coercive treatment under any circumstances and that therefore, instead of an alternative to incarceration, restitution has become an extra burden on some offenders.[41]

Beyond these problems, some juvenile probation officers view restitution programs as a threat to their authority and to the autonomy of their organizations. It is interesting to note that courts believe police officers view restitution more positively than social workers because the police are quick to grasp the retributive nature of restitution.

Another problem restitution programs must deal with is the charge that they foster involuntary servitude. For the most part, the courts have upheld the legality of restitution even though it has a coercive element. Some people believe that restitution is inherently biased against indigent clients. A person who is unable to make restitution payments can have probation revoked and thus face incarceration. It is necessary to determine why payment has stopped and to suggest appropriate action for the court to take rather than simply treat nonpayment as a matter of law enforcement.

Finally, restitution orders are subject to the same abuses of discretion as traditional sentencing methods. The restitution orders one delinquent offender receives may be quite different than those given another similarly situated youth. To remedy this situation, a number of jurisdictions have been using restitution guidelines to control orders.

It is possible that restitution programs are an important alternative in incarceration, benefiting the child, the victim, and the juvenile justice system. H. Ted Rubin, a leading juvenile justice expert, even advocates that courts placing juveniles in day-treatment and community-based residential programs also include restitution requirements in their orders and expect that these requirements be fulfilled during placement.[42]

However, all such programs should be evaluated carefully to answer such questions as what type of offenders would be most likely to benefit from restitution, when is monetary restitution more desirable than community service, what is the best point in the juvenile justice process to impose restitution, what is the effect of restitution on the juvenile justice system, and how successful are restitution programs? The evidence does indicate that restitution is inexpensive, avoids juvenile stigma, and helps compensate victims of crime.

PRIVATIZATION OF JUVENILE PROBATION

No discussion of innovative juvenile probation programs would be complete without mention of the private sector's role in correctional services.

Juvenile probation is a major component of the juvenile justice system, and one that is finding its resources strained by growing caseloads. With juvenile courts placing more than 80 percent of adjudicated delinquents on some form of probation, these agencies represent the most significant area of juvenile corrections. Many juvenile probation programs, however, have been unable to maintain quality and cost-effective services. At the same time, the juvenile justice system is overwhelmed by such problems as illegal drug use, youth gangs, school violence, and serious juvenile crime. To assist the juvenile courts in expanding their efforts and coping with these problems, the Office of Juvenile Justice and Delinquency Prevention has funded a $1.7 million Private Sector Probation Initiative Program.[43]

Its purpose is to have private companies and institutions offer probation services to selected juveniles. Under this program, a number of jurisdictions contract out probation services to private sources. In the Third Judicial District of Utah, for example, the private-public partnership offers a 90-day intensive supervision program, with a significant reduction in recidivism rates. In Cleveland, Ohio, private-sector court services are provided to status offenders and delinquents at a cost per youth of $80 compared to $1,200 for public-sector probation services. Kenosha County, Wisconsin, contracted for central case management and weekend adventure programs, which has enabled the state to close one of its training schools. And San Francisco County was able to retain its status offender services by private contract when budget cuts threatened to eliminate them from the public sector.[44] What these programs demonstrate is that juvenile probation services can be improved by transferring some of the functions and responsibilities to the private sector. In the future, the private sector is expected to offer more juvenile justice services previously performed by government.

COMMUNITY-BASED INSTITUTIONS

To many juvenile justice experts, the institutionalization of even the most serious delinquent youths in a training school, reform school, or industrial institution is a great mistake. A period of confinement in a high-security juvenile institution usually cannot solve the problems that brought a youth into a delinquent way of life, and the experience may actually help to amplify delinquency once the youth returns to the community. Surveys indicate that about 30 percent to 40 percent of adult prison inmates had been juvenile delinquents and many have been institutionalized as youths. There is often little reason to believe that an institutional experience can have a beneficial effect or reduce recidivism.[45]

Because of the problems associated with institutional care, such influential policy-making bodies as the National Council of Juvenile and Family Court Judges have recommended that, whenever possible, treatment of serious offenders be community based. While recognizing the problems presented by the chronic offender, the council maintains that adequate security can be maintained in community-based programs.[46] Similar initiatives have been promoted by state governments. For example, Florida requires its state correctional department to "develop nontraditional, innovative, and diversified commitment programs for youth."[47]

Since the early 1970s, Massachusetts has led the movement to keep juvenile offenders in the community. In the mid-1960s, its Department of Youth Services housed over 1,000 youngsters in secure training schools. Under Jerome Miller, who became the commissioner of the department in 1969, Massachusetts closed most of its secure juvenile facilities and began a massive deinstitutionalization of juvenile offenders.[48] Today, twenty years after the institutions were closed, the Massachusetts Department of Youth Services operates a community-based correctional system. The vast majority of youths are serviced in nonsecure settings, while the relatively few committed youth are placed in some type of residential setting ranging from group and foster homes to secure facilities and forestry camps.

Initially, many of the early programs suffered from residential isolation and limited services. Over time, however, many of the group homes and unlocked structured residential settings were relocated in residential community environments and became highly successful in addressing the needs of juveniles presenting little or no security risk to themselves or others.

Roxbury Youthworks, an inner-city program in Boston, Massachusetts, is such a private community-based agency controlling juvenile delinquency through a comprehensive range of resources that include: (1) evaluation and counseling at a local court clinic; (2) employment and training; (3) detention diversion; and (4) outreach and tracking to help youth reenter the community. Youthworks is one of twenty-four independent programs—both residential and nonresidential—contracted with by the state youth services department to provide intensive community supervision for almost 90 percent of all youths under its jurisdiction.[49]

There are other dramatic examples of jurisdictions that have attempted to reduce the need for high-security institutions to treat delinquent offenders. Similar to the Massachusetts experience, Vermont closed the Weeks School—the only training school in the state—in 1979 and moved to a noninstitutional system. As of 1985, Vermont did not operate a juvenile facility. In 1975, Pennsylvania removed youths from the Camp Hill Penitentiary, which had been used to house the most hard-core juvenile offenders. Three-quarters of the juvenile inmates were returned to programs in their home communities. The remainder were transferred for short periods to small, secure institutions, then released. In 1978, Utah established a system of seven community-based programs as an alternative to traditional institutionalization in the state's Youth Development Center. An evaluation comparing the recidivism rates of comparable groups showed higher rates of success for the alternative program.

Today, among the states with the lowest incarceration rates for juvenile offenders are Pennsylvania (76 per 100,000) and Utah (73 per 100,000). In neither of these states did the deinstitutionalization effort cause an increase in either the amount or the seriousness of juvenile crime.[50]

The deinstitutionalization movement is still alive. Most recently (1988), Maryland closed its Montrose Juvenile Training School, a facility that had been in operation for nearly three-quarters of a century. Over two hundred youths were released from the school in less than a year. Many of them should not have been there in the first place since they had not committed serious or violent crimes. Nearly half of the youths were released with services and supervision in their own homes. Most of the others were safely placed in smaller, nonsecure residential programs.[51]

In the last two decades, we have seen a number of states reduce the use of institutionalization in favor of nonsecure facilities and community-based programs.[52] Recently, West Virginia, Oklahoma, Oregon, and Louisiana have either closed training schools or reduced the juvenile population in such institutions. The following "Case in Point" highlights the need for such programs and the difficulty in obtaining services for children in the juvenile justice system.

CASE IN POINT

You are a juvenile corrections consultant doing a study to determine if dispositional decisions are meeting the needs of children in juvenile courts.

Jamie B., age 15, was adjudicated a juvenile delinquent. Placed on probation for one charge of shoplifting, he failed to report to the probation officer. Brought into the juvenile court on a second petition, namely being intoxicated and disruptive in public, Jamie admitted to having a substance abuse problem.

At the dispositional stage of the court process, Jamie's attorney asked the court to place him in a drug rehabilitation program. The judge suggested that such services could be obtained in a state training school since other less-restrictive dispositional alternatives were not available. Concluding that Jamie's behavior constituted a threat to the community and to his own welfare, the court committed the youth to a state training school for an indeterminate period of time not to exceed two years.

A wide variety of dispositional alternatives are listed in the juvenile code of this jurisdiction. Among these are: supervised probation; participation in a supervised day program; placement in a residential or nonresidential treatment program; and commitment to a state training school. The legislative preference for a community-based solution to Jamie's problem is reflected throughout the code. Jamie's lawyer challenges the dispositional decision, claiming that the commitment to a training school without first examining the appropriateness and availability of community-based services was judicial error.

Do you think the commitment order should be vacated and Jamie's case remanded for a new dispositional hearing?

Encouraging Community Corrections

A number of factors have affected the placement of juvenile offenders in nonsecure community-based facilities. At first, reformers such as Jerome Miller revealed the futility of exposing youths to the hardships of high-security institutions. Then in 1974, the Juvenile Justice and Delinquency Prevention Act tied the receipt of federal funds for juvenile justice programs to the removal of status offenders from institutions. Consequently, many states reformed their juvenile codes to support new community-based treatment programs and to remove status offenders from institutions. Most states now have provisions banning the institutionalization of status offenders with delinquents. In some states, however—for example, Missouri and Alaska—repeat status offenders may be placed in secure facilities while in other states—such as Connecticut and North

Dakota—offenders cannot be held in public facilities but may be held in privately run institutions. A few states—Alabama and Ohio—allow status offenders to be institutionalized with delinquents if their behavior is so unruly that the court finds them unamenable to any other kind of treatment.[53]

The second factor fueling the deinstitutionalization movement was an effort to grant children the general right to services and, in particular, the legal **right to treatment.** This concept recognizes the principle that when the juvenile justice system places a child in custody, basic concepts of fairness and humanity suggest that the system supply the child with rehabilitation. The right to treatment (see Chapter 19) often meant providing counseling, education, adequate food and medical care, and so on. Consequently, the cost of maintaining youths in secure treatment facilities has skyrocketed. A national survey conducted in 1985 found that the average cost of maintaining one youth for one year was $25,000.[54] In 1987, the figure was $27,000.[55] Considering these costs and the assumed ineffectiveness of institutional treatment, "the least restrictive alternative available" has been sought to treat juvenile offenders, and in many cases this means placement in community-based programs.

A word of caution: while the movement to place juveniles in nonrestrictive, community-based programs continues, *the actual number of incarcerated youths has increased in recent years.*[56] The population of juveniles, for instance, held in secure public juvenile facilities increased 54 percent from 29,000 in 1977 to more than 53,000 ten years later.[57]

During the same ten-year period, the number of children in halfway houses or group homes doubled from 11,000 to about 21,000.[58] Nonetheless, secure institutional programs still make up over 32 percent of public and private facilities and house 58 percent of the total juvenile population, in spite of all the emphasis placed on community corrections in the last two decades.[59] Community corrections truly has supplemented and not replaced institutionalization.

Residential Community Treatment

How are community corrections implemented with delinquent youths? In some cases, adjudicated children are placed under probation supervision, and the probation department maintains a residential treatment facility. Or placement can be made to the department of social services or juvenile corrections with the direction that the youth be placed in a residential nonsecure facility.

Residential programs can be divided into four major categories: (1) group homes, including boarding schools and apartment-type settings, (2) foster homes, (3) family group homes, and (4) rural programs.

Group homes are nonsecure, structured residences that provide counseling, education, job training, and family living. They are staffed by a small number of qualified persons, and they generally hold twelve to fifteen youngsters. The institutional quality of the environment is minimized, and children are given the opportunity for a close but controlled interaction and relationship with the staff. Children reside in the home, attend public schools, and participate in community activities in the area.[60] Over the past two decades, extensive work has been done on group home settings. The Focus on Delinquency entitled "Residential Treatment Programs" illustrates two pioneering community-based residential treatment programs in the field of juvenile corrections that have served as models for many other programs.

Residential Treatment Programs

The Highfields Project

Highfields was a short-term residential nonsecure program for boys that began in 1950. Boys in the program were kept at Highfields, New Jersey, for periods of three or four months. They were permitted to leave the grounds under responsible adult supervision. They were also granted furloughs over weekends to visit their families and to continue to relate to the community. The youths lived in groups of no more than twenty boys in a large home on an estate. They also worked twenty to forty hours a week at a neuropsychiatric clinic. The most important treatment technique was peer pressure exerted through active participation in guided group interaction sessions.

The Highfields project was evaluated by using a controlled group of boys sent to Annandale, a juvenile reform school in the same state. One year after release, Highfields boys had a lower recidivism rate than Annandale boys. The Highfields project was considered as successful as any training school and was much less expensive to operate. However, the validity of the recidivism rates was questioned because of the difficulties associated with matching the control and treatment groups.

The Silverlake Experiment

The Silverlake experiment occurred in Los Angeles County in the mid-1960s. Like Highfields, this program provided a group home experience seeking to create a nondelinquent culture for male youths between the ages of 15 and 18. Seriously delinquent youths were placed in a large family residence in a middle-class neighborhood. Some of them attended local high schools, and many returned to their homes on weekends. Only twenty boys at a time lived in the residence. They were responsible for maintaining the residence and for participating in daily group interaction meetings. These sessions were the major formal treatment approach for implementing programs goals. The Silverlake program sought to structure a social system with positive norms by discussing the youths' problems and offering positive alternatives to delinquent behavior in the group sessions.

To evaluate the Silverlake experiment, experimental and control groups were selected at random from the youths participating in the program. There was no significant difference in the recidivism rates of the two groups tested, and it was unclear whether one program reduced recidivism more than the other. Since both control-group youths and treatment youths lived in the facility, the researchers concluded that the experimental group receiving guided group interaction and the control group were positively affected by the program. Recidivism rates twelve months after release indicated a general reduction in delinquent behavior on the part of participants.

Source: H. Ashley Weeks, Highfields (Ann Arbor: University of Michigan Press, 1956); LaMar T. Empey and Stephen Lubeck, The Silverlake Experiment: Testing Delinquency Theory and Community Intervention (Chicago: Aldine, 1971).

Foster care programs typically involve one or two juveniles who live with a family—usually a husband and wife who serve as surrogate parents. The juveniles enter into a close relationship with the foster parents and receive the attention, guidance, and care that they did not receive before. The quality of the foster home experience depends on the foster parents and their emotional relationship with the child. Foster care for adjudicated juvenile offenders has not been extensive in the United States. It is most often used for orphans or for children whose parents cannot care for them. Welfare departments generally handle foster placements, and funding has been a problem for the juvenile justice system. However, foster home services for delinquent children and status offenders have expanded as an approach in the area of community treatment.[61]

Family group homes combine elements of both foster care and group home placements. Children are placed in a private group home that is run by a single family rather than a professional staff. This model can help troubled youths learn to get along in family-type situations and at the same time help the state avoid the start-up costs and neighborhood opposition often associated with public institutions. Family group homes can be found in many jurisdictions throughout the United States.[62]

Rural programs include forestry camps, ranches, and farms that provide specific recreational activities or work in a rural setting. Individual programs handle from thirty to fifty children. Such programs have the disadvantage of isolating children from the community, but reintegration can be achieved if the child's stay is short and if family and friends can visit.

Most residential programs use group counseling techniques as the major treatment tool. Although group facilities have been used less often than institutional placements in the years past, there is definitely a trend toward developing community-based residential facilities.

NONRESIDENTIAL COMMUNITY TREATMENT

In **nonresidential programs,** youths remain in their homes or in foster homes and receive counseling, education, employment, diagnostic, and casework services. A counselor or probation officer gives innovative and intensive support to help the child remain at home. Family therapy, educational tutoring, and job placement may all be part of the program.

Nonresidential programs are often associated with the Provo program begun in 1959 in Utah and the Essexfields Rehabilitation Project started in the early 1960s in Essex County, New Jersey.[63] Today, the most well-known approach is **Project New Pride,** which has been replicated in a number of sites around the United States. The accompanying Focus on Delinquency describes the Project New Pride program.

CRITICISMS OF THE COMMUNITY TREATMENT APPROACH

The community treatment approach has limitations. Public opinion may be against community treatment, especially when it is offered to juvenile offenders who pose a real threat to society. Institutionalization may be the only answer for the violent young offender. Even if the juvenile crime problem abates, society may be unwilling to accept reforms that liberalize policies and practices in the field of juvenile corrections. For example, it is common for neighborhood groups to

Glen Ostergard stands on a corner in a predominantly gay area in San Francisco, California known as Polk Gulch. At the age of 17, he was hustling as a teenage gay prostitute in order to survive. He has since pulled his life together with the help of a local counseling service and now helps other kids on Polk Street.

actively oppose the location of corrections programs in their community. The thought of a center for young drug users being located across the street can send shivers down the spine of many property owners.

Evaluations of recidivism rates do not show conclusively that community treatment is more successful than institutionalization. Some experimental programs indicate that young people can be treated in the community as safely and as effectively as children placed in an institution. However, commitment to an institution guarantees that the community will be protected against further crime, at least during the time of the child's placement. More research is essential to evaluate the success of community treatment programs.

Much of the early criticism of community treatment was based on poor delivery of services, shabby operation, and haphazard management, follow-up, and planning. In the early 1970s, when Massachusetts deinstitutionalized its juvenile correction system, there was a torrent of reports about the inadequate operation of community treatment programs. This was caused by the absence of uniform policies, different procedures in various programs, and the lack of accountability.[64] The development of needed programs was hampered, and available resources were misplaced. Today's community treatment programs have generally overcome their early deficiencies and operate with more expertise than in the past.

It is also possible that deinstitutionalization will result in the increased use of pretrial detention for children, because judges fear that dangerous children will

Project New Pride

One of the most well-known community-based treatment models is Project New Pride. Begun in Denver, Colorado, in 1973, it has served as a model for similar programs around the country.

The target group for Project New Pride is serious or violent youthful offenders from 14 to 17 years old. They have at least two prior convictions for serious misdemeanors and/or felonies and are formally charged or convicted of another offense when referred to New Pride.

The percentage of females in the New Pride population is generally low, ranging from 10 percent in Denver New Pride to 15 percent in the Juvenile Resource Center in Camden, New Jersey, one of the replication sites.

Will any hard-core youths be accepted into New Pride? The only youths not eligible for participation are those who have committed forcible rape or are diagnosed as severely psychotic; New Pride believes this restriction is necessary in the interest of the safety of the community and of the youths themselves.

The project's specific goals are to work these hard-core youths back into the mainstream of their communities and to reduce the number of rearrests. Generally, reintegration into the community means reenrolling in school, getting a job, or both.

Schooling

New Pride youths receive alternative schooling and are then reintegrated into the public school system or directed toward vocational training. Some youths get jobs and pursue a GED certificate. Some of them complete high school in the alternative school (certified by the public school system). Those with learning disabilities receive specific attention to their problem within the alternative school. The program encourages all youths to obtain a high school diploma, and it urges those who must work to participate in a GED program.

Jobs

New Pride places specific emphasis on vocational training. The staff recognizes that money is the key to independence for these youths, and the most socially acceptable way to get money is to work for it. On coming to New Pride, few know how to apply for a job, much less keep one. New Pride finds jobs for the majority of its youths, and many of them work very successfully in project-owned small businesses. Most of the jobs are part-time to allow the youths to continue their education.

Getting a job is crucial to these young people— not only to their ability to become self-sufficient but also to their emotional and psychological well-being. This need is borne out by the fact that Denver New Pride youths without jobs get rearrested at three times the rate of those with jobs.

Family

Not only do the youths benefit from intensive counseling, but counselors are also available for their families. New Pride encourages family members to visit the project facility in order to observe the daily operation, involve themselves in their child's treatment, and to get to know the staff. Often, by understanding and supporting the objectives of the program, the family is helped to remain together as a unit. For example, it is not atypical for family members to demand most of a youth's pay; this can reduce motivation to work. But New Pride does feel that a youth's contributing to his or her own support can play an important role in preparing for independent living. Family members some-

continued

times need guidance in financial assistance and in dealing with domestic violence, alcoholism, or drug abuse.

Community

New Pride community-based programs are extremely cost-effective when compared with the cost of placing a child in an institution. In Colorado and New Jersey, for example, it costs approximately $28,000 per year to incarcerate a youth; the cost for Denver New Pride and the Juvenile Resource Center in Camden is approximately $4,500. Through successful treatment of these youths, they become taxpayers and put dollars back into the community rather than being supported by taxpayers.

An overall benefit to the community is New Pride's ability to reduce juvenile crime, to reduce illiteracy, to reduce the number of troublemakers in the public schools, and to increase the work force.

The Services of the Program

Participation in New Pride involves six months of intensive involvement and a six-month follow-up period, during which the youth slowly reintegrates into the community. During the follow-up period, the youth continues to benefit from as many services as necessary and works closely with counselors.

The integrated delivery of all services is extremely important in meeting all of the needs of juvenile delinquents in New Pride. Youths with poor vision will not perform well in school; those not able to read or write well may not be able to get a job.

Alternative Schooling

The majority of New Pride youths have dropped out of school at the time of referral to the program. Many have at least one learning disability. Participation in the alternative education provided by New Pride is encouraged, and the youths are generally required to show progress in school before being considered for job placement. As a result of years of negative feedback, these youths fear and avoid educational activities.

A focus of New Pride is to develop a more positive attitude toward learning. In a relaxed, casual setting, the youths benefit from a five-to-one student-to-teacher ratio—with volunteers, a one-to-one ratio is achieved—where the staff is strongly supportive of student efforts and encourages their strengths. All youths participate in some form of New Pride alternative education; some work toward reintegration back into the public schools (academic credit is awarded for New Pride schools); some study in a GED program while working part-time; some need treatment for specific learning disabilities while increasing their academic achievements; and most need to get jobs and require vocational training.

Job Placement

Job preparation is a key function of Project New Pride since most youths are without skills and have unrealistic expectations in regard to the demands of a job. Before attempting to place youths in jobs, New Pride guides them in such basics as filling out a job application form and interviewing. The employment component is designed to introduce the youths to the expectations of the work world first, then to provide them with on-the-job training under close supervision, and finally to place them in jobs when they have developed some marketable skills.

Economic Development

To supplement opportunities for pre-vocational training and to return some profit for the program, New Pride successfully developed its own small businesses. The types of business operated vary with the location of the site, the needs of the local community (based on a market analysis), and the extent of volunteer support by local business people. These profit-oriented businesses include housing renovation, a pizzeria, lawn maintenance, a bakery, janitorial services, a vegetable farm, and a garden nursery.

Source: Project New Pride (Washington, D.C.: U.S. Government Printing Office, 1985).

be treated leniently. Also, it may cause more children to be transferred to adult courts and subsequently to be committed to adult prisons. Finding out if this is actually happening is a difficult task, but there is no question that law-and-order forces are seeking to turn more children over to the adult system.[65]

The Hidden Correctional System

In a very important article, sociologist **Paul Lerman** described the growth of a "hidden" private-sector correctional system.[66] He found that American society has developed three major systems of juvenile social control: child welfare, mental health, and juvenile corrections. The mental health and public welfare systems became increasingly involved in juvenile justice in the 1960s and 1970s because opportunities, in terms of federal funding, developed to implement their preexisting concern with children in trouble. This development coincided with an increased federal role in developing a "welfare state," exemplified by such programs as Medicaid, Medicare, and aid to education. Lerman concluded that community corrections has evolved into another example of net-widening. Although deinstitutionalization had been implemented, the actual number of youths committed to some form of treatment, albeit community-based, had increased.

A similar conclusion was reached by Barry Krisberg and Ira Schwartz in their study of the influence of deinstitutionalization on juvenile justice policy.[67] They also warn of a hidden juvenile justice system involving juveniles admitted to private psychiatric settings, chemical dependency treatment programs, and residential centers for mentally ill youth.

Drug paraphernalia is shown against a 1-800-COCAINE poster at the drug abuse hot line at Fair Oaks Hospital in Summit, New Jersey, part of the "hidden" correctional system.

General Effectiveness of Community-Based Programs

Beyond these criticisms, has community treatment generally proven successful? Some research efforts have shown success. Lloyd Ohlin and his associates found that youths in nonsecure placements were less likely to recidivate than those placed in more secure institutions.[68] However, other reviews of community corrections reached the opposite result. Dennis Romig's national survey of community treatment programs concluded that few were effective in helping youths, and Malcolm Klein's analysis showed that community corrections has many pitfalls.[69]

The dilemmas faced by community treatments are illustrated by the **Community Treatment Project (CTP)** of the California Youth Authority. The purpose of the project was to determine whether intensive supervision of juveniles in the community would be more successful than the normal program of institutionalization.[70] The project, established in 1961, served as a model in juvenile justice for more than two decades. The study took children committed from the juvenile courts of the cities of Sacramento, Stockton, San Francisco, and Modesto and classified them according to a measure of interpersonal maturity (I-level). The children were divided into a control group treated in a traditional institutional program. Those in the experimental group were placed in a community institution for eight months. Individual treatment plans were developed for each child in the experimental group. Certain types of youths did especially well; others did not respond to community treatment.

Numerous researchers have examined the data from the California Community Treatment Project.[71] On the whole, recidivism rates seemed to be lower for those in community treatment than for those in traditional programs. However in an important analysis, Paul Lerman showed that the original CTP success was more a function of the way recidivism rates were computed than the actual success of the program. While youths in the CTP were as likely to commit new crimes and get arrested as those in the comparison groups, their control agents were less likely to bring formal action against them. What appeared to be a change in the behavior of clients was actually a result of change in the behavior of their supervisors.[72] Lerman found that the CTP project was no more effective than traditional institutionalization, nor was it any more cost effective. Thus, the track record of community-based corrections is still open for debate.

Despite such dilemmas, the greatest advantage community corrections has is its cost. A national survey of the costs of treating youths found that the average annual expenditure per child in a training school was $27,000, while a community-based program may cost half as much. If community-based correction were only equally successful as secure institutional care, it could be justified on the basis of savings to the taxpayer alone.[73]

SUMMARY

Community treatment represents efforts by the juvenile justice system to keep offenders in the community and spare them the pains and stigma of incarceration in a secure facility. The primary purpose of community treatment is to address the individual needs of juveniles in a home setting, employing any combination of educational, vocational, counseling, or employment-related services.

The most widely used method of community treatment is probation. Approximately 400,000 youths are currently on probation. They must obey rules given to them by the court and partake in some sort of treatment program. Probation officers monitor their behavior in the community. If rules are violated, youths can have their probation revoked and suffer more punitive means of control, such as secure incarceration.

Probation departments have developed restitution programs as a type of community treatment. These involve having the delinquents either reimburse the victims of their crimes or do community service. While these programs appear successful, critics accuse them of widening the net of social control over young offenders.

Other forms of community treatment are day programs and residential community programs. The former allow youths to live at home while receiving treatment in a nonpunitive community-based center; the latter require that youths reside in group homes while receiving care and treatment.

Critics of community corrections charge that rather than reducing the offender population in custody, community corrections *increase* it because the sum total of youths in some form of treatment has increased rather than decreased. Thus, a "hidden" juvenile justice system that includes mental health, chemical dependency programs, and social welfare programs now exists.

Despite criticisms, the cost savings of community treatment, coupled with its benign intentions, are likely to keep these programs growing. They are certainly no worse than secure institutions.

KEY TERMS

community treatment

restitution

probation

juvenile probation officer

social investigation report

conditions of probation

revoke

intensive supervision

house arrest

electronic monitoring

wilderness probation

balanced probation

monetary restitution

victim service

community service restitution

Alternative Work Sentencing Program (Earn-It)

widening the net

right to treatment

residential programs

group homes

foster care programs

family group homes

rural programs

nonresidential programs

Project New Pride

Paul Lerman

Community Treatment Project (CTP)

QUESTIONS FOR DISCUSSION

1. Would you want a community treatment program in your neighborhood?

2. Is "net-widening" a real danger, or are treatment-oriented programs simply a method of helping troubled youths?

3. If a youngster violates the rules of probation, should he or she be placed in an institution?

4. Is juvenile restitution fair? Should a poor child have to pay back a wealthy victim, such as a store?

5. What are the most important advantages to community treatment for juvenile offenders?

6. What is the purpose of juvenile probation? Identify some conditions of probation and discuss the responsibilities of the juvenile probation officer.

7. Discuss the recent trends in community treatment of juvenile offenders?

NOTES

1. American Bar Association, *Standards Relating to Probation*, Standard 1.2 (New York: Institute of Judicial Administration, 1968), p. 10; see also Dean J. Champion, *Probation and Parole in the United States*, (Columbus, Ohio: Merrill Publishing Co., 1990), Chap. 11.

2. Sanford Fox, *Juvenile Courts* (St. Paul: West Publishing Co., 1984), pp. 227–28.

3. See Ralph Brendes, "Interstate Supervision of Parole and Probation," in *Probation, Parole, and Community Corrections*, eds. Robert Carter and Leslie Wilkins New York: Wiley, 1970).

4. George Killinger, Hazel Kerper, and Paul F. Cromwell, Jr., *Probation and Parole in the Criminal Justice System* (St. Paul: West Publishing Co., 1976), p. 45.

5. National Advisory Commission on Criminal Justice Standards and Goals, *Corrections* (Washington, D. C.: U.S. Government Printing Office, 1983), p. 75.

6. Bureau of Justice Statistics, *Report to the Nation on Crime and Justice*, 2nd ed. (Washington, D.C.: U.S. Government Printing Office, 1988), p. 95.

7. For a general review of the organization of probation services in the United States, see National Council on Crime and Delinquency, *Probation and Parole Directory* (Hackensack, N. J.: NCCD, 1976).

8. Patricia Torbet, *Organization and Administration of Juvenile Services* (Pittsburgh: National Center for Juvenile Justice, September 1989).

9. *Ibid:* p. 12.

10. American Bar Association, *Standards Relating to Juvenile Probation Function* (Cambridge, Mass.: Ballinger Publishing Co., 1977), p. 124.

11. "Correction in the United States—A Survey for the President's Commission on Law Enforcement by the National Council on Crime and Delinquency," **Crime and Delinquency Journal 13**:44 (1967).

12. *Ibid.*

13. Paul Piersma, et al., *Law and Tactics in Juvenile Cases* (Philadelphia: American Law Institute—American Bar Association Committee on Continuing Education, 1977), pp. 358–67.

14. See *Morrissey v. Brewer*, 408 U.S. 471, 92 S. Ct. 2593, 33 L.Ed.2d 484 (1972); and *Gagnon v. Scarpelli*, 411 U.S. 778, 93 S.Ct. 1756, 36 L.Ed.2d 655 (1973).

15. See, generally, James Byrne, "The Control Controversy: A Preliminary Examination of Intensive Probation Supervision Programs in the United States," *Federal Probation* 50:4–16 (1986).

16. See Mass.Gen.Laws Ch. 119, 52–83; Martin Levin and Rosemary Sarri, *Juvenile Delinquency: A Comparative Analysis of Legal Codes in the United States* (Ann Arbor, Mich.: National Assessment of Juvenile Corrections, 1974).

17. For a review of these programs, see James Byrne, ed., *Federal Probation* 50:2 (June 1986); see also Emily Walker, "The Community Intensive Treatment for Youth Program: A Specialized Community-Based Program for High-Risk Youth in Alabama," *Law and Psychology Review* 13:175–99 (1989).

18. Edward Latessa, "The Cost Effectiveness of Intensive Supervision," *Federal Probation* 50:70–74 (1986); see also John Ott, "Bibliotherapy as a Challenging Condition to the Sentence of Juvenile Probation," *Juvenile and Family Court Journal*, 40:63–67 (1989).

19. S. H. Clarke and A. D. Craddock, *Evaluation of North Carolina's Intensive Juvenile Probation Program*, (Chapel Hill, N.C.: University of North Carolina Institute of Government, 1987).

20. T. L. Armstrong, *National Survey of Juvenile Intensive Probation Supervision* (Washington, D.C.: U.S. Department of Justice, Criminal Justice Abstracts, 1988).

21. "Volunteers in Probation," *Newsletter of the National Information Center on Volunteerism*, ed. Ivan Scheier (Boulder, Colo.: Boulder County Juvenile Court, 1972).

22. Richard Ball and J. Robert Lilly, "A Theoretical Examination of Home Incarceration," *Federal Probation* 50:17–25 (1986); Joan Petersilia, "Exploring the Option of House Arrest," *Federal Probation* 50:50–56 (1986); Annesley Schmidt, "Electronic Monitors," *Federal Probation* 50:56-60 (1986); Michael Charles, "The Development of a Juvenile Electronic Monitoring Program," *Federal Probation* 53:3–12 (1989).

23. Joseph B. Vaughn, "A Survey of Juvenile Electronic Monitoring and Home Confinement Programs," *Juvenile and Family Court Journal* 40:1–36 (1989).

24. Robert Callahan, "Wilderness Probation: A Decade Later," *Juvenile and Family Court Journal* 36:31–35 (1985).

25. "Wilderness Programs in Probation," *Juvenile and Family Court Newsletter,* Vol. 19 (1989), p. 5.

26. Steven Flagg Scott, "Outward Bound: An Adjunct to the Treatment of Juvenile Delinquents: Florida's STEP Program," *New England Journal on Criminal and Civil Confinement* 11:420–37 (1985).

27. Dennis Mahoney, Dennis Romig, and Troy Armstrong, "Juvenile Probation: The Balanced Approach," *Juvenile and Family Court Journal* 39:1–59 (1988).

28. *Ibid;* also Charles McGee, "Measured Steps Toward Clarity and Balance in Juvenile Justice System," *Juvenile and Family Court Journal* 40:1–24(1989).

29. Anne L. Schneider, ed., *Guide to Juvenile Restitution* (Washington, D.C.: U.S. Department of Justice, 1985); Anne Schneider and Jean Warner, *National Trends in Juvenile Restitution Programming* (Washington, D.C.: U.S. Government Printing Office, 1989).

30. See Anne Newton, "Sentencing to Community Service and Restitution," in *Criminal Justice Abstracts* (Hackensack, N.J.: National Council on Crime and Delinquency, September 1979), pp. 435–68.

31. Anne Schneider, "Restitution and Recidivism Rates of Juvenile Offenders: Results from Four Experimental Studies," *Criminology* 24:533–52 (1986).

32. Linda Szymanski, *Juvenile Restitution Statutes* (Pittsburgh: National Center for Juvenile Justice, 1988).

33. N.C. Gen.Laws 7A, 649.

34. Descriptive materials can be obtained from the Earn-It Program, District Court of East Norfolk, Quincy, MA 02169; see also Jean Warner, Vincent Burke, and Anne L. Schneider, *Directory of Juvenile Restitution Programs* (Washington, D.C.: National Criminal Justice Reference Service, 1987).

35. Peter Schneider, "Research on Restitution: A Guide to Rational Decision Making," in Schneider, *Guide to Juvenile Restitution,* p. 137.

36. Peter Schneider, William Griffith, and Anne Schneider, *Juvenile Restitution as a Sole Sanction or Condition of Probation: An Empirical Analysis* (Eugene, Ore.: Institute for Policy Analysis, 1980).

37. Anne Schneider, "Restitution and Recidivism Rates."

38. Burt Galaway, "Restitution as Innovation or Unfilled Promise," *Federal Probation* 52:3–15 (1989).

39. Willaim Staples, "Restitution as a Sanction in Juvenile Court," *Crime and Delinquency* 32:177–85 (1986).

40. *Ibid.,* p. 183.

41. Barry Krisberg and Jame Austin, "The Unmet Promise of Alternatives to Incarceration," *Crime and Delinquency* 28:374–409 (1982).

42. H. Ted Rubin. "Fulfilling Juvenile Restitution Requirements in Community Correctional Programs," *Federal Probation* 52:32–43 (1988).

43. "Privatizing Juvenile Probation Services: Five Local Experiences,"*National Institute of Justice Reports* (Washington, D.C.: Office of Justice Programs, December, 1989), p. 10.

44. *Ibid.* p. 12.

45. Bureau of Justice Statistics, *Report to the Nation on Crime and Justice* (Washington, D.C.: U.S. Government Printing Office, 1988), pp. 44–45.

46. National Council of Juvenile and Family Court Judges, "The Juvenile Court and Serious Offenders," *Juvenile and Family Court Journal* 35:16 (1984).

47. Fla. Stat.Ann. 959.011 (West Supp., 1983).

48. Commonwealth of Massachusetts, *Department of Youth Services Annual Report of 1978* (Boston: State Purchasing Agency, 1978).

49. "Roxbury Agency Offers a Map for Youths at the Crossroads," *Boston Globe,* 18 February, 1990, p. 32.

50. National Council on Crime and Delinquency, *Juvenile Justice: Tough Enough* (San Francisco: National Council on Crime and Delinquency, n.d.), p. 10.

51. Jeffrey Butts, *Youth Corrections in Maryland: The Dawning of a New Era* (Ann Arbor, Mich.: Center for Study of Youth Policy, University of Michigan 1988).

52. J. Blackmore, M. Brown, and B. Krisberg, *Juvenile Justice Reform—The Bellweather States* (Ann Arbor, Mich.: Center for Study of Youth Policy, University of Michigan, 1988).

53. W.N. Paul and H.S. Watt, *Deinstitutionalization of Status Offenders: A Compilation and Analysis of State Statutes* (Denver, Colo.: State Legislative Leaders Foundation, 1980), pp. 54–57.

54. Bureau of Justice Statistics, *Children in Custody, 1985* (Washington, D.C.: U.S. Government Printing Office, 1986).

55. Bureau of Justice Statistics, *Children in Custody Series 1975–85 Census of Public and Private Juvenile Detention, Correctional, and Shelter Facilities* (Washington, D.C.: U.S. Department of Justice, May 1989), p. 2.

56. *Ibid.,* p. 10.

57. *Ibid.,* p. 2; see also Bureau of Justice Statistics, *Children in Custody—Public Juvenile Facilities—1987.* (Washington, D.C.: U.S. Department of Justice, 1989).

58. *Ibid.,* p. 2.

59. *Ibid.,* p. 2.

60. American Bar Association, *Standards Relating to Disposition* (New York: Institute of Judicial Administration, 1968), p. 68.

61. See E. Lawder, R. Andrews, and J. Parson, *Five Models of Foster Family Group Homes*, Report of Child Welfare League of America (New York: Child Welfare League, 1974); Yitzhak Bakal, *Closing Correctional Institutions* (Lexington, Mass.: D.C. Heath, 1973); Andrew Rutherford and Osman Berger, *Community-Based Alternatives to Juvenile Incarceration* (Washington, D.C.: U.S. Government Printing Office, 1976), pp. 10–35.

62. Joseph Rowan and Charles Kehoe, "Let's Deinstitutionalize Group Homes," *Juvenile and Family Court Journal* 36:1–4 (1985).

63. Lamar Empey and Maynard Erickson, *The Provo Experiment* (Lexington, Mass.: D.C. Heath, 1972); Paul Pilnick, Albert Elias, and Neale Clapp, "The Essexfields Concept: A New Approach to the Social Treatment of Juvenile Delinquents," *Journal of Applied Behavioral Sciences* 2:109–21 (1966).

64. Rob Wilson, "The Legacy of Jerome Miller," *Corrections Magazine*, September 1978, p. 11.

65. Barry Krisberg and Ira Schwartz, "Rethinking Juvenile Justice," *Crime and Delinquency* 29:333–64 (1983).

66. Paul Lerman, "Child Welfare, the Private Sector, and Community Based Corrections," *Crime and Delinquency* 30:5–38 (1984).

67. Krisberg and Schwartz, "Rethinking Juvenile Justice."

68. Lloyd Ohlin, Alden Miller, and Robert Coates, *Juvenile Correctional Reform in Massachusetts* (Washington, D.C.: U.S. Government Printing Office, 1976).

69. Dennis Romig, *Justice for Our Children* (Lexington, Mass.: Lexington Books, 1978); Malcolm Klein, "Deinstitutionalization and Diversion of Juvenile Offenders: A Litany of Impediments," in *Crime and Justice*, vol. 1, ed. Norval Morris and Michael Tonry (Chicago: University of Chicago Press, 1979), pp. 145–201.

70. Marguerite Q. Warren, "The Community Treatment Project: History and Prospects," *Law Enforcement Science and Technology*, ed. S.A. Yafsky. Proceedings of the First National Symposium on Law Enforcement Science and Technology (Washington, D.C.: Thompson, 1967), p. 191.

71. See Paul Lerman, "Evaluating the Outcome of Institutions for Delinquents," *Social Work Journal* 13:68–81 (1968).

72. Paul Lerman, *Community Treatment and Social Control* (Chicago: University of Chicago Press, 1975).

73. "Juvenile Correctional Programs: Some Cost Comparisons," *Investigative Newsletter on Institutions and Alternatives* 4:4–6 (March 1981).

19 Institutionalization and Aftercare

If, after a dispositionary hearing, the juvenile court judge finds that community treatment is inadequate to deal with the special needs of a delinquent child, the child may be referred to the state department of youth services for a period of confinement in a state-run treatment center. Or where appropriate, the child may be referred to a privately run treatment program that specializes in dealing with a particular social problem (for example, drug abuse or violent juvenile crime). Such programs are often long-term facilities that hold adjudicated delinquents in environments that limit access to the community.

Today, correctional institutions operated by federal, state, and county governments are generally classified as secure and nonsecure facilities. Secure facilities contain the movement of residents through staff monitoring, locked entrances and exits, and interior fence controls. Nonsecure institutions, on the other hand, generally do not restrict the movement of the residents and allow much greater freedom of access in and out of the facility.[1]

There has been a general movement in the past twenty years toward the use of fewer and smaller secure facilities, on the theory that these programs allow more freedom and a greater chance of rehabilitating young offenders than do large bureaucratic institutions. States such as Utah and Vermont have for the most part closed their large training schools and now rely on smaller institutions of less than forty youths. Violent youths and chronic serious offenders are placed in a few small, high-security treatment units.

This approach uses a diverse network of community-based programs that allow for specialized individual treatment and are generally offered by private providers under contract with the state.[2] One of the most talked about of these private-sector programs is the **Paint Creek Youth Center** (PCYC) in Bainbridge, Ohio. Since its beginning several years ago, PCYC has been the focus of considerable discussion within the juvenile justice community because it offers an alternative to traditional public correctional services. In a small, open setting, PCYC combines proven program components, including a highly structured environment, intensive aftercare, low client-staff ratio, job training and work experience, and many other comprehensive services.[3]

Beyond the secure and nonsecure classifications, there are at least six different categories of correctional institutions in the United States: (1) detention centers that provide restrictive custody pending adjudication or disposition, (2) shelters that offer nonrestrictive temporary care, (3) reception centers that screen juveniles placed by the courts and assign them to an appropriate facility, (4) training schools or reformatories that are for adjudicated youths needing a long-term, secure setting, (5) ranch or forestry camps that provide special, long-term residential care in a less restrictive setting, and (6) halfway houses or group homes where juveniles are allowed daily contact with the community.[4] Youth correctional systems often incorporate virtually all of these programs.

Many experts believe that institutionalizing young offenders generally does more harm than good. It exposes them to prison-like conditions and to more experienced delinquents without giving them the benefit of constructive treatment programs. In contrast, offenders in the less costly community-based programs often have recidivism rates at least as low as (if not lower than) those in institutions. Nonetheless, secure treatment in juvenile corrections is still being used extensively around the country, and the populations in these facilities are continuing to grow.

In this chapter, we analyze the current state of secure juvenile corrections. A brief history of juvenile corrections is undertaken, and then discussion turns to such issues as the extent of correction, the juvenile client, life in institutions, and treatment issues.

THE HISTORY OF JUVENILE INSTITUTIONS

Until the early 1800s, juvenile offenders as well as neglected and dependent children were confined in adult prisons. Physical conditions in these institutions were horribly punitive and inhumane, a fact that led social reformers to create a separate court system in 1899 and eventually to open correctional facilities solely for juveniles.[5] These early juvenile institutions were industrial schools modeled after adult prisons but designed to protect children from the evil influences in adult facilities. The first was the New York House of Refuge, established in 1825.

Not long after this, states began to establish **reform schools** for juveniles. Massachusetts was the first to open a state reform school—the Lyman School for Boys in Westborough—in 1846. New York opened the State Agricultural and Industrial School in 1849, and Maine opened the Maine Boys' Training School in 1853. By 1900, thirty-six states had reform schools.[6] While it is difficult to precisely measure the total population of these institutions, Margaret Werner Cahalan has impressively reviewed historical corrections statistics in the United States. She found that by 1880, there were approximately 11,468 youths in correctional facilities, a number that more than doubled by 1923 (see Table 19.1).[7] Early reform schools were generally punitive in nature and were based on the concept of rehabilitation or reform through hard work and discipline.

In the second half of the nineteenth century, emphasis shifted from the massive industrial schools to the **cottage system.** Juvenile offenders were housed in a series of small cottages in a compound, each one holding twenty to forty children. Each cottage was run by cottage parents, who attempted to create a home-like atmosphere. It was felt that this would be more conducive to rehabilitation than the rigid bureaucratic organization of massive institutions.

The first cottage system was established in Massachusetts in 1855, the second in Ohio in 1858.[8] The system was generally applauded as being a great improvement over the earlier industrial training schools. The general feeling was that by

TABLE 19.1 Youths in Correctional Facilities, 1880-1980

	1880	1890	1904	1910	1923	1980
Number	11,468	14,846	23,034	25,038	27,238	59,414
Per 100,000 population aged 10-20	97	100	126	125	125	136

Source: Margaret Werner Cahalan, *Historical Corrections Statistics in the United States, 1850–1984* (Washington, D.C.: U.S. Department of Justice, 1986), pp.104–105.

moving away from punishment and toward rehabilitation, diagnosis, and treatment, not only could known offenders be rehabilitated, but crime among dependent and unruly children could be prevented.[9]

Twentieth-Century Developments

The early twentieth century witnessed important changes in the structure of juvenile corrections. Because of the influence of World War I, reform schools began to adopt military styles. Living units became barracks; cottage groups, companies; housefathers, captains; and superintendents, majors or colonels. Military-style uniforms became standard.[10]

As the number of juvenile offenders increased, the forms of institutions varied to include forestry camps, ranches, and educational and vocational schools. Beginning in the 1930s, for example, camps became a part of the juvenile correctional system. Modeled after the camps run by the Civilian Conservation Corps, the juvenile camps centered on conservation activities, outdoor living, and work as a means of rehabilitation.

Los Angeles County was the first to utilize camps during this period.[11] Southern California had problems with transient youths who came to California with no money and then got into trouble with the law. Rather than filling up the jails, the county placed these offenders in conservation camps, paid them small wages, and then released them when they had earned enough money to return home. When the camps proved more rehabilitative than training schools, California established forestry camps in 1935 especially for delinquent boys, and the idea soon spread to other states.[12]

Also during the 1930s, efforts at reforming the juvenile correctional institution were taken under the U.S. Children's Bureau. The Bureau did studies and conducted projects to determine the effectiveness of the training school concept. Little was learned from these early programs because of limited funding and bureaucratic ineptitude, and the Childrens Bureau failed to achieve any significant change in the juvenile correctional field. But such efforts recognized the important role of positive institutional care in delinquency prevention and control.[13]

Another innovation came in the 1940s, with the American Law Institute's Model Youth Correction Authority Act. This act emphasized the use of reception-classification centers. California was the first to try out this new idea, opening the Northern Reception Center and Clinic in Sacramento in 1947. Today, there are seventeen such centers scattered around the United States.[14]

Since the 1970s, the major change in institutionalization has been the effort by the federal government to remove status offenders from institutions housing juvenile delinquents. This initiative also includes removing status offenders from secure pretrial detention centers and removing all juveniles from contact with adults in jails.

This "decarceration" policy mandates that courts use the **least restrictive alternative** in providing services for status offenders. This means that a noncriminal child should not be put in a secure facility if a community-based model will do. In addition, the federal government prohibits states from putting status offenders in separate custodial care facilities that are similar in form and function to those used for delinquent offenders. This is to prevent states from merely shifting their institutionalized population around so that one training school houses all delinquents and another houses all status offenders, but actual conditions remain the same.

The decarceration movement has had some dramatic results. At the end of 1977, some 3,376 status offenders were being held in public short- and long-term institutions; by 1985, the number declined to 2,293, and in 1987 (the latest available data), the figure stood at 2,523.[15] This initial decline may signify a shift in court policy and judicial decision making; judges may be more likely to encourage prosecutors to charge youths with delinquency rather than status offenses. Or as Paul Lerman warns, removing status offenders from secure public institutions may mean involving them in privately administered mental health and/or community-based programs.[16] According to Lerman, it is difficult to determine whether federal initiatives have resulted in a decline in the custodial population or merely a shift in its whereabouts. The increase of nine percent from 1985 to 1987, on the other hand, may result from the fact that private facilities are more likely to house younger youth, who seem to be coming into the correctional system in increasing numbers.

JUVENILE INSTITUTIONS TODAY

There are approximately 1,107 public and 2,195 private juvenile facilities in operation around the United States, holding a one-day count of approximately 91,646 youths (the latest available data at the time of this printing).[17] In 1985, there were 1,040 public and 1,996 private juvenile facilities, with 83,402 juveniles in custody. Overall, the number of youth and institutions has increased by about nine percent in this period, possibly due to a "get tough" policy with juvenile offenders (see Figure 19.1).

The majority of these institutions are small, nonsecure facilities holding less than twenty youths. However, there are also about seventy facilities that house over two hundred juveniles. While about 80 percent of the public institutions can be characterized as "closed" and secured, only 20 percent of private facilities are high security.

Public institutions for juveniles can be administered by any number of state agencies: child and youth services; mental health, youth conservation, health, and social services; corrections; and child welfare.[18] Social service departments administer juvenile institutions in twenty states and the District of Columbia, while corrections agencies have this responsibility in fourteen states, and youth services departments in thirteen states. In three jurisdictions, delinquent institutions are administered by a specialized department of family and children's services.[19] Recently, a number of states have created separate youth service organizations and removed juvenile corrections from an existing adult corrections department or mental health agency. Virginia, for instance, created a new Department of Youth Services as of July 1990, while Arizona's juvenile corrections program has become an independent agency after it split from the Department

FIGURE 19.1
Growth in institutional
care, 1975 to 1987

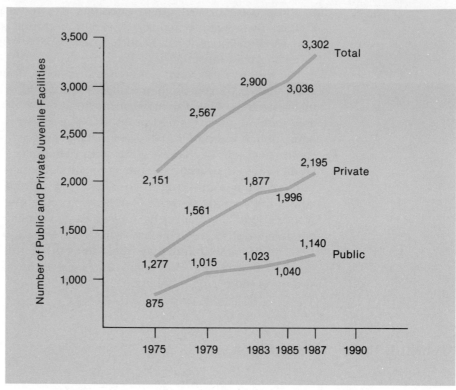

Source: Bureau of Justice Statistics, *Children in Custody 1975–85* and *Fact Sheet 1987*
(Washington, D.C.: U.S. Department of Justice, 1989).

of Corrections.[20] The institutions in some states fall under a centralized corrections system that covers adults as well as juveniles. Other states operate separate adult and juvenile systems. Maryland has enhanced its juvenile corrections program by the creation of its Juvenile Services Agency, whose director reports directly to the governor. It has 1,800 employees and an $87,000 million budget. In 1988, the agency serviced over 29,000 juveniles. It operates a secure facility, five youth centers, and four detention centers. These facilities are augmented with contractual residential and nonresidential programs for troubled youths as well as a variety of community-based services.[21]

Administrative Arrangements

A wide diversity of administrative arrangements characterize the organization of institutional juveniles corrections in the United States today. According to experts, there is a preference for a single statewide department of juvenile corrections.[22] This form of organization seems best able to carry out the courts' dispositions, appropriate monies, and implement effective institutional programs for children.

For the most part, institutional administration is not an easy task. It must cover business management (budgeting) and program planning. The quality of administration often determines the effectiveness of a particular facility.

At the present time, the physical plants of juvenile institutions across the nation vary tremendously. Many of the older training schools are tremendously outdated. Older facilities still tend to place juvenile offenders in a single building.[23] More acceptable structures today include a reception unit with an infirmary, a security unit, and dormitory units or cottages. Planners have concluded that the most effective design for training schools is to have facilities located around a community square. The facilities generally include a dining hall and kitchen area, a storage warehouse, academic and vocational training rooms, a library, an auditorium, a gymnasium, a laundry, maintenance facilities, an administration building, and other basic facilities, such as a commissary, a barbershop, and a beauty shop.[24]

Physical conditions of individual living areas vary widely, depending on the type of facility and the progressiveness of its administration. In the past, most training school conditions were appalling, with children living in unbelievable squalor. Today, most institutions provide children with toilet and bath facilities, beds, desks, lamps, and tables. Following the recommendations of various standards, new facilities usually provide single rooms for each individual. A national survey described the typical juvenile institution:

> Institutions for the delinquent child usually have vastly different characteristics than those holding adults. Often they are located on a campus spreading over many acres. The housing units provide quarters for smaller groups invariably less than sixty and frequently less than twenty. Often they also provide apartments for cottage staff. Dining frequently is a function of cottage life, eliminating the need for the large, central dining rooms. Grills seldom are found on the cottage doors and windows, although sometimes they are covered by detention screens. Security is not the staff's major preoccupation.[25]

Most experts recommend that juvenile facilities have indoor and outdoor leisure areas, libraries, academic and vocational education spaces, chapels, facilities for youths to meet with their visitors, a reception and processing room, security fixtures (which, when necessary, are normal in appearance), windows in all sleeping accommodations, and fire safety equipment and procedures.

Another approach has been the coeducational training school, which lessens the shock of being separated from society in a single-sex institution. However, Clemens Bartollas and Christopher Sieverdes's evaluation of coed training schools found that residents still felt "scared" within them and were victims of sexual and physical violence.[26]

The physical conditions and architecture of secure facilities for juveniles have come a long way from the training schools of the turn of the century. However, many administrators and state legislators have not yet realized that more modernization is necessary to meet even minimum compliance with national standards for juvenile institutions. Correctional administrators have described conditions as horrendous, and health officials have cited institutions for pollution by vermin, rodents, asbestos, and so on.[27] While some positive changes have taken place, there are still enormous problems to overcome.

Extent of Juvenile Corrections

There is little question that tremendous variation exists among the states in the use of juvenile correction. California is by far the leading state in both its use and variety of juvenile correctional facilities. It alone houses almost 20 percent of all residents of public and private facilities (about 16,000 currently).[28] The California incarceration rate for juveniles is over 540 per 100,000 population. In contrast, Texas holds almost 4,200 youths in public and private facilities and has an incarceration rate of about 235 per 100,000 juveniles in the population. New York, another populous state, has almost 5,400 youth in custody and averages an incarceration rate of 350 per 100,000 population.[29] In 1987, the national average was 208 juveniles per 100,000 in public custody. These numbers indicate that states address the problems of institutional care in different ways.

One major problem facing the juvenile correctional system is overcrowding. Many juvenile institutions contain more residents than they are designed to hold. Overcrowding—and its attendant problems—is one reason that some states, including Idaho, Utah, and Connecticut, have made determined efforts to close public facilities and house most of their juvenile populations in small, privately run facilities. Colorado, West Virginia, Oregon, Pennsylvania, and North Dakota also are attempting to reduce their secure populations and rely more heavily on community-based programs.

Changes are also anticipated in the juvenile institutions of Arizona and Arkansas. The impetus for change in Arizona has been a class-action lawsuit brought on behalf of minors confined in the Catalina Mountain Juvenile Institution that challenges the inadequate conditions of confinement at the institution. In Arkansas, an investigation into abuses at the state's two training schools could lead to reductions in that state's juvenile correctional population.[30]

The rise in the correctional population has caused many juvenile institutions to suffer from overcrowding.

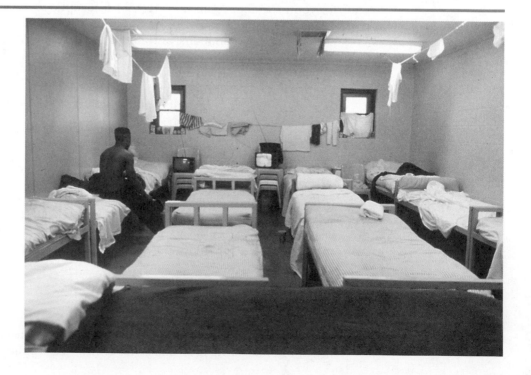

Overcrowding has made some states reluctant to increase the number of juvenile residents in their publicly run facilities. Another reason for the reluctance is the enormous expense involved. The average cost of housing one resident for one year in 1987 was $27,000. New York ($54,000), Rhode Island ($78,000), Connecticut ($45,000), Idaho ($43,100), Minnesota ($39,100), and Oklahoma ($43,000) were among the top states in the cost of housing juveniles. Pennsylvania averaged $44,000 per juvenile resident, giving credibility to the old correctional saying, "It's a lot cheaper to send a kid to Penn State than to the state pen." Costs range from a low of $16,500 to a high of $78,000.[31]

Today, the average cost to house one resident for one day is about $75 and can be as high as $125 per day in the Northeast, where operating costs are substantially greater.[32] In addition, the cost of constructing a thirty-to-forty bed secure treatment facility for juvenile offenders can be $6 million or more, or $50,000 to $60,000 per juvenile per year compared to an operating cost of $5,000 to $10,000 per year in most delinquency prevention programs.

PROFILE OF THE INSTITUTIONALIZED JUVENILE

The best source of information on institutionalized youths is the federal government's *Children in Custody* (CIC) series. This survey provides timely information on the number and characteristics of children being held in public and private facilities around the nation.

FIGURE 19.2
Rate for incarcerated
children, 1985 to 1987

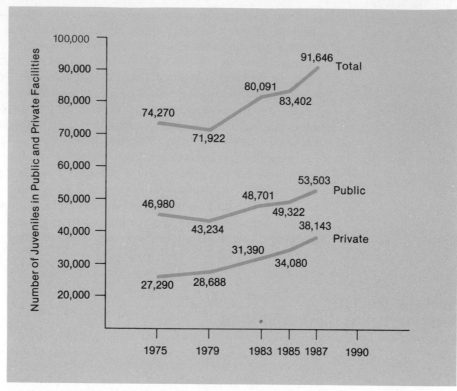

Source: Bureau of Justice Statistics, *Children in Custody 1975–85* and *Fact Sheet 1987* (Washington, D.C.: U.S. Department of Justice, 1989).

The latest CIC survey indicates that about 92,000 youths were being held in all types of facilities as of 1987 (see Figure 19.2).[33] Of these, approximately 66,000 were long-term commitments, 16,000 were preadjudication detainees, and the remaining 10,000 youths were admitted voluntarily to receive some type of treatment (mostly in private institutions). The census also found that over 63,000 juveniles were confined for delinquent acts, 11,000 as a result of status offenses, and 18,000 were nonoffenders.[34]

The number of youths in public facilities remained virtually unchanged between 1980 and 1985 (about 50,000) but increased seven percent between 1985 and 1987 (53,500). Private-sector institutions experienced an increase of approximately 10 percent between 1983 and 1985 (from 31,000 to 34,000), as well as another 10-percent increase from 1985 to 1987 (from 34,000 to 38,000).[35]

The data suggest that after a decade of decarceration efforts, the number of youths in some form of incarceration has increased, a trend that reflects the dominance of a conservative, control-oriented policy. Even the effort to remove status offenders from secure public facilities has slowed, and the number of incarcerated status offenders increased to over 2,500 in 1987.[36]

The Hidden Correctional System

While the number of institutionalized youths appears to be on the increase, the CIC data may reveal only the tip of the correctional iceberg. For example, the data does not include many of the minors who are incarcerated after they are waived to adult courts or who have their cases tried there because of exclusion statutes. Most states do place underage juveniles convicted of adult charges in youth centers until they reach their majority, whereupon they are transferred to an adult facility. In addition, as Ira Schwartz and his colleagues point out, there is a "hidden" system of juvenile control that places wayward youths in private mental hospitals and substance-abuse clinics for behaviors that could easily have brought them a stay in a correctional facility or community-based program. Schwartz found that in a single year (1983), Minneapolis hospitals admitted more than 2,000 teenage psychiatric patients for an average stay of thirty-eight days; the numbers of admissions doubled between 1976 and 1983.[37]

This "hidden system" is an important community resource for mentally ill children and substance-abuse offenders. During the past few years fourteen states have made changes in their laws relative to the civil commitment of children. Wyoming, for example, created the State Hospital Juvenile Treatment Program and allowed any adjudicated delinquent or person in need of supervision to be committed to the program. Montana established a Youth Treatment Center for the care of seriously mentally ill children between the ages of 12 and 18, including those committing delinquent acts. Michigan and Nebraska have enacted similar comprehensive statutes addressing the placement needs of minors. Other states, such as North Dakota and Missouri, are easing admission procedures for juvenile drug users in order to expand treatment options for them.

These efforts suggest that the number of institutionalized children may be far greater than is reported in the CIC surveys. Undoubtedly, private-sector juvenile corrections in the form of contract services or other institutional support has become a significant part of the juvenile justice system.[38]

Personal Characteristics

The data from the *Children in Custody* report gives some personal background information on children in custody. The "typical" resident is a 15- to 16-year-old white male who is incarcerated for an average stay of approximately five months in a public facility or 6 months in a private one. Almost 80 percent of all the residents in public and private facilities were males and about 20 percent were female.

With regard to racial characteristics, over 52 percent of all juveniles held in custody were white, 34 percent were black and 12 percent were Hispanic. Also, private and public facilities differed widely in the racial makeup of the youth they held. Over 63 percent of those in private institutions were white, while over 54 percent of the juveniles held in public facilities were black or Hispanic. Only about 34 percent of the juveniles held in private settings were of minority origin.[39] While the number of white juveniles held in public facilities decreased slightly between 1985 and 1987, the number of black and Hispanic juveniles increased by 15 and 20 percent respectively.

While the data shows that a majority of juvenile correctional inmates are white, recent research by Barry Krisberg and his associates found that minority youths are incarcerated at a rate three to four times that of white youths and that this overrepresentation is not a result of differentials in their arrest or crime rates. Of equal importance, minorities are more likely to be confined in secure public facilities rather than in open private facilities that may provide more costly and

TABLE 19.2 Demographic Characteristics and Adjudication Status of
Juveniles Held in Public Juvenile Facilities, 1983, 1985, and 1987

	NUMBER OF JUVENILES		
	1983	1985	1987
Total	48,701	49,322	53,503
Sex			
Male	42,182	42,549	46,012
Female	6,519	6,773	7,491
Race and ethnicity			
White	27,805	29,969	24,631
Black and Hispanic	23,747	24,820	28,890
Other	1,104	1,084	0
Age on census date			
9 years and under	42	60	73
10–13 years	3,104	3,181	2,675
14–17 years	39,571	40,640	42,802
18–20 years	4,804	5,409	6,955
21 years and over	86	32	0
Adjudication status			
Detained	13,156	14,474	11,566
Committed	35,178	34,549	38,522
Voluntarily admitted	367	299	535

Source: Bureau of Justice Statistics, *Children in Custody 1975-85* and *Fact Sheet 1987* (Washington,
D.C.: U.S. Department of Justice, 1989). (Data for 1987 computed from *Fact Sheet*.)

effective treatment. The authors found that racial disparity in juvenile disposition
was a growing problem that demanded immediate public scrutiny.[40]

Most juveniles committed to institutions were between 14 and 17 years old.
Private facilities tend to house younger youths, while public institutions provided
custodial care for older children, including a small percentage between 18 and 21
years old (see Table 19.2).

What did juvenile offenders have to do in order to wind up in a correctional
facility? Contrary to popular belief, the great majority of residents were not committed for violent crimes. Most incarcerated youths were property offenders. In fact, the
number of nondelinquents committed to public and private institutions—including
status offenders, neglected, dependent, and emotionally disturbed youths—was
greater than the number of youths committed for violent acts. The image of the
incarcerated delinquent as a violent menace to society is somewhat misleading.

Institutionalized Males

More than a decade ago, shocking exposés of the treatment of institutionalized
children focused public attention on the problems of juvenile corrections.[41] To-

day, some critics believe that the light of public scrutiny has moderated conditions within training schools. There is now greater professionalism among the staff, and staff brutality seems to have diminished. Status offenders and delinquents are for the most part held in separate facilities. Finally, confinement length is shorter and programming has increased.

Despite such improvements, the everyday life of male inmates still reflects institutional values. Clemens Bartollas, S. J. Miller, and Simon Dinitz have identified an inmate value system that in many ways resembles the "inmate social code" found in adult institutions. The general code revolves around the following principles:

- Exploit whomever you can.
- Don't play up to staff.
- Don't rat on your peers.
- Don't give in to others.
- Be cool.
- Don't get involved in other inmates' affairs.
- Don't steal "squares" (cigarettes).
- Don't buy the treatment games of the staff.[42]

In addition to these general rules, there were separate norms for black inmates—"exploit whites," "no forcing sex on blacks," "defend your brother"—and for whites—"don't trust anyone," "everybody for himself."

The male inmate code still seems to be in operation. More recent research conducted in five juvenile institutions confirmed the notion that residents formed cohesive groups and adhered to an informal inmate culture in an effort to "do time" gracefully.[43] The more serious the youth's delinquent record and the more secure the institution, the greater the adherence to the inmate social code.

Today, male delinquents are more likely to form allegiances with members of their own racial group and attempt to exploit others less favored. They also scheme to manipulate staff and take advantage of weaker peers.[44] However, in institutions that are treatment-oriented and where staff-inmate relationships are more intimate, residents are less likely to adhere to a negativistic inmate code.

Institutionalized Females

Females have traditionally been less involved in criminal activities than males. As a consequence, the number of females in institutions has been lower than the number of males. However, the growing involvement of girls in criminal behavior and the feminist movement have drawn more attention to the female juvenile offender. This attention has revealed a double standard of justice. For example, girls are more likely than boys to be incarcerated for status offenses, such as truancy, running away, and sexual misconduct. Institutions for girls are generally more restrictive than those for boys. They have fewer educational and vocational programs and fewer services. They also do a less-than-adequate job of rehabilitation. It has been suggested that this double standard operates through a chivalrous male justice system that seeks to "protect" young girls from their own sexuality.[45]

According to *Children in Custody*, 19,320 females are being held in public and in private juvenile facilities.[46] Girls account for approximately 21 percent of the total institutional population.

Over the years, the number of females held in public institutions has generally declined. This represents the continuation of a long-term trend to remove girls, many of whom are nonserious status offenders, from closed institutions and place them in less restrictive private or community-based facilities. So while a majority of males are today housed in private facilities, most female delinquents reside in private facilities. Over 31 percent of female incarcerated youth, for instance, are in private facilities, while only 14 percent are held in public facilities.[47]

Institutionalized girls are often runaways seeking to escape intolerable home situations that can involve abusive or incestuous relationships. Some are pregnant and have no means of support. Only a few are true delinquents. Many are the "throwaways" of society—those whom nobody wants. Recent studies also estimate that between 200,000 and 300,000 or more female adolescents are involved in prostitution nationally.[48] These numbers continue to grow because the number of runaways keeps increasing.

The same double standard and inequality that bring a girl into an institution continue to exist once she is in custody: there, she receives training in "womanly arts" and is incarcerated for a longer term than most males receive. Institutional programs for girls tend to be strongly oriented toward the reinforcement of traditional roles for women. How well these programs rehabilitate young girls and ready them for life in a quickly changing society is questionable.

Often many of the characteristics of juvenile female offenders are similar to those of their male counterparts. These include poor social skills, low self-esteem, and poor home environment. Other problems are more specific to the female juvenile offender, such as sexuality issues, victimization, educational and vocational inequity, and the lack of placement options.

Although there is a recent movement toward the use of coed institutions for juveniles, most girls remain incarcerated in antiquated, single-sex institutions that are usually isolated in rural areas and rarely offer adequate rehabilitative services. Results of a recent federally sponsored survey of training schools across the nation revealed a definite pattern of inequality in services for boys and girls.[49]

Several factors account for the different treatment of girls. One is sexual stereotyping by administrators, who feel that "girls should be girls" and that teaching them "appropriate" sex roles in prison will help them adjust on the outside. These beliefs are often held by the staff as well. Many of them have only a high-school education, as well as rigid and highly sexist ideas of what is appropriate behavior for adolescent girls. Girls' institutions tend to be smaller and less filled than boys' institutions. As a result, they simply do not have the money to offer as many varied programs and services as do the larger male institutions.[50]

Make-Believe Families

A unique characteristic of incarcerated girls is their tendency to form surrogate or **make-believe families**. Because the girls have little or no contact with their real families during their incarceration, these relationships often provide substitutes for the affection and support they are lacking:

> The make-believe or prison family is . . . a form of structured peer group interaction that is characterized by role-taking among the participants. Prison family members normally adopt roles traditionally assigned to family members in the larger society, e.g., father,

mother, sister, brother, cousin, etc., and interactions between role-players often resemble those which occur in an actual extended family. Strong in-group loyalties typify inmate family relationships and a functional diversion of responsibility and labour characteristically takes place among family members. Family members also are likely to lend each other mutual advice and assistance, look out for one another's interests, and participate in institutional activities together.[51]

These kinship groups sometimes involve homosexual relationships between the girls. Each institution is different in its tolerance of such activities. Some matrons understand the need their girls have for human companionship and love and permit such families to exist as long as they are not detrimental to any member. Others display an active fear of homosexuality by forbidding close contact between the girls and by drumming into their minds the evils and dangers of lesbianism. An important study by **Rose Giallombardo** compared three institutions for female delinquents and found that the courtship, marriage, and kinship relationships established by the adolescent inmates represented an attempt to provide a solution to personal and social deprivations by duplicating the external world. According to Giallombardo, the prison homosexual marriage alliance and the larger kinship network created structures that provided the female residents with emotional fulfillment and expression during the period of incarceration.[52]

Similarly, Alice Propper's study of homosexual behavior in seven institutions found that about 14 percent of the girls reported they were "married to" or "going with" another girl: 10 percent engaged in "passionate kissing"; 10 percent wrote love letters; and 17 percent reported having at least one homosexual experience.[53] Propper found that prison homosexuality was independent of the make-believe family. That is, a girl could be part of a family relationship without necessarily engaging in homosexual activity and vice versa. The factors Propper found to be most predictive of homosexual relationships within female institutions were prior homosexual experience in the outside world, poor heterosexual relationships, and positive, supportive, same-sex relationships within the institution setting.

In general, it appears that society is more concerned about girls who act out and less concerned about their rehabilitation because the crimes they commit are not serious. These attitudes get translated into fewer staff, less modern buildings, and poorer vocational, educational, and recreational programs than those found in boys' institutions. Ilene Bergsmann points out that little time and effort has been devoted to the female offender in the last century. She concludes that differential treatment of females and males in the juvenile justice system begins with the schools, continues with law enforcement, and is perpetuated by the correctional system.[54]

CORRECTIONAL TREATMENT FOR JUVENILES

Nearly all juvenile institutions utilize some form of treatment program for the children in custody—counseling on an individual or group basis, vocational and educational training, recreational programs, and religious counseling. In addition, most institutions provide medical and dental health programs of some kind, as well as occasional legal service programs. Generally, the larger the institution, the greater the number of programs and services offered.

The purpose of these various programs is to rehabilitate the youths within the institutions—to reform them into well-adjusted individuals and send them back into the community to be productive citizens. Despite generally good intentions, however, the goal of rehabilitation has rarely been attained. National statistics show that a significant number of juvenile offenders commit more crimes after release from incarceration.[55]

One of the most common problems is a lack of well-trained staff members to run programs. Budgetary limitations are a primary concern when it comes to planning for institutional programs. It costs about $27,000 per year to keep a child in an institution—a staggering amount that explains why institutions generally do not employ large staffs of professionals.[56]

It is also not clear which programs provide the most effective treatment. Some often-cited studies indicate that few of the treatment programs presently being utilized in juvenile institutions are effective in preventing future delinquency.[57]

The most glaring problem with treatment programs is that they are not being utilized effectively.[58] While the official goals of many institutions may be treatment and rehabilitation, the actual programs may center around security, control, and punishment.[59] Whether juveniles who respond to a structured setting should be released without knowing if they have been really rehabilitated is exemplified in the situation outlined in the following "Case in Point."

CASE IN POINT

You are an aftercare worker responsible for evaluating and recommending the release of juveniles from institutional confinement.

William G. was 15 and a half years old when he was committed for eighteen months to a secure juvenile institution after being adjudicated delinquent for breaking and entering and larceny. William resided with his aunt and uncle and two cousins. His mother died three years ago, and he has had no contact with his father for ten years. Initial psychological testing indicated that William was a hostile, angry youth with borderline intelligence, poor controls, and no guilt. The psychiatrist believed that William was likely to recidivate in the future. Considering the fact that William was before the juvenile court on two prior occasions (for truancy and drug use), he seemed like a youth out of control.

Recent evaluations of William's institutional progress are in marked contrast to his behavior while living in the community. He has been cooperative and personable and has maintained a positive attitude during his twelve months at the institution. William seems to have benefited from the structural controls and constant monitoring offered in such a setting. On the other hand, he does require special education, but because of his poor and inconsistent school record, the public school system is reluctant to take him back.

William is approaching his seventeenth birthday. The prosecutor's office and institutional personnel recommend that William complete his sen-

continued

tence. William's attorney suggests that the youth is ready for some form of residential placement.

How would you decide William's case?

What programs are needed to meet his needs?

Can both the doctrine of *parens patriae* and public protection be served here?

Individual Treatment Techniques

One common treatment approach is **individual counseling**. It is estimated that over 90 percent of juvenile institutions utilize this approach to some extent.[60] This is not surprising, since psychological problems such as depression are a real and present problem in juvenile institutions.[61] Individual counseling does not attempt to change a youth's personality. Rather, it attempts to help individuals understand and solve their present adjustment problems. The advantage in individual counseling is that institutions can utilize it on a superficial basis with counselors who may not be professionally qualified.

Highly structured counseling can be based on psychotherapy or psychoanalysis. **Psychotherapy** is an outgrowth of Freudian psychoanalytic techniques and requires extensive analysis of the individual's past childhood experiences. An effective therapist attempts to help the individual solve conflicts and make a more positive adjustment to society through altering negative behavior.

Although individual counseling and psychotherapy are used extensively in institutions and may work well for certain individuals, there is little indication that these treatments are even marginally effective. In a review of ten such programs, Dennis Romig reported that eight had completely negative results.[62]

Another highly utilized treatment approach for delinquents is **reality therapy**.[63] This approach, developed by William Glasser, emphasizes the present behavior of offenders by making them completely responsible for their actions. Glasser feels that a psychoanalytical emphasis on the past may lead children to excuse present and future misbehavior by encouraging them to think of themselves as sick and unable to change their actions.[64] The success of reality therapy depends greatly on the warmth and concern of the individual counselor. Unfortunately, many institutions rely heavily on this type of therapy because they assume that highly trained professionals are unnecessary. Actually, a skilled therapist is essential. The individual must be knowledgeable about the complexity of personalities and be able to deal with any situation that may come up in the counseling.

The object of reality therapy is to make individuals more responsible people. This end is accomplished by giving them confidence and strength through developing their ability to follow a set of expectations as closely as possible.

Another treatment, **transactional analysis** (TA), has been used in the past primarily for adult offenders. However, its developer, Eric Berne, feels that it may have special value for adolescents.[65] Transactional analysis is based on certain assumptions:

1. Human relationships consist of competitive acts of social maneuvering that serve a defensive function and yield gratification. Berne calls these acts *games.*

2. All persons manifest three different ego states: the *child*, a relic of the child's past; the *parent*, whom the person has incorporated through identification with parents; and the *adult*, who is the mature and responsible self.

3. Each of these ego states perceives reality differently; the child prelogically, the parent judgmentally, and the adult comprehensively on the basis of past experience.

4. The three states operate constantly in response to the person's need and the games in which the person indulges at a given time.[66]

Through transactional analysis, an attempt is made to show the individual that his or her behavior falls into these categories and that childish and undesirable behavior can be altered into more mature behavior.

Behavior modification, another method of treatment, is used in almost three-quarters of all institutions.[67] It is based on the theory that all behavior is learned and that present behavior can be shaped through a system of rewards and punishments. This type of program is easily utilized in an institutional setting that offers points and privileges as rewards for such behaviors as work, study, or the development of skills. It is a reasonably effective technique, especially when utilized on a contractual basis.[68] When youths are aware of what is expected of them, they plan their actions to meet these expectations and then experience the anticipated consequences. In this way, they can be motivated to change.[69] Behavior modification is effective in controlled settings, where a counselor can manipulate the situation, but once the youth is back in the real world, it becomes difficult to use.

In general, effective individual treatment programs are built around many of the following specific counseling techniques: (1) psychotherapy, (2) reality therapy, (3) transactional analysis, and (4) behavior modification. Other less formal approaches include personal growth counseling, substance-abuse treatment, assertion training, and self-image and ego development counseling.

Group Treatment Techniques

Group therapy is more economical than individual therapy because one therapist can handle more than one individual at a time. Also, the support of the group is often highly valuable to the individuals in the group, and individuals derive hope from other members of the group who have survived similar experiences. Another advantage of group therapy is that a group can often solve a problem more effectively than an individual.[70]

There are some disadvantages to group therapy. For one, it provides less individualized attention. Some individuals may be different from the other group members and need more highly individualized treatment. Others may be shy and afraid to speak up in the group and thus fail to receive the benefits of the group experience. Some individuals may dominate group interaction, and the leader may be ineffective in handling this situation. Finally, group condemnation may seriously hurt rather than help a child.

More than any other group treatment technique, group psychotherapy probes into the personality and attempts to restructure it. Relationships in these groups tend to be quite intense. The group is used to facilitate expression of feelings, to solve problems, and to teach members to empathize with one another.

Unfortunately, as Irving Schulman suggests, "the components necessary for an effective group psychotherapy situation, such as personal interaction, cooperation, and tolerance, are in direct conflict with the antisocial, antagonistic, and exploitive orientation of delinquents."[71] This type of technique is often effective when the members of the group are there voluntarily, but institutionalized delinquents are often forced to attend.

Guided group interaction (GGI) is a fairly common method of group treatment. It is based on the theory that through group interactions, a delinquent can begin to realize and solve personal problems. A group leader facilitates interaction among group members, and a group culture develops. Individual members can be mutually supportive and can help develop more acceptable behavior. Guided group interaction was an instrumental factor in the success of programs at Highfields, New Jersey, and Provo, Utah.[72] In the 1980s, a version of GGI called **Positive Peer Culture** (PPC) became popular in juvenile corrections. PPC programs utilize groups in which peer leaders get other youths to conform to conventional behaviors. The rationale for PPC is that if negative peer influence can encourage youths to engage in delinquent behavior, then positive influences can help them conform.[73]

Milieu therapy seeks to make all aspects of an inmate's environment a part of his or her treatment and to minimize differences between the custodial staff and the treatment personnel. It also emphasizes peer influence in the formation of constructive values.[74] Milieu therapy attempts to create an environment that encourages meaningful change, increased growth, and satisfactory adjustment. This is often accomplished through peer pressure to conform to group norms.

One early type of milieu therapy based on psychoanalytic theory was developed in Chicago during the late 1940s and early 1950s by Bruno Bettleheim.[75] This therapy attempted to create a conscience, or superego, in delinquent youths by getting them to depend on their therapists to a great extent and then threatening them with loss of the loving and caring relationship if they failed to control their behavior.

Today, institutional group counseling often focuses on drug and alcohol group counseling, self-esteem development groups, and role-model support sessions. In addition, because juveniles are entering the system considerably more violent than in years past, group sessions are used in dealing with appropriate expressions of anger and rage and methods to understand and control such behavior.

Vocational, Educational, and Recreational Programs

In addition to individual and group treatment programs, most institutions utilize vocational and educational treatment programs designed to teach juveniles skills that will help them adjust more easily when they are released into the community. Educational programs for juveniles are required in long-term facilities because children must go to school until they are of a certain age. Since educational programs are an important part of social development and have therapeutic value in addition to their instructional values, they are an essential part of most treatment programs. What takes place through education is related to all other aspects of the institutional program—the work activities, cottage life, recreation, and clinical services.[76]

Educational programs are probably some of the best-staffed programs in training schools, but even at their best, most are inadequate. Training programs must contend with a myriad of problems. Many of the youths coming into these institutions are mentally retarded or have low IQs or learning disabilities. As such, they are educationally handicapped and far behind their grade levels in basic academic areas. Most of these youths dislike school and become bored with any type of educational program. Their boredom often leads to acting out and subsequent disciplinary problems.

Ideally, institutions should allow the inmates to attend a school in the community or offer programs that lead to a high school diploma or GED certificate. Unfortunately, not all institutions offer these types of programs.[77] Ironically, more secure institutions, because of their large size, are more likely than group homes or day-treatment centers to offer supplemental educational programs, such as remedial reading, physical education, and tutoring.[78] Some more modern educational programs offer computer learning and programmed learning modules.

Vocational training has long been utilized as a treatment technique for juveniles. Early institutions were even referred to as industrial schools. Today, vocational programs in institutions are varied. Programs offered to boys include auto repair, printing, woodworking, mechanical drawing, food service, beauty shop techniques, secretarial training, and data processing. One obvious problem here is sex-typing, and the recent trend has been to allow equal access to all programs offered in institutions that house girls and boys. This is more difficult in single-sex institutions, because funds often cannot be found to offer all types of training.

A review of twelve studies of vocational programs for youths concluded that "job placement, vocational training, occupational orientation, field trips, and work programs alone do not positively affect juvenile delinquency."[79] Dennis Romig points out:

> Job advancement skills, support educational programs, a career-ladder frame of reference, or skills for starting new and competing businesses all work to involve youths or inmates positively in careers. It is not simply vocational training or a job that counts; it is giving the individual a job where he or she can have hope for advancement. Programs are needed for delinquent youths that give them skills to advance, thus fostering a more positive outlook for the future.[80]

The Ventura School for Female Juvenile Offenders under the California Youth Authority has been a pioneer with this concept. Private industry contracts with the youth authority to establish businesses on the institutional ground. The businesses hire, train, and pay scale wages for work. Wages are divided into a victim's restitution fund, room and board fees, and forced savings, and a portion is given to the juvenile to purchase canteen items. Trans World Airlines (TWA), for example, has established a ticket reservation center on school grounds. The center handles the overflow phone calls from Los Angeles. Many juveniles have been trained and a significant number have been employed by TWA or travel agencies upon their release. Ventura also has a program that involves private industry in the manufacture of uniforms at the school, particularly for the petroleum industry. The development of these skills are often marketable to employers in need of trained workers.[81]

Recreational activity is also an important way to help relieve adolescent aggressions, as evidenced by the many diversionary and delinquency prevention programs that focus on these activities as the primary treatment technique. A recreation program should include active and sedentary activities, both indoor and outdoor, for teams and individuals. Adequate equipment and supplies should be provided for a comprehensive program. In the case of nonsecure facilities, maximum use of recreational facilities in the community—swimming pools, parks, bowling lanes, and gymnasiums—should be made.[82]

A survey by the National Assessment of Juvenile Corrections asked youths in institutional programs to respond to the statement, "most of the time it is boring here." Some 77 percent responded that the statement was true.[83] It is an unfortunate reality that many of the training schools in the United States do not offer adequate recreational facilities for institutionalized youths. Many are stark and furnished only with televisions and a few chairs. Little organized activity is available. On the other hand, many newer facilities have recreational programs and equipment for a wide variety of leisure-time activities.

Treating Chronic Delinquents

Treating the **chronic juvenile offender** has become a major concern in recent years. While significant efforts are being made to deinstitutionalize and decarcerate the nonserious and status offender, the question remains what to do with the more serious juvenile delinquent who commits such crimes as rape or robbery. One answer has been to ease waiver rules and standards so that younger children can be transferred to the adult court. A number of states have created concurrent jurisdiction laws, which enable prosecutors to choose whether to bring a case to the adult court or juvenile court.

Another approach has been to incarcerate serious offenders in intensive juvenile treatment programs, where their problems can be dealt with while they are isolated both from society and from other juvenile offenders. This policy received impetus from a controversial book by **Charles Murray** and **Louis B. Cox,** *Beyond Probation*.[84] Murray and Cox compared chronic delinquents sent to traditional Illinois training school programs with those in an innovative community-based program, the Unified Delinquency Intervention Services. They discovered a **suppression effect,** a reduction in the number of arrests per year of the incarcerated youths. Moreover, the suppression effect for youths sent to training school was higher than for those in less-punitive treatment programs. Murray and Cox concluded that the juvenile justice system must choose which policy alternative its programs are aimed at achieving: prevention of delinquency or the care and protection of needy youths. If the former is a proper goal for the juvenile justice system, then institutionalization or the threat of institutionalization is desirable.

Similarly, Andrew Vachss and Yitzhak Bakal argue that a secure treatment center is necessary to deal with what they call **life-style violent juveniles.**[85] If secure placements were not available, there would be (1) increased use of waiver; (2) a dangerous mixing of offender types within an institutional setting (that is, nonviolent youths would become exposed to more serious offenders); (3) collapse and failure of alternative programs, because they would become contaminated by chronic offenders; and (4) the continuing problems of a system that returns dangerous juveniles to communities in far more dangerous condition and at the same time continues to incarcerate nondangerous juveniles within its "programs."[86]

Specialized Programs

Many states have set up specialized programs to deal with the chronic, violent offender. These efforts have been aided and funded by the federal government's Violent Juvenile Offender program, which tests innovative strategies for reintegrating chronically violent offenders back into the community.[87] For example, Pennsylvania's Southeast Secure Treatment Unit is devoted specifically to the treatment of small groups of mentally retarded, violent teenagers.[88] The Closed Adolescent Treatment Center was set up in Colorado to handle hard-core juvenile offenders through the use of behavior modification techniques.[89] Clients in the Colorado center are aggressive violent youths who have repeatedly sabotaged any efforts to help them. The program awards points for positive behavior, such as good relationships with peers or adults, that can then be used to obtain privileges.

Another approach that seems to show promise is the outdoor education and training programs (known collectively as **Outward Bound** programs). Two of these programs are described in the Focus on Delinquency entitled "Juvenile Rehabilitation Strategies: Wilderness Programs."[90]

While incarcerating the serious offender does have the near-term advantage of incapacitating a threat to the community, what are the long-term consequences? According to Murray and Cox, there is a "suppression effect" on the future arrests. However, not all research supports this contention. Donna Hamparian and her associates found that institutionalizing chronic offenders actually increased both arrest probability and the seriousness of future crimes.[91] Hamparian states:

> The most obvious conclusion to draw is that the less intrusive the intervention, the better for all concerned. "Getting tough" seems to simply increase the velocity from one arrest to the next. Institutionalization may just promote some careers since there is little left to lose.[92]

Hamparian's results are evidence that secure treatment for violent chronic offenders may not be the answer to halting serious delinquency.

Similarly, Martin Forst, Jeffrey Fagan, and T. Scott Vivora suggest that the public protection benefits of transfer statutes that result in the placement of chronic juvenile offenders in secure institutions may be offset by the social costs of imprisonment. According to the authors, the increased exposure of juveniles to violence in secure adult facilities may increase the chances that they will exhibit violent behavior upon release.[93]

In the future, juvenile corrections agencies may implement shock incarceration programs. These feature high-intensity military discipline and physical training for short periods of time. The expectation is that the offender will be "shocked" into going straight. These programs are now being used with young adult offenders and juveniles who have been waived to the adult system in Mississippi, Kansas, Florida, Georgia, and other jurisdictions. (See chapter opening photo.)

How Effective Is Treatment?

Without question, the primary justification for incarcerating juvenile offenders is the hope that they will one day be rehabilitated and become productive members

Youths in the VisionQuest program engage in camping and physical activities.

Juvenile Rehabilitation Strategies: Wilderness Programs

Camping or wilderness adventure has usually played a peripheral role in juvenile rehabilitation programs. In the 1930s, the Chicago Area Project developed a summer camping component as part of its delinquency prevention efforts. Many states rotated selected wards from the state training schools through forestry camps, where they worked in fire crews or at maintaining trails. The difference with these newer programs is that the outdoor education component has now assumed a central role. Two well-established and respected programs using these concepts are VisionQuest and the Associated Marine Institutes. Many more use similar techniques.

VisionQuest

VisionQuest, a for-profit contractor with headquarters in Tucson, Arizona, is probably the largest program of its type, with annual commitments in ex-

cess of five hundred delinquent youths. VisionQuest typically takes youths committed directly by juvenile courts in Pennsylvania, California, and several other states. The length of stay is usually between one year and eighteen months.

To enter the program, each candidate youth must agree to (1) abstain from drugs and sex during his or her commitment, (2) not run away, and (3) complete at least two impact programs, which can include residence in a wilderness camp, cross country travel on a wagon train, or voyaging on a sailing vessel. In addition to its impact programs, VisionQuest conducts counseling sessions with other family members while a youth is in the program and operates several group homes that facilitate reentry into the community. While they are on the wagon train or in wilderness camp, each youth is assigned to a small group (tepee) of about eight other youths and two junior staff. Each wagon train or wilderness camp consists of about thirty to forty-five youths and a similar number of staff. Jun-

continued

of society. If successful rehabilitation were not the ultimate goal of juvenile corrections, the use of residential facilities would be an expensive exercise in futility. In fact, the concept of rehabilitation has received significant criticism for the past twenty years. Several reviews of correctional treatment for juveniles (and adults) have concluded that the occasionally successful rehabilitation effort was a rare exception to the general rule of failure; when rehabilitation efforts worked, it was in special settings with hand-picked offenders.[94] All too often treatment efforts seem misguided and poorly planned, staffed, and funded. And while high hopes may have been held out for a particular treatment modality, those who implement it often fail to take into account the background of their clients, which is frequently marked by emotional trauma and low self-esteem.

Can the treatment of youthful offenders by the juvenile correctional system be written off as a lost cause? Those who favor the treatment philosophy believe it is still too early to close the book on rehabilitation and that even partial success is still better than the alternative. While no single program may be able to help all ior staff members sleep in the tepees with the juveniles and are off duty two days in every seven.

In addition to the wagon trains and sailing programs, VisionQuest is also known for its confrontational style. Committed youths are not allowed to slide by and just "do time." Rather, an individual program is worked out to ensure that each youth is challenged intellectually, physically, and emotionally. When juveniles do not perform up to expectations or begin to "act out," they are "confronted" by one or more senior staff members in an attempt to get them to deal with whatever issues underlie the poor behavior.

Associated Marine Institutes

Associated Marine Institutes (AMI) is the parent agency for a group of nonprofit programs (institutes) located in Florida that use various marine projects as a means of motivating and challenging delinquent youths. Most of AMI's programs are nonresidential, picking up participating youths in the morning and returning them home in the evening, five days a week. During a typical stay of six months in the program, a participating youth will attend remedial classes, learn scuba diving and related safety procedures, study marine biology, and participate in some constructive work project,

such as refurbishing an old boat or growing ground cover for some commercial site.

AMI also operates a long-term residential program at Fisheating Creek in south-central Florida. In this program, boys committed by the Dade County Juvenile Court spend six months to a year in an isolated work camp. During the first phase, their living conditions are extremely primitive, and their working conditions are rather hard (digging out stumps to clear an airstrip). Graduation to Phase 2 earns participants the right to sleep in air-conditioned quarters and have better work assignments. The last two phases of the program are spent in one of the nonresidential institutes near their home.

One of the distinctive characteristics of the nonprofit AMI is its heavy reliance on the capitalist spirit. Employee performance is periodically assessed by computerized measures (such as GEDs obtained, program completion rate, or subsequent recidivism rate) applied to all of the youths. End of the year staff bonuses, based on these performance measures, can exceed 10 percent of regular salary. Committed youths can also earn money by participating in various work projects, such as clearing brush, that AMI has contracted to undertake.

Source: Adapted from Peter Greenwood and Franklin Zimring, One More Chance (Santa Monica, Calif.: Rand Corp., 1985), pp. 41-42).

delinquents, and though some hard-core offenders may be immune to all efforts to rehabilitate them, even the most die-hard anti-rehabilitation foe would grant that many programs provide effective treatment to a great number of clients. For example, a national review of delinquency prevention projects by the Rand Corporation found that some innovative programs featuring outdoor work projects have produced dramatic results with even hard-core delinquents.[95] And some studies, including a recent review by Carol Garrett, indicate that the success of juvenile treatment may be greater than previously believed.[96]

Garrett reviewed the findings of 111 methodologically sound juvenile corrections studies conducted between 1960 and 1983. They included programs that stressed either psychological counseling, behavior modification, life-skill improvement, or other treatments (for example, the use of megavitamins). Her conclusion: institutional treatment can work. While there was no clear-cut evidence that one particular treatment strategy was the most effective, the great majority showed change in a positive direction. And while Garrett does not conclude that successful correctional treatment alone can prevent delinquency, she does find it has important consequences for the psychological adjustment of offenders and their improved academic achievement.

On the other hand, a recent analysis of juvenile correctional treatment research between 1975 and 1984 by Steven Lab and John Whitehead indicates that treatment has little impact on recidivism.[97] The authors report that the state of the evidence concerning correctional treatment presents a vast disparity in opinion regarding whether treatment actually works.

One of the real problems with obtaining effective treatment involves adapting programs to the changing character of the juvenile offender population. In response to changes in race, gender, age, and even offenses over the last twenty years, changes must be made in program goals. For example, competency-based education, employment skills, and public service programs may be more relevant today than traditional counseling programs.

Another effort to improve treatment results is by developing valid objective classification systems in juvenile corrections. Susan Guarino Ghezzi and James Byrne have identified a classification model for structured decision making in this area. Using classifications for risk, treatment, and control, these researchers believe a hierarchy of sanctions could increase accountability and control in juvenile justice policy making and lead to the development of more effective treatment programs in the future.[98]

THE RIGHT TO TREATMENT

The goal of placing children in institutions is basically to prepare them for a positive adjustment in the community. Therefore, lawyers in the field of juvenile justice claim that children in state-run institutions have a legal **right to treatment.**

The concept of a right to treatment was first introduced to the mental health field in 1960 by Morton Birnbaum.[99] He theorized that individuals who are deprived of their liberty because of a mental illness serious enough to require involuntary commitment are entitled to treatment to correct that condition. People for whom treatment is not provided are entitled to release from the institution.[100]

Not until 1966 did any court acknowledge any such right to treatment. That year, in *Rouse v. Cameron*, the District of Columbia Circuit Court of Appeals held that mentally ill individuals were entitled to treatment, an opinion based on interpretation of a District of Columbia statute.[101] Although the court did not expressly acknowledge a constitutional right to treatment, it implied that it could have reached the same decision on constitutional grounds:

> Had appellant been found criminally responsible, he could have been confined a year, at most, however dangerous he might have been. He has been confined four years and the end is not in sight. Since this difference rests only on need for treatment, a failure to supply treatment may raise a question of due process of law. It has also been suggested that failure to supply treatment may violate the equal protection clause . . . .Indefinite confinement without treatment of one who has been found not criminally responsible may be so inhumane as to be "cruel and unusual punishment."[102]

The constitutional right to treatment suggested by the *Rouse* decision was further recognized in 1971 in *Wyatt v. Stickney*.[103] This case was particularly important because it held that involuntary commitment without rehabilitation was a denial of due process of law. There is an "unquestionable . . .constitutional right" for those in noncriminal custody "to receive such individual treatment as will give each of them a realistic opportunity to be cured or to improve his or her mental condition."[104]

Of greater significance, however, is the U.S. Supreme Court's decision in the case of *O'Connor v. Donaldson* in 1975.[105] This case concerned the right to treatment of persons involuntarily committed to mental institutions. The court concluded that, except where treatment is provided, a state cannot confine persons against their will if they are not dangerous to themselves or to the community. In his concurring opinion, however, Chief Justice Warren Burger rejected the idea that a state has no authority to confine a mentally ill person unless it provides treatment. He also denied that commitment is the *quid pro quo* for treatment.

The right to treatment argument has expanded to include the juvenile justice system. One of the first cases to highlight this issue was *Inmates of the Boys' Training School v. Affleck* in 1972.[106] This case analyzed conditions that allegedly violated juvenile constitutional rights to due process and equal protection and that constituted cruel and unusual punishment. *Affleck* was one of the first cases to describe some of the horrible conditions existing in many of the nation's training schools. The court argued that rehabilitation is the true purpose of the juvenile court and that without that goal, due process guarantees are violated. It condemned such devices as solitary confinement, strip cells, and the lack of educational opportunities and held that juveniles have a statutory right to treatment. The court also established the following minimum standards for all juveniles confined in training schools:

- A room equipped with lighting sufficient for an inmate to read by until 10:00 P.M.
- Sufficient clothing to meet seasonal needs
- Bedding, including blankets, sheets, pillows, pillow cases, and mattresses, to be changed once a week
- Personal hygiene supplies, including soap, toothpaste, towels, toilet paper, and toothbrush
- A change of undergarments and socks every day
- Minimum writing materials: pen, pencil, paper, and envelopes
- Prescription eyeglasses, if needed
- Equal access to all books, periodicals, and other reading materials located in the training school
- Daily showers
- Daily access to medical facilities, including provision of a twenty-four-hour nursing service
- General correspondence privileges[107]

These minimum requirements were expanded in *Martarella v. Kelly*, which analyzed juvenile treatment facilities and the confinement of persons in need of supervision in New York. The court held that failure to provide these juveniles with adequate treatment violated their right to due process and to be free from cruel and unusual punishment.[108]

Nelson v. Heyne

Facts

In a class civil rights action on behalf of juvenile inmates of the Indiana Boys' School, a state institution, a complaint to the district court alleged that defendants' (Robert Heyne, commissioner of corrections; Robert Hardin, director of the Indiana Youth Authority; and Alfred Bennett, superintendent of Indiana Boys' School) practices and policies at the school violated the Eighth and Fourteenth Amendment rights of the juveniles under their care. The alleged practices included the use of corporal punishment, solitary confinement for periods ranging from five to thirty days, intramuscular injections of tranquilizing drugs, and censorship of inmate mail.

The school itself was a medium-security state correctional institution for boys 12 to 18 years of age, where about one-third were noncriminal offenders. The average length of stay at the institution was about six and a half months, and although the school's maximum capacity was under three hundred boys, the usual population was about four hundred. The counseling staff included twenty persons, three of whom were psychologists with undergraduate degrees, and one part-time psychiatrist who spent four hours a week at the institution. The medical staff included one part-time medical physician, one registered nurse, and one licensed practical nurse.

The district court in this case found that it had jurisdiction over the case and thereafter held that the use of corporal punishment and the method of administering tranquilizing drugs by the defendants constituted cruel and unusual punishment in violations of the plaintiffs' Eighth and Fourteenth Amendment rights. In a separate judgment, the court found that the juveniles had a right to a affirmative treatment and that the school had not satisfied the minimal constitutional and statutory standards required by its rehabilitative goals. The defendants appealed on January 31, 1974, before the final relief was granted. The Seventh Circuit of the U.S. Court of Appeals granted review.

Decision

In *Nelson v. Heyne*, the circuit court dealt with the issue of a juvenile's constitutional affirmative right to treatment within a closed institution. Specifically, the questions were (1) whether the practices

continued

In 1974, the case of *Nelson v. Heyne* was heard on appeal in the Seventh Circuit Court of Appeals in Indiana. Because of its significance for the right to treatment issue, the case is outlined in the Focus on Delinquency entitled "*Nelson v. Heyne.*"

In *Morales v. Turman*, the court held that all juveniles confined in training schools in Texas have a constitutional right to treatment. The court established numerous criteria for assessing placement, education skills, delivery of vocational education, medical and psychiatric treatment programs, and daily living conditions.[109] In a more recent case in New York, *Pena v. New York State Division for Youth*, the court held that the use of isolation, hand restraints, and tranquilizing drugs at Goshen Annex Center was punitive and antitherapeutic and therefore violated the Fourteenth Amendment right to due process and the Eighth Amendment right to protection against cruel and unusual punishment.[110]

alleged by the defendants were violations of the cruel and unusual punishment clause of the Eighth Amendment and (2) whether defendants had a constitutional right to rehabilitative treatment, and if so, whether the treatment as provided by the school was adequate. The court discussed the practices of corporal punishment in light of the cruel and unusual punishment standard suggested in *Furman v. Georgia*, 408 U.S. 238, 279 (1971). By that standard, punishment is excessive if it is unnecessary, and it is unnecessary if less severe punishment would serve the same purpose.

Although the court did not find corporal punishment to be cruel and unusual per se, it did find that on the basis of undisputed expert testimony the beatings as applied were unnecessary and therefore excessive, thus violating the Eighth Amendment proscription against cruel and unusual punishment. The court next looked at the school's practice of administering tranquilizing drugs "to control excited behavior" without individual medical authorization and without first trying oral medication. Based on expert testimony at trial that established the possible serious side-effects of these drugs, the court rejected the school's assertion that the use of drugs was not punishment. After stressing the need to balance the school's desire to maintain discipline with the child's right to be free from cruel and unusual punishment, the court held that the school's interest in reforming juveniles through the use of drugs in maintaining a rehabilitative atmosphere did not justify the cruel and unusual dangers resulting from poorly supervised administration of tranquilizing drugs.

Turning to the crucial holding by the district court that incarcerated juveniles have an affirmative right to rehabilitative treatment, the Seventh Circuit noted that the Supreme Court has assumed, although it has not explicitly stated, that the state must provide treatment for incarcerated juveniles. In light of this, the court looked at several recent cases concerning the impact of the *parens patriae* doctrine on this right, most notably the case of *Martarella v. Kelly*, 349 F. Supp. 575 (S.D.N.Y.1972), in which the court found a clear constitutional right to treatment for juveniles based on the Eighth and Fourteenth Amendments. The Seventh Circuit agreed then with the lower court that the juveniles did indeed have a constitutional as well as a statutory right to rehabilitative treatment. Last, the court held that the Quay system of behavior classification utilized by the school was not treatment. Subsequently the case was remanded to allow the lower court to determine the "minimal standards of care and treatment for juveniles" needed to provide them with their "right to 'individualized' care and treatment."

Nelson v. Heyne is significant in that it is the first federal appellate court decision affirming that juveniles have a constitutional as well as a statutory right to treatment. It is also the first to hold that federal judges can require standards by which to judge minimal adherence by institutions to individualized treatment.

Source: Nelson v. Heyne, 491 F.2d 353 (7th Cir. 1974).

The Current Status of the Right to Treatment

Although the U.S. Supreme Court has not yet ruled that juveniles have a constitutional right to treatment, the cases described above have served as a basis for many substantive changes in the juvenile justice system, most notably in the improvement of physical conditions in juvenile institutions and in the judiciary's recognition that it must take a more active role in the juvenile justice system.

The principle theories used by the courts for the right to treatment doctrine include: (1) arguments under the due process clause of the Fourteenth Amendment; (2) the use of the Eighth Amendment's prohibition against cruel and unusual punishment; (3) and the application of state statutory or constitutional provisions where rehabilitation is the purpose for which the juvenile offender has been confined.

However, the right to treatment has not been advanced in all instances, and the case law does not totally accept a legal right to treatment for juvenile offenders. For example, in *Ralston v. Robinson*, the Supreme Court rejected a youth's claim that he should continue to be given treatment after he was sentenced to a consecutive term in an adult prison for crimes committed while in a juvenile institution.[111] In reaching its decision, the Court rejected the concept that every juvenile offender, regardless of the circumstances, can benefit from treatment. In the *Robinson* case, the offender's proven dangerousness outweighed the possible effects of rehabilitation.

Similarly, in *Santana v. Callazo*, the influential U.S. First Circuit Court of Appeals rejected a suit brought by residents at the Maricao Juvenile Camp in Puerto Rico on the grounds that the administration had failed to provide them with an individualized, comprehensive rehabilitation plan or adequate treatment. The circuit court concluded that it was a legitimate exercise of state authority to incarcerate juveniles solely to protect society from them and that therefore the offender does not have a right to treatment per se. However, courts can evaluate each case individually to determine whether the youth is receiving adequate care.[112]

The future of the right to treatment for juveniles is somewhat uncertain. The courts have not gone so far as to order the creation of new programs, nor have they decided what constitutes minimal standards of specific individual treatment. However, federal courts have continued to hear on a case-by-case basis complaints that treatment is not up to minimal standards or that inappropriate disciplinary methods were being used. In one such case, *Gary H. v. Hegstrom*, a federal judge ruled that isolation punishments at the McClaren School for Boys in Oregon were excessive and that residents were being denied their right to treatment.[113]

The circuit court of appeals affirmed the lower court's judgment regarding the existence of unconstitutional conditions at the school and ordered due process hearings prior to confinement in excess of twenty-four hours and minimum sanitary, health, educational, and medical resources for the residents. But the wholesale adoption of various professional association standards for model institutions was not constitutionally mandated. The court also held that it was not appropriate to mandate dispositions that were so costly that other children be deprived of services. Some experts believe that a case like *Hegstrom* may eventually reach the Supreme Court and provide an avenue for a definite decision on the right to treatment.[114] Thus far, minimum standards of care and treatment have been mandated on a case-by-case basis, but some courts have limited the constitutional protections regarding the right to treatment. In light of the new hard-line approach to juvenile crime, it does not appear that the courts will be persuaded to expand this constitutional theory further.

INSTITUTIONAL RULES AND DISCIPLINE

All secure institutions for juveniles must maintain a relatively high level of security within the facility. Consequently, most maintain lengthy sets of rules governing the daily activities of the inmates. Failure to abide by them results in serious consequences, such as loss of privileges, a longer sentence, isolation, or transfer to a more secure facility.

The following are examples of rules used at secure institutional programs for female juvenile offenders:

- Do not be disrespectful to any staff member.
- Do not fight in or out of the cottage.
- Do not become involved in negative campus activities, in or out of the cottage.
- Do not bring, take out, or deliver bed and clothing issues in or out of the cottage.
- Keep your room, dresser drawers, closets, beds, and personal belongings clean and neat at all times.
- Never under any circumstances enter another girl's room.
- Do not talk or yell out your window at any time to anyone.
- Do not go upstairs, downstairs, to the basement, outdoors, or to another girl's room without first getting permission from the staff member on duty.
- Never leave your room without first getting permission of the staff member on duty (knock on door).
- Do not use profanity at any time.
- Do not talk to girls in room confinement at any time.

Rule infractions at the Indiana Girls School for which brief detention can be utilized are: being absent without leave; escaping or attempting to escape; attacking a staff member; attacking, threatening, or bullying other inmates; fighting; destroying property; theft; possessing cigarettes and matches; refusing to report for work assignment or leaving work assignment without permission; using very foul, abusive language to a staff member or another inmate; consistently refusing to obey any rule or regulation; consistent violent outbursts of temper, sass, or impudence; and participating in illicit sexual activity.[115]

Juvenile institutions have a history of punishment practices that often reads like a horror story. Cases have been reported of brutal beatings, extended solitary confinement, and other inhumane practices in juvenile institutions across the nation.[116] As recently as the early 1970s, major newspapers have published reports on conditions in these institutions. Kenneth Wooden's *Weeping in the Playtime of Others* shocked the public's conscience with tales of beatings, deaths, and deprivations in the nation's training schools.[117] The conditions of juvenile confinement and some of the important case decisions regarding juvenile institutions are discussed below.

Legal Rights of Juveniles in Institutions

Several court cases and a large amount of publicity have led a number of federal and state groups to develop standards for the juvenile justice system, including its institutions.[118] The most comprehensive standards are those of the Institute of Judicial Administration-American Bar Association's joint project on juvenile justice standards; the American Correctional Association; and the National Council on Crime and Delinquency. These standards provide appropriate guidelines for conditions and practices in juvenile institutions. They call on juvenile corrections administrators to maintain a physically safe and healthy environment for incarcerated youth.

Today, state-sponsored brutality has been for the most part outlawed. The use of restraints, solitary confinement, and even medication for unruly residents has certainly not been completely eliminated. The courts, however, have consistently ruled that corporal punishment in any form, other than for one's own protection, is constitutionally unacceptable and violates standards of decency and human dignity.

Disciplinary systems are an important part of any institutional program. Most institutions maintain disciplinary boards that regulate and hear appeals by juvenile inmates on their disciplinary procedures. The case of *Wolff v. McDonnell* focused on due process requirements for disciplinary proceedings in adult institutions.[119] To provide the same rights for juveniles, several sets of standards have recommended similar rules and regulations governing juvenile institutional boards, including notice, representation by counsel, and the right to a written record of proceedings and decision.[120] Many state court decisions involving children have affirmed the principles in *Wolff v. McDonnell*. Ideally, rules and discipline should have two purposes. First, they should maintain security and control within the institution only to the level necessary to provide a sense of well-being to staff and inmates. Second, they should be therapeutic by teaching inmates to "understand the wisdom and necessity of a postponement of or substitution for immediate pleasure and gratification of a wish or need."[121]

Isolation or "administrative segregation" is also an issue that has been subject to court review. The leading case, *Lollis v. New York State Department of Social Services,* concluded that confining a female status offender to a small room for a two-week period was unconstitutional.[122] Virtually all courts have generally reached similar conclusions. If juveniles are confined under such conditions, it is only if they are a serious threat to themselves or others, and even then they should be released as soon as possible.

In the past twenty years, there has been considerable litigation over conditions of confinement. Most of the litigation results from the violations of the constitutional rights of the residents and has become the basis for institutional reform.

JUVENILE AFTERCARE

Aftercare in the juvenile justice system is the equivalent of parole in the adult criminal justice system. When juveniles are released from an institution through an early-release program or after completing their sentences, they may be placed in an aftercare program of some kind. The feeling is that children who have been institutionalized should not be abruptly returned to the community without proper help and supervision. Whether individuals who are in aftercare as part of an indeterminate sentence remain in the community or return to the institution for further rehabilitation depends on their actions during the aftercare period.

In a number of jurisdictions, the early release of juveniles resembles the adult parole process. A paroling authority that may be an independent body or part of the corrections department or some other branch of state services makes the release decision. Like adult parole, juvenile aftercare authorities look at the youth's adjustment within the institution, whether he or she is chemically dependent, what the crime was, and so on.

Some authorities are even making use of **parole guidelines** first developed with adult parolees. Each youth who enters a secure facility is given a recommended length of confinement that is explained at his or her initial interview with parole authorities. The stay is computed on the basis of the offense record influenced by aggravating and mitigating factors. The parole authority is not required to follow the recommended sentence but instead uses it as a tool in making decisions.[123] Whatever approach is used, several primary factors are considered by virtually all jurisdictions when recommending a juvenile for release. They are (1) institutional adjustment, (2) length of stay and general attitude, and (3) likelihood of success in the community.

Supervision

One purpose of aftercare is to give an individual some extra assistance during the readjustment period in the community. The institutionalized minor is likely to have a difficult time coping with life in the community after release. The experience of being in the institution generally has negative effects. First, the minor's activities have been tightly regimented for some time; once such restraints are removed, the youth may not find it easy to make independent decisions. Second, peers in the institution may have convinced the minor that he or she has been scapegoated by an unforgiving society. Furthermore, the community itself may view the returning minor with a good deal of prejudice; adjustment problems may reinforce a preexisting need to engage in bad habits or deviant behavior.[124]

Juveniles in aftercare programs are supervised by a parole caseworker or counselor whose job is to provide surveillance by maintaining contact with the juvenile, to make sure that a corrections plan is followed, and to show interest and caring in order to help prevent further mistakes by the juvenile. The counselor also keeps the youth informed of available services that may assist in reintegration and counsels the youth and his or her family on the possible reason for the original problems.

Unfortunately, aftercare caseworkers, like probation officers, often carry such large caseloads that their jobs are next to impossible to do adequately.

Research has generally questioned the effectiveness of traditional juvenile parole programs (those involving casework and individual or group counseling).[125] In one of the most impressive research efforts on the effectiveness of juvenile parole, Patrick Jackson randomly assigned subjects from the California Youth Authority to parole or outright discharge.[126] He found that youths under formal parole supervision were actually more likely to become reinvolved in serious offenses than those simply discharged and left on their own. However, there was relatively little difference between the two groups with respect to the chance of being rearrested or serving time in another institution. Jackson found that the longer a person was retained on parole, the greater the chance of his or her being rearrested. Thus, Jackson finds that there are few beneficial elements of parole supervision and many potentially harmful side-effects.

Despite the less-than-encouraging results of the Jackson research, there are indications that juvenile aftercare can be very effective if it is combined with innovative treatment efforts. For example, the Violent Juvenile Offender program discussed earlier utilized short-term incarceration with intensive follow-up in what appears to be a successful rehabilitory effort. Jeffery Fagan and his colleagues found that highly structured efforts to reintegrate youths into society can have better results than previously thought possible.[127] The Albuquerque Girls Reintegration Center in Albuquerque, New Mexico, is an excellent example of a successful community-based program that prepares female juvenile offenders for their eventual release to their home community.[128] The program provides participants with positive role models, involvement in community activities, and realistic school and work experience.

Aftercare Revocation Procedures

A final issue in aftercare for juveniles concerns revocation procedures. Although adult parolees have been entitled to certain procedural rights in revocation proceedings since 1972, the Supreme Court has not yet extended the same rights to juveniles.[129] However, most states have extended these rights to juveniles on their own initiative.[130] In addition, appellate courts that have considered juvenile aftercare revocation procedures have found that juveniles are entitled to the same due process as adult offenders. To avoid revocation, a juvenile parolee must meet the following conditions, among others: adhere to a reasonable curfew set by youth worker or parent; refrain from association with persons whose influence would be detrimental, including but not limited to persons convicted of crimes or persons of a known criminal background; attend school in accordance with the law; abstain from drugs; abstain from alcohol; report to the youth worker when required; refrain from acts that would be crimes if committed by an adult; refrain from operating an automobile without permission of the youth worker or parent; refrain from being habitually disobedient and beyond the lawful control of parent or other legal authority; refrain from running away from the lawful custody of parent or other lawful authority.

Certain procedural safeguards have been set up to ensure that revocation of parole is handled fairly:

1. Parolee must be notified of the specific conditions of parole.
2. Before proceeding, parole workers and legal personnel must agree about the need to revoke and the sufficiency of the evidence.
3. Parolee must receive notice of allegations.
4. Parolee has the right to legal counsel at state expense if necessary.
5. Parolee has the right to confront and cross-examine witnesses.
6. Parolee has the right to introduce documentary evidence and witnesses.
7. Parolee has the right to a hearing before an independent hearing officer who shall be an attorney but not an employee of the revoking agency.
8. Parolee has the right to a speedy hearing to be held within twenty days from mailing notice of hearing where the releasee is not taken into custody.
9. Parolee has the right to a verbatim record of the hearing.
10. The decision must be based on substantial evidence.
11. Parolee has the right to a judicial review. Successful completion of an aftercare program generally marks the end of a juvenile's involvement with the juvenile justice system.

The use of these procedures has led to sound administrative discretion and adequate due process safeguards for juveniles in revocation hearings.

SUMMARY

The juvenile institution was developed in the mid-nineteenth century as an alternative to placing youths in adult prisons. Youth institutions developed over the years from large, closed institutions to today's open, cottage-based education- and rehabilitation-oriented institutions. Most institutions for youths feature libraries and recreational facilities and are low security.

The juvenile institutional population has increased in recent years to more than 90,000 residents, despite efforts to decarcerate status offenders and petty delinquent offenders. Although there has been a shrinking youth population and a stabilization in juvenile arrest rates, there appears to be evidence of higher rolls of incarceration in the future. In addition, increasing numbers of youths are being "hidden" in private mental centers and drug-treatment clinics.

Most institutions maintain intensive treatment programs featuring individual or group therapy. Although a wide variety of techniques are used around the nation, there has been little evidence that any single method is effective in reducing recidivism. Yet, the philosophy of treatment and rehabilitation remains an important goal of juvenile practitioners.

The right to treatment is a major issue in juvenile justice. This refers to legal decisions that mandate that a child cannot simply be warehoused in a correctional center and must be provided with proper care and treatment to aid rehabilitation. What constitutes proper care is still debated, and recent federal court decisions have backed off from holding that every youth can be rehabilitated. Gender is also a factor in access to treatment resources: institutions for females generally have fewer vocational and educational programs than those exclusively for male delinquents.

Most institutions have a standard set of rules and discipline. There have been many exposés of physical brutality in youth institutions, and courts have sought to restrain the use of physical punishment on inmates.

Most juveniles released from institutions are placed on juvenile parole or aftercare. There is little evidence that this type of community supervision is actually more beneficial than simply releasing youths on their own. Many jurisdictions are having success with community halfway houses and reintegration centers.

The chronic offender has come to be recognized as a major social problem. A number of states have set up intensive programs to deal with these hard-core offenders.

KEY TERMS

Paint Creek Youth Center

reform schools

cottage system

"decarceration"

least restrictive alternative

make-believe family

Rose Giallombardo

individual counseling

psychotherapy

reality therapy

transactional analysis (TA)

behavior modification

group therapy

guided group interaction (GGI)

Positive Peer Culture (PPC)

chronic juvenile offender

Charles Murray

Louis B. Cox

suppression effect

life-style violent juveniles

Outward Bound

right to treatment

Nelson v. Heyne

Lollis v. New York State Department of Social Services

aftercare

parole guidelines

QUESTIONS FOR DISCUSSION

1. Should status offenders ever be institutionalized with delinquents? Are they really different?

2. What kinds of programs would you implement in a juvenile correctional center?

3. Do you believe that juveniles have a right to treatment? Should all offenders receive psychological counseling? What court decisions give credence to your position?

4. Is the use of physical punishment ever warranted in an institution? If not, how do you reconcile the fact that the Supreme Court has upheld the use of corporal punishment in public schools?

5. Identify and explain the current problems and issues in juvenile corrections. What possible solutions might you suggest?

6. In light of the extensive use of incarceration for juvenile offenders, do you think the trend toward determinate sentences for serious juvenile crime is desirable? Isn't such an approach in direct conflict with our decarceration policy?

7. How should society deal with the chronic juvenile offender? Is incarceration the only practical solution?

NOTES

1. Bureau of Justice Statistics, *Children in Custody 1975-85—Census of Public and Private Juvenile Detention, Correctional and Shelter Facilities* (Washington, D.C.: U.S. Department of Justice, 1989), p. 4.

2. Edward Loughran, et al., *Reinvesting Youth Corrections Resources—A Tale of Three States* (Minneapolis: Hubert Humphrey Institute of Public Affairs, 1986).

3. Office of Justice Programs, *Private Sector Corrections for Juveniles—Paint Creek Youth Center* (Washington, D.C.: Office of Juvenile Justice and Delinquency Prevention Update, 1988).

4. Office of Justice Programs, *Children in Custody 1975-85* (Washington, D.C.: U.S. Department of Justice, 1989), p. 4.

5. For a detailed description of juvenile delinquency in the 1800s, see J. Hawes, *Children in Urban Society: Juvenile Delinquency in Nineteenth Century America* (New York: Oxford University Press, 1971).

6. D. Jarvis, *Institutional Treatment of the Offender* (New York: McGraw-Hill, 1978), p. 101.

7. Margaret Werner Cahalan, *Historical Corrections Statistics in the United States, 1850-1984* (Washington, D.C.: U.S. Department of Justice, 1986), pp. 104–5.

8. Clemons Bartollas, Stuart J. Miller, and Simon Dinitiz, *Juvenile Victimization: The Institutional Paradox* (New York: Wiley, 1976), p. 6.

9. LaMar T. Empey, *American Delinquency—Its Meaning and Construction* (Homewood, Ill.: Dorsey, 1978), p. 515.

10. National Conference of Superintendents of Training Schools and Reformatories, *Institutional Rehabilitation of Delinquent Youth: Manual for Training School Personnel* (Albany, N.Y.: Delmar, 1962), p. 4.

11. Edward Eldefonso and Walter Hartinger, *Control, Treatment, and Rehabilitation of Juvenile Offenders* (Beverly Hills, Calif.: Glencoe, 1976), p. 151.

12. *Ibid.*, p. 152.

13. M. Rosenthal, "Reforming the Justice Correctional Institution: Efforts of U.S. Childrens Bureau in the 1930s," *Journal of Sociology and Social Welfare* 14: 47–73 (1987).

14. National Criminal Justice Information and Statistics Service, *Children in Custody: Advance Report on the Juvenile Detention and Correctional Facility Census of 1975* (Washington, D.C.: U.S. Government Printing Office, October 1977), p. 17.

15. Bureau of Justice Statistics, *Fact Sheet on Children in Custody* (Washington, D.C.: U.S. Department of Justice, 1989).

16. Paul Lerman, "Child Welfare, the Private Sector, and Community-Based Corrections," *Crime and Delinquency* 30:5-38 (1984).

17. Data in this and the following section comes from the federal government's *Children in Custody* series, published on a biennial basis by the U.S. Department of Justice's Bureau of Justice Statistics. (*Fact Sheet on Children in Custody, 1989.*)

18. Mark M. Levin and Rosemary C. Sarri, *Juvenile Delinquency: A Study of Juvenile Codes in the U.S.* (Ann Arbor, Mich.: National Assessment of Juvenile Corrections, 1974), p. 55.

19. Patricia Torbet, *Organization and Administration of Juvenile Services: Probation, Aftercare, and State Delinquent Institutions* (Pittsburgh: National Center for Juvenile Justice, September 1989), p. 4.

20. *Ibid.*

21. L. Rossi, "Maryland's Juvenile Services Agency: Giving Youths a Chance to Change," *Corrections Today* 51:130 (1989).

22. American Bar Association, Project on Standards for Juvenile Justice, *Standards Relating to Corrections Administration* (Cambridge, Mass.: Ballinger Publishing Co., 1977), Standard 2.1.

23. American Bar Association, Project on Standards for Juvenile Justice, *Standards Relating to Architecture of Facilities*, Standard 5.1, Commentary (Cambridge, Mass.: Ballinger Publishing Co., 1977), p. 50.

24. Eldefonso and Hartinger, *Control, Treatment, and Rehabilitation of Juvenile Offenders*, p. 162.

25. National Advisory Commission on Criminal Justice Standards and Goals, *Corrections* (Washington, D.C.: U.S. Government Printing Office, 1973), p. 348.

26. Clemens Bartollas and Christopher Sieverdes, "Coeducational Training Schools: Are They a Panacea for Juvenile Corrections?" *Juvenile and Family Court Journal* 34:15–20 (1983).

27. Cited in Alan Breed and Barry Krisberg, "Is There a Future?" *Corrections Today* 48:14–26 (1986).

28. Office of Justice Programs, *Children in Custody*, 1989, p. 10.

29. *Ibid;* p. 13; see also Office of Juvenile Justice and Delinquency Prevention, U.S. Department of Justice, *Children in Custody*, Public Juvenile Facilities, 1987.

Reported in *Juvenile Justice Bulletin*, October 1988, p. 2.

30. Breed and Krisberg, "Is There a Future?"; Terry Demchak, "Changes Anticipated in Arizona and Arkansas Juvenile Institutions," *National Center for Youth Law News* 10:8-10 (December 1989).

31. Edward Loughran, "How to Stop Kids from Going Bad," *Boston Globe*, 11 February 1990, p. A21.

32. Bureau of Justice Statistics, *Fact Sheet on Children in Custody*, p. 1.

33. Data is from *Fact Sheet on Children in Custody: Public and Private Juvenile Facilities, 1989* (Washington, D.C.: U.S. Government Printing Office, 1989).

34. Office of Juvenile Justice and Delinquency Prevention, U.S. Department of Justice, "More Juveniles Held in Public Facilities" from *Children in Custody*, September 1989, p. 2.

35. *Ibid.;* also see unpublished paper by David Shichor and Clemens Bartollas California State University, San Bernardino, Calif. entitled "Comparison of Private and Public Placements" (1990), which calls for a nationwide effort to evaluate private placements for juvenile offenders.

36. Bureau of Justice Statistics, *Fact Sheet on Children in Custody*, September 1989, p. 2.

37. Ira Schwartz, Marilyn Jackson-Beck, and Roger Anderson, "The 'Hidden' System of Juvenile Control," *Crime and Delinquency* 30:371-85 (1984).

38. Rebecca Craig and Andrea Paterson, "State Involuntary Committment Laws: Beyond Deinstitutionalization," *National Conference of State Legislative Reports* 13:1-10 (1988).

39. Bureau of Justice Statistics, U.S. Department of Justice, "More Juveniles Held in Public Facilities" from *Children in Custody*, September 1989, p. 1.

40. Barry Krisberg, et al., "The Incarceration of Minority Youth," *Crime and Delinquency* 33:173-205 (1987).

41. Kenneth Wooden, *Weeping in the Playtime of Others: America's Incarcerated Children* (New York: McGraw-Hill, 1976).

42. Clemens Bartollas, S.J. Miller, and Simon Dinitz, *Juvenile Victimization: The Institutional Paradox* (New York: Halsted Press, 1976).

43. Christopher Sieverdes and Clemens Bartollas, "Security Level and Adjustment Patterns in Juvenile Institutions," *Journal of Criminal Justice* 14:135-45 (1986).

44. *Ibid.*, p. 143.

45. Several authors have written of this sexual double standard. See E.A. Anderson, "The Chivalrous Treatment of the Female Offender in the Arms of the Criminal Justice System: A Review of the Literature," *Social*

Problems 23:350-57 (1976); G. Armstrong, "Females under the Law: Protected but Unequal," *Crime and Delinquency* 23:109-20 (1977); M. Chesney-Lind, "Judicial Enforcement of the Female Sex Role: The Family Court and the Female Delinquent," *Issues in Criminology* 8:51-59 (1973) and "Juvenile Delinquency: The Sexualization of Female Crime, "*Psychology Today* 19:43-46 (July 1974); Allan Conway and Carol Bogdan, "Sexual Delinquency: The Persistence of a Double Standard," *Crime and Delinquency* 23:13-135 (1977).

46. Bureau of Justice Statistics, U.S. Department of Justice, "More Juveniles Held in Public Facilities" from *Children in Custody*, September 1989, p. 1.

47. Data derived from the Bureau of Justice Statistics, *Children in Custody* series, 1989.

48. Patricia Hersch, "Coming of Age on City Streets," *Psychology Today*, January 1988, p. 28; Daniel Campagna and Donald Puffengerger, *The Sexual Trafficking in Children: An Investigation of the Child Sex Trade.* (Dover, Mass.: Auburn House, 1988).

49. "A Look at Juvenile Female Offenders," *Juvenile Corrections and Detention Newsletter,* 2:6 (1988).

50. For a historical analysis of a girls' reformatory, see Barbara Brenzel, *Daughters of the State* (Cambridge, Mass.: MIT Press, 1983).

51. Thomas W. Foster, "Make-Believe Families: A Response of Women and Girls to the Deprivations of Imprisonment," *International Journal of Criminology and Penology* 3:71 (1975).

52. Rose Giallombardo, *The Social World of Imprisoned Girls: A Comparative Study of Institutions for Juvenile Delinquents* (New York: Wiley, 1974), pp. 15-16.

53. Alice Propper, *Prison Homosexuality* (Lexington, Mass.: Lexington Books, 1981), pp. 15-16.

54. Ilene R. Bergsmann, "The Forgotten Few Juvenile Female Offenders," *Federal Probation* 53:73-79 (1989).

55. Wooden, *Weeping in the Playtime of Others.*

56. Bureau of Justice Statistics, U.S. Department of Justice Children in Custody, 1975–1985, May 1989.

57. K. Daniel O'Leary and O. Terence Wilson, *Behavior Therapy: Application and Outcome* (Englewood Cliffs, N.J.: Prentice-Hall, 1975), quoted in Robert C. Trojanowicz, *Juvenile Delinquency: Concepts and Control,* 2nd ed. (Englewood Cliffs, N.J.: Prentice-Hall, 1978), p. 303.

58. For an interesting article highlighting the debate over the effectiveness of correctional treatment, see John Whitehead and Steven Lab, "Meta-Analysis of Juvenile Correctional Treatment," *Journal of Research in Crime and Delinquency* 26:276-95 (1989).

59. See, for example, Edward Rolde, et al., "The Maximum Security Institution as a Treatment Facility for Juveniles," in *Juvenile Delinquency: A Reader,* ed. James E. Teele (Itasco, Ill.: Peacock, 1970), pp. 437-44.

60. Robert D. Vinter, ed., *Time Out: A National Study of Juvenile Correction Programs* (Ann Arbor, Mich.: National Assessment of Juvenile Corrections, 1976), pp. 20-53.

61. Louise Sas and Peter Jaffe, "Understanding Depression in Juvenile Delinquency: Implications for Institutional Admission Policies and Treatment Programs," *Juvenile and Family Court Journal* 37:49-58 (1985-1986).

62. Dennis A. Romig, *Justice for Our Children: An Examination of Juvenile Delinquent Rehabilitation Programs* (Lexington, Mass.: Lexington Books, 1978), p. 81.

63. See Vinter, *Time Out.* Vinter reports that reality therapy is utilized in 80 percent of the institutions surveyed.

64. See, generally, William Glasser, "Reality Therapy: A Realistic Approach to the Young Offender," in *Readings in Delinquency and Treatment*, ed. Robert Schaste and Jo Wallach (Los Angeles: Delinquency Prevention Training Project, Youth Studies Center, University of Southern California, 1965); see also Richard Rachin, "Reality Therapy: Helping People Help Themselves," *Crime and Delinquency* 16:143 (1974).

65. See Eric Berne, *Transactional Analysis in Psychotherapy* (New York: Grove, 1961).

66. Lewis R. Wolberg, *The Techniques of Psychotherapy* (New York: Grune & Stratton, 1976). p. 257.

67. See Helen A. Klein, "Towards More Effective Behavior Programs for Juvenile Offenders," *Federal Probation* 41:45-50 (1977); Albert Bandura, *Principles of Behavior Modification* (New York: Holt, Rinehart & Winston, 1969); H.A. Klein, "Behavior Modification as Therapeutic Paradox," *American Journal of Orthopsychiatry* 44:353 (1974).

68. See Robert B. Rutherford, "Establishing Behavioral Contracts with Delinquent Adolescents," *Federal Probation* 39:29 (1975). For examples of token economics within institutions, see E.L. Phillips, "Achievement Place: Token Reinforcement Procedures in a Home-style Rehabilitation Setting for Predelinquent Boys," *Journal of Applied Behavior Analysis* 1:213 (1968); D. Wexler, "Token and Taboo: Behavior Modification, Token Economics, and the Law," *California Law Review* 61:81 (1973).

69. Romig, *Justice for Our Children*, pp. 20-24.

70. See J.N. Yong, "Advantages of Group Therapy in Relation to Individual Therapy for Juvenile Delinquents," *Corrective Psychiatry and Journal of Social Therapy* 17:37 (1971).

71. Irving Schulman, "Modifications in Group Psychotherapy with Antisocial Adolescents," *International Journal of Group Psychotherapy* 7:310 (1974).

72. See LaMar T. Empey and Steven Lubeck, *The Silverlake Experiment* (Chicago: Aldine, 1971); H. Ashley Weeks, *Youthful Offenders at Highfields* (Ann Arbor, Mich.: University of Michigan Press, 1958); LaMar T. Empey and J. Rabow, "The Provo Experiment in Delinquency Rehabilitation," *American Sociological Review* 26:679 (1961).

73. Larry Brendtero and Arlin Ness, "Perspectives on Peer Group Treatment: The Use and Abuses of Guided Group Interaction/Positive Peer Culture," *Child and Youth Services Review* 4:307-24 (1982).

74. Maxwell Jones, *Social Psychiatry in Practice* (Baltimore: Penguin, 1968); Loren Crabtree and James Fox, "The Overthrow of a Therapeutic Community," *International Journal of Group Psychotherapy* 22:31 (1972).

75. Bruno Bettleheim, *The Empty Fortress* (New York: Free Press, 1967).

76. U.S. Department of Health, Education, and Welfare, Children's Bureau, *Institutions Serving Delinquent Children* (Washington, D.C.: U.S. Government Printing Office, 1983), p. 73.

77. Vinter, *Time Out*, p. 15.

78. *Ibid.*, p. 152.

79. Romig, *Justice for Our Children*, p. 51.

80. *Ibid.*, pp. 51-52.

81. See *California Youth Authority Newsletter*, Ventura School for Juvenile Female Offenders, (Ventura, Calif.: California Youth Authority, 1988).

82. National Advisory Commission on Criminal Justice Standards and Goals, *Report of the Task Force on Juvenile Justice and Delinquency Prevention*, Standard 24.12 (Recreation and Leisure Time Activities), Commentary (Washington, D.C.: U.S. Government Printing Office, 1976), p. 721.

83. Vinter, *Time Out*, p. 181.

84. Charles Murray and Louis B. Cox, *Beyond Probation* (Beverly Hills, Calif.: Sage, 1979).

85. Andrew Vachss and Yitzhak Bakal, *The Life-Style Violent Juvenile* (Lexington, Mass.: Lexington Books, 1979).

86. *Ibid.*, p. 11.

87. Robert Mathias, Paul DeMuro, and Richard Allinson, eds., *Violent Juvenile Offender* (San Francisco: National Council on Crime and Delinquency, 1984).

88. "SESTU Spells Special Treatment for Special Offenders," *Youth Forum* 6:6-8 (1982).

89. V.L. Agee, *Treatment of the Violent Incorrigible Adolescent* (Lexington, Mass.: Lexington Books, 1979).

90. Peter Greenwood and Franklin Zimring, *One More Chance, The Pursuit of Promising Intervention Strategies for Chronic Juvenile Offenders* (Santa Monica, Calif.: Rand Corp., 1985).

91. Donna Martin Hamparian, Joseph Davis, Judith Jacobson, and Robert McGraw, *The Young Criminal Years of the Violent Few* (Washington, D.C.: U.S. Department of Justice, 1985), p. 8.

92. Donna Hamparian, Richard Schuster, Simon Dinitz, and John Conrad, *The Violent Few* (Lexington, Mass.: Lexington Books, 1975).

93. Martin Forst, Jeffrey Fagan, and T. Scott Vivana, "Youth in Prisons and Training Schools: Perceptions and Consequences," *Juvenile and Family Court Journal* 40:1-15 (1989).

94. See, for example, Robert Martinson, "What Works—Questions and Answers about Prison Reform," *Public Interest* 32:22-54 (1974); Romig, *Justice for Our Children*.

95. Greenwood and Zimring, *One More Chance*.

96. Carol Garrett, "Effects of Residential Treatment on Adjudicated Delinquents: A Meta-Analysis," *Journal of Research in Crime and Delinquency* 22:287-308 (1985).

97. S. Lab and J. Whitehead, "Analysis of Juvenile Correctional Treatment," *Crime and Delinquency* 34:60-83 (1988).

98. Susan Guarino-Ghezzi and James Byrne, "Developing a Model of Structured Decision Making in Juvenile Corrections: The Mass Experience," *Crime and Delinquency* 35:270-303 (1989).

99. Morton Birnbaum, "The Right to Treatment," *American Bar Association Journal* 46:499 (1960).

100. Discussed in Adrienne Volenik, "Right to Treatment: Case Developments in Juvenile Law," *Justice System Journal* 3:292-307 (1978).

101. 373 F.2d 451 (D.C.Cir. 1966).

102. *Ibid.*, p. 453.

103. 325 F. Supp. 781 (1971); see also Note, "Wyatt v. Stickney—A Constitutional Right to Treatment for the Mentally Ill," *University of Pittsburgh Law Review* 34: 79-84 (1972).

104. 325 F. Supp. 373, 784 (1972).

105. 422 U.S. 563 (1975).

106. 346 F. Supp. 1354 (D.R.I. 1972).

107. *Ibid.*, p. 1343.

108. 349 F. Supp. 575 (S.D.N.Y. 1972).

109. 383 F. Supp. 53 (E.D. Texas 1974).

110. 419 F. Supp. 203 (S.D.N.Y. 1976).

111. 102 S. Ct. 233 (1981).

112. 714 F. 2d 1172 (1st Cir. 1983).

113. 831 F. 2d 1430 (1987); see also David Lambert, "Children in Institutions," *Youth Law News* 8:10-14 (1987).

114. *Ibid.*

115. Statement of Dorothy VânBrunt, superintendent, Indiana Girls School, Indianapolis, Indiana, in "Juvenile Confinement Institutions and Correctional Systems," *Hearings before the Subcommittee to Investigate Juvenile Delinquency of the Committee of the Judiciary*, U.S. Senate, 92nd Congress, 1st sess., 1971.

116. See, generally, Edward Wakin, *Children without Justice—A Report by the National Council of Jewish Women* (New York: National Council of Jewish Women, 1975), pp. 43-55; Howard James, *Children in Trouble—A National Scandal* (New York: Pocket Books, 1971), pp. 102-25; *Martarella v. Kelly*, 349 F. Supp. 575 (1972).

117. Wooden, *Weeping in the Playtime of Others.*

118. Harry Swanger, "Juvenile Institutional Litigation," *Clearinghouse Review* 11:219-21 (1977). Swanger reports that the National Juvenile Law Center in St. Louis has been involved in litigation since 1972 that has sought and obtained reform of such practices as solitary confinement, disciplinary procedures, corporal punishment, forced drugging, and institutional rules. Examples of the litigation include the following cases: *Nelson v. Heyne*, 355 F. Supp. 451 (N.D. Ind. 1972); *Inmates v. Affleck*, 346 F. Supp. 1354 (D.R.I. 1972); *Morales v. Turman*, 383 F. Supp. 53 (E.D Tex. 1974).

119. 418 U.S. 539 (1974).

120. American Bar Association, Project on Standards for Juvenile Justice, *Standards Relating to Corrections Administration*, (Cambridge, Mass.: Ballinger Publishing Company, 1977), Standard 8.9.

121. Eldefonso and Hartinger, *Control, Treatment, and Rehabilitation of Juvenile Offenders*, p. 195; see also Brother Christian Hynes, "Discipline in a Treatment-Oriented School for Delinquent Boys," *Federal Probation* 33:29 (1969), for a discussion of purposes of discipline and how to administer it.

122. 322 F. Supp. 473 (1970).

123. Michael Norman, "Discretionary Justice: Decision Making in a State Juvenile Parole Board," *Juvenile and Family Court Journal* 37:19-26 (1985-1986).

124. William R. Arnold, *Juveniles on Parole* (New York: Random House, 1970), p. 87.

125. See Romig, *Justice for Our Children*, pp. 185-94.

126. Patrick Jackson, *The Paradox of Control: Parole Supervision of Youthful Offenders* (New York: Praeger, 1983).

127. Jeffrey Fagan, Cary Rudman, and Eliot Hartstone, "Intervening with Violent Juvenile Offenders: A Community Reintegration Model," in *Violent Juvenile Offenders*, ed. Robert Mathias, Paul DeMuro, and Richard Allinson (San Francisco: National Council on Crime and Delinquency, 1984), pp. 207-31.

128. "Girls Reintegration Center—Albuquerque, New Mexico," *Juvenile and Corrections Newsletter* 2:6 (1988).

129. See *Morrissey v. Brewer*, 408 U.S. 471, 92 S. Ct. 2593, 33 L.Ed.2d 484 (1972). Upon revocation of parole, a defendant is entitled to the due process rights of (1) a hearing, (2) written notice of charges, (3) knowledge of evidence against him or her, (4) opportunity to present ad cross-examine witnesses, and (5) a written statement of reasons for parole revocation.

130. See Malcolm S. Goddard, "Juvenile Parole Revocation Hearings: The New York State Experience," *Criminal Law Bulletin* 13:552-73 (1977).

Concluding Notes: American Delinquency

This text has reviewed in great detail current knowledge of the nature, cause, and correlates of juvenile delinquency and society's efforts to bring about its elimination and control. In accumulating this information, we have analyzed research programs, theoretical models, governmental policies, and legal cases. Taken in sum, this information presents a rather broad and complex picture of the youth crime problem. Delinquents come from a broad spectrum of society; kids of every race, gender, class, region, family type, and culture are involved in delinquent behaviors. To combat youthful law violations, society has tried a garden variety of intervention and control strategies: tough law enforcement; counseling, treatment and rehabilitation; provision of legal rights; community action; educational programs; family change strategies. Yet, despite decades of intense effort and study, it is still unclear why delinquency occurs and what, if anything, can be done to control its occurrence.

Though uncertainty prevails, it is possible to draw some inferences about youth crime and its control. After reviewing the material contained in this volume, certain conclusions seem self-evident. Some involve social facts; that is, particular empirical relationships and associations have been established that have withstood multiple testing and verification efforts. Other conclusions involve social questions; there are issues that need clarification, and the uncertainty surrounding them has hampered progress in combating delinquency and treating known delinquents.

To sum up, we have assembled some of the most important social facts in this volume and some of the most important social questions that still remain to be answered.

1. The statutory concept of juvenile delinquency is in need of review and modification. Today, the legal definition of a juvenile delinquent is a minor child usually under the age of 17 who has been found to have violated the criminal law (juvenile code). The concept of juvenile delinquency occupies a legal position falling somewhere between criminal and civil law in most jurisdictions. Some states, for example, end juvenile court jurisdiction at age 18, while others treat juveniles as adults when they are younger, such as 16 or 17 years of age. Serious consideration must be given to a redefinition of the jurisdictional aspects of juvenile criminality.

2. The concept of the status offender (PINS, CHINS, and MINS) needs to be clarified. When a child is subject to state authority because of school truancy, incorrigibility, or being a runaway, such behavior is considered noncriminal but consistent with the *parens patriae* philosophy of giving the state jurisdiction to protect the best interest of the child. Separating the status offender from the juvenile delinquent avoids the stigma associated with the delinquency label. However, reforming the treatment for status offenders and the possibility of eliminating the juvenile court's jurisdiction over such behaviors needs to be evaluated.

3. *Measuring juvenile delinquency requires that all methods of data collection be evaluated, including official statistics from the Uniform Crime Reports, self-report studies, and victimization data.* Official statistical information dealing with juvenile delinquency rates in the United States indicate that about 1.5 million youths were arrested by the police in 1988. Uniform Crime Report data indicates that the number of juveniles arrested has declined for more than a decade. While the general public has been skeptical of this conclusion, national crime survey data and victimization reports also agree that delinquency rates have either declined or stabilized. However, the disturbing news is that young people are committing proportionally more criminal behavior than those in any other age category.

4. *Substance abuse is closely associated with juvenile crime and delinquency.* Today, there is great uncertainty about the trends in teenage substance abuse. Although the total number of arrests involving legal minors has declined, those held for substance abuse have increased by 50 percent since 1985. Surveys of arrested juveniles indicate sizable numbers of young people are involved with drugs and alcohol throughout the United States. Most efforts in the juvenile justice system to treat young offenders involved with substance abuse seem to be unsuccessful. Traditional prevention efforts and education programs have not had encouraging results.

5. *The chronic violent juvenile offender is a serious social problem for society and the juvenile justice system.* Chronic male delinquent offenders commit a disproportionate amount of antisocial behavior as well as a significant amount of the most serious juvenile crimes, such as homicides, rapes, robberies, aggravated assaults, and serious drug offenses. Many chronic offenders become adult criminals and eventually end up in the criminal court system.

Chronic juvenile delinquency has unquestionably become a major concept within the field. The best approach to dealing with chronic offenders remains uncertain, but concern about such offenders has shifted juvenile justice policy toward a punishment-oriented philosophy.

6. *There is basic disagreement in the juvenile justice system over the relationship between social class and juvenile crime.* In addition, there is uncertainty as to the relationship between race and juvenile delinquency. While some experts believe that class position influences crime rates, others disagree that lower class structure predetermines juvenile delinquent behavior. Furthermore, the existing data does not conclusively suggest that racial differences in the crime rate can be explained by an association between race, class, and antisocial behavior. Thus, research continues to be needed to determine what the true relationship is between these variables.

7. *No single scientific theory adequately explains the problem of juvenile delinquency.* Despite years of research, no theory or combination of theories provides conclusive insight into the onset and location of delinquency and the causation

of youth crime. While social psychological theories, such as those involving learning and social control, can help us better understand why some youths become delinquent and criminal, they fail to fully account for differences in delinquency rates across ecological areas, ranging from neighborhoods within a city to different regions throughout the country. These theories also fail to explain important individual differences between children who commit crime in high crime areas and those who do not.

8. Integrated theoretical concepts are an emerging force in the study of delinquent and antisocial behavior. Theories involving social interaction, social process, and delinquency prevention and interactional theories addressing the lifestyle changes of delinquents, are also important ingredients in the search for understanding juvenile criminality by theoretical construction.

9. Environmental influences, such as family relationships, affect patterns of behavior. Over the years, family relationships have long been linked to the problem of juvenile delinquency by many experts. Broken homes, for instance, are not in and of themselves a cause of delinquency, but there is some evidence that single-parent households are more inclined to produce delinquency-promoting behavior. In addition, there seems to be a strong association in family relationships between child abuse and delinquency. Cases of abuse and neglect have been found in every level of the economic strata. And a number of studies have linked child abuse and neglect to juvenile delinquency. While the evidence is not conclusive, it does suggest that a strong relationship exists between child abuse and subsequent delinquent behavior. Some experts believe that a major effort is needed to reestablish parental accountability and responsibility.

10. Female delinquency has become a serious topic of concern to experts in the juvenile justice system. The nature and extent of female delinquent activities changed in the late 1980s, and it now appears that girls are engaging in more frequent and serious illegal activity. Female crime rates have increased in recent years, and the nature of female juvenile delinquency and youth crime is now similar in some respects to that of male delinquency.

11. Juvenile gangs have become a serious and growing problem in many major metropolitan areas throughout the United States. Ethnic youth gangs, mostly males aged 14 to 21, appear to be increasing in such areas as Los Angeles, Chicago, Boston, and New York. Sound empirical data on what causes gang delinquency is currently unavailable. One view of gang development is that such groups serve as a bridge between adolescence and adulthood in communities where adult social control is not available. Another view suggests that gangs are a product of lower-class social disorganization and that they serve as an alternative means of advancement for poorly motivated and uneducated youth. Today's gangs are more often commercially than culturally oriented, and profit from the drug trade is generally a significant motive for gang behavior.

12. Many of the underlying problems of youth crime and delinquency are directly related to education. Numerous empirical studies have confirmed that educational success is an important contributing factor in delinquency. Today, young people spend considerable time in school. Educational institutions are obviously one of the primary instruments of socialization. Since a great deal of delinquent activity takes place on school grounds and since dropping out of school is associated with antisocial behavior, there is general agreement that children who are unsuccessful in school are more likely to commit delinquent acts. School-based crime control projects have not been very successful, and a great deal more effort is needed in this critical area of school-delinquency prevention control.

13. *Today, no single ideology or view dominates the direction, programs, and policies of the juvenile justice system.* Throughout the past decade, numerous competing positions regarding juvenile justice have emerged. As the liberal program of the 1970s has faltered, more restrictive sanctions have been imposed. The "crime control" position seems most formidable today. However, there remains a great deal of confusion over what the juvenile justice system does, what it should do, and how it should deal with youthful antisocial behavior.

14. *Today's problems in the juvenile justice system can often be traced to the uncertainty of its founders, the "child savers."* Such early twentieth-century groups formed the juvenile justice system on the misguided principle of reforming wayward youth and remodeling their behavior. The "best interest of the child" standard has long been the guiding light in juvenile proceedings, calling for the strongest available rehabilitative services. Today's juvenile justice system is often torn between playing the role of social versus crime control agent.

15. *In recent years, the juvenile justice system has become more legalistic by virtue of U.S. Supreme Court decisions that have granted children procedural safeguards in various court proceedings.* The case of *In re Gault* of the 1960s motivated state legislators to revamp their juvenile court legal procedures. Today, the Supreme Court is continuing to struggle with making distinctions between the legal rights of adults and minors. Recent Court decisions that allowed children to be searched by teachers and denied their right to a jury trial showed that the Court continues to recognize a legal separation between adult and juvenile offenders.

16. *Despite some dramatic distinctions, juveniles have gained many of the legal due process rights adults enjoy.* Among the more significant elements of due process are the right to counsel, evidence efficiency, protection from double jeopardy and self-incrimination, and the right to appeal.

17. *The death penalty for children has been upheld by the Supreme Court.* According to the *Wilkins v. Missouri* and *Stanford v. Kentucky* cases in 1989, the Supreme Court concluded that states are free to impose the death penalty for murderers who commit their crimes while age 16 or 17. According to the majority decision written by Justice Antonin Scalia, society has not formed a consensus that such executions are a violation of the cruel and unusual punishment clause of the Eighth Amendment.

18. *One of the most significant changes in American law enforcement has been the emergence of community policing in the field of delinquency prevention.* Community participation and cooperation, citizen crime prevention programs, and education programs such as Project DARE (drug education) have become a mainstay of law enforcement in the 1980s and have had a particularly significant impact on improving perceptions of community safety and the quality of community life in many areas.

19. *The use of detention in the juvenile justice system continues to be a widespread problem.* After almost two decades of work, virtually all jurisdictions have passed laws requiring that status offenders be placed in shelter care programs rather than detention facilities. Another serious problem related to the use of juvenile detention is the need to remove young people from lockups in adult jails.

The Office of Juvenile Justice and Delinquency Prevention has given millions of dollars in aid to encourage the removal of juveniles from such adult lockups. But eliminating the confinement of children in adult institutions remains an enormously difficult task in the juvenile justice system.

20. *The use of waiver, bind-over, and transfer provisions in juvenile court statutes has been growing.* This trend has led toward a criminalization of the juvenile system. Since there are major differences between the adult and juvenile court systems, transfer to an adult court exposes youths to more serious consequences of their antisocial behavior and is a strong recommendation of those favoring a crime-control model.

21. *The role of the attorney in the juvenile justice process requires further research and analysis.* Most attorneys appear to be uncertain whether they should act as adversaries or advocates in the juvenile process. In addition, the role of the juvenile prosecutor has become more significant as a result of new and more serious statutory sentencing provisions.

22. *Juvenile sentencing procedures now reflect the desire to create uniformity and limited discretion in the juvenile court, and this trend is likely to continue.* Many states have now developed such programs as mandatory sentences, sentencing guidelines, and limited-discretion sentencing to bring uniformity into the juvenile justice system. As a result of the public's fear about serious juvenile crime, legislators have amended juvenile codes to tighten up juvenile sentencing provisions.

23. *In the area of community sentencing, new forms of probation supervision have become commonplace in recent years.* Intensive probation supervision, balanced probation, wilderness probation, and electronic monitoring have become important community-based alternatives over the last few years. Probation continues to be the single most significant intermediate sanction available to the juvenile court system.

24. *Victim restitution is another widely used and programatic method of community treatment in today's juvenile justice system.* In what is often referred to as monetary restitution, children are required to pay the victims of their crimes or in some instances provide some community service directly to the victim. Restitution provides the court with an important alternative sentencing option and has been instituted by statute in virtually every jurisdiction in the country.

25. *The concept of deinstitutionalization has become an important goal of the juvenile justice system.* The Office of Juvenile Justice and Delinquency Prevention has provided funds to encourage this process. In the early 1980s, the deinstitutionalization movement seemed to be partially successful. Admissions to public juvenile correctional facilities declined in the late 1970s and early 1980s. In addition, the number of status offenders being held within the juvenile justice system was reduced. However, the number of institutionalized children in recent years has increased, and the deinstitutionalization movement has failed to meet all of its optimistic goals.

26. *The number of incarcerated youths continues to rise despite declining arrest rates.* Today, there are over 90,000 youths in some type of correctional institution. The juvenile courts seem to be using the most severe of the statutory dispositions, that is, commitment to the juvenile institution, rather than the "least restrictive statutory alternative." In addition, there seems to be a disproportionate number of minority youths incarcerated in youth facilities. The mi-

nority incarceration rate is almost four times greater than that for whites, and minorities seem to be placed more often in public than in private treatment facilities.

27. *Despite the growth of alternative treatment programs, such as diversion, restitution, and probation, the number of children under secure institutional care has increased, and there continues to be much uncertainty about the success of such programs.* Nearly all juvenile institutions utilize some form of treatment program for the children in their care. Despite generally positive intentions, the goal of rehabilitation in an institutional setting is very difficult to achieve and rarely attained.

28. *The future of the legal right to treatment for juveniles remains uncertain.* The appellate courts have established minimum standards of care and treatment on a case-by-case basis, but it does not appear that the courts can be persuaded today to expand this constitutional theory to mandate that incarcerated children receive adequate treatment. Eventually, this issue must be clarified by the Supreme Court.

There is serious crisis in the American juvenile justice system. How to cope with the needs of large numbers of children in trouble remains one of the most controversial and frustrating issues in our society. The magnitude of the problem is such that over 1.5 million youths are arrested each year; over 1.3 million delinquency dispositions and one million status offense cases are heard in court; and drug abuse is a significant factor in more than 60 percent of all the cases referred to the juvenile courts. Today, the system and process seems more concerned with crime control and willing to ignore the rehabilitative ideal. Perhaps the answer lies outside the courtroom in the form of greater job opportunities, improved family relationships, and more effective educational systems.

GLOSSARY

A

acquittal Release or discharge, especially by verdict of a jury.

action Lawsuit; a proceeding taken in a court of law. Actions are either civil (to enforce a right) or criminal (to punish an offender).

adjudicated Having been the subject of completed criminal or juvenile proceedings and having been convicted or declared a delinquent, a status offender, or a dependent.

adjudication (juvenile) Juvenile court decision, terminating a hearing, that the juvenile is a delinquent, a status offender, or a dependent or that the allegations in the petition are not sustained.

adjudicatory hearing In juvenile proceedings, the fact-finding process wherein the juvenile court determines whether there is sufficient evidence to sustain the allegations in a petition.

adjustment Settlement or bringing to a satisfactory state so that parties are agreed without official intervention of the court.

adversary system Procedure used to determine truth in the adjudication of guilty or innocence, which pits the defense (advocate for the accused) against the prosecution (advocate for the state), with the judge acting as arbiter of the legal rules. Under the adversary system, the burden is on the state to prove the charges beyond a reasonable doubt. This system of having the two parties publicly debate has proved to be the most effective method of achieving the truth regarding a set of circumstances. (Under the accusatory, or inquisitorial, system that is used in continental Europe, the charge is evidence of guilt that the accused must disprove; the judge takes an active part in the proceedings.)

affidavit Written statement of fact, signed and sworn to before a person having authority to administer an oath.

aftercare Supervision given children for a limited period of time after they are released from a training school but still under the control of the school or of the juvenile court.

age of onset Age at which youths begin their delinquent careers. Early onset of delinquency is believed to be linked with chronic offending patterns.

aging out Refers to the phenomenon in which people spontaneously reduce the rate of their criminal behavior as they mature.

aggregate measures Data collected on groups of people rather than individuals. A good example of aggregate data is the Uniform Crime Reports index crimes; though the number of criminal incidents that occur in a given area can be counted, little data is provided on the offenders who commit them or the circumstances in which they occurred. Self-report surveys are usually considered individual-level data, since subjects' responses can be examined on a case-by-case basis.

alienation Mental condition marked by normlessness and role confusion.

androgens Male sex hormones.

anomie Normlessness that is produced by rapidly shifting moral values. An anomic person has few guides to what is socially acceptable behavior. According to Merton, anomie is a condition that occurs when personal goals cannot be achieved by available means.

appeal Review of lower court proceedings by a higher court. There is no constitutional right to appeal. However, the "right" to appeal is established by statute in some states and by custom in others. All states set conditions as to type of case or grounds for appeal, which appellate courts may review. An appellate court does not retry the case under review. Rather, the transcript of the lower court case is read by the judges, and the lawyers for the defendant and for the state argue about the merits of the appeal—that is, the legality of lower court proceedings, instead of the original testimony. Appeal is more a process for controlling police, court, and correctional practices than for rescuing innocent defendants. When appellate courts do reverse lower court judgments, it is usually because of "prejudicial error" (deprivation of rights), and the case is remanded for retrial.

appellant   Party who initiates an appeal from one court to another.

appellee   Party in a lawsuit against whom an appeal has been taken.

arrest   Taking of a person into the custody of the law, the legal purpose of which is to restrain the accused until he or she can be held accountable for the offense at court proceedings. The legal requirement for an arrest is probable cause. Arrests for investigation, suspicion, or harassment are improper and of doubtful legality. The police have the responsibility to use only the reasonable physical force necessary to make an arrest. The summons has been used as a substitute for arrest.

arrest warrant   Written court order by a magistrate authorizing and directing that an individual be taken into custody to answer criminal charges.

atavistic   According to Lombroso, the primitive physical characteristics that distinguish born criminals from the general population. Lombrosian theory holds that characteristics of criminals are throwbacks to animals or primitive people.

Augustus, John   Individual credited with pioneering the concept of probation.

authoritarian   Person whose personality revolves around blind obedience to authority.

B

bail   Amount of money that has to be paid as a condition of pretrial release, normally set by a judge at the initial appearance. The purpose of bail is to ensure that people accused of crimes will return for subsequent proceedings. If they are unable to make bail, they are detained in jail.

Beccaria   Eighteenth-century Italian philosopher who argued that crime could be controlled by punishments only severe enough to counterbalance the pleasure obtained from them.

behaviorism   Branch of psychology concerned with the study of observable behavior rather than unconscious motives. It focuses on the relationship between particular stimuli and people's responses to them.

beyond a reasonable doubt   Degree of proof required for conviction of a defendant in criminal and juvenile delinquency proceedings. It is less than absolute certainty but more than high probability. If there is doubt based on reason, the accused is entitled to the benefit of that doubt by acquittal.

biosocial   The view that thought and behavior have both biological and social bases.

booking   Administrative record of an arrest made in a police station. It involves listing of the offender's name, address, physical description, date of birth, employer, time of arrest and offense and the name of arresting officer.

Photographing and fingerprinting of the offender are also part of booking. The *Miranda* warning is given again (the first time was at the scene of the arrest). In addition, the accused is allowed to make a telephone call.

burden of proof   Duty of proving disputed facts on the trial of a case. The duty commonly lies on the person who asserts the affirmative of an issue and is sometimes said to shift when sufficient evidence is furnished to raise a presumption that what is alleged is true.

bourgeoisie   In Marxist theory, the owners of the means of production; the capitalist ruling class.

C

capital punishment   Use of the death penalty to punish transgressors.

career criminal   Person who repeatedly violates the law and organizes his or her life-style around criminality. A chronic offender.

case law   Law derived from previous court decisions; opposed to statutory law, which is passed by legislatures.

certiorari   Literally, "to be informed of, to be made certain in regard to." The name of a writ of review or inquiry.

chancery court   Court proceedings created in fifteenth-century England to oversee the lives of high-born minors who were orphaned or otherwise could not care for themselves.

child abuse   Any physical, emotional, or sexual trauma to a child for which no reasonable explanation, such as an accident, can be found. Child abuse can also be neglecting to give proper care and attention.

child savers   Nineteenth-century reformers who developed programs for troubled youth and influenced legislation creating the juvenile justice system. Today, some critics view them as being more concerned with the control of the poor than with their welfare.

chivalry hypothesis   View that the low female crime and delinquency rates are a reflection of the leniency with which police treat female offenders.

choice theory   The school of thought that holds that people will engage in delinquent and criminal behavior after weighing the consequences and benefits of their actions.

chronic delinquent   Youth who has been arrested five or more times during his or her minority. This small portion of the offending population are believed to engage in a significant portion of all delinquent behavior.

chronicity   State of being a chronic recidivist.

classical theory   Theoretical perspective suggesting that (1) people have free will to choose criminal or conventional behaviors; (2) people choose to commit crime for reasons of greed or personal need; (3) crime can be deterred through fear of punishment.

clearance Crime reported to the police that is "solved" by an arrest.

cognitive theory Study of the perception of reality; the mental processes required to understand the world we live in.

cohort study Study utilizing a sample of people who share a single characteristic, such as place of birth, and whose behavior is followed over a period of time.

commitment Action of a judicial officer ordering that an adjudicated and sentenced adult or adjudicated delinquent or status offender who has been the subject of a juvenile court disposition hearing be admitted to a correctional facility.

common law Basic legal principles that developed in England and became uniform (common) throughout the country. Judges began following previous court decisions (precedent) when new but similar cases arose.

community facility (nonconfinement facility, adult or juvenile) Correctional facility from which residents are regularly permitted to depart, unaccompanied by an official, to use community resources, such as schools or treatment programs, or to seek or hold employment.

community policing Police strategy that emphasizes fear reduction, community organization, and order maintenance, rather than crime fighting.

concurrent sentences Literally, running sentences together. The condition set for serving sentences of imprisonment for multiple charges. When people are convicted of two or more charges, they must be sentenced on each charge. If the sentences are concurrent, they begin the same day and are completed after the longest term has been served. (*See also* consecutive sentences.)

conduct norms Behaviors that are expected of social group members. If group norms conflict with those of the general culture, members of the group may find themselves described as outcasts or criminals.

conflict theory View that conflict among interest groups, especially those of opposing socioeconomic classes, is the main determinant of human behavior.

consecutive sentences Literally, sentences that follow one another. Upon completion of one sentence, the other term of incarceration begins. (*See also* concurrent sentences.)

consent decree Decree entered by consent of the parties. Not properly a judicial sentence but in the nature of a solemn contract or agreement of the parties that the decree is a just determination of their rights based on the real facts of the case, if such facts are proved.

containments According to Reckless, internal and external factors and conditions that help insulate youths from delinquency-promoting situations. Most important of the internal containments is a strong self-concept, while external containments include positive support from parents and teachers.

constitutional law Branch of public law of a state that maintains the framework of political and government authorities and functions in accordance with the state's constitution.

conviction Judgment of guilt; verdict by a jury, plea by a defendant, or judgment by a court that the accused is guilty as charged.

correctional institution Generic name for long-term adult confinement facilities that are often called prisons, federal or state correctional facilities, or penitentiaries, and for juvenile confinement facilities that are often called training schools, reformatories, boys' ranches, and the like.

correctional institution (juvenile) Confinement facility having custodial authority over delinquents and status offenders committed to confinement after a juvenile disposition hearing.

corrections Generic term that includes all government agencies, facilities, programs, procedures, personnel, and techniques concerned with the investigation, intake, custody, confinement, supervision, or treatment of alleged or adjudicated adult offenders, delinquents, or status offenders.

court Agency of the judicial branch of government authorized or established by statute or constitution and consisting of one or more judicial officers that has the authority to decide on controversies in law and disputed matters of fact brought before it.

crime Offense against the state; behavior in violation of law for which there is prescribed punishment.

crime control Model of criminal justice that emphasizes the control of dangerous offenders and the protection of society. Its advocates call for harsh punishments as deterrents to crime, such as the death penalty.

criminal justice process Decision-making process from the initial investigation or arrest by police to the eventual release of offenders and their reentry into society; the various sequential criminal justice stages through which offenders pass.

criminal justice standards Models, commentaries, or recommendations for the revision of criminal justice procedures and practices; for example, the American Law Institute's Model Penal Code, the American Bar Association's Standards for Criminal Justice, and the recommendations of the National Advisory Commission on Criminal Justice Standards and Goals.

criminal justice system Group of agencies and organizations—police, courts, and corrections—as well as the legislation and appellate courts responsible for the administration of criminal justice and crime control.

criminal law Body of law that defines criminal offenses, prescribes punishments (substantive law), and delineates criminal procedure (procedural law).

criminal sanction Refers to the right of the state to punish people if they violate the rules set down in the criminal code. The punishment is connected to commission of a specific crime.

criminology Study of the causes and treatment of criminal behavior, criminal law, and the administration of criminal justice.

critical criminology Branch of criminology that reviews and analyzes historical and current developments in law and justice in order to expose the interests of the power elite and ruling classes.

cross-sectional data Survey data that involves all age, race, gender, and income segments of the population measured simultaneously. Since people from every age group are represented, age-specific crime rates can be determined. Proponents believe that this is a sufficient substitute for the more expensive longitudinal approach that follows a group of subjects over time in order to measure crime rate changes.

culpable Implication of a wrongful act but one that does not involve malice. It connotes fault rather than guilt.

culture conflict Condition brought about when the rules and norms of an individual's subcultural affiliation conflict with the role demands of conventional society.

cultural deviance Condition that exists when obedience to subcultural norms conflicts with the rules and laws of the larger, general culture.

cultural transmission Concept that conduct norms are passed down from one generation to the next so that they become stable within the boundaries of a culture. Cultural transmission guarantees that group life-style and behavior are stable and predictable.

culture of poverty View that lower-class people form a separate culture with its own values and norms that are in conflict with conventional society; the culture is self-maintaining and ongoing.

D

dark figures of crime Incidents of crime and delinquency that go undetected by police.

degenerate anomalies According to Lombroso, the primitive physical characteristics that make criminals animalistic and savage.

deinstitutionalization Closing of institutions and moving inmates to community-based programs.

delinquency Juvenile actions or conduct in violation of criminal law and, in some contexts, status offenders.

delinquent Juvenile who has been adjudicated by a judicial officer of a juvenile court as having committed a delinquent act.

delinquent act Act committed by a juvenile for which an adult could be prosecuted in a criminal court. A juvenile who commits such an act can be adjudicated in a juvenile court or prosecuted in a criminal court if the juvenile court transfers jurisdiction.

dependency Legal status of juveniles over whom a juvenile court has assumed jurisdiction because the court has found their care by parents, guardians, or custodians falls short of a legal standard of proper care.

dependents Juveniles over whom a juvenile court has assumed jurisdiction because the court has found their care by parents, guardians, or custodians falls short of a legal standard of proper care.

desert-based sentences Principle of basing sentence length on the seriousness of the criminal act and not the personal characteristics of the defendant or the deterrent impact of the law. Punishment based on what people have done and not on what others may do or what they themselves may do in the future.

desistance Phenomenon that relates to the decline in the crime rate as a person matures; synonymous with the aging-out process. Desisters are youths who spontaneously terminate their delinquent careers.

detached street workers Program that places social workers in the community in order to reach fighting gangs.

detective Police agent who is assigned to investigate crimes after they have been reported, to gather evidence, and to identify the perpetrator.

detention Temporary care of a child alleged to be delinquent who requires secure custody in physically restricting facilities pending court disposition or execution of a court order.

detention center Government facility that provides temporary care in a physically restricting environment for juveniles in custody pending court disposition.

detention facility (juvenile) Confinement facility having custodial authority over juveniles confined pending and after adjudication.

detention hearing In juvenile proceedings, a hearing by a judicial officer of a juvenile court to determine whether a juvenile is to be detained, to continue to be detained, or to be released while juvenile proceedings are pending in the case.

determinate sentence Involves "fixed" terms of incarceration, such as three years' incarceration. It is felt by many to be too restrictive for rehabilitative purposes; the advantage is that offenders know how much time they have to serve, that is, when they will be released.

deterrence Act of preventing a crime before it occurs by means of the threat of criminal sanctions.

developmental theory View that personal characteristics guide human development and influence and control behavior choices.

differential association Theory positing that criminal behavior is learned when an individual encounters an excess of definitions favoring law violations over those that support conformity to law; also learned in primary groups characterized by intimacy.

discretion Use of personal decision making and choice in carrying out operations in the criminal justice system. For example, police discretion can involve the decision to make an arrest, whole prosecutorial discretion can involve the decision to accept a plea bargain.

disposition For juvenile offenders, the equivalent of sentencing for adult offenders. The theory is that disposition should be more rehabilitative than retributive. Possible dispositions may be dismissal of the case, release of the youth to the custody of his or her parents, placement of the offender on probation, or sending him or her to an institution or state correctional institution.

disposition hearing Hearing in juvenile court conducted after an adjudicatory hearing and subsequent receipt of the report of any predisposition investigation to determine the most appropriate disposition of a juvenile who has been adjudicated a delinquent, a status offender, or a dependent.

district attorney County prosecutor who is charged with bringing offenders to justice and enforcing the laws of the state.

diversion Official halting or suspension of formal criminal or juvenile justice proceedings against an alleged offender at any legally prescribed processing point after a recorded justice system entry and the referral of that person to a treatment or care program administered by a nonjustice public agency or a private agency or the recommendation that the person be released.

dower Middle Ages custom of monetary compensation being given the groom by the bride's family before a marriage could take place.

drift According to Matza, the view that youths move in and out of delinquency and that their life-styles can embrace both conventional and deviant values.

Drug Enforcement Administration (DEA) Federal agency that handles enforcement of federal drug control laws.

due process Basic constitutional principle based on the concept of the primacy of the individual and the complementary concept of limitation on governmental power; a safeguard against arbitrary and unfair state procedures in judicial or administrative proceedings. Embodied in the due process concept are the basic rights of a defendant in criminal proceedings and the requisites for a fair trial. These rights and requirements have been expanded by appellate court decisions and include (1) timely notice of a hearing or trial that informs the accused of the charges against him or her; (2) the opportunity to confront accusers and to present evidence on the accused's own behalf before an impartial jury or judge; (3) the presumption of innocence under which guilt must be proven by legally obtained evidence and the verdict must be supported by the evidence presented; (4) the right of an accused to be warned of constitutional rights at the earliest stage of the criminal process; (5) protection against self-incrimination; (6) assistance of counsel at every critical stage of the criminal process; and (7) the guarantee that an individual will not be tried more than once for the same offense (double jeopardy).

E

ecological theory View that the interrelationship between people and their environment influences behavior.

ego identity According to Erikson, ego identity is formed when persons develop a firm sense of who they are and what they stand for.

electroencephalogram (EEG) Device that can record the electronic impulses given off by the brain, commonly called "brain waves."

emancipation Relinquishment of the care, custody, and earnings of a minor child and the renunciation of parental duties.

equipotentiality View that all people are equal at birth and are thereafter influenced by their environment.

exclusionary rule Principle that prohibits using evidence illegally obtained in a trial. Based on the Fourth Amendment "right of the people to be secure in their persons, houses, papers, and effects, against unreasonable searches and seizures," the rule is not a bar to prosecution, as legally obtained evidence may be available and may be used in a trial.

F

family court Court with broad jurisdiction over family matters, such as neglect, delinquency, paternity, support, and noncriminal behavior.

Federal Bureau of Investigation (FBI) Arm of the U.S. Justice Department that investigates violations of federal law, gathers crime statistics, runs a comprehensive crime laboratory, and helps train local law enforcement officers.

felony Criminal offense punishable by death or by incarceration in a state or federal confinement facility for a period whose lower limit is prescribed by statute in a given jurisdiction, typically one year or more.

finding of fact Court's determination of the facts presented as evidence in a case, affirmed by one party and denied by the other.

fine The court-imposed penalty requiring that a convicted person pay a specified sum of money.

focal concerns According to Walter Miller, the value orientations of lower-class cultures whose features include the need for excitement, trouble, smartness, fate, and personal autonomy.

free will View that people are in charge of their own destinies and are free to make personal behavior choices unencumbered by environmental controls.

G

general deterrence Crime-control policy that depends on the fear of criminal penalties. General deterrence measures, such as long prison sentences for violent crimes, are aimed at convincing the potential law violator that the pains associated with crime outweigh its benefits.

graffiti Inscription or drawing made on a wall or structure. Used by delinquents for gang messages and turf definition.

group home Nonconfining residential facility for adjudicated adults or juveniles or those subject to criminal or juvenile proceedings, intended to reproduce as closely as possible the circumstances of family life and, at minimum, provide access to community activities and resources.

guardian *ad litem* Court-appointed attorney who protects the interests of a child in cases involving the child's welfare.

H

habeas corpus Literally, "you have the body." A variety of writs whose objective is to bring a party before a court or judge. The function of the writ is to release the person from unlawful imprisonment.

halfway house Nonconfining residential facility for adjudicated adults or juveniles or for those subject to criminal or juvenile proceedings, intended to provide an alternative to confinement for persons not suitable for probation or in need of a period of readjustment to the community after confinement.

hearing Presentation of evidence to the juvenile court judge, the judge's consideration of it, and the decision on disposition of the case.

helping professions Occupations such as social work, mental health, and family care that are dedicated to the health and welfare of the needy and indigent.

I

incarceration Putting a person in prison. The basic purposes of such confinement have been punishment, deterrence, rehabilitation, and integration into the community.

identity crisis Psychological state, identified by Erikson, in which youth face inner turmoil and uncertainty about life roles.

index crimes Crimes used by the FBI to indicate the incidence of crime in the United States and reported annually in the Uniform Crime Reports. They include murder and nonnegligent manslaughter, robbery, rape, aggravated assault, burglary, larceny, and motor vehicle theft.

indictment Written accusation returned by a grand jury that charges an individual with a specified crime after determination of probable cause. The prosecutor presents enough evidence to establish probable cause.

indigent Person who is needy and poor or who lacks the means to provide a living.

inmate Person in a confinement facility.

innocents Youths who have never been apprehended for a delinquent act.

insanity Unsoundness of mind that prevents one from comprehending the consequences of one's acts or from distinguishing between right and wrong.

instrumental Marxist theory View that capitalist institutions such as the criminal justice system have as their main purpose the control of the poor in order to maintain the hegemony of the wealthy.

intake Process during which a juvenile referral is received and a decision is made to file a petition in juvenile court, to release the juvenile, to place the juvenile under supervision, or to refer the juvenile elsewhere.

intake unit Government agency or unit of an agency that receives juvenile referrals from police, other government agencies, private agencies, or individuals and screens them, resulting in closing of the case, referral to care or supervision, or filing of a petition to juvenile court.

interactionist perspective View that one's perception of reality is significantly influenced by one's interpretations of the reactions of others to similar events and stimuli.

interrogation Method of accumulating evidence in the form of information or confessions from suspects by police; questioning that has been restricted because of concern about the use of brutal and coercive methods and interest in protecting against self-incrimination.

interstitial Space that separates things. In criminology, a space or separation in the social fabric. An interstitial area encourages the formation of gangs.

investigation Inquiry into suspected criminal behavior for the purpose of identifying offenders or gathering further evidence to assist the prosecution of apprehended offenders.

J

jail Confinement facility, usually administered by a local law enforcement agency, that is intended for adults but sometimes also contains juveniles. It detains persons pending adjudication and persons committed after adjudication for sentences of a year or less.

judge Judicial officer who has been elected or appointed to preside over a court of law. The position is created by statute or by constitution, and the officer's decisions in criminal and juvenile cases can be reviewed only by a judge of a higher court.

judgment Statement of the decision of a court that the defendant is convicted or acquitted of the offense(s) charged.

judicial officer Any person exercising judicial powers in a court of law.

jurisdiction Every kind of judicial action; the authority of courts and judicial officers to decide cases.

just deserts Idea that penalties to be given to convicted offenders should be decided chiefly by reference to the seriousness of the offense and the number and seriousness of prior convictions.

juvenile courts Courts that have original jurisdiction over persons defined by statute as juveniles and alleged to be delinquents, status offenders, or dependents.

juvenile delinquency Participation in illegal behavior by a minor who falls under a statutory age limit.

juvenile justice agency Government agency or subunit thereof whose functions are the investigation, supervision, adjudication, care, or confinement of juveniles whose conduct or condition has brought or could bring them within the jurisdiction of a juvenile court.

Juvenile Justice and Delinquency Prevention Act of 1974 Federal law establishing an office of juvenile justice within the Law Enforcement Assistance Administration to provide funds for the control of juvenile crime.

juvenile justice process Court proceedings for youths within the "juvenile" age group that differ from the adult criminal process. Under the paternal *(parens patriae)* philosophy, juvenile procedures are informal and nonadversarial, invoked *for* the juvenile offender rather than *against* him or her; a petition instead of a complaint is filed; courts make findings of involvement or adjudication of delinquency instead of convictions; and juvenile offenders receive dispositions instead of sentences. Recent court decisions *(Kent* and *In re Gault)* have increased the adversarial nature of juvenile court proceedings. However, the philosophy remains one of diminishing the stigma of delinquency and providing for the youth's well-being and rehabilitation, rather than seeking retribution.

juvenile record Official record containing, at a minimum, summary information pertaining to an identified juvenile concerning juvenile court proceedings and, if applicable, detention and correctional processes.

L

labeling theory Theory that views society as creating deviance through a system of social control agencies that designate certain individuals as deviants. The stigmatized individual is made to feel unwanted in the normal social order. Eventually, the individual begins to believe that the label is accurate, assumes it as a personal identity, and enters into a deviant or criminal career.

latchkey children Children left unsupervised after school by working parents.

law Method for resolving disputes. A rule of action to which people obligate themselves to conform, via their selected representatives and other officials. The principles and procedures of the common law, as distinguished from those of equity.

law enforcement agency Federal, state, or local criminal justice agency whose principal functions are the prevention, detection, and investigation of crime and the apprehension of alleged offenders.

law enforcement officer Employee of a law enforcement agency who is an officer sworn to carry out law enforcement duties or a sworn employee of a prosecutorial agency who performs primarily investigative duties. Also called police officer.

law guardian Person with the legal authority and duty of taking care of someone and managing the property and rights of that person, if the person is considered incapable of administering the affairs personally.

Law Enforcement Assistance Administration Unit in the U.S. Department of Justice established by the Omnibus Crime Control and Safe Streets Act of 1968 to administer grants and provide guidance for crime prevention policy and programs.

learning disabilities Neurological dysfunctions that prevent people from learning up to their potential.

lineup Pretrial identification procedure in which a suspect is placed in a group for the purpose of being identified by a witness.

M

mandamus Literally, "we command." A legal, not an equitable, remedy. When issued, it is an inflexible peremptory command to do a particular thing.

mandatory sentence Statutory requirement that a certain penalty shall be set and carried out in all cases on conviction for a specified offense or series of offenses.

manslaughter Voluntary (nonnegligent) killing; intentionally causing the death of another with reasonable provocation.

masculinity hypothesis View that women who commit crimes have biological and psychological traits similar to those of men.

medial model View that the justice system should help rehabilitate offenders rather than punish them. Advocates of the medial model liken criminality to a "disease" that can be "cured" through proper treatment.

mens rea Guilty mind; the mental element of a crime or the intent to commit a criminal act.

middle-class measuring rods According to Cohen, the standards with which teachers and other representatives of state authority evaluate lower-class youths. Because they cannot live up to middle-class standards, lower-class youths are bound for failure, which brings on frustration and anger at conventional society.

minor Person who is under the age of legal consent.

***Miranda* warning** Result of two Supreme Court decisions (*Escobedo v. Illinois*, 378 U.S. 478 (1964) and *Miranda v. Arizona*, 384 U.S. 436 (1966), that require police officers to inform individuals under arrest of their constitutional rights. Although aimed at protecting individuals during in-custody interrogation, the warning must also be given when the investigation shifts from the investigatory stage to the accusatory stage—that is, when suspicion begins to focus on an individual.

misdemeanor Offense punishable by a fine or by incarceration for not more than one year in a county jail. There is no uniform rule; an offense can be a misdemeanor in one jurisdiction and a felony in another.

Model Penal Code Generalized modern codification of that which is considered basic to criminal law, published by the American Law Institute in 1962.

moral entrepreneurs Interest groups that attempt to control social life and the legal order in order to promote their own personal set of moral values.

murder Intentionally causing the death of another without reasonable provocation or legal justification, or causing the death of another while committing or attempting to commit another crime.

N

National Council on Crime and Delinquency Private national agency that promotes efforts at crime control through research, citizen involvement, and public information efforts.

National Crime Survey Ongoing victimization study conducted jointly by the U.S. Justice Department and the Census Bureau that surveys victims about their experiences with law violation.

neurological Pertaining to the brain and central nervous system.

neutralization Ability to overcome social norms and controls. Neutralization theory holds that delinquents adhere to conventional values while "drifting" into periods of illegal behavior. In order to drift, delinquents must first neutralize legal and moral values.

nonjudicial disposition Rendering of a decision in a juvenile case by an authority other than a judge or court of law. Often an informal method used to determine the most appropriate disposition of a juvenile.

nonresidential program Program enabling youths to remain in their homes or foster homes while receiving services.

nonsecure setting Setting in which the emphasis is on the care and treatment of youths without the need to place constraints on them and to worry about the protection of the public.

O

official data Incidents of crime and delinquency that are recorded by police agencies.

official records Data kept by police, courts, and correctional agencies.

Office of Juvenile Justice and Delinquency Prevention (OJJDP) Branch of the U.S. Justice Department charged with shaping national juvenile justice policy through the disbursement of federal aid and research funds.

P

parens patriae Power of the state to act in behalf of the child and provide care and protection equivalent to that of a parent.

parole agency Correctional agency that may or may not include a parole authority and whose principal functions are the supervision of adults or juveniles placed on parole.

parole authority Person or correctional agency having the authority to release on parole adults or juveniles committed to confinement facilities, to revoke parole, and to discharge from parole.

parolee Person who has been conditionally released from a correctional institution prior to the expiration of his or her sentence and placed under the supervision of a parole agency.

paternalism Male domination. A paternalistic family, for instance, is one in which the father is the dominant authority figure.

part I offenses Eight index crimes whose incidence is reported to the FBI by local police.

part II offenses All other crimes other than part I offenses. Arrests for these crimes are reported to the FBI.

patriarchy Legal or social institution dominated or ruled by a male.

penalty Punishment meted out by law or judicial decision on the commission of a particular offense. It may be death, imprisonment, a fine, or loss of civil privileges.

persistence Refers to the offending patterns of youths who continue in a delinquent career despite repeatedly being apprehended and sanctioned by legal authorities.

petition Document filed in juvenile court alleging that a juvenile is a delinquent, a status offender, or a dependent and asking that the court assume jurisdiction over the juvenile or that the juvenile be transferred to a criminal court for prosecution as an adult.

petition not sustained Finding by a juvenile court in an adjudicatory hearing that there is insufficient evidence to sustain an allegation that a juvenile is a delinquent, a status offender, or a dependent.

person in need of supervision Person usually characterized as ungovernable, incorrigible, truant, and habitually disobedient.

plea-bargaining Discussion between the defense counsel and the prosecution by which the accused agrees to plead guilty for certain considerations. The advantage to the defendant may be in the form of a reduction of the charges, a lenient sentence, or, in the case of multiple charges, dropped charges. The advantage to the prosecution is that a conviction is obtained without the time and expense of lengthy trial proceedings.

police discretion Refers to the ability of police officers to enforce the law selectively. Police officers in the field have great latitude to use their discretion in deciding whether to invoke their arrest powers.

police officer style Refers to the belief that the bulk of police officers can be classified into ideal personality types. Popular style types include: supercops, who desire to enforce only serious crimes, such as robbery and rape; professionals, who use a broad definition of police work; service oriented, who see their job as that of a helping profession; avoiders, who do as little as possible. The actual existence of ideal police officer types has been much debated.

population All people who share a particular personal characteristic, for example, all high school students or all police officers.

positivism Branch of social science that uses the scientific method of the natural sciences and that suggests that human behavior is a product of social, biological, psychological, or economic forces.

presentence report Investigation performed by a probation officer attached to a trial court after the conviction of a defendant. The report contains information about the defendant's background, education, previous employment family, his or her own statement concerning the offense, prior criminal record, interviews with neighbors or acquaintances, and his or her mental and physical condition (i.e., information that would not be made record in the case of a guilty plea or that would be inadmissible as evidence at a trial but could be influential and important at the sentencing stage). After conviction, a judge sets a date for sentencing (usually ten days to two weeks from date of conviction), during which time the presentence report is made. The report is required in felony cases in federal courts; in some states, it is optional at the discretion of the judge, while in others, it is mandatory before convicted offenders can be placed on probation. In the case of juvenile offenders, the presentence report is also known as a social history report.

primary deviance According to Lemert, deviant acts that do not help redefine the self and public image of the offender.

primogeniture Middle Ages practice of allowing only the family's eldest son to inherit lands and titles.

probable cause Reasonable ground to believe the existence of facts that an offense was committed and the accused committed that offense.

probation Sentence entailing the conditional release of a convicted offender into the community under the supervision of the court (in the form of a probation officer) subject to certain conditions for a specific time. The conditions are usually similar to those of parole. (Probation is a sentence, an alternative to incarceration; parole is administrative release from incarceration.) Violation of the conditions of probation may result in revocation of probation.

probation agency Also called probation department. Correctional agency whose principal functions are juvenile intake, the supervision of adults and juveniles placed on probation status, and the investigation of adults and juveniles for the purpose of preparing presentence or predisposition reports to assist the court in determining the proper sentence or juvenile court disposition.

probation officer Employee of a probation agency whose primary duties include one or more of the probation agency functions.

probationer Person required by a court or probation agency to meet certain conditions of behavior; person who may or may not be placed under the supervision of a probation agency.

procedural law Rules that define the operation of criminal proceedings. The methods that must be followed in obtaining warrants, investigating offenses, effecting lawful arrests, using force, conducting trials, introducing evidence, sentencing convicted offenders, and reviewing cases in appellate courts. Substantive law defines criminal offenses; procedural law delineates how the substantive offenses are to be enforced.

prosecutor Representative of the state (executive branch) in criminal proceedings; advocate for the state's case—the charge—in the adversary trial, for example, the attorney general of the United States, U.S. attorneys, attorneys general of the states, district attorneys, and police prosecutors. The prosecutor participates in investigations both before and after arrest, prepares legal documents, participates in obtaining arrest or search warrants, decides whether to charge a suspect and, if so, with which offense. The prosecutor argues the state's case at trial, advises the police, participates in plea negotiations, and makes sentencing recommendations.

prosecutorial agency Federal, state, or local criminal justice agency whose principal function is the prosecution of alleged offenders.

public defender Lawyer who works in a public agency or under private contractual agreement as defense counsel to indigent defendants.

psychoanalytic (psychodynamic) Branch of psychology that holds that the human personality is controlled by unconscious mental processes developed early in childhood.

psychopath Person whose personality is characterized by lack of warmth and affection, inappropriate behavior responses, and an inability to learn from experience. While some psychologists view psychopathy as a result of childhood trauma, others see it as a result of biological abnormality.

psychotic Person who has lost control of his or her thoughts, moods, and feelings.

R

random sample Sample selected on the basis of chance so that each person in the population has an equal opportunity to be selected.

rationale choice View that crime is a function of a decision-making process in which the potential offender weighs the potential costs and benefits of an illegal act.

recidivism Repetition of criminal behavior; habitual criminality. Recidivism is measured by (1) criminal acts that resulted in conviction by a court when committed by individuals who are under correctional supervision or who had been released from correctional supervision within the previous three years and (2) technical violations of probation or parole in which a sentencing or paroling authority took action that resulted in an adverse change in the offender's legal status.

referral to intake In juvenile proceedings, a request by the police, parents, or other agency or person that a juvenile intake unit take appropriate action concerning a juvenile alleged to have committed a delinquent act or status offense or to be dependent.

reform school Institution in which efforts are made to improve the conduct of those forcibly detained within. Educational and psychological services are employed to achieve this goal.

rehabilitation Restoring to a condition of constructive activity.

relative deprivation Condition that exists when people of wealth and poverty live in close proximity to one an-

other. Some criminologists attribute crime rate differentials to relative deprivation.

release (pretrial) Procedure whereby an accused person who has been taken into custody is allowed to be free before and during trial.

release from detention Authorized exit from detention of a person subject to criminal or juvenile justice proceedings.

release on bail Release by a judicial officer of an accused person who has been taken into custody upon the accused's promise to pay a certain sum of money or property if he or she fails to appear in court as required. The promise may or may not be secured by the deposit of an actual sum of money or property.

release on own recognizance Release, by a judicial officer, of an accused person who has been taken into custody upon the accused's promise to appear in court as required for criminal proceedings.

residential child-care facility Dwelling other than a detention or shelter care facility that provides living accommodations, care, treatment, and maintenance for children and youths and is licensed to provide such care. Such facilities include foster family homes, group homes, and halfway houses.

residential treatment center Government facility that serves juveniles whose behavior does not necessitate the strict confinement of a training school, often allowing them greater contact with the community.

resource deprivation Effect of growing up under conditions lacking adequate care, custody, and material goods.

responsible Legally accountable for one's actions and obligations.

restitution Restoring of property, or a right, to a person who has been unjustly deprived of it. A writ of restitution is the process by which a successful appellant may recover something of which he or she has been deprived under a prior judgment.

revocation Administrative act performed by a parole authority that removes a person from parole or a judicial order by a court removing a person from parole or probation, in response to a violation on the part of the parolee or probationer.

right to counsel Right of the accused to assistance of defense counsel in all criminal prosecutions.

right to treatment Philosophy espoused by many courts that offenders have a statutory right to treatment. A federal constitutional right to treatment has not been established.

rights of defendant Powers and privileges that are constitutionally guaranteed to every defendant.

role diffusion According to Erikson, role diffusion occurs when youths spread themselves too thin, experience personal uncertainty, and place themselves at the mercy of leaders who promise to give them a sense of identity they cannot develop for themselves.

routine activities   View that crime is a "normal" function of the routine activities of modern living. Offenses can be expected if there is a suitable target that is not protected by capable guardians.

runaway   Juvenile who has been adjudicated by a judicial officer of a juvenile court as having committed the status offense of leaving the custody and home of his or her parents, guardians, or custodians without permission and failing to return within a reasonable length of time.

S

sample   Limited number of persons selected for study from a population.

schizophrenia   Type of psychosis often marked by bizarre behavior, hallucinations, loss of thought control, and inappropriate emotional responses. There are different types of schizophrenia: catatonic, which characteristically involves impairment of motor activity; paranoid, which is characterized by delusions of persecution; and hebephrenic, which is characterized by immature behavior and giddiness.

search and seizure   U.S. Constitution protects against any search or seizure engaged in without a lawfully obtained search warrant. A search warrant will be issued if there is probable cause to believe that an offense has been or is being committed.

secondary deviance   According to Lemert, deviant acts that redefine the offender's self and public image. Acts become secondary when they form a basis for self-concept, for example, when a drug experimenter becomes an addict.

secure setting   Setting that places constraints on youths for care and treatment and for the protection of the public.

security and privacy standards   Set of principles and procedures developed to ensue the security and confidentiality of criminal or juvenile record information in order to protect the privacy of the persons identified in such records.

selective incapacitation   Policy of putting suspected chronic offenders behind bars for long periods of time. Advocates suggest that special laws be created to heavily penalize persistent offenders.

self-fulfilling prophecy   Deviant behavior patterns that are a response to an earlier labeling experience. People act in synch with social labels, even if the labels are falsely bestowed.

self-report   Research approach that requires subjects to reveal their own participation in delinquent or criminal acts.

sentence   Sanction imposed by the court upon a convicted defendant, usually in the form of a fine, incarcera-tion, or probation. Sentencing may be carried out by a judge, jury, or sentencing council (panel of judges), depending on the statutes of the jurisdictions.

sentence, indeterminate   Statutory provision for a type of sentence to imprisonment, in which, after the court has determined that the convicted person shall be imprisoned, the exact length of imprisonment and parole supervision is fixed within statutory limits by a parole authority.

sentence, suspended   Court decision postponing the pronouncing of sentence upon a convicted person or postponing the execution of a sentence that has been pronounced by the court.

short-run hedonism   According to Cohen, the desire of lower-class gang youths to engage in behavior that will give them immediate gratification and excitement but that in the long run will be dysfunctional and negativistic.

shock probation   Sentence that involves a short prison stay to impress the offender with the pains of imprisonment before he or she begins a probationary sentence.

skinhead   Member of white supremacist gang, identified by a shaved skull and Nazi or Ku Klux Klan markings.

social bond   Ties a person has to the institutions and processes of society. According to Hirschi, elements of the social bond include commitment, attachment, involvement, and belief.

social control   Ability of social institutions to influence human behavior. Among the primary agencies of formal social control are the school and the justice system.

social disorganization   Neighborhood or area marked by culture conflict, lack of cohesiveness, transient population, insufficient social organizations, and anomie.

socialization   Process of human development and enculturation. Socialization is influenced by key social processes and institutions.

social process   Operations of formal and informal social institutions. Elements of the social process include socialization within family and peer groups, the educational process, and the justice system.

social structure   Fabric of society. Within the social structure are the various classes, institutions, and groups of society.

sociobiology   Branch of science that views human behavior as being motivated by in-bred biological urges and desires. The urge to survive and preserve the species motivates human behavior.

sociopath   Person whose personality is characterized by lack of warmth and affection, inappropriate behavior responses, and an inability to learn from experience. Used interchangeably with psychopath.

specific deterrence   Crime-control policy that suggests that punishment should be severe enough to convince previous offenders never to repeat their criminal activity.

spontaneous remission Another term used for the aging-out process.

standard of proof Proof beyond a reasonable doubt—the standard used to convict a person charged with a crime. Many U.S. Supreme Court decisions have made the beyond a reasonable doubt standard a due process and constitutional requirement.

stare decisis "To stand by decided cases." The legal principle by which the decision or holding in an earlier case becomes the standard with which to judge subsequent similar cases.

status offender Juvenile who has been adjudicated by a judicial officer of a juvenile court as having committed a status offense.

status offense Act that is declared by statute to be an offense but only when committed by a juvenile. It can be adjudicated only by a juvenile court.

statutory law Laws created by legislative bodies to meet changing social conditions, public opinion, and custom.

stigma Social disgrace or condemnation. Stigmatized persons feel they are outsiders or outcasts from society.

stop and frisk Practice of police officers who are suspicious of an individual to run their hands lightly over the suspect's outer garments to determine if the person is carrying a concealed weapon. Also called a "patdown" or "threshold inquiry," a stop and frisk is intended to stop short of any activity that could be considered a violation of Fourth Amendment rights.

stardom formations According to the Schwendingers, adolescent social networks whose members have distinct dress, grooming, and linguistic behavior.

strain Social psychological condition that is created when a person's social goals cannot be achieved by available legitimate means. Lower-class youths might feel strain because they are denied access to adequate educational opportunities and social support.

stratified Grouped according to social strata or levels. American society is considered stratified on the basis of economic class and wealth.

street crime Illegal acts designed to prey on the public through theft, damage, and violence.

structural Marxist theory View that the law and justice system is designed to maintain the capitalist system and that members of both the owner and worker classes whose behavior threatens the stability of the system will be sanctioned.

subculture Group that is loosely part of the dominant culture that maintains a unique set of values, beliefs, and traditions.

substantive criminal laws Body of specific rules that declare what conduct is criminal and prescribe the punishment to be imposed for such conduct.

subterranean values According to Sykes and Matza, the ability of youthful law violators to repress social norms.

summons Alternative to arrest usually used for petty or traffic offenses; a written order notifying an individual that he or she has been charged with an offense. A summons directs the person to appear in court to answer the charge. It is used primarily in instances of low risk, where the person will not be required to appear at a later date. The summons is advantageous to police officers because it frees them from spending time on arrest and booking procedures; it is advantageous to the accused in that he or she is spared time in jail.

surplus value Marxist view that the laboring classes produce wealth that far exceeds their wages and goes to the capitalist class as profits.

T

take into custody Act of the police in securing the physical custody of a child engaged in delinquency. Avoids the stigma of the word *arrest*.

tongs Chinese gangs.

totality of the circumstances Legal doctrine that mandates that a decision maker consider all the issues and circumstances of a case before judging the outcome. For example, before concluding whether a suspect understood his or her *Miranda* warning, a judge must consider the totality of the circumstances under which the warning was given. The suspect's age, intelligence, and competency may be issues that influence his or her understanding and judgment.

training school Correctional institution for juveniles adjudicated to be delinquents or status offenders and committed to confinement by a judicial officer.

transfer hearing Preadjudicatory hearing in juvenile court for the purpose of determining whether juvenile court jurisdiction should be retained or waived over a juvenile alleged to have committed a delinquent act and whether he or she should be transferred to criminal court for prosecution as an adult.

transfer to adult court Decision by a juvenile court resulting from a transfer hearing that jurisdiction over an alleged delinquent will be waived and that he or she should be prosecuted as an adult in a criminal court.

transitional neighborhood Area undergoing a shift in population and structure, usually from middle-class residential to lower-class mixed use.

treatment Rehabilitative method used to effect a change of behavior in an inmate, juvenile delinquent, or status offender. It may be in the form of therapy programs or educational or vocational training.

triads Chinese self-help groups.

trial Examination of issues of fact and law in a case or controversy, beginning when the jury has been selected in a jury trial or when the first witness is sworn or the first evidence is introduced in a court trial and concluding when a verdict is reached or the case is dismissed.

Type I offenses Another term for index crimes.

Type II offenses All crimes other than index and minor traffic offenses. The FBI records annual arrest information for Type II offenses.

U

UCR Abbreviation for the Federal Bureau of Investigation's uniform crime reporting program.

V

verdict In criminal proceedings, the decision made by a jury in a jury trial or by a judicial officer in a court trial that a defendant is either guilty or not guilty of the offenses for which he or she has been tried.

victim Person who has suffered death, physical or mental suffering, or loss of property as the result of an actual or attempted criminal offense committed by another person.

victim survey Crime-measurement technique that surveys citizens in order to measure their experiences as victims of crime.

victim precipitated Describes a crime in which the victim's behavior was the spark that ignited the subsequent offense, for example, the victim abused the offender verbally or physically.

W

waiver Voluntary relinquishment of a known right.

widening the net Phenomenon that occurs when programs created to divert youths from the justice system actually involve them more deeply in the official process.

writ of certiorari Order of a superior court requesting that the record of an inferior court (or administrative body) be brought forward for review or inspection.

writ of habeas corpus Judicial order requesting that a person detaining another produce the body of the prisoner and give reasons for his or her capture and detention. Habeas corpus is a legal device used to request that a judicial body review reasons for a person's confinement and the conditions of confinement. Habeas corpus is known as "the great writ."

writ of mandamus Order of a superior court commanding that a lower court or administrative or executive body perform a specific function. It is commonly used to restore rights and privileges lost to a defendant through illegal means.

Y

youth services bureau Neighborhood youth service agency that coordinates all community services for young people and provides services lacking in the community or neighborhood, especially those designed for the predelinquent or the early delinquent.

youthful offender Person adjudicated in criminal court who may be above the statutory age limit for juveniles but who is below a specified upper-age limit for whom special correctional commitments and special record sealing procedures are made available by statute.

Appendix: Excerpts from the U.S. Constitution

Amendment I (1791)

Congress shall make no law respecting an establishment of religion, or prohibiting the free exercise thereof; or abridging the freedom of speech, or of the press; or the right of the people peaceably to assemble, and to petition the government for a redress of grievances.

Amendment II (1791)

A well regulated militia, being necessary to the security of a free state, the right of the people to keep and bear arms, shall not be infringed.

Amendment III (1791)

No soldier shall, in time of peace, be quartered in any house, without the consent of the owner, nor in time of war, but in a manner to be prescribed by law.

Amendment IV (1791)

The right of the people to be secure in their persons, houses, papers, and effects, against unreasonable searches and seizures, shall not be violated, and no warrants shall issue, but upon probable cause, supported by oath or affirmation, and particularly describing the place to be searched, and the persons or things to be seized.

Amendment V (1791)

No person shall be held to answer for a capital, or otherwise infamous, crime unless on a presentment or indictment of a grand jury, except in cases arising in the land or naval forces, or in the militia, when in actual service in time of war or public danger; nor shall any person be subject for the same offense to be twice put in jeopardy of life or limb; nor shall be compelled in any criminal case to be a witness against himself, nor be deprived of life, liberty, or property; without due process of law; nor shall private property be taken for public use without just compensation.

Amendment VI (1791)

In all criminal prosecutions, the accused shall enjoy the right to a speedy and public trial, by an impartial jury of the state and district wherein the crime shall have been committed, which district shall have been previously ascertained by law, and to be informed of the nature and cause of the accusation; to be confronted with the witnesses against him; to have compulsory process for obtaining witnesses in his favor, and to have the assistance of counsel for his defense.

Amendment VII (1791)

In suits at common law, where the value in controversy shall exceed twenty dollars, the right of trial by jury shall be preserved, and no fact tried by a jury shall be otherwise reexamined in any court of the United States, than according to the rules of common law.

Amendment VIII (1791)

Excessive bail shall not be required, nor excessive fines imposed, nor cruel and unusual punishment inflicted.

Amendment IX (1791)

The enumeration in the Constitution of certain rights shall not be construed to deny or disparage others retained by the people.

Amendment X (1791)

The powers not delegated to the United States by the Constitution, nor prohibited by it to the states, are reserved to the states respectively, or to the people.

Amendment XIV (1868)

Section I. All persons born or naturalized in the United States, and subject to the jurisdiction thereof, are citizens of the United States and of the state wherein they reside. No state shall make or enforce any law which shall abridge the privileges or immunities of citizens of the United States; nor shall any state deprive any person of life, liberty, or property, without due process of law; nor deny to any person within its jurisdiction the equal protection of the laws.

Table of Cases

Name Index

Sickmund, Melissa, 491nn.5, 6
Siegel, Larry, 184n.36
Siegel, Leslie, 75n.4
Sieverdes, Christopher, 567
Silva, Phil, 98, 110, 123n.149
Simcha-Fagan, Ora, 152n.21
Simon, Rita, 226−27
Simonsen, C., 121n.62
Simpson, John, 213n.70, 235nn.73, 75
Simpson, Sally, 234n.68
Singer, Simon, 46, 49n.44, 235n.72, 521, 527n.69
Sitt, B. Grant, 249
Skinner, B. F., 102
Skinner, William, 184n.24
Skovron, Sandra Evans, 23nn.46, 50, 426n.61
Slaughter, Ellen, 526n.28
Slawson, John, 109−10
Smetena, Judith, 272n.54
Smith, Beverly, 382, 395n.35
Smith, Charles, 447, 448, 456n.63
Smith, Douglas, 49n.35, 64, 76n.27, 77nn.43, 44, 233n.2, 448−49, 456n.57
Smith, Richard, 246
Smith, Robert, 425n.27
Snyder, Eloise, 212n.34
Snyder, Howard, 18, 23n.41, 70−71, 72, 75n.11, 77n.64, 78n.70, 491n.6
Snyder, Phyllis, 17−18, 23n.35
Solar, Mark, 476
Solnit, Albert, 518
Somerville, Dora, 223
Sorrell, James, 102
Spergel, Irving, 282, 299, 305n.27
Spitzer, Stephen, 207, 213n.78
Sprague, John, 120n.31
Staples, William, 543−44
Steffensmeier, Darrell, 48nn.9, 10, 75n.3, 228
Steffensmeier, Renee Hoffman, 228
Stern, Susan, 272n.44
Stewart, David, 49n.49
Stinchcombe, Arthur, 313
Stone, Karen, 274n.96
Stouthamer-Loeber, Magda, 243, 272n.35
Strasburg, Paul, 444
Straus, Murray, 242, 251−52, 254−55, 265, 271n.1
Streib, Victor, 444, 521, 522, 527n.71
Streifel, Cathy, 75n.3
Strodtbeck, Fred, 184n.35, 279
Sullivan, Dennis, 491n.6
Sutherland, Edwin, 110, 157−58, 159, 160
Sutherland, Mary, 469
Sutton, John R., 395n.16
Svikis, Dace, 366n.19
Swanger, Henry, 492n.35
Sykes, Gresham, 162, 163
Szymanski, Linda, 455n.16, 508, 526n.33

Tangri, Sandra, 185n.44
Tannenbaum, Frank, 193
Tardiff, Kenneth, 87, 119n.24
Taylor, Carl, 297
Templer, Donald, 366n.19
Tennenbaum, David, 108
Tennyson, Ray, 153n.64
Terry, Robert, 447
Thatcher, Robert, 96, 121n.82
Thomas, Charles, 18, 23nn.40, 44, 196, 212n.38, 482, 493n.73
Thomas, W. I., 55, 218−19
Thompson, Kevin, 77n.45, 235n.74
Thornberry, Terence, 48n.3, 57, 77n.47, 176−77, 272n.44, 317, 333n.53, 348, 366n.28, 447
Thrasher, Frederick, 282, 283, 286
Tifft, Larry, 49n.29
Timrots, Anita, 49n.38
Titchener, Edward, 105
Tittle, Charles, 64, 77n.44, 152n.19, 184nn.12, 16, 197, 212n.44, 245
Toby, Jackson, 207, 213n.80, 244, 313, 318−19, 320
Tonry, Michael, 75n.1
Tontodonato, Pamela, 73, 78n.76
Torbet, Patricia, 557n.8, 597n.19
Tracy, Paul, 69, 76n.24, 77nn.45, 60
Tracy, Sharon, 18, 23n.42
Tuck, Mary, 119n.10
Turnquist, Dawn, 274n.112

Uchida, Craig, 454n.3

Vachss, Andrew, 581
Van den Haag, Ernest, 119n.4
Van Voorhis, Patricia, 172, 185n.56
Vasta, Ross, 49n.45
Vaughn, Joseph B., 539−40, 558n.23
Vedder, Clyde, 223
Villemez, Wayne, 64, 77n.44
Vigil, James Diego, 305n.40
Visher, Christy, 448, 456n.57
Vivora, T. Scott, 582, 599n.93
Voeller, Kytja, 121n.69
Volavka, Jan, 97
Volenik, Adrienne, 512
Von Hirsch, Andrew, 72
Voss, Harwin, 60, 76n.21, 317

Wakefield, James, 121n.65
Waldo, Gordon, 108

Walker, Samuel, 431
Walters, Glenn, 113, 124n.159
Walters, James, 246
Walters, Richard, 103
Warren, Earl, 507
Warren, Keith, 272n.43
Watson, John B., 102
Wattenberg, William, 224
Watts, W. David, 367n.49
Webb, James, 152n.23
Webster-Stratton, Carolyn, 273n.88
Weeks, Ashley, 243
Weiner, Neil Alan, 185n.77
Weis, Joseph, 38, 139, 174−75, 228
Weisfeld, Glen, 288
Wellford, Charles, 197
Wells, L. Edward, 168, 185n.47
Wells, Richard, 256, 274n.105
Wertham, Frederic, 8
West, D. J., 70, 247, 312
Wheeler, Stanton, 212n.25
White, Helene Raskin, 76n.17, 108, 123n.132, 149, 173, 185n.65, 356, 367n.53
White, Jennifer, 110
White, Lynn, 152n.39
White, Thomas, 113, 124n.159
Whitehead, John, 22n.4, 186n.82, 586, 598n.58
Whyte, William, 289
Wiatroski, Michael, 185n.59
Widom, Cathy Spatz, 267, 276n.153
Wilbanks, William, 76n.29
Wilkinson, Karen, 249
Williams, Jay, 58, 64, 76n.19
Willis, Cecil, 256, 274n.105
Wilson, Edmond O., 91
Wilson, James Q., 56, 57, 84, 110, 111, 245
Wilson, William Julius, 305n.39
Winfree, L. Thomas, 349, 366n.37
Winick, Charles, 366n.26
Winn, Russ, 469
Wish, Eric, 333n.54, 346, 356
Wolfgang, Marvin, 57, 66−69, 75n.10, 77n.60, 139, 312
Wooden, Kenneth, 593
Wooden, Wayne, 299, 306nn.77, 82
Wormith, J. Stephen, 123n.123
Wright, Lloyd, 367n.49
Wundt, Wilhelm, 105

Yablonsky, Lewis, 107, 281, 293, 299−300

Zigler, Edward, 241, 271n.7
Zimmerman, Joel, 96, 121n.77

Subject Index

California
  camps in, 564
  community-based institutions in, 549,
    555
  correctional institutions in, 567–69
  probation in, 545
  reception-classification centers in, 564
Cambridge-Somerville Youth Study, 116,
  181
Camps, 564
Capital punishment for children, 20, 88,
  422, 521–22, 604
Chancery court system, 376, 377
Chicago Area Project, 129, 146, 303, 584
Chicago Bar Association, 14
Chicago Reform School, 381–82
Child abuse
  alcohol and drug abuse and, 255–56
  battered child syndrome, 250
  causes of, 253–57
  child protection system, 258–64
  children attending court hearings,
    261–63
  in colonial America, 378
  delinquency and, 265–67
  description of abusive parent, 254–55
  difference between neglect and, 251
  early steps to prevent, 249–50
  economic conditions and, 255, 256–57
  extent of, 242, 251–52, 254–55
  by gender, 255
  legal processing of abuse cases, 259
  number of reported cases, 252–53
  origin of term, 250–51
  by parents, 249
  rights of parents, 264–65
  separation/removal of children from
    parents, 263–64
    social class and, 256–57
    state intervention, 259–60
Child Abuse Prevention and Treatment
  Act, 258
Child care
  in colonial America, 377–78
  development of concern for, 374–76
  in the 1800s, 378–84
  in the Middle Ages, 372–73
  in the 1600s and 1700s, 373–74
Children
  abduction of, 43
  rights of, 392–93, 403, 414, 420–22,
    506–11, 516–18, 591–92
  sexual abuse of, 253, 257
Children in Custody (CIC) series, 569–70,
  571, 573
Children in Need of Supervision (CHINS),
  391, 418
Children's Aid Society, 383
Child savers, 11, 379–81, 386–88
Chivalry hypothesis, 219–20

Choice theory
  definition of, 82
  development of, 83–85
  educational impact on delinquency
    and, 309
  family structure and delinquency and,
    240
  integrating developmental theory and,
    111–13
Chronic career offenders, 6
Chronic delinquents, 6
  categories of, 71
  controlling, 413–14, 602
  Delinquency in a Birth Cohort, 66–69
  offense specialization, 71–72
  predicting who will become, 70–71
  selective incapacitation, 72
  solutions for dealing with, 72–73
  treating, 581
  versus conventional delinquents, 66
Chronic recidivists, 68
Cities in Schools (CIS), 330
Classical criminology, 83–84
Clearance, 29
Cliques, 278
Cocaine, 337
Cognitive theory, 105–6, 177
Cohort studies
  child abuse and delinquency and use
    of, 266–67
  Delinquency in a Birth Cohort
    (Wolfgang), 66–69
  research studies using, 69–70
Collateral review, 517–18
Colorado
  correctional institutions in, 568
  correctional treatment in, 582
  nonresidential community treatment
    programs in, 550, 552–53
  probation in, 538
Comic books, impact of, 8
Community
  delinquency and change in the, 132
  drug controlling programs, 360
  policing, 430, 451–52, 604
  school crime and crime in the, 321–22
Community Research Center, 467
Community treatment
  community-based institutions, 545–50
  criticisms of, 550–51, 554–55
  definition of, 532
  effectiveness of, 555
  hidden correctional system, 554
  nonresidential, 550, 552–53
  privatization of probation, 544–45
  probation, 532–41
  residential, 548–50
  restitution, 541–44, 605
Community Treatment Project (CTP),
  555

Comprehensive Employment Training
  Act, 179
Compulsory school attendance, 323–24
Concurrent jurisdiction statutes, 486
Conduct norms, 139
Conflict
  criminology, 200
  effects of family, 242–43
  female delinquency and, 223
  parental/intrafamily, 247
Conflict theory
  concept of delinquency in, 202–4
  demystification, 202
  description of, 189, 199–201
  educational impact on delinquency
    and, 309
  elements of, 201–2
  evaluation of, 207
  instrumental theory, 205–6
  integrated structural Marxist theory,
    206–7
Conformity
  social adaptation, 136
  weak commitment to, 167
Congress of National Black Churches,
  360
Connecticut
  community-based institutions in,
    547–48
  correctional institutions in, 568, 569
Containment theory, 166–68
Control theories. See Social control
  theories
Correctional institutions. See also
  Institutions
  administrative arrangements of,
    566–67
  categories of, 562
  cost of, 569
  development of juvenile institutions,
    382–83
  during the 1900s, 564–65
  early history of, 563–64
  hidden correctional system, 554,
    570–71
  overcrowding in, 568–69
  profile of institutionalized juveniles,
    569–75
  rules and discipline in, 590–92
  statistics on, 563, 565, 568
Correctional treatment
  behavior modification, 578
  for chronic delinquents, 581
  educational programs, 579–80
  effectiveness of, 582, 584–86
  general description of, 575–76
  group treatment techniques, 578–79
  individual counseling, 577
  Outward Bound programs, 582, 584–85
  psychotherapy, 577